The Most Southern Place on Earth

THE MOST SOUTHERN PLACE ON EARTH

The Mississippi Delta and
the Roots of Regional Identity

JAMES C. COBB

OXFORD UNIVERSITY PRESS
New York   Oxford

Oxford University Press

Oxford New York Toronto
Delhi Bombay Calcutta Madras Karachi
Kuala Lumpur Singapore Hong Kong Tokyo
Nairobi Dar Es Salaam Cape Town
Melbourne Auckland Madrid

and associated companies in
Berlin Ibadan

Copyright © 1992 by James C. Cobb

First published in 1992 by Oxford University Press, Inc.,
198 Madison Avenue, New York, New York 10016-4314

First issued as an Oxford University Press paperback, 1994

Oxford is a registered trademark of Oxford University Press

Library of Congress Cataloging-in-Publication Data
Cobb, James C. (James Charles), 1947 –
The most southern place on earth:
the Mississippi Delta and the roots of regional identity /
James C. Cobb.
p. cm. Includes bibliographical references (p.) and index.
ISBN 0-19-504540-8
ISBN 0-19-508913-8 (pbk.)
1. Delta (Miss. : Region)—Civilization.   2. Delta (Miss. : Region)—Social conditions.
3. Delta (Miss. : Region—Economic conditions.
I. Title. F347.D38C63 1992 976.2'4—dc20 91-46181

10 9 8 7

Printed in the United States of America

To Lyra

▽ Preface
▽
▽

In May 1985 I appeared on a Center for the Study of Southern Culture vid-eotape, standing in a cotton field on the outskirts of Marks, Mississippi, describing the Mississippi Delta as a land of astounding economic and social disparity and declaring it "the most southern place on earth." Although at the time I felt terribly pleased with the cleverness and originality of my observa-tion, I soon learned that I was actually but one of a host of commentators who over the years have treated the Mississippi Delta as an isolated, time-warped enclave whose startling juxtaposition of white affluence and black poverty sug-gested the Old South legacy preserved in vivid microcosm.[1]

Since my undergraduate days, I had envisioned the Mississippi Delta as the distilled essence of the Deep South—the last stronghold of the plantation and the only place in Dixie where cotton would always be King. Before I came to the University of Mississippi in 1981, however, my actual knowledge of the Delta was by no means extensive. When I arrived in Oxford, I was uncertain even of the area's exact location, although I soon learned that the "Mississippi Delta" is actually the Yazoo-Mississippi Delta and is not the true delta of the Mississippi but the common flood plain of the Yazoo and Mississippi rivers. Only later would I encounter David Cohn's oft-quoted and occasionally pla-giarized insistence that "the Mississippi Delta begins in the lobby of the Pea-body Hotel in Memphis and ends on Catfish Row in Vicksburg." Further investigation on my part would reveal that as an exercise in physical geography Cohn's identification of the northern and southern termini of the Delta was somewhat imprecise. When it came to cultural geography, however, Cohn's description of the symbolic socioeconomic extremities of the Delta proved to be right on the mark.[2]

Cohn stressed the uniqueness of his native Delta, describing it as "a strange and detached fragment thrown off by the whirling comet that is Amer-ica," and sure enough, I soon noticed that in Mississippi one spoke not of going to Clarksdale, Greenville, or Greenwood, but of traveling "into the Delta," the implication being that of passage back in time, to a setting that—if such a thing were possible—seemed even more southern than the rest of the state. The more I read and observed—the social self-assurance and Fraternity and Sorority Row prominence of Ole Miss's Delta-bred white students, the refusal of a Delta civic club to accept a black faculty colleague as a luncheon speaker, the well-publicized contrasts between poverty and affluence in the Delta's notorious Tunica County, the literary and musical creativity that abounded in the area—the more convinced I became that the story of the Delta might afford the opportunity to study in sharply defined geographical miniature the rich history and culture of the Deep South.[3]

Fueled by exuberance and restrained by neither significant research nor serious reflection, I proceeded at this point to offer my cotton-patch exposition on the Delta's intense and uniquely enduring southernness. Although I was hardly alone in making such an assessment, as my research progressed I grew to regret my impressionistic observations, not because I had exaggerated the Delta's southernness, but because I had oversimplified and, to some extent, trivialized it. The Delta that ultimately emerged from my study was no mere isolated backwater where time stood still while southernness stood fast. Indeed, many of the major economic, political, and social forces that have swept across the American landscape during the last 150 years have actually converged in the Mississippi Delta.

Although it would one day come to symbolize the Old South, with only 10 percent of its land cleared in 1860, the Yazoo Delta was little more than a sparsely inhabited plantation frontier as the antebellum era drew to a close. Its inexhaustible soils and year-round work demands made the Delta an optimum environment for large-scale cotton cultivation and the employment of slave labor. But although it seemed like the answer to every planter's prayers, the oft-flooded, thickly forested Delta's formidable physical disadvantages effectively reserved its tremendous wealth-producing potential for those with the sizable labor and capital or credit resources necessary to exploit it. The upheaval of the Civil War and Reconstruction destroyed the Delta's prospects as a large slave-holder's paradise and confronted its planters with the reality of their dependence on a huge black labor force suddenly free to exert its newfound economic leverage and exercise its recently acknowledged political rights as well. In 1875 the desire of whites in the Delta and throughout Mississippi to regain control of their labor and reassert white political supremacy manifested itself in the violent, unlawful, but ultimately successful effort to redeem the state from Republican rule.

Redemption brought no immediate restoration of planter hegemony in the economic or political arenas, however. Freedmen continued to use demand for their labor to secure more advantageous terms from their employers, while their participation in biracial fusion arrangements raised questions about the future of white political supremacy as well. Not until the 1880s, when federally funded levee rehabilitation and privately financed railroad expansion triggered a land and population boom, did the region begin to reclaim its antebellum identity as the undisputed domain of the planter.

By the turn of the century, self-styled planter aristocrats once again presided over the Mississippi Delta, but for all their pretensions these planters were a far cry from the stereotypical squires who inhabit the Old South legend. Even in the antebellum era, successful Delta planters had been far more concerned about matters of profits and costs than their seigneurial airs seemed to suggest, but the Delta's New South planter elite were considerably more sophisticated and dynamic than their antebellum predecessors had been. They not only stood ready to court federal funds, as well as northern and foreign investment capital, in the interest of the overall development of the Delta's economy, but they embraced and adapted theories and strategies of management and supervision modeled after those currently in fashion in the industrial North. Meanwhile, soaring land prices, disfranchisement, and a socially and legally imposed redefinition of sharecropping that effectively reduced croppers to wage laborers enabled Delta planters to regain control over their black workers. With a comprehensive and rigidly enforced system of caste further guaranteeing their dominance, the Delta's white elite entered the twentieth century presiding over a social order reminiscent of the Old South while adhering to an economic philosophy rooted firmly in the New.

The New Deal brought major changes to the Delta's economy, but the region's white leadership drew on its experience in manipulating federal relief during the 1927 flood and managed to use many New Deal programs to sustain and even strengthen its socioeconomic and political grip on the Delta. World War II brought a massive dislocation of labor and induced considerable social ferment, but the ability of Delta whites to utilize their continuing influence over federal agencies and programs proved crucial to their efforts to resist the rising civil rights pressures and black political challenges of the 1960s and 1970s. Only in the 1980s did Delta blacks begin to gain political influence consistent with their numerical strength, and even then it was by no means clear whether blacks were actually capturing political control or whites were simply surrendering it, effectively abdicating any responsibility for the leadership of an economically depressed Delta sustained primarily by federal life support systems and threatening to become little more than a vast rural ghetto.

The foregoing overview by no means suggests that my original perception of the Delta as a potential window on the historical and cultural experience of the Deep South was inaccurate. The Delta's story incorporates numerous elements crucial to understanding the broad sweep of southern history. It begins with the westward spread of slavery and affords an excellent perspective on the operation of large-scale slave estates as well as the economic and social implications of emancipation, Reconstruction, and the emergence of postbellum plantation tenancy. In the wake of these developments came disfranchisement and the imposition of an inflexible and remarkably effective system of repression and racial control. The Delta also provides a superb setting for studying the effects of the New Deal and subsequent federal farm, relief, and welfare programs on the South. The region was on the front lines of the civil rights struggles of the fifties and sixties and witnessed the gradual expansion of black political influence in the 1970s and 1980s. The post–New Deal Delta's economic transformation and the struggle to create nonagricultural opportunities for its impoverished and undereducated black population reflect the recent experience of much of the rural and small-town South. As the cradle of the blues and the greatest single subregional contributor to the stream of southern black migrants to the urban North, the Delta was indeed, as Tony Dunbar observed, "a primary taproot of black culture and history in America." Finally, as a remarkably rich source of inspiration to writers and artists of various sorts, the Delta's socioeconomic and cultural milieu may hold the keys to a better understanding of the flowering of creativity that sparked the post–World War I southern literary renaissance.[4]

Like the South at large, the Delta presented a fascinating saga of continuity amid change, but if its story was certifiably southern, it was by no means exclusively so. Despite its image as an isolated Old South enclave holding out to the last against the besetting forces of change, the Delta's postbellum experience has been characterized by close and consistent interaction with prevailing national and international economic influences and trends. Although its white leaders dedicated themselves to the maintenance of the social and political status quo within the region, since the Redemption Era they have worked assiduously to promote the Delta's economic expansion and secure its effective integration into the world and national economy. For more than a century, socioeconomic and political conditions in the Delta have reflected no more formative influence than that of the programs and policies of the federal government, and at no time during the twentieth century has the Delta been without at least one powerful and influential voice in Washington.

In 1990 Tony Dunbar wrote of a struggle between "powerful forces from outside the Delta" and a "deep cultural bedrock that refuses to give way." No visitor who observes the corporate-owned megaplantations, shiny new Wal Marts, or video rental outlets housed in old plantation commissaries is likely to quibble with Dunbar's up-close assessment of the contemporary scene. On the other hand, to take a longer view and survey the entire historical experience of the region is to discover that "powerful forces from outside the Delta" have often reinforced rather than undermined its resistance to change. In fact, much of what Dunbar and a host of others have seen as a simple indigenous "cultural bedrock" is actually the multilayered and remarkably complex long-term historical product of the Delta's interaction with a variety of external influences.[5]

Lawrence Levine has argued that culture is less "a fixed condition" than "a process: the product of interaction between past and present." In Levine's view, therefore, cultural persistence depends less on the ability to defend the status quo than the capacity to "react creatively and responsively to the realities of a new situation." If Levine is correct, it is time to rethink the familiar concept of southern culture as a free-standing set of exotic and immutable beliefs, rituals, and relationships mysteriously persisting in outright defiance of the powerful innovative influences of American mass society. As Immanuel Wallerstein has observed, the problem with this traditional approach is that "it forces one's vision inward." My experience in studying the Delta suggests the need to do just the opposite, to look outward and reexamine the South's socio-economic and cultural characteristics within the context of its interaction with, rather than its isolation from, the larger national and global setting. Approached in this fashion, the Delta became a part of the world rather than a world apart, a place where questions about the heart and soul of a region often produced answers about the conscience and character of a nation as well.[6]

Townsend, Tenn.   J. C. C.
March 1992

▽ Acknowledgments
▽
▽

An adequate list of acknowledgments for this book might well require publication of a separate volume. In the space available, I can only begin to scratch the surface of my indebtedness.

Research for this project was supported in part by a National Endowment for the Humanities Fellowship for Individual Research and a Summer Research Fellowship from the University of Mississippi, as well as funds provided in conjunction with the Bernadotte Schmitt Chair of Excellence at the University of Tennessee.

An earlier version of Chapter 11 appeared in the December 1990 issue of the *Journal of American History* and an earlier version of Chapter 13 appeared in the winter 1989 issue of the *Southern Review*. I wish to thank the editors of these journals for granting permission to reprint this material.

I also wish to thank Leon J. Millner for permission to quote from David L. Cohn's *Where I Was Born and Raised* (Houghton Mifflin, Co., © 1948).

The following publishers have granted permission to quote from the works listed below:

Harper Collins Publishers, Inc.: Richard Wright, *Black Boy*, © 1945; Richard Wright, *Uncle Tom's Children*, © 1969.

Oxford University Press: Lawrence Levine, *Black Culture and Black Consciousness: Afro-American Folk Thought from Slavery to Freedom*, © 1977.

University of Wisconsin Press: John Dollard, *Caste and Class in a Southern Town*, © 1949.

Yoknapatawpha Press, Willie Morris, *North Toward Home*, © 1982.

I am especially grateful for the cooperation of Thomas Verich and the staff of Archives and Special Collections at the University of Mississippi; Richard Schrader and other members of the staff at the Southern Historical Collection at the University of North Carolina; and Sammy Cranford, who oversees the Sillers Family Papers at Delta State University. Ann Wells of Virginia Military Institute proved unfailingly knowledgeable and helpful when she was a member of the Special Collections staff at Mississippi State University. Clint Bagley of the W. A. Percy Library in Greenville, Mississippi, was wonderfully cooperative and hospitable as well. Ann Lipscomb, Hank Holmes, and other members of the staff of the Mississippi Department of Archives and History made every trip to Jackson seem like a visit with old friends.

Shirley Culp of the University of Alabama endured the dreary task of retyping numerous drafts of the manuscript. India Cooper did a superb job of copyediting. Sheldon Meyer of Oxford University Press was marvelously patient, supportive, and wise. From the beginning, he perceived far better than I what a complex and demanding project I had undertaken.

Charles East offered indispensable information and advice on the literary culture of the Delta. Lance Walters provided a wonderful index to the Mississippi slave narratives. Neil McMillen graciously shared his data on lynching in Mississippi.

A number of individuals provided information, encouragement, suggestions, and criticism. These include Clarence Mohr, Pete Daniel, David Sansing, Bill Ferris, Alan Lomax, Todd Diacon, Paul Mertz, Mike and Tana McDonald, Jerry Thornbery, Tom Boschert, Bud Bartley, Bob Haws, Hardy Jackson, Tom Dyer, and Jack Kirby. I am especially indebted to my colleagues at the University of Tennessee, who gave me the opportunity to enjoy the beauty of East Tennessee while completing this project and made our entire family feel at home from the moment we arrived.

During the seven years that I was absorbed in researching and writing this book, I experienced the joy of watching our son Ben grow from wide-eyed skateboarder to sophisticated collegian, remaining all the while just about the finest son any parent could hope to have. I also felt the deep sorrow of losing my beloved mother, Modena Cobb, the greatest person I have ever known or expect to know. The primary constant during a period when I changed jobs twice and made two more stops on my teaching tour of the Southeastern Conference has been my wife Lyra. Although I have never met anyone more steadfastly self-effacing, she has always performed brilliantly in any role—be it wife, mother, editor, or construction supervisor—that she has undertaken. When it comes to outwitting obstructionism, she has no equal, and, despite her gentle demeanor, she is a ferocious campaigner against snobbery and pretense in any form. Because I love and admire her so much and because I am so grateful for the sweetness of our life together, I dedicate this book to Lyra Cobb.

▽ Contents
▽
▽

The Most Southern Place on Earth

▽ Introduction:
▽ "Pure Soil, Endlessly Deep,
▽ Dark, and Sweet"

Approximately fifteen thousand years ago, during the final cycle of worldwide glaciation, the Mississippi River and its tributaries cut deep valleys within the Lower Gulf coastal plain. As the glaciers melted and the level of the sea around the mouth of the Mississippi rose, these engorged and sediment-laden streams backed up, flooding the lower Mississippi valleys over an area as much as eighty miles wide at some points and covering them with a thick coating of alluvium drained from a land area encompassing what now amounts to 41 percent of the continental United States. One of the many basins marking the irregular surface of this vast alluvial bed is the Yazoo-Mississippi Delta, which is actually more diamond or oval than deltoid in shape. The Mississippi River, which runs southwestward from Memphis to Greenville, where it then bends slightly eastward toward Vicksburg, forms the western boundary of the area. On the east, the Yazoo Delta is defined by a line of bluffs, some reaching two hundred feet in height. These bluffs run from slightly below Memphis south to Greenwood and thence southwesterly along the Yazoo River, which meets the Mississippi at Vicksburg. The Yazoo-Mississippi Delta is approximately two hundred miles long and seventy miles across at its widest point. The area within its boundaries is approximately 7,110 square miles.[1]

Although it appears flat to the naked eye, the surface of the Delta is actually the somewhat uneven result of centuries of flooding and sedimentation by the Mississippi and its tributaries. When confined to its normal channel, the Mississippi dumped its rich load of silt in its true delta at its mouth. During floods, however, when the great stream climbed out of its channel, it also slowed and lost more of its suspended soils to its expanded bed. Its first losses were its heavier, coarser soils, which accumulated near the normal river bed, while the lighter, finer particles were not deposited until the rising waters reached further inland.[2]

In a typical late winter and spring before white settlers tried to tame the river with levees, the Mississippi, swelled by rapidly melting snows that had

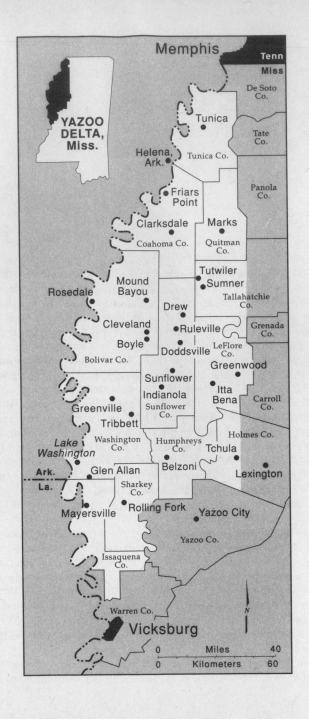

YAZOO DELTA, Miss.

Memphis

Tenn
Miss

De Soto Co.

Tunica

Tate Co.

Helena, Ark.

Tunica Co.

Panola Co.

Friars Point

Clarksdale

Marks

Coahoma Co.

Quitman Co.

Tutwiler

Sumner

Mound Bayou

Tallahatchie Co.

Rosedale

Drew

Cleveland

Ruleville

Grenada Co.

Boyle

Doddsville

LeFlore Co.

Bolivar Co.

Greenwood

Sunflower

Indianola

Itta Bena

Carroll Co.

Sunflower Co.

Greenville

Tribbett

Holmes Co.

Lake Washington

Washington Co.

Humphreys Co.

Tchula

Ark.
La.

Glen Allan

Belzoni

Lexington

Sharkey Co.

Mayersville

Rolling Fork

Yazoo City

Issaquena Co.

Yazoo Co.

Warren Co.

N

Vicksburg

0   Miles   40
0   Kilometers   60

blanketed the area to the north, would also cause the waters of the Yazoo and its tributaries to rise, thereby flooding the surrounding lowlands and triggering a similar, though scaled-down, flooding effect along the backed-up feeder streams of the Yazoo. With slightly over 50 percent of its rainfall occurring in the months from December to May, when the Mississippi and its tributaries were already most likely to be at their highest levels, flooding, with the accompanying deposit of fertile organic material, was but part of a natural, recurrent cycle of life in the Delta.[3]

The Yazoo Delta, wrote David L. Cohn, "was the land of the loins of the river. It had sprung from the body of the Mississippi in a gestation eons long. Untold centuries ago it began to deposit here rich detritus of mountains and plains borne on its bosom, as it flowed from the north to the south to sea. Accretion by slow accretion, without foundation of rock or shale, it laid down this land . . . pure soil endlessly deep, dark, and sweet."[4]

The basin's humid subtropical climate nurtured a lush blanket of vegetation on this rich land that the river had built. Cypress, tupelo, and sweet gums, averaging four to six feet in diameter, dominated forests also dotted with sycamore, poplar, pecan, maple, hickory, walnut, ash, hackberry, black gum, cottonwood, honey locust, and slash pine. Between these trees spread what William Alexander Percy envisioned as "a chaos of vines and cane and brush." As the centuries passed, flood after flood spread blankets of rich alluvium over accumulating layers of decomposing vegetation, and the Delta's soil only grew richer. ("Taken as a whole," reported a geologist from the Delta in 1906, "the plant food percentages in this soil are probably unexcelled by any soil in the world thus far examined.")[5]

Disturbed but little by the mound-building Indians who dwelt primarily on the sedimented high ground along the banks of rivers and streams, the rich Delta jungle was slumbering still when Hernando de Soto began an excursion from Florida to the Mississippi in 1539. De Soto claimed the area including the Yazoo Delta for Spain, but the Spanish made no effort to establish settlements in the southern coastal portions of Mississippi, and the Delta continued its sleep. At the conclusion of the French and Indian War, the Yazoo Delta fell into British hands as a result of the general cession of French lands required by the Peace of Paris in 1763. The British promptly declared most of the area part of the Illinois territory and therefore off limits to white settlers. The territory passed to the United States at the end of the Revolutionary War. Georgia's claims to all the lands between it and the Mississippi River led to abortive attempts by land speculators to promote the settlement of this area, but the way was not fully clear for white occupation on a significant scale until the United States organized the Mississippi Territory in 1798.[6]

Among the handful of whites who actually visited the Delta at this point, none disputed the incredible fertility of its soil. Neither, however, was any observer unaware of the formidable physical challenges posed by the oft-flooded Delta wilderness. As early as the 1720s, when the lower Mississippi

Valley still lay in the hands of the French, the area already enjoyed a reputation as what one scholar described as "a seething lush hell." One traveler who passed through the Delta in 1805 or 1806 reported in his diary that "all the country, or nearly so between the Yazoo and the Mississippi to the mouth of the Yazoo, overflows annually and renders it of no value."[7]

Writing in his *Emigrant's Directory* in 1817, Samuel Brown predicted great things for the fourth Chickasaw Bluff, destined to "become the site of a handsome town," and for Walnut Hills at the southern end of the basin. Memphis and Vicksburg eventually vindicated his optimism, but even the zealous and imaginative Brown found it difficult to conjure up much of a future for the swampy interior wilderness of a Delta that lay covered with forests and "impervious and widespreading canebrakes." Given the preponderance of such testimony, it was hardly surprising that even after Mississippi gained statehood in 1817 the rich, dark alluvial soil of the Delta continued to lie, in Cohn's words, "as in a dream" awaiting the arrival of those who would rip it from "the passionate embrace of deep-rooted trees and close-clinging vines" and exploit its richness to the fullest.[8]

1 ▽ Plantation Frontier
   ▽
   ▽
   ▽

Early travelers' accounts did not exaggerate the difficulties inherent in clearing and settling such a swampy wilderness, but those who wrote off the Yazoo-Mississippi Delta's long-term prospects for development failed to appreciate the importance that the remarkable fertility of its continually replenished alluvial soil would assume in a regional, national, and international economy grown ravenous for cotton. More than that, however, those who doubted that the Delta could ever be cleared, tamed, and farmed efficiently failed to take into account the determination, rapacity, and cruelty that humans could exhibit if the proper incentives were in place. Scarcely three decades after Mississippi joined the Union, though still a largely uncleared wilderness, the Yazoo Basin had already emerged as the most attractive new planting region in the Cotton South.

When Mississippi became the nation's twentieth state in 1817, the Delta region was still in the hands of the Choctaw. White migration to other areas of Mississippi soon generated pressure for Indian removal, which was accomplished in a series of three treaties between 1820 and 1832. The Treaty of Doak's Stand in 1820 marked the sale of part of the southwestern holdings of the Choctaw. These lands were quickly organized into Hinds County. Hinds begat Yazoo in 1823, and five years later Washington County, which then included much of the Yazoo Delta, was carved from Yazoo and the part of Warren County north of Vicksburg. Elsewhere within the Yazoo Basin, Bolivar, Coahoma, and Tunica Counties were formed in 1836, and Issaquena and Sunflower were created in 1884.[1]

Initial settlement in the Yazoo region was concentrated primarily on or near the Mississippi River. The almost impenetrable interior of the basin presented would-be pioneers with too many obstacles, and except for the high banks of a few interior streams and the Lake Washington area south of the present site of Greenville, it was virtually unpopulated. The first white settlers who came to the area probably arrived between 1825 and 1827. One such pioneer was Junius Ward of Kentucky, who traveled down the Natchez Trace and, after hearing of a beautiful lake in the Yazoo Wilderness, persuaded some Choctaws to take him there. Ward determined to locate on the banks of what would become Lake Washington. He returned the next year, bringing his slaves down the Mississippi by flatboat and building a raft to carry his possessions up a bayou to his new lakeside home. When he arrived he found he already had a neighbor in Princeton engineering graduate Frederick Turnbull, who had constructed a flatboat and floated up a bayou to the lake. Turnbull surveyed his land, built a cabin, and left, returning the following year with his family, his remaining slaves, and other possessions.[2]

The accounts of Ward's and Turnbull's settlement near the lake illustrated the isolated frontier conditions that prevailed in the Mississippi Delta in the 1820s. Because there were no roads, both chose locations that provided access by a water route to the Mississippi, where they could connect via steamboat with the outside world. The Lake Washington area soon became a magnet for others as early settlers convinced friends and relatives to move to the Delta.[3]

Despite the almost universal tendency to associate the conquest of the frontier with the hardworking, upwardly mobile yeoman farmer, the Delta was destined from the beginning to be the domain of substantial planters—"pioneers with means," as David Cohn described them—who possessed both the financial resources and the slaves required to clear and drain the land and take full advantage of its fertility. By 1830 Washington County's population stood at 1,976—of whom 1,184 were slaves.[4]

Swelled by purchase, natural increase, and immigration, the slave population continued to multiply, increasing almost sixfold between 1830 and 1840. In the latter year, there were already more than ten slaves for every white in Washington County. By 1850 this ratio would stand at 14.5 to 1. Individual slaveholdings expanded rapidly. Andrew Turnbull, who owned 26 slaves in 1830, held 96 five years later. Of nineteen planters who owned more than 100 slaves in 1855, ten had owned fewer than 50 slaves in 1838. The average number of slaves held by members of this group in 1838 was only 54, while the average for 1855 was 151. The average white family in Washington County held 81.7 slaves in 1850. (Across the Delta, by 1850 slaves outnumbered whites by 5 to 1.)[5]

Because the legislature carved Issaquena out of Washington County in 1844, 1850 census figures for Washington County are misleading. They do show, however, that 85 percent of the farms were valued at ten thousand dollars or more and that 67 percent of Washington County's white residents had moved to the Delta from outside the state.[6]

The Delta county of Bolivar, created in 1836, followed a comparable pattern of settlement and economic development. Its population grew significantly in the 1840s but expanded most dramatically in the 1850s, when the white population increased by 253 percent and the slave population by 332 percent. Most of the whites who came to the county were born outside Mississippi. In 1860 only 19 percent of white heads of households were Mississippi natives.

Only ten of Issaquena County's heads of households in 1860 had been born in Mississippi, whereas thirty-four were from Kentucky, Tennessee, or Alabama. Many of the Delta's wealthiest planters had come from outside the state. Only eight of twenty Issaquena planters whose wealth exceeded a hundred thousand dollars in 1860 had been born in Mississippi. This pattern was even more pronounced in Coahoma and Tunica, where every such planter in 1860 had come from outside the state.[7]

Rumors of the Delta's unhealthiness and reasonably accurate depictions of its jungle-like vegetation and climatic unpredictability may have delayed settlement of the area, but larger economic and demographic forces ultimately pushed settlers into the Yazoo Basin. In the non-Delta counties in Mississippi and in the cotton-growing states to the east, wornout lands insufficient to support extended families with an expanding slave force dictated a move to the richer lands of the Southwest. Burdened by debt and with his Claiborne County plantation "fast failing," Benjamin G. Humphreys determined to transfer his planting activities to the Delta in the 1840s. In 1854 a Holly Springs planter noted "a great feeling manifested by the planters of the hill country to go to the bottom lands, for our hill country is exhausting so fast they will be compelled to send their force to better lands."[8]

For many residents of areas suffering from soil depletion, a move to the rich lands of the Delta offered the only hope of maintaining the accustomed standard of living. A large number of Tallahatchie County settlers, among them two nephews of John C. Calhoun, came from South Carolina. Another group of Scotch-Irish descent left the Abbeville district of South Carolina and settled together in Tallahatchie.[9]

A survey of the birthplaces of heads of households in several Delta counties in 1850 shows the river counties of Tunica, Coahoma, Bolivar, and Washington, those most readily accessible by water to migrants from Kentucky and Tennessee, absorbing more immigrants from those than any other states. Meanwhile, the inland, part-Delta counties like Carroll, Holmes, Panola, and Tallahatchie, reachable by overland routes, drew more heavily from the Carolinas and Georgia.[10]

Concerned about his ability to advance beyond "common mediocrity" in his native state of North Carolina, Paul Carrington Cameron began to consider relocating in the Southwest during the 1830s. When Cameron expressed a desire to begin a planting operation in Mississippi but outside the Delta, James Williamson urged him to reconsider. "There are," Williamson wrote, "but few upland plantations I would select to locate a large negro force upon permanently. They must all in time tire or wear out and as for reclaiming them for planting purposes it is out of the question." He also challenged Cameron's "apprehension" about the "healthfulness" of the Delta, "especially for negroes." A well-fixed plantation with a good cistern, he thought, was "about as healthy as the uplands and the production, of course, much greater." Williamson insisted that the best parts of the Delta constituted "the most certain cotton planting area in the world."[11]

A move into the rich Delta lands certainly offered the chance to improve an individual's or a family's fortunes, but the Delta presented an almost insurmountable challenge to anyone who did not have the capital and slave labor required to establish a plantation in that wilderness area. One estimate put the investment in clearing typical Delta land for cultivation at a hundred dollars per acre. An ideal Delta plantation, as described by a correspondent for the *National Intelligencer* in 1855, would have included sixteen hundred acres with a thousand of them under cultivation. With 750 acres in cotton and 250 more in corn, peas, or sweet potatoes, at least seventy-five field-working slaves would be needed. Allowing for children and the elderly, this would have meant a total slave population of approximately 135. With livestock and equipment, including a gin but no steam engine, the cost of outfitting this operation would run in the neighborhood of $150,000. This was a sizable outlay, one beyond the reach of most planters in the antebellum South. Properly managed, however, such a plantation would produce eight bales to the hand or a bale to the acre, ultimately yielding a net return of about twelve thousand dollars, or 8 percent on the initial investment.[12]

The largest slaveholding plantation in the Delta area belonged to absentee planter Stephen Duncan of Natchez, who began in the early 1850s to shift more of his planting operations to the fertile new ground of the Delta. By February 1851 more than 700 of his 1,036 slaves were on his plantations in Issaquena County, and by the eve of the Civil War Duncan's Issaquena property was valued at well over $1.3 million.[13]

In the mid-1840s the Hampton family of South Carolina began acquiring property in Washington and Issaquena counties. Wade Hampton II purchased a twenty-seven-hundred-acre plantation in Issaquena, and his sons Wade Hampton III and Christopher F. Hampton also purchased plantations in Washington County. By 1860 Wade Hampton III had assumed control of the family's Mississippi holdings, including approximately nine hundred slaves in Washington and Issaquena counties. (Hampton also assumed more than $400,000 in his father's debts, more than $170,000 of which was accounted for in notes held by the hard-nosed and financially astute Stephen Duncan.)[14]

Although a move into the "Yazoo bottoms" might reinvigorate and expand family fortunes, there were no guarantees in a region where a planter's quest for quick riches always involved considerable risk and uncertainty. In 1854 Andrew J. Polk reported to Paul Cameron on his planting experience in the Delta: "I went there with about six hundred acres of open land and negroes enough to work one thousand acres. That first year we planted 600 in cotton and cleared for the corn. I had a splendid stand and all seemed going on prosperously when about the 25th of May my slaves were attacked with cholera in a most malignant form." This five-week epidemic cost Polk twenty of his valuable slaves and left weeds and grass overgrowing the cotton. The result was a disappointing crop of only 275 bales. The following year a hailstorm totally destroyed the first crop and Polk was able to get only a half-crop replanted.[15]

Bad weather and flooding proved a constant threat to Delta planters. "Backwater" delayed J. W. Fowler's planting in 1847. The first seeds went in on April 28, and the last were not planted until May 20. It was not until February 3, 1848, that the whole crop had been gathered. Fowler speedily began preparations for planting the next year's crop, which also suffered from both high water and a killing frost that came on April 19, 1848.[16]

In October 1858 Everard G. Baker noted that "a bad spell of weather would injure the crop very materially. . . . The planter's bosom is full of solicitudes and foreboding this season of the year with the clouds lowering as they are at present." The Delta's climate presented planters with formidable extremes. In March 1855 Wade Hampton II described the drought conditions in Issaquena County as "truly appaling [*sic*]." In April 1858 Wade Hampton III warned that "if the river does not fall very soon, we shall have the most disastrous freshet ever known in this valley. . . . My plans were in good order and I had hopes of making the best crop I ever have made, but now I fear I will have none."[17]

The accounts for J. W. Fowler's Coahoma County plantation reflect the extent to which the fortunes of the Delta planter were at the mercy of not only weather conditions but volatile cotton prices as well. In 1850 Fowler made only 123 bales, but cotton prices averaged over eleven cents per pound. As a result, he netted $5,839.84 as opposed to the $5,504.53 he cleared the following year, when he made forty-seven more bales but the price was three cents lower. The truly prosperous years, of course, were those when a large yield was accompanied by high prices. In 1856 Fowler produced 304 bales, which brought 11.5 cents per pound, leaving him a net sales income of $16,467.34. This figure was impressive, but the fact that it was approximately 80 percent higher than the income for the preceding and succeeding years illustrates the tremendous annual variations in income among cotton planters in the Delta.[18]

Until all the cotton was picked and sold, many planters had little notion of how well they had fared in any year. In early November 1857, William Worthington wrote his brother at the University of Virginia that "our cotton crops are turning out tolerably well, rather better than we expected." The price of cotton fell, however, from a high of 16.25 cents per pound for early bales to 9.5 cents for later ones. The financial panic of that year temporarily halted sales, but a few days after Christmas, Amanda Worthington wrote her son in Charlottesville that with picking substantially completed and "a goodly number of bales of trashy stuff in the market yet," the family had sold 698 bales for $21,585.23. A few weeks later the verdict was in and somewhat different from William's earlier assessment. Amanda Worthington sent the news northward that "our cotton has fallen far short of what we expected, not much exceeding 1,100 bales on both places and the latter part selling for little or nothing."[19]

The correspondence relating to the financial and planting activities of the W. H. E. Merritt family reveals the high stakes that rode on cotton-planting ventures in the Delta. The family lived in Virginia, and its plantations in the

Delta were operated by the sons of W. H. E. Merritt. With heavy debts to
meet, the Merritts were understandably concerned with large cotton yields.
H. E. Merritt announced plans in February 1857 to leave Vicksburg and travel
up the Yazoo to the plantation "to have everything pushed." "Up there," Merritt explained, "everything depends on energy and good judgment." Hoping to
divest themselves of some of their lands, the Merritts anxiously awaited the
arrival of another Virginian, Philip St. George Cocke, who reportedly had a
hundred thousand dollars to invest in Delta land.[20]

Another acquaintance, Sterling Neblett, was a wealthy planter to whom
the Merritts often went in search of loans. Neblett estimated his 1857 cotton
crop at about twenty-three hundred bales; he had expected three thousand, but
due to bad weather his hands were only able to pick fifteen days in November,
and December proved little better. To make matters worse, the crop had been
very late in maturing. "We have made the largest crop I ever made if we can
save it," he wrote W. H. E. Merritt, "but too late—we have from 140 to 160
acres never picked over and now to pull not pick." Despite Neblett's gargan-
tuan crop, he wound up having to market 286 bales of cotton in a great hurry
to meet expenses.[21]

The quest for riches so intoxicated many Delta planters that they became
all but unmindful of their mounting financial obligations. In 1857 Andrew
Jackson Donelson pronounced his cotton crop "almost a complete failure, not
turning out more than one-third of what we had a right to anticipate in the
beginning of the season." Undaunted, he vowed to plant for five hundred bales
the following year, explaining to his children that, while his Bolivar County
plantation generated "a good deal of debt," it promised to "make you all rich
in a few years if I can pay for it, and improve it properly."[22]

Sterling Neblett complained of a son, to whom he had loaned more than
twenty thousand dollars, who had become "Mississippianized" and "careless
of debt." The financial pressures and responsibility took their toll on young
H. E. Merritt, who complained, "My stay in Mississippi has been the most dis-
agreeable part of my life." Martha Rebecca Blanton worried in 1859 that her
husband, Orville, had "a mania for buying negroes." Having bought seventeen
slaves, Orville set his sights on making a 500-bale cotton crop. "Well, I hope
he may," his wife wrote, "but it makes me feel very poor to go so in debt."
Orville assured her that if conditions did not change, he would soon be free of
debt, and he began to clear new ground in earnest. Two years later Orville made
a 535-bale crop, but by then he was already aiming for 650 bales the following
year. Still, according to his wife, two more such large crops would give them
only "a glimpse of the light of day, but not put us out of debt quite."[23]

After considerable deliberation, Paul Cameron finally purchased land in
the Delta in Tunica County, and in March 1857 he sketched out his plans to
plant a hundred acres in cotton and two hundred in corn, expecting a harvest
of a hundred bales and ten thousand bushels, respectively. He expressed the
hope that his total debt of approximately thirty-one thousand dollars for the

new operation would be paid out by the end of the year. Looking back on his harvest a year later, Cameron was sorely disappointed: "Of corn a plenty is made, of cotton but a little. . . . It will not exceed 35 bales. This is a poor beginning: cotton stalks higher than my head on horseback—late planting—wet season—new land—and early frost caused so short a crop—of pork I shall make a little more than half a supply. So you see that I shall have to draw largely for cash at some other point to supply wants here." Cameron still held property in North Carolina and owned a place in Alabama as well, and his response to his setback was to invest more heavily in his operation by purchasing more mules and transferring more slaves from North Carolina to Mississippi.[24]

In addition to the pressures of financial risk and unpredictability, the Delta's climate was a constant source of concern. In 1833 North Carolinian James H. Ruffin explained why he was avoiding the Delta:

> Well authenticated accounts from the Yazoo concur in representing that whole section of country as very sickly, though it is very productive. . . . The prices of land in the nation vary from 6 to 10$. It is calculated that in the county of Yazoo lying between the Yazoo and Big Black River, the negroes die off every few years, though it is said that in time each hand also makes enough to buy two more in place. This state of things will take place throughout the whole extent of country lying between these two rivers as they both run through a very low flat region, and are subject to frequent floods by which they rise above their banks and spread over an immense quantity of land.

Ruffin described the remainder of Mississippi eastward to the Alabama line as "barren and wholly worthless." To settle outside of the Delta would be to choose, in Ruffin's view, "as poor a region as in North Carolina," while settling in the Yazoo area meant being "liable at any moment to be taken off by diseases of every kind."[25]

Though its overall unhealthiness was probably exaggerated, the Delta's climate did prove a challenge to early immigrants. Perpetual bouts with disease finally forced Methodist circuit rider John G. Jones to give up his Delta ministry. Jones found that in addition to malaria, cholera and typhoid fever raged in the Delta throughout the 1830s. The pioneering Worthington family endeavored each year to spend the weeks from early May to early October in Louisville, Kentucky, visiting kinfolk and escaping the mosquitoes and the heat and humidity. In April 1838 Amanda Worthington informed her Kentucky kin that her family hoped to leave Washington County within the next few weeks. As she looked back on a beautiful spring and a growing crop of cotton, corn, and vegetables, she observed, "This would be the most delightful country in the world if it were not for the months June, July, August, and September." Complaining of mosquitoes that even in April "seem like they would devour us," she reported that her baby, Tom, "rolls on the floor, scratches and screams every evening as if he would go crazy—he is as badly marked as one just recovering from the small-pox." In a short time, Tom would be dead.[26]

A severe epidemic of dysentery struck J. W. Fowler's slaves in June and July 1854. Many required constant attention from a physician, whom Fowler finally paid five hundred dollars after the doctor had agreed to reduce his original bill of seven hundred dollars. The Delta plantation of Everard G. Baker was plagued constantly by both overflows and sickness. Fever hit the Baker family extremely hard in 1860, striking almost every family member, killing Baker's twenty-six-year-old wife and leaving him with six small children. A year later he lost one of those, a daughter, and five years thereafter yet another.[27]

Although many believed it was "almost worth a man's life to cast his lot in the Swamp," for every report of illness and death in the Delta, there were numerous accounts of six-foot cotton and guaranteed riches. William Otey wrote exultantly from his plantation near Yazoo City in 1852: "I have got the best crop I ever saw in my life. The cotton is about as high as my head and opened to the top, it looks like a snowbank, the prettiest site [sic] I ever saw."[28]

In the Mississippi hills, the Oxford *Mercury* accepted at face value the report of a Bolivar County planter that "an acre of ground is just as good for a bale of cotton this year as a six pence is for ginger cake in Bolivar." The *Mercury* noted the story of one planter with sixteen hands who expected to make 250 bales at sixty dollars per bale and calculated that a plantation with a hundred hands might gross ninety thousand dollars. Such a calculation, the writer argued, "will give you some idea of planting cotton in the Mississippi bottoms."[29]

On March 11, 1855, Wade Hampton II had complained of a three-month drought and deemed it "perfectly useless to plant" because "the ground is so perfectly dry." Yet in November, Hampton claimed that his 2,529-acre Walnut Ridge Plantation in Issaquena County was producing more than two bales per acre and described his bountiful crop as "beyond all description." The year 1855 was also a good one for Washington County planter William R. Elly, who averaged 7.5 bales of cotton per hand. In the same year, a Yazoo City planter claimed that his plantation had been averaging a bale per acre and ten bales per hand for several years. In 1856 on Daniel O. Williams's Deer Creek Plantation, forty hands picked 321 bales. In 1859 some Issaquena planters enjoyed even higher yields per hand, and, according to one estimate, in 1860 these planters grossed an average of $350 per slave between the ages of ten and seventy, including house servants and others who seldom worked in the field. During the 1850s the Issaquena plantations of Stephen Duncan yielded more than three thousand bales of cotton annually, bringing in an average net income of approximately $105,000. Paul Cameron's willingness to risk so much on his Delta venture sprang in part from the success of his Tunica County neighbor who repeatedly made ten bales to the hand and had used his profits to purchase two sections of land at thirty dollars per acre. Lands to the south of Cameron were reportedly going in some cases for ninety dollars per acre in 1858.[30]

Such news should have been heartening to Cameron, but the pressures he faced and the risks he took nonetheless weighed heavily on him, as did the isolation and separation from his family that he endured in "the low grounds of sorrow." Noting that "it is a dull life here," Cameron confessed his wish that "my lands in Mississippi and Alabama with the slaves here" were "all in North Carolina 6 percent bonds and I was with my good wife and little ones at my dear old home."[31]

Cameron's homesickness was hardly unusual for a resident of what remained essentially an isolated frontier wilderness throughout the antebellum period. Life was not so dull for everyone, however. The rough-and-tumble existence in frontier Washington County came through in Amanda Worthington's report to her family in Kentucky in 1838. The nearby town of Princeton, she feared, "will be as noted as Sodom or Gomorrah in a little time." It had been only a few days, she explained, since the son of the sheriff and his companion were both killed with a Bowie knife by a third young man "whom they were trying to make drunk by way of a frolic." The young assailant was jailed immediately, but Mrs. Worthington noted that "it has been with the utmost difficulty that his friends have been able to prevent his being hung right up." With election day approaching, however, she anticipated that "there will be a strong enough party to finish him I fear without judge or jury."[32]

Fifteen years later, the Delta seemed to have changed but little. "This is a very civil country," wrote a sarcastic J. F. Griffin from Washington County in 1853. "There has been 5 murders committed within 5 miles of this place within 7 months, no talk of preaching—O yes, the negroes preaches, and some being a dancing [sic] at the same time, in the quarter."[33]

With the Delta still largely an uncleared wilderness, its pioneer residents displayed an absolute passion for hunting. In April 1855 Wade Hampton II reported that hunters from his Issaquena County plantation had killed two bears one day and three more the next. A six-day hunt in November of that same year yielded ten bears. J. F. Griffin complained about the incessant "reigns" in the Delta, but he did delight in telling of "catching 500 pounds of fish per day, when high waters brought 15 to 30 pound buffalo fish" up into the ditches on the plantation. "This is no fish story," Griffin insisted. "We shut up the ditches and ketch [sic] them when we please." Ex-slave Mark Oliver recalled the plentiful game and fish in antebellum Washington County: "The woods was full of game, deer, bears, wild cows, panthers, turkeys, geese, ducks, possums, rabbits, squirrels, birds and everything. . . . Bout the only thing my young master thought about was hunting. When I was big enough, he took me with him. Me and him sure had good times. We has killed turkeys in the new plowed field. The wild cows and deer would come to the houses to get water and it wasn't nothin' to see bears everyday."[34]

In 1850 Alabama-born Amelia Glover assured her fiancé, James L. Alcorn, that she had no qualms about joining him in a log cabin in the "wilds of Coahoma." She reminded him that her parents had begun their marriage in a log cabin. Nonetheless, Amelia had to endure considerable teasing about her impending move to the "Swamps of Mississippi."[35]

After their marriage that same year, Alcorn and his bride left for the Delta accompanied by twenty slaves, a gift from her father. Despite her assurances, Amelia Alcorn did find life in the Delta a genuine challenge. Not long after their marriage, she narrowly escaped drowning when the steamboat carrying her and her husband caught fire. Alcorn saved her life by throwing her overboard and jumping in after her. Amelia could not swim, but Alcorn caught her by the hair and pulled her to some willows to which they clung until rescued.[36]

Amelia's family was comfortably ensconced among Alabama's planting aristocracy, and her marriage to Alcorn marked, as Lillian Pereyra observed, not only "a great social step upward for Alcorn," but a genuine "meeting of the new frontier aristocracy with the older established class which had preceded it by a generation." The couple gradually adjusted to life in a Delta wilderness that had to be cleared and conquered, all the while pursuing an aggressive social life that befitted their status as members of a new regional aristocracy.[37]

The region seemed more suited to the frontiersman than to the planter patrician, but despite the fact that they lived in a largely unconquered wilderness, Delta planters wasted no time in cultivating the airs and lifestyle of an aristocratic leisure class. In March 1857 Martha Rebecca Blanton complained of a "violent cold," which she attributed to living in a house where drying gum planks split, leaving widening cracks "that you could run your hand through." Still, she added that, despite having to subsist on pork, bread, and milk and live "in a sort of shanty," she would be happy if only she could find "a good cook." Slightly more than a week later, however, she had received her new carpet and was already looking forward to moving into a new house scheduled to be completed in June.[38]

An especially revealing description of the antebellum Delta's self-styled aristocracy came from Samuel Worthington, whose family were pioneer settlers of Washington County. In Worthington's words, "a feudal aristocracy reigned supreme" in antebellum Washington County, where there were "practically no poor white people who worked (except the learned professions)" and those who did were "wholly outside the pale of this charmed circle. The Medes and the Persians had no more inexorable law."[39]

According to Worthington, whose father owned thirty-five hundred acres and 182 slaves in 1850, the Delta slavocracy lived "the good life," journeying northward each May to mountain and seaside resorts, accustomed to having "'the pregnant hinges of the knee' bent to them everywhere." These planters returned to the Delta in October, just in time to hunt deer, bear, or even panther. The fall and winter season was a whirl of dinners "to which all their neighbors for miles around were invited."[40]

A similar description of the lifestyle of the Delta's antebellum aristocracy came from planter-politician Walter Sillers, who described the early Delta settlers as "all wealthy, as wealth was rated in that day and age. Better still, they were educated, cultured people, with manners patterned from the English gentlemen . . . whose chief aim was to build up a country worth living in, and to enjoy it to the fullest. . . . Every lady had her carriage and pair of fine horses and coachman at her command; this meant much visiting, many picnics, 'fish frys,' dinner parties, and balls."[41]

Nostalgic recollections of the glorious antebellum years are hardly unusual. They abound in the privately published histories of the poorest red-dirt counties in the South. In the case of the Mississippi Delta, however, the early white settlers did, for the most part, come from at least the middling ranks and above of the society from which they departed. They did generally improve their fortunes within a short period of time so that they were, or at least thought themselves to be, affluent enough to live "the good life" and to amass the material possessions that went with it.

Younger members of the Delta aristocracy gave so many parties that such entertainment was often available several nights a week. These elaborate affairs served to acquaint "eligible" young adults of comparable social standing, and the Delta's gentry thought nothing of a forty-mile roundtrip if a good party awaited them in the middle of it. European travel was also a favorite for wealthy planting families in the Delta. James B. Allen saw to it that his son Charles received part of his schooling in Europe, where Charles traveled widely and from which he made it a point to correspond in French.[42]

Their lifestyles and material wealth seemed to encourage some members of the Delta's plantation elite to indulge in considerable social pretense. Former slave Prince Johnson (a house servant, he was named for Prince Albert) described the family tragedy caused by the haughtiness of his owners, who considered themselves such "quality" folks that they bought up all the neighboring small farms in order to avoid having "poor white trash neighbors." His master and mistress would not allow their daughter to marry the young man of her choosing, and to spite them she ran off with the son of the Irishman who dug all the ditches on the plantation. The result, as described by the ex-slave, was that "Old Miss wouldn't have nothing more to do with her, same as if she wasn't her own child, but I would go over to see her, and carry her milk, and things out of the garden. It was pitiful to see my little miss poor." Ultimately Prince took advantage of his privileged status as a houseboy to at least talk his mistress into giving her exiled daughter a cow.[43]

Given the opportunity, most Delta planters who read Faulkner's *Absalom, Absalom!* would have identified with the aristocratic General Compson rather than the parvenu Thomas Sutpen. Although, like Sutpen, early Delta planters had to carve their estates out of the wilderness, few of them sprang from origins as humble as Sutpen's, and most could claim a greater degree of sophistication and a more polished set of manners. On the other hand, however, as with Sutpen, there was a distinct inclination among Delta planters to rely heavily on ostentatious displays of material wealth as the basis for their claims to superior social standing.[44]

Samuel Worthington's description of the physical possessions of Washington County planters emphasized wealth and conspicuous consumption and suggested as well a people bent on owning and doing what was considered stylish and fashionable in white society at large: "My father's house at Wayside cost him, with the furniture, thirty-five thousand dollars, and the chandeliers some three thousand more." Worthington himself was born in a more humble dwelling, but true to his tendency to equate wealth and physical possessions with social standing, he based his own identity as one "to the manner [sic] born" on the fact that he lived as a child "in the house that had the first brick chimney ever built in Washington County."⁴⁵

In order to document further the advanced state of culture among the planter elite, he pointed out that they owned only the most costly jewelry, tableware, and furniture: "Solid mahogany and rosewood furniture was used generally; I never saw any veneered furniture before the war in the planters' houses. There were pianos in every home, and accomplished musicians and well trained voices were by no means rare. *To show the cultured state of society*, Mrs. Ben Smith of Longwood Plantation had what was considered in that day one of the finest and *most costly* collections of statuary in the United States" (italics mine).⁴⁶

A Choctaw chieftain and the owner of approximately four hundred slaves, Delta planter Greenwood Leflore ordered ten thousand dollars' worth of furnishings from France for a single room in his lavish home, replete with "Louis XIV furniture and clocks and candelabras inlaid with brass and ebony." Elsewhere, Washington County planter Henry Johnson gave his daughter a new house as a wedding present. Construction began in 1855 and was not completed until four years later. Built of bricks made on the place, the house incorporated French, Spanish, and Georgian Colonial styles and featured iron grill work on the balconies of both stories. Its walls were two feet thick, its thirty rooms had ceilings fourteen feet high, and its semicircular parlor projected beyond the front line of the entrance porch. Within the walls were niches appropriate for statuary and "objects [sic] d'art."⁴⁷

Disappointing news did little to temper the affinity of the Worthingtons and other members of the Delta's planter class for high living. In the wake of the panic of 1857 and a disappointing crop, Amanda Worthington complained to her son Albert that she had never "known such tight times about a little money." She then went on to describe a "gorgeous" wedding supper that included "oysters, ice cream and all that sort of thing" and a wedding party that broke up after midnight and left a slightly tipsy Worthington clan to find their way home in a blinding rainstorm. Most got lost, wandered over ditches and levees, and arrived home in the predawn hours "the muddiest folks you ever saw" but otherwise still in high spirits. Albert's mother closed her letter with a good-natured complaint about his brother William, who had just taken an expensive steamboat to New Orleans instead of waiting for a cheaper one and who, despite the family's recent economic setbacks, had taken a large amount of money with him "to spree on." "You know," she wrote, "he is a 'monsus' [monstrous] fellow for that."⁴⁸

J. F. Griffin reported on a grand Fourth of July celebration on the Sunflower River in 1855. Griffin made the thirty-mile trip from Greenville, having heard "there was plenty of white gals over that way." For the first sixteen miles of his journey, Griffin encountered not a single dwelling. When he found a host, however, he found female companionship in the person of his host's daughters: "I tell you I didn't have to be rapped [*sic*] up in a blanket to keep from freezing, you know." Griffin feasted on bear, venison, and other meats and drank his share of Kentucky whiskey and wine (after toasting "a union between the gents of Washington and the young ladies of Sunflower.") A dance ensued, accompanied by "only 10 fiddlers," and Griffin danced "till broad Daylight." Griffin enjoyed Sunflower hospitality for five days before going home reluctantly "for want of clean close" [*sic*].[49]

Recently recovered from a severe case of chills, Martha Rebecca Blanton reported to her parents on a two-night "frolic" held in her new house at Belle Air Plantation near Greenville in 1857. This affair featured dancing until 3:00 a.m. and a feast of oysters, chicken salad, jelly, charlotte, pound cakes, sponge cakes, oranges, apples, nuts, and raisins. The feast, supplemented by a huge batch of eggnog, was provided despite Blanton's intention to be "economical," and her guests "did not seem afraid to eat." This revelry came in the wake of a severe storm that had done considerable damage around Greenville and in the midst of a severe outbreak of influenza that had caused several deaths in the vicinity.[50]

Among many Delta planter families, a casual attitude toward overindulgence in alcohol came with their determined pursuit of the good life. Wade Hampton II noted in January 1855 that he had declined to attend two recent parties at which there had been both dancing and some drinking. Amanda Worthington treated excessive consumption of alcohol matter-of-factly in her correspondence, reporting with amusement on a recent wedding where one of the male attendants "was so drunk when he got there that he could barely stand up." She also noted that George Ward, son of pioneer settler Junius Ward, had married his cousin "Miss Williams" and asked, "Won't she have a jolly time of it unless he quits the bottle?" Another Washington County woman recalled a riotous party where all the young men became intoxicated. When her drunken suitor offered to take her home, she demanded to be accompanied instead by another gentleman, who proved to be even more inebriated than her original escort.[51]

Further evidence of widespread consumption of alcohol among the Delta area's better element appears in the diary of plantation mistress Minerva Cook. A devout Catholic, Mrs. Cook noted in December 1857 the sad case of a Methodist minister's wife whose four sons were "quite dissipated, drunken, good for nothing gamblers, and black legs, unbelievers, perfect infidels." The woes of the minister's wife did not end there, however, for her daughters were also "very fond of their good liquors, wines, brandies, etc." Mrs. Cook professed sympathy for the poor mother but added with pious condescension that Mrs. Ford would not feel so badly "had she have begun with them whyle [*sic*] in early life to love religion, fear God, watched over their morals," and "kept them from bad associates."[52]

As to the rearing of her own children, Mrs. Cook commended herself and her husband, who "assists me in every respect with regards to advice, prayer, or instruction instilled in their minds." She had felt less confident in her husband's parental example a few months earlier when he returned from Vicksburg accompanied by their teenage son and "could not stand strait [sic] he was so tight." Unable to sleep, she pondered "the fate of my beloved husband . . . if he continued in that awful and sinful vice, and the dreadful and horrid example of the father before his dear little sons."[53]

In assessing her husband's weakness for alcohol, Mrs. Cook blamed not his upbringing, as she had with her friend's children, but the society that condoned such behavior: "I do not believe that he would drink much but association is everything. The company he now keeps are all drunkards, the misfortune is they are all called respectable men and shaken hands with by the devout."[54]

Mrs. Cook was also critical of the aversion to labor and the absence of thrift she observed among her status-conscious neighbors. She supervised a regular routine of churning, egg gathering, poultry raising, truck gardening, berry picking, and even hunting that brought in a regular petty-cash income from local sales. She confessed that "anyone to see me and my domestic habits would at once say that I was avaricious and craving after property and love money and riches." Explaining her energy and thrift, she continued: "It is a great mistake I think when any one has property and do not try to increase it. I think it is a great sin and that God will punish us for it. I do not think that we ought to let our property by any means be on a stand because we think we have plenty or because we think our children will squander it." As for her own children, Mrs. Cook announced her intention to "learn them to labor and do every kind of work, it is no degradation but a reconciliation I think and I intend to learn mine to work."[55]

The Delta's reputation as a land where planters generally led a leisurely existence was in sharp contrast to its image as a region where the lot of the slave was an especially hard one. Frederick Law Olmsted felt that slaves generally were forced to "labor harder and more unremittingly" in the southwestern states like Mississippi and Alabama than in the other slave states. Within these states, Olmsted added, "I found the lives and comfort of the negroes, in the rich cotton-planting districts especially, habitually regarded, by all classes, much more from a purely pecuniary point of view than I had ever supposed they could be; and yet that, as property, negro life and negro vigor were generally much less carefully encouraged than I had always before imagined them to be."[56]

A Mississippi planter believed that on the large, expensive estates in the Delta and elsewhere in the Mississippi black belt "everything has to bend, give way to large crops of cotton, land has to be cultivated wet or dry, negroes to work, hot or cold." Certainly, part of the perception that the slave's existence on a Mississippi Delta plantation was a harsh one stemmed from the reality of a heavy and pressurized year-round work schedule. The typically large investment in land and slaves meant that the land had to be cleared, drained, and cultivated as quickly and extensively as possible.[57]

With the later opening date for cotton in the Delta, picking could continue well into January. Once the cotton was picked, there was usually time for a few weeks of clearing, repairing, and ditching before preparations for planting began. On the Newstead Plantation in Washington County in 1858, clearing and burning proceeded at a rapid pace despite the summer's heat and widespread illness among the slaves. On Paul Cameron's Tunica County plantation in 1860, the slaves continued to pick cotton despite the raining and freezing conditions that prevailed in late November. A concerned overseer reported that picking would probably go on until Christmas. On an icy and snowy January day in 1862, Everard G. Baker had his male slaves chopping down cotton stalks while the females cleaned out the bayou.[58]

In the first year of its existence, Panther Burn Plantation was the scene of an ongoing effort to hack cotton fields and corn patches out of forests and swamps. The year 1859 began with the slaves engaged in splitting rails, building quarters, and cutting cane. An expanding slave force spent January and February clearing, cutting, and building, foul weather notwithstanding. On March 28, 1859, the virgin earth of Panther Burn received its first planting of cotton. Planting continued through April and into May, delayed somewhat by spring floods. All the while, cutting and clearing occupied whatever spare minutes or spare hands might be available. Despite a midsummer attack of fever that took many of the hoe hands and plowmen out of the fields, the first year's picking yielded 133 bales of cotton averaging approximately 550 pounds per bale.[59]

On the William Elley Plantation in Washington County, the slave work force labored throughout the winter, clearing new ground, ditching, and splitting rails. As spring approached, plowing began, followed by the planting of corn and cotton. The frenzied pace of cotton picking left the slaves restless and the overseer short-tempered. In a single week in early November, six slaves received whippings, two for fighting, two for "changing their places at the wagons," one for "telling lies," and another for picking "trashy cotton." Whatever slack time afforded itself during the cultivation and harvest of crops was devoted to more clearing and preparation of new ground. Snow or cold was no deterrent, and all work appears to have been pursued at a brisk pace. On "hogkilling" day, December 10, 1855, the slaves had slaughtered thirty-seven hogs by 8:00 a.m. and had finished cutting up and salting the meat by midday.[60]

On Doro, the Charles Clark plantation, the slaves might be given six to ten Saturday afternoons off each year if conditions permitted, but these holidays rarely came during cotton season. Slaves enjoyed little leisure under the supervision of Minerva Cook, who expressed disappointment at the performance of her seamstress Jane for succeeding in washing and ironing only 140 "pairs of clothes" in a three-day span. On another occasion she had Jane punished for ironing only 60 pairs in a two-day span. Pregnant women were far from pampered on the Cook place. Charlotte, a slave woman, was working in the late May heat when she went into labor, gave birth "about a mile from the house, picked it up, climbed a fence, walked up a hill and packed it in her arms, afterbirth and all."[61]

Mrs. Cook described the workday of her house servant Mary in her diary. Mary's first chore was milking fourteen cows. She then cooked breakfast, swept the house, made the beds, dusted, washed the dishes, prepared meals for some of the other servants, nursed her own infant, and, at last, ate breakfast. Immediately thereafter, she cleaned the kitchen, prepared a huge midday meal, washed dishes, cleaned the dining room, washed a large batch of clothes and hung them out, and began preparing supper. After supper she milked for the second time that day, nursed her child, cleaned the kitchen, and retired.[62]

The arduous work routine in combination with the susceptibility of the low-lying Delta to malaria, dysentery, and a host of "fevers" of various strains no doubt contributed to the belief that, as J. H. Ruffin put it, the slaves in the Delta "die off every few years." Charles Sydnor concluded that there was little difference in the black-white life expectancy rate among twenty-year-olds in antebellum Mississippi. Sydnor's failure to consider infant mortality was significant; however, for the state as a whole in 1850 the infant death rate among slaves was more than twice as high as the rate for whites. One critical planter who lived outside the area claimed that slave mortality was much higher in the Delta than elsewhere in the state and estimated that "not one-fourth of the children born are raised" on many of the plantations in the "rich planting portion of Mississippi." J. W. Fowler's journal entries made throughout the 1850s contain numerous references to stillborn infants or the deaths of infants before their first birthdays. In November 1857 Wade Hampton III expressed his pleasure over a good cotton crop at his Washington County plantation, but noted as well that there had been "in all 37 deaths this year" and added, "I am greatly distressed at this mortality." In February 1858 Paul Cameron complained that during the previous year among his slaves "all suffered much from chills," and although there had been no deaths, there had been "only two births in a family of 35!"[63]

Observers generally believed that the lot of the slave was hardest throughout the Delta on large absentee-owned plantations supervised solely by overseers. Sydnor suggested that about half of the plantations with more than fifty slaves that lay along the Mississippi River fell into this category. In 1860, 55 percent of Bolivar County's slaveholders were absentees. Olmsted quoted at length the observations of a small planter in the Delta as reported by the London *Daily News* in 1857. The English traveler who filed the report described his host as "a fast friend of slavery" who nonetheless "drew for my benefit one of the most mournful pictures of a slave's life I have ever met with." According to this man's account of the lives of slaves on large estates, "a vast mass" spent their lives "from the moment they are able to go afield in the picking season till they drop worn out in the grave in incessant labor, in all sorts of weather, at all seasons of the year without any other change or relaxation than is furnished by sickness, without the smallest hope of any improvement either in their condition, in their food, or in their clothing indebted solely to the forbearance of good temper of the overseer for exemption from terrible physical suffering."[64]

Because large and often absentee-owned planting operations were so numerous in the region, the overseer was indeed a crucial figure on Delta plantations. Noting the difference between the master's treatment of the slaves and that afforded them by the overseer, a former slave on a Delta plantation explained: "You know when a man owned you he had to be careful not to kill you or even bruise you, but the poor white overseer didn't own nothing and didn't have anything to loose [*sic*]." Such was apparently the case, for example, with the overseer who threw a fork that lodged in Delia Hill's eye after the young slave fell asleep as she fanned the flies away from him while he ate.[65]

Fearing that an overzealous or cruel overseer might abuse his slaves and neglect his livestock and other property, J. W. Fowler prepared written instructions for the overseers on his Coahoma County lands in 1857. Fowler stressed "health, happiness, good discipline and obedience; good sufficient and comfortable clothing, a sufficiency of good wholesome and nutritious food for both man and beast" as "indispensably necessary for successful planting, as well as for reasonable dividends for the amount of capital invested, without saying anything about the master's duty to his dependents, to himself and his God." He proceeded to instruct his overseers to see first to the health, clothing, religious instruction, and morale of his slaves and threatened dismissal should any slave be abused. Only after outlining these responsibilities and encouraging the overseer to make "(if practical) a sufficient quantity of corn, hay, fodder, meat, potatoes and other vegetables for the consumption of the plantation" did Fowler stress the desirability of producing "as much cotton as can be made by requiring good and reasonable labor of operations and teams."[66]

Another Delta planter saw a good crop in terms of a number of factors such as "hands, breeding women, children, mules, stocks, provisions, farming utensils of all sorts and keeping up land, ditches, fences and etc." Therefore, he wrote, the overseer's object was "not to make a given number of bags of cotton but as many as can be made without losing as much or nearly as much in these particulars as is gained in cotton." As to the punishment of his slaves, the planter wrote, "They must be flogged as seldom as possible yet always when necessary."[67]

In the mind of Daniel O. Williams, humanitarianism and sound management went hand in hand. He urged his son, who managed their Deer Creek Plantation, not to worry about "a few dollars expense in getting garden seed for the negroes. A great deal less meat will do them when they are well suplied [*sic*] with vegetables." Williams's correspondence with his son suggested that other Delta planters or overseers may have been overworking their slaves: "I would feel better satisfied to make 5 bales to the hand under such [humane] treatment than to make 10 bales to the hand under the driving cruel system." On another occasion he urged his son never to "be led astray by reflections of your own, or by the force of bad example to treat your negroes unkindly. They are very ignorant, treacherous, and agravating [sic], thieving and lieing [sic], but they take all the hard work off of you, and deserve kind and humane treatment."[68]

Like their counterparts elsewhere, Mississippi planters expected a great deal for what they paid their overseers. For an annual average salary of approximately $450 plus housing, provisions, and, perhaps, a servant, the overseer was expected to care for, supervise, and discipline the slaves, provide for the livestock, keep up the implements, and produce a bountiful crop of corn and grain as well as cotton.[69]

J. F. Griffin was luckier than most. He signed on as an overseer on a Washington County plantation working fifty-one hands. He received seven hundred dollars in wages and his own horse. He also had the benefit of "old Zack," a driver with fifteen years experience. The land was excellent, some of it recently cleared of cane. Old Zack rang the bell forty-five minutes before dawn each day. Griffin's fire was made for him, his horse saddled, and his boots blacked and standing by the door. The work routine was vigorous: "I tell you things rattles these frosty mornings." Griffin was in the fields from "morning till knight [sic]." The place had ten miles of ditches that had to be maintained, in addition to planting, cultivating, and harvesting the cotton and corn. Griffin's greatest complaint stemmed from the fact that his landlady, her attractive daughters, and sister-in-law would leave the place on May 1 and head for Kentucky for the summer, leaving him as the only white on the place. The co-owner of the plantation was a Kentucky lawyer and legislator who paid only infrequent visits to the Delta.[70]

On an absentee-owned plantation the overseer might well be the only white resident. Although sometimes scorned by the slaves as poor white trash, the overseer was often of yeoman origins. Still, as a domain of large, socially self-conscious planters, the Delta offered him little opportunity for contact with other whites of his class. Planters discouraged fraternization with the area's small marginal, "po-white" population, and the doors of the big house were, for the most part, closed to him socially. Not surprisingly, an overseer on Charles Clark's Doro Plantation wrote in 1861: "I am very lonesome today. I think I shall have to get me a wife and where shall I find her. Ladies seem to be as scarce as chicken teeth in this vicinity."[71]

Under such conditions, it was small wonder that effective overseers were hard to find. No planter in the Delta area was more cognizant of this reality than Charles Allen of Warren County, who hired three overseers between the end of 1859 and the beginning of 1861. One resigned, and he discharged the other two, one for drunkenness and the other for "gross inefficiency." When he engaged "Mr. Beale," a fourth, in August 1861, Allen agreed to pay him fifty dollars per month plus "meat and bread." This was a relatively generous salary by Mississippi standards, but Allen noted that he wanted "a good overseer bad."[72]

Mr. Beale ultimately proved unsatisfactory as well, however; Allen insisted that Beale should be getting forty acres of corn planted per day, but Beale protested that thirty acres was the maximum he could achieve. Allen told Beale that he could be replaced with someone who could get more work out of the slaves, but he confessed to his diary, "Overseers are scarce and I will remain at home, I may get along with him." Mr. Beale's performance improved briefly, but a month later Allen complained that his overseer "does nothing on the plantation without wanting orders" and generally neglected the health of the slaves and the livestock. In essence, Beale proved unsatisfactory because, in Allen's view, he neither drove the slaves hard enough nor saw adequately to their welfare. When Allen discovered eighty-nine pieces of meat missing from the smokehouse, he finally discharged Beale, for letting the "smokehouse leak" and "for his utter incapacity to carry on the place—he not only lacks ability but energy and is perfectly indifferent to the interest of the place."[73]

With so much of their wealth concentrated in their slaves, Delta planters, like their counterparts elsewhere, were understandably concerned about the health and especially the natural increase of their slaves. Hence, if a plantation showed high mortality or low birth rates among the slaves, the planter was certain to inquire as to the causes. On the other hand, however, the Delta planter who made a huge investment in acquiring, clearing, draining, and cultivating his land did so with an eye primarily toward exploiting the remarkable productive potential of the soil. The Delta's unhealthy climate and the strenuous year-round labor demands of its plantations made it a less than optimum location for fostering a high rate of natural increase in one's slaveholdings. Such growth was certainly welcome, but the records and correspondence of Delta planters indicate that large cotton crops were their primary concern.

Financially overextended planters like the Merritt brothers did not hesitate to fire overseers whose crops fell short of expectations. In February 1857 H. E. Merritt explained that he had just dismissed two overseers because he was determined to do something about his "present situation" of indebtedness. "If an overseer will not answer," Merritt wrote, "he must be dismissed." The pious pronouncements of the planter notwithstanding, the self-interested Delta overseer did everything in his power to squeeze every possible bale of cotton out of the plantation and the work force he supervised. His job and his prospects for a bonus or a raise depended almost entirely on the plantation's cotton yield. If the owner was an absentee, the overseer knew full well that his employer would be much more likely to judge him solely on the size of the cotton crop. At the same time, the owner was certain to be less aware of how hard the overseer had to drive the slaves to produce the maximum yield. As one contemporary writer noted, when seeking new positions, overseers made their case by pointing to "the number of bags they have heretofore made to the hand and generally the employer recognizes the justice of such claims."[74]

As a small planter, the Deltan who discussed the overseer's treatment of slaves may have been somewhat biased, but he reasoned that "whether the owner be resident or non-resident, if the plantation be large, and a great number of hands be employed upon it, the overseer gets credit for a large crop, and blamed for a small one." As for the slaves on such a plantation, the overseer's goal was "to get as much work out of them as they can possibly perform. His skill consists in knowing exactly how hard they may be driven without incapacitating them for future exertion. The larger the plantation, the less chance there is, of course, of the owner's softening the rigor of the overseer, or the sternness of discipline by personal interference."[75]

Conditions varied from one plantation to another, but testimony from the WPA slave narratives indicates that the majority of the slaves on Delta plantations worked long, hard hours the year round and enjoyed little relief from the physical rigors and emotional hardships of their condition. Charity Jones's mother and father were sold to separate masters, neither of whom would sell either parent to the other owner. Charity's father died before emancipation would have reunited the family. Slave women on Delta plantations found themselves no less vulnerable to the advances of white men than were their counterparts elsewhere in the South. The pious Minerva Cook noted without comment that one of the slave women on her plantation had given birth in July 1855 to "a fine son of a yellow complexion." Claiming that most of the advances came from owners' overseers and "de outside white folks," Joe Clinton, who had been a slave on a Coahoma County plantation, acknowledged that the masters simply "'lowed it without trying to stop all sich stuff as dat." "Course de wimmens," Clinton explained, "dey just had to put up with it." Noah Rogers, a mulatto, believed his master was his father. As a slave, Rogers was treated much like his playmate, the master's son, who was allowed to teach Rogers to read. When war came, Rogers went along as a body servant to his former playmate and, probably, half-brother. After the war, Rogers actually took into his home and cared for the impoverished and senile master whom he thought to be his father.[76]

Not many such stories had so tender an ending. Ellen Cragin, whose own mother was used as a "breeder," recalled that her master "would have children by a nigger woman and then have them by her daughter." The daughter of her owner, and therefore resented and unwanted by the plantation mistress, Elvira Boles was sold to another man, who fathered her first child. Boles lost another child who died when her owner tried to march his slaves to Texas to evade the Yankees.[77]

Direct, overt resistance to whippings and other forms of punishment was relatively rare, but it did occur, and the rebellious slave achieved permanent heroic status among his or her peers. Cragin recalled that her mother, Luvenia Polk, who worked as a weaver, once fell asleep at her task. When her mistress's son told his mother, he was ordered to whip her. As she awoke to a hail of blows, Luvenia "took a pole out of the loom and beat him nearly to death with it." When her young assailant begged for mercy, she told him, "I'm going to kill you. These black titties sucked you and then you came out here to beat me." Fearing reprisal, Luvenia Polk fled the plantation and did not see her daughter again until "after freedom."[78]

When her grandmother was about to be whipped, Marie Hervey's grandfather "got an ax and told them that if they did he would kill them." "They never could do anything with him," Hervey claimed. Ruben Laird recounted an incident in which an overseer pursued a woman he intended to whip only to have her turn on him with a hoe. The overseer, according to Laird, went directly and resigned his position, telling the owner that the slaves on this particular plantation were "too ambitious" for him to manage.[79]

A more common reaction to punishment and abuse was running away. Susan Jones's brother, Henry, fled after one whipping only to be pursued by the master's coon dogs and recaptured. He was placed in a barrel with a slat nailed over his shoulder and one between his legs. Henry whittled his way out of the barrel, escaped again, suffered another whipping on recapture, but then escaped for good by making his way to some nearby Union troops.[80]

Despite the assertions of many whites that they held the undying affection and trust of their slaves, blacks on Delta plantations created and sustained a separate community that functioned, insofar as possible, as a cushion against the potentially devastating impact of slavery. Slaves warned each other of the master's or the overseer's approach. Of necessity, they often worshipped and learned to read in secret and stole from the smokehouse or the corn crib when the occasion arose. Delia Hill remembered being sent to church services where the preacher urged her and her fellow slaves to inform upon each other for thievery and other offenses and to provide whites with other details of life in the quarters. Delia and her peers ignored this admonition, however, "'cause, honey, if we did de niggah get a killin', and our mammy tie up our feet and hang us upside down by our feet, build a fire under us and smoke us, scare us plum to death. We swear mammy goin' to burn us up. Lord, child, dat was an awful scare."[81]

Although Delta slaves were sustained emotionally by a strong sense of community, their physical comfort and security lay wholly in the hands of their white owners and overseers. On the other hand, however, nowhere in the antebellum South was white dependence on their black laborers greater than in the Mississippi Delta. In order to illustrate the humble origins of the antebellum South's "ruling class," Wilbur J. Cash told the story of a "stout young Irishman" (perhaps Cash's great-grandfather) who came to the South Carolina up-country around 1800. In the beginning, the ambitious pioneer owned no slaves, but through backbreaking day and night toil, he managed to hack a plantation out of the wilderness. He accumulated a slave force, built a rude, boxlike big house, sent his sons to college, and died "a gentleman of the old school" and "a noble specimen of the chivalry at its best," leaving an estate that included "two thousand acres, a hundred and fourteen slaves, and four cotton gins."[82]

Cash's parable may have been applicable to the slave society of the Carolinas and Georgia and even some portions of Alabama and Mississippi, but the Delta was another story. On the one hand, the Mississippi Delta seemed in every respect a cotton planter's wildest fantasy fulfilled. Its self-replenishing alluvial earth promised bountiful crops without fear of the soil depletion that was becoming common throughout the eastern cotton belt. Yet, although it presented potential settlers with even greater opportunities for quick wealth, its physical challenges were also more formidable. The enormous task of clearing and draining the Delta wilderness, in addition to the cost of acquiring the land, was simply beyond the resources of those without substantial slaveholdings. As a result, if the slave society of the older southern states sprang from a frontier where opportunity abounded for any white farmer with sufficient energy and ambition, the antebellum Delta offered a frontier that was far less economically "democratic" or socially fluid, one whose massive cotton yields and rapidly accumulating riches seemed reserved primarily for those—including, perhaps, the sons of Cash's Irishman—who already possessed not just the financial resources (and the nerve to risk them on an annual basis) but the sizable slave labor force needed to clear, maintain, and operate a plantation under physically demanding and disadvantageous circumstances.

By the middle of the nineteenth century, the Delta had already assumed an enduring identity as a region where a wealthy, pleasure-seeking, and status-conscious white elite exploited the labor of a large and thoroughly subjugated black majority. The planter's grip on both the economy and the society of the Delta seemed completely secure in 1850. Yet, from the earliest days of the region's settlement and for well over a century thereafter, regardless of how affluent they became, Delta planters never lost sight of the fact that their capacity to harness and maximize the wealth-producing potential of their land—and, hence, their freedom to indulge their legendary addiction to material finery and high living—was wholly dependent on their success in retaining and controlling a large supply of black labor.

2 ▽ "The Stern Realities
▽ of War"
▽

As its plantation economy boomed in the 1850s, the Yazoo Delta seemed to offer nothing less than the answer to a cotton planter's prayers. Its self-replenishing soils could never be worn out, and its year-round work demands made it the ideal environment for the maximum exploitation of slave labor. Near the end of the 1850s, the state geologist of Mississippi predicted that within a century "whatever the Delta of the Nile may once have been, will only be a shadow of what the alluvial plain of the Mississippi will then be. It will be the central point—the garden spot of the North American continent—where wealth and prosperity culminate." Such optimism flowed not only from the proven fertility of Delta cotton land—described by a correspondent for *Debow's Review* as "the best land which our globe is able to produce"—but from an apparent breakthrough in efforts to establish an effective, centralized system of flood control that would give more protection against the annual overflows that had so often destroyed cotton crops and frightened away potential investors and settlers in years past. In 1858 the General Levee Board was established and charged with directing and coordinating the construction of 262 miles of levees at an estimated cost of $6.25 million.[1]

These higher levees would almost certainly subject the other side of the river with its lower banks and sizable tributaries to catastrophic flooding, but one Delta planter estimated in 1858 that a good flood-control system could bring local property values in the basin up to an aggregate total of approximately $150 million over the next decade. As to the consequences for those on the Arkansas side, he wrote: "If both sides of the river cannot be leveed, then we must protect ourselves, and let our neighbors in Arkansas suffer." This obsession with personal and regional self-interest, which would characterize Delta planters for more than a century, was rooted in the Delta's dramatic emergence in the 1850s as a region whose wealth-producing potential appeared to know no limits.[2]

As Table 1 shows, both the slave and white population of the six Delta counties expanded dramatically between 1850 and 1860. Table 2 indicates that

TABLE 1. Population, White and Slave, Yazoo-
Mississippi Delta, 1850-1860

County	White Population		Slave Population	
	1850	1860	1850	1860
Bolivar	395	1,393	2,180	9,078
Coahoma	1,387	1,521	1,391	5,085
Issaquena	366	587	4,105	7,244
Sunflower (est.)	348	1,102	754	3,917
Tunica	396	883	917	3,483
Washington (est.)	546	1,212	7,836	14,467
	3,438	6,698	17,183	30,274
Percent Increase 1850-1860	94.8		76.2	

Source: *Seventh Census of the United States*, vol. 1, *An Appendix Embracing Notes upon the Tables of Each of the States, etc.* (Washington, 1853), 447; *Eighth Census of the United States*, vol. 1, *Population* (Washington, 1864), 270.

average farm real estate values per acre more than tripled in Bolivar, Coahoma, Issaquena, and Tunica counties over the same period. At thirty-four dollars this figure was more than three times as high as the average for fifty-two non-Delta counties in 1860. By 1860 the average value of a farm in Tunica, Coahoma, Bolivar, Washington, and Issaquena counties was in excess of thirty thousand dollars. The number of planters in these counties whose total wealth exceeded one hundred thousand dollars rose from fourteen to eighty-one during the 1850s. Meanwhile, cotton production increased by more than 1,700 percent in Tunica and over 600 percent in Bolivar during the 1850s. At the end of the decade, the Delta counties were averaging 5.7 bales of cotton per hand as compared to the 3.8 bales harvested per hand in the older river counties and the 3.4 bales produced in adjoining counties with less productive soil.[3]

TABLE 2. Average Farm Real Estate Values Per Acre, 1850-1860

County	1850	1860
Bolivar, Coahoma, Issaquena, Tunica*	$11.00	$34.00
Remaining non-Delta counties for which data were available (N = 52)	$ 4.50	$10.20

*Data for Sunflower and Washington counties were not available.
Source: Thomas J. Pressly and William H. Scofield, eds., *Farm Real Estate Values in the United States, 1850–1860* (Seattle, 1965), 54–55.

According to the 1860 census, 18.3 percent of the slaveholders in Bolivar, Coahoma, Issaquena, and Tunica counties owned fifty or more slaves. (Figures for Sunflower and Washington counties were unavailable.) In comparison, across the sixteen slave states an average of only 2.8 percent of the slaveholders owned more than fifty slaves; for the remainder of Mississippi, the figure was 5.0 percent. In the same year, ten of nineteen Mississippi planters who held three hundred slaves or more owned plantations in counties lying wholly or partly in the Delta.[4]

By 1860 mean total wealth per freeman in Bolivar, Coahoma, Issaquena, and Tunica counties was $18,438 as compared to a southwide mean of $4,380. For Issaquena this figure stood at $26,800, making it the second richest county in the nation. All four counties were listed by Lee Soltow among the thirty-six wealthiest in the United States for 1860. These statistics reflected not so much the value of Delta lands, the size of landholdings, or their remarkable productivity, as the value of the slave property held by Delta planters. When Soltow factored out the slave-value component (at nine hundred dollars per slave) and simply computed the wealth per adult male (free or slave), the mean total in the four Delta counties fell to $1,623.[5]

With so much of their wealth concentrated in their slaves and so much of their capital and credit resources invested in clearing and improving their lands, Delta planters had no choice but to temper their optimism with a growing concern as the slavery controversy grew more heated during the 1850s. Reflecting what William L. Barney called "the understandable conservatism of a planter class which supervised one of the greatest concentrations of wealth in the South," many of the Delta's planters first supported Whig party presidential candidates and then joined with various dissident groups in the "American" or "Know Nothing" party as Whig strength declined during the 1850s. As the likelihood of secession grew, a number of Delta leaders expressed grave misgivings about the prospect of leaving the union.[6]

As large slaveholders, Delta planters had a greater stake than most in maintaining the South as what Gavin Wright called "an economic entity unified by the market for slave labor." Certainly, with work proceeding on its levee system and with the influx of settlers in the 1850s, the Delta's economy stood to suffer greatly from any action that might lead to war or disruption of normal commerce. Delta planter William Kirkland warned that in the event of secession, "property, I think, will go down, especially in the South."[7]

Barney identified young, upwardly mobile planters as the most likely advocates of secession in Mississippi. The Delta, on the other hand, was home to a large number of planters whose families had been well established in the planting class before they moved into the Delta. These planters had been well served by the status quo, and for many of them the best hope for maintaining their wealth and status seemed to lie in remaining within the Union and, perhaps, seeking further constitutional guarantees to preserve slavery. From his residence in North Carolina, absentee Delta planter Paul C. Cameron expressed his hope that the South might "attain justice" through "unrepealable provisions of the Constitution." In the election of 1860, the Delta counties of Issaquena, Washington, Bolivar, Coahoma, and Tunica gave the Southern Rights candidate John C. Breckinridge less than 50 percent of their votes. When the elections for the secession convention of 1861 were held, only Issaquena selected a delegation favoring immediate disunion, while the others chose representatives leaning toward secession only in cooperation with the other southern states.[8]

Among the prominent opponents of immediate secession elected to represent Delta counties at the convention were J. Shall Yerger of Washington County and James L. Alcorn of Coahoma. A native of Maryland who owned 101 slaves and twenty thousand dollars in real property in 1850, Yerger pleaded for a final effort through a southern state convention to preserve southern rights short of secession. His own aggregate wealth valued at $250,000 in 1860, Alcorn warned that the wages of secession might be subjugation. He foresaw a South with its cotton fields trampled by northern soldiers and a future "when the slave should be made free and the proud southerner stricken to dust in his presence." Alcorn actually voted against Yerger's proposal for a southern convention, apparently hoping to win the confidence of the less committed disunionists and secure their support for an amendment delaying secession until Alabama, Georgia, Florida, and Louisiana had seceded. This amendment failed, however, as did an attempt by a delegate from Warren County to subject any ordinance of secession to popular ratification. At that point, Alcorn spun on his heels to cast the first vote in favor of secession, playing to a packed, pro-secession gallery with his emotional announcement that "the die is cast; the Rubicon is crossed; I follow the army that goes to Rome."[9]

Agreeing with Alcorn, another Deltan observed in the wake of the passage of the ordinance that there was "now no choice." Remaining in the Union would be "as great an evil as to secede from it." By his own account, Alcorn had hoped that by ingratiating himself with the secessionists, he would be in a position to lead the state back into the union should cooler heads ultimately prevail. With the attack on Fort Sumter, however, this slim likelihood disappeared entirely, and Alcorn, like most other Deltans who had expressed their reservations, accepted the inevitability of armed conflict.[10]

Across the Delta, local companies were raised, drilling began, and, in the words of a Washington County matron, "business was almost forgotten, every nerve was strained to the utmost, waiting. . . . Women whose hands had known no heavier work than some dainty trifles blistered their fingers making tents and haversacks. We knitted socks and comforters, and made clothes for the soldiers."[11]

One of these sewing sessions provided the backdrop for a scene worthy of inclusion in *Gone with the Wind*. As the young ladies sat making a tent, a young enlistee burst in to announce: "We have orders to march; we leave in the morning." He exchanged glances with one of the seamstresses, and the two disappeared briefly, returning to announce that they would be married that evening. The sewing circle broke up and wedding preparations began. Caught up in the excitement, another couple decided to marry. The next day, the two bridegrooms boarded a steamboat for Memphis, one of them never to return. About a year later, a young diarist reported that "there are only two young men left in our neighborhood now and one of them, Dr. Smith, is lame and can't well go; the other is Mr. Meriweather who ought to be thrashed and made to leave."[12]

When the Union commanders decided to emphasize the strategic importance of the Mississippi River, the Yazoo Delta found itself on the front lines of the Confederacy. Still largely a frontier wilderness, the Delta presented a formidable physical challenge to both its invaders and its defenders. Shelby Foote described the Delta in 1862 as "nearly roadless throughout its flat and swampy expanse, subject to floods in all but the driest seasons, and—except for the presence of a scattering of pioneers who risked its malarial and intestinal disorders for the sake of the richness of its forty-foot topsoil—was the exclusive domain of moccasins, bears, alligators, and panthers. It was, in short, impenetrable to all but the smallest of military parties engaged in the briefest of forays. An army attempting to march across or through it would come out at the other end considerably reduced in numbers and fit for nothing more strenuous than a six-month rest, with quinine as the principal item on its diet."[13]

Confederate General Samuel Wragg Ferguson testified from unpleasant experience to the difficulties of moving troops through the Delta and to the general unhealthiness of the climate: "The pull through the mud of the swamp was a hard one, the wheels crushed thousands of crayfish, left in puddles and in the puddles could be seen many large rusty moccasin [*sic*] snakes, attracted by the fish." Having been "exposed to the worst malarial influences," Ferguson was soon battling "a severe and protracted case of bilious dysentery" and the "first attack of fever I can remember to have had."[14]

When New Orleans and Memphis fell to Union gunboats in the spring and early summer of 1862, the only significant obstacle remaining to their free run of the Mississippi River was the strategically crucial city of Vicksburg. It was the Delta's location as the hinterland of Vicksburg that would bring the tangible reality of the war home to the Old South's last plantation frontier. Union gunboats, with virtual free run of the river north and south of Vicksburg, were a common sight on the Mississippi by the summer of 1862. After Memphis fell into federal hands in early June 1862, residents of the northernmost Delta counties existed, according to one Greenvillian,

> in a state of intense anxiety and suspense. Each day there was circulated some rumor of the approach of the enemy. Sometimes they were reported a few miles up the river, again, the smoke of the gunboats had been seen just around the bend, and they would be on us directly. These cries of "wolf" eventually induced a cer-

tain complacency until "Boom! Boom! Boom!" the earth seemed to quake as to our terrified ears the sound reverberated from every quarter of the universe. . . . It is useless to tell you how frightened we really were. The gunboats had really come. We flew to our homes, hitched up every available vehicle, to make what we believed to be a race for life.

Fleeing in her carriage with her children, this Greenville matron encountered her minister and an old planter on horseback headed for a patch of woods from which to observe the gunboats. In a short while, this once-bold pair flew back past her, Yankees in hot pursuit. When the preacher passed her she noted, "His pants had worked up nearly to his knees, his hat was gone, and he was a most unclerical looking person." Eventually, the Yankees withdrew, only to return and withdraw on numerous other occasions. Stragglers and unsupervised troops were a recurrent threat, however, and the riverfront areas of the Delta were never far from being an occupied territory.[16]

By early December 1862, Union troops were burning plantations, gins, farms, and slave cabins in Coahoma County. Every home in the tiny town of Delta was torched. James L. Alcorn reported that the Yankees had not only broken up all of a neighbor's fine furniture and thrown it in the yard but had stolen ten thousand dollars from the house and killed most of the stock on the plantation as well. With Confederate troops under orders to destroy all cotton likely to fall into Union hands and inclined on occasion to torch not only the cotton but the gins and warehouses that held it, planters at times found it difficult to distinguish friend from foe. One plantation mistress expressed dismay that "the Yankees are right in the midst of us, when we thought ourselves very secure." She voiced the fear as well that "our own soldiers will eat us out of house and home while they are camped so near."[17]

In late December 1862, Everard G. Baker was arrested by Union troops and held for several days. In his absence federal troops took off three fine horses valued at a thousand dollars, while the Confederates had burned all of his cotton held over from the previous year as well as most of his 1862 harvest. To make matters worse, Baker fell ill after his release and spent ten days in bed. He faced a "dull gloomy Christmas" in 1862 as he saw his country "overrunning and ruin and want staring us in the face."[18]

Baker's experience was repeated time and again. J. W. Fowler of Coahoma County kept meticulous records of his losses at the hands of federal troops. On August 14, 1862, he charged up $29,162 for cotton lost at fifty cents per pound. Fowler also added, for good measure, $500 for "perishable property taken and wanton damage." By 1864 he was losing slaves as well as livestock and equipment. Yet Fowler continued stubbornly to record every loss, including that of seven turkeys, which he valued at two cents each. By the end of the war, his figures showed that the Federals "owed" him $73,788.09. Until the fall of a besieged Vicksburg on July 4, 1863, the Delta continued to be the scene of chaotic skirmishing, foraging, and property destruction as Union troops were employed to draw Confederate troops away from the defense of Vicksburg and to cut the city off from its hinterland.[19]

Union vessels traversing the Delta's serpentine waterways usually did so tentatively, subject to snags, low-hanging branches, and rapid changes in water levels. Gunboats operating from the Mississippi could shell towns, landings, or plantations, but inland they more often simply carried detachments of troops who scoured the surrounding countryside, burning what cotton the Confederates had not burned themselves and seizing whatever livestock, provisions, or other property met their needs or struck their fancy.[20]

Washington County proved to be a persistent source of aggravation to Union forces. Snipers consistently harassed gunboats on the river, and Confederate forces rematerialized whenever Yankee troops were withdrawn. In retaliation, General William T. Sherman made Washington County one of the war's earliest victims of his scorched-earth approach to warfare. In his orders he noted that "Greenville has been a favorite point from which to assail our gunboats and one object of your expedition is to let the planters and inhabitants . . . see and feel that they will be held accountable for the acts of guerrillas and Confederate soldiers who sojourn in their county." Union soldiers seized even more stock and took what slaves they could with them, eventually organizing a black regiment numbering about five hundred. Writing from Greenville, R. L. Dixon reported in March 1863 that the area was overrun with two thousand troops "committing depredations." Washington County lost its strategic importance with the fall of Vicksburg, but on August 23, 1863, a recalcitrant sniper who fired on a gunboat finally brought the full wrath of the Union forces down on the city of Greenville itself, and all but two of the town's houses and buildings were burned to the ground.[21]

With so many white men away at war, the women of the Delta's planter families assumed responsibility for managing plantations, maintaining control of their slaves, and dealing with numerous unwelcome Yankee visitors. While her husband was serving the Confederate cause in Virginia, Mildred Humphreys ran the family plantation on Roebuck Lake. In February 1863 she warned her husband that federal troops might soon be in the area in numbers sufficient to "devastate the whole country." She promised her husband that "if they come to Roebuck Lake, they will be sure to find me at home. I think my presence may check them in the destruction of property. I will have the meat, hogs, and cattle taken to the woods and put in houses or pens and watched day and night." As she prepared for the Yankee onslaught, Humphreys ran the plantation with a determination to maintain business as usual. She supervised the planting of 200 acres of cotton and the clearing of 350 acres of new ground. She oversaw as well the construction of fences to prevent the loss of cattle and the spinning of yarn into fabric to be used to clothe the slaves. Humphreys struck a deal with a cobbler to trade him cowhides for shoes, and, anticipating the destruction of her crops, she planned to stockpile a large reserve of corn. Within a short time, she was supplying a hundred bushels of meal to the Confederates per day, and she readily donated every cotton bale on the place to serve as the foundation for the breastworks at Fort Pemberton.[22]

When Union soldiers did threaten the plantation, it fell to the plantation mistress to defend the family's property however she could. Louisa McGhee Burrus did her best to prevent Yankee troops from taking her cattle and finally pleaded with their commanding officer "to leave one cow for the sake of the children," only to be told, "Madam, my orders are to take all."[23] In retaliation for the burning of a Union gunboat, Yankee troops torched the Bolivar County home of Major W. E. Montgomery, son-in-law of Confederate general and future governor of Mississippi Charles Clark. The ranking Union officer had orders not to destroy any of General Clark's belongings and gave Mrs. Montgomery forty-five minutes to empty the house. Reinforced by the arrival of her aunt, Matilda Sillers, matriarch of the Sillers clan, Mary Delia Montgomery succeeded in enlisting the aid of her adversaries in emptying the house even down to the piano, the carpets, and the trunk where the silver was hidden. Her charm failed her, however, as she entreated the commander not to destroy the family's food pantry, and as she and her children continued to retrieve belongings amid the smoke, the soldiers set fire to the house. Mrs. Montgomery managed to save the smokehouse and loom house, where the family established a temporary residence. Years later, Walter Sillers, who as a ten-year-old observed the torching of the Montgomery house, reflected on the event with the observation that "not often did our ladies give vent to their indignation over the actions of the federals, but during the burning of this home the faces of my mother and cousin showed such anger and scorn as to deeply impress me, a boy of ten years." As a footnote to the story, the music-loving Mrs. Sillers, at whose behest Mrs. Montgomery's piano had been saved, had that very day dispatched three men on a flatboat to the home of a neighbor to fetch a borrowed piano back to her place. Unfortunately, Yankee soldiers intercepted this would-be cultural mission, set the flatboat on fire, and demolished her piano.[24]

Mrs. Sillers led her own family to an abandoned interior plantation, hid what little she could in the woods, and generally "made do" with what she had. With powder at twenty dollars per pound, ammunition was scavenged from unexploded shells at no little peril to the scavenger. The family survived on sorghum molasses, sweet potatoes, and corn bread along with meat from livestock herded into the woods. Mrs. Sillers supervised the slave women in spinning some of their hoarded cotton into clothing material dyed with maple bark. She even succeeded in spinning the thread, weaving and dying the cloth, and making her husband the grey shirt he was wearing when captured. News of this capture led Sillers and her children to attempt to see their husband and father before he was transported north, but they arrived just as the transport sailed. Sillers never saw her husband after his capture, learned how he died, or located his grave.[25]

Lettie Vick Downs began hearing rumors of Yankee troops near her Deer Creek home as early as March 1863. As the siege of Vicksburg intensified, the

Union presence in the area became even more pronounced, and she and her family fled to the interior of the Delta on a flatboat. Troops took all but the oldest slaves, torched her home, and tore her carpets into saddle blankets. "I wonder," she confided to her diary, "if the Yankees would feel complimented if they knew what low estimate was placed on their character (if they have any and I think it doubtful) by the ladies of the South."[26]

Mrs. Downs and her family were soon beset by rumors of Yankee-incited blacks roaming about the country murdering and raping as they pleased. She wondered how southern whites could ever forgive "a people who instigate a race that have been raised and cared for as children to rise and slay their owners in cold blood." She was even more distressed when Union troops visited her father's home and "suffered a negro to threaten his life and insult him as he never was before." Mrs. Downs finally made her way to Kentucky as 1863 came to an end, but reflecting on the war's effect on her, she noted that she felt far older than her twenty-three years: "My afflictions and anxiety of mind have left their traces on my brow. Trouble has added many years to my feelings and the Spring of youth has passed, never to be recalled."[27]

For all the distress suffered by Delta whites, the physical hardships caused by the war often fell most heavily on the slaves. Ruben Laird remembered that when local planters fed Confederate troops and clogged the river with trees to impede Yankee pursuit, the Federals retaliated by raiding the slave quarters where he lived and eating or destroying all the food they could. As a result, Laird and the other slaves had nothing to eat but peas, which they eventually even ground into flour to use in making bread. Henrietta Gooch recalled the Yankees coming to burn the cotton and take all the meat on the plantation. Lizzie Dunn remembered that although the Yankees treated her white folks politely, "they et them out time and again." Elvira Collins never forgot that a Yankee soldier used his sword to decapitate her pet rooster.[28]

Anxious to avoid such losses and none too keen about secession in the beginning, James L. Alcorn wrote his wife that he had made many "agreeable acquaintances" among "the Feds," with whom he had carried on a flourishing illicit trade in cotton. In late November 1862 he reported that he had sold eighty bales for more than twelve thousand dollars and hoped to sell an additional hundred bales worth fifteen thousand dollars more. Alcorn received his payments in greenbacks, with which he hoped he could buy "in Memphis, Confederate money by the sacks full at from thirty to forty cents on the dollar." A few weeks later, he reported that he had sold fifteen bales for thirty-two hundred dollars and that he now held ten thousand dollars in greenbacks and another thousand in gold. Alcorn estimated that if he could prevent the Confederates from burning his cotton, he would probably receive an additional twenty thousand dollars. He also predicted that if things went his way he could, within the space of five years, "make a larger fortune than ever."[29]

The fact that Alcorn's daughters by his first wife were able to go on a two-week, fifteen-hundred-dollar shopping spree in the spring of 1864 suggested that he was not suffering financially, as did his habit of sending money to his beloved Amelia, who had removed to Alabama during the war. Alcorn's repeated assurances that he would not allow his wife to fall below her accustomed station in life may explain his motive for dealing in contraband, but he was by no means a lone smuggler. Delta planters faced a choice between selling their cotton illegally and having it confiscated by the Federals or burned by the Confederates. It was small wonder, then, that Alcorn could report to his wife on a scene on the riverbank "when nearly four hundred bales of cotton were openly sold and fully fifty men on the bank participating." "You remember how they once talked," a cynical Alcorn recalled. "It would astonish you to witness the reaction. The authorities out in the hills, I am told, are furious." As time passed and conditions in the Delta became more desperate, would-be smugglers often ran afoul of ruthless Confederate guerrillas who made a practice of preying on smugglers and demanding a bribe in exchange for allowing the citizen to continue his forbidden commerce. Still, selling cotton to the Yankees became so commonplace that one observer estimated as of March 1864 that as many as five hundred bales of cotton per day were passing through Vicksburg, coming out of the Delta via the Yazoo River.[30]

Many Deltans may have been reduced to smuggling only by the desperate circumstances into which they fell by the end of the war. Yet the level of smuggling activity documented in the region while the conflict was still relatively young reflected not only the initial misgivings of many Delta planters about secession but a proclivity for independent, self-interested behavior that would characterize the region's white elite in the decades that followed. In 1863 J. D. B. Debow, acting as special agent for the Confederate Congress, travelled through the Delta to investigate charges of cotton smuggling and unwarranted destruction of cotton by Confederate troops. With so many federal greenbacks flowing into the Delta, Debow could not secure transportation through the area with Confederate currency and had to resort instead to bartering for it with sugar and salt.[31]

Although smuggling and consorting with guerrillas sustained a few Delta planters, for most the wartime experience was a classic example of going quickly from good to bad to worse. As Christmas neared in 1863, Washington County matron Myra Smith reflected on the rapid decline in her fortunes: "When the year 1863 entered, I was a happy wife with an abundant home; its close finds me a houseless, homeless widow with an afflicted family." At the end of the war, Smith summarized the war's result as "defeat and bankruptcy to very many, we among the number. Our home is burned, our property gone, scattered to the winds."[32]

Sixteen-year-old Amanda Worthington kept a diary that reflected the South's failing fortunes during the war and her bitterness toward the Yankees, first as distant enemies, then as invaders, and finally as the slayers of her brother Albert. She noted on February 25, 1862, that "our people are having a dreadful time now, we have been defeated in six successive battles. Everybody has the blues and feels out of heart." On December 6 the war become even more of a reality for Amanda. She noted the presence of a great many Confederate soldiers but obviously felt threatened by the Yankee gunboats, which moved "up and down our dear river displaying the hated flag of the Union with enough impudence to provoke a saint almost. I have seen several of them and it does make me mad whenever I do, to think of the invaders being on our river unmolested."[33]

By the following April, Yankee soldiers were frequent visitors to the Worthington Place. One such visitor requested a song, and an enraged Amanda complied most reluctantly: "I marched myself in never even speaking to the man and seated myself at the piano; my face was burning like fire and I was so agitated and mad that I could hardly sing." A few days later, about fifteen Union soldiers returned, gathering up 160 Worthington slaves and the livestock and leaving but one blind mule for her father to ride. The sight of the elder Samuel Worthington, described by his son as a man "whose pleasant lot had ever been to command and be obeyed," on a blind mule and his subsequent arrest by the Yankees led Amanda to express her "bitter hatred" toward them. The loss of the servants was especially painful to Amanda, who grieved "that my dear father and mother should be deprived of every luxury and almost every necessity of life." Amanda was also horrified that because of the departure of their house servants, her cousins Sallie and Mary "have had to cook for the last day or two!! I think that's coming down to the stern realities of war sure enough."[34]

The realities of war became considerably sterner when Amanda's brother Albert came home on furlough. When a slave warned of approaching Yankee soldiers, Albert fled through the back pasture only to have his escape announced by the family's hunting dogs, who took out after him in full cry. A rifleman brought down young Worthington with a single shot, and the wounded young man's mother and brother arrived in time to hear one of the soldiers urge the man who fired to "beat the rebel's brains out with your gun before the lieutenant comes up. It will never do to let him hear you say you shot him after he surrendered." They threw themselves across the wounded Albert to shield him, but they succeeded only in postponing the inevitable. Nearly fifty years later Samuel Worthington still remembered the incident vividly, explaining that "it would be impossible, even if desirable, to describe my brother Albert's suffering, and death a few hours later, and the bitter grief of the family." Worthington cited this incident as but one example of the extent to which "the planters and their families were made to drink the cup of bitterness to its very dregs."[35]

In addition to the insults, indignities, and personal tragedies brought on by the war, the greatest blow to the material fortunes of Delta planters came with the demise of slavery, the fabric of which deteriorated rapidly under wartime conditions. On January 29, 1862, sixteen slaves rebelled against the overseer and quit Charles Clark's Doro Plantation. By the end of 1862, James L. Alcorn and his neighbors were already losing their slaves in great numbers.

Several of these wound up across the river in federally occupied Helena, Arkansas, where they regularly confronted their former owners but showed no inclination to rejoin them. On December 18, 1862, Alcorn expressed pleasure that none of his slaves had run away recently, although he noted that only ten days had passed since he had been forced to administer a whipping to several of them. In general, however, Alcorn felt that even at this early stage of the war blacks in Coahoma County had become "thoroughly demoralized" and were "no longer of any practical value to this vicinity."[36]

Virginia Harris claimed that the Yankees carried off her father, while her sister fled to a refugee camp. On one of the many sojourns by Union troops in his neighborhood, one of Letha Taylor Meek's fellow slaves took her owner's carriage and two mules and escaped with three female companions to Memphis. When Union troops sacked the plantation where R. H. Howard lived, the slaves cooperated by running off the livestock. On the Burrus Plantation, the stockman rounded up the cattle for the Yankees. Elsewhere, Mildred Humphreys realized that she not only had to hide her animals but her slaves as well; otherwise, the slaves were certain to reveal the place where the livestock had been taken. Walter Sillers admitted that all but twenty of his father's slaves "fled to freedom" before the war's end.[37]

In January 1864 Wade Hampton III warned that "no Negroes should be left near the river, as they act as spies for the Yankees." In June 1864 a slave directed federal troops to two Delta plantation homes where Confederate officers were staying. After the Confederates had been rounded up, the Union commander learned that local blacks had known of the Union movement into the area for some time but had deliberately withheld the information from local whites.[38]

When the Union soldiers set fire to Mary Delia Montgomery's smokehouse, she succeeded in putting out the fire but received little help from her slaves, most of whom "seemed paralyzed." Her slaves also took "as much as they were able" from the piles of clothing and other material hurriedly removed before the Montgomery home was burned. In order to recover these purloined goods, Mrs. Montgomery called on the "few remaining white men" in the neighborhood to assist her in a search of the slave cabins. The search turned up a large number of items, "toys and foolish trinkets as well as articles of value." "Aunt Hannah," one of the oldest of the slaves, claimed to be bedridden with illness. She cried that she had belonged to Mrs. Montgomery's mother and expressed dismay that she, of all people, was under suspicion. Yet a curious lump in her mattress yielded "a butter dish, a silver goblet, handsome dresses and so forth." All over the plantation "along the bank of the Bogue, under logs, and covered up with brush was hastily hidden plunder."[39]

Realizing the threat that the Yankees posed to their control over their slaves, many masters hid their slaves or evacuated them. Adeline Hodge remembered that after her owner left for the war "de nigger drivers an' o'seer began to drive us round like droves ob cattle. Every time dey hyar dat de Yankees war cuming dey would take us out in de woods an hide us." Finally, the slaves were marched to Demopolis, Alabama, and sold. Families were torn apart, and Hodge told her interviewer, " I don't know any more whar my own folks went to den you does."[40]

Milly Henry's owner told his slaves: "De Yankees am a comin' to take my slave 'way frum me 'n I don't 'pose dat dey am gwine ter do dat. Fer dem reasons we leaves for North Carolina 'day att termorrer an' I ain't gwine ter hyar no jaw 'bout hit." With that he picked out about five hundred of his slaves to make the trip, separating Milly from her grandmother, whom he left because "she am so old 'n feeble." "I hates dat," said Milly, "but I don't say nothin' at all." Many slaves did refuse to cooperate with efforts to evacuate them. One Delta planter claimed in November 1863 that every planter who tried to move his slaves "lost nearly if not all the men and many of the women and children." As for his own slaves, the planter wrote, "I believe every Negro on this place will go to the Yankees before they go to the hills."[41]

When the slaves on the plantation where Charity Jones lived learned they were free, they "got together and laughed and sang and danced all night rejoicing." Mark Oliver remembered a similar celebration: "They jumped and hollered and carried on something terrible. The boys in blue came by to excite them more." Ellen Cragin recalled her elderly aunt, Nancy, who refused to work and was forced to spend her days seated on an ant-infested log. On the day when the slaves learned they were free, however, the old woman leapt off her log and ran about the plantation "shouting and hollering." According to Cragin's account, the slaves understood her actions immediately: "The people all said, 'Nancy's free; they ain't no ants biting her today.'" The reality of emancipation was not so pleasant for the former owners, like Cindy Anderson's "Marster Cain," who "came stompin' around cussin' an' tol us to git out."[42]

Although he apparently told them nothing, the blacks on William Cooper's plantation clearly knew of the war's end. Many of them refused to work, and others left at the first opportunity. From fighting and bickering among themselves, they moved to open defiance and flight. Cooper noted on May 16, 1865, that "Old Mary, Ann, and Billie were demoralizing all the slaves they could." A short time later, he was denouncing a "dirty little chicken-thieving boatman" who had tried to lure away some of his "darkey girls." A week later he noted that "Ruth declines to plow" under the advice of Charlie, who had refused to work for a week. By mid-July Cooper was lamenting the departure of two men and two women who "left in the night about 10 pm," on July 16, 1865.[43]

By way of contrast, many former slaves reached by WPA interviewers indicated that they did not learn about freedom for some time. One ex-slave in Bolivar County claimed that some blacks had been legally free for three years before they discovered it, and Ruben Fox of Coahoma County insisted that it was nearly four years after the war before he and his fellow slaves heard about it. Needham Love recalled bitterly that he worked incessantly to cut trees and cane on his master's new plantation near the Tallahatchie River and that most of his toil had taken place after he was actually a free man.[44]

In addition to their slave property, Delta planters lost legal and social status as well. Well before the end of the war itself, the once-dominant planters in the Delta found themselves in the unfamiliar role of semi-subjugation to military authority. In their new circumstances, they often found that their former habits of command now counted for little and that what they had thought was genuine deference and respect from the slaves had vanished, often to be replaced by defiance and open contempt.

When A. G. Paxton returned to his plantation near Greenville at the end of the war, he ordered former slave Israel Gillespie to spread out recently picked cotton to dry. Gillespie replied: "Mr. Paxton, I want to tell you that the thing is played out." Paxton said nothing but "went back to the house and reflected on Israel Gillespie's speech and all that it implied." James L. Alcorn reported gleefully the capture of the "old Scamp Gipson," a Confederate lieutenant who had once spied on Alcorn. Gipson hid in an old hollow stump, only to be discovered by a black soldier who ordered him to "come outen dis hole you damn old secesh son of a bitch." A number of Alcorn's neighbors were taken prisoner, including "Fowler" (perhaps J. W. Fowler), who was charged with threatening to shoot one of his departing slaves. When Fowler denied the charge, the Union commandant informed him that the United States government regarded him as "meaner, lower, and more contemptible than the most villainous negro in the State of Mississippi, and there is no negro however low whose word would not be preferred to yours."[45]

A number of other Delta planters wound up, at least temporarily, as prisoners, while their slaves went free. Alcorn recounted the story of a fellow planter who addressed a former slave as "uncle" only to have the man curse him and tell him that he did not allow such men to claim kinship with him. As the planter moved out of earshot, he exclaimed loudly, "Oh my God! How long before my a———will be kicked by every negro that meets me?" A sarcastic Alcorn concluded that, generally, "the poor downtrodden people make not the slightest resistance. They beg daily for an audience with the General and when he graciously permits this, if he will grant them permission to sell a few bales of cotton (upon which they pay a tax of twenty six percent on the proceeds of sale, besides a tax on the goods purchased) they go away with many thanks and other flattering words are expressed to the General for his clemency and humanity."[46]

As for himself, Alcorn had been "graciously granted . . . the privilege of staying a time at my own house, provided I shall demean myself as a good boy." The "negroes of the neighborhood" were to be the witnesses to Alcorn's conduct. Alcorn concluded that only perhaps the "Lacademonian Helotes" were ever "lower in their degradation and even more cruelly treated by their masters than on the border southward." Otherwise, he wrote, "I am unacquainted with any race who has sunk lower—and none who have descended with such rapidity."[47]

As she struggled to keep her family's ravaged plantation in operation in the wake of the war, Jean Smith mocked a friend's invitation to visit her in Greenville and attend a series of social affairs: "I look like attending a party when half the time I am in the kitchen and the other half in bed. My hands are outlandishly rough, and I am a mixture of yellow and gentle brown." Smith noted that she had no party dress, "nor money to buy one—having sold all to get bread and meat."[48]

Although they escaped some of the wartime indignities decried by Alcorn and others, those who had fled the Delta during the war were in for a shock when they returned. Young Annie Jacobs described her demoralized family's return to the Delta. Before they reached their beloved Doro Plantation, they learned that it was no longer on the Mississippi. The river had shifted its course, leaving Doro on a large lake. As the family made its return, creaking along ingloriously in an oxcart through the Delta mud, the Doro that came into view was a changed place indeed: "Home! What a shock to find such desolation! For three years the river, having its way, had swept through the levees and overflowed the whole Delta at every flood. Our fences were all gone, weeds blackened by frost, and cockleburs waist high, covered the lawn, yard and gardens." Squatters had taken refuge in the house, "a bare frame, curtainless windows, one section of the gallery railing gone." The overall scene reminded the young girl of Nehemiah's return to Jerusalem: "Everything gone to rack and ruin. Cattle trampling down and swarming orchards and shrubbery. All the rare and delicate plants and trees that had made Doro such a beauty spot were dead."[49]

Henry T. Ireys recalled his impressions of Washington County immediately after the war:

> From a scene of plenty and prosperity there was presented destructions waste [sic] from a well stocked plantation, with horses, mules, negroes and cattle, to a dearth of labor and no stock. I went to Vicksburg and rounded up a few of our old people but most of them had scattered and were never to be heard from.

As these accounts suggest, a number of difficulties accompanied the resumption of cotton planting after the war. In addition to the transition from slave to free labor, stock, equipment, and, in some cases, housing were needed. The floods that had gone unchallenged after the neglect and destruction of the levees during the war created yet another frustration as farm land quickly retrogressed to swampland. Scarcely 10 percent of Delta land had even been cleared in 1860, and by 1865 the area was scarcely distinguishable from the frontier wilderness that had greeted the region's first settlers.[51]

Robert Somers described the postbellum Delta as a region still lightly touched and certainly not tamed by the hand of man. Noting that fully three-fifths of the land along the Mississippi River could not be cultivated because of flooding, he explained: "The ordinary annual flood covers large spaces of the soil with deep water." The result was insects in "pestiferous abundance." The uncultivated majority of the land was covered with forest and canebrake, the latter being the haunt of black bears and panthers. Swans, pelicans, and other wild birds abounded. The streams and lakes were home to trout and "a few alligators."[52]

Somers described a plantation near Austin that had been purchased in 1860 by a planter who had abandoned his wornout lands for "the fat virgin soil" of the Delta. His first planting produced huge green stalks but less lint than he expected. The next year's crop was abundant, but by that time "the hurly burly of armed men" had rendered the plantation virtually inoperative, and so it remained for the balance of the war. Chills and fever forced the planter away from the plantation in 1865, and the land was first rented and then sold. "This," Somers wrote, "is the general course of property in 'the bottom.'"[53]

Somers concluded with the somber assessment that "the reclamation of the 'bottom land' in Mississippi is a work of time, and the efforts made, in the spirit of American adventure, will render it by successive stages much more habitable than it is at present. Yet one must look at existing conditions, and, in the light of these, it must be owned that the superior productiveness per acre of such regions as this is attended with some formidable disadvantages."[54]

One new settler described a postbellum Bolivar County blanketed by cane and briers, where bears played havoc with the corn crop and alligators preyed on pigs so regularly that the children of the field hands had to be warned constantly to be on their guard. Mosquitoes and buffalo gnats added to the general anxiety and discomfort. When Dan Sessions, his wife, and baby first arrived at Australia Landing in Bolivar County, they drove through thick cane and briers to reach their new home. Mrs. Sessions confessed that her "heart fell" as she confronted a two-room log house, its unwhitewashed walls chinked with mud. "This contrasted with the handsome home from which we came," she wrote, "gave me a feeling of having dropped from high aspirations to dire reality."[55]

In testimony to the frontier conditions that prevailed in the Delta at the close of the war, plantation manager Henry Crydenwise cited

> bears, panthers, wildcats and wolves, besides a large variety of other less danger-
> ous animals. . . . Anyone may kill a wildcat almost any time here. They even some-
> times come up into or about the quarters. They are larger than a domestic cat of
> a dark gray color. Several bears have been killed about here. They come out into
> the cornfields at night and tear down and eat the corn like a great hog. The colored
> man who hunts a great deal has killed three panthers this fall. Two of them in the
> woods a short distance back of our house. Their appearance is something like a
> cat only they are nearly as large as a young calf. With all they are the most savage
> looking animal I ever saw. Their strong sinewy legs with large hooked claws like
> a cat could tear a man in pieces in a trice if they choose to.

Although the year was 1866, the work routine on the Issaquena County plantation where former Union officer Crydenwise was employed was reminiscent of the antebellum years and reflected the extent to which the Delta's postbellum plantations continued to operate under frontier conditions. Sixty to seventy hands were busily engaged in plowing (with fifteen plows operating at a time) on the place where six to seven hundred acres would be planted in cotton and the remainder in corn. Awakened at daylight by one bell and sent to the fields at 7:00 a.m. by another, the hands divided according to their tasks. Women and children chopped down head-high weeds to clear the way for plowing. While some of the men—and some of the women as well—did the plowing, another crew rolled logs and cleared new ground. All of this proceeded under the supervision of the three or four white men normally employed on the place.[57]

Busy with his everyday responsibilities about the plantation, Crydenwise painted an attractive portrait of a pleasant, bucolic existence in the postbellum Delta. He assured his parents that he and his wife, Sarah, had "considerable society" and spent their leisure "quite pleasantly." Sarah told a somewhat different story. "Anxious for the year to wear away," she complained of mosquitoes, gnats, and fleas: "One has to scratch to live here." Fearing a rumored cholera epidemic, she described severe rains and heat "so oppressive I can barely write half a dozen lines at a time." As to Henry's claim that the Delta offered "considerable society," Sarah confessed that the couple had recently ridden some sixteen miles to pay a social call. "You would probably think that much too far for pleasure," Sarah suspected.[58]

Despite these conditions, however, when would-be planters like Henry Crydenwise looked at the Delta, they saw not swampland and wilderness, but the chance to make their fortunes: "There is no place where I could do better than here. Had I a farm all stocked at the North I could not, with good success, make beside expenses more than a few hundred dollars a year, while here, with no capital invested and my money at interest, I can probably make three or four times as much."[59]

Hearing promises of yields of four to seven hundred pounds of lint cotton per acre, northern investors flocked into the Delta. George C. Benham was moved to abandon his pharmacy for an eleven-hundred-acre plantation with nine hundred acres in cultivation. The asking price was $75 per acre, but Benham and his partner calculated that with a minimum crop of nine hundred bales of cotton (which should sell for $120 per bale), the plantation should gross approximately $108,000 the first year. Not only did the venture seem a "short cut" to a fortune, but it offered Benham the chance to escape his pharmacy for "the grand sweep of an eleven-hundred acre plantation, with a roll of laborers running up in the hundreds; riding on a fine horse, with a broad Panama hat, and a ringing spur, under a Southern sky." Such prospects spurred a number of ambitious northerners to take the plunge, and land prices rose dramatically in late 1865 and early 1866. Whitelaw Reid reported that by the end of 1865 riverfront plantations were being leased at $12 to $14 per acre and already heavily indebted landholders were trying desperately "to borrow money on almost any conceivable terms to carry on operations for the next year."[60]

In the wake of the Civil War, as on its eve, there was no shortage of those who could stare at what others saw as nothing more than an undeveloped malarial wilderness and envision it as the future "garden spot" of the North American continent. Effective systems of flood control and transportation remained vital to the realization of the Delta's true potential, but an even more immediately crucial need was a supply of labor adequate to the task of clearing, draining, and cultivating the Delta's rich earth. In the antebellum era, both labor and land had been counted as property, and both the value (as a source of capital) and the exertions of labor could be utilized to enhance the value and productivity of land. As a result, before the war the Delta's future lay largely in the hands of the established planter whose ample slaveholdings and ready access to capital enabled him to transform a swampy wilderness into a plantation. Well before the war's end, however, James L. Alcorn warned that "our negroes will soon be ashes in our hands, our lands valueless without them." In the wake of the war, just as Alcorn had predicted, Delta planters faced the challenge of making their lands valuable again without the guaranteed benefit of labor either as collateral or even as a stable source of manpower under their control.[61]

As postbellum Delta planters struggled to make the transition, in the words of Gavin Wright, from "laborlords" to "landlords," they would have to contend with the efforts of the freedmen to use their mobility and much-needed services as laborers not only to resist resubjugation but to pursue economic independence as well. This struggle between former slaves and former masters to determine whose interests would prevail would quickly emerge as the dominant influence on both economic and political developments in the Delta during the early postbellum decades.[62]

3 ▽ A "Harnessed
  ▽ Revolution"
  ▽

Recognizing the Delta's potential as a perpetually fertile plantation paradise, ambitious antebellum planters had envisioned vast fields of head-high cotton tended by legions of servile blacks while projecting themselves as members of an omnipotent white gentry whose affluence allowed them to live as graciously and extravagantly as they chose. The destruction of slavery interrupted this dream for whites but created a new one for blacks, that of a rich cotton region where demand for their unfettered labor might provide them with opportunities for significant progress toward independent land ownership and facilitate their social and political advancement as well.

Noting the scarcity of labor in the Delta in 1866, plantation manager Henry T. Crydenwise predicted that with every passing year more blacks would take advantage of demand for their services to gain access to "the means of setting up for themselves." The ultimate result, Crydenwise believed, would be a subdivision of the plantations into smaller tracts and a move toward something resembling "our northern mode of farming." Crydenwise underestimated the difficulties that blacks would encounter as they sought to become independent farmers, but, however wishful, his prophecy largely anticipated the strategy pursued by blacks in the postbellum Delta. Between Delta blacks and the realization of their goal of economic as well as political independence, however, lay the determination of the region's planters, who throughout the upheaval of war, emancipation, and Reconstruction fought to regain their political, racial, and economic dominance and, insofar as possible, recapture the dream of a Delta where the planter's power was absolute and his wealth unrestricted.[1]

At the close of the war, confusion was rampant, not just among the freedmen, but also among the former masters, who faced the disquieting prospect of relying on free labor to grow and harvest their cotton. Vernon L. Wharton provided an insightful assessment of planter attitudes: "For the first time in their lives, they found it necessary to deal and bargain with their laborers. Negroes who had worked for them for twenty years were simply walking off the place. How did one go about getting new workers under this abominable system? There was a strange and unhappy silence around the old slave auction blocks."[2]

Distressed at the prospect of negotiating with his former slaves, a Delta planter wrote Governor William Sharkey in July 1865 pointing to the need for "some systematic plan to be adopted in the State or at least in the management of the large estates in the river counties." The major problem, in this planter's view, was making the freedmen "understand their condition and that they will have to work." He called on the governor to send "discreet commanders to read the law to the Negroes and to show them an officer (in blue) that would be left to carry it out by the aid of the citizens if he had to use force."[3]

The system proposed by this anxious planter hardly presented blacks with a free-labor market or the freedom to withhold their labor. Institutionalized coercion was vital to his plan; hence his correspondent reminded Sharkey that "it will be absolutely necessary to have some mode of punishment." This might be accomplished, he suggested, by having every plantation "declared a town" with the "planter as Judge of Police to hear complaints and decide according to law and evidence with power to sentence and inflict—Or the neighborhood physician might be best, as feigned sickness will be one of the greatest causes of complaint and he could decide better in such cases—It might by all means be generally understood amongst planters and negroes, that a discharge of a negro without a recommendation would be equivalent to a sentence on the public works for the balance of the year."[4]

Such blatantly coercive plans to restore white supremacy over black labor suggested not only that many Delta planters had not truly accepted emancipation as a necessarily permanent condition, but that they believed that military authorities might actually assist them in reversing the war's results. Initially, at least, official army policy gave planters some cause to feel this way. When the United States Army assumed control of Mississippi at the end of May 1865, the state's military commandant immediately urged the freedmen to contract to work with their old masters, so long as they received fair treatment and reasonable wages. He then dispatched provost marshals to enforce his orders. Colonel William E. Bayley, a provost marshal with unmistakably proplanter sympathies, reported from Bolivar County that the freedmen were unwilling to settle down to a sedentary existence as farm labor: "Their idea of freedom is: that they are under no control; can work when they please and go where they wish. Many after contracting to work until January 1st, 1865, [sic] leave on the most trifling pretext. If it is not stopped and they made to work as they agreed the crops of this county will be lost to the county and the revenue and taxes to the Government. Also hundreds of Negroes thrown as paupers on the Government, next year."[5]

Affirming his intention to hold employees to their obligations, Bayley expressed his desire to apply military discipline to the freedmen "to make them do their duty." He also requested that boats on the Mississippi be forbidden to transport Bolivar County blacks without his permission. "This," he assured his superiors, "will prevent injustice and crime, for whenever they steal or become tired of their contract they go to the river, hail a boat and leave." Bayley's observation affirmed the generally recognized preferences of newly emancipated blacks for plantations near the riverfront, where they not only secured better terms from their employers but felt they ran less risk of reenslavement than in the more remote, interior regions. At any rate, Delta planters were soon praising Bayley's efforts to stabilize labor conditions in the area.[6]

Created by Congress in March 1865 to oversee "all subjects" relating to the condition of freedmen in the South, the Freedman's Bureau began to assume this responsibility in June of that year. For the most part, the bureau continued the army's policy of encouraging the former slaves to seek employment with local whites, although its agents were more likely to take note of cases where the freedmen had been coerced or abused. For example, one Freedman's Bureau agent reported that Greenwood planter W. P. Atkins had beaten one of his former slaves and tied her up by her thumbs because she had tried to board a boat from Vicksburg. From the lower end of the Delta in Issaquena County, Lt. C. B. Foster encountered "a deep rooted feeling of hate, and a desire to show enmity, by the white towards the black." Foster observed freedmen "with cheeks pounded, eyes badly injured, with teeth knocked out and other evidences of maltreatment." His efforts to help them secure legal redress had been "thrown aside" by the courts, and the only instance of justice being done in a case concerning a black was one in which a freedman was jailed for attempting to raise a small amount of cotton on a plantation that had been abandoned since the war began.[7]

Foster reported "illy disguised hostility" toward the Freedman's Bureau and recounted an incident wherein a white citizen armed with a pistol chased a black man past his office, threatening to kill the freedman because the man, though not in his employ, had refused to work for him. Contrary to Bayley's report of freedmen breaking their contracts, Foster cited the common practice whereby the ignorance of the freedmen "was imposed upon," and they were induced to sign documents "the force of which they were not cognizant of."[8]

Elsewhere, Illinois-born planter P. F. Howell reported that as soon as federal troops were withdrawn from the vicinity of his plantation near Yazoo City, "the citizens organized themselves, patrolled the road leading into the city, and would not allow the negroes to come to town or travel from place to place. They were thus virtually compelled to hire to their former masters." To counter this coercive advantage enjoyed by those against whom they competed for labor, Howell and Edward Ellet paid their hands one-fourth of their wages each quarter. For rations, their workers received cornmeal, pork, and a pint of molasses per week. "The latter," Howell explained, "is a luxury and is given as a premium to obtain hands."[9]

Northerners like Howell often met with a less than cordial reception from local whites. Returning from a hunting trip to the Delta, Samuel G. Swaim observed that "anyone who thinks that the war is over should go through the country between the Yazoo and Mississippi rivers. The southern people are determined to drive northern people out of the country. . . . All the northern men planting in that part of the country bar their doors at night and have their firearms where they can lay their hands on them at any moment." A year after the war, Howell reported that local whites had nothing but "curses both loud and deep" for what they called the "beastly black Republicans."[10]

Though northerners were far from popular with local white planters, many of these same planters hired former Union soldiers (like Crydenwise) and compensated them handsomely for their work as plantation supervisors because of the general feeling that blacks were far more likely to sign on to work for a northern white than a southern one. C. B. Foster reported a great reluctance on the part of the freedmen to make contracts "with native planters" but "entire willingness to do so with northerners." A prospective plantation owner recently returned from the Delta told J. T. Trowbridge that "the Negroes everywhere I went have been shamefully abused. They had been promised that if they would remain and work the plantations, they should have a share of the crops; and now the planters refuse to give them anything. They have no confidence in Southern men, and will not hire out to them; but they are very eager to engage with Northern men." Wade Hampton III bragged of his cleverness in engaging "Yankee tenants," explaining, "It will be a good thing for my negroes to have Yankees so near them, and this will be sure to make them more contented."[11]

Early hopes of high postwar cotton prices had encouraged new investors and surviving planters to take whatever steps necessary to assure adequate labor. Cash wages, a system more familiar and appealing to northern-born planters than their southern counterparts, prevailed immediately after the war, with the planters often withholding half the wages until the end of the season. Desperate for labor, a few Delta planters offered as much as twenty-five dollars per month for prime field hands, although when Freedman's Bureau officials suggested a basic wage of fifteen dollars per month, with planters also providing quarters, medical service, and some rations, most planters rejected such terms as too generous.[12]

At the end of 1865, with planters looking ahead to the ensuing crop year, freedmen who had remained with their former masters and had been the victims of either fraud, abuse, bad crops, or unrealistic expectations balked at signing new labor contracts. Rumors of free land as a Christmas gift from the government also served as a deterrent to contract making. Confusion was rampant, not just with the freedmen, but also with the former masters for whom the prospect of a future pinned to free-labor agriculture was anything but attractive. The editor of the Friars Point *Coahomian* reported in November 1865 that local planters generally agreed "that labor is now in too disorganized a state to attempt to raise cotton." Planters talked of stabilizing the labor situation and gaining control of wages and terms offered to freedmen by joining together to establish uniform labor policies, but their talk produced no tangible results.[13]

By the beginning of 1866, the pressing need for labor and the greater leverage accruing to newly mobile blacks were apparent in contracts that offered rations, housing, and clothing as well as wages ranging from fifteen to twenty dollars for men and twelve to fifteen dollars per month for women, with lesser amounts for children. The contract for 1866 between Robert E. Woods, Jr., and the freedmen family of William S. Slider provided for rations, housing, and fuel as well as annual wages of five hundred dollars for the six adults and their children. All of the wages were to be withheld until the end of the year. Nathan Bedford Forrest employed about 140 hands on two Coahoma County plantations in 1866. Forrest's terms, reputedly the most generous in the vicinity, offered twenty dollars per month with the costs of supplies for dependents deducted from wages for first-class hands.[14]

Although the wage system spread rapidly in 1866, a Department of Agriculture report concluded that this approach "generally proved unprofitable" because the freedmen had tried "to use too freely their newly found liberty," while the planters had proven themselves "little at home in the management of free labor." The overall result was inefficiency, idleness, neglect, and violence or the threats thereof, the upshot being that at year's end "the cotton fields were in many cases left in the lurch."[15]

Hoping to restore white control over black labor, in November 1865 the Mississippi legislature had enacted statutes so restrictive of the rights of blacks that they came close to reviving the state's old slave code. In fact, the Mississippi lawmakers went so far as to declare "in full force and effect" all the old laws pertaining to "crimes and misdemeanors committed by slaves, free negroes or mulattoes." Under the new Mississippi "Black Code," the ability of blacks to lease land, carry weapons, bring legal action or provide legal testimony, consume or dispense alcohol, or preach the gospel was severely limited. By prohibiting blacks from leasing land outside cities and towns, the Black Code sought to prevent them from becoming independent farmers and thereby force them to return to their former masters. A further effort to restore white control of black labor came in the form of a provision requiring all freedmen to sign an annual labor contract or be arrested as vagrants and have their services sold to the highest bidder. In addition, orphans of freedmen or freedmen under the age of eighteen could be apprenticed to any competent white, provided the former owner was given preference.[16]

Although officials in Washington objected to many provisions of the Black Code, a number of these laws were enforced by local officials until federal officials threatened to prosecute anyone who violated the nondiscrimination provisions of the newly enacted Civil Rights Act of 1866. Still, it was apparent well before the legislature repealed the most obnoxious provisions of the Black Code in January 1867 that the determination of the freedmen would make the restoration of white control of black labor a far more difficult and complex process than many whites had imagined.[17]

One of the ways in which blacks exerted their newfound leverage as free laborers was by insisting on an exemption from labor after noon on Saturdays.

A black folktale from the Delta explained how it came to pass that blacks expected to take Saturday afternoons off. Despite the advice of the "high boss," a "mean straw boss" insisted that blacks on a certain plantation work on Saturday. In a dream, the straw boss saw his two children trapped on a lake in a sinking boat. His first reaction was that there was no cause for alarm because some of the blacks were bound to be fishing nearby and were certain to come to the rescue of the children. However, he fell into a panic as he realized that he had all the blacks on the place at work. At that point, he cursed himself for "not letting the Negroes off on the day they loved so well" and vowed that if one black worker had slipped off to go fishing and saved his children, none of the blacks on the place would ever have to work on Saturday again. At this point, the "high boss of all the lands" intervened, telling him "You have been a fool, but your wish is granted. I made seven days and said rest on Sunday, but knowing the Negro had to work so much harder I want him to have Saturday so that he can make his arrangement to rest."

One planter who was surely not amused by this story was Everard G. Baker, who complained on July 17, 1866, that he was still unable to "lay by" his cotton. He blamed his "backward" condition on his black laborers, who refused to work on "Saturday evenings." In reality, freedmen sought not so much freedom from labor as from white supervision when they refused to work on Saturdays. As Leon F. Litwack observed, "The idea of a five-day work week . . . imparted to many freedmen a greater feeling of independence even as their economic situation remained the same." Few whites, however, were ready to surrender their supervisory prerogatives, and most claimed that blacks would not work without oversight and prodding from whites. Baker complained that the freedmen on his place worked only "tolerably," resisted early morning chores, and sought to take "2 to 3 hours at 12M." Baker vowed that he would not be "bothered" with freedmen in the future, but when he came back and reviewed his diary a year later, he wrote, "I had better have adhered to the above resolution. I did not and much regret it."[18]

Describing the reaction of his workers to their settlements in 1866, Tunica County planter George Collins noted that "the poor creatures were much disappointed and I think dissatisfied with the result. They seem to forget all that they have received during the year and only look on the balance due them as their entire wages." Elsewhere, a Freedman's Bureau agent noted from Coahoma County in 1866 a remarkable sense of unity among black workers: "I find that when one or more freedmen becomes dissatisfied, others are very liable to sympathize with them, and in case one leaves, others will follow."[19]

Hoping to avoid such disappointments and desertions without relinquishing the upper hand in their dealings with their workers, planters tried to make their labor contracts as clear and specific as possible. In an effort to standardize the work day, contracts specified a predawn to postdusk schedule. On Sunflower Plantation, in exchange for one-third of the crop, the contract in 1867 required workers to "feed the stock, get their breakfast, and be at work in the field by sunrise and to work until sunset." The agreement allotted "the usual time" to the noon meal and stipulated that during the picking season, hands must "put away their day's work after sunset." Like many of the contracts being issued by this time, this agreement threatened deductions for time lost to sickness and a threefold deduction for "absence without leave."[20]

Organizing his workers into gangs, J. W. Fowler kept meticulous records of his transactions with his free laborers, much as he had with his slaves. He deducted fifty cents for every work day lost and charged as well for supplies, medical expenses, and transportation. These bills often mounted up. Henry Clay and his wife earned $39.30 in 1868 after having $38.25 deducted for time lost, mostly by the wife, who was charged for missing 67.5 days of work. Fowler's charges for transportation could be harsh. He docked one hand five dollars because the man used his wagon to go to Friars Point and declined to haul cotton on the trip. He charged another four dollars for the use of his carriage to go to church. Fowler's workers probably subjected themselves to such punitive charges because they put a premium on their ability to move about without supervision or obligation to the landlord.[21]

Elsewhere, labor contracts for a Washington County plantation threatened forfeiture of one day's wages for even a momentary absence from work. Workers also faced the loss of a month's wages for using cotton for pillows or bedding. An agreement used on the Cold Spring Plantation in Washington County in 1868 was even more specific, calling for not just a sunrise to sunset schedule but a ten-hour work day during all but the three winter months, when nine hours were expected. Absence or indolence would be assessed at two dollars per day, half of which went to the land owner and half to the offender's co-workers. The contract stipulated that fifteen minutes of lost time would be charged as one-fourth day lost, half an hour as half a day, and an hour as an entire day. Workers' gardens were limited to one-eighth of an acre, and whereas early contracts had stipulated "sufficient" rations, this one specified the exact amount of pork, beef, and cornmeal allotted to each man, woman, and child. This particular contract, five pages in length, sought to cover every aspect of the mutual obligation between employer and employee. While the document seemed to restrict the laborer's freedom and exact from him the maximum amount of work, cooperation, and deference, in this and similar contracts employers also offered specific performance incentives like a new suit of winter clothes or a share of the livestock raised on the plantation during the contract year.[22]

The fact that employers felt they had to offer such rewards suggested that their best efforts to coerce and restrict labor with specific performance requirements and/or threats of punishment were often less than successful. In fact, the very extensiveness of the contracts, which on the surface had seemed to return the laborer to a near enslaved status, was also a reflection of the difficulties that Delta planters experienced in trying to reestablish control of labor that was no longer enslaved.

Labor scarcity and instability combined with disappointing crops to bring ruin to a number of those who sought to make a fortune planting in the Delta. John A. Andrew, a former governor of Massachusetts, lost thirty thousand dollars in 1866, which also became "a year of wreck" for George Benham and his partner, who had expected their new plantation to produce a gross income of $108,000 on nine hundred bales of cotton but found instead that their yield was only sixty-five bales and their total proceeds a disastrously puny $6,564.[23]

The disappointments of 1866 led many landowners to put their plantations up for sale or lease. Among the estates on the market was a twelve-hundred-acre place on the Yazoo River that had not only a house but "the old set of hands are on it, and everything is ready to commence work." The sixty hands on the plantation were former slaves "who are unwilling to leave their old home." In December 1866, *Debow's Review* listed eighty-one "estates" for sale in Mississippi, nineteen of them in the Delta. The price of the Delta plantations ranged from five to thirty-seven dollars per acre. In only three cases had as much as half the land been cleared. The owners in some areas did take pains to claim, truthfully or not, that the place was "free from overflow" and made it a point to inform readers if there was already labor on the plantations. To establish the loyalty of his labor, one seller advertised: "Freedmen on the place to work it and have remained on it during the war."[24]

With three hundred thousand acres in the Delta remaining under water during a good part of the 1866-1867 season, land prices held up reasonably well, but many owners still put their lands up for sale or lease at rates that were "not only moderate but cheap." George W. Humphreys offered "Sligo," his 609-acre plantation, for lease in 1867 in return for six bales of cotton "weight 450 pounds each."[25]

In addition to bad weather and disappointing crops, the economic difficulties and uncertainties besetting both blacks and whites in the Delta were rooted in a complex set of problems that plagued the entire postbellum South. Chief among these was the scarcity of capital and/or credit, a condition that derived both from the shortage of banks across the rural South and a reluctance on the part of merchants and financiers to advance credit when farmers had nothing more than severely devalued land to offer as collateral. Mississippi lawmakers had responded to this problem in 1867 with the passage of the state's soon-to-be infamous "crop lien" law. Entitled "An Act for the Encouragement of Agriculture," the measure sought to facilitate the financing of postbellum agriculture by guaranteeing a first lien on the crop to anyone providing loans or advancing supplies for the production of that crop. The law was aimed primarily at merchants and investors, but it also granted lien rights to landlords who provided advances to their laborers. For the laborers themselves, however, there were no such guarantees, and a number of them complained that their claims for wages and/or a share of the crop were all but worthless after an indebted planter's entire crop had been applied to pay off his financial obligations.[26]

The problem of credit and capital scarcity encouraged planters and freedmen to enter into sharecropping arrangements wherein laborers farmed a specified acreage in exchange for a share of the crop from which the costs of varying levels of support in the form of food, clothing, and supplies had been deducted. Most blacks were unable to pay cash rent or purchase their own supplies and pay rent in the form of a portion of the crop or, for that matter, secure advances from a furnishing merchant without the endorsement of a white landlord. At the same time, the lack of capital and the exorbitance of the interest rates on agricultural credit made it difficult for planters to make regular cash payments to workers before the crop was harvested. Finally, sharecropping seemed to shift some of the risks of cotton growing onto the laborers and provide greater incentives for the workers to give their best efforts (so as to increase their earnings) and remain on the plantation until the harvest was complete (in order to collect their earnings).

For their part, freedmen not only hoped to use sharecropping as a springboard to some more desirable renting arrangement which could lead to independent land ownership, but saw it as a chance to escape the close supervision, all too reminiscent of slavery, that they associated with gang labor for wages. Sharecropping therefore emerged from what Gavin Wright called a "market process" that produced a compromise between "the freedmen's desire for autonomy and the employer's interest in extracting work effort and having labor when it was needed." A number of Delta freedmen had contracted to work for a share of the crop as early as 1865, and observers generally held that the "short crops" of 1866 and 1867 speeded the demise of the wage system. Sharecropping was a common labor arrangement in some areas of the Delta by 1868, a year that saw a dramatic expansion of such activity statewide.[27]

Even as they looked to sharecropping as a step toward independent landownership, Delta freedmen clung to the belief that the government was going to give them "forty acres and a mule" or, at least, acreage in some quantity. Under the provisions of the Freedman's Bureau Act, abandoned, confiscated, or purchased lands could be assigned for the use of the freedmen; at the close of the war, the Freedman's Bureau did in fact hold approximately eighty thousand acres of farm land in Mississippi. On July 1, 1865, however, President Andrew Johnson ordered that all such property be returned to owners who had either received a pardon from him or taken the amnesty oath. By the end of 1867, all lands formerly held by the bureau had been duly restored to their former owners. Still, for several years after the war, the expectation that land would be redistributed at year's end, as a Christmas present of sorts, discouraged freedmen from making contracts for the next year. In the immediate aftermath of the war, tales of freedmen measuring off their plots on the plantation had elicited mirthful reactions from some planters, but the continued faith of the former slaves in this notion soon took on sinister implications among whites who feared that their laborers might elect to take by force what the government declined to award them by law.[28]

Such was the fear of Everard G. Baker, who blamed black troops for telling the freedmen that the government would "give them lands, provisions, stock, and all things necessary to carry on business for themselves, and are constantly advising them not to make contracts with white persons, for the next year." "Strange to say," wrote an ostensibly puzzled and definitely perturbed Baker, "the Negroes believe such stories in spite of facts to the contrary told them by their masters employers [*sic*]." Worse still, Baker claimed black troops were stirring up fears of reenslavement among the freedmen and urging them to engage in a Christmastime massacre of local whites. Baker charged that the freedmen were being told that by wiping out the white population, they would clear the way for the Delta to "be given to them by the northern people forever as an inheritance." "To ignorant persons situated as the Negro is such arguments seem quite plausible," the alarmed planter concluded.[29]

Baker was by no means alone in his fears. Other nervous whites warned Mississippi governor Benjamin G. Humphreys of an imminent racial upheaval, "expressing serious apprehensions that combinations and conspiracies are being formed among the blacks to seize the lands and establish farms, expecting and hoping that Congress will arrange a plan of division and distribution." If Congress failed to act, the freedmen were allegedly ready to "proceed to help themselves, and are determined to go to war, and are confident that they will be victors in any conflict with whites." Humphreys responded with a warning to the freedmen that "if any such hopes or expectations are entertained, you have been grossly deceived, and if any such combinations or conspiracies have been formed to carry into effect such purposes by lawless violence . . . you cannot succeed."[30]

Henry M. Crydenwise assured his concerned parents that there was no cause to worry about his safety, rumors of black uprisings notwithstanding: "I am in just as much danger of being murdered by father as by the Negroes." Still, worrying about a black revolt was second nature to the white residents of the South's black majority areas. It had haunted whites in the Delta since the antebellum era and had surfaced repeatedly during the war, when so many white males were absent. In the early postbellum years, the trauma of confronting their former slaves as freedmen exacerbated these fears, which were also compounded by the frustrations of trying to farm with free labor. Throughout the Delta, whites displayed an absolute mania for disarming blacks. Noting that Wade Hampton III's son "Kit" (Christopher F.) was active in the effort, C. B. Foster reported that Issaquena whites were confiscating any firearms the freedmen possessed and had no qualms about kicking down doors and breaking open trunks to seize these weapons. Explaining that he had heard of no example of a freedman misusing his firearm and citing the need for guns for hunting, he deemed it a "flagrant injustice" to deny them their weapons.[31]

The tensions between former slaves and former masters were such that occasional violence was almost inevitable. Nathan Bedford Forrest killed a freedman with an ax on one of his Delta plantations, claiming self-defense after a knife attack. Tom Edwards, the deceased, had a reputation for beating his wife but was also widely known as an agitator among the workers. The plantation's carpenter claimed that Edwards threatened anyone who interfered with his whipping of his wife, vowing that he did not "care a God-dam for General Forrest or any other God-dam man." The carpenter testified that Edwards was a notorious wife beater, but neither Edwards's wife nor an eye-witness to the slaying corroborated Forrest's claim that he had been attacked with a knife. A few weeks earlier, Edwards had led a group of angry blacks who gathered on another of Forrest's plantations, "armed with a Spencer rifle or other warlike weapons," to protest an overseer's threat to hang an insubordi-nate freedman up by the thumbs. Such efforts by whites to employ physical coercion against an ostensibly free labor force were far from uncommon in the Delta. One Freedman's Bureau agent reported that "it is the practice of planters in Coahoma and Bolivar Counties, Mississippi, to systematically tie up and whip the hands (freedmen) employed by them for any, and all causes. . . . Num-bers of them have reported that they are worse off now than when they were slaves."[32]

Continuing reports of such incidents indicated that whites were experi-encing considerable difficulty as they sought to regain control over their black laborers. In February 1867 a frustrated George Collins complained: "The Negro is so uncertain, and it takes such caution and care to avoid continual conflicts with them and to keep them from fighting among themselves." "It is so different," Collins complained, "working now and formerly when we had control of the labor."[33]

Shortly after Collins offered his gloomy assessment, the challenge of regaining control of black labor became more formidable still. The blatant bad faith embodied in Mississippi's Black Code—and those of the other southern states as well—and persistent reports of white abuse of the freedmen had strengthened the hand of congressional Radicals and contributed significantly to the onset of congressional Reconstruction in the old Confederacy. The pas-sage of the Reconstruction Act of March 2, 1867, brought not only military government and the threat of further federal interference with white efforts to coerce or intimidate their black workers, but the prospect of black political empowerment as well.[34]

The first duty of the military governors in the South was to register vot-ers—about sixty thousand blacks were quickly added to the voter rolls in Mis-sissippi—and make preparations for elections to choose delegates to draw up new state conventions. With its black majority, the Delta played a key role in the establishment of Republican political control in the state. Led by northern whites and old-line Mississippi Whigs, the Republicans drew up a new state constitution in 1868, won the elections in 1869 to fill the offices created under the new constitution, and assumed their new posts in 1870. These events brought nothing but dismay to Delta planters because, instead of shuffling com-pliantly back to the fields, their former slaves were voting and holding office in addition to playing an active role in Republican ascendance in both local and state politics.[35]

Black political participation made Delta whites even more paranoid about the prospect of a black insurrection, and they complained that the military presence in the Delta had renewed black hopes of receiving free land from the government as a Christmas present in 1867. Crop conditions remained poor, thereby contributing to the general anxiety and instability. Describing the crop of 1867, a Freedman's Bureau official noted that it had not "exceeded half of what was regarded as an average crop" and had "commanded but one-half of the prices of the previous year," thus reducing the proceeds to one-fourth of what was anticipated by the planter and freedmen as the proceeds of the year's labor. The result was "the financial ruin of the planter and capitalist and discontent to the laborer." With the measly crop harvested, at the end of 1867 this official reported, "The freedmen are now idle, and without, in a great majority of instances, the means of support. The result is great depreciations being committed on livestock, hogs, sheep, and cattle." One military commander reported from the river counties, where little corn or other foodstuffs had been produced over the last two years, that bands of armed blacks were "plundering for food" while white landlords fled for their lives. "There's reason to fear a war of the races if the blacks are not fed," the report concluded.[36]

Hoping to regain the upper hand in their treatment of black laborers, the Deer Creek Planters Association proposed in January 1868 that local landlords act collectively to establish uniform wages, hours, and contract terms. They enclosed a resolution blaming "the great and increasing distress prevailing all over our country" on the "inattitude on the part of freedmen to discharge their duties as laborers in the fields." In an effort to compensate for the failure of the contract system, "to protect themselves from loss," and to promote the welfare of the freedmen, in whom they professed a deep interest, they proposed a list of a dozen rules and stipulated monthly wages (plus provisions) of six dollars per man and four dollars per woman. An alternative was to feed and house each laborer in exchange for three bales of cotton. Proposed working hours were daylight to dark, six days per week with Sundays free, although religious assemblies by blacks were not encouraged. Failure to perform as expected would bring immediate dismissal without compensation for past labor. Renting land to freedmen was deemed acceptable only in "exceptional cases." Members also agreed not to employ freedmen who had been discharged by fellow members.[37]

Many planters did apparently take a hard line in their dealings with the freedmen in 1868. As the year began, a number of blacks spurned labor contracts either because they felt they had been cheated in the previous year's settlements or because the wages they were offered were in some cases no more than one-third of what they had been promised (though not always paid) in 1867. Writing from Greenville in January 1868, a Freedman's Bureau official noted that the attitude of local whites toward the freedmen was "by no means good. . . . They show every disposition to oppress them when in their power." One estimate suggested that as many as six thousand blacks faced utter destitution in Washington County alone in 1868. A Freedman's Bureau official reported that he had found sixty to seventy persons both homeless and without more than a few days' supply of food. Having refused to sign a contract or having been denied the opportunity to sign one, these former laborers found themselves turned out of the cabins where they had lived previously. Such reports suggested that the supply of freedmen exceeded demand for their services, but this was not necessarily the case. In March 1868 a Freedman's Bureau official reported that in the Delta "the demand for labor is greater than the supply, there being applications in this office for several thousand more laborers than can possibly be processed."[38]

Not surprisingly, the treatment afforded the freedmen varied according to the season and the availability of labor. Some Greenville-area planters often showed "kindness and forbearance" toward their workers early in the year "in order to retain them as laborers," but at settlement time some freedmen received payment in the form of dead stock or broken equipment or found themselves losing a larger part of their anticipated wages to "lost time charged at unheard of rates." A Freedman's Bureau official reported in 1868 that planters exhibited "a good disposition" toward those who worked "but were very bitter to those who make politics their profession and advocate the present plan of Reconstruction." Andrew Jackson Donelson found it "terrible to contemplate the future if what is called democracy in the South succeeds in giving office and power to the Negroes." George Collins attended a political rally in Tunica County in 1871 at which he heard speakers of both races deliver remarks "characterized by low, vulgar language . . . calculated to stir up bad feeling between the races." Alarmed at the preponderance of blacks among local officials and the influence of "whites worse than negroes" and "carpetbaggers of the vilest kind," Collins predicted glumly that there would be "no control of labor and no way of collecting debts."[39]

On July 5, 1872, Everard G. Baker noted that his family spent the preceding day "in the cotton field at hard work." "So much," wrote Baker, "for the 4th of July, which once was an honored anniversary with us, but now we are so oppressed with carpetbag and negro rule and with all the yankees, that we the southern people feel we have quite gone out of existence except to work very hard for bare subsistence."[40]

Whites exaggerated the extent of black officeholding during Reconstruction, but blacks were elected sheriff in four Delta counties, and they held other key local posts as tax collectors or members of the board of supervisors. A number of blacks also represented Delta counties in both houses of the legislature. In Bolivar County, Blanche K. Bruce held simultaneously the offices of sheriff, tax collector, and superintendent of education. Bruce used this power base to obtain a seat in the United States Senate in 1874.[41]

At the grassroots level, the activities of the Loyal League provided the means of maintaining political enthusiasm among the black masses of the Delta and promoting organized, unified activity on the economic front as well. Loyal League meetings and parades boosted morale and gave blacks a sense of common interest and destiny with their counterparts on other plantations. The Loyal League seems to have been heavily involved, for instance, in the efforts of black workers to force landlords to allow them to rent land, an arrangement that promised greater independence and economic progress than working for wages in gangs or squads. Complaining that freedmen seemed increasingly intent on becoming "*landholders* and *tenants*, and not *hirelings*," a Delta planter attributed this trend to "Loyal League teachings."[42]

For a time, at least, the election of black officials and widespread political activity at the local level seemed to go hand in hand with economic progress for blacks. The 1868 crop was nearly a hundred thousand bales larger than that of 1867, and cotton prices rose sharply as well. Cotton productivity rose even more dramatically in 1869 and 1870; the latter year's crop of approximately 650,000 bales was well over twice the size of the 1867 crop in Mississippi. One of the state's Republican newspapers bragged in 1870 that "the colored people . . . were never so well off as at present." Intense poverty remained the rule rather than the exception in the Delta, of course, but the impression of progress was nonetheless widespread among blacks. Writing from Vicksburg early in 1873, a correspondent described local blacks as a people who "appreciate their new condition thoroughly and flaunt their independence."[43]

No such optimism was apparent on the other side of the color line. Although they exaggerated, and in some cases manufactured, the hardships they faced, economically and emotionally, the Reconstruction Era was a time of shock and upheaval for Delta whites. The story of the misfortunes that befell the Smith family who resided on Live Oak Plantation not far from Vicksburg was in many ways reminiscent of the fictional experience of the O'Haras in *Gone with the Wind*. Dr. George Smith lived on Live Oak with his three daughters. Smith's failing health and lack of business acumen left responsibility for maintaining the place in the hands of his daughter Jean, who also had to look after her two younger sisters, one of whom seemed subject to both depression and hypochondria. As conditions grew steadily worse on the place, Jean waded a swollen bayou to confirm her suspicions that a tenant family was stealing cotton. When the tenants proved uncooperative and "impertement [*sic*]," she tried without success to get her father to take action in the matter. "Everyday," she wrote, "I am convinced how foolish it is for us to look for Pa to provide for us." She tried to convince her father that the family should move out and rent the place to someone willing to farm it. Instead, her father wanted to put a new roof on the leaky old house and purchase some swamp lands for cotton planting, despite the fact that the family had only four bales of cotton to use to pay taxes, buy winter clothes, and purchase food for an entire year. Although her father was a physician, he found his bills impossible to collect. The girls were reduced finally to selling articles of clothing in order to raise money.[44]

Her husband had become "accustomed to the feeling of having no country," wrote J. R. Dixon from Greenville in 1867. As for herself, she determined "as there is no bright side, not to look at the picture." The Dixons also complained bitterly about the difficulty they faced in controlling their black labor force: "The Negroes are not working to make a crop. They seem indifferent to whether they make anything over a comfortable living—and seem to think they are obliged to have this whether they work or not. Despairing of finding "good help" in the Delta, Dixon returned from a visit to Virginia with three black servants, but she feared they would quickly become "demoralized here where the negroes are so independent and are behaving so badly." She recounted the activities of the Loyal League, whose members dressed in military garb and paraded about on "fat prancing horses." She discounted these activities as little more than an attempt to "imitate white folks," but, nonetheless, "it looked to me very much like equality and was of course very distasteful."[45]

The Dixon family finally decided to abandon the Delta for California, but J. R. Dixon remained bitter about Delta blacks, who were "becoming more worthless every year." She expressed pleasure that "we will have nothing more to do with the ungrateful creatures." As she looked ahead to California, however, she by no means considered the possibility of life without blacks and actually inquired as to "what wages are paid the negro women in the neighborhood." She anticipated that some of her servants might accompany her, but she also asked her son who had preceded her to California, "How many negroes are in the neighborhood?" So general was the dismay among local whites that a number of the Dixons' friends vowed they were also ready to head to California. Mrs. Dixon cited no less an example than "Will Percy"—Colonel William Alexander Percy, who would eventually play a significant role in overthrowing Republican rule in Mississippi—who reportedly claimed in 1870 that he would make such a move to California or elsewhere if only he could sell his property for cash and thereby secure enough money on which to live until "he could become established in his profession."[46]

If many Delta whites found it difficult to adjust to living and working with free blacks, a number nonetheless realized that a certain amount of interracial cooperation was vital to their hopes of restoring prosperity to the region and to their own political ambitions as well. As a large landholder and the first Republican governor of Mississippi, James L. Alcorn had doubly good reason to adopt a conciliatory stance toward blacks. Alcorn advocated limited black suffrage in 1865 and supported ratification of the Fourteenth Amendment in 1866. He warned whites that their only hope of maintaining political control and ensuring that Reconstruction remained a "harnessed revolution" was to acknowledge the civil and political rights of blacks. Alcorn urged other Delta whites to follow his lead and "vote with the Negro, discuss politics with him, sit, if need be, in council with him, and form a platform acceptable to both, and pluck our common liberty and prosperity from the jaws of inevitable ruin."[47]

By no means were all Delta whites as candid or enthusiastic as Alcorn about cooperating with blacks, but pro-Republican sentiment among native whites in the Delta and other black majority counties was perceptibly stronger than elsewhere in the state. After analyzing such "scalawag" support for the Republican party in Mississippi during the first half of the 1870s, Warren C. Ellem concluded that "the bulk of the scalawags were located in the Delta counties." Ellem's analysis of the 1871 election for district attorneys in Mississippi showed that in the five Delta counties for which figures were available, the scalawag vote accounted for an average of 97 percent of the total white vote. Ellem linked the strength of the native white Republican vote in the Delta to the region's traditionally Whiggish inclinations during the antebellum era, but he might have cited as well the overwhelming desire of self-interested Delta planters to stabilize race relations and secure the black workers needed to grow their cotton and clear their land.[48]

Simultaneously pursuing the Alcorn family's economic and political interests, James A. Alcorn's cousin Robert adopted an especially conciliatory approach and praised local blacks in an article entitled "A Talk with the Freedmen," noting that they had "agreeably disappointed" their former owners "by the praiseworthy exertions you have put forth to obtain an honest livelihood." Instead of lapsing into "barbarism" the freedmen had "in the main" been "frugal, law-abiding, and industrious." For their "commendable bearing," Alcorn wrote, "the white people accord to you a high mode of praise."[49]

Despite such overtures, however, the Delta did not escape racial violence during Reconstruction. Controversial black political leader William T. Combash led an uprising in Sunflower and Carroll counties in November 1869. When Combash marched a band of twenty blacks into Greenwood only to be repulsed by local whites, he threatened to return with five hundred men. The local carpetbag sheriff organized a posse and gave pursuit. Two of Combash's crew were killed, and the others scattered. Combash soon perished at the hands of a squad of troops sent by Governor Adelbert Ames to restore order to the area.[50]

The Combash incident demonstrated the fearful possibilities of a full-scale explosion of racial tension in the black-majority Delta. Next to the restoration of white supremacy, the most fundamental consideration of Delta whites during Reconstruction—as it would be for decades to come—was that of labor stability. As a result, although Delta whites sought on the one hand to regain dominance over black workers, many of them also tried, insofar as possible, to avoid the most extreme forms of repression and abuse that could lead to polarization, racial conflict, and a black exodus from the Delta. Moreover, the realities of black voting and Republican influence on local politics dictated as cooperative an attitude toward blacks as white leaders could muster. As a result, for example, in contrast to a wave of white vigilantism that left thirty blacks dead in Meridian, leaders of a black uprising that followed the shooting of a black girl in Tunica County in 1874 were not even tracked down.[51]

Even among white Republicans, however, the inclination to make concessions or behave in conciliatory fashion toward blacks had its limits, especially where the extension of black political influence on a significant scale was concerned. In fact, by 1873 the primary source of friction within Republican ranks was the matter, as Wharton described it, "of the extent to which Negroes were to be allowed to hold offices and to dominate the councils of the party." This divisive question manifested itself in 1873 at both the state and county conventions and in the decision of James L. Alcorn to run for governor as an "Independent Republican" against the duly nominated and staunchly problack Adelbert Ames. Even Alcorn's own black laborers refused to support him, and Ames won the election handily, but the scalawag vote declined substantially in the Delta. Statewide, the 1873 vote broke sharply along racial lines, and the fact that Alcorn had received the endorsement of the state's "Democratic-Conservative" organization suggested that Republican rule in Mississippi might soon be a thing of the past.[52]

Other danger signs included the overall slump in cotton prices during the 1870s. The average price for middling cotton at New Orleans between 1866 and 1869 was twenty-five cents, while the average price for the period 1870-1875 was only seventeen cents. In fact, between 1872 and 1877, cotton prices fell by 50 percent. The Depression of 1873 affected the Delta so severely that by early 1874 even big-time planter and former governor Charles Clark was scrambling to secure supplies and credit. "Bankruptcy and ruin seem inevitable," wrote another planter, "and only those who can get away stand a chance to repair their losses."[53]

Against the backdrop of the Depression of 1873, the fall in cotton prices not only, in Eric Foner's words, "arrested the modest progress of the late 1860s and early 1870s toward the growth of a class of independent black farmers," but also helped to neutralize the effects of the dramatic expansion of black political power in Mississippi in 1873. With blacks proving instrumental in the election of Governor Adelbert Ames, increasing substantially their representation in the legislature, and reaffirming their grip on local offices throughout the black majority counties, the time should have been ripe for an all-out campaign for new policies attuned to their economic, social, and political needs. Unfortunately for blacks, however, the depressed farm economy spurred cries for retrenchment and intensified the demands of white landowners for drastic reductions in taxation. Even Governor Ames, sorely indebted to black voters though he was, promised to practice "rigid economy and a strict accountability" in his new administration.[54]

Moreover, instead of responding to black complaints that the crop-lien system was preventing them from receiving "the complete benefit of our labor," when the legislature repealed the state's controversial crop-lien law, Ames expressed concern about the possible loss of credit for both landlord and laborer and proceeded to veto the repeal measure. In his inaugural address, Governor Ames had condemned the existing agricultural system in Mississippi and thereby raised hopes among blacks that he planned some action to facilitate their efforts to acquire land. Ames offered no specific proposals, however, although the legislature took steps to open state-held lands for private acquisition. This move proved a boon for railroads and timber companies, and the passage in 1875 of an Abatement Act, providing for the restoration of property surrendered before 1874, opened the way for whites to recover their tax-delin-quent lands, but neither of these developments significantly aided the cause of blacks, who had never held land in the first place.[55]

As the depression deepened, the planters of the Delta became the state's most vocal advocates of tax reduction and governmental retrenchment. Faced with a dramatic decline in crop income, Delta planters found themselves paying taxes at rates they found exorbitant to support a new political order that, if suc-cessful, might make it impossible for them to regain control over their labor. The Constitution of 1868 set assessments of land at market value, and after a series of similarly Republican-inspired reforms and improvements to roads, schools, and other public properties and governmental agencies and institu-tions, the tax rate stood at $26 per $1,000 valuation by 1874. In the same year, the state auditor estimated that one-fifth of the state's total land area had been forfeited by owners seeking to avoid the tax obligations associated with large-scale land ownership. In the Delta the tax problem was compounded by the additional burden of levee taxes, which by the end of 1874 cost the typical Delta planter approximately $4.15 per acre. More frustrating still was the fact that much of this tax debt resulted from an effort to restore the credit rating of the old General Levee Board by paying off its debts dating back to its bond issue of 1858. Most Delta planters saw a suitable levee system as a prerequisite for the restoration of the Delta's prosperity, but not all were ready or able to accept the sacrifices that accompanied the pursuit of this goal.[56]

In response to what they saw as excessive state and local property and levee taxes, planters had to invest more and more money in opening lands to cultivation. At the end of 1871, George Collins complained of having paid out nearly fourteen hundred dollars in taxes in the last eight months. To meet such an obligation, Collins felt he had to work at least four hundred acres, and he saw no hope of lessening his tax load so long as "the lawmakers are not tax payers." In 1872 Collins reported on a prevailing impression that the levee board would soon own most of the land in the area. He even suggested that some landowners had deliberately let their lands go, hoping later to buy up levee bonds at a reduced rate and thereby recover their former holdings. Still others continued to live on and farm their forfeited lands, paying no taxes at all to either the state or local levee boards. Meanwhile, representatives of the state found it difficult to convince potential buyers that even the rich lands of the Delta were worth the risk involved in purchasing and paying delinquent taxes on lands to which they might never secure a clear title.[57]

By 1871 seven Delta counties accounted for 1.4 million acres in forfeited land. The 1875 Abatement Act voided all state claims on back taxes, but it did nothing about local taxes or a bewildering tangle of levee board obligations. The foreclosure of Delta lands became a self-accelerating phenomenon because the lands that continued on the tax rolls had to take on the additional revenue burdens once borne by those that had been forfeited.[58]

A number of observers believed that, in addition to a desire to restore white supremacy, it was distress over the tax situation that led many fence-sitting former Whigs and politically active former scalawags to join forces with the Democrats to overthrow Republican rule in Mississippi. The taxation issue figured prominently in the successful effort spearheaded in 1873 by influential planter and lawyer William Alexander Percy to reclaim control of Washington County government from the Republicans. This move allowed white planters to take over the county Board of Supervisors, which set property and other tax valuations. More important, however, the restoration of local planter supremacy gave Percy and his Delta cohorts a base from which to battle Republican governor Adelbert Ames for control of state politics. When a heated contest for sheriff between two local black Republicans erupted into a gun battle that left one of them dead and the other driven into hiding by a speedily assembled white militia unit, the fugitive candidate withdrew, and Percy skillfully assembled a biracial fusion ticket on which he appeared as a candidate for the legislature.[59]

This successful fusion effort involved cooperation with a group of Republican bolters whom the Democrats had once denounced as the "damnedest scoundrels and vagabonds in the county." Local Democrats had also brought in former abolitionist Cassius M. Clay to urge local blacks to overthrow Republican rule. After these elections, a Washington County Democratic leader boasted that victory had been achieved in that county through "honest hard work" and without "intimidation" or "lost ballot boxes." This claim was suspect at best, and certainly the same could hardly be said for the Democratic effort statewide. The violent ouster of Republican officials in Vicksburg in 1874 was reinforced by a subsequent effort on the part of Warren County planters to rid the area of "all bad and leading negroes" and gain stricter control "over tenants and other hands." Foreshadowing the bloody Redemption campaign of the following year, the violence in Vicksburg and its environs mushroomed and led ultimately to the deaths of as many as three hundred blacks and the temporary ouster of the local black sheriff, although in January 1875 a detachment of federal troops finally restored the sheriff to office.[60]

Meanwhile, the serious floods of 1874 also contributed to general dissatisfaction, and taxpayers' leagues blossomed in every county. Moreover, Mississippi Democrats clearly interpreted their party's landslide victory in the 1874 congressional elections as an indication that Republican Reconstruction policies had fallen into general disfavor in the North. The Depression of 1873 had actually played a major role in the outcome of the election, but in the words of a Mississippi Democrat his party's triumph in 1874 "satisfied us that if we succeeded in winning control of the government of Mississippi we would be permitted to enjoy it." Thus assured, the Democrats showed little hesitation in 1875 in launching a campaign of violence and intimidation against potential Republican voters. Given the refusal of the Grant administration to intervene in Mississippi's affairs, these terror tactics proved crucial to the restoration of Democratic political control.[61]

In September 1875 a white mob broke up a Yazoo County meeting and drove out controversial carpetbag sheriff A. T. Morgan in addition to murdering several blacks, one of them a state legislator. Morgan had married a northern-born black teacher, but, as Eric Foner pointed out, his greatest offense was probably that of assisting a large number of blacks in becoming property owners as well as expanding and improving schools and other public facilities.[62]

Elsewhere, the chameleon-like James L. Alcorn denied ever having been a "black Republican," put together a ticket to unseat local pro-Ames incumbents, and led a white invasion of a black political meeting in Coahoma County. As Alcorn ordered the group to disperse and the black sheriff fled, shooting erupted, mortally wounding several blacks and whites. "Without bloodshed," Richard N. Current wrote, "Alcorn could not have hoped to elect his anti-Ames ticket, for the county was overwhelmingly black and had given Ames a landslide victory over Alcorn in the election of 1873."[63]

By election day, observed Current, the level of bloodshed was such in some areas of the state that Republican leaders "were hiding out in the woods and swamps." With many Delta planters still concerned about forestalling violence, the Republican vote actually increased in some counties in 1875, but in areas where violence had occurred Republican turnout fell precipitously. Only seven Republican ballots—as compared to more than four thousand for the Democrats—were counted in Yazoo County (where total turnout exceeded the number of registered voters), and in Coahoma Republican totals fell by eight hundred. Statewide, a Democratic landslide turned five of six congressional seats over to the Democrats, who also gained a four-to-one majority in the legislature.[64]

The newly assembled Democratic legislature quickly impeached and removed Lieutenant Governor Alexander K. Davis. Davis was black, and the Democrats did not want to see him elevated to the governorship when Republican governor Ames was removed from office. With Davis out of the way, Ames was forced to resign or face impeachment charges himself. John M. Stone, the Democratic president pro tempore of the state senate, became governor, Mississippi was "redeemed" from Republican rule, and Reconstruction, whose promise of economic, political, and social advancement for blacks had seemed so genuine only two years before, drew to an abrupt and disappointing close.[65]

As he surveyed a variety of reasons for the failure of Reconstruction to secure permanent recognition and protection of "blacks' rights as citizens and free laborers," Foner cited "the early rejection of federally sponsored land reform" as a move that "left in place a planter class far weaker and less affluent than before the war," but one "still able to bring its prestige and experience to bear against Reconstruction." "While hardly an economic panacea," Foner argued, "land distribution would have had profound consequences for southern society, weakening the land-based economic and political power of the old ruling class, offering blacks a measure of choice as to whether, when, and under what circumstances to enter the labor market, and affecting the former slaves' conception of themselves."[66]

As suggested by the excitement over rumors of free land at Christmas that swept across the early postbellum Delta each year, the quest for economic independence through land ownership was indeed, as Foner saw it, "central to the black community's effort to define the meaning of freedom." Without sustained governmental support and intervention on a scale wholly unthinkable to most observers in the 1870s, unfavorable credit and cotton market conditions—not to mention white hostility—might have sufficed to wreck the aspirations of black landowners in the Delta in any event. Still, as landowners the freedmen would have at least had the opportunity to take their chances as individual producers or, as Barbara J. Fields has suggested, to explore communal or cooperative arrangements that might have given them a measure of insulation from disadvantageous credit and/or market conditions. Instead, as the case of the Delta demonstrates so well, in the absence of any significant attempt to bolster the economic position of the freedmen, Reconstruction dissolved into little more than another disappointing attempt to institute democratizing social and political reforms in a society without fundamentally altering its existing economic order. (A contemporary observer described Republican policy as an effort "to promote political equality in a society characterized by equality in nothing else.")[67]

Such an experiment could have succeeded only if the force of federal authority stood squarely and consistently behind the freedmen in the exercise of their political rights. Once they became convinced, however, that Washington considered it politically inexpedient to intervene in behalf of those whom it had encouraged to assert their full rights as citizens, white opponents of Reconstruction did not hesitate to unleash a bloody, broad-daylight campaign of violence that, in Foner's words, "turned the electoral tide in many parts of the South." (This would not be the Delta's last experience along these lines. Nearly a century later, the region would be caught up in the "Second Reconstruction," wherein Washington would busily engage itself in the cause of civil rights for blacks even as its economic and welfare policies buttressed the position of the segregationist white elite. Significantly, the earliest successful effort to organize a county-level black population for effective political action in the civil rights–era Delta came in Holmes County, where a number of blacks had become landowners in the 1930s through the tenant purchase program of the New Deal's Farm Security Administration.)[68]

For all its disappointing aspects, the Reconstruction experience nonetheless left Delta blacks considerably better off than they would have been otherwise. John R. Skates concluded that Redemption in Mississippi "represented an effort by the whites to place the freedmen once more under the political and social control of their former masters." Redemption was indeed a step toward the restoration of white control over black labor in the Delta, but it was only a step. So long as blacks constituted a majority of the population and continued to vote and hold office, Delta whites could not escape the fear that political equality might lead inevitably to economic and social equality, especially in light of the disunity and factionalism among whites that the experiences of secession, war, and Reconstruction had brought to light and exacerbated as well.[69]

Other problems stood in the path of those whites who hoped to reverse the effects of fifteen years of military occupation and economic upheaval and restore to the Delta the momentum and promise it had enjoyed in the years immediately preceding the war. In addition to the overhanging cloud of unpaid taxes and title disputes that helped to depress the market for land, there was the matter of restoring the Delta's flood-control system and establishing a transportation network that would facilitate further development of the region's interior lands. Finally, the rebuilding of the Delta would require both a great deal of capital and a great deal of labor as well. White leaders would have to look elsewhere, to both public and private sources, for most of the capital. For the labor, meanwhile, planters could look only to the Delta's blacks.

Consequently, even in the wake of Redemption, the Delta's future by no means lay wholly in the hands of its white landlords. In addition to their crusade for internal improvements and their quest for external financial assistance, Delta whites faced the task of restoring labor stability and regaining their dominance over a black population determined to use demand for its labor to safeguard its freedom and enhance its prospects for socioeconomic and political advancement. The process of establishing a viable system of labor would play a major role in determining the nature not only of the economy but of the society that emerged on what remained in 1875, as it had been two decades earlier, a promising but largely undeveloped agricultural frontier.

4 ▽ Conquering the Plantation
▽ Frontier
▽

Many Delta planters had blamed Reconstruction, with its military supervision and Republican rule, for their inability to secure an adequate, dependable supply of controllable labor. Even in the wake of Redemption, however, Delta planters were unable to rely simply on coercion and intimidation as a solution to their labor problems. Instead, they continued their struggle to regain control of their labor and searched for a labor system that would guarantee them a stable, dependable work force of the size and type they needed. Beyond that, they faced the ongoing challenge of restoring and expanding the region's flood-control system and establishing a transportation network that would facilitate the clearing and development of the Delta's interior wilderness while connecting all of its planters more directly and efficiently to the world cotton market. Only when all these goals had been achieved would the Delta be in a position to fulfill the economic promise it had shown in the antebellum years.

It soon became apparent that the restoration of Democratic political supremacy in 1875 was by no means a panacea for the labor woes of Delta planters, who continued to find black workers difficult to attract, retain, or control. In 1879 thousands of blacks flocked to the Mississippi River to catch boats that would carry them on the first leg of an "exodus" to Kansas. Fearful that some northern philanthropist might try to provide blacks "crazed with the fever of immigration" with a boat offering free passage to Kansas, the planters of Washington County issued a memorial warning that such an act would be ruinous. The likely result, according to the planters, would be a wholesale desertion by the freedmen of their worldly possessions as well as their contractual obligations to their benevolent landlords. The boat would be able to carry only a tiny fraction of the assembled throng; the rest would be left disappointed and utterly destitute on the riverbank, while "in the meantime the loss of the bulk of the cotton crop and bankruptcy of all dependent on it would result. The final destruction, pilfering, and violence that would ensue can better be imagined than described."[1]

Although Delta planters had relied on violence as well as legal and extra-legal coercion in order to stem the exodus, they denied that "the negro in the Valley of the Lower Mississippi is subjected to the prejudice of race, any personal abuse, any extortion, any denial of political, legal, or social rights, any personal discomforts of want, to which he would in his condition be subjected in a greater degree at any other place on the American Continent." In order to lend as much plausibility as possible to this assertion, they pointed out that, given the planter's investment in his crop and his desperate need for labor, "it is idle and preposterous to assert" that white landlords would take the risk of running off their hands "by unkindly treatment." However lacking in credibility it may have been, this memorial nonetheless revealed the continuing anxieties of Delta planters about an unstable labor supply on which they were so obviously dependent.[2]

Because it seemed to be the most attractive alternative available to ambitious but impoverished freedmen and labor-hungry but capital-strapped planters, the sharecropping system became noticeably more widespread in the Delta in the wake of the Depression of 1873. Planters and freedmen continued to experiment with a number of labor arrangements throughout the 1870s, however, and even at the end of the decade, sharecropping was by no means the dominant labor system in the Delta.

For reasons both economic and racial, whenever possible many Delta planters clung to some form of wage labor. Some believed that sharecropping was neither profitable nor efficient. From Carroll County in the edge of the Delta, C. M. Vaiden warned that if planters persisted "in this folly . . . in ten years their ruin will be the result." Others quickly found that the sharing of risk with the tenants under sharecropping was often more theoretical than real. As Wharton observed: "Under whatever system the Negro might work, even under those in which he was supposed to furnish rations for himself and feed for the stock, his penniless condition practically always made it necessary for the planter to furnish him and to charge the supplies, deducting their cost from the worker's share at the end of the season." This reality meant that less of the actual risk of sharecropping was transferred to the tenant than might have seemed the case. The wording of the contract notwithstanding, the need to keep the cropper alive, fed, and clothed in order to hope for a reasonable return on the sharecrop arrangement left the landlord in a position where his expenditures to sustain the tenant could exceed the proceeds due the tenant, the result being a debt that, if of any consequence at all, was likely to be uncollectible. It was true that the tenant's assets could be confiscated and liquidated, but in many cases these would suffice to wipe out only the smallest of debts.[3]

Debts might at least serve to hold tenants in place from year to year, but especially in the years before the state's enticement laws were in place, many labor-hungry planters were not above recruiting their neighbors' hands, be they indebted or not. The complaint of a Hinds County landowner in 1879 was even more applicable to the Delta: "I have a good hand; my neighbor offers him a higher price, and also tells him I will cheat him out of his wages. I have had this done by the richest men in the neighborhood."[4]

In order to minimize their risks, Delta planters had stood ready as early as 1869 to offer three-fourths of the crop to tenants who could furnish themselves. Emphasizing the risks sharecropping entailed for the planter in the uncertain economic circumstances of the 1870s, in 1875 a friend advised Bolivar County planter John Burrus to "make your contracts so as to throw as much expense on the laborer as possible. This is certainly the safest. Those who farm here next year say they will take a mortgage to start on or they will advance nothing until the crop is ginned out." Vowing that he would not "stay here and risk living or starving with free negroes," Burrus's friend reported that "very many planters in this section are abandoning the business altogether and many others renting to the negroes themselves and paying no part of the expense." To emphasize the abandonment of cotton planting, he informed Burrus, "You never saw so many mules for sale in your life." Elsewhere, learning in January 1879 that a number of his hands would be leaving, Frederick Metcalfe predicted, "I will lose over $100 this year in advancing."[5]

Given the demand for labor in the Delta, there was some risk for the planter in any system involving material or cash advances or investments in incentives that would make laborers more desirable or attractive as tenants to other landlords. Although they began their experiences as nonslave agricultural labor with few advantages, the blacks on George Collins's plantation became, in his words, "sharper every year." As time passed, a number of them accumulated livestock and equipment from working with him and used their acquisitions to bargain for better terms elsewhere in the labor-hungry Delta. "Most of them I have built up," Collins explained, "but others offer them inducements and now and then one of them leaves." Collins found that the risks involved in outfitting tenants were so great that in 1877 he set out to find as many hands as possible who could furnish themselves. He also decided to work as much as 150 acres with wage hands. This approach he found not very profitable "but better far I think than the miserable share plan."[6]

As an 1870 Department of Agriculture report explained, from the perspective of planters, sharecropping emerged at least in part as an "unwilling concession to the freedman's desire to become a proprietor." In addition to their concerns about the economic implications of sharecropping, whites clearly resented and feared the feelings of independence that many black sharecroppers seemed to exhibit. Although white landlords insisted they were merely wage laborers whose earnings were not due until after the harvest, many black sharecroppers considered themselves part-owners of the crop and reserved their right to work at their own pace and to reject what they considered excessive white supervision.[7]

Although they consistently opted for sharecropping over wage labor, Delta blacks saw sharecropping primarily as a step toward independent landownership. Hence, when their own economic circumstances permitted or when they enjoyed the leverage to bargain with their employers, many blacks sought a rental arrangement because they felt renting afforded them a better opportunity than sharecropping to acquire the means to purchase their own land. Finding their labor at a premium after the improved cotton crop of 1868, a number of blacks abandoned sharecropping in 1869 and persuaded landowners to allow them to rent instead, the rent being payable after the sale of the crop.[8]

Planters who rented land to blacks often faced ostracism or worse from other whites who feared that this practice might lead to a loss of labor control or, worse yet, widespread acquisition of Delta lands by blacks. Observed one Tunica County planter of another's decision to rent to blacks at a hundred pounds of lint per acre, "I fear Judge Wright has made a bad step, one that is injurious to him, and also the country generally." The Black Codes had attempted to outlaw renting or leasing of farm land by blacks, and in the spring of 1869 James L. Alcorn's home at Yazoo Pass had been torched after he announced that he would rent the land to a black family.[9]

Such "warnings" notwithstanding, throughout the Reconstruction Era planters with no hope of securing labor by other means had little choice but to rent all or part of their lands to blacks. Harry St. John Dixon learned from his mother that his father was planting one more crop before trying to rent his place "if he should find anyone fool enough to try planting again." Taylor Rucks could not understand why his hands had refused to sign labor contracts for 1867. He finally concluded that local blacks were trying to force planters to rent to them in small lots. The move to pressure whites into renting to blacks was in many cases broad-based and well organized. During Reconstruction, leaders of the Loyal League had openly expressed the belief that through collective action blacks could compel whites to rent land to them.[10]

George Collins understood that his tenants aspired to become "independent of me and each other," but he remained frustrated in his efforts to deal with them, particularly at settlement and contracting times. When he resorted to black renters, he found them largely unwilling to rent the most productive but also most expensive lands, preferring instead the cheaper, unimproved forest edge and "deadened" lands "back there among the wolves and other wild things." Not only was the rent lower under this arrangement, but direct supervision by the planter was more difficult, and tenants could supplement their rations from the game that the forest harbored. As Sydney Nathans explained, "For a black with resources, interested in making money but also eager to be self-sufficient, the unimproved land provided an ideal place to practice the mixed economy of the yeoman farmer." In years when there were no floods and the market for cotton was good, hardworking blacks paying ten dollars per acre in rent cleared as much as two hundred dollars.[11]

Despite their misgivings, many planters soon realized that renting unimproved land could benefit them in the long run by increasing their cultivatable acreage, so long as they required black renters to assume responsibility for

clearing some of the land they rented. James L. Alcorn built groups of cabins
in areas that he hoped to clear. These vacant cabins attracted itinerant black
laborers, who soon made contracts at Alcorn's commissary and proceeded to
deaden the trees and hack away the underbrush. The results, described by a
contemporary observer, were that "within a brief period cotton and corn grow
luxuriantly about the congeries of white cottages not long before hidden in the
foliage of the matted vines and among great towering oak and cypress tress."[12]

The percentages of farms listed by the 1880 Census of Agriculture as cultivated by the owners were almost identical for the Delta (57.9) and for the
remainder of the state (56.6), but because the average farm size in the Delta
stood at 440 acres as compared to a state average of only 156 acres, Delta landowners who farmed their own land were forced to rely much more heavily on
hired labor than were their counterparts elsewhere in the state. Whether they
preferred the wage or sharecrop system, many Delta planters found that in
order to procure enough workers, they actually had to enter into a variety of
labor arrangements on a single plantation. The Dixons experienced perpetual
problems with labor on their Washington County plantation, finding that they
could not depend on "squad leaders" to recruit sufficient labor to harvest their
cotton. They quickly resorted to a combination of sharecropping and standing
rental arrangements at five acres per bale of cotton. Elsewhere, James L. Alcorn
retained a large force of sharecroppers, whose labor he supplemented at picking time with that of poor whites from the hills who received a fixed wage for
their labor.[13]

On many plantations, while ambitious blacks with tools and mules or oxen
became "the planter's temporary pioneers" at the edge of the forest and in the
new grounds, other blacks worked for wages or sharecropped on the better
land. Although the former were farther along than the latter, the common goal
of both was to achieve landowning status and gain as much independence from
whites as possible.[14]

The diversity of labor arrangements in the Delta led to some confusion in
agricultural census reports. This confusion was exacerbated by the fact that
prior to 1910, census reports made no distinction between sharecropping
(where the laborer supplied only his labor and received a portion of the crop as
his compensation) and sharerenting (where the laborer generally received
housing but provided his own supplies and simply paid the landlord a portion
of the crop as rent). In their analysis of the 1880 census, Roger L. Ransom and
Richard Sutch found that only eleven of the nation's major cotton-growing
counties reported less than 5 percent of their farms operating under a sharecropping or share-rental arrangement. Two of these—Issaquena, the only
county that reported no sharecropping or sharerenting whatsoever; and Sunflower, which showed less than 3 percent of its farms operating on such a
basis—were in the Delta. Three more counties—Washington (the state's largest cotton producer in 1880), Sharkey, and Quitman—reported less than 10
percent of their farms involved in sharecropping or sharerenting. A sudy of

cotton production included in the 1880 census described a strong year-round market for wage labor at seventy-five cents to one dollar per day in Issaquena and indicated that any system other than wage labor resulted in "shiftlessness" and "serious neglect of the crops." One estimate put production at three bales per hand for renters and eight to ten per wage hand.[15]

Although the county's official census report showed no sharecropping or sharerental arrangements, another Issaquena observer praised the "half crop" system for producing the best cotton because "the owner or his agent sees that the crop is properly tilled." Meanwhile, a group of planters from Washington County, which reported only 7.5 percent of its farms rented for shares in 1880, described nonetheless a system popular throughout the county wherein the laborer supplied his labor, rations, and, perhaps, half the feed in exchange for half the crop. Despite the low levels of sharecropping or renting reported in some counties, when all the farms in the nine core counties of the Delta were considered together, the percentage of those reported as rented for a share of the crop in 1880 was 17.2 as compared to an average in the remainder of the state of 26.6 percent. When farms rented for cash were considered, the results were practically reversed. In the Delta, 25 percent of the farms were operating under this method as compared to 16.8 percent in non-Delta counties.[16]

The upper echelons of white society in the postbellum Delta were reserved for those who could trace their roots in the region to the antebellum period, and families who managed to hold on to their land throughout the war and the Reconstruction Era enjoyed a definite economic advantage over those who came later. However, the key to achieving genuine prosperity in the late nineteenth-century Delta was less a matter of pedigree or persistent land ownership than of the ability to attract and retain the requisite number of dependable workers. In 1866 John A. Andrew blamed his bankruptcy on his labor problems, and the Hinds County *Gazette* reported gleefully that, despite his Yankee background, the former Massachusetts governor now stood ready to fight to put blacks back "in slavery again." W. W. Williams, who had agreed to look after his cousin's place in Yazoo County, urged her to sell in September 1869. Williams explained that the previous renter had been unable to get hands and had made barely enough to pay the rent. Williams thought he had a prospective buyer lined up, but he warned her that, although he had sold land at ten dollars per acre the year before, she would be lucky to get half that for her holdings in the current market.[17]

Although he encountered all manner of adversity, Andrew Jackson Donelson felt his problems with his labor were his most serious. At the end of 1868, he hoped that the departure of one of his most troublesome tenants would leave the others "more contented" and easily managed. In order to retain an adequate labor supply for 1869, Donelson had to double the supplies for his hands. He attributed his difficulties with the hands to the activities of "Windly," who had "done what he could to destroy the place, corrupting the negroes and lessening the product at least ½."[18]

Donelson counted on a large crop to "repair damages" to his finances. By April 1, however, he was less hopeful of getting out of debt, citing "enormous" taxes and "bad faith" on the part of those who managed his affairs. Still, he predicted, "all will be right if we are not badly overflowed." By December, however, Donelson was forced to admit that "the weather is so unfavorable for gathering the crop in the bottom that I shall fall below my calculation." After two more disappointing years, Donelson's health began to fail in the spring of 1871, and his death in June of that year left his creditors no choice but to sell his Bolivar County estate, including crops and livestock, in order to collect on a twenty-six-thousand-dollar debt.[19]

Wade Hampton III had bragged in June 1866 that his and his brother Kit's were "the only hands in the county who work." The situation had changed markedly, however, by 1875, when a wistful, debt-ridden Hampton admitted, "I do not greatly fancy the idea of becoming an overseer," but, he added, "nothing can be made unless I remain on the place." Plagued by debt, Frederick Metcalfe complained, "The labor of my life is coming to naught." Metcalfe had also to contend with thievery, malingering, fighting, and outright defiance by his hands. After seeing his interest in Newstead Plantation sold for debt on March 1, 1875, Metcalfe returned from Greenville and "as usual found the servants out of kilter." Metcalfe discharged one of his squads and noted with resignation, "If I leave home everything goes wrong."[20]

The classic case of tragedy and failure in a land of bright promise and high hopes was that of George Collins, who found the Delta no more to his liking than had his father-in-law, Paul Cameron. On January 19, 1871, Collins reported on one of the many labor shortages that befell him in his ill-starred tenure as the operator of Cameron's Delta plantation. Not only did he have more than fifty bales of cotton still in the field, but he feared that when he finally settled his accounts he would have "nothing to start on for another year," especially since he would have to buy all the corn consumed on the place. Moreover, with the late harvest, no arrangements could be made for labor for the next year. A distressed Collins begged Cameron to come to the plantation: "I feel so much like giving up everything, it seems so hopeless and perhaps you might cheer us up and give us advice that would help us some."[21]

The Collins family met personal as well as financial tragedy in the Mississippi bottoms. Their daughter, Mary, fell sick and died at Christmas in 1871. Though her parents remained in Mississippi, they refused to bury her in "the land of strangers" and shipped her body back to North Carolina for burial. Still grieving over his daughter's death, Collins poured out his heart to his mother-in-law, Annie Cameron, in January 1872 as he sought to console her about her son Duncan's decision to give up cotton planting and take a job on a steamboat. "I think he is wise," wrote Collins, "to trust to his own head and hands to keep clear of the free negro. . . . My own bitter experience here shows me that nothing is to be expected here except a dog's life and a bare pittance." Noting that "every year my capital gets less and less," Collins added, "It is hard to give up after all I have gone through here, but I see no other hope. There is nothing to live for here."[22]

Continually threatening to leave the Delta, Collins nonetheless hung on. In February 1879, still depressed and frustrated, he wrote Paul Cameron, ostensibly to thank him for his "very liberal action" in paying the tuition of Collins's children. Quickly, however, Collins's letter of thanks became an apologia, one that revealed the many problems and challenges faced by postbellum Delta planters. Collins reminded Cameron that when he took over management of the Tunica County plantation in 1866, it had no fences, ditches, cribs, or stables. Only thirty acres were ready for cultivation at that time. Collins calculated that in a fourteen-year span, much of it under "the infamous radical rule," he had paid more than ten thousand dollars in taxes. During the same period Collins claimed to have cleared five hundred acres of land at a cost of five dollars per acre and spent about four thousand dollars on buildings, paying high lumber costs in addition to five to eight dollars per day per carpenter. The hard-luck planter had also lost about twenty-five-hundred dollar's worth of mules. He had been forced to pay exorbitant costs for food (pork at $40.00 per barrel and flour at twenty dollars) all the while forking over interest at 12 percent or higher. The difficulties and expense involved in clearing land had left Collins unable to work more than 25 percent of the property on which he paid taxes.[23]

That Collins was by no means alone in his difficulty was clear enough: "I am the only one left of all who settled here when I did and the year after; every one broke and gone and I no better off." Collins noted that a single Memphis merchant currently offered for sale thirty-seven plantations taken through foreclosure. The fact that other merchants had also become large landholders only proved, in Collins's mind, "the general bankruptcy of planters in this section."[24]

On their twentieth wedding anniversary in 1880, a miserably lonely Collins wrote his wife that, except for the love they shared, the previous two decades had consisted of little but "lost labor and mistaken effort" on his part. Two years later Collins offered a familiar refrain: a hundred bales of cotton open in the field, not nearly enough hands to pick it, and the entire corn crop yet to be gathered—a crisis desperate enough, in Collins's words, "to make me tremble."[25]

After seventeen years of such crises, Collins finally gave up and left Mississippi in 1883. Noting the "whining tone of self-defense and self-pity" that characterized Collins's letters, David Donald has suggested that Collins personified a "Southern Civil War generation . . . cut off from its roots by the war experience and doubly traumatized by a sense of defeat and betrayal." Donald noted as well that despite their economic woes the Collinses persisted in trying to live in the style to which they had become accustomed in the 1850s and simply "could not adjust their scale and style of living to postwar circumstances." Arguably, an emotionally tougher, more experienced, and financially astute planter might have done better, but Collins's monumental difficulties with labor were by no means unique in the Delta in the two decades after the war and before the establishment of a relatively efficient and complete rail and levee network. Indeed, the renters who took over the operation of the Cameron place the year after Collins departed soon warned Paul Cameron of the need to invest more money in the upkeep of the plantation, which needed new ditches, new fences, and new cabins. "Reliable and desirable tenants will only go into good houses," they wrote Cameron, and they informed him that they might want to rent his place for the following year if it were fixed up but offered no assurances "that we will want it even then."[26]

Such difficulties notwithstanding, an adequate supply of labor and some reasonably good luck could mean great wealth for a Delta planter. James L. Alcorn estimated his damages from a tornado and a fire in 1871 at a hundred thousand dollars. Yet he fully expected to make up for his losses with a single crop and bragged that "not a dozen men in all the South could have lost so much and again risen under that loss." A skillful recruiter and manager of labor who had carried on a brisk trade in smuggled cotton during the war, Alcorn managed to avoid the heavy debt that crushed so many of his contemporaries. By 1876 he owned approximately twenty thousand acres and paid one-ninth of the taxes collected in Coahoma County. His 1879 tax bill of $5,101 led him to complain about being "land poor," but he apparently met his obligation without difficulty. Keeping alive the Delta planter's tradition of ostentatious materialism through the lavish furnishings and decorations he acquired for Eagle's Nest, his home near Jamestown, Alcorn also paid twenty-two hundred dollars for a marble statue of himself.[27]

Alcorn was by no means the only large landowner in the Delta. Across the region in 1880, 293 farms exceeded a thousand acres. This figure represented 16 percent of the state's total for farms this size, although the Delta accounted for only 3 percent of the state's farms. Despite the setbacks suffered by a number of planters, the post-Reconstruction Delta soon produced enough success stories to reclaim its reputation as the most profitable cotton-growing region in the South. By 1880 the region had already taken its place as the state's leading cotton producing area. With less than 13 percent of its land area under cultivation, the planters in eleven Delta or part-Delta counties harvested more than one-fourth of all the state's cotton. Washington, the state's leading cotton growing county, accounted for nearly fifty-five thousand bales, while Issaquena led the state in productivity with an average yield of 0.88 bales per acre in 1879. Overall, the Delta counties averaged 0.73 bales to the acre as compared to an average in the remainder of the state of only 0.41 bales.[28]

The Delta achieved its impressive level of aggregate cotton production with a crop density of only 48.1 acres per square mile, as compared to 81.4 acres per square mile in the tableland counties that made the next largest percentage contribution (21.0) to the state's total cotton production. With less than 12 percent of the state's tilled acreage and barely 16 percent of its cotton acreage, the Delta led the way because its soils were so fertile and its farmers were concentrating so heavily on cotton production. Whereas approximately 41 percent of the cropland statewide was planted in cotton, Delta planters devoted 59 percent of their cultivated acreage to the crop. In the remainder of the state, the ratio of corn acreage to cotton acreage was 0.81, while this figure for the Delta was only 0.41.[29]

These figures reaffirmed the Delta's identity and promise as a cotton kingdom, but they provided only a hint of what the Delta might one day become. In 1880 the region remained, as Sydney Nathans put it, "suspended between plantation and frontier." As of 1880 there were but two towns between Vicksburg and Memphis with a population greater than one thousand. Visitors to the region found relatively little cleared land except along the bayous, lakes, and rivers, and some of the land that had been cleared in the antebellum area was rapidly returning to forest. The rich Delta soil was still covered in many places with blue cane "fifteen to twenty feet high," and clearing the land was so arduous and expensive that many purchasers quickly gave up and sold out. Will Dockery recalled forty-acre plots that were swapped for livestock or rifles. With no roads "worth considering," Dockery often traveled through the woods or in open sloughs as he made his way about the county, where, in true frontier fashion, the saloons far outnumbered the churches and schools. Bear remained plentiful as the 1880s began, and bear hunting was a favorite sport among Delta planters, two of whom claimed to have killed three in a single day during 1881.[30]

The Delta frontier was an exciting place, but not nearly so exciting in the minds of some as the area's unfulfilled potential as a thoroughly developed plantation region. Between the Delta and the realization of its rich promise, however, lay a number of unresolved problems. Flood control remained a pressing concern. Many would-be planters shied away from a region that, despite the richness of its soil, was still subject to massive annual overflows, especially since the investment required to buy or rent land and claim or reclaim it from the wilderness was such a sizable one. There was also the related matter of a transportation system adequate for the needs of a region whose full potential could be realized only if its isolation could be overcome and it could be linked securely to the major cotton markets of the world. Many believed that if these problems could be solved, laggard development and labor shortages would become a thing of the past because the Delta would attract large numbers of ambitious settlers and workers of both races.

With the Yazoo Basin moving toward a uniform system of flood control, the Civil War had interrupted levee construction and the collection of the taxes needed to support it. A major flood hit the Delta in 1862, breaking the levees in many places and forcing many families inland. Union gunboats had also taken their toll on the levee systems during 1863 and 1864.[31]

In addition to dynamiting the Yazoo Pass levee in the hope of reaching Vicksburg from the north via the Coldwater, Tallahatchie, and Yazoo rivers, federal troops had also inflicted heavy damage on levees up and down the Mississippi. James L. Alcorn reported on January 1, 1865, that the war- and water-ravaged Delta had "reverted back to substantially the condition of waste from which it had been reclaimed in the fifties." In the massive flood of April 1865, more than a mile of levee caved into the river and numerous crevasses opened elsewhere. Flood waters covered the Delta for months, destroying livestock and thwarting efforts to get a crop in the ground.[32]

There was little sentiment for reviving the old 1858 levee district, but planters in Bolivar, Washington, and Issaquena counties formed their own such district and financed it with a ten-cent-per-acre tax on land and a one-cent-per-pound levy on the cotton it produced. Individual planters also financed levee repairs and construction and accepted levee board bonds as reimbursement, often relying on special subscription campaigns to fund major projects. The flood of 1874 devastated crops so thoroughly that levee taxes had to be cut in half. The board reorganized in 1877 to include all of Bolivar, Washington, Issaquena, and Sharkey counties. This revamped group became known as the Mississippi Levee Commission, but efforts to form basinwide flood-control organizations came to naught. Planters in the northern Delta counties of Tunica, Coahoma, Tallahatchie, Panola, DeSoto, and part of Sunflower set up a separate levee district complete with a taxing provision calling for a 2 percent annual assessment on all lands within the district. Corruption and mismanagement prevented this group from making headway in flood control, but, as had been the case in the counties to the south, the willingness of planters to burden themselves with heavy taxation indicated that they realized the importance of flood control to the future of the Delta as a cotton kingdom.[33]

Valiant and costly as they were, the flood prevention efforts of Delta planters were too primitive and localized to be effective. Experts generally agreed that sufficient protection from overflows would come only with significant federal involvement and support. The efforts of Delta representatives played a key role in the creation by Congress in 1879 of the Mississippi River Commission. After the severe flood of 1882, the commission made federal funds available to repair some of the larger crevasses in the levees. From this point on, the commission contributed annually to flood control. In the same year, Congress authorized army engineers to assist local boards with levee construction if such construction would improve navigation. With the benefit of such strong external support, levee construction proceeded apace. By 1896 a district engineer for the Corps of Engineers at Vicksburg wrote that "it would be difficult to find another portion of the country of like area where improvement and development have been so marked. By the cooperation of the River Commission, state Levee Commissions, and the Yazoo and Mississippi Valley Railway Company, a basin some 200 miles long by about 60 miles broad . . . has been secured against overflow." Subsequent floods would disprove this assertion, but the support of the federal government for the inconsistent, inadequate, piecemeal efforts of state and local interests to protect the Delta from devastating inundations was nonetheless sufficient to energize and accelerate the further settlement of the Delta and exploitation of its rich lands.[34]

With its abundance of interconnected waterways, the Delta seemed well blessed with adequate means of transportation. In fact, however, the area's streams were hardly ideal avenues for travel and transport. Spring floods meant caving banks and brought water levels up near overhanging tree branches. Submerged snags pulled into the streams by high, rushing waters posed a threat as levels fell in autumn. These snags were a serious problem, often blocking streams at harvest time when water traffic was likely to be heaviest. When creeks and rivers became impassable, planters had little choice except to store their cotton near the stream and wait for high water in the spring or, in the likely event that debts were too pressing to allow such delay, haul their cotton over swamp and thicket to the Mississippi, where it could be loaded on riverboats for transport to New Orleans or Memphis. The Delta's dependence on water transportation clearly hindered the settlement, clearing, and cultivation of its interior lands.[35]

Prior to the 1880s, Delta planters viewed railroads primarily as supplementary links to the major north-south streams that ran up and down the region. By the end of the 1870s, planter capital had built two narrow-gauge, single-track lines that, despite their ambitious "Greenville, Columbus and Birmingham" and "Mobile and Northwestern" titles, totaled scarcely seventy miles in length. In 1882 railroad magnate Collis P. Huntington joined forces with New York banker Richard T. Wilson to purchase several Mississippi railroad franchises with an eye toward completing a Memphis to New Orleans link, on which only 25 of 454 track miles had been laid. Part of the package was 774,000 acres of Delta land owned by the two franchises, but the prime attraction for the purchasers was the right-of-way through the nearly level Yazoo Delta, a route that promised relatively low construction and operating expenses.[36]

By the fall of 1884, the new Louisville, New Orleans, and Texas Railway Company was handling traffic between the Delta's two major market outlets, giving its planters their first taste of the advantages of a modern long-haul rail line and its superiority to the steamboat as a means of transporting their crops. The railroad ran regardless of weather or season, and enthusiastic planters scrambled to subsidize the LNO&T's expansion into their vicinities by granting right-of-ways across their land. Most plantations received their own station, and gins and loading areas quickly materialized along the line. By 1892 more than half of the railroad's 807 miles of track lay within the Yazoo Delta.[37]

LNO&T officials launched energetic efforts to promote settlement along its right-of-way. To that end they contacted Isaiah T. Montgomery, who had headed the abandoned all-black colony at Davis Bend near Vicksburg, about the possibility of establishing a black settlement in the Delta. Envisioning an environment where blacks could enjoy economic, social, and political opportunities unavailable elsewhere in 1887, Montgomery chose a location in Bolivar

County. The group, headed by Montgomery and his cousin Benjamin T. Green, purchased fifteen hundred acres of land, and the all-black town of Mound Bayou was soon thriving. Its population had reached six hundred by 1890, and it eventually formed the core of a larger agricultural colony of four thousand blacks.[38]

Meanwhile, the LNO&T literally prospered itself out of existence. By 1886 the railroad was turning a profit of $1,257 per mile on the single track line running south through Clarksdale to Vicksburg. Its gross receipts tripled between 1887 and 1891, and some of its officials complained that their volume of traffic was more than the railroad was equipped to handle. Its success, as well as the aggressiveness of its management, quickly brought the railroad into competition with the massive Illinois Central line for the bulk of the north-south traffic out of New Orleans. When accumulating debts forced Huntington to part with his holdings piece by piece, the Illinois Central suddenly had an opportunity to acquire a serious and profitable competitor, and in 1892 it purchased the LNO&T, tying it quickly and securely into its system and renaming it the Yazoo and Mississippi Valley Railroad. As Robert L. Brandfon put it, "A more satisfactory purchase had never been made." Despite the depression that gripped the nation during the period, the Yazoo and Mississippi Valley's gross receipts per mile rose from $4,111.55 in 1892 to $5,901.00 in 1898. The latter figure exceeded the total earnings of the parent company itself in any year from 1887 to 1890. Over the decade the gross receipts of the Y&MV grew by 51 percent.[39]

Officials of the Illinois Central tried initially to encourage immigration to the Delta by small farmers, but the economic and social ambitions of its white landholders and, ironically, the credit policies of the railroad itself combined to ensure that the resurgent Delta would retain its status as a plantation kingdom. As Brandfon wrote:

> The old formulas did not apply because farming in the Yazoo Delta was unlike farming in most areas of the country; it was a state of mind. No sooner did a man set foot into the Yazoo Delta than 'his eyes . . . opened upon the fair prospect.' . . . This was the infection of the Yazoo Delta; more than a place to earn a better living, it represented an opportunity to attain the very heights of the South's agricultural social status—to be a planter.[40]

The desire to attain planter status and amass all the wealth, power, and prestige that status implied drove most landholders to strive constantly to enlarge their holdings, despite the enormous costs of clearing, draining, and cultivating the expanded acreage. Banking on the remarkable productive capacity of the rich alluvial soil, the planters plunged repeatedly and often more deeply into debt. Dealing with his factor on terms that amounted to an approximate interest rate of 13 percent in addition to the factor's commission of 2.5 percent on each purchase and each sale, the planter often wound up paying up to 20 percent per year in interest and commission charges. Despite the apparent exorbitance of this rate, heavy indebtedness was a way of life in the Delta, and in order to capitalize on the planter's demand for more land, the Illinois Central adopted a more than liberal credit policy. Selling its lands at from seven to fifteen dollars per acre with 20 percent down and the balance payable at 6 percent in from two to five years, the railroad also offered a warranty title deed on the basis of the down payment alone. Meanwhile, the rise in land values accompanying the breakthroughs in levee construction and rail expansion and the stabilization of cotton prices in the 1880s had enhanced the attractiveness of land as collateral. As a result, explained Brandfon, "with a title deed in his pocket," the ambitious Delta planter "found it easier to raise large amounts of cash by mortgaging his land rather than by tenuous crop liens or personal cognizance." In the long run, the railroad had actually undermined its own efforts to populate the Delta with small farmers, because its credit policies had simply reinforced the acquisitive impulses of Delta planters by allowing them to extend their indebtedness significantly with only a 20 percent downpayment for new lands.[41]

Once it was connected fully by rail to the nation's greatest markets, the cotton economy of the Delta grew explosively in the 1880s. Clear-cutting as they went, a number of timber companies began to follow railroad trunk lines into the interior of the region. Cultivatable acreage doubled, and cotton production in 1889 was more than 160 percent of the 1879 crop. Planters took a second look at some of the less desirable, swampy lowlands they had spurned formerly, and by the end of the 1880s cotton and corn were planted "down to the water's edge of the bayous." The growth of the railroad not only encouraged more widespread cultivation of cotton, but it increased the value of all land, improved or not, in the Delta counties, where, on the average, land prices rose by nearly 50 percent between 1880 and 1890.[42]

The stabilization of cotton prices encouraged those with access to sufficient capital to rent for cash, and the percentage of farms operating under this agreement grew from 25 percent in 1880 to 41.2 percent in 1890. The dominant trend, however, was toward sharecropping, and the percentage of farms rented for a share of the crop in 1890 (42.4) was 2.5 times as great as the figure for 1880 and significantly higher than the figure (30.6) for the remainder of the state in 1890. The rapid growth of the sharecropping system was traceable to the expanded labor requirements of the Delta's booming plantation economy and to the resultant efforts of Delta planters to recruit impoverished black refugees fleeing the failing soils and stagnant economies of the hill counties in Mississippi.[43]

In 1879, as Delta planters wrung their hands at the prospect of a mass exodus of Mississippi blacks to Kansas, a number of newspapers in the rest of the state had hailed this development: "We hope they will better their condition and send back so favorable a report from the 'land of promise' that thousands will be induced to follow them; and the immigration will go on till the whites will have a numerical majority in every county in Mississippi." As the black population of the Delta swelled with immigrants, however, the region's attractiveness to blacks began to take its economic toll in the hill and prairie counties. In a single week, Fannie Cromwell, a black labor recruiter, was reported to have enticed over a hundred workers from the Columbus, Mississippi, area to the Delta. Early in 1880 the Hinds County *Gazette* reported that five hundred blacks had been led from Oktibbeha County to a single plantation in the Delta.[44]

Soon planters in the rest of the state were threatening to "shoot on the spot" or "tar and feather" the first person they discovered trying to "decoy away" their labor. For whites in other counties, it was one thing for blacks to leave the rich, black-majority counties of the Delta for Kansas or elsewhere. It was quite another for them to enrich the Delta further, both politically and economically, by deserting other parts of the state for the richer soils of the Yazoo Basin. The objections of hill-county whites led finally to the passage, over the long-standing objections of the Delta planters, of an anti-enticement law in 1884. This law fell to gubernatorial veto, but an 1890 measure provided penalties—a heavy fine and damages equal to twice the crop lost by the first employer—for anyone who knowingly employed a worker who was already under contract to someone else.[45]

Black labor continued to flow into the Delta in the wake of the 1890 law, but the real black influx had come in the 1880s, when a booming economy triggered black population growth in excess of 60 percent across the nine "core" counties of the region. While significant at slightly less than 18 percent, white population increase during the 1880s was not nearly so striking; with blacks outnumbering whites by seven to one in 1890, the dependence of Delta whites on black labor clearly had diminished but little over the course of three tumultuous decades. Moreover, the rapidly expanding black population, whose labor was vital to the economic preeminence of the white landowner, seemed to pose a serious threat to white supremacy in the social and political sector.[46]

During Reconstruction labor-hungry Delta planters had on several occasions urged their friends and neighbors to refrain from the wholesale repression and violence against blacks that was so common in other parts of the state. Even in the violent context of Redemption in 1875, after the black followers of John Brown had been stampeded in Coahoma County, the leader of a group of whites crouched in ambush reportedly ordered his troops to hold their fire and "let the poor devils go. We need them to pick our cotton." Reporting to the New York *Tribune* on the affair, James L. Alcorn assessed the incident in terms wholly pragmatic: "We have lost a week's work, but believe there will be no future trouble."[47]

Assessing the more moderate response of white Deltans to the efforts of blacks to exercise their newly won freedom, William C. Harris concluded that "in Redemption as in Reconstruction, the concern for social order and labor stability frequently surmounted any desire by planters of these counties to maintain a rigid subordination of blacks." Harris noted further that "compared to the tyranny existing in the interior, in most river counties blacks continued to exercise a surprising degree of freedom and political action."[48]

After Redemption the white leadership in several heavily black Mississippi plantation counties continued the practice of limited interracial political cooperation as the most expedient means of furthering their own political interests while controlling black political activity and pacifying blacks sufficiently to maintain a stable plantation labor force. Under these "fusion" arrangements, blacks were normally allotted some minor political posts in exchange for their support for the white candidates who headed the fusion ticket. One white participant in the system described fusion as a means by which blacks could have "some of the offices, and the whites, of course, the best ones." The fusion ticket in Coahoma County in 1883 featured a white candidate for state senate, a white and a black candidate for the state house of representatives, whites for sheriff and clerk of court, and blacks for treasurer and assessor. At one point, all but one of the elected officials in Bolivar County were black.[49]

In Coahoma County's elections in 1881, two factions competed for black votes. A candidate for sheriff on an all-white slate, William A. "True Blue" Alcorn, offered cynical assurances that, regardless of what their white employers who were supporting his fusion ticket opponent might tell them, blacks could behave "as they pleased." Blacks were in this enviable position because, as Alcorn saw it, the local planters loved "to see cotton grow too well to let Mr. Nigger suffer." In 1881 the Friars Point *Gazette* courted blacks with a special front-page column entitled "News Notes and Items of Interest about Colored People." The paper also used courtesy titles—Mr. and Mrs.—for blacks.[50]

The desire of the white planting interests for economic and social stability played a major role in encouraging black-white fusion efforts. So long as fusion produced such stability, its proponents were satisfied. With elections scheduled at peak labor times on the plantations, blacks were less likely to participate in significant numbers. This suited local whites quite well, and the Friars Point *Gazette* noted that work had won over politics in both the spring and fall elections in 1881, the result being "no time is wasted by the laboring classes."[51]

Fusion allowed Delta whites to use their influence over the black vote to their advantage in statewide political contests, but its most disconcerting aspect was its tendency to encourage white political factions within the Delta to compete for black votes. This competition led to efforts by whites to discredit certain other whites in the eyes of black voters, often with bitter results. The Greenville *Times* warned blacks, for example, that one local aspirant seeking their support had not only supported the Black Code but urged planters to respond to the Exodus of 1879 by arming themselves and going to the riverbank. Such an effort by a white candidate to win black support by attacking another white candidate threatened only to create deep and permanent political divisions among whites in the Delta.[52]

J. Morgan Kousser explained that, as long as blacks retained political bargaining potential, "whites had to fear Negro domination." In 1888 candidates from two white factions created considerable excitement among Bolivar County blacks, courting them ardently and reportedly offering bribes for the support of influential blacks. Spectacles such as both white candidates for the legislature appearing before a crowd of fifteen hundred gathered for the laying of a cornerstone at a black church in Coahoma County were also alarming to whites, and by the end of the 1880s, whites were sternly advising blacks to tend to their farming and leave politics to their white benefactors. In October 1889 the Bolivar County *Review* asserted that the only way our civilization can be preserved is by whites uniting for "the common good." The writer credited white unity for the "splendid political management" he observed in nearby Washington County. Planter-politician Walter Sillers saw no end to "politics" in the Delta so long as blacks maintained the right to vote.[53]

Political discontent festered throughout Mississippi at the end of the 1880s as the Farmer's Alliance movement capitalized on the growing dissatisfaction of small farmers, both black and white. To conservative Delta Democrats, the alliance movement posed the threat of a biracial coalition of have-nots capable of ousting the Delta's planter-business elite from its dominant position in state and local politics. Ironically, many of those whites who supported the alliance, including those in the Delta where the movement enjoyed relatively little success, blamed the manipulated black vote for the ability of their upper-class white antagonists to retain their dominant political influence. Thus blacks were often damned by those who opposed the alliance movement as well as by those who supported it.[54]

Beyond the matter of white unity, there was also the fear of a unified black majority seizing physical as well as political control throughout the Delta. In January 1889 rumors of an impending riot by blacks swept across Coahoma County. One writer urged white authorities to "make short work" of "those who fired the mind of the ignorant and consequently prejudiced Negro," but he also cautioned against a repeat of the "bloody scenes" of the Redemption Era as he reminded readers of both races that their interests were still "closely allied."[55]

Antiblack sentiment erupted tragically in Leflore County in September 1889, illustrating the growing fear among whites of a black takeover in the Delta. After controversial Colored Farmer's Alliance organizer Oliver Cromwell enjoyed considerable success among Leflore County blacks, he received a number of stern warnings, including death threats from local whites. Leflore blacks rallied to Cromwell's defense, presenting whites with a statement of defiance said to represent the feelings of "3,000 Armed Men." Rumors of blacks arming themselves for an insurrection led the Leflore County sheriff to call on the governor to send in national guardsmen to keep the peace. In fact, however, a posse of local whites apparently killed as many as twenty-five blacks, a number of whom were involved neither with the Colored Farmer's Alliance nor the alleged insurrection. There were numerous reports of whites invading black homes, and one observer even claimed to have seen a white youth "beat out the brains of a little colored girl" while another white held a gun on the girl's parents.[56]

After the alliance leaders had been killed or had fled the area, white planters reportedly offered refuge to local blacks who feared further mob action because, despite their racial anxieties, as one historian put it, "white landowners nonetheless opposed annihilating people who within a few weeks could pick their cotton." The "Leflore County Massacre" provided a violent illustration of the mounting anxieties among Delta whites, whose labor needs had once encouraged them to accept black political participation but who faced by the end of the 1880s the reality of a black population explosion sufficient to threaten the future of white supremacy in the Delta.[57]

Observing this phenomenon, Washington County Democratic leader J. S. McNeily agreed with Walter Sillers in 1890 that "the handwriting was on the wall for every black county ultimately" unless white supremacy could be assured. Destined to play a major role in the disfranchisement movement, McNeily joined those who argued that only by denying the ballot to blacks could whites hope to retain control of an economically resurgent Delta.[58]

Many Delta whites had initially opposed a constitutional convention to consider disfranchisement, because they believed that stripping the vote from blacks would undermine their region's political influence in the state at large. Delta whites also feared that their dirt-farmer antagonists in the hills would use the convention to pursue a populistic anti-Delta agenda of legislative reapportionment, prohibition, and railroad regulation. Haunted by still-vivid memories of the lengthy period of military occupation their region had already experienced, many Delta whites worried as well that too brazen an attempt to disfranchise blacks might lead to an abhorrent Reconstruction-like renewal of federal interference in the internal politics of the state. On the other hand, the flood of blacks into the Delta (symbolized by the establishment of the black colony in and around Mound Bayou) posed the threat of racial upheaval to a white population that was itself absorbing a smaller though significant influx of racially antagonistic, lower-income whites from the hills. As for more affluent whites, J. Morgan Kousser explained that "the plantation elite's reasons for wanting to disfranchise blacks were obvious. The end of Negro voting would solidify their control over their tenants and free them of having to deal with elected or appointed black officials—a type of contact almost all southern whites found distasteful."[59]

Partisan concerns also played a major role in moving the Delta's white Democrats to support disfranchisement. Mississippi senator Hernando de Soto Money admitted that the goal of the disfranchisers was "to maintain a civilization that is dependent very largely upon the Democratic Party being in control." Walter Sillers saw disfranchisement in terms of the opportunity it presented for white Democrats to "organize a majority and freeze out factions." With factionalism out of the way, the Delta's Democratic political leaders could claim to speak for all Deltans and therefore present a truly united front that would greatly enhance their efforts to protect and advance their region's interests in state politics.[60]

Some Delta whites hoped that a portion of the Delta's numerical losses in black votes resulting from disfranchisement would be offset by the number of white voters elsewhere in the state who would also be disqualified by the various restrictions imposed on suffrage. At the constitutional convention called to consider disfranchisement in 1890, hill-county leaders objected strenuously that the means proposed to take the vote from blacks would also deny the franchise to fifty thousand whites. A Delta delegate retorted that "to avoid the disfranchisement of a lot of white ignoramuses we can't have an educational qualification and to pander to the prejudices of those who have no property, we cannot have a property qualification." Many Delta whites also actively opposed the "understanding clause," which was added to the constitution to provide a registration loophole for the illiterate whites of the hills.[61]

J. S. McNeilly believed that the Australian ballot might provide a second line of defense against the hill-county white vote by "separating the voter from the mass and the mass manager," although he feared that the introduction of a secret ballot might encourage blacks to seek more education. When the convention's work was finally done, however, the poll tax, literacy test, and secret ballot had their desired effect, while the understanding clause proved no particular boon to the white counties. (Of the scarcely two thousand registrants who gained the vote through this provision in 1892, nearly half were black.) The results of the 1895 gubernatorial election outlined the effects of disfranchisement in Mississippi. The percentage of adult black males who did not vote rose from 71 percent in the 1888 presidential election to nearly 100 percent in 1895. The fact that nonvoting by whites was 7 percent higher in 1895 than in 1888 also suggested that the new constitution would serve Delta whites well as they battled their upland adversaries in the hills for control of state politics.[62]

By 1895, with Republican opposition in disarray and the disfranchisement provisions working to near perfection, the Bolivar *Journal*, ecstatic that Walter Sillers's dream of white unity in the Delta had been realized, acknowledged differences among Democrats but rejoiced that "they will be settled within the party ranks, and whenever the black brigade appears within the field, it will be met and vanquished by a united Democracy." Even Sillers's old political nemesis, Charles Scott, who had often benefited from black support, celebrated the death of fusion in "Bolivar the Blessed."[63]

In addition to a new sense of partisan unity, the 1890 constitution yielded other benefits for Delta whites. Although white-county representatives had succeeded in their efforts to use the 1890 convention to reapportion the legislature, a new reapportionment plan based ostensibly on "voting" population (adult male) rather than total population ultimately did little to undermine the disproportionate influence enjoyed by whites from black-majority counties in the state legislature. Prior to the ratification of the new constitution, the white-majority counties with a total adult white male population of 73,010 were allotted only 51⅔ seats in the state house of representatives and 17⅔ seats in the state senate, while the black-majority counties with 47,600 adult white males held 68⅓ seats in the house and 22⅓ seats in the senate. Framers of the new constitution finally fashioned a compromise wherein white-majority counties were to be given thirteen new house seats, and additional white-majority house districts were to be carved out of black-majority counties. These latter counties, on the other hand, were to receive more favorable apportionment in the state senate, and their leaders expected as well that a requirement stipulating three-fifths approval of all revenue measures would give them effective veto power over all tax increases.[64]

In the immediate aftermath of the convention, hill-county leaders were jubilant over the new apportionment scheme, and some Delta leaders were so distressed that they talked openly of seceding from the state. (Actually, the Delta delegates to the convention had backed the apportionment proposal by a vote of eight to seven, although some of those who supported the move to strengthen white-county representation were apparently motivated by a concern for maintaining white supremacy should the constitution's disfranchising provisions be voided by the courts or by Congress.) Despite these initial impressions to the contrary, however, the new apportionment plan continued to favor the white minority that ruled the Delta. In the lower house, the nearly 17-seat advantage formerly enjoyed by the black counties in 1882 shrank to 8 seats under the 1890 plan, but the black-county advantage in the senate actually rose slightly, from 4⅔ seats in 1882 to 5⅓ seats in 1890.[65]

Albert Kirwan found it "almost unbelievable" that white-county leaders had not realized that the reapportionment plan did them no favors. Kirwan pointed out that, according to the census of 1890, if every adult male in every legislative district created by the 1890 constitution had voted for a candidate of his own race, sixty-nine blacks would have gained office as compared to sixty-four whites.[66]

As Table 3 indicates, the 1890 plan did little to equalize per capita representation of white males between the black-majority counties—where practically all of the black males were disfranchised—and white-majority counties. After 1890 each member of the house of representatives from a black-majority county had a constituency of 675 adult white male voters as compared to the average of 1,168 for each representative from a white county. In the senate, members from black-majority counties represented only 1,891 white males, as compared to the 3,681 white males represented by senators from white-majority counties.

In the long run, disfranchisement allowed the Delta's Democratic leadership to consolidate its local power base, while continued malapportionment facilitated its efforts to advance its Delta-oriented agenda in state politics. C. Vann Woodward concluded that "instead of redressing the gross inequality of representation that penalized the white counties and was their main reason for

TABLE 3. White Males per Representative in the House of
Representatives and State Senate, 1882 and 1890

	House of Representatives		*State Senate*	
	—1882—	*—1890—*	*—1882—*	*—1890—*
White-majority counties	1,413	1,168	4,133	3,681
Black-majority counties	697	675	2,131	1,891

Source: Clark L. Miller, "Let Us Die to Make Men Free" (Ph.D. diss., University of Minnesota, 1983), 625.

agreeing to the convention and submitting to the poll tax and disfranchisement
plan, the Mississippi convention actually perpetuated and solidified the power
of the Black Belt oligarchy. Its work was, therefore, doubly undemocratic: It
disfranchised the race that composed a majority of the population, and it delivered a large majority of whites into the control of a minority of their own race
in the black counties."[67]

Although Delta whites could hardly have asked for a better result, available
evidence gives little hint of a conspiracy on their part. Many Delta leaders who
supported disfranchisement did so with great apprehension that such action
might bring a renewal of federal interference in their racial affairs and only after
making a difficult choice between the anticipated loss of political influence in
the state legislature and their urgent concerns about the future of white
supremacy both in their region and in the state at large. If Delta representatives
at the 1890 convention realized at the time that the new apportionment plan
would actually preserve their political advantages in the legislature, they gave
no such indication. Instead, however, they managed to exact significant concessions, such as the three-fifths vote requirement for the passage of revenue
measures, in exchange for their acceptance of a reapportionment plan that,
despite their fears, ultimately proved beneficial to them. As a result, instead of
forcing them to give ground politically to protect their racial preeminence, the
1890 constitution actually enhanced the economic and political standing of
affluent Delta whites even as it made their racial position within the Delta more
secure.[68]

Disfranchisement proved every bit as injurious to the interests of the Delta's blacks as it was beneficial to those of its whites. In 1891 Mississippi senator
E. C. Walthall had bragged on the floor of Congress that thirty-one of forty-
four Bolivar County officeholders were black. His remarks found their way
into the national press, and one Kansas City paper pointed out that "Bolivar
County alone boasts more colored elected officeholders than any whole northern state, possibly a series of northern states." A few blacks continued to vote
in Bolivar after the 1890 disfranchisement provisions were in place, but whites
knew full well that black voting could be shut off whenever it became troublesome. As white political leaders embraced the white primary system, which

allowed them to settle their differences within the confines of the Democratic party, black political fortunes declined proportionately. The poll tax gradually eased most black registrants off the rolls, and those who remained voted only sporadically and in negligible numbers after 1895.[69]

The waning political influence of blacks manifested itself in a number of ways. Whereas in 1890 roughly equal numbers of blacks and whites had been summoned for jury duty in Bolivar County, no blacks were called by 1902. In 1872 J. C. Crittendon, a black man, had presided as a Bolivar County supervisor over the construction of a new courthouse. By 1915 Crittendon was working as a porter in that same courthouse. Unworried about black objections, white landlords in Coahoma County rejected federal flood-relief assistance in 1897, dismissing blacks who complained as "incapable of comprehending the true import of government aid."[70]

In the final analysis, the effort to secure the Delta's future as a land of economic and political opportunity for whites led directly to an era of drastically diminished economic, political, and social prospects for blacks. Surveying the postbellum Delta, Sydney Nathans explained that "during the first twenty years after emancipation, a standoff [between blacks and whites] prevailed on the plantation frontier." Nathans observed that "although their chances were drastically different" during the early postbellum years, when the Delta was an expanding but only partially developed region, both the planter and the black worker had seen "an opportunity to make money."[71]

Although whites had generally enjoyed the upper hand in their dealings with blacks throughout the late nineteenth century, during the early postbellum decades the desire of Delta planters to achieve dominion over their workers was in many cases tempered by their fears that heavy-handed, abusive behavior could cost them the labor they needed to cultivate and harvest their cotton. The rapid growth of the black population during the 1880s eased concerns over the labor supply, however, even as it exacerbated white fears of social and political inundation. The black population boom therefore spurred whites to impose extensive political restraints on a black majority that had once been able to parlay the planter's need for labor into at least some limited political and economic gains. In the long run, disfranchisement supplanted fusion as a means for ensuring white political supremacy and labor control and took its place alongside flood protection and railroad construction as a key element in the effort to secure the Delta's future as the South's preeminent plantation region. When Nathans concluded that "reclamation of the Delta from the swamp . . . sealed its destiny as the domain of the planter," he might have noted the role of the 1890 constitution in this process as well.[72]

The United States government also bore a certain amount of responsibility for the declining political fortunes of Delta blacks. By failing to suppress the terrorism of 1875, the Grant administration had actually set the stage for the restoration of white supremacy, while the Supreme Court offered its stamp of approval to the primary means by which this goal was achieved with its 1898

Williams v. Mississippi decision upholding the constitutionality of the 1890 disfranchisement statutes. When John Sharp Williams observed in 1907 that "the danger of political negro domination in Mississippi has passed away," he traced the demise of the black political threat back not to 1890 but to 1898, when "the Supreme Court of the United States held our State Constitution not be violative of the Constitution of the United States."[73]

Despite the political setbacks they suffered, through shrewdness and determination some Delta blacks continued to make economic advances well into the twentieth century. By 1900, for example, black landowners in Tunica County outnumbered white ones by nearly three to one. This statistic seems remarkable in light of the obstacles black farmers encountered, but their holdings were concentrated overwhelmingly in less desirable, marginal areas, and despite their numerical superiority, when total acreage was considered, black farmers held only 10 percent of the county's land. Moreover, land prices rose in the Delta from an average of thirteen dollars per acre at the beginning of the boom decade of the 1880s to more than forty dollars in 1910, a trend that quickly moved even the less desirable Delta acreage out of the reach of would-be black landowners. Delta planters who had once rented their roughest lands to blacks as a means of getting them cleared had less incentive to provide blacks with even this narrow avenue of upward mobility once the completion of the railroads and the levee network facilitated the penetration of the region by the timber companies, who often paid as little as twenty-five cents per acre for the privilege of clearing the planter's lands of timber.[74]

As the plantation economy became more stable, the fabled agricultural ladder grew steeper and more slippery, and the racial climate deteriorated rapidly as well. The Delta's white leaders continued to express a desire to see blacks treated fairly, but, with its burgeoning black population and numerous examples of escalating racial tensions, the Delta stood at the forefront of a wave of racial violence that saw Mississippi move quickly to claim gruesome distinction as the lynchingest state in the nation. Between 1888 and 1901, seventeen counties wholly or partially within the Delta accounted for thirty-four of the ninety-three lynchings recorded by the NAACP for all of Mississippi's eighty-two counties.[75]

Historians have long debated the matter of whether the passage of blatantly discriminatory legislation at the end of the nineteenth century brought an end to a period of flexibility and fluidity in race relations or merely institutionalized a prevailing white sentiment that had already blocked social and political advances by blacks. In the Delta the first two postbellum decades had been marked by significant examples of socioeconomic and political gains by blacks. Yet changes in the economic and demographic conditions in the region during the 1880s triggered a sharp decline in the overall fortunes of blacks and set the stage as well for the legal and extralegal measures whereby whites regained control over black workers in the Delta. Prior to the 1880s, Delta freedmen had been able to capitalize on the demand for their labor to advance themselves not only materially but politically and, to a much more limited extent, even socially as well. These advances first slowed and then ceased altogether, however, as publicly funded improvements in the Delta's flood-control system acted in combination with its expanded railroad network to move the region into what Brandfon called "the mainstream of national commerce." Although it ultimately contributed to diminished opportunities for blacks, more effective integration into the world and national economy brought a dramatic increase in the Delta's black population and thus shaped the context in which white leaders took steps to ensure that the already uphill struggle between a landless black labor force and a landed white elite would never take place on level ground.[76]

With its black labor force expanded and politically neutralized and its transportation and flood-control network vastly improved, the Delta's white planters and businessmen were in a position to capitalize more fully on world demand for their cotton. The overall result was impressive statistical evidence of aggregate economic expansion. The benefits of this growth, however, went primarily to a tiny segment of the population, while the dramatic curtailment of economic and political opportunities for the Delta's huge black majority stamped upon the region an image of material and human disparity that would remain its trademark for more than a century.

If the events of the 1880s and 1890s ultimately helped to seal the gloomy fate of the Delta's black laborers, they had precisely the opposite effect on the fate of its planter elite. The question of the fortunes of the planter class in the wake of the Civil War and Reconstruction has attracted considerable scholarly attention, with most of the debate revolving around the matter of whether the former slaveholders gave way to a new, more dynamic generation of business-minded merchants and industrialists. Since the publication in 1951 of his *Origins of the New South*, C. Vann Woodward has remained steadfast in his contention that the planter class "took a terrific tumble" as a result of the Civil War. The Delta certainly presented numerous examples of planters who lost their land either to excessive operating debt or an inability to pay their taxes or a combination thereof. A number of Delta planters also managed to somehow retain or reclaim their lands, but Woodward questioned whether a planter's ability merely to hold onto land should necessarily serve as an indication of his enduring preeminence. He observed that those who "hung onto or inherited land and prospered are known to have moved to town, opened stores, run gins, compresses, and banks, invested in railroads and mills, and played the speculative markets." His suggestion that these resourceful planter-businessmen "transformed themselves into members of the new class that was creating a commercial revolution and fostering an industrial revolution" may have exaggerated their achievements, but his general blueprint for survival or success as a planter described the experience of many prominent late nineteenth-century Delta planters whose interests and holdings actually made them some combination of planter and merchant, banker, or lawyer.[77]

Take, for example, the case of John Clark, who came to the Delta in the antebellum era and managed to retain his land after the war. Clark founded the town of Clarksdale in 1869, opened a store, and profited handsomely as land values rose during the railroad boom of the 1880s. By the early 1890s, Clark owned five thousand acres of land, two gins, a sawmill, and a merchandising operation. He also held an interest in a cotton compress and was an organizer of the Clarksdale Bank and Trust as well as a director of the Clarksdale Brick and Manufacturing Company. Another example was that of William H. Dickerson of Friars Point, who owned eight thousand acres of land by the 1890s, operated a mercantile establishment, and was a large stockholder in a box and woodwork factory, an oil mill, and a land company. Dickerson also owned a hotel and an entire block in the town of Friars Point. Finally there was Henry T. Ireys, who became Greenville's first cotton factor after playing an active vote in railroad development in the Delta. Ireys not only owned extensive planting and town properties but also served as president of the Delta Insurance Company.[78]

As a Reconstruction Era governor and senator, wealthy planter James L. Alcorn was a prominent former Whig who worked energetically to secure state and federal funds for levee construction, and his desire, in the words of a contemporary, to see "the old civilization of the South modernized" rather than overthrown clearly put him in the ideological mainstream as far as the Delta's white leaders were concerned. Elsewhere, men like W. L. Nugent, a planter-lawyer whose clients included a Jackson bank, also achieved at least temporarily heroic status through their efforts to promote land sales to railroads and British land speculators.[79]

Many of the Delta's economic and political leaders had close ties to the railroad. No less a planter aristocrat than Colonel William Alexander Percy, the "Gray Eagle of the Delta," took the lead in promoting centralized levee rehabilitation and railroad expansion in the Delta. Percy was also a prominent lawyer, as was his son, LeRoy, who found it no particular disadvantage to serve as chief counsel to the Illinois Central Railroad while he pursued his career as a planter. LeRoy Percy's income from his law practice, as well as from his partnership in a cotton factorage firm and his holdings in stock and bonds, helped to supplement his income from cotton growing and cushion the impact of bad crop years. Feeling less pressure during such years, Percy was less tempted to squeeze his tenants for debts or cheat on their settlements. Consequently, he had less trouble retaining labor than did many of his contemporaries. In addition to his efforts to win federal support for levee construction and flood control, Percy subsequently won acclaim among his Delta peers for his efforts to bring Italian labor to the Delta as a means of furthering the region's economic development.[80]

Percy's friend Charles Scott of Bolivar County was the consummate planter-lawyer-banker-businessman-politician; his gracious manner and aristocratic appeal made him an effective spokesman for Delta planters in their efforts to enlist the help of the Illinois Central Railroad in bringing an adequate supply of labor to the area. Although Scott had moved to the Delta after the war, by 1883 his individual holdings included more than nine thousand acres of land, and he was co-owner of several hundred more. Combining what Brandfon called "the appeal of the Southern romantic past" with "the success-ful business virtues of the twentieth century," Scott not only promoted the interests of the railroad but was a leader in the move to secure congressional funding for the Delta's levee system as well. He also served as president of the Bank of Rosedale. Scott and his brother Daniel, also an attorney, married two of the daughters of Colonel Alexander Yerger, a prominent figure in Bolivar County politics. (This pattern of kinship and intermarriage was by no means unusual among the Delta's political elite at the end of the nineteenth century. John Clark was married to the sister of James L. Alcorn, and his daughter was the wife of J. W. Cutrer, a prominent lawyer and member of the state senate.)[81]

In keeping with the aims of its prominent citizens, the Delta's newspapers were, for the most part, unfailingly boosterist in outlook. In April 1877 the Greenville *Times* unloosed a torrent of praise for the energy and pluck of the local populace in Greenville and throughout Washington County. With "more land in cultivation in Washington County than ever before," local enterprises were popping up everywhere. Most notable was the oil mill erected by Edmund S. Richardson at his Refuge Plantation. The paper reported that the machinery alone cost $40,000 and described the mill as the "most complete" such opera-tion between Greenville and New Orleans. With twenty-five hundred acres in cultivation, Refuge was reportedly the largest on the river, and Richardson held four other adjoining plantations encompassing nearly four thousand acres of improved land. In addition, he operated other plantations in Washington County and others still in Coahoma, Bolivar, and Holmes. Richardson, accord-ing to the *Times*, was the largest cotton planter in all of creation, except, per-haps, for "the Khedive of Egypt."[82]

In March 1882 the Greenville *Times* paid tribute to the Calhoun Land Company, which had just acquired seven plantations totalling twelve thousand acres on the Arkansas side of the river. The editor praised "Colonel" Calhoun, who had moved to the Delta from Pendleton, South Carolina, in 1867 and who had pioneered in bringing in black labor from the South Atlantic states. The editor also acknowledged the accomplishment of Calhoun, whose "pluck and energy" had enabled him to bring northern capital to the Delta, "thus making the initial movement which may result in our material advantage, that is, the assistance of capital to give the rich lands of the South their 'antebellum' value." Such enthusiasm was not only contagious but mandatory for a politically ambi-tious young newspaperman like James K. Vardaman, who as editor of the Greenwood *Enterprise* led his town's crusade for federally funded levee expan-sion, industrial development, and a variety of growth-oriented civic improve-ments. David Donald sensed defeatism and an absence of "entrepreneurial leadership" among George Collins and some of his planter contemporaries, but this was clearly not a problem for the leading men of the Delta by the end of the nineteenth century.[83]

A great many of the Delta's planter-businessmen-boosters were politically active. This was the case not only with LeRoy Percy, Charles Scott, and Walter Sillers, but with lesser known figures such as Will Collins of Issaquena County, who actually moved from merchandising to serving as deputy sheriff to appointment as a levee-tax collector to election to the county board of supervisors. In Tunica County, Richard F. Abbay owned two thousand acres of land and a merchandising operation in addition to serving in the general assembly.[84]

Woodward noted that anyone who foreclosed on land in the postbellum era could call himself a planter. In the case of the Delta, he might have added that most did. William Alexander Percy described his father LeRoy's circle of friends and political allies as the men who worked to "protect the country from overflow . . . bore the brunt of the Delta's fight against scalawaggery and Negro domination during reconstruction, . . . stole the ballot boxes which, honestly counted, would have made every county official a Negro," and "helped to shape the Constitution of 1890, which, in effect and legally disfranchised the Negro." Percy's recitation of these achievements read like a chronology of major developments in the restoration of the Delta as a vibrant plantation region, and he identified these men as members of the class "which traditionally had led in the South." In fact, however, whatever their pedigrees, these political leaders were not only planters but merchants, lawyers, journalists, and businessmen as well.[85]

The primary power base for Percy's boyhood heroes was the levee board, whose political influence within the Delta derived from its control of lucrative construction and repair contracts as well as remunerative positions for lawyers, engineers, and other employees. Percy cited the loss of levee board dominance by his father's friends as a sign of the declining influence of the old "intelligent, disinterested" Delta aristocracy, but, in reality, when Percy and his cohorts were forced to yield power, it merely passed to a competing faction of like-minded planter-businessmen and professionals.[86]

Even the free silver controversy that arose in the 1890s failed to produce much in the way of class-based political divisions among white leaders in the Delta. In fact, the conflict merely reflected the factional allegiances that had emerged from the often bitter struggle for levee board control. Like their "gold bug" opponents, such as LeRoy Percy and Charles Scott, free silverites like Walter Sillers and J. W. Cutrer were by and large successful lawyers and planters. Sillers owned a thousand acres of land in 1890, as did his law partner, Fred Clark. (In keeping with the Delta pattern, Sillers and Clark were also first cousins.) Sharing common economic pursuits and often ties of kinship as well, both of these elite factions also maintained an overarching commitment to flood control and the economic development of the Delta.[87]

C. Vann Woodward stressed the ties to the Whig party that characterized Redemption Era political leaders in Mississippi and throughout the South.

Although their upper-class white, pro-business "New South" orientation and their advocacy of government funding for internal improvements in the form of the levee rehabilitation and expansion suggested at least a neo-Whiggish political orientation, the individual political histories of the Delta's turn-of-the-century leaders are too convoluted to support such a generalization. Like many of their scalawag predecessors, the emergent post-Reconstruction power elite in the Delta were not so much persisting in the region's inclinations to Whiggery as upholding a long-standing Delta tradition of independent, self-interested, and largely pragmatic political behavior. They were less concerned about partisan labels or a consistent political philosophy than a narrowly focused policy agenda designed specifically to promote the development of the Yazoo Delta in a manner that would serve their own ends as well.[88]

Robert L. Brandfon described the common outlook and goals of the leaders of a turn-of-the century Delta that he called the "Cotton Kingdom of the New South." Brandfon neatly summarized the hopes of the Delta's leaders that "through the improvement of river transportation; the building of levees to protect these lands; the stimulation of land values by appreciation; and the introduction of capital, immigrant labor, and railroads, the Cotton Kingdom would become as efficient as any northern factory system, make profits as never before, and thus provide general prosperity for a New South."[89]

The planter remained an influential figure in the Mississippi Delta of the late nineteenth and early twentieth centuries, but the growing complexity of the region's economy made it more difficult (and less useful) to make distinctions among planters, lawyers, merchants, industrialists, and bankers. As David Cohn explained, "There were differences between townsmen and planters, but lines were not sharply drawn. . . . Sharing a common tradition . . . they were drawn closer by intermarriages. It was inescapable, then, that the town should become marked by the planter morality and the plantation point of view." Cohn was correct, of course, but despite their aristocratic airs and often lavish lifestyles, by the turn of the century the Delta's leading planters hardly fit into the restrictive mold of gentleman farmer, and while their social and political philosophies might be classified as "conservative" or "traditionalist," they were by no means committed to the status quo in the economic arena. Not only had they diversified their own activities, but they had played a leading role in efforts to bring in outside capital—both public and private—to develop the Delta's economy, upgrade its transportation network, and render it safer from overflow.[90]

In the 1850s the Delta had given every indication of becoming a cotton planter's paradise. The upheaval of civil war and the social and political restructuring of the Reconstruction Era interrupted the region's movement in this direction and introduced a new possibility—this one of a Delta that seemed to hold out attractive opportunities for blacks as well as whites. In the wake of Reconstruction, the restoration of conservative white political supremacy combined with the infusion of large amounts of public and private capital to create an economically dynamic Delta poised to enter the new century. The Delta that emerged from this process was not the open, competitive agricultural society that had been the promise of the early 1870s, however, but the undisputed domain of an ambitious and grasping planter-business-professional elite. Fancying themselves heirs to an aristocratic antebellum tradition, this cadre of white leaders sought to create through an ironic combination of economic modernization and racial resubjugation a prosperous and politically insulated cotton kingdom where the Delta planter's longstanding obsession with unfettered wealth and power could be transformed from Old South fantasy to New South reality.

5 ▽ New South Plantation
  ▽ Kingdom
  ▽

As a booming plantation kingdom, the turn-of-the-century Delta shrouded the ruthless efficiency and ambition of the New South in the romantic, laid-back, precapitalist imagery of the Old. Having long since abandoned the dream of populating the Delta with small farmers, officials of the Illinois Central Railroad marketed the Delta in 1910 as the Old South reincarnate: "Nowhere in Mississippi have antebellum conditions of landholding been so nearly preserved as in the Delta." The railroad's brochures described magnificent plantations "several hundred to several thousand acres in extent" worked by blacks who performed their duties in an atmosphere of Tara-like contentment: "The Negro is naturally gregarious in instinct, and is never so happy as when massed together in large numbers, as on the Delta plantations."[1]

Many of the Delta's plantations were indeed large, but in their modes of operation they more closely resembled modern factories than Old South estates, and despite their earnest efforts to emulate the lifestyle of Ashley Wilkes, big-time Delta planters showed a clear preference for the management style of Andrew Carnegie. Meanwhile, for the masses of blacks who toiled on the great estates of the Delta, the first quarter of the twentieth century was a period of unrelenting frustration during which the inverse relationship between their own socioeconomic and political status and that of their prosperous white employers became inescapably apparent. Despite continuing demand for their services, even the most determined blacks soon faced the facts of life in a region that had once tantalized them with promises of independence and opportunity but now taunted them with the reality of poverty, repression, and hopelessness that would be their true lot in life so long as they remained in the Delta.

The 1910 Census of Agriculture concluded that "the plantation system is probably more firmly fixed in the Yazoo-Mississippi Delta than in any other area of the South. The fertile soil and climatic conditions favorable for cotton raising, together with the large negro population, make the plantation the dominant form of agricultural organization in the Delta." In 1910 nine Delta counties representing but 11 percent of the state's land area accounted for 28 percent of the value of its total cotton crop. (Despite minimal expenditures for fertilizer, Delta planters achieved consistently higher yields than farmers in the rest of the state who were trying to combat both soil depletion and the boll weevil. In fact, between 1909 and 1915, as the rest of the state reeled under the boll weevil's onslaught, cotton yields rose in the Delta by 20 percent. In the latter year, the Delta accounted for half the state's total cotton production. The much greater natural fertility of the Delta soil not only reduced the cost of growing cotton but increased the value of the region's land. Outside the Delta, farm land ranged in value from $5.88 to $21.00 per acre, while in the nine "core" counties the lowest average value per acre was $31.67 and the highest $47.76.)[2]

By 1890 about one-quarter of Mississippi's blacks already lived in the Delta. Across the region blacks outnumbered whites nearly seven to one, with the ratio in Issaquena County standing at almost sixteen to one. By 1990 seven of the twelve blackest counties in the nation were in the Yazoo-Mississippi Delta. By 1910 Issaquena (94.1 percent) and Tunica (90.6 percent) were the nation's first and third blackest counties, and only Quitman at 76.5 had a black population percentage below 80 percent.[3]

Farm tenancy was widespread in Mississippi by the turn of the century, but it flourished in the Delta as nowhere else. As of 1910, 92 percent of the area's farms were operated by tenants, as compared to 63 percent outside the Delta. Approximately 95 percent of the Delta's tenants were black, as compared to 77 percent statewide.[4]

A Department of Agriculture study provided considerable insight into the tenancy system as it existed in the Delta on the eve of World War I. Utilizing data from nine counties for 1913, the authors examined cash renting (where the landlord provided land, house, and fuel and the tenant paid a fixed rent per acre in cash or in lint cotton), sharerenting (where the landlord provided land, house, fuel, and a portion of the fertilizer and the tenant paid as rent a share of the crop, usually one-third or one-fourth) and, finally, the sharecropping system (where the landlord supplied everything except one-half the fertilizer and the tenant divided the crop with the planter).[5]

The authors concluded that for the tenant, the higher the investment (and thus the tenant's share of the risk) the larger the potential return. Hence, whenever possible, tenants preferred some form of cash or share rental arrangement to sharecropping, although the latter remained preferable to day labor for wages. The cash renter, with the largest investment of any of the three tenant classes, stood by far the best chance of clearing a significant amount of money at the end of the year. Average incomes ranged from $333 for sharecroppers to $398 for share renters to $478 for cash renters. For the landlord, the average return on his investment, without an adjustment for local taxes, was 6.6 percent with cash renters, 11.8 percent with share renters, and 13.6 percent with sharecroppers. The overall average return to the landlord stood at 10.6 percent.

Whereas the sharerenting arrangement was the most risky but also potentially most rewarding for the tenant, the opposite was true for the planter, who took the greatest risk but stood to reap the greatest reward from contracting with a sharecropper.[6]

Regardless of the the contract terms, both parties naturally fared better if the crop yield was good. For the landlord, an average sharecropper income of three hundred dollars or better was good news indeed, for it meant a return of at least 15.5 percent, and in the isolated cases where the cropper earned at least a thousand dollars, the landlord received more than a 25 percent return on his investment.[7]

As one of the "most highly specialized cotton producing areas in the world," the Delta was well positioned to take advantage of the rapid growth of cotton demand that occurred during the first years of the twentieth century. With the introduction of twelve million new spindles in the British textile industry alone between 1900 and 1904, as well as the opening of new textile markets by the world's imperialist powers, there was a widespread concern that world cotton demand might have outgrown the supply. Moreover, as Britain relinquished its role in the spinning of lower-grade cotton to competitors like France, Germany, Japan, and the United States, its textile magnates sought new sources of higher quality cotton to augment its imports from Egypt and India. Delta boosters responded to concerns about the cotton supply by pointing out that only 30 percent of their region's land was even in cultivation in 1900. They boasted that once it was fully cleared and drained, the Delta alone might be capable of producing as much cotton as the rest of the nation's cotton-growing areas combined. Citing the move to establish modern drainage systems in the region, spokesmen pointed out that a better-drained Delta would be healthier for humans and less hospitable to the much-feared boll weevil that had already ravaged other less fortunate areas of the Cotton South. Finally, by maintaining drier, better-drained soil, Delta planters could experiment with some of the finer, higher quality strains of cotton comparable to those produced in Egypt and suitable to the needs of British spinners intent on producing higher grades of cloth.[8]

A number of British investors proved receptive to the claims of Delta spokesmen that their region was indeed a new Nile Valley. Early in 1911 a British consortium purchased from thirty to forty thousand acres of Delta land at a price estimated to be between two and three million dollars. These lands ultimately became the property of the Delta and Pine Land Company, which turned them into the world's largest cotton-planting operation.[9]

The Delta never became a competitive producer of the long-fibered, higher-quality cotton that flourished in Egypt and the American Southwest, but the British entrepreneurs had little reason to regret their investment. From the beginning, in fact, more than the incredibly fertile soil and the potential for producing a higher grade of cotton fiber, the "superior type of farm organization" these astute businessmen had seen in the Delta had impressed them. The efficiency they observed on Delta plantations seemed to ensure "profits without exception." As cotton prices rose in proportion to the growth of world demand, Delta planters had adopted increasingly sophisticated management techniques. Like the successful northern industrialists whose profits they envied so much, these planters had discovered that true efficiency derived not just from larger yields but from lower costs of production as well. As a result, although promoters touted the Delta as the second coming of the Old South, what the British investors actually saw in the region was a modern plantation system geared to achieving what Robert L. Brandfon called "the businesslike efficiency of industrialism."[10]

Despite its facade of personalism and paternalism, the system of plantation management that characterized large plantations by the second decade of the twentieth century was keyed wholly to profitable operation through close supervision and minimal cost outlays. Describing such plantations, Harold Woodman wrote: "A centralized office made all major management decisions, determining hours of work, the amount and kind of fertilizer and such used, the maintenance and improvements required, the tools, equipment and mules to be used, the boll weevil poisoning to be applied. Supervisors or overseers directed the work and saw to it that the workers followed the routine set by the manager."[11]

The refinement of these management techniques was perhaps the final stage in the process whereby the sharecropper's status was redefined from partner in the crop to what Woodman called "a wage worker paid in kind." Because Mississippi's crop-lien laws accorded priority to landlords and/or merchants to cover reimbursement for rent and advances, the cropper's claim for his share of the crop became valid only after the lien of the planter (and possibly the merchant as well) had been satisfied. Since the crop remained the property of the landlord until he divided it, and since other laws treated the cropper as a wage worker "subject to the rules and regulations set by his employer," landlords retained the prerogative of marketing the cotton and simply distributing the appropriate shares to their croppers. Under such circumstances the cropper was not actually a tenant who paid rent to the landlord but a worker who received from the landlord a post-harvest wage drawn from the proceeds of his crop.[12]

Moreover, despite having once entered into sharecropping arrangements in order to achieve personal autonomy as well as economic advancement, by the second decade of the twentieth century sharecroppers on the Delta's massive business plantations were, except for day laborers, its most tightly supervised farm workers. The greater opportunities for profit afforded by sharecropping made it the labor arrangement of choice for operators of the large plantations, where centralized management and close attention to every detail of cotton growing helped to reduce the risks that had once made Delta planters so leery of sharecropping. On a number of Delta plantations, tenants were actually charged fifty cents per acre annually under the heading of "Insurance" or

"Information" in order to defray the costs of hiring an overseer to inspect their crops. Also, in the Delta the average tenant plot was only 23.1 acres as compared to 38.3 acres for such plots outside the region. The smaller size of these plots allowed Delta planters and foremen to supervise their croppers more closely.[13]

At the same time, the desire to minimize his risks also encouraged the planter to hold down the advances he issued to his croppers. In bad times or in periods when prospects were less than bright, the cropper's allowance was certain to shrink. Since not even the planter could predict accurately the size of the upcoming crop or how rapidly the harvest would proceed, planters considered it especially prudent to keep early advances as low as possible. In so doing, they reduced their own chance of losses, both from a poor crop that might leave tenants unable to repay their debts or from croppers who moved away before crops were finished and settlements made.[14]

Many planters claimed that they anticipated a 10 to 15 percent loss on all advances. As a result, not only were advances held down, but for sharecroppers they seldom came in cash. Instead, they were confined to the fundamental necessities of food and clothing. A cropper living on advances was almost certain to be wearing the cheapest shoes and clothing available and subsisting on a diet of fat salt pork, cornbread, and canned goods, mostly beans. If the plantation operated a commissary, the decision as to whether a family received new shoes might be made by the overseer rather than the tenant himself. Advances generally ran from fifty cents to a dollar per acre worked by the cropper and his family, although allowances for groceries might be made separately. On Bledsoe Plantation at Shellmound in Leflore County, grocery advances seldom exceeded fifty cents per acre per month. If in any month this limit was surpassed, the excess went into the books in red ink, to be subtracted from the next month's advance.[15]

To the renter and a rare sharecropper who received them, cash advances meant lower prices for the goods they bought (credit prices reflected an interest charge) and in some cases the chance to purchase merchandise that was of higher quality than what was available on credit advance. On Alfred H. Stone's Washington County plantation, there were actually two plantation stores— one for credit customers and one for those who could pay cash. Those who made their purchases at the "cash" store bought better merchandise at close to the market price, but they also paid 20 percent interest on their cash advances. On Runnymede Plantation in Leflore County, special cash advances cost 25 percent for money used to purchase food and 35 percent for that used to buy clothing. Presumably, such exorbitant interest rates would not only serve as a deterrent to heavy indebtedness on the part of the tenant but also allow the planter to recoup from those tenants who paid off their debts the losses the planter incurred when other tenants could not.[16]

As a rule, regular advances ran from March 1 to August 1, dates that corresponded roughly to the period of soil preparation, planting, and cultivation.

Thereafter, advances were reduced or curtailed altogether, and the payment received for cotton seed during the fall picking season became the cropper's primary means of subsistence.[17]

Planters reported that in years past landowners had competed for labor by giving large "Christmas" advances, but by 1913 this practice was frowned upon because it gave tenants too much independence, the consensus among planters being that the larger such an advance, the longer the period during which a tenant would refuse work. Said one observer: "After a Negro gets his settlement at Christmas, he will not do a stroke of work until the money is gone. When it is spent they come again for advances. This is apt to be along in January or February for they soon spend their money."[18]

This reported penchant for such "high living" among black sharecroppers was in all likelihood the result of a five-month existence on a noncash income limited largely to the absolute necessities of food and clothing as defined by the landlord. However, too large a Christmas advance or partial pre-Christmas settlements could mean that harvesting the remainder of the crop would be delayed or that insufficient day labor would be available to perform necessary repairs and maintenance prior to the spring cotton-planting season. From the standpoint of the planter, the optimum strategy in dealing with tenants was to keep them economically dependent enough to ensure that they would be ready to work whenever labor was needed without creating a sense of hopelessness and frustration great enough to cause them to seek employment elsewhere. Individual acts of paternalism masked fundamentally cold and impersonal calculations that lay behind the planter's every management decision. Complain as they might about the fines and medical bills they had to pay for their tenants, few planters appeared to allow the economic costs of supporting and retaining labor to cut into their profits.[19]

Although Delta planters had successfully adopted modern, centralized management techniques to maximize the efficiency and profitability of these operations, they continued to struggle with labor turnover even as the black population grew and the Delta emerged as the most productive cotton growing region in the South. Given the high stakes involved and the obsession of Delta planters with retaining labor, it was not surprising that the Mississippi Delta accounted for an inordinate number of peonage complaints. Mississippi senator and Delta planter John Sharp Williams conceded in 1907 that strict enforcement of federal antipeonage statutes would be "to the detriment of southern plantation interests." Ironically, many planters resorted to peonage in order to prevent the loss of labor to other planters. Mississippi's 1890 enticement law was used liberally—primarily against planters—but the law also limited a tenant's options by discouraging planters from contracting with him if there was the slightest question as to whether he was under contract to another employer.[20]

In an attempt to restrain labor further, in 1900 the legislature passed a law to punish severely any tenant who entered into a second written contract

"without giving notice of the first." In 1904 the legislature enacted a new
vagrancy law aimed at driving "negro loafers to the field." In 1906 the lawmakers added the "false pretense law," providing criminal punishment for tenants who abandoned a contract after accepting even the smallest of advances.
Describing the false pretense law, Neil McMillen wrote: "Together with the
state's other restrictive labor statutes, it served as a legal framework for involuntary servitude. Not least of all, it reflected a social ethos that winked at even
the less subtle forms of latter-day bondage and that accepted some degree of
force as a requirement of black labor." In response to federal court decisions,
the state's supreme court voided the two-contract law in 1912, but the false
pretense law remained on the books until 1930. Meanwhile, during World
War I a number of towns enacted "work or fight" laws in response to white
perceptions of a war-induced labor shortage.[21]

   Although state and local statutes supplied the legal framework to support
peonage, neither coercion nor law nor a combination of the two was sufficient
to relieve the planter's concerns about labor turnover. Explaining how he had
dealt with a tenant who, he claimed, had left the plantation owing him $400, a
planter reported matter-of-factly that he had "caught up with the man and
whipped him till he couldn't stand up. Thought that would hold him for a while.
But the next morning he was gone. Never got a trace of him. I'd sure like to
know how he got off. He couldn't stand up when I got through with him."
Through manipulation of the crop lien and the furnish system, planters could
generally hold on to labor from planting through harvest, but at year's end there
was almost certain to be substantial movement from plantation to plantation.
As McMillen observed, "Annually, during the postsettlement reshuffling process, perhaps as many as one in three tenant families chose, in the plantation
idiom, to 'hit the grit' or 'light a shuck.'" This was true whether the cropper
had "come out ahead," "just lived" (broken even), or "gone in the hole."[22]

   One observer sympathetic to the planter contended in 1913 that widespread evidence of peonage notwithstanding, "a negro with a debt does not
hesitate long if he desires to halt the debt." The Jackson *Clarion-Ledger* claimed
that an indebted black laborer fleeing his obligation raised the cry of
"peenage" anytime he was "stopped and made to work out his indebtedness."
A number of planters managed to fill their labor needs by "buying" the debts
of black tenants from other landlords. Planters were more likely to make such
a "purchase" if the tenant owned a mule or implements. (Such a tenant required
less support from the landlord, and his property could be attached if he
attempted to move while indebted to the planter.) Hence LeRoy Percy was prepared to pay a fellow planter $289.96 so that a tenant with mule and implements
could move to his place while Walter Sillers, Jr., received $483.00 in return
for releasing a tenant who also owned his own mule.[23]

   A close observer of the plantation system in the Delta observed in 1907
that "plenty of men" had "gotten wealthy during the last six years of prosperity, good crops, and good prices by taking from helpless Negro tenants on his

plantation that which was rightfully theirs." Clearly, many "debts" were mere fabrications of the planter or the bookkeeper, but, given the questionable wisdom of a black tenant's disputing the word of a white planter, in the Delta an imaginary debt was as effective as a real one in restricting labor mobility, although in neither case was actual or alleged indebtedness an absolute guarantee that a worker would stay put.[24]

If real or imaginary debt did not serve to hold tenants in place, neither did relative prosperity. Delta planter and amateur race theorist Alfred H. Stone described an experiment in which the goal was the creation of a stable, "assured" tenantry by attracting to the plantation through "ties of self-interest" enough renters "to make us in turn measurably independent of the general labor situation." The plan was to offer a selected group of black tenants the opportunity to rent acreage at a uniform, fixed level and to purchase stock, implements, and wagons upon "exceptionally favorable" terms. The plantation management would supervise the planting, cultivation, harvest, and sale of the crop according to a detailed contract outlining the obligations of both parties. "The problem before us," explained Stone, "was to place in the hands of the people the means of acquiring something for themselves, and then, in every instance of deficient individual initiative, by proper supervision make them acquire it."[25]

The results of the experiment proved anything but satisfactory to Stone. In no year did the number of tenants who left fall below 22 percent of all the families on the plantation. Forty-five percent of the renters left in 1899 after an average earning of only $373.50 per family, but 41 percent also moved on in 1903, when incomes were nearly twice that high, and more than a quarter of the tenants left the plantation in 1901, when family income was approximately $1,000.00. In the end the experiment led to a large-scale outflow of equipment and property purchased on liberal credit terms, a result not unlike the one lamented by the luckless George Collins several decades earlier. Realizing what was happening, Stone began to replace his renters with sharecroppers, who were not offered such easy terms or urged to purchase stock or equipment. Noting a family that came on the plantation in 1900 bringing $108 worth of possessions and left in 1903 with $1,000, Stone concluded that this family, like most of the others who left, did so "to get rid of the supervision incident to plantation management." Few who participated in Stone's experiment achieved this goal, however; most became tenants on other plantations, and many lost what they carried away, slipping back to sharecropper status.[26]

Stone's observation concerning the desire of Delta blacks to escape supervision was particularly revealing. In the wake of the Civil War, Delta blacks had seen sharecropping as a means of escaping constant and close scrutiny by whites. The expert centralized management and supervision that characterized large plantations in the Delta worked to the economic benefit not only of the planter but often of the cropper as well. (Stone's experiment had sought to overcome "deficient individual initiative" with "proper supervision," and one planter bragged years later, "When I loan a man [cropper] money, I make him make good.") Close supervision by plantation management might result in a good settlement for the cropper, but a prospering cropper might nonetheless choose to move on because he felt that the economic benefits of submitting to such supervision did not outweigh its damaging emotional and psychological effects.[27]

An observer of the plantation system in the Delta noted that "the average negro prefers to be as free from the overseer as he can." Stone attributed the failure of his tenants "to respond to the influence of the most economic conditions with which it was possible to surround them" to both their "migratory instinct" and "a characteristic easy-going indolence, which seeks freedom to assert itself, and chafes under restraints which measurably restrict its enjoyment." Stone offered a racial explanation for a phenomenon that, as Gavin Wright pointed out, derived from a combination of economic and psychological factors. As Wright explained: "The freedom from minute supervision, orders and punishment has always been a basic human goal and historically a dimension of economic class, just as it is a measure of social standing in our own day." Hence, while black sharecroppers had little choice but to "work or starve," they at least possessed the "right to quit," and the assertion of this right provided at least a temporary relief from the frustrations of life as a closely monitored peasant in a planter's kingdom. Even if the move was confined to a small geographic area where there was little choice as to how one's living was made, mobility was the only advantage a black sharecropper could exercise in defense of his dignity, and exercise it he did, even if doing so was often not in his economic best interest.[28]

January was "movin' month" for sharecroppers in the Delta. A common joke about a restless Delta sharecropper was that he moved so often that on the first of January "his oldest chickens just lay down and cross dey legs to be tied." As reported by a WPA worker, the comments of black tenants about their reasons for moving so frequently were revealing. Some complained of having to buy provisions they had helped to grow. Others accused the landlord of cheating them: "I'se been cheated outen my rights, short weighted at de gin, short weighted at de store on de place and my account has been tampered wid. I can't read nor write but I made a mark every time I bought something but de man at de store on de place out marked me, my old 'oman and nine children worked and went naked all of de year, we didn't an [sic] I born to die so I am lighting a shuck off of dis place."[29]

Another respondent complained of "white folks" demanding to know too much about the affairs of their tenants, including not only social activities but "what you orders from de mail-houses" (as opposed to buying at the commissary). Another departing tenant vowed that, because his current landlord felt that his tenants were "uppity" if "you don't spit your guts out to them," he was moving to a place "where folks don't be so nosey."[30]

Another Delta tenant offered no complaint about his landlord but explained that he moved every year because he feared that, if he did not, others might suspect that he seldom cleared any money and simply could not move. For those anxious to avoid a confrontation (or settlement) with the landlord, Sunday night between eight and midnight was prime moving time. One such nocturnal mover shifted his family between town and country every six months, always settling in the country by March 1 in order to "git finished" and then heading back to the city, only to return at cotton picking time.[31]

Though blacks enjoyed little legal protection, many landlords who mistreated their tenants often found it difficult to recruit or retain labor from year to year. As Vernon Lane Wharton noted: "So long as the great mass of the Negroes were practically without worldly goods, nothing could keep them from moving off in the middle of the night, carrying a small bundle of personal effects, to seek a better opportunity or a more liberal employer." As a plantation manager charged with securing labor, LeRoy Allen had to contend with his employer's reputation for being especially quick to resort to the lash. On another occasion Allen had difficulty signing up hands because he had been mistaken for a planter who was known for brutal and dishonest treatment of his labor.[32]

In their dealings with their tenants, planters clearly held the upper hand in every sense of the word, but the rootlessness of the labor force posed a problem. There was no guarantee that the annual relocation of labor would distribute workers evenly according to the needs of the region's planters, for whom adequate labor was not only a necessity but an absolute obsession. Hence even the most tolerant and benevolent of Delta planters often found themselves involved in a yearly scramble to secure or retain dependable labor. This reality demanded that planters exercise both firmness and restraint in just the right proportions so as to maintain control of their laborers without repressing them so severely as to drive them away to another plantation.

Although he combined an aristocratic demeanor with a hard-nosed management style, LeRoy Percy was by no means a typical Delta planter. His inherited wealth and steady income as a successful lawyer allowed him to deal more generously and fairly with his tenants than did many of his counterparts. Despite the economic advantages he enjoyed, however, Percy also harbored the Delta planter's typically obsessive concern with maintaining an adequate supply of labor. This was true at least in part because, for all of his sensitivity to the need for labor, Percy often had difficulty retaining and attracting dependable workers himself. Percy appeared to show genuine compassion for George Nathan, a black man accused of refusing to surrender two bales of cotton on which his creditors held a lien. He instructed one of his employees to "see George at once and explain the matter to him, and tell him that we cannot protect him if he does not ship the cotton." Percy counseled patience in dealing with Nathan, "as it already seems a pretty hard case for the negro, as they took everything he had from him, including a house and lot in Leland, and I suppose he tried to save these two bales of cotton."[33]

Percy's concern for this unfortunate black man may well have been genuine, but he did not act totally out of compassion, as he revealed when he urged that Nathan be offered a rental or share contract and noted that his former landlord had described him as "the best negro for getting labor on the place that he ever saw." Percy concluded: "You might be able to utilize him in this particular." Percy also relied on the tactic of retaining black women as sharecroppers in order to procure the services of their husbands and boyfriends as day laborers.[34]

Percy's rule of thumb in managing his plantation was to maintain as much stability and continuity as possible. He urged his plantation and store managers to do all that they could to keep the tenants satisfied and to treat them fairly, the variations in their dispositions and attitudes notwithstanding. On the other hand, when a significant financial risk was involved, Percy consistently took a stern, businesslike approach. In December 1905, when Green Walker, one of his black tenants, asked for a hundred-dollar Christmas advance, Percy was aghast: "We simply can't afford to advance Christmas money on this scale." Estimating that such advances would force him to "put out" fifteen hundred to three thousand dollars in the weeks remaining before Christmas, he instructed his plantation manager to talk the hands "out of the idea of Christmas money. Talk short crops and hard times." "Here and there it may be necessary to put out a few hundred dollars," Percy conceded, "but a Negro like Green Walker ought not to think of getting a hundred dollars and should learn to cut his Christmas spending according to his means and should not expect to spend a hundred dollars, when he already owes over $400.00. If he can get $25.00 to throw away for Christmas, he ought to be satisfied." Percy realized the economic consequences of the loss of labor, but there were limits to the financial risks he was willing to take to retain it. "I know it is hard to satisfy labor and I realize the danger of losing them; but we must take a stand somewhere, and if necessary, I would rather lose him than to give him that much."[35]

On another occasion Percy stubbornly advised against letting one of the tenants get his supplies anywhere other than the Tralake Commissary: "The fact of it is, it will lessen your control over him, and then it puts notions in the heads of the other negroes." When informed that a local black man was stirring up trouble on Tralake, Percy informed his manager: "I don't mind your being rough with Toler if you catch him on the place."[36]

Although he sometimes "purchased" from other planters the debts of tenants with mules and implements who desired to move onto his place, Percy was almost resigned to having some of his hands leave without settling their debts. They often moved to plantations only a few miles away, but Percy claimed that it was his policy to ask no payment from the new landlord for a hand who left without mules or implements and to decline to provide such a payment should such an already-indebted hand move onto his place. When another planter requested compensation for a tenant who had left his place for Percy's, Percy informed him of his policy, which, he claimed, had cost him "something like twenty thousand dollars" in 1906 alone, when practically every hand had left his two-thousand-acre Tralake place. Percy also chided his neighbor for making threats against the wayward tenant and advised him that, while he could not protect the man in question, "I don't think it would be the right thing for you to carry out the threats."[37]

Percy's own labor was his primary concern, but he disliked any hint of instability among the Delta's black tenants. He was not above intervening in a neighbor's affairs in order to stave off a dispute that could put laborer and landlord in court and perhaps induce a contagion of "lawing" by the local tenants. In one instance, when a black tenant desired to leave a friend's place, Percy urged his friend to "make the best arrangement you can with him" in order to keep him on the place. He warned that any number of lawyers might take the man's case or that some labor-hungry planters might provide him "any assistance that he wants." The only winner in a legal fight would be the lawyer, and not only would the planter lose his tenant but "the balance of the labor on your place would be demoralized by it."[38]

By no means all Delta planters took as philosophical a view of the matter as did Percy, but his attitude toward the migration of labor from plantation to plantation reflected his realization that the landlord's control over tenant mobility was, after all, less than absolute. Dealing too severely with a cropper who desired to leave could cost the planter several other prized tenants. Moreover, trying to recoup relatively minor losses when an indebted cropper fled to another plantation was to run the risk of coming into conflict with a fellow planter. Hence the planter's most viable policy in these situations was to do his best to keep his tenants in place. At any rate, Percy saw as a dangerous precedent any landlord-tenant dispute that threatened to expand into a landlord-landlord dispute. Too many such incidents would destroy the sense of unity that the white planter minority tried to project and, perhaps, open the door to such intense open competition among planters that the goal of labor stability would become even more difficult to achieve.

Always concerned about black out-migration, Percy cautioned against creating a panic by voicing fears of an invasion of the Delta by the boll weevil. Such talk might, he feared, cause a "stampede" of black labor that would do more harm than the actual damage inflicted by the insect itself. Hoping to calm fears about the boll weevil, he championed a crop diversification plan, experimented with weevil-resistant cotton, and played a key role in the establishment of a boll weevil research center for the Delta.[39]

Despite his fear of a black exodus, Percy was by no means satisfied with blacks as a farm labor force. Frustrated by what he saw as the poor quality as well as the instability of the black labor force, Percy told the State Bar Association in 1907 that white Mississippians might be caricatured "as standing with both heels firmly planted in the earth, and with both hands firmly clasping the coat tails of the fleeing negro, in one breath upbraiding him for worthlessness and inefficiency and in the other vowing that no other laborer should be allowed to replace him."[40]

Hoping to reduce his region's dependence on blacks, Percy spearheaded efforts to promote immigration to the Delta by Italian farmers. As an attorney for the Illinois Central Railroad, he was in a good position to assist that company's efforts to encourage immigration to the Delta. He began his own personal experiment with Italian labor by recruiting Italians to work on the eleven-thousand-acre Sunnyside Plantation across the river in Arkansas. This plantation had been leased by O. B. Crittenden and Company, the cotton factorage firm in which he was a partner. An early such experiment had been all but destroyed by malaria, but Percy determined to try again, recruiting only from the agricultural provinces of northern Italy, bringing in qualified managers, and, ironically, scattering among the Italians a few "model" black tenants.[41]

Early results were impressive. The Italians rented good land at $6.50 to $7.00 per acre, worked in family groups from sunup to sundown six days a week, and grew their own vegetables. Responding to an inquiry from a correspondent in New York, Percy claimed that some of the Italians who worked no more than forty acres of land had managed to save over an eight- or nine-year span as much as fifteen thousand dollars in cash. In 1905 approximately five hundred Italians had cleared an aggregate sum of approximately forty-six thousand dollars. Moreover, Percy described them as "industrious, peaceable and thrifty" as well as "healthy, hearty and virtuous, there never having been a bastard born on the property."

Percy was less upbeat when he wrote a Mississippi associate explaining why the Italians were not allowed to handle the sales of their own crops. He noted their inexperience in such matters as well as the loss of work attendant to their coming to Greenville to negotiate the sale. Most important, however, Percy noted, if they were allowed to sell their cotton before their accounts were paid, "it would require a regiment of Pinkerton Detectives to prevent them from stealing it. They are industrious, but no more honest than the negro, and much more enterprising."[42]

Percy's comments revealed that, for all their allegedly superior work habits, the Italians found it difficult to accept the restrictions that Delta planters attempted to impose on their tenants. For example, whatever its practical advantages, the Italians saw the system of marketing their cotton through their employers as an infringement on their freedom. Realizing that such treatment was similar to that accorded blacks, they soon became resentful, having grasped quickly the mores of a society where the actual physical cultivation of cotton bore the stigma of "nigger work." In fact, one Italian correspondent complained from Greenville that "legions of Italians" were forced to go into the cotton fields "and waste their time and good labor on work which the negroes do not want to do anymore." Immigrants soon found that newspapers and public speakers were making distinctions between "Italians" and "whites," and in at least one instance Italian children were suspended from a white Delta school because they were deemed racially inferior to the other students.[43]

Percy and other planters who experimented with Italian labor soon faced a barrage of criticism from disenchanted Italian officials and journalists. An investigation by Justice Department Special Agent Mary Grace Quackenbos led her to conclude that contrary to their announced intentions, Delta planters were less interested in creating an Italian colony than in securing a large supply of "cheap docile labor." Quackenbos found widespread evidence of peonage and rampant profiteering and dishonesty on the part of Delta planters in dealing with their Italian tenants. Her findings showed, for example, that the typical charge for ginning a five-hundred-pound bale of cotton was $2.50, while the actual cost usually ran somewhere near forty cents. She also pointed out that Italian laborers were forced to surrender their cotton seed to be charged against the costs of ginning, whereas black tenants maintained the option of retaining their seed. Finally, Quackenbos offered numerous examples of excessive charges for transportation and handling of cotton as well as for medical supplies and treatment by physicians. Quackenbos also observed that, although Delta planters lauded Italian farmers as vastly superior to their black counterparts, "there was little disposition to separate them from the negro race or differentiate in their treatment."[44]

Quackenbos's report led to an unsuccessful attempt by the Justice Department to gain a peonage indictment against the Sunnyside operation. Percy asked President Theodore Roosevelt to suppress Quackenbos's report, but his public attacks on her led to the report's being leaked to the press. Percy blamed the ensuing uproar on the Italian government, unscrupulous Italian labor agents, and a specially imported priest. "Without the Priest," Percy believed, "they are without a leader. Some of them may leave or make unreasonable demands, but a united movement upon their part need not be apprehended; nor any demand from a great number of them."[45]

Percy's analysis was decidedly off the mark. The Italian tenants simply did not "fit in" with the Delta's tenant farming system, because they were too independent and aggressive. For example, Percy blamed the burning of a huge barn full of corn and hay on discontented Italians whose request to move from Sunnyside to his Tralake Plantation had been denied. Ultimately, however, many Italians also manifested their frustrations with the tenancy system in much the same fashion as blacks did, moving from place to place unpredictably and often without clearing up their accounts with the landowner.[46]

Those Delta planters who complained about the absence of thrift, industry, and loyalty among their black laborers and who hoped to remedy this deficiency by encouraging foreign immigration were foredoomed to fail in their efforts because, for all the advantages that these immigrants seemed to have as tenants, they were far less vulnerable than blacks to coercion or intimidation. Not only were Italians and other immigrants less likely to work without protest for minimal wages—Delta planters were much like their South Carolina counterparts described by Gavin Wright as wanting the best of both worlds, i.e., "the highest type of immigrant" but "at the scale of wages paid the Negro"— but they were not inclined to accept the restrictions that went with being a tenant farmer in the Mississippi Delta. These restrictions, including credit only at the plantation commissary and selling cotton only to the owner or his agent, not only conflicted with what appeared to be a tenant's economic best interest, but they carried with them the stigma of subservience and inequality and thus lumped together all tenants, black and white. Such a situation was unacceptable, socially and economically, to the Italians who had moved to Delta plantations, and they made no secret of their resentment at being treated like blacks.[47]

Delta planters were sometimes driven to what seemed, by Mississippi standards at least, extreme conciliatory measures to attract and retain the labor they needed. Their paternalism and relative benevolence found its limits, however, at the point of entering into a truly coequal economic relationship with anyone, black or white, who grew the cotton that was the key to the planter's wealth and power. The best of these planters were guided by conscience, religious beliefs, and their sense of noblesse oblige to treat tenants fairly and sometimes compassionately. Even this better element, however, believed that their ability to maintain their wealth and influence depended on the Delta's remaining a region where, by virtue of his skin color alone, any white planter could, after the fashion of one Tunica County landlord, matter-of-factly tell any sharecropper, "This is a place for me to make a profit, not you."[48]

With its cotton economy booming, the Delta continued to attract large numbers of black in-migrants throughout the first three decades of the twentieth century (its black population increased by nearly 50 percent between 1900 and 1930), but despite the fertility and productivity of the Yazoo Basin, the great majority of blacks found only frustration and disappointment as they confronted the cold-blooded realities of a repressive racial climate and a modernized and depersonalized plantation economy where their opportunities for advancement were minimal. As Harold Woodman explained: "Many blacks increasingly found that the measure of independence they had achieved was slipping away with the consolidation of the centralized business plantation."[49]

As we have seen, by 1910 croppers were little more than wage laborers with no control whatsoever over the production or marketing of the cotton they grew. In fact, instead of offering both day-to-day autonomy and greater promise of upward mobility, by the second decade of the twentieth century sharecropping had evolved on the large plantations of the Delta into a system that offered little promise of progress, either economic or personal—in either the short or long run.

As the Delta's black population swelled, the percentage of black farmers who owned their own land shrank from 7.3 in 1900 to 2.9 by 1925, while this figure (maintained in part, no doubt, by the continuing migration of landless blacks to the Delta or out of the state entirely) hovered near 20 percent for the remainder of the state throughout the period. Further evidence of declining opportunity for blacks in the Delta lies in the fact that the number of black cash tenants had fallen by 1925 to barely one-fifth the number for 1900.[50]

The fortunes of Mound Bayou, once described by its proud founders as "the Jewel of the Delta" and by Theodore Roosevelt as an "object lesson full of hope for the colored people," seemed to embody the fate of Delta blacks in general. As late as 1910, the Bank of Mound Bayou had claimed resources in excess of a hundred thousand dollars, and the town had also once been home to a thriving oil mill. By 1915 the bank had been reorganized in order to save it, and the oil mill had closed. Land values in the area fell by more than 50 percent in response to the depression in cotton prices that occurred between 1920 and 1922. As the financial picture became increasingly gloomy, overextended independent farmers fell back into tenancy, and their wives and other women in the community turned to domestic service.[51]

The outbreak of World War I and the ensuing disruption of the world cotton market contributed to an especially sharp downturn in black fortunes, but behind the declining status and dashed aspirations of its black residents lay the reality of the Delta's true identity, in the words of Sydney Nathans, "not as a democratic frontier eager for settlers, but as a plantation country hungry for labor." By 1920 the small window of opportunity the Delta had once afforded ambitious blacks was firmly shut. It had actually begun to close in the 1880s as railroad and levee construction stimulated development and settlement and brought in a huge influx of black farm workers. Delta planters gave the closing window a firm shove with their support for disfranchisement, and the first two decades of the twentieth century witnessed the final stages of the transformation of a labor-hungry frontier into a modern plantation region that afforded its rigorously supervised black workers little reason to hope for a better, more satisfying tomorrow.

The few blacks who managed to claim for themselves even a small piece of the expanding prosperity of the Delta in the late nineteenth and early twentieth centuries found themselves by 1920 caught up in a web of indebtedness and credit scarcity, and, lacking the resources to maintain the modest upward momentum of the previous decades, many fell back among fellow blacks who had long ago relinquished their hopes for a brighter future in the Delta.

Along with economic decline, Delta blacks lived with the reality of a racial climate that, like their political and economic circumstances, worsened as the twentieth century unfolded. Although many Delta planters recoiled from the bloodthirsty, race-baiting rhetoric that had won James K. Vardaman a growing number of followers around the state, any Delta black who stepped too far out of line risked the real possibility of facing a lynch mob. In June 1903 Harry Ball reported the lynching in Greenville of a "miserable negro beast" who allegedly attacked a telephone operator as she left the office. After a suspect was captured, a mob stormed the jail, carried the "wretched creature" to the telephone exchange, and strung him up in full view of an applauding group. The mob consisted of many respected citizens, among them a close friend of Ball's who insisted that he go and view the body. "Everything was very orderly," Ball explained. "There was not a shot, but much laughing and hilarious excitement. . . . It was quite a gala occasion, and as soon as the corpse was cut down, all the crowd betook themselves to the park to see a game of baseball."[52]

Many lynch mobs acted with less restraint. In 1904 Luther Holbert, a black man who lived at Doddsville in Sunflower County, was accused of killing James Eastland, a white planter, as well as two other blacks. Accompanied by his wife, Holbert attempted to escape. A mob formed, and in the course of its pursuit two innocent blacks were shot. When the mob overtook the couple, its leader quickly tied both to trees. The Vicksburg *Evening Post* offered the following account of what was to be one of the most brutal episodes in the state's long history of racial atrocities:

> While the funeral pyres were being prepared, they were forced to suffer the most fiendish tortures. The blacks were forced to hold out their hands while one finger at a time were chopped off. The fingers were distributed as souvenirs. The ears of the murders [*sic*] were cut off. Holbert was beaten severely, his skull was fractured, and one of his eyes, knocked with a stick, hung by a shred from the socket. . . . The most excruciating form of punishment consisted in the use of a large corkscrew in the hands of some of the mob. This instrument was bored into the flesh of the man and woman, in the arms, legs, and body, and then pulled out, the spirals tearing out big pieces of raw, quivering flesh every time it was withdrawn.

Twenty-five years later, the lynching of Charley Shepherd in Bolivar County was just as horrible. Over a seven-hour period, reported the Jackson *Daily News*, "the enraged farm and townspeople of the Delta went about their work of torturing." Shepherd's body was soaked with gasoline, but before he was ignited the mob saw to it that his mouth and nose were partially filled with mud so that the inhalation of the gas fumes would not bring his agony to a premature end. "It was 45 minutes," the *Daily News* added, "before the powerfully built negro finally quit his convulsive twitching and agonized fighting at the ropes and flames. . . . The blackened skull smoked in a ditch beside the road this morning, tossed there by a souvenir hunter."[54]

According to statistics compiled by the NAACP, during the first three decades of the twentieth century, the seventeen counties lying wholly or partly in the Delta witnessed a total of sixty-six lynchings. This figure accounted for over 35 percent of the 188 confirmed lynchings in the state (for which the county where they occurred could be identified) during this period. From 1900 through 1930, this seventeen-county area averaged a lynching every 5.5 months.[55]

In terms of the number of lynchings per ten thousand blacks, Delta blacks were actually "safer" than those in some of the majority-white counties. Still, as Neil McMillen has pointed out, "because lynching, as object lesson, touched the entire black community and not merely the victims and their families, the larger total number of mob deaths in the Delta may have produced more fear than the higher statistical probability of lynching in the white counties. To the Washington County blacks who in the course of one lifetime could have witnessed at least thirteen vigilante executions in their county alone, there was cold comfort in the fact that they were somehow statistically safer than their hill county counterparts." McMillen and others have noted the lingering shock effects of a lynching. A Delta black recalled that in the wake of one such example of mob violence, the local black community was terrorized: "None of em would come out on the streets."[56]

A combination of fear, frustration, disillusionment, and anger drove Delta blacks to join in large numbers the great northward migration, which saw a hundred thousand blacks leave the state between 1915 and 1920 alone. As this exodus unfolded, the Illinois Central Railroad, which had played the vital role in sealing the Delta's future as a modern plantation region, also became the avenue of escape for disillusioned blacks headed to Chicago—often with the encouragement of the militant Chicago *Defender*, which was itself borne south by the porters who worked on the trains. The number of Mississippi-born blacks living in Illinois grew by 400 percent between 1910 and 1920, and during the same period the percentage of Chicago blacks who had been born in Mississippi increased fivefold. Many Delta blacks went north in response to reports of industrial employment opportunities left vacant by the cessation of European immigration during World War I. Many were also enticed to Chicago and elsewhere by the stories of recently departed friends and kin, much as the parents or grandparents of the northbound out-migrants had been lured to the Delta by tales of rich black soil, head-high cotton, and the ostensibly greater opportunities available to blacks on the postbellum South's labor-scarce plantation frontier.[57]

The northward migration of blacks from the Delta was for many only the second leg of a journey that had originated elsewhere in Mississippi. Hence, although the Delta became what one historian called a "staging area" for the Great Migration, the offsetting influence of a continuing black influx actually caused the Delta's black population to rise by 17 percent between 1910 and 1920 and to remain constant over the decade that followed. A reporter observed that in the Clarksdale area it was "difficult to observe the exodus" because people were "continually moving in from the hills to fill their places." In this reporter's view, however, "the 'hill' people came hoping to make more money. When they had settled in this section they found that they did not get what they earned."[58]

For many black emigrés, the Delta became less a home than a temporary place of abode; the plantation where they sharecropped was not where they lived but where they "stayed," and "ramblin'" or escape became a dominant theme of the blues, an expressive new musical form that the Delta gave to the nation in the late nineteenth and early twentieth centuries. Sydney Nathans linked the contrasts between the Delta's image as a promised land and its reality as "the closed world of the plantation" to the themes of alienation and disillusionment that permeated the blues. William Barlow went further, insisting that "even as they grew and prospered in close proximity to their folk roots, the rural blues articulated the call for urban migration." This certainly appeared to be the case with Big Bill Broonzy, whose "Keys to the Highway" seemed to describe the urgency with which he made his way to Chicago in 1920:

> I got the keys to the highway;
> I'm booked out and bound to go.
> Got to leave here running;
> Walking's got most too slow.[59]

Like Broonzy's, the decision of most blacks who fled the Delta was absolute and irrevocable. The comments of those who left the Delta during the Great Migration indicated that, despite what they had been told, in actual practice the Delta's system of large-scale plantation agriculture required laborers whose disadvantageous economic, social, political, and legal circumstances made it difficult for them to press landlords for better terms or fairer settlements. At the same time, the small-town mercantile and service economy that existed in mutual dependence with the plantation system demanded a work force adaptable to wages and working conditions that were comparable to those on the plantation.

Former tenants who had left the Delta complained of unfair treatment by their landlords, who often refused to let them sell their cotton off the plantation and who paid them twenty to twenty-five cents per pound for it when the true market price might be as high as forty. The inflated prices that accompanied credit purchases were also an exceedingly sore point with black tenants, as were settlements that were often delayed or based on dubious arithmetic.[60]

The inadequacy of schools for blacks was yet another problem. Greenwood blacks cited teacher salaries of thirty dollars per month (as compared to those of whites at fifty dollars). In Clarksdale a large percentage of black teachers were believed to be prostitutes, and the school board certainly saw no need to seek out college graduates to serve as teachers. In Leland three teachers taught 350 black students, and in Indianola, where black teachers earned only fifteen to twenty dollars per month, some of the teachers were also students— in the fifth grade. A common complaint across the Delta concerned the refusal of white officials to open the black schools until the cotton harvest was substantially complete. A reporter found that in Leland black schools were still not operating on November 17.[61]

To the suggestion of a black minister that migrants were fleeing the Delta because of their fear of "the mob," an indignant Walter Sillers asserted that "no law-abiding Negro is afraid of mob violence. . . . He not only knows he is valuable to the white man, more so than his mules and fine horses, but he also relies upon the kindly feeling and sense of justice of the white man." Given the frequency of lynchings in the area, blacks must have wondered whether Sillers was referring to the same Delta they knew all too well. In addition to lynchings and other forms of violence, there were numerous reports of intimidation. When an Indianola black threatened to sue his landlord over his settlement, the planter responded, "So you are one of those lawsuit niggers—if you sue I'll kill you." After he eventually won an out-of-court settlement, the tenant judiciously left for the North.[62]

Greenwood whites had an especially bad reputation for mistreating blacks at the train station. Not only were suspected out-migrants roughed up and threatened by law enforcement officials, but train porters were harassed as well. Often such incidents led to flight by not only the aggrieved party but his or her friends. In Greenville a policeman, aware that a friend needed a cook, saw a young woman on a porch and ordered her to accompany him to a friend's house, where she was forced to begin cooking. She prepared one meal before boarding the train for the North.[63]

Delta blacks also complained about the absence of legal protection. White offenses against blacks—including homicide—went not only unpunished but often unprosecuted. One planter who was accused of killing a tenant for selling cotton off the plantation was never brought to trial. On the other hand, woe be unto the black person charged with an offense against a white. A Greenwood black related a conversation between a black physician, arrested for operating his automobile without headlights, and a prominent white. The white man allegedly admitted that, if he were black, he "would rather appear in a Russian court than appear before a court here for trial."[64]

Faced with little hope of legal protection from whites and even less chance for a fair trial for any transgression across racial lines, blacks had little choice but to suppress their anger and frustration or to leave the Delta for good. Apprehensive of their plans being discovered, blacks seldom talked to whites or even other blacks about leaving. One black explained: "People said they were going to Memphis, when you next heard from them they would be in Chicago, St. Louis or Detroit." When blacks confided to friends that they were planning to leave, large crowds assembled at the train station to see them off. When a departed person's absence was detected, a typical response was, "Oh, he got off last night!" With Delta whites threatening to take such action "as may be necessary" to protect their labor supply, nocturnal departures were the safest means of ensuring a safe getaway. In order to avoid confrontations with whites at the train station, a number of Greenville blacks walked the twelve miles to Leland to board the train. Once they had made up their minds to leave, however, most blacks were not to be dissuaded by a few threats. "Our pepel [*sic*] are tole that they cannot get anything to do up there and they being snatched off trains . . . ," wrote one black Deltan, "but in spite of this they are leaving every day and night."[65]

Such determination came through in the words of a Greenville black who resolved "to get my famaly [*sic*] out of this cursed South land down here a Negro man is not good as a white man's dog." An investigator found two hundred abandoned houses in Greenville by the end of 1917. In addition to simply dragging blacks off trains, Delta whites also tried more positive approaches to stemming the flow of out-migrants. Blacks noted a general rise in wages in the wake of the exodus. Around Greenville, cotton pickers received two dollars per hundred in 1917 as compared to the sixty to seventy-five cents they had been paid the year before. Planters spoke to meetings of black leaders, often hoping that ministers and other black professionals could be convinced or coerced to urge other blacks to stay put. This approach was seldom successful, however, for even though black professionals saw their livelihoods slipping away as the northward traffic increased, they perceived that the anger and frustration among blacks was too volatile to be tampered with.[66]

In one Delta community, a prominent black leader from elsewhere in the state who had been invited to speak against the exodus thought better of it and changed his topic at the last minute. Various biracial committees were formed to discuss the problem and publicize the opportunities available to blacks in the Delta counties, and individual planters, such as the one who bought several automobiles to sell to tenants on "easy terms," took steps to preserve their own labor supplies. In the wake of racial disturbances in northern cities, Greenville whites sent an agent up to offer recent migrants free transportation back to Mississippi. For the most part, however, such advances were spurned. Not even parents whose children had left for the North were quick to encourage their offspring to return. An Urban League investigation noted that "parents who allow their children to go are afraid to permit them to come home. They want to feel that their children are manly and they assert that it means considerable danger to resent an insult."[67]

Although whites were overjoyed to find a black who had returned because of dissatisfaction with the North, such cases were apparently rare. Having moved to an area "where the people at least made a pretense at being civilized," a Mississippi migrant vowed that he would return to Mississippi only "when a man's home is sacred; when he can protect the virtue of his wife and daughter against the brutal lust of his alleged supervisors; when he can sleep at night without the fear of being visited by the Ku-Klux because he refused to take off his hat while passing an overseer. . . ."[68]

One interviewee conceded that "everything they say about the North ain't true but there's so much of it true you don't mind the other." This particular migrant had found work quickly in Chicago but moved to Gary, Indiana, where he and other workers not only earned forty-five cents per hour but "called the foreman by his first name and didn't have to be bowing and scraping for our jobs neither." In addition to much greater economic opportunity, Chicago offered dignity and self-esteem: "I tell ya a man's a man there. My children were in Chicago going to Wendell Phillips school, setting down with somebody who is going to be president some day." Citing the large salaries made by some of his friends, he concluded, "They spends a lot of it . . . [but] they could save it if they wanted to." As far as he was concerned, there was no comparison between his new home and his old one: "You couldn't pay me to live home now." A Mississippi woman expressed the difference between her new home and her old one in terms that she knew her friends could appreciate when she simply wrote, "Honey, I got a bathtub."[69]

In the aftermath of the Great Migration, concern about labor shortages became so intense that many planters were driven to desperate measures. LeRoy Allen advanced a prospective tenant $425 to return to the hills and discharge his debts there. As "collateral" the man left a young man he claimed was his son. Only later, when it became obvious that his prospective worker would not return, did Allen discover that the boy was not even related to the man who had absconded with Allen's money.[70]

For all such stories suggesting that they were at the mercy of their prospective tenants, however, when planters talked of a scarcity of labor, they often meant a scarcity of labor willing to accept whatever terms the landlord offered. By the end of the 1920s, most Delta blacks lived in severe economic deprivation, politically and legally powerless to improve their material circumstances or even protect themselves from violence, coercion, or unlawful incarceration bordering on slavery. A study of eighty black tenant families conducted in early 1927 revealed an average annual gross income of $579. Actually focused on the nutritional habits of the tenants, the study was conducted during February, traditionally the leanest month for Delta tenants because they had received their settlement in December, and March, which was usually the month when regular advances began anew. Not surprisingly, the researchers found deficiencies in the energy and nutritive values of the diets of the black subjects. Nearly 13 percent of those studied consumed no milk whatsoever. Fats provided more than 25 percent of the total calories ingested, and with molasses as a staple, sweets also contributed heavily. On the other hand, more than half of the families were at least 10 percent below recommended levels of protein, calcium, phosphorous, and iron. Typical weekly menus were heavy on biscuits, fried pork, and cornbread, and one of the poorest families subsisted for an extended period on an unchanging menu of rice, cornbread, and coffee for breakfast and a dinner (served in this case at 4:00 p.m.) of cornbread and peas cooked without benefit of even the traditional piece of salt pork.[71]

Experts related these dietary problems to the high death rate among Delta blacks as well as to the incidence of pellagra and rickets. One health officer, who explained that his department lacked the personnel to examine black children, nonetheless estimated that these two diseases were twice as prevalent among blacks as among whites. Twenty of the families studied accounted for sixty-one visits to the doctor during a single year.[72]

The problem was in large part one of income. Tenants who received their settlements in cash exhibited better dietary habits than did those on plantations where settlements were in supplies. Ignorance and illiteracy played a role as well. Observers claimed that many blacks were unaware of nutritious, low-cost dishes like macaroni and cheese. A black home demonstration agent explained that she had met Delta blacks who had never tasted ice cream.[73]

Improper diet among Delta sharecroppers was not, however, solely a function of low income and educational levels. The value of garden products per farm in the Delta in 1929 was less than $15.00 compared to a state average of $46.49. Planters blamed this failure to grow more foodstuffs on the shift-

lessness of their black tenants, but when Kathleen Knight's family joined other
Alabama whites in migrating to the Delta, they found that their landlord refused
to allot them any land for a garden.[74]

Competition for labor appeared to have contributed to some few improvements in tenant housing as the unpainted, one-room cabin gave way to the
whitewashed, three-room house. Still, a black home demonstration agent
offered this description of the interior of a typical black tenant farmer's home
in the Delta at the end of the 1920s:

> The average home has only the furniture they cannot do without, such as beds,
> chairs (usually not more than four), possibly a dresser and wash-stand, more often
> a dresser than a wash-stand. It is a rare case to find books. Few take a monthly
> paper. Most of the houses are papered with newspapers which are bought by
> solicit. Magazines are used for pictures only. Many of these are posted on the
> walls of the homes. The women have learned through club work to make inex-
> pensive rugs from discarded stockings and clothing. Aside from these, there are
> no rugs. Nine out of every ten have no window shades. All have some kind of
> curtains.[75]

Richard Wright, who spent a part of one childhood summer traveling
through the area filling out applications for illiterate customers of an illiterate
insurance salesman, found little that was appealing about the Delta: "I saw a
bare bleak pool of black life and I hated it; the people were alike, and their farms
were alike." He remembered "sleeping on shuck mattresses, eating salt pork
and black-eyed peas for breakfast, dinner and supper." Wright was also "aston-
ished" at the ignorance of black children in the Delta: "I had been pitying
myself for not having books to read, and now I saw children who had never
read a book. Their chronic shyness made me seem bold and city-wise; a black
mother would try to lure her brood into the room to shake hands with me and
they would linger at the jamb of the door, peering at me with one eye, giggling
hysterically!" Wright obviously felt considerable guilt when sharecropper
families, struck by his command of word and pen, would "stand and gape" as
he filled out forms for insurance they had purchased in the pathetic hope of
"connecting themselves with something that would make their children "write
'n speak lak dat pretty boy from Jackson.""[76]

Although she was by no means unsympathetic to planters, Beulah Ratliff
painted an equally dreary portrait of black life in the post-World War I Delta:
"The life of the Mississippi plantation Negro is toil, ignorance, hopelessness,
animal stupidity and bestiality. He is a filthy, stolid, unloved and unloving creature, as far from the 'merry, singing hoehand' of fiction as is the dirty, diseased
reservation Indian from Cooper's 'noble redman.'"[77]

Such conditions went a long way toward explaining why the steady northward flow of blacks from the Delta continued throughout the 1920s until it was
finally slowed temporarily by the effects of the Great Depression. This ongo-

ing exodus of labor and the inability of whites to induce even those blacks who remained in the region to stay put for any length of time suggest as well why accounts of peonage and involuntary servitude continued to filter out of the Delta. Sunflower County blacks complained that employers prevented them from leaving their plantations, even to see their children. In 1928 a Greenville white wrote the Justice Department concerning the case of Dave Ross, an elderly black sharecropper he described as "hardly able to do a day's work." A local planter had apparently advanced Ross some money in order to induce him and his family to work a crop with him. At the last moment, however, Ross's family balked at the move. The planter confiscated Ross's furniture, leaving his family to sleep on the floor while Ross went to jail. The complainant explained that his only interest in the matter was "to see justice done as a former employer of the old negro who is broken in health." He added that if his action in contacting the Justice Department were to become known locally, "it will make it very hard on me in a business way."[78]

Sam Edwards, a black coast guardsman returning on leave to visit his mother in Greenwood, ran into trouble in Tchula; he was arrested for "trespassing without money" and hauled into a grocery store "courtroom" where, when it was discovered that he did indeed have money, the charge was changed to vagrancy. For this offense he was sentenced to thirty days at hard labor and a twenty-dollar fine. The judge, incredulous that a Mississippi black actually did not know how to pick cotton, promised to send Edwards to a place where he "could learn." That place turned out to be a plantation owned by the father of the man who had arrested him. Thirty-six days later Edwards was released, having been beaten on several occasions with a "seven pound strap," once for writing a letter to his commanding officer and on other occasions for picking less than a hundred pounds of cotton within a specified period, drinking two cups of water instead of one, and breaking a hoe handle. Although his "sentence" had expired, Edwards secured his release only by agreeing to sell his watch for seven dollars to "Captain Brown," a black straw boss. Edwards reported "about 16 or 17" black men were being held on the farm and treated in the same manner.[79]

Nothing activated the planter's concerns about losing his labor more than the threat of flood. Throughout the 1920s the planters around Yazoo City fretted with each overflow that they would not be able to retain enough labor to work another crop. Reporting on the 1922 overflow, J. W. McRaven observed that "business is at a standstill and everybody got the blues over high water conditions. The river is higher than it has been in years—Holly Bluff, Louise, Midnight and all that section of county are under water and it is feared that the water will not go down in time to make a crop this year. This means the Negroes will all leave and labor will be hard to get back another year." A year later McRaven told a similar story: "A great many of the Negroes have become discouraged and abandoned their crops and gone North to work in the industrial plants." With blacks fleeing the Delta in such numbers, McRaven sensed "a general feeling of uneasiness as to what the future prospects on these large plantations will be."[80]

Having caused massive dislocation of labor, the catastrophic flood of 1927 left numerous charges of involuntary servitude in its wake. In *Lanterns on the Levee*, William Alexander Percy cast his father, LeRoy, as a courageous, benevolent aristocrat defending helpless blacks against the vicious racism of the poor whites. During the 1927 flood, however, when the younger Percy decided to evacuate the seventy-five hundred blacks who were crowded onto the levees at Greenville, he ran into opposition from local planters, among them his father, who warned him, in Will's words, "that if we depopulated the Delta of its labor, we would be doing it a grave disservice." When Will refused to relent, LeRoy convinced him to recanvass the relief committee, which had already agreed to the need for evacuation. Before the committee reconvened, however, LeRoy had lobbied each member so effectively that its opinion was reversed, much to the distress of a frustrated Will.[81]

LeRoy Percy explained his attitude on this question with the admission that he appreciated the fact that "if I were a negro living in a tent on Trail Lake [his plantation], looking over thousands of acres with not an acre of cotton, and would go for a visit to the fertile lands of Coahoma County and reside in a well equipped cabin on prosperous land for a few weeks, those few weeks would be indefinitely prolonged." After LeRoy's death, when Will learned of the last-minute lobbying effort that prevented the evacuation, he rationalized LeRoy's actions with the observation that his father had known "that the dispersal of our labor was a larger evil to the Delta than a flood."[82]

Lewis Baker explained the differences in the way father and son viewed the matter of evacuation, arguing that Will had actually tried to uphold the planter aristocrat's vaunted sense of noblesse oblige by trying to protect the defenseless blacks. LeRoy, on the other hand, having "grown up in the impoverished postwar south," realized that the Delta's "way of life," which both men sought to preserve, "depended on economic prosperity, the vagaries of the weather, the cotton market, and the labor of a race of people he never claimed to understand." LeRoy's insistence on holding the blacks on the levee indicated that he saw them as but one "segment of the Delta whose welfare must be considered in relation to the good of the whole." Above all else, one thing was certain. No thought was given by either of the Percys, at any point, to the idea of consulting the blacks themselves. "They had no capacity to plan for their own welfare;" Will explained, "planning for them was another of our burdens."[83]

As the months passed, it became apparent that most of the blacks huddled together in the refugee camps would work no cotton in 1927—at least not in the Delta. Labor agents from the North and other parts of the South as well descended on the Delta despite the warnings of Governor Dennis Murphree concerning "the serious result which can be brought about if refugees are allowed to be taken from the refugee camps for selfish interest." As Pete Daniel noted, Murphree apparently ignored the fact that the blacks "were systematically being denied the right to search for a new job" in order to serve the "selfish interest" of labor-hungry Delta planters.[84]

One investigator described the plight of the refugee, who was forced to register when he entered the camp and restrained from leaving "unless some outside person makes application for his release with the promise of giving him a home and seeing that he is not a Public Charity Ward. The Labor Agents have no access to the Camps and the Planters have, hence they are able to offer homes to many of our people in the Delta and on the Plantation from which they came." Planters also took steps to discourage labor agents. Whites around Yazoo City promised to deal with such people according to the old "Yazoo plan," which consisted of hot pursuit and heavy punishment if that pursuit proved effective. Delta planters, who had shown few qualms about enticing laborers from the neighboring hill counties, had no sympathy for such activities when others were attempting to take their workers away from them.[85]

The national guardsmen charged with camp security appeared to have the dual mission of keeping the refugees in and others—particularly labor agents— out. In his short story "Down by the Riverside," Richard Wright used the evacuation and incarceration of Delta blacks as the backdrop for the story of a black man who loses his wife during childbirth and his own life at the hands of soldiers charged with "guarding" the black evacuees.[86]

At the end of June 1927, a Hazlehurst, Mississippi, attorney described the case of John and Willie Douglas, who had recently slipped away from a plantation at Thornton, leaving behind six children, the youngest only two years old. They claimed that their letters to their children were intercepted by the plantation owner. Myron McNeil cited this case as "one instance in hundreds of instances where negroes from the hill counties are being forced to remain in the Delta against their wills." "These negroes," NcNeil wrote, "were all originally from the hill counties, and when the boll weevil struck the hill counties, the Delta farmers and planters came into the hills and solicited all this labor to go to the Delta, and it was released without objection by the hill farmers." McNeil added that the boll weevil's invasion of the hills was "far more disastrous, financially speaking, than when the flood struck the Delta." In the wake of the flood, however, the hills had become relatively attractive again, but some of the would-be returnees were being held against their will by a group of unscrupulous planters.[87]

Planters not only worried about losing labor but feared as well the possibility that flood-induced shortages would drive up labor costs. At the end of June 1927, Delta Farms Company president Oscar Johnston wrote V. E. Cartledge at the Deeson refugee camp to express his concern that "some of our neighbors are paying more than $1.25 a day for day labor which they are taking out of the camp." Noting that his company had pegged the wages it paid for day labor at $1.25, he explained to Cartledge that "if we permit outsiders to pay more than this, I imagine it will be hard to get labor on Delta Farms."[88]

Despite ongoing complaints about the labor supply, Delta planters exercised firm control of both the economy and the society of the Yazoo Mississippi Delta at the close of the 1920s. Conditions in the Delta at this point actually reflected the culmination of trends that spanned the transitional half-century during which the region had moved from an essentially untamed wilderness frontier to a modern plantation kingdom. The more effective integration of the Delta into the national economy began with the incorporation of the area's railroad network into the national transportation system during the 1880s and continued with the adoption of modern industrial management techniques in the first decades of the twentieth century. (The fact that these developments brought a steady decline in the fortunes of the Delta's black workers simply affirmed Ralph Ellison's contention that "the welfare of the most humble black Mississippi sharecropper is affected less by the flow of the seasons and the rhythms of natural events than by the fluctuations of the stock market.") In addition to their sophisticated, depersonalized management techniques, planters also relied on both legal and extralegal coercion to strengthen their control over their labor. Abortive efforts to utilize white or immigrant labor to replace blacks only demonstrated that, as it was practiced in the Delta, the system of plantation agriculture could not function to the satisfaction of the landlord with a labor force that enjoyed anything approaching social or political equality.

This reality had become fully and finally apparent to the blacks who left the area in large numbers after 1915. Meanwhile, those blacks who remained could expect little more than a lifelong existence as members of a forever-shifting, essentially rootless labor force; their frequent jumps from one plantation to another provided the only means of asserting their limited autonomy, while the emergent musical tradition of the blues became the primary emotional outlet for their feelings of alienation and disaffection. The localized instability of the work force sometimes discouraged individual planters from engaging in consistently abusive and outrageously unfair treatment of their tenants, but blacks enjoyed little in the way of formal legal protection. Although whites had clearly retained the upper hand, in 1880 a suprisingly competitive relationship had prevailed on the plantation frontier of the Delta between whites desperate for labor and blacks intent on exploiting that desperation in order to achieve economic independence and enhanced social and political status. By 1930, however, the Delta's politically and economically thwarted and socially repressed blacks stood little chance of escaping a lifetime of labor on someone else's land and, for the most part, on someone else's terms as well.

6 ▽ A World Apart
▽
▽

At the middle of the nineteenth century, the Yazoo Delta was already known as the domain of an exceptionally prosperous, powerful, and socially and politically conservative planter elite. War, emancipation, and Reconstruction temporarily loosened the planter's grip on the region, but by the end of the century, the dynamic plantation kingdom of the Delta once again presented a stark contrast to the economically stunted piney woods and red-dirt counties of Mississippi that Robert L. Brandfon described as "less than an underdeveloped area." The Delta's vibrant plantation economy with its unrelenting appetite for labor encouraged its white leaders to adopt a less militantly negrophobic public posture on the race question and nurtured as well an enduring and distinctive social structure, moral code, political philosophy, and policy agenda which fostered a sense of uniqueness that Delta whites were as quick to assert as their hill-county antagonists were to assail.[1]

From the earliest days of its settlement, the Delta's physical environment encouraged its residents to believe they were different from other Mississippians. A frontier mentality pervaded the thinking of many Deltans because, for all the efforts to tame the river and crisscross the region with railroads, much of the Yazoo Basin remained uncleared timber- and swampland well into the twentieth century. With less than a third of the land in cultivation in 1900, every large plantation was the scene of frenetic efforts to deaden timber and clear more land. Elizabeth Spencer's *This Crooked Way* describes a turn-of-the-century Delta where "the land was black and tough. There were fields and swampy woods and nothing else. The fields, toothed with smoking stumps in the middle of the cotton rows and continually threatened with wire hard vine, had the tattered look of having been rent from the woods. Wild and jungle-like to the edge of the fields, the great trees stood, oak and sycamore and elm, and always in the marsh and swamp water, the cypress, pillared spider-like among its great knees and ragged with moss."[2]

Bear, deer, and other wild game remained so abundant in the Delta that in November 1902 President Theodore Roosevelt went bear hunting near the little Sunflower River in an area described by a correspondent as a practically "unbroken wilderness." (It was on this hunt that Roosevelt won fame as a sportsman by refusing to shoot or allow to be shot a bear that had been clubbed and roped to a tree. This incident was commemorated by the creation of the "Teddy bear.")[3]

One of the keys to clearing and settling the Delta was curbing the massive overflows that came, or threatened to come, every year. To that end, levee crews worked from daylight to dusk with a half-hour for breakfast and an hour and half at noon. Writing in 1905 about his experiences as a member of such a crew, William Hemphill, a young South Carolinian, sketched a portrait of the young, brawling, exploitive frontier society that was the Mississippi Delta. A native of the Piedmont, Hemphill was fascinated by the Delta's large black population: "Fact is, there is hardly anything else in this Delta but negroes—about six or eight to every white man." Hemphill was more than a little uneasy among so many blacks. "Every white man here virtually carries his life in his hands for it is a place where the long arm of the law does not reach. If a white man gets into trouble with a negro he has got to shoot and shoot quick or get shot. Everybody carries a gun however contrary to the laws of the state it may be and is always in a state of preparedness."[4]

With violence so common around the levee camps, whites hardly took note of the killing of a black man. In fact, Hemphill wrote, "the way these levee niggers shoot one another is something fearful." He cited a shooting the previous evening which only briefly interrupted the crap game that prompted it. Clearly scandalized by such behavior, Hemphill also reported on an incident that might well have formed the material for a first-rate blues song. A levee worker was shot, and his "woman" visited the scene to view his remains. "Poor old Jim, done dead," she remarked, "guess I have to get me another man tonight." Hemphill added that if a white foreman shot "a couple of niggers," something that was "by no means an unheard of or infrequent thing," work on the levee continued without interruption. Hemphill explained this swift resort to gunfire in terms of the "veritable jungle" along the river, which would provide virtually impenetrable cover for any black tempted to defy or assault his white overseer. For "one white foreman miles from anywhere working a hundred or a hundred and fifty of the most reckless niggers in the world," it was, in Hemphill's view, "a plain case of which you'd rather do or get shot."[5]

Hemphill was struck by the profiteering that he encountered among Delta merchants and what he felt was far too tolerant an attitude toward racial intermingling. After discovering "a big fat greasy negro wench . . . revelling in the delights of an ice cream soda" in an establishment where he had just consumed one himself, the thoroughly discomfited Carolinian went to a hardware store and purchased "a shooting iron" of his own.[6]

Hemphill's experience in the turbulent, untamed Delta called to mind the words of William Faulkner's Issac McCasklin, who described it as a region "where white men rent farms and live like niggers, and niggers crop on shares and live like animals, where cotton is planted and grows man-tall in the very cracks of the sidewalks, and usury and mortgage and bankruptcy and measureless wealth, Chinese and African and Aryan and Jew all breed and spawn together until no man has time to say which one is which and no one cares." Certainly this Delta was no place for the timid or faint of heart. Elizabeth Spencer's pioneer planter Mays Johnson came across as a hardened frontiersman who "wore a gun openly at his hip and a limber black whip coiled around his forearm, the handle at rest in his grasp. He spoke to the white men like niggers and to the niggers like dogs."[7]

If the conditions described by Hemphill and depicted by Faulkner and Spencer suggested the frontier, the fact that the levee-building effort failed to bring the Mississippi River fully under control only added to the instability and uncertainty of Delta life in the late nineteenth and early twentieth centuries. Flood, fear of flood, and memory of flood were influential realities for everyone who lived in the region.

Florence Sillers Ogden remembered watching as a child the approach of floodwaters "coming in great white waves." Taking a "last stand" on the kitchen steps, Florence and the other children watched the water rise, fearing it would actually enter the house. Suddenly it stopped—two inches short of invading the Sillers home—and there remained for six weeks of what Florence called "hell in high water."[8]

Like many others, the Sillers family resolved to make the best of their plight; because their house remained dry and Florence's father was hospitable to a fault, their home was on occasion a refuge for as many as thirty-five people. All about town, young men went foraging, picking up chickens from trees and rooftops. The levee teemed with people who rode their skiffs out to socialize and enjoy the feel of solid earth beneath their feet. In the Sillers home, Florence's Aunt Mamie played the piano, which had been placed on a scaffold just in case the water did invade the house. Elsewhere, young people held "overflow parties" and went boating or swimming in an effort to turn the inconvenience into a frolic.[9]

On the one hand, Deltans eagerly anticipated the recession of the flood waters. On the other, they knew that the frustrating, discouraging, and distasteful process of cleaning up and returning to normalcy awaited them once the flood was over. Sillers described the scene in the wake of the 1897 flood as the town of Rosedale lay "plastered in slimy mud. The streets and lawns were littered with the corpses of dead animals washed in by the current. Broken remains of fences and plankwalks lay helter-skelter over the town. The stink of dead things, drying mud, rotting plant life, and human refuse lay thick on the air. The streets were bogs of greenish mud. Crawfish squirmed about in the mud and as it dried, they died and added their bit to the stench." Such conditions were hardly conducive to good health, and the period after the waters fell was considered the most dangerous part of any overflow. Mosquitoes, horseflies, and buffalo gnats flourished, as did malaria and dysentery and various other diseases that affected both humans and livestock. Just as the waters began to fall, Sillers lost her baby sister to a sudden attack of fever.[10]

In mid-March 1890 levees broke around Greenville, leaving the city protected only by a hastily erected embankment that threatened to give way at any minute. In the face of an impending immersion, nearly the entire populace turned out to shore up the defenses against the river. Harry Ball described the "strange scene": "Here a little squad of Irishmen working like clockwork, gangs of negroes shouting and singing over their labor, bunches of clerks, coats off, and elegant young dudes, white handed and dressed in flannel shirts and boots like comic opera choruses, with solid business men wielding spade and shovel and puffing and perspiring with the unwonted toil."[11]

Ball claimed to have earned his share of blisters in this effort, which, as was often the case, proved "all in vain." On March 31, while heading for lunch, Ball met a young man yelling, "Levee's busted." Reaching home, he found his sister struggling to save their rosebushes even as the water came "rolling and whitening" toward their house. Soon the water was knee deep in their yard and the family was hurriedly pulling up carpets, although they never imagined that the water would ever "rise high enough to run us out of the house." As the water rose, so did Ball's uneasiness, but he contrasted the calm of his family, "old overflow campaigners," with the "terror" among those less accustomed to high water: "Shouts for help were heard on every hand, and through the pouring rain boat load after boat load went by—bedding, clothing, provisions, drenched and forlorn women in hysterics, and shrieking children." One by one Ball's neighbors left, and eventually so did the rest of his family; at last he "held the fort alone" save for an old hen with twenty-six chicks who occupied a box on the kitchen table. The next morning Ball discovered the old hen perched on the teakettle as her dead chicks floated about the kitchen.[12]

A week after the overflow began, the waters appeared to be receding in the Ball house. Ball began bailing water out of his hall with a washbasin only to discover, after considerable effort, that the volume of water was greater than when he began. The waters were rising again, and he fell furiously to stacking up books, which he had piled on the floor the day before. He collapsed exhausted into bed at midnight and awoke the next morning to find six inches of water under his bed. He soon discovered that another levee had broken, leaving the entire town of Greenville flooded and the population living in boats for two months, "the waters being constantly covered with craft of every possible description, from sloop rigged sailboats and amateur steam launches to a raft made of two planks." Ball relied for transportation on a "very perilous little skiff," which he paddled straight into the hall of his house. There he pulled off shoes and socks, waded to the bed, undressed, and lay reading and smoking until he fell asleep. The worst part of his routine was "the anguish of getting up in the morning and stepping out of bed into a half a foot of cold water!"[13]

Often frightening and always massively disruptive, floods were simply a fact of life throughout the nineteenth and early twentieth centuries—the Delta suffered major floods eleven times between 1858 and 1922—but no one living at the time had ever experienced such an overflow as came in 1927. The 1927 flood cost the lives of from 250 to 500 people and left more than 16.6 million acres and 162,000 homes under water. At one point, over an area thirty miles wide and a hundred miles long, water stood in depths of from four to fifteen feet. Harry Ball described the flood as "the greatest natural calamity in the history of the nation," and few Delta residents born since the Civil War could recall any worse event in their lives.[14]

Ball recalled the scene in Greenville on the night of April 21, 1927, as that of "a whole population fleeing for refuge to the levee, many half-naked and shrieking in the midst of a chaos of terrified livestock." For many Deltans the 1927 flood left only memories of tragedy. Such was the case with a black woman who had given birth the day before the 1927 overflow began. Her husband went out in search of help to evacuate his wife and baby and apparently drowned. The woman and her infant spent four days on the roof of their house before they were discovered, the infant dead and the mother wild with fear and grief.[15]

Ball recorded the sad case of the Hilliards, who fled to Cleveland when the overflow came but attempted to return by barge when the waters began to fall. A change in current caused the barge to capsize, drowning two Hilliard children and three black adults who had accompanied the family. The remainder of the party survived by clinging to a pier until rescued. When the family finally reached home, they found twenty dead cows and mules in their yard and the house "a ruin." A cow had managed to wedge itself in a window, where it perished, and a large dead hog lay in the middle of a bed. The Clark family lived on the outskirts of Greenville, and when the levee broke, the current swept mother, grandmother, son, and daughter out of the house. Only the mother escaped drowning, clinging all night to a floating log.[16]

In addition to tragedy, the 1927 flood produced circumstances both comic and bizarre. Joe Rice Dockery recalled opening the bathroom door in one flood-besieged house only to find the family's prize heifer comfortably ensconced therein. A few days later, Dockery entered a flooded home near Webb where the water was so deep that it threatened to enter his hip boots. He was fascinated by what appeared to be the tinkling of tiny chimes until he finally realized that the sound came from teacups clinking against each other as they floated about in a flooded china cabinet and rocked on waves created by Dockery and others wading about in the house. During the 1927 flood, James Hand shaved by dipping his razor in the water that stood in the house where he was staying, and at one point he took a bath on a friend's kitchen table. Hand also reported that he had seen a man navigate a rowboat through the local courthouse.[17]

Perhaps the most onerous duty Joe Rice Dockery performed in 1927 was "burying" the dead from among the refugees on the levee. Dockery recalled going "off shore out in the Mississippi River, and right in sight of these thousands of refugees who were singing and all that kind of thing there. There were many preachers in charge, well not in charge, but there to see that it was a very dignified thing, not just throwing some boxes overboard or anything like that. I did that one whole afternoon. I don't know how many bodies we tucked away out there in the Mississippi River."[18]

The 1927 debacle finally led to more effective congressional action on flood control in the lower Mississippi Valley in the form of a 1928 flood control act that appropriated $325 million for a flood-control system. Still, no amount of after-the-fact assistance could erase the imprint of the flood on the Delta or its inhabitants. After the flood receded, a visitor to Greenville reported that, although the water was gone, its mark remained in the form of "deeply seared scars upon the face of the fair land, and more deeply still upon the hearts, and the minds, and the hopes, and the very futures of the young and the old." Those who had survived the flood and struggled to rid their stench-ridden homes of mud, snakes, crawfish, and frogs took heart in the news of an extensive flood-control effort, but with each new spring came an irrepressible anxiety that this might be the year when another "watery Armageddon" would come.[19]

The challenge of facing and surviving flood after flood was but one of the experiences that created a bond among residents of the Delta and imbued them with a sense of impending crisis as well. As David Cohn saw it, Deltans shared not only the "pains of pioneering" and "the perils of the river" but the experience of life in "a cotton-intoxicated area" where "cotton-growing was a secular religion." "Cotton starred our folklore, was the staple of our talk, the stuff of our dreams, the poesy of many of our songs."[20]

Court was often suspended until hoe hands could get the grass out of the cotton, and a field hand experienced and proficient in growing cotton was almost certain to best a wandering, relatively unknown "strange nigger" if the two took their conflict of interest before a jury. Rumors of army worms and boll weevils could set off a panic followed by wholesale emotional depression throughout the Delta. On the other hand, projections for a good crop set off a flurry of activity: "Railroads assembled freight cars. Gins, cottonseed oil mills, and compresses looked to their machinery. Bankers dusted off old promissory notes. Then they made calculations, half actuarial and half dreamful, of the possibilities of payments. Merchants ordered goods from drummers or went on buying trips to St. Louis or New York. Negro household servants anticipated their annual cotton-picking expeditions to the fields. Posters flamed on country barns and town walls announcing the coming of Gentry's Dog and Pony Show."[21]

With cotton as the staff of economic life in the region, the cotton planter was quite naturally the dominant figure in both the economy and the society of the Delta. LeRoy Percy's dealings with a group of Greenville physicians illustrated the economic leverage wielded by a big-time Delta planter. Not only was Percy able to secure a 15 percent rebate for all drugs purchased or services requested, but he could evaluate the validity of the charges assessed and scale down his payments accordingly. At one point, for example, he clashed with some local physicians over their bill for services provided for his plantation. He pointed out that some of the patients listed were not his tenants and that their charges seemed "quite excessive." Percy demanded a revised bill and instructed the physicians to supply it in short order so that the appropriate deductions could be "charged against the tenants before any settlements are made."[22]

Even the scaled-down bill, however, fell short of satisfying Percy, who still found "charges much in excess of the ordinary charges for attendance on negroes." Percy cited the fifty-dollar fee assessed for delivering a black tenant's baby. Such a charge, in Percy's view, was appropriate for "white people able to stand the expense for similar services," while the "ordinary charge" for blacks was usually about fifteen dollars. Most of the charges involved tenants who were "absolutely unable to pay anything," and although this was no fault of the physicians, Percy refused to pay them the $393.75 they requested. He deducted the 15 percent rebate, reducing the bill to $348.00, and then sent a check for $250.00. "If this is not satisfactory," Percy wrote, "you better come in to see me about the bill. I will not be willing to pay unless we make some adjustment of it before the tenants having something coming to them receive such a balance."[23]

Although most leading economic and political figures in the Delta pursued a variety of business and investment interests, most of them preferred to be identified as planters. Among whites in the Delta, the appeal of cotton planting was symbolic of social as well as economic supremacy: "The Delta owner of extensive lands lived, not on a farm, but on a Plantation. He was known, not as a farmer, but as a planter. 'Farmer' then connoted among us a cautious, small landowner, with a bit of the overalled, goateed hick about him." On the other hand, "planter" linked one with "the antebellum past, reminiscent of the dream, if not always the reality, of what had been. It conjured up a certain lordliness of living and a touch of the romantic. . . . The planter occasionally died in a duel; the farmer of lockjaw got by stepping on a rusty nail." "Planter" suggested aristocracy and inherited wealth, the habit of command, and "a cavalier dash that mocked at the dull virtue of caution and scorned the pedestrian uses of compound interest piling up in a bank."[24]

Arguments for agricultural diversification held little sway against the appeal of a vocation that afforded such a "gracious, spacious way of earning a living." Cotton was, after all, the "lordliest" and most "spirit-pleasing" of crops: "No still life was so dear as jute-wrapped bales on the gin's platform awaiting transfer to railroad station or steamboat landing. No sight was so stirring as the silvery flashing of hoes in the hands of a hundred Negroes getting the cotton out of the grass. No encounter was so warmly pleasant as, riding homeward on a horse at first dusk, to meet field hands riding the mules to the lot, each politely tipping his cap to the boss man and saying softly, 'Good evenin', Mistuh Ed.' "[25]

Exhilarating as it was, planter status was by no means a guarantee of financial solvency. In fact, Delta whites often seemed more concerned about maintaining the former condition than the latter. In 1887 Bolivar County's John C. Burrus received a stern warning to cut back his orders and expenses so that they would be "more in proportion to the crop you have." Burrus faced especially intense pressure in 1899, when bad weather left many planters unable to pay their debts. His factor assured him that all of his cotton was on the market but added that "nearly all of it is low in grade and hard to sell. Cotton that we sold in Feb. at 5¼ cents now brings 4¼ cents to 4 cents and the demand even at these prices is extremely poor." The factor added more unwelcome news: "At these prices you know the cotton reported by you will not be sufficient to pay you out with us." He asked, "What is to be done about the balance you will owe us?"[26]

In the same year, a concerned Charles B. Allen, Jr., urged his father to avoid borrowing more money in order to sustain his planting operations. Informing his father that he could not sign another note for him, Allen asked, "Can't you get mules and supplies by mortgaging this year's crop? I hate like everything to see you get more money. If you don't mind you will loose [sic] everything."[27]

Nearly a decade later, LeRoy Percy complained that "economic conditions" remained "fundamentally wrong" in the Delta: "Ninety-five percent of the planting operations of this section of the Delta are carried on upon borrowed money. Easy credit has been the curse of this section." With money so readily available, "men without any experience, ability, and pecuniary resources" had become involved in cotton planting on a large scale.[28]

By 1930 more than 61 percent of Delta farms were mortgaged, as compared to 38 percent in the rest of the state. Owing money was so common in the Delta that it was by no means a source of shame or even embarrassment. On the contrary, indebtedness was a status symbol of sorts, as indicated by the admission of a Delta black who told David Cohn: "It ain't what I owes that worries me. It's gittin' to owe." In a society where everybody was likely to be somebody else's debtor, suing to recover a debt was considered "boorish" and was certain to earn one "social ostracism." Foreclosure on a note might set off a chain reaction that would lead eventually to the forecloser's being called to account for his own financial obligation. A good cotton crop might lead to a general "scaling down" of debts, but the "clear receipt" indicating freedom from financial obligation, though "a novel document," was one that carried no social prestige whatsoever.[29]

Even when cash flow shrank to a trickle, there was little belt-tightening among Delta planters, who chose instead to live on what local blacks called "credicks." Universal indebtedness was what Cohn called "the economic equivalent of the Indian rope trick," but magic was preferable to logic in a society that chose to look not at today's deficits but at the "next cotton crop," which was certain to bring high prices and prosperity." "The future," Cohn wrote, "was an inexhaustible bank upon which we drew constantly to make up the deficits of the present." Cohn also relished the irony in the fact that it was not until the Great Depression of the 1930s that the rest of the nation discovered "the magic of the freezing of debts."[30]

The apparent ease with which fortunes were made in the Delta seemed to make some planters almost oblivious not just to debt but to the ease with which their riches could be lost. Two incidents from the early career of LeRoy Allen illustrate the volatile nature of cotton planting in the Mississippi Delta. In 1919 the owners of the plantation where Allen served as manager agreed, in advance of cotton picking, to sell the first hundred bales at fifty cents a pound. At the time, this price seemed extremely good, but by the end of picking season, cotton was going for a much higher price. Not only did the owners miss out on a chance to boost their profits, but they had to face a host of disgruntled tenants, whose counterparts on other plantations bragged of settlements nearly twice as high as what they had received.[31]

Within a few months, Allen was a planter himself. Along with two partners, he had purchased an eleven-hundred-acre plantation near Tutwiler with other associated properties and interests at a price of $360,000. In addition to the purchase of seed and other necessities, the partners quickly spent more than fifty thousand dollars on equipment, livestock, and advances to tenants. Still, their optimism ran high; at a real estate agent's insistence, Allen took possession of a Model T Ford, to be paid for with the proceeds from the crop. Before picking began, high-grade cotton was selling at $1.25 per pound, and two of the three partners disdained an offer to divest themselves of their holdings at a forty-five-thousand-dollar profit. They spurned as well early offers of 87.5 cents per bale on their first hundred bales.[32]

By mid-September the partners had ginned 155 bales of cotton for which they were offered not $1.00, but 45 cents per pound. A shocked Allen called his tenants together, had the buyer repeat his offer, and promised to credit their accounts for the amount that they would receive from a sale at such a price. He warned, however, that few, if any, of the tenants would clear any money if their entire crop were sold at that price. Not surprisingly, he had no takers. Three weeks later, however, he sold the same cotton for 31.75 cents per pound, and by the end of the picking season the price was down to 12.5 cents. This financial disaster brought the partnership to an end, leaving Allen with less than a hundred dollars to his name. He was far from alone, however, as he noted: "Planters whom I had known to be in excellent financial condition before the 1920 collapse had either lost their property or were struggling mightily to hold on in a struggle in which the odds were likely against them."[33]

John Faulkner captured the panic and frustration of the 1920 cotton debacle in *Dollar Cotton*. Planter Otis Town refuses to sell his mortgaged crop until the price returns to a dollar per pound. Outraged, he finally invades the New York Stock Exchange and accosts its president, insisting that "hit ain't right fer no one nor nuthing to say cotton is wuth a dollar one year and then turn right around and say better cotton ain't wuth as much the next year. You never picked no crop from plants that you had growed yourselves. They ain't even a bale of cotton setting on that floor where them fellers is saying what it's worth."[34]

Tough times brought considerable "po'-moufin'," but the spending habits of Delta whites changed but little. As David Cohn explained, in the Delta the word *budget* smacked of "unbecoming niggardliness and skimpiness; a thin cake baked without a fat abundance of eggs and butter." A budget entailed "a constant counting of pennies and complicated calculations that are weariness of the mind" and demanded as well "a constant discipline of denial that is weariness of the flesh."[35]

Delta planters lived from crop to crop, and as a result they exulted one minute over what was surely the finest stand of cotton they had ever seen and agonized over weather, worms, or weevils the next. On November 19, 1889, planter Clive Metcalfe complained that it had been raining for the last forty hours. "My God!" Metcalfe asked, "what is to become of us?" Two days later he fretted that more rain was on the way and admitted that he just didn't know "what poor folks will do." In Metcalfe's case, "poor folks" soon threw themselves into a whirl of Christmas season partying and entertaining in Greenville.[36]

In 1887 a young Delta woman reported on the ever-present cycle of optimism and gloom that characterized Delta planting regardless of chronological era. Early in the year, she told of "half crops" that "sold for nothing." Still, the young people continued to have their usual round of parties, and Christmas was "dull" for her only because she was struggling to overcome a prolonged illness. Five years later she complained that low cotton prices had "really ruined her family." The "ruin" actually amounted only to a delay in building a new house, however, and she noted that, although local planters were "very blue," they were busily getting ready to plant more cotton.[37]

Walter Sillers reflected the characteristic good cheer that swept the Delta in prosperous years when he bragged in 1916 that Bolivar County was the second greatest cotton-growing county in the nation and asserted flatly that "the boll weevil does not bother us in the least." With the best crop the county had ever raised ready to be laid by and cotton prices high, he predicted that soon "there will be so much money in this section, people will not want to sell at any prices and lands will be so high it will be hard to get a place at a low figure."[38]

Sillers's buoyant mood may have derived in part from his interest in finding a buyer for a certain piece of land in the Delta, but it more likely simply reflected the prevailing mood in his section, just as it did five years later when he reported that the area he had described previously as a lush, boll weevil-free cotton-growing paradise now suffered under "very poor" crop conditions. Sillers described a cotton crop "so small that I don't believe it will ever amount to anything." This stunted crop resulted from "the heavy infestation of the boll weevil" that was destroying 30 to 50 percent of the squares and fruit "as fast as it is put on the cotton." The Delta's only hope for economic survival, Sillers believed, was a stretch of extremely hot, dry weather, which would kill much of the boll weevil population.[39]

Even as Sillers described the impending crop failure, however, he touted the creation of Bogue Phalia Outing Club, where younger members of the Delta's gentry could gather for boating, swimming, golf, and tennis. Sillers also reported that the people of Rosedale had put aside their boll weevil worries to celebrate the Fourth of July in fine fashion, with a baseball doubleheader against the Delta town of Shelby. (In a particularly telling passage, Sillers added that "this is the first time that I can recall that I have ever celebrated the Fourth of July, or have ever seen the people of Rosedale observe the Fourth and celebrate it in holiday spirit. Something unusual for this section.")[40]

However meager their harvests or the income they produced, Glen Allan planters gathered at The Highland Club for the regular Thursday evening poker games, which were often still going on on Monday or even Tuesday. Summertime poker games, illegal but not unknown even in the courthouse, ran almost continuously—tablestakes stud with everything based on the bettors' judgment. After Shelby Foote's family moved to Greenville in 1910, his father "did little but play poker at the Elks Club there." According to Foote, "men used to get in fist fights for a seat at the table because he always lost, and he wound up broke."[41]

Willingness to risk everything at the poker table was second nature to those who gambled so heavily from year to year on the cotton crop. Such flamboyance was integral to the extravagant, romantic lifestyle of the stereotypical Delta planter. To young Joe Rice Dockery, LeRoy Percy was nothing short of the ideal role model for a young Delta planter: "I never saw a man that I thought was as attractive as Senator LeRoy Percy . . . one of the handsomeness [*sic*] men I've ever seen . . . charm personified . . . he was my idol." Dockery remembered a Greenville lady who told him that "some men have the ability to make money. Some of them are very glad-handers, good fellows, well-met. Some of them are sportsmen entirely, men's men. Some of them are ladies' men entirely. . . . Senator Percy had just about everything you could mention, and he had it in the right way." Dockery's father, Will, a teetotaler save for an occasional glass of wine at Antoine's, nonetheless appreciated Percy's zest for life and admitted to his star-struck son, "If I could get as much pleasure out of a drink as Senator Percy does, then I could have one myself every now and then."[42]

With the admiration of the planter ideal came the dedicated pursuit of the "good life." Several times a year Dockery and his father would join LeRoy Percy and another friend from Natchez on a duck-hunting excursion to Louisiana that began with a day in New Orleans. Percy would spend the day playing poker or bridge at the Boston Club, while the remainder of the group would hire "a tremendous car" with a chauffeur and tour the city. Dinner was always at Antoine's, and "there was no attempt to save a nickel or anything like that." The next day the group would be off to Lake Charles for several days of duck hunting. Dockery also enjoyed playing tennis and shooting craps—"a very well-run type of gentlemanly game." As a young man working on his father's plantation, Dockery spent a month to six weeks each year in Mexico, fishing, hunting, riding, and partying "with all that international oil crowd down there."[43]

Travel was a favorite pastime for the Delta elite. In July 1889, for example, Clive Metcalfe and his mother began an extensive tour that took them first to Italy; they visited Venice ("No carriages . . . a peculiar city"), Milan, Florence, and Rome ("Hot as Tom Turkey!"), where they visited the Vatican ("That is the place where the Pope stays"). From Italy it was on to France and then to London, where they visited Madam Toussaud's wax museum and Metcalfe nearly lost his hat to a monkey at the "zoological gardens."[44]

In 1907 LeRoy Percy planned a hunting trip to Wyoming that would take him away from Mississippi for at least a month. He planned the trip with his brother, Walker, and their wives accompanied them on the jaunt, which also included a tour of Yellowstone. Obviously disappointed that his son Will preferred "European travel" to "communing with nature in the Golden West," Percy nonetheless urged Will to "let me know what kind of a European trip you have been figuring on and then I will figure on it." When Will returned from Europe, he received a letter from his father, who enclosed a check for five hundred dollars because it had occurred to him that "between mountain climbing and opera in Munich, a few suppers with champagne trimming in Paris, and other accessories of foreign travel and sightseeing you will undoubtedly reach your alma mater in a very depleted pecuniary condition." Percy assured his son that, if the check was not sufficient to cover his initial school expenses, he would send more.[45]

The following year the elder Percy sailed for Europe on the *Lusitania*. Percy planned to "knock around England and Scotland" and then "take a look at Holland." He proposed a rendezvous with a friend either in Paris, the south of France, or Switzerland. Percy was also intrigued by the possibility of "autoing the chateux district" as well, and he concluded that "with such a good field to pick from, we can't go very far wrong."[46]

In 1924 Percy and his wife, Camille, cruised the Mediterranean and the Nile. The next summer they visited the South Seas, and the following year they toured Italy and the Riviera. Percy indulged his wife's expensive tastes by paying a 90 percent duty on Venetian linen brought back from Italy. He lamented her "disregard of the value of figures" but paid the stiff duty in order to allow her to have the "real Venetian stuff" and "laud [*sic*] it over the inferior women who have been content with domestic purchases."[47]

Percy did not deny himself by any means when it came to what he thought were the finer things in life. He settled for none but the best wine, brandy, or whiskey and delighted in nothing so much as a good all-night poker game. He described with great glee one such affair hosted by his brother, Willie, in Memphis: "The result was disastrous to the host. I left him with a sincere spell of repentance on, which I think will run until somewhere near frost time. The cigars were said to be good and his whiskey excellent, and outside of these incidentals the sitting put him to the bad about twenty five hundred, disarranged all his summer plans. . . . Fortunately for the family I grabbed a good slice of it, and kept it from going among strangers."[48]

Despite their penchant for travel, Delta planters had no objection to pursuing a good time at home. Wealthy Delta alumni provided guarantees that brought football teams from Ole Miss and Mississippi A&M to play at rickety high school stadiums before a few hundred spectators. In the wake of "dollar cotton" prices the previous year in 1920, Delta planters even bankrolled the Delta Independent League, a minor league baseball organization that paid its top players, many of whom would soon be in the major leagues, as much as a thousand dollars per month.[49]

As had been the case since the antebellum era, the Delta's aristocracy were ready to traverse their entire region at a moment's notice, provided a good time lay at the end of their journey. On July 2, 1884, Delta plantation maiden Kate Burrus reported to her cousin on a dazzling series of parties and dances that she had recently attended in Bolivar County, which remained at that point a largely uncleared wilderness. She had just returned that morning at six "not the least fatigued or sleepy" from an all-night dance where she had "an immense time." In September 1890 Walter Sillers reported that the "young folks" of Bolivar County had been holding parties at the rate of three per week. Clive Metcalfe threw himself into the Christmas festivities in Greenville, noting on December 28, 1888, "another [second consecutive] night's dissipation—had a delightful time." Metcalfe seldom missed a party, but he admitted on March 31, 1889, that he had attended church for the first time in a year.[50]

Frequent dances and parties served as courtship opportunities for the young men and women of the Delta aristocracy. At age fifteen Florence Sillers and her escort rode on horseback for fifteen miles in a rainstorm to attend her first picnic in a late nineteenth-century Delta whose roads were sometimes impassable even in good weather. Her escort's horse fell on him, leaving him muddy and bruised as well as wet, but they pressed on. The rain continued, and the picnic moved indoors. Dancing began with four or five men to one girl, and despite the discomfort of being muddy and wet, Sillers recalled the evening as "one of the grandest times of my life." After this introduction to Bolivar County society, she could remember "no more dull moments in our lives." Men were "plentiful" and girls "scarce." Sundays meant visits from suitors, and the twelve-mile trip to the town of Bolivar soon seemed like no distance at all, especially if a dance or party beckoned. The weather was never too hot or wet for young Florence, who, despite her active social life, married Walter Sillers, the "first white man" she met after arriving in Bolivar County.[51]

So much enthralled with dancing were the good white folk of Bolivar County society that they used the courthouse as a dance hall, clearing out furniture and waxing the floors. Turkey, ham, chicken, ice cream, cake, and bis-

cuits were prepared in abundance. Long gowns were the order of the day for
ladies, as were bouquets of roses. The men wore swallowtails, high silk hats,
and patent-leather shoes. A midnight supper provided an intermission, and
dancing often continued until dawn.[52]

Without question, one of the Delta's leading bon vivants in the late nineteenth century was Harry Ball of Greenville, whose extensive diary recorded
in detail the social life of Washington County during the late nineteenth and
early twentieth centuries. In the space of six days in 1887, Ball attended three
all-night parties. After the first one, he reported that "notwithstanding the heat
we all danced furiously until 4 o'clock in the morning, and I enjoyed it very
much." The hard-partying Ball fortified himself with a few hours' sleep and
then boarded a train for Leland. There he and his friends were met by wagons
that transported them to a party on Deer Creek, where "a perfectly uproarious
dance was inaugurated, terrifying the baby into ceaseless yells, and shaking the
house to the foundation." The men dressed in "spike tails" and the women in
"fine low-necked dresses" enjoyed "a big country supper," and Ball reported,
"Notwithstanding the all night dance of the night before we kept up the ball
until 5½ a.m."[53]

Two days later the irrepressible Ball was at it again, this time at "a most
tremendous shindig," where "flowers bloomed, diamonds and pearls flashed
and glimmered . . . gorgeous silks and satins rustled in the dance . . . champagne
sparkled . . . and . . . hours were danced away until the sun rose in cloudless
splendor over the glittering beauty of Lake Washington." Ball had escorted
Miss Prudence Hunt to the affair—"Ah, Miss Prue! Those hours upon the dark
gallery among the palmetto branches! Where was thy Prudence?" Dancing
began at 9:00 p.m. and continued until 6:00 a.m., when the exhausted band was
dismissed, although many of the revelers stayed on and "gyrated" to the music
of the piano until 8:00 a.m. Ball proclaimed the party "a glorious victory" and
proceeded to sleep away the entire day. Two days later he had to forego another
party because of sore feet, and four days after his third all-night spree he complained: "My feet won't endure shoes yet."[54]

Ball's diary is dominated by descriptions of such ostentatious celebrations:
a full-dress ball at the local Jewish club attended by two hundred persons ("the
largest public ball we have ever had"); a party at which he "launched" a young
widow "anew in the social scene" (once in the swing, the young lady "danced
continually until we broke up at 4"); a leap-year ball in 1888, where guests
attended in fullest possible war paint and he danced "from 9 until 3, refusal
being impossible"; and a ball the following year, attended by three hundred
people, at which he danced forty-three dances "with all sorts, ages, sizes, and
conditions." After the Christmas-New Year's season of 1887-1888, Ball confided to his diary on January 6 that he had not been in bed before 1:00 a.m. since
Christmas and made the empty vow that he was "done with all manner of dissipation for some time to come."[55]

Ball clearly enjoyed the social whirl of Greenville and Washington

County. He attended not only parties but plays and operas as well and partook of what appeared to be the prevailing custom of paying calls on friends (married or single, male and/or female) in the evenings. After one stretch of partying followed by a trip to the opera, he exulted: "What a frivolous life we lead for sure!"[56]

In addition to parties and dances, another favorite form of entertainment was an excursion on the *Kate Adams*, perhaps the most famous steamboat in the Delta and certainly the favorite means (though slower than the train) of getting to Memphis. Rosedale residents loved the ten-to-twelve-hour roundtrip excursions to Arkansas City on "the Kate." Florence Sillers recalled that the boat's captain "liked the Rosedale crowd. . . . The young ladies were beautiful. The young men good spenders, good poker players and crap shooters, good company." Such excursions usually meant a band was on board, and a night of dancing ensued.[57]

A trip to Memphis took a day and a night on the Kate or five hours on the train, and it often meant a stay at the city's famous Peabody Hotel. Even for the high-living white folk of the Delta, the trip to Memphis was something of an event, for it was only worthwhile if a two-night stay was involved. For the ladies and children, such a trip was a grand outing of shopping and sightseeing. When a man went alone, however, his intentions were suspect, and the too-frequent male visitor to Memphis could well find himself the unnamed, but by no means unknown, subject of a blistering Sunday sermon.[58]

If, on the one hand, the social and cultural life of the Mississippi Delta seemed impressive for a region scarce removed from the wilderness, it also had its limitations. Much of the entertaining amounted to little more than competitively conspicuous consumption; the quality of the affair was judged by how much it must have cost. Both the imported and home-grown entertainment often left a great deal to be desired. Harry Ball reported on the performance of the play *Sea of Ice* by the local "Amateur Company," noting that "it was very heavy spectacular drama, and far too much for inexperienced players. The audience went wild, and laughed uncontrollably, even in the most affecting scenes, entirely ruining the good effect. The costumes were splendid, and most of the absurdity was due to Mrs. Ferguson, at her ripe age, assuming the part of a young Indian maid, in very, very inadequate clothing . . . her . . . kirtle . . . only coming down to the knees on one side, and not that far on the other, with bare arms, bare bosom, bare legs, and big bracelets round her ankles."[59]

Critics of the Delta often charged that many of its residents became irresponsible or overindulgent in the pursuit of a good time. Like a number of prominent Deltans, Senator John Sharp Williams made no secret of his love of good whiskey. During one of Williams's Prohibition Era visits with one of his favorite bourbon-sipping companions, LeRoy Percy, Percy's secretary complained that the bottle of bourbon that Percy and Williams were emptying had cost twenty-five dollars. "At last," Williams exulted, "we've found a place where they appreciate the true value of liquor."[60]

Williams's reputation as a drinker was well known. When Lem Motlow of the Jack Daniels distillery sent him four bottles of his prized product for evaluation, Williams quickly pronounced it "the best whiskey that I have yet saw." Although opponents endeavored to use his well-known affection for liquor against him, they gained little by their efforts. In the 1907 senatorial campaign, James K. Vardaman alluded to Williams's drinking habits, but Williams dismissed "this little whispered slander," assuring a supporter that any man who was "fool enough to suppose that a man who could do the work that I have done in the last ten years and be either a drunkard or a constant drinker, has too little sense to vote."[61]

After a rancorous exchange with Alabama senator Thomas Heflin over Heflin's resolution to bar airplanes from flying over public assemblies in the District of Columbia (Heflin had been distracted during an outdoor speech by a low-flying plane), Williams asked, "Why should anybody quarrel with anything which makes a noise in competition with a Senator making a noise? They are both equally noisy and between the two, the airplane is the more scientific noise." Questioning Williams's sobriety, the frustrated Heflin asserted that "whatever else may be said of me, when I come into the Senate chamber, I always come in full possession of my faculties." "Well," Williams snapped in quick reply, "what difference does that make?"[62]

Delta representatives seldom showed any enthusiasm for statewide prohibition, and the issue of national prohibition created a serious dilemma for a whiskey-loving senator whose state had already outlawed the sale of alcohol. Although he voted, albeit with great reluctance, for Prohibition, Williams took no personal vows of temperance. As he confronted the gloomy reality of prohibition, he wished for "enough liquor stored away to last me a life time." And when, on occasion, his stock dwindled to two and a half quarts, he did not know whether to get a good friend "and finish what I have left on hand and each shoot the other or to expatriate ourselves and go to France or Cuba." Such shortages were probably infrequent; when Prohibition began, saloon-keeper-turned-bootlegger Phillip J. Roche, a longtime confidant, assured Williams, "I have enough whiskey saved to do you until you die; just tell me when you want it." Williams responded by instructing Roche to bring him "a quart every Monday and every Friday afternoons."[63]

From the standpoint of their moralistic antagonists in the hills, the problem with Delta whites was not just that they drank so much but that they made no effort to conceal it. After LeRoy Percy's candidate had bested the Klan's choice for sheriff in 1922, four kegs of whiskey—supplied by LeRoy but not drawn from his own private stock of good liquor—fueled "a party never to be forgotten" where, in Will Percy's view, "there were few inhibitions and no social distinctions" and the "banker's wife hobnobbed with the hot tamale man, a lawyer's careened with a bootlegger. People who hadn't spoken for years swore deathless loyalty on one another's shoulders." At the conclusion of this "memorable evening," departing guests "fell off bicycles and into gutters, ran over street signs and up trees."[64]

For Klan supporters, this celebration simply confirmed their estimates of the sorry state of morality in the Delta. Elsewhere, a participant in a well-known Christmas party held annually on a plantation near Glen Allan reported matter-of-factly that the affair was always a tremendous success because the children went outside to play while the adults gathered inside to "get drunk and sing."[65]

Moral laxity and aristocratic social pretension were but part of an overall regional identity that bred resentment and conflict as it became increasingly apparent to less fortunate whites living elsewhere in a state mired in deepening poverty that, despite its sins, the Delta was enjoying consistent and expanding prosperity. Stories of fortunes won through diligence not in the fields but at the poker table were abundant in Delta lore. Legend had it that the Delta village of Midnight had gotten its name when Jimmy Dick Hill, scion of an already wealthy Delta family, won himself a huge parcel of prime Delta land at "straight up twelve o'clock" during one of the area's famous high-stakes, all-night poker games.[66]

Such tales of undeserved good fortune explained why, as John Faulkner put it, "the individual and collective mind of the hillman was stubbornly set in condemnation of anyone who lived in the Delta." Certainly many political conflicts in Mississippi reflected the bitter antagonism between a flourishing cotton kingdom and the economically declining and morally disapproving "redneck" counties of the remainder of the state.[67]

Animosity toward the Delta had manifested itself in Mississippi politics even before the Civil War as legislators debated the matter of state funding for levee construction. By the end of the 1880s, levee and railroad expansion contributed to an even sharper divergence of interests between a resurgent Delta and the economically distressed hill counties.[68]

Robert L. Brandfon linked the Delta's destiny as a plantation kingdom to its infectious appeal as a place where, still clad in brogans and overalls, even the most horny-handed white emigré from the hills could call himself a "planter," and therefore "immerse himself in the heady myths and pretensions of King Cotton, the overlordship of Negro tenants, and the imagery of an antebellum southland that never was." Paradoxically, however, the Delta's dramatic emergence as the New South's Old South was largely attributable to the rapid modernization of its economy and transportation network during the 1880s. Moreover, the Delta's increasing socioeconomic and political isolation from the remainder of Mississippi was actually traceable to its strengthening ties to the world and national economy and its greater exposure to the ways of the world at large. As Brandfon noted, while the economic prospects of the remainder of the state grew ever more dismal, because of its attachment "to the major north and south rail artery of the nation," the Delta became "part of one of the great mainstreams of national commerce."[69]

By providing swift and convenient access to New Orleans, the railroad also nurtured what Brandfon called "a sense of cosmopolitanism" among Delta whites. "In other words," he explained, "it was during this period of the 1880s, a period of expansion stimulated by the railroad, a period of prosperity and rising land values, that the Delta farmer was separated from his brother in the hills. One became a planter, the other remained a farmer, and with the passing years, as the differences became more marked, so the enmity between them grew in like proportion."[70]

Elsewhere, it was dismay over the existing apportionment system that so clearly favored the Delta and other black majority counties that led many hill-county representatives to accede to the call for a constitutional convention in 1890, and the promise of a more equitable apportionment plan encouraged a number of these same spokesmen to acquiesce to provisions that ultimately disfranchised as many as fifty thousand whites. The tensions between the majority-black "coon counties" and the majority-white "cow counties" were more than obvious to a journalistic observer at the 1890 convention.[71]

By the end of the nineteenth century, political conflict in Mississippi often followed the geographic, economic, and class lines that separated the Delta from the hills. For example, the controversy over the infamous convict-lease system in Mississippi actually fed on the hill-county antagonism toward the Delta. Delta landlords had utilized convict labor as early as the late 1860s, when planter-speculator Edmund Richardson struck a deal with Fourth District military commandant Alvin C. Gillem whereby he secured control over the state's convicts for several years. Instead of paying the state, however, Richardson was reimbursed annually in the amount of nearly thirty thousand dollars for their upkeep and transportation. With such a labor force to command, it was small wonder Richardson soon cleared thousands of acres of fertile Delta cotton land and became known as "the greatest cotton planter in the world." In 1876 the legislature authorized the Penitentiary Board to relieve overcrowding at the state prison by leasing the convicts as laborers to individuals at a monthly rate of $1.10 per convict. The lessee was to provide food, shelter, and medical care. Utilizing a brokerage firm, the state quickly leased 321 convicts to planters in the Delta. Subsequently convicts were also leased to private employers to build railroads and levees, both of which were vital to expanding the prosperity of the Delta.[72]

The convict-lease system was replete with opportunities for abuse and neglect. Lessees had no interest, either personal or financial, in the health or well-being of the worker. Efficiency demanded the most work at the lowest outlay for upkeep. There was none of the incentive for solicitude prompted by the need to retain tenants from year to year or even that prompted by the desire to protect one's investment in slave property. Atrocity after atrocity found its way into public view despite the fact that many of the convicts labored in the virtual isolation of the Delta's malarial swamps. One report described convicts leased to the railroad laboring in knee-deep water "held together by chains that fretted in their flesh, compelled to attend to the calls of nature in line as they stood day in and day out and their thirst driving them to drink the water in which they were compelled to deposit their excrement."[73]

The fact that a large number of the abused convicts were black may have worked to prevent a greater outcry over the system, but many of its outrages were so horrendous that the color of the victim became almost irrelevant. In 1894 Julius Adams, a black convict convicted of petty larceny and unable to pay his fourteen-dollar fine, was leased to Delta landowner J. H. Foltz. When Adams escaped and fled to the Leflore County sheriff's office, he told his story to then-newspaper editor James K. Vardaman. Adams charged that he had been forced to work outdoors in bitter cold, the result being that his fingers froze, the skin bursting and peeling off to expose the bones. According to Adams, Foltz not only failed to provide medical care, he required Adams to continue working. When his hands became gangrenous, Adams was taken to the chopping block, where each of his fingers was cut off at the first joint. Foltz subsequently locked Adams in a log cabin and chained him down each night. When he was finally able to work in the fields again, Adams eluded Foltz's dogs and made his escape. The race-baiting Vardaman seemed an unlikely champion for a black convict, but Vardaman cited "the mutilated disfigured hands of Adams" as evidence of "deeds of barbarity that would outrage the bloody instincts of the most conscienceless savage that ever roamed the wilds of the West!"[74]

For all their expressions of humanitarianism and moral outrage, Vardaman and other hill-county political champions who sought to curb the convict-lease system were not unmindful of the fact that the practice clearly benefited powerful Delta corporate and planting interests. An investigating committee reported in 1902 that the Yazoo Delta Railroad had at one time employed two hundred convicts, but no record of payment could be found. As the state initiated a policy of leasing private lands, working them with convict labor, and splitting the profits with the landowner, the large planters of the Delta continued to be the prime beneficiaries.[75]

As Robert L. Brandfon noted, many of the denunciations of the convict-lease system "were not predicated on its barbarity, but rather on the Delta planters' monopoly over it." Governor Vardaman, who succeeded in bringing the system of leasing to an end, captured this sentiment in his annual message in 1906: "While the state has realized a very considerable revenue from the work of the convicts, it has also contributed a very large revenue—the products of the convicts' toil—to swell the fortunes of favored private individuals. It is an easy matter to make money planting cotton in the Yazoo Mississippi Delta when you own the labor, pay no taxes or interest, and the products sell for a good price." Ironically, Vardaman's crusade to end the brutal convict-lease system led to the establishment of an almost equally infamous "plantation prison" in the Delta at Parchman.[76]

Taxation and the distribution of revenue provided another basis for conflict between the Delta and the hills. The constitution of 1890 called for the distribution of school funds according to the number of educable children in the county. The common school fund was augmented by poll tax collections. Both factors favored the Delta counties with large numbers of blacks who were counted as part of the school-age population but who paid no poll taxes. Nowhere in Mississippi did whites make even a pretense of an equal allocation of school funds between the races, but because many black children seldom attended school and were less likely to remain in school as they grew older, whites enjoyed obvious educational advantages over their counterparts in white-majority counties. For example, Washington County, with a more than eight-to-one black majority, operated its white schools for seven months in 1893 and paid its teachers an average salary of thirty-seven dollars per month. At the same time, predominantly white Smith and Jones counties struggled to maintain a three-month term and paid their teachers only sixteen dollars per month.[77]

Not surprisingly, in 1900 when the state's voters approved overwhelmingly a constitutional amendment providing for distribution of the school fund according to actual attendance, opposition was concentrated in the Delta, where spokesmen such as LeRoy Percy condemned this and other such equalization measures as efforts to capitalize on "a latent feeling of hostility on the part of the balance of the state towards the Delta."[78]

With local tax boards allowed to set their own assessment levels, each year brought a new effort to reduce each county's contributions to the state treasury. As the richest counties in the state, those in the Delta stood to gain the most by undervaluing property, and, as a rule, gain they did. In most years, the poor, underdeveloped counties of the piney woods paid larger amounts in taxes than most of those in the Delta. In 1916 an angry legislator complained about wealthy Delta planters who were not paying their "just proportion of the state's obligations" and cited one such county where three-fourths of the land was assessed at less than one dollar per acre.[79]

In response to this inequity, in 1916 the legislature created a new state board of equalization, which promptly set tax assessments at 100 percent of estimated values. With this move came a pledge that the next legislature would reduce the tax levy, but it nonetheless brought angry protests from the Delta. The self-interested nature of those protests quickly became apparent as assessments fell in most of the state's sixty-five poorest counties but rose by 464 percent in Bolivar and 434 percent in Coahoma.[80]

Much of the Delta-hills squabbling revolved around the issue of control of state politics. The 1890 constitution left in place a system in which nominations for statewide office were made by a state convention. A county's voting strength at the convention reflected the number of representatives it sent to the lower house of the legislature; because legislative apportionment continued to favor the black majority counties after 1890, hill-county leaders were soon complaining that the Democratic party's nominating process was unduly influenced by political leaders from the Delta. By 1902 sentiment for a statewide nominating primary had grown so strong that such a measure passed both houses of the legislature with a total of only six dissenting votes, although a number of Delta representatives abstained.[81]

By forcing Delta candidates to campaign for nomination to statewide office, the primary system only highlighted the economic and class differences between whites in the Delta and those in the rest of the state. For example, although once a Vardaman supporter, LeRoy Percy grew increasingly contemptuous of the hill-county favorite's belief "that money is an evil to be guarded against; that the people of the state would be happier and better if they were deprived of all opportunity of acquiring money; that Spartan simplicity, virtue, and poverty are the virtues which should be emulated." Vardaman's error, Percy concluded, resulted from "an untrained mind grappling with economic questions and trying to be original. Carried to its logical conclusion, it would mean a return to barbarism; and between barbarism and Wall Street I think he rather leans toward barbarism."[82]

Percy's sarcasm underscored the economic differences that lay behind the Delta-hills schism. Dependent on banks and the railroad, their fortunes shaped by the fluctuations of the world cotton market, and their surplus capital invested heavily in stocks and bonds, Delta planters had good reason to associate their interests with those of Wall Street, whereas many of their economically strapped hill-county brethren saw banks and large corporations as nothing short of anathema. For big-time planters such as Percy, bigger was definitely better. Explaining his personal investment philosophy, Percy wrote, "I have never felt disposed to take small dabs of stock in different enterprises, the amount invested is not sufficient to warrant personal attention, and the dividends come in in driblets so as not to be of value. My rule has been to confine myself to enterprises where I could make substantial investments." On another occasion Percy explained that he did little business with Mississippi banks because "we usually get what money we need in New York at a lower rate than they offer."[83]

Delta leaders who aspired to positions of influence in state politics realized they suffered from their socioeconomic and geographic isolation from the rest of the state. When Charles Scott queried LeRoy Percy about Scott's chances of being elected governor, Scott's primary concerns were his name recognition "in the interior of the state" and "prejudice against a large landowner." Percy replied almost proudly that his judgment in the matter was probably of "small value" because, like Scott, he had "no wide state acquaintances, and have never been, in any way, in touch with the feeling of the masses of the people throughout the state outside of the Delta."[84]

Between the lines, the Scott-Percy exchange centered on the question of whether the people of Mississippi had the good sense to take advantage of the leadership a Delta aristocrat could offer. Scott confided: "I have always thought that I would not care to hold office unless I was entirely independent of the salary. My affairs now are getting in better shape financially and if I have no unexpected backset, I might be able to spend $10,000 or $15,000 a year in the Governor's mansion, while I believe that the salary does not exceed $4,500.00." Scott reportedly owned thirty thousand acres of land by the turn of the century, but Percy urged him not to hesitate because of his wealth. In Percy's view the people had supported "back scrubs and short-horses because there is no thoroughbred running." Percy assured Scott that Mississippians "would welcome the opportunity of placing in the Governor's office a man who seeks the office, inspired only by laudable and patriotic ambition."[85]

The direction and tenor of Mississippi politics in subsequent decades cast considerable doubt on Percy's assertion. As V. O. Key, Jr., once observed, "It is a puzzling characteristic of southern politics that candidates can at times get themselves elected by their skill in advocacy of something on which everyone is agreed." Although there was never at any point any sign of significant disagreement between Delta and hill-county whites about the necessity of maintaining absolute and ironclad supremacy over blacks, there were some major differences in the tactics the two groups employed in pursuit of this goal.[86]

These differences manifested themselves in the attempts of Delta politicians to shield their black laborers from the most malignant aspects of the intense racism of the Klan or of hill-county politicians, who, in turn, scorned their Delta adversaries as, in Key's words, "less devout communicants" in the faith of white supremacy. There was considerable irony in this view, given the lynching rate in the Delta, but Lewis Baker explained that the region's planters simply took a "more businesslike approach to the race issue" than was typical among Mississippi farmers: "Mississippi's woods were full of hill farmers who spent one month a year rounding up blacks to pick their cotton, and the other eleven hatching schemes to ship them all to Africa or Saint Louis. In the Delta, on the other hand, the shortage of year-round agricultural labor was one of the chief impediments to economic growth, and the planters knew it."[87]

Alfred H. Stone, who considered himself an expert on the "race question," was especially candid when it came to the Delta's dependence on blacks. "Every step taken in the development of this section has been dependent upon, and marked by, an increased negro population," Stone concluded. Consequently, he foresaw that "the future of this territory will inevitably be linked with the future of the American negro."[88]

Although he had experimented with immigrant labor with an eye toward reducing his region's dependence on blacks, like Stone, LeRoy Percy recognized the threat to the Delta posed by racial agitation, which might put black labor in flight. Percy was distressed by any turn of events that aggravated "the inflammable and extreme element among the Southern people; making the Negro more difficult to reason with and control, and, arraying against him all of the vicious and ignorant of our own race, intensifying in every way the burden, heavy enough already, of the thinking, conservative element of our suffering people." Percy associated himself and his fellow Delta planters with this "conservative element," which bore the burden of "not only the future prosperity and development of the South, but its very civilization."[89]

The attitudes of Stone and Percy seemed to conflict directly with those of Vardaman. A Greenwood resident who nonetheless emerged as the political champion of the hill-county whites, Vardaman regularly described blacks as a bigger and more costly curse to the country than "all the wars it has waged added to the ruin wrought by flood and fire." According to Vardaman, a black man's nature resembled that of the hog. He was "a lazy, lying, lustful animal which no conceivable amount of training can transform into a tolerable citizen." Seemingly obsessed by his visions of lust-crazed black beasts stalking virginal white women, Vardaman asserted, "We would be justified in slaughtering every Ethiop on the earth to preserve unsullied the honor of one Caucasian home."[90]

Reporting on the 1907 campaign for the Senate between John Sharp Williams and Vardaman—during which Vardaman called for the repeal of the Fifteenth Amendment, which had given blacks the vote—Percy recalled that in his race for governor Vardaman had won the support of the hill counties "by talking about the impossible things he was going to do in reply to the Negro question." "There is," Percy wrote, "the decided possibility that the same old hobby horse may serve to ride into the Senate." Percy also attacked Vardaman's efforts to create "horrible pictures of the assaults of negroes upon the white women . . . only to inflame the passions and hatred of his audience. . . . Playing with dynamite, arousing the bitterest of race feelings, to accomplish nothing—only to get a few votes." Clearly disturbed by the ascendance of other demagogic politicians around the region, Percy concluded: "Arkansas has her Jeff Davis, Tennessee her Bob Taylor, South Carolina her Tillman." He supposed it was only fitting that Mississippi "have a Vardaman in order to show how far the South has wandered from the guidance of her forefathers."[91]

Their disdain for Vardaman's race-baiting did not prevent either John Sharp Williams or LeRoy Percy from reasserting their own commitments to white supremacy whenever they were challenged. Williams announced that if he believed it could be accomplished, he would be as willing as Vardaman to have the Fifteenth Amendment repealed "and much more capable of it." Williams also expressed opposition to the establishment of a training school for blacks because it would bring them "into competition with white mechanics and artisans." He squelched rumors that he had forced a white servant to eat with his black servants by explaining that he had actually discharged his white servant because she was willing to eat with blacks. Both Percy and Williams worked to have blacks removed from federal appointments, and Williams castigated President Woodrow Wilson for appointing a black justice in the District of Columbia, warning that a number of southern politicians would "welcome it as an opportunity to flim-flam and demagogue on the negro problem."[92]

Clearly, neither Williams nor Percy harbored any sympathy for notions of racial equality. When Percy lamented the fact that practical handling of the race question had become "infinitely more troublesome and dangerous to all concerned" because of the attempts of politicians "to make political capital out of it," he spoke from a realization that such demagoguery posed a constant threat to the stability of the Delta's labor supply. Percy's concerns on this point

were particularly acute in years like 1907, when, by his estimate, "fully 10 percent of the land in the Delta" was not being farmed due to bad weather and
"insufficient labor."[93]

After the 1907 election, Percy wrote President Theodore Roosevelt
explaining that in supporting the victorious Williams he had been working to
"keep Mississippi from practically vetoing my ideas on the race question by
sending Vardaman to the Senate." Although Williams won, the decision was
"uncomfortably close, and not a tribute to the intelligence of the state."[94]

Ironically, Vardaman had supported Deltan Charles Scott in the 1907
gubernatorial race, but Vardaman's hard core of supporters from the hill counties refused to back the Delta conservative despite their champion's endorsement of him. Scott's strength resided instead in the relatively more affluent
counties, where Vardaman fared poorly in his contest with Williams. Vardaman's support of Scott demonstrated a surprising degree of ideological flexibility on his part, but many of his wool-hat supporters could not bring themselves to vote for an affluent Delta planter and corporate lawyer like Scott.[95]

This anti-Delta sentiment played a key role in Percy's defeat at the hands
of Vardaman in the 1911 senatorial primary. Percy was the incumbent in this
race, having been chosen by a legislative caucus in 1910 to fill the seat vacated
by the death of Anselm McClaurin. Percy's status as a wealthy Delta planter
was the dominant theme of Vardaman's campaign. As Lewis Baker has
explained, Vardaman was exceptionally adept at convincing his followers that
their poverty was the fault of wealthy planters like Percy. The result in the
1911 campaign was, in Baker's words, that "LeRoy was attacked for opposing
prohibition, for bringing Italians to the Delta, for hunting and playing cards on
Sunday, for representing the black Knights of Pythias Lodge in a lawsuit against
the white lodge of the same name, and for being a tool of the railroads." Try as
he might to respond to or refute these statements, Percy had no hope of coun-
teracting the hostility generated among voters outside the Delta by "the fact
that he was a wealthy corporate attorney and planter with little sympathy for
the religious zeal and malignant racism of Vardaman supporters."[96]

When it came to class-based contempt, Percy's supporters gave as good
as they got. It was during the 1911 campaign that an armed and extremely nervous Will Percy surveyed a hill-county crowd that he described as "ill-dressed,
surly . . . unintelligent and slinking . . . the sort of people that lynch Negroes,
that mistake hoodlumism for wit and cunning for intelligence, that attend
revivals and fight and fornicate in the bushes afterwards . . . undiluted Anglo-
Saxons . . . the sovereign voter. It was so horrible it seemed unreal." After the
election, which also saw another redneck champion, Theodore G. Bilbo, gain
the lieutenant governorship, LeRoy Percy insisted that "with Vardaman
elected, I consider Bilbo's election fortunate for the state. The more nauseous
the dose, the sooner will vomiting relieve the patient."[97]

With his defeat in 1911, LeRoy Percy's career in state politics was over,
but he continued to warn that overt repression and abuse of blacks could lead
to economic disaster for his region. The Great Migration seemed to confirm

his worst fears, and Percy became especially alarmed as post-World War I tensions over the liberating effects of their wartime experience on black soldiers, especially their access to European women, fed the resurgence of the Ku Klux Klan.

Percy believed that Klan agitation made the "'brother in black' hard to hold and easier to move." Confessing the obvious—that he was "intensely uneasy about the labor"—Percy called the Klan "a menace to the prosperity and welfare of my people" and dismissed the contention that the group meant no harm to blacks: "You can make three parades in the county of Washington of your Ku Klux Klan and never say an unkind word and you can start the grass growing in the streets of Greenville."[98]

Percy noted the high level of black out-migration from the Delta in 1922 and felt certain matters would only get worse if Klan activity continued. He condemned the organization for destroying "the feeling of community harmony which had always prevailed in this county more than in any place I have ever known." Percy's definition of "harmony" came through in his glowing description of "five or six thousand free negroes" working on a flood-threatened levee under the supervision of a few whites "without the slightest friction and of course without any legal right to call upon them for work, and yet the work is done not out of any feeling of patriotism but out of a traditional obedience to the white man." Percy also failed to acknowledge that the fear of lynching and other forms of violence and intimidation may have contributed to the ostensibly docile behavior on the part of blacks that he cited as evidence of "harmony." Finally, as we have seen, the same concern for the Delta's labor supply that lay behind Percy's effort to defend blacks against the demagogic assaults of hill-county politicians and the threats of the Ku Klux Klan also led him to expose many of these same blacks to the risks and hardships of incarceration on the levees during the 1927 flood.[99]

However pragmatic his motives, Percy's written and verbal attacks on the Klan and his successful campaign to keep a Klansman out of the sheriff's office in Washington County nonetheless won him praise from fellow planters who recognized the threat that the Klan posed to their labor supply. One Percy admirer wrote from Issaquena County that "every farmer in the Delta should feel very grateful to you for what you did; someone put up posters in re [*sic*] to organizing here and it literally scared the negroes crazy; a certain element in Mayersville were in favor but your speech made 'Christians of them.'"[100]

The rout of the Klan in 1922 was the last major political triumph for LeRoy Percy. The same year marked the end of the political career of Percy's friend John Sharp Williams. Williams declined to seek reelection to the Senate in 1922, despite the fact that one of the candidates was his old antagonist James K. Vardaman. Williams left public life readily expressing a desire "to be left free and untrammeled from the insolent interference of every little two by four fool who thinks he has a right to advise me because I am in office and he has a vote."[101]

When his supporters urged him to run again in order to prevent Vardaman from returning to the Senate, Williams replied, "If it be true that there is nobody in Mississippi except me who can beat Vardaman, then Vardaman won't be beaten, because I can not make a vicarious offering of my peace of mind and contentment the balance of my life just to keep Vardaman out of office. The people of Mississippi ought to have honor and sense enough to keep him out." To another supporter, Williams declared that if he was the only man in Mississippi who could defeat Vardaman (who ultimately lost in the primary runoff to Hubert Stephens), "then Mississippi has sunk to a very low level and doesn't deserve to be represented by anybody better than Vardaman."[102]

Shortly before LeRoy Percy's death in 1929, Williams wrote Percy, hoping to revive Percy's spirits after the recent loss of his beloved wife, Camille, but Williams's letter also carried a sense of resignation to the political demise of the Delta aristocrat. Williams saw few others like Percy left in "this mean old world," but he sought to encourage his old friend by expressing his own determination to remain in the world, "even if only on its outskirts." After Percy's death Williams mourned the loss of a fellow "gentleman" who was "true as steel." Although Williams's own physical health remained good, he admitted that his "sap, vigor, vitality and interest in life" were gone.[103]

Even before William's decision to withdraw from politics, the Delta's declining influence in statewide elections was clear enough. Deltan Oscar Johnston lost the 1919 gubernatorial primary to Lee M. Russell, the hand-picked successor to Theodore G. Bilbo, in a campaign that featured attacks on Johnston as a privileged planter aristocrat. After Johnston's defeat, it was nearly thirty years before another gubernatorial candidate from the Delta even made it into a runoff.[104]

Despite their inability to get one of their own into the governor's mansion, however, Delta whites remained committed to a political agenda that reflected the region's distinctive economic orientation. Between 1919 and 1943, Delta voters consistently backed candidates who espoused fiscal conservatism and promised policies not only favorable to large landholders but conducive to corporate expansion as well. By the mid-1920s, Delta politico Walter Sillers, Jr., sounded much like Henry Grady reciting his famous "Pickens County Funeral" oration as he spun the tale of the "average Mississippian" who slept under a blanket from Baltimore, on a mattress from Pittsburgh, and a bed from Indianapolis. He wore a New York suit, a Boston shirt, and St. Louis shoes, and, like Grady's famous Georgian, when he died, he was placed "in a Cincinnati coffin made out of white pine, and put in a hearse that came from Detroit, to which is hitched a pair of Kansas City horses, and laid away in a grave that is dug with a Pittsburgh spade." Sillers concluded his remarks by praising a legislature (probably 1924) that had passed a number of proindustry measures designed to remove limitations on land ownership and otherwise facilitate corporate investment. More such legislation, Sillers believed, would be enormously beneficial to Mississippi in "building up her industries and creating opportunities for our people."[105]

Such sentiments translated into strong Delta support for gubernatorial aspirants Henry L. Whitfield in 1923 and Hugh L. White in 1931, both of whom were openly probusiness and energetic advocates of industrial development. When Martin S. Conner campaigned for governor as the friend of the common man in 1931, he collected relatively few votes in the Delta. On the other hand, however, Conner's endorsement of the sales tax during his first administration and his call for fiscal responsibility in government won him the Delta's backing in his unsuccessful gubernatorial bid in 1939.[106]

In their battle to serve their own peculiar regional and class interests in the legislature, Delta whites enjoyed a number of benefits conveyed by the 1890 constitution, which had stripped the vote, via the poll tax and other provisions, not only from practically every black but from thousands of hill-county whites as well. The 1902 primary law had made it more difficult for a Deltan to win the governorship, but the chief executive's powers were also severely limited by the 1890 constitution. Such power to govern as existed in Mississippi largely resided with the legislature, where uncorrected malapportionment helped to maintain the Delta's influence. A stable, unified political agenda and a tendency to return incumbents to office enabled Delta representatives to control key posts and committee assignments in both legislative chambers and thereby protect the Delta's economic and social interests from the attacks of hill-county champions. Only three times between 1916 and 1940 did the Speaker of the Mississippi House of Representatives reside in other than a black-majority county. Given the appointment powers accorded the Speaker, it was hardly surprising that black-majority county lawmakers enjoyed an all but total domination of house committees like Ways and Means and Appropriations.[107]

Bolstered by the three-fifths requirement for approval of all revenue measures, powerful Delta representatives consistently opposed the efforts of hill-county leaders to provide expanded and improved schools, hospitals, and other public facilities and services for low-income whites. Moreover, Delta politicians fought every effort to introduce a more equitable, progressive tax structure. In 1932 Mississippi became the first state to establish a statewide sales tax, a move that gladdened the hearts of Delta planters, who always stood ready to embrace regressive taxation in any form. Oscar Johnston defended the sales tax as "the fairest and most equitable form of taxation that has yet been conceived . . . less socialistic than the income tax, and certainly more equitable than the ad valorem tax." Making little effort to conceal the regional self-interest that lay behind his position, Johnston complained that "the farmers in the delta are now paying a tax equal to approximately twenty percent of the gross sales value of the agricultural products being marketed by them."[108]

By the early years of the twentieth century, the Delta's prosperous and efficient plantations and planter-dominated social structure set it apart from the remainder of a Mississippi struggling for economic survival. Ironically, the Delta's socioeconomic and political isolation from the rest of the state was in large part the result of its integration into the nation's primary commercial, financial, and transportation network. The essentially pragmatic, labor-conscious racial paternalism and rigid fiscal conservatism of Delta whites also offered a stark contrast to the rabid race-baiting and the populistic policy orientation of hill-county representatives. The same was true of the cosmopolitan perspectives and hedonistic lifestyles of the Delta's self-styled planter aristocrats when compared to the austere circumstances and fire-and-brimstone fundamentalism of the hill-county whites. The mutual stereotypical contempt with which these two groups regarded each other helped to sustain a sharp class-based division of interests and outlooks that dominated politics and society in Mississippi for much of the first half of the twentieth century and reinforced a widespread perception of the Delta as not just a region but a world and a way of life apart.

7 ▽ "The Deepest South"

▽

▽

By the 1930s the Mississippi Delta's distinctive economic and cultural identity had attracted the attention of observers well beyond the boundaries of Mississippi. In 1935, for example, Rupert Vance identified the "cotton obsessed, Negro obsessed" Delta as "the deepest South," a region where one found "the highest economic range the South, with its peculiar social organization of black and white, may be expected to attain without industrialization." To Vance, however, the Delta was above all a land of contrasts. He was struck by both the "mansions" and the manners of the region's planter aristocracy— "affable and courteous with equals, commanding and forceful with inferiors"—but he noted as well that in the Delta the "Negro" was "to be found at his lowest level in America."[1]

The Delta Vance described was indeed a region where extremes of white affluence and privilege were sustained by equally striking levels of black deprivation and powerlessness. The ability of the Delta's white minority to subjugate and exploit its black majority depended in large part on a system of caste-based social control that was rigid, pervasive, and self-perpetuating. Only if members of both races played their well-defined caste roles with inerrant consistency and an almost exaggerated vigor could white dominance of such a racially and economically imbalanced society be maintained.

Fortunately the caste system of the Mississippi Delta attracted the attention of two social scientists, who recorded their detailed impressions of life on both sides of the color line in the Delta town of Indianola at the end of the 1930s. Taken together, the observations of John Dollard and Hortense Powdermaker provide an excellent starting point for an examination of the racial and class structure of the Delta as it was before economic, social, and political change began to undermine the stability of the South's premier plantation region.[2]

Both Dollard and Powdermaker realized that the anachronistic, contradictory, and exceedingly complex social system they studied was linked inextricably to the Delta's plantation-based economy. Dollard presented a number of examples that demonstrated the economic advantages offered whites by the caste system. In one case, a sixteen-year-old black girl served during the summer as a children's nurse in a white home. She worked from six in the morning until seven in the evening for $1.50 per week. In order to improve her hours and her salary, she was seeking employment as a maid, a job she hoped might pay as much as $2.00 per week. In another case, which Dollard conceded was extreme, a white woman boasted of being able to ring for her maid to bring her a pitcher of ice water at three in the morning. She explained that such obedience was what made her "love" blacks. Still, when her maid, who received $2.50 per week plus food and housing, asked for a twenty-five-cent raise, the woman responded with "You go to hell" and laughed in her face.[3]

David Cohn described the benefits accruing to middle-class whites under the Delta's peculiar socioeconomic arrangements. Servants were "cheap, plentiful, and cheerful except during cotton-picking times in the fall." At that point, "by a convention well understood on both sides," domestic servants temporarily deserted their urban employers for the cotton fields. Deft pickers, after all, might bring in up to two dollars per day, whereas a cook was paid three to six dollars a week, her wages supplemented by the universal custom of "'totin', whereby she took home food to her family from the white folks' kitchen." "Hardly plagued with leisure," the cook arrived at six to start fires, cooked, washed, and baby-sat. A black youth mowed the lawn for a quarter, "stoked at noon with a pork chop sandwich, hot biscuits, and a jug of cold buttermilk provided by his employer," and a washwoman did the family laundry for $1.25.[4]

While whites enjoyed the benefits of this system, severe economic disadvantage was the lot of blacks in the countryside as well as the town. One black woman in her fifties told Powdermaker that over the course of thirty-six years of farming she and her husband had actually cleared money only six times. Another couple who sharecropped and rented for fourteen years achieved this goal only three times, their largest profit being $110, which they used to make a payment on a house in town because they had given up on farming.[5]

As a matter of course, many banks refused to loan money to blacks, referring them instead to a merchant, who might well demand interest as high as 25 percent. A wholesale grocer told Dollard that prior to 1930 some local planters had provided cash furnishes, but as the Depression deepened, they had responded to their own diminished reserves by opening commissaries and advancing groceries and supplies, often at 20 to 25 percent interest. Interest on advances ran from 15 to 25 percent, and although planters complained about the interest costs they faced, Dollard found no planter paying more than 12 percent and most paying considerably less. One particularly enterprising planter bought corn in the fall at sixty cents per bushel and sold it to his tenants in the spring at ninety cents. He also purchased "duck" bagging for cotton-picking sacks at ninety-nine cents per bag and sold them to tenants at a dollar and a quarter.[6]

Hortense Powdermaker marveled at the candor of those planters who admitted, and even boasted about, cheating their tenants. Others rationalized their dishonesty by asserting that the only hope of getting blacks to work was to keep them in debt or at a bare subsistence level. Prior to her arrival in Indianola, Powdermaker had known that southern blacks effectively had no political or legal rights, but she found it a "minor shock" that they had no economic rights either. "I had not before known of such a society.... Tribal societies had their well-defined rules and customs of reciprocity. The Middle Ages, of which the South reminded me in some ways, had an established system of duties and responsibilities between lords and serfs. But the rules on which the share-cropping system was based were broken more often than followed."[7]

Frank Smith recalled being told by a plantation bookkeeper of the time when the planter who employed him had ordered him to charge all the tenant families on his place with another barrel of flour, rationalizing this cheating with the explanation that he had lost heavily at poker the night before and could not bear the thought of his wife and children having "to pay for last night." Smith also offered the oft-retold account of a black sharecropper who has been told that his debits and credits balanced exactly. (This statistically improbable occurrence was remarkably commonplace on Delta plantations.) In this case, the cropper asks the "Cap'm" to double-check his figures and is reassured, "You don't owe me a cent." When the black man asks, however, what is to be done with "them two bales I ain't done hauled in yet," the "Cap'm" suddenly discovers that two pages of his account book are stuck together "Well, what do you know! ... I'll just have to add this whole account up again." Given the outrageousness of such landlords, it was small wonder that rural black teachers and home demonstration agents were often forbidden to teach tenants how to compute their share of the crop, or that blacks with what Neil McMillen called "a propensity to figure" were viewed as potential troublemakers.[8]

A black folktale from the Delta offered a wry commentary on the readiness of white planters and merchants to manipulate the figures in the accounts of their tenants. Entitled "De Wite Man Boun Ter Cut Yer Down," the story dealt with a black man and a white man who simultaneously came up on two boxes, one large and one small, at a crossroads. The black man raced ahead to claim the larger one, only to find it filled with shovels and hoes, while the smaller box, opened by the white man, contained the pencils and paper that whites have used ever since to "outfigger" blacks.[9]

Just as it bolstered whites in their dishonesty, the caste system protected them from black economic competition in any form. One white merchant who sold illegal, "bootleg" beer was able to force black bootleggers to adhere to the same price scales because those who refused to do so invariably faced a raid by white deputies, who normally ignored white bootlegging activities.[10]

In the rare instances when blacks did manage to make some headway in spite of the disadvantages they faced, they had to exercise extreme caution lest their success engender white resentment. One reasonably well-to-do black landowner credited his success not only to "hard work" and "slow saving" but to "staying in my place, acting humble." Regardless of one's humility, obvious upward mobility on the part of blacks could be harmful to their health and safety. Ralph Ellison told of a black man who was lynched for painting his house. Fannie Lou Hamer recalled that her father had risen from sharecropper to cash tenant, painted his house, and acquired his own livestock and implements, only to have a white man poison his livestock and send the family plummeting black into sharecropping.[11]

In addition to the economic benefits provided by the caste system, Dollard also noted the advantageous sexual position occupied by white males under this system. Actually, however, despite the fact that white males enjoyed a high level of access to black women while black males were ostensibly forbidden so much as a glance in the direction of white females, white males in the Delta confronted a complex set of sexual anxieties and concerns that even their dominant position in the caste system could not alleviate.

Winthrop D. Jordan traced the stereotype of the beast-like, lustful, oversexed black man and the totally unchaste, sexually promiscuous black woman back to earliest European contact with Africa. Jordan saw the remarkable durability of these stereotypes as evidence that "'ideas' persist according to the measure of their deep-rootedness in psycho-social necessities." Jordan noted that the belief that black males possessed exceptionally large penises "was a venerable one which easily predated the settlement of America." Seventeenth-century accounts of travel to west Africa included references to the "extraordinary greatness" of the "members" of the native males or of their large "propagators." By the eighteenth century, the abnormal length of the black man's penis had become, in Jordan's words, "something of a commonplace in European scientific circles." This notion remained both viable and pervasive among Delta whites in the 1930s, lending credence to the belief that a white woman raped by a black man would not only undergo terrible agony but would be ruined "socially." Observers differed as to whether this reference was to the loss of chastity and racial purity or whether it revealed a deeper fear on the part of white males that, after a sexual encounter with a black man, no white woman could ever be satisfied by a white lover.[12]

Certainly, Delta white men discussed the matter of the length of the black man's penis with both anxiety and envy. One planter told Dollard of entering a sharecropper cabin unannounced and discovering a black man preparing for intercourse. Dollard's informant was shocked by the size of the man's penis "and gave an indication by his arm and clenched fist of its great length and diameter." Local legend also had it that the belief in the greatness of the black man's penis was confirmed by those who conducted preinduction physical examinations in the county in 1917. (Dollard added that the same notion of genital prowess had been applied to Jews in Nazi Germany as a means of stirring up anti-Semitism.)[13]

Closely related to the question of penis size was the matter of sexual potency, and here again the black man was accorded superhuman qualities. The local jailer told Dollard of a black man who "swung praying" after requesting female companionship on the night before his execution. Bound by custom, local officials honored this last request and secured a woman who spent the night with the condemned man. The young man's hanging ultimately made less of an impression on them, however, than what Dollard called his "virility-in-the-face of death."[14]

Powdermaker reported a similar incident although she used it to illustrate the prevailing stereotype of promiscuity attached to lower-class black women in Indianola. In the episode described by Dollard, it had been difficult to secure a nocturnal companion for the condemned man, and when she was found, she demanded $2.50 in view of the "gruesome" nature of her assignment. In the story told by Powdermaker, however, the black prisoner himself offered forty dollars, and one notoriously "loose" woman sped to the jail so rapidly that "the rest of the town was rather disgusted by her open and indecorous haste."[15]

Like the belief in the lustfulness and superior sexual endowment of the black man, the lasciviousness of the black female was also an enduring article of faith among whites. Jordan quoted English travelers to Africa concerning "hot constitution'd Ladies" with a "temper hot and lascivious, making no scruple to prostitute themselves to the Europeans for a very slender profit, so great is their inclination to white men." The functionality of this belief was readily apparent in that it salved the guilt of the white men who used their physical, material, and psychological advantages as a means of exploiting sexually vulnerable black women whether in Africa, the antebellum South, or the caste-dominated society of the Mississippi Delta.[16]

As a boy in the Delta, Willie Morris believed that only black women engaged in the sex act with white men "just for fun," because they alone possessed "the animal desire to submit that way." The result was that for the young Morris, black girls and women were "a source of constant excitement and sexual feeling," filling his "fantasies and daydreams" with "delights and wonders."[17]

Although white leaders claimed that white men who sought to fulfill their fantasies with a black woman did so at the risk of their good name, such behavior seemed as much winked at as frowned upon. Its tolerance for miscegenation won the Delta the condemnation of hill-county whites, whose attitudes John Faulkner captured in *Dollar Cotton*: "Sleep with your black cooks if you want to. Sleep with them one night and your wives the next. Live in your rotten ungodliness and raise mongrel brats in your front parlors. But keep your scum out of the hills."[18]

As a black youth in Glen Allan, Clifton Taulbert observed that, "even though strict racial segregation was the order of the day, it somehow seemed to have slipped at night." An aunt whom he described as "part Jewish" told Taulbert that "nearly ever' peckerwood got a nigger in his closet." Endesha Ida Mae Holland noted that, during her childhood in Greenwood, some black women "aspired to become the woman, the mistress, of some wealthy white man." This practice was common enough that "for those girls that were light enough, it was a fairly simple process."[19]

Some black women may have seen the role of mistress to a white man as a chance to advance themselves socially or economically, but many others may have felt they had little choice. Spurning the advances of a white employer could mean the loss of one's job; if a white man offered money for sex, an impoverished black woman had to weigh her own feelings of revulsion against the needs of her family.

The hypocritical nature of white racial and sexual attitudes in the Delta often led cynical observers to venture that white men had no objection to sleeping with black women so long as they were not forced to eat breakfast with them the next morning. A popular joke involved two planters who took their teenage sons to New York in order to initiate them in the ways of women and the world. The two men summoned a bellhop and ordered him to procure a prostitute for each of them and to have room service deliver the biggest steaks the cook could prepare. The bellhop returned with steaks for each of the men and for the prostitutes as well, but when four black women rang the doorbell shortly thereafter, he was hastily summoned back to the room and accosted by one of the planters "What do you mean, son? Don't you know we can't eat with these women?"

The irony of an absolute taboo against interracial eating juxtaposed with a considerably more tolerant attitude toward interracial sex was not lost on the black women interviewed by Dollard. "Repeatedly," Dollard wrote, "in dreams of Negro women I noticed the manner in which eating with a white man symbolized other intimacies. Eating together is the sort of act which can be done in a normal courtship situation and is a sign of legitimate social contact which might lead to legitimate sexual contact." In the case of white men and black women in the Delta, the first, less intimate, level of activity—dining together—was forbidden while the ultimately intimate activity of intercourse was readily tolerated. To the black women, eating with a white man carried with it the connotation of equality and mutual respect that intercourse did not.[20]

The matter of mulatto offspring was a particularly delicate and embarrassing one, especially if the prevailing gossip could be confirmed through the child's physical resemblance to its father. In one such case, the resemblance was so striking and the child so fair that the white man's wife persuaded city officials to forbid the child from passing anywhere near his father's house on the way to school. In another case, when a black woman had a son by a man who was a member of a prominent white family and insisted on naming the child after him, influential whites forced her to leave town. Dollard's explanation was that the cook had "defied caste etiquette," not by having the child, but by suggesting that it was legitimate and "that it could expect status classification according to its father, which was implied in taking his name."[21]

Many students of race relations in the South have suggested that the paranoia of whites concerning the threat of the rape of white women by black men arose from a deep-seated horror that black men might retaliate in kind for the sexual aggressiveness of white men toward black women. As Hortense Powdermaker put it, the white man's fear "that the negro desires, and may succeed in exercising, the right enjoyed by the white man, keeps him in constant danger and in constant dread."[22]

Although even the minutest evidence of black ambitions toward economic, political, or social equality was likely to bring swift and violent retribution, the prevention of sexual relations between black men and white women was the absolute, all-consuming obsession of white males in the Delta. A breach of the sexual color barrier by a black man was perceived by white men as tantamount to the instantaneous achievement of equality, more so than if the black man had purchased the largest plantation in the county, cast his ballot for governor, or dined in a white restaurant. As Dollard explained, "Behind the actual or posited desires of Negro men for white women is seen also the status motive, the wish to advance in social rank, to be as good as anyone else, and to have available what anyone else has." As a result, Dollard concluded, "The race-conscious white man has a proprietary interest in every white woman, he also acts as if an attack upon or an approach to the white woman were an attack on himself."[23]

A resolution adopted at a mass meeting of the leading white citizens of Bolivar County was especially revealing. Those in attendance declared themselves "unalterably opposed to lynch law, except for the crime which in the South puts its perpetrator on a level with the beasts of prey, and beyond the pale of human sympathy and protection of law."[24]

Under the sexual and racial double standard imposed by the Delta's caste system, a white male's own interracial sexual activities did not prevent him from enforcing what Cohn called the "iron taboo." Powdermaker related the story of a young black man who joined a crowd of men watching a dogfight. As he walked away afterward, he was accosted by a white man who accused him of staring not at the warring canines but at a white woman who had walked by during the fight. The angry white man threatened to shoot the young black if he caught him looking at white women again. Bystanders later warned the young man that this was no idle threat—his accuser had a "bad reputation" and had already "shot several people." Powdermaker learned that he was also reportedly having an affair with a black mistress.[25]

A white woman voluntarily consorting with a black man risked banishment from the community or even death. For the black man in such a case, death was a certainty, the degree of its horror the only variable. Rumors of relationships between white women and black men quickly attracted the attention of the police. Cohn reported an incident in which an officer who found a white girl and a black man together did not hesitate to kill the black man on the spot. The white girl's parents sent her away and warned her never to return.[26]

As the foregoing incident suggests, although white women appeared to occupy an enviable and exalted position within Delta society, the sexual and color taboos imposed by the system of caste actually bore down on them with considerable force. Along with their reputation for chastity and purity came the stereotype of inhibition and frigidity. As a youth in the 1940s, Willie Morris claimed that not until he was twelve years old did he even entertain the possibility that white women actually engaged in the sex act for pleasure. Dollard suggested that this belief inhibited white males when they were engaged in sex with their wives. Unmarried white females, in turn, received repeated warnings against behavior even remotely suggestive of passion on their part, lest their overheated boyfriends respond by seeking an outlet for their pent-up desire through a visit to "niggertown."[27]

Despite their efforts to conceal it, white females in the Delta evinced considerable resentment of the sexual double standard that allowed their husbands to treat them, in Dollard's words, as "sexual property" by accepting "gratification elsewhere" while refusing "the like privilege" to their wives. Dollard identified a particular genre of humor that suggested white women also envied the sexual freedom of black women. One such joke concerned a black woman who appeared in court and told the judge she had been a widow for ten years. The judge then looked at a row full of children behind her and asked, "Whose children are these?" When the woman explained that they were hers, the judge said, "What, you say these are your children!" "Yes, sir," the woman replied, "I said, 'He's dead', not 'I'm dead!'"[28]

In addition to documenting the persistence of white sexual stereotypes of blacks, Dollard and Powdermaker found other examples of the stereotypical mythology traced by Winthrop Jordan to earliest European contact with Africa. A prime example was the inclination to link blacks with apes. Dollard recalled a popular joke among whites concerning a planter who imported African apes and trained them to pick cotton. Despite the apparent success of his experiments, his friends warned him that his efforts would come to nothing, because as soon as "the Yankees" learned of what he had done, they would come down and free the apes. This story, Dollard noted, was a favorite even among those who considered themselves less racially biased than most of their peers.[29]

The view of blacks as insensitive inferiors with severely underdeveloped senses of perception was a highly functional one, because it allayed white guilt and helped to rationalize what to an external observer appeared to be cruel and insulting behavior toward blacks. Likewise, seeing blacks as less ambitious and more readily satisfied with a humble status in life made it easier to justify deliberately underpaying them, holding down their advances on their crops, or providing them with only a feeble excuse for an education. In such a context, whites could behave in a way that was actually insulting or demeaning to blacks and transform that behavior into a grand or generous gesture on their part. Dollard reported the story of a white man who proudly showed him a group of his tenants who were eating soured ice cream. The man had purchased the ice cream for a picnic, and the unused portion had gone bad. To offer spoiled ice cream to whites would have been unthinkable, but in this man's view, the blacks thought "they were getting a whole-hearted treat," and he told his story with what Dollard described as "a certain self-righteous glow."[30]

While it is conceivable that this man's tenants were so unfamiliar with the taste of ice cream that they were unaware that what they were eating was spoiled, it is more likely that they simply realized that to refuse this "treat" would displease their employer and get them into trouble. Hence their overt response was automatic, much the same as their reaction to inadequate salaries or furnish or questionable crop settlements. The real insight provided by the incident was not into the inability of blacks to differentiate between edible and inedible ice cream, but into the tightness of the Delta's caste system and its ability to provide the dominant whites with a self-satisfying response to what was actually an ungenerous and degrading act on their part.

Willie Morris's recollection of his youth in Yazoo City was laced with references to blacks, whom he and his friends alternately pitied, imitated, and tormented. As a twelve-year-old, Morris had attacked a three-year-old black boy from ambush, slapping, shoving, and kicking him. After he thought about what he had done, Morris felt a "secret shame," but in the immediate aftermath of the incident, he confessed, "My heart was beating furiously, in terror and a curious pleasure. . . . For a while I was happy with this act, and my head was strangely light and giddy." In retrospect Morris realized that what he had done was more than "a gratuitous act of childhood cruelty," something "infinitely more subtle and contorted." Morris also recalled taunting and chasing three ragged, hungry black children who were searching for food in garbage cans. A favorite form of amusement among Yazoo City's white youth was riding by the bus station and opening the car door so as to topple blacks "like dominoes" off the concrete banister where they were seated, awaiting the buses.[31]

With the cruelty and sadism came at least momentary impulses of "pity and sorrow." Morris described an incident wherein he and a group of high school friends went on a July fourth picnic only to discover a black family which had been burned out of its shack the night before and had taken refuge in a dirt-floored cabin near the picnic site. Having saved nothing but themselves and the clothes they wore, the family could only sit in hungry silence as the young whites ate and swam. Morris and his girlfriend took up a collection for the family and gave them food, but, uncomfortable under the continuing gaze of the blacks, the young whites soon packed up and went back to Yazoo City, where they resumed their picnic on the grounds of one of the big houses in Morris's neighborhood.[32]

In Delta society, where the treatment accorded blacks by whites might shift suddenly from paternalistic benevolence to gratuitous cruelty, whites showed little inclination to reflect on the assumptions about blacks and the proper relationship between blacks and whites. For example, like other white youths, Morris simply assumed that he would be treated with "generosity and affection" by any and all black adults he encountered. To Willie and his friends, blacks were "ours to do with as we wished. I grew up with this consciousness of some tangible possession, it was rooted so deeply in me by the whole moral atmosphere of the place that my own ambivalence—which would take mysterious shapes as I grew older—was secondary and of little account." As an adult, Morris was better able to assess the impact of this environment on blacks after his New York encounter with a young black woman from the Delta who began sobbing in the midst of their conversation and left abruptly. A white civil rights worker later explained, "She told me you're the first Mississippi white person she was ever with socially. You made her nervous as hell. Her emotions got the better of her."[33]

Delta whites prided themselves on their acts of kindness and indulgence toward individual blacks, but when it came to the welfare of blacks as a group, white attitudes personified the indifference that seemed so typical of white southerners at large. David Cohn acknowledged that at the end of the 1930s there were pitifully few hospital beds for blacks in the ten core counties of the Delta. Charity hospitals where care might be available were from 50 to 150 miles away, and their facilities were severely limited. Hence any serious health emergency became a matter of life and death for a Delta black. Cohn related the story told by a planter who had put a desperately ill black woman in the back of a truck and sent her to a charity hospital 125 miles away. When she arrived, no room was available and the driver took the suffering woman 50 more bone-rattling miles to another charity hospital, where she was also turned away. The truck that had left the plantation as an ambulance returned as a hearse.[34]

On both sides of the color line there was concern that with the passage of time even the individual acts of kindness that might occasionally save a suffering black from the fate of the rejected, dying woman were becoming increasingly rare. Dollard cited the case of a white family who moved an ailing elderly black man out of his servants' quarters on Monday, put him in a wagon, and sent him to his sister's house, where he died on Wednesday morning.[35]

In theory, the Christianity and and essential kindness of whites were supposed to provide sufficient guarantee of the safety and comfort of blacks in the Delta. The problem was that individual whites were normally satisfied that they had fulfilled their obligation to blacks by simply treating fairly those with whom they dealt personally. Rarely did one white criticize, much less interfere with, another's methods of dealing with blacks. The notion, with roots in the era of slavery, that the weight of public opinion served as a powerful force against the mistreatment of blacks was as dubious in the Delta in the 1930s as it had been a century before. For all the hushed expressions of regret at the way a certain white man treated "his niggers," the same man, especially if he was successful economically, could easily be considered a pillar of his church and his community.

In Powdermaker's view, "the passivity of 'good white folks' in the face of behavior openly at odds with their own ideals and practices hardly required

explanation, considering some of the special inducements to inertia." The
more "tolerant" and "socially secure" white might deplore certain "evils," but
those evils, as Powdermaker noted, "are part of the *status quo* which it is in his
interest to maintain. It is therefore to his interest to consider them inevitable."
This pragmatic acquiescence of the white better element extended in practice,
if not in rhetoric, to the tragedy of lynching, which they publicly deplored but
seldom acted to prevent. In fact, when questioned, a number of them expressed
the belief that an occasional lynching was necessary to keep blacks in line. Dollard observed that, even in cases where the lynch mob killed and tortured the
wrong man, the message to blacks was clearer than if the victim was actually
guilty of a crime. In Clarksdale a black youth falsely accused of rape and actually
exonerated in court by the alleged victim's husband was seized as he walked
from the courthouse by a gang of whites who tied his feet to the back of their
car and dragged him, with his head bouncing on the road, all the way to Marks.
This brutal incident suggested that all blacks, particularly males, were vulnerable to such atrocities and therefore should be doubly careful to avoid the
slightest misstep where the delicate matter of caste-based propriety was concerned.[36]

In addition to living each day with the knowledge that any action that even
seemed to challenge white authority might cost them their lives, Delta blacks
endured daily humiliation and denigration and constant reminders of their subservience each time they came into contact with whites. For example, blacks
were never addressed by whites as "Mr." or "Mrs." and were often referred
to by their first names, no matter how prestigious their position within black
society. In fact, the use by whites of black surnames was all but unknown. Some
whites deliberately avoided learning even the first names of blacks, thereby
denying them even the slightest recognition as individuals. Blacks were particularly sensitive on this point, often responding with only weakly suppressed
disdain to the use of terms like "Uncle" and "Aunty." So hurtful was the refusal
of whites to grant even the slightest personal courtesy that one black woman
dreamed repeatedly of standing in a crowd of whites and asserting her right to
be addressed as "Mrs." A black couple was said to have named their daughter
"Mis Julia" in order to assure that she would be addressed politely by whites.
Handshakes were never proffered to blacks, and white males remained seated
in the presence of standing black females.[37]

In addition to the absolute avoidance of "Sir" and "Ma'am" in conversations with black adults, Willie Morris learned "as a matter of course that there
were certain negative practices and conditions inherently associated with being
a nigger." Morris explained:

> "Keeping a house like a nigger" was to keep it dirty and unswept. A "nigger car"
> was an old wreck without brakes and with squirrel tails on the radio aerial.
> "Behaving like a nigger" was to stay out at all hours and to have several wives or
> husbands. A "nigger street" was unpaved and littered with garbage. "Nigger talk"

was filled with lies and superstitions. A "nigger funeral" meant wailing and shouting and keeping the corpse out of the ground for two weeks. A "white nigger
store" was owned by a white man who went after the "nigger trade." There were
"good niggers" and "bad niggers" and their categories were so formalized and
elaborate that you wondered how they could live together in the same town.[38]

Whites refused as an absolute point of principle to refer to blacks as
"Negroes," preferring "colored" or "nigra" if they did not use the more offensive "nigger." Whites also insisted that, regardless of the status of the caller or
the nature of his or her call, all blacks must come to the back door. Failure to
do so would almost certainly bring a strong rebuke if not a severe "cussin' out."
Even courtesy by blacks did little to undermine caste etiquette. A sincere
"thank you" from a black might be expected to elicit at best an "all right," or
more likely a simple grunt, but almost never the "you're welcome" that connoted a favor willingly done by one friend for another.[39]

This taboo operated from the other direction as well. Etiquette demanded
that all men, especially blacks, remove their hats in an elevator. Finding himself
in an elevator and carrying a load of packages, Richard Wright was assisted by
a white man who took his hat off for him and placed it upon his packages.
Wright explained that

> the most accepted response for a Negro to make under such circumstances is to
> look at the white man out of the corner of his eye and grin. To have said: "Thank
> you!" would have made the white man think that you thought that you were
> receiving from him a personal service. For such an act I have seen Negroes take
> a blow in the mouth. Finding the first alternative distasteful, and the second dan-
> gerous, I hit upon an acceptable course of action which fell safely between the
> two poles. I immediately—no sooner than my hat was lifted—pretended that my
> packages were about to spill and appeared deeply distressed with keeping them
> in my arms. In this fashion I evaded having to acknowledge his service, and in
> spite of adverse circumstances, salvaged a slender shred of personal pride.[40]

Because interaction with whites was so fraught with potential for either
physical or emotional harm, or both, blacks placed great stock in the value of
their own autonomous organizations and institutions. There was little doubt
that the black church played a major role in insulating blacks from the psychological trauma inflicted by the caste society of the Delta. Although some observers thought it actually served the interests of whites by providing blacks with
a convenient nonthreatening outlet for their frustrations and ambitions, the
black church also offered an opportunity for the expression of both community
and individuality and thereby helped blacks, as a group and as individuals, to
transcend at least in part the potentially devastating impact of the racially
restrictive Delta environment.[41]

Hortense Powdermaker saw the black church helping to maintain black self-respect "in a situation geared to destroy it." Powdermaker explained that in the black church "the equality of all people before God and their importance to Him was the theme of sermons and Sunday school lessons. Negroes could even regard themselves as superior because they thought they were following Christ's precepts far better than were the white people, whose behavior was called 'unchristian.'"[42]

In short, the black church was the one institution in the community that was controlled by blacks. Powdermaker noted the contribution of the church to "the sense of respect and esteem from others which is so consistently refused to Negroes by the white society which dominates most of their lives." As Clifton Taulbert explained, the black church was "more than an institution, it was the very heart of our lives. Our church was all our own, beyond the welfare of whites, with its own societal structure." On Sunday morning blacks in Glen Allan were transformed when they entered their churches: "Today, field hands were deacons, and maids were ushers, mothers of the church, or trustees." To Taulbert the church "provided the framework for civic involvement, the backdrop for leadership, a safe place for social gatherings, where our babies were blessed, our families married, and our dead respected."[43]

Dollard described the sense of unity and collective strength he found when he was asked as a white, and therefore honored, guest to address a vocal and responsive black congregation: "Helped by appreciative murmurs which began slowly and softly and became louder and fuller as I went on, I felt a great sense of elation, an increased fluency, and a vastly expanded confidence in speaking. There was no doubt that the audience was with me, was determined to aid me in every way." When he finished his talk, which focused on the sorrows and hopes shared by all humanity, he felt that "the crowd had enabled me to talk to them much more sincerely than I thought I knew how to do; the continuous surge of affirmation was a highly elating experience. For once I did not feel that I was merely beating a sodden audience with words or striving for cold intellectual communication. . . . No less with the speaker than with the audience there is a sense of losing the limitations of self and of unconscious powers rising to meet the unbound, unconscious forces of the groups."[44]

Like the church, the black family played an important role in providing insulated space for self-expression and growth. Yet the pervasiveness and complexity of the Delta's caste system presented black parents with the painful but absolutely necessary task of educating their children to the racial realities of their everyday existence. Many parents simply advised their children to refrain from playing with whites, and when the children asked why, the usual response was "That's just the way it is." One mother admonished her children to "always treat white people nice and never give them any sass." Another went further: "Them's white children and if you hit them, they'll kill you."[45]

Endesha Ida Mae Holland remembered that her mother offered the same warning to her brothers each morning: "Don't y'all look into no white woman face, cause all she got to say is y'all look like y'all want to rape her." The result of the caste-conditioning, according to Holland, was that "my brothers to this day don't know one white woman from the other by her facial features." (Given the widespread insistence by southern whites that "all niggers look alike to me," Holland's observation was an especially ironic commentary on the double-edged impact of caste.)[46]

Such lessons in the complex realities of caste were always painful, as was the necessity of warning children against responding in kind to white harassment or abuse. Failure to take such action could easily lead to tragedy, however, as suggested in the case of an eleven-year-old son of prominent black parents. After fighting with a young white boy, the young black pursued him with a butcher knife. Soon a mob of whites, led by the white boy's father, appeared at the black boy's house. The cursing mob ransacked the house and left, but the father telephoned shortly thereafter, warning the parents that they should surrender their son. The boy finally appeared, having hidden for twenty terror-filled hours in the chimney. Eventually the excitement died down, and the family was able to ignore earlier warnings to leave town.[47]

One of the most embittered informants contacted by Powdermaker related the story of his twenty-first birthday party. On that day he was accosted by two white men who lashed him with a whip. Just as he secured a gun to go after them and seek revenge, his father arrived, took the gun, and sought out the two men, one of whom shot him. As the family made final preparations for the arrival of the guests for the son's birthday party, the father's body arrived instead.[48]

Life under such a system seemed to require nothing so much as an unlimited capacity to maintain self-control in the face of constant humiliation and abuse. One method of coping with this stress was the practice of playing the "the dozens," a test of wits centering on the ability to give and absorb verbal abuse. Ritual insult was widely practiced in west Africa, and the dozens doubtless descended from this practice. Playing the dozens was most common among adolescent males, but it was far from uncommon among adult males, or women, especially adolescents or young adults. Like an affinity for the blues, expertise in the dozens, despite their obscenity and vulgarity, did not preclude a high religious and moral profile within the black community. Brethren and sisters of the church, so humble, attentive, and polite in the company of whites, took on an entirely different demeanor once the dozens began. The insults in the dozens could be personal:

> Your breath smell like a gallon of gas,
> Or a cool breeze off a cheese's ass.[49]

More commonly, however, the derision was directed at the competitor's family, often at the mother; presumably, to insult another person's mother was the ultimate, all but unbearable, offense against the rival and thus the supreme test of one's ability to control his emotions and keep his wits in order to make a response. The insults might begin with physical caricature:

> Talking about Paul's mamma,
> She's so poor, you can see her main gristle.
> Ever time she walks, her ass hole whistles.[50]

As the abuse level escalated, the next step was the inevitable claim to sexual intimacy with the rival's mother. This claim could be made even more insulting by the suggestion that many men enjoyed such intimacy:

> I know your mamma.
> She can wiggle, she can wobble, she can throw it so good.
> She got the best damn pussy in the neighborhood.[51]

In his analysis of the dozens, William Ferris concluded that unlike a number of black folk tales that exhibited hostility toward whites, "aggression in the dozens is directed toward other blacks, and there is no overt expression of protest toward forces—such as the church and whites—outside the group." The danger of violence arising from the dozens resulted largely from the inability of the participants to view them as a competition, a test of wits and self-control. Dollard suggested that the dozens served primarily as an outlet for hostilities that could not be vented against whites. Such an explanation seems logical and in keeping with the theory that the high level of violence among Delta blacks was the simple manifestation of their thwarted anger toward whites.[52]

Lawrence Levine gave this theory of redirected aggression some credence, noting the general popularity of ritual insult humor during the angry years of the Great Depression. Levine conceded as well that the dozens might well reflect the sexual identity crisis confronting black males in a society where matriarchal influences often dominated black family life. Certainly the fact that the mother bore the brunt of direct insult in the dozens supports this point of view. Yet Levine also emphasized the importance of the dozens as training in self-discipline: "Developed at a time when black Americans were especially subject to insults and assaults upon their dignity to which they could not safely respond, the dozens served as a mechanism for teaching and sharpening the ability to control emotions and anger; an ability which was often necessary for survival."[53]

Like the dozens, black folklore and mythology also offered important psychological and emotional support to those on the lowest level of Delta society. Rooted in the African heritage and set against the backdrop of slavery, trickster tales centered on the successful efforts of "weaker" beings, such as the rabbit or the slave, to outwit "stronger" ones, such as the fox or the master. Trickster stories featuring Brer Rabbit outwitting foxes and alligators circulated freely among Delta blacks, as did the exploits of "John," the wily slave who always

bested his master. In one such tale, collected in Bolivar County, John declined
to carry out his owner's instructions to hitch up the mules so that the wagon
could be used to haul firewood. When John continued to refuse to obey, Old
Master warned him, "Don't be so sassy, old nigger, because if I had my pistol
I would blow your brains out." Learning his master was unarmed, John
responded, "Master, you don't have your pistol? I'm going to whip you this
morning." This story suggests not only the slow-wittedness of the white man,
who revealed to John that he was unarmed, but the difficulties masters faced in
forcing compliance from their slaves when the latter knew that the threat of
physical harm could not be carried out.[54]

Although trickster tales continued to circulate, trickster-like behavior
become a less viable response to the circumstances in which Delta blacks found
themselves by the end of the nineteenth century. For example, malingering
only hurt one's family or one's co-workers once blacks were pursuing autonomy and economic independence as free laborers. Likewise, stealing could
bring imprisonment or dismissal, neither of which would benefit any black person in any fashion. In the twentieth century, black ambivalence about reliance
on trickery as opposed to more direct, confrontational strategies began to man-
ifest itself in a number of tales in which the trickster won only a Pyrrhic victory
at best. A tale collected in Bolivar County reflected this trend. In this story, a
"tapin" (terrapin) outwits a deer and bests him in a race only to be trampled by
the deer.[55]

As time passed, the trickster figure gave way to the "badman," who
taunted, tortured, robbed, and killed without remorse. Perhaps the most
famous mythical black badman was "Stagolee," whose exploits circulated
throughout the Delta. Fearless and compassionless, Stagolee was bad to the
bone:

> Back in '32 when the times was hard,
> I carried a sawed-off shotgun and a crooked deck of cards,
> Wore blue-suede shoes and carried a diamond cane,
> Had a six inch peck with a bebop chain. . . .
> I'm that mean son-of-a-bitch they call "Stagolee."[56]

In one episode Stagolee kills a man for stealing his Stetson hat, ignoring
the man's pleas in behalf of his children and his wife. Both the sheriff and the
judge are intimidated by him. Stagolee laughs off his lengthy prison sentence,
and in the version where he is executed, he terrifies the occupants of hell,
including Satan himself: "Stand back, Tom Devil, I'm gonna rule Hell by
myself."[57]

Lawrence Levine has noted that, unlike the legends and ballads surrounding white outlaws, black lore presented these "bad" men as totally bad—without compassion and totally devoid of socially redeeming features or intent.
Whereas white outlaw figures like Robin Hood or Jesse James robbed from

the rich and gave to the poor, black outlaws showed no favoritism, victimizing the weak just as readily as the strong. Their badness spoke for itself, and their heroic status derived from the feeling among occupants of what Levine called "the most oppressed and deprived stratum" of society that "within the circumstances in which they operate, to assert any power at all is a triumph."[58]

Eric Hobsbawn has linked the socially conscious white outlaw to a nostalgic popular desire to return to the "good old days" of a bygone but more just era, but for blacks in North America no such era had ever existed. What they needed was not a restoration but a revolution, a total rebuilding of society from the ground up. Since there was no real hope or prospect of such a development, black outlaws spent their energies in acts of "pure vengeance" and "explosions of fury and futility." The black outlaw had no more sense of himself as a potential force for change than did the bluesman, whose energies seemed to go largely into drinking, gambling, and rambling. For black audiences the outlaw story or song might prove cathartic and vicariously inspirational, but the pleasure, the sense of release, was wholly temporary, and the return to reality was swift and inevitable.[59]

Another perspective on the black badman holds that his heroic status in black folklore reflected "a general perception of the law and the institutions that it supported as persecutorial." In this view the concept of the heroic badman derives from both the trickster and conjurer figures so celebrated in black lore under slavery. In this view as well, the truly heroic black "badmen" actually took action not against helpless victims, but against the "bad niggers" who victimized them and who, along with those who sought to enforce the restrictions imposed by the white man's laws, were the real enemies of innocent blacks. In fact, however, black badmen represented rebellion against not only white law but white values as well. This undercurrent of rebellion among blacks also manifested itself, for example, in ill-concealed contempt for those black ministers who often seemed to endorse a status quo highly beneficial to whites (and to themselves as well) while they encouraged their congregations to focus their hopes for justice and deliverance primarily on the hereafter. The black minister is frequently the object of contempt in both black humor and the blues (where he is often portrayed as a lazy, hypocritical adulterer and fornicator), while the heroic badman—and, as we shall see, the bluesman as well— was actually linked more closely to the forces of Satan or, at any rate, like his slave conjurer ancestors, possessed supernatural powers that clearly did not derive from Jehovah. (Witness the fearless Stagolee's ability to intimidate Satan himself.) Hence the badman's popularity rested on his capacity to symbolize rejection of white values whether codified by law or sanctified by the church.[60]

Mythical heroic badmen had their flesh-and-blood counterparts among Delta blacks. One such example was reported in a study of Natchez, but a similar incident might have occurred anywhere in the Delta. It was standard practice for condemned criminals (who were almost always black) to seek forgiveness for their sins publicly, and often ostentatiously. The condemned was actually requesting forgiveness not only from God but from whites for disturbing the order and the sanctity of caste society. In essence the repentant offender was condoning the punishment he was about to receive for breaking laws made and enforced primarily for the benefit of whites. When "Roy," a black man facing execution, declined to "get religion" and went out into "eternity" as an "unprepared man," both the white and black communities in Natchez took note, the former shaking their heads at the actions of the bad or "bitter" negro and the latter making little secret of their admiration for the man's courage in the face of death (and white authority).[61]

Admiring blacks circulated numerous rumors of Roy's bravado: "A man tol' me that when Reverent Daniels was praying ovah him jus' befo' they hung him, he asked Roy: 'Brother will I see you again [meaning in heaven]?' Roy tol' him: 'I see you now.' . . . They tell me that when they tol' Roy about the Devil he said he wuz goin' to hell an' bus' in de do' and break off de Devil's horns." (Roy's alleged threat to terrorize Hell and its inhabitants suggests that with retelling this incident began to merge with the legend of Stagolee.)[62]

A huge crowd appeared at the funeral home to view the defiant Roy's body, and he profited by comparison with Nathan, who "got religion" before he was hanged: "Dis man [Nathan] wuz chicken-hearted and scary. But dat Roy was de man. He went down like uh man. . . . Dis guy Nathan, he was chicken-hearted lak 'n he wuz sorry awright. Dey tell me he couldn't get enough religion. But dat other guy, he was hard, jus born hard 'n ben lak dat all his life didn't care about nuthin; he never been sorry for nuthin' he done." One of Nathan's leading detractors and Roy's most ardent admirers was Jerry, who observed, "That man [Roy] went up on dem galluhs with jus' what he had in himself. . . . Not what preachin' an a lot of singin' and prayin' an stuff had put in him, but jus with what he had of his own." Despite his admiration for Roy's ability to face death without using religion as a crutch or anesthesia, Jerry was a well-known churchman among local blacks. The anthropologists who studied this incident concluded that local blacks viewed Roy's hanging as "a caste matter rather than a matter of punishment or control of crime. To them, the Negro murderer who confesses and makes his piece with god accepts the white authority and acquiesces in his caste role. On the other hand, the Negro who refuses the consolation of religion achieves the heroic role of one who dares to defy and deny the white authority even in the face of death."[63]

Delta whites were reluctant to admit that blacks such as Roy lived in their midst. Writing in 1938, David Cohn assured his readers that "the present relatively untutored Negro of the Delta harbors no feelings of bitterness or revenge against the whites unless the disabilities under which he labors are too cruelly pressed upon him. If he is able to earn a living and seek happiness among his own people, he is content."[64]

Clearly one of the most enlightened and realistic white observers of Delta life, Cohn just as clearly had little appreciation of the bitterness bottled up inside many Delta blacks. For example, Cohn himself recalled a homicide wherein a black man had apparently killed a white man and his pregnant wife and badly beaten their son just before Christmas in 1934. Cohn described the gory scene: "The man lay face downward stretched across the bed, a bullet hole in the back of his head and his eye torn out where the bullet emerged. The woman's body was dismembered. Her brains, beaten out of her head, splattered a pillowcase. Scattered about the room were portions of her intestines, uterus, and vagina. Her abdomen yawned an empty hole. Great slabs of flesh had been sliced from her legs and thighs. Blood stained the floors, the walls and bedclothing."[65]

Rumors that cannibalism was involved were fueled by the discovery of slabs of the woman's flesh and leathery strips of her skin in the defendant's corn crib. When asked whether he was sorry for what he had done, the condemned man, James Coyner, expressed no more regrets "than if I had spilled a glass of milk. What's done is done, what's bothering me right now is that this jailhouse is cold." The strong sexual connotation of the crime became all the more alarming in view of the fact that the killer was apprehended because police were able to link him to a series of obscene letters to white women. The level of white horror and outrage generated by the killing was such that a certain lynching was avoided only by the presence of a large contingent of machine-gun-equipped national guardsmen. The attention and excitement generated by the incident among Delta blacks indicated that Coyner, like Roy, had achieved celebrity status in their eyes.[66]

Although acts of aggression and defiance toward whites were likely to bring swift and often terrible retribution, it may have seemed to the casual observer that even the most blatant, brutal, and unprovoked acts of violence went unpunished and almost unnoticed in the Delta so long as both the perpetrator and the victim were black. In fact, however, as blacks who found vicarious fulfillment in the remorseless defiance of a Roy or a James Coyner knew all too well, this was not always the case, particularly if, in the eyes of whites, the victim of the crime was a "white man's nigger." So imperative was the maintenance of white supremacy in the Delta that the legal system took note of, and offered a limited amount of protection to, those blacks who enjoyed the approval of whites. Planters might even take care to retain capable legal counsel for such a black. For example, a white employer urged Walter Sillers to do his best to keep the case of one of his hands from coming to trial, explaining that the man was a "hard working negro" and he wanted "to get him out of this trouble."[67]

On the other hand, a Delta prosecutor secured a death sentence for a black defendant by telling the white jury that "this bad nigger killed a good nigger. The good nigger was a white man's nigger, and these bad niggers like to kill that kind." The defendant's attorney explained that "the average white jury would take it for granted that the killing of a white man's nigger is a more serious offense that the killing of a plain, every-day black man."[68]

White influence in these matters was so strong that the status of the white man with whom the black was linked could well affect his fate in the courtroom. "Whose nigger are you?" was often the first question a black defendant was asked. The lesser the status of his white benefactor, the greater the likelihood of a harsh sentence. This system was roughest on a black who shifted about a great deal and might be between employers at the time. The lesson here was "attach yourself to a white man and stay put." As David Cohn explained, the fate of a black who had "no white folks at all" was surely "in the lap of the gods." Confronted with a legal system that served the interests of whites even in cases where both the aggressor and the victim were black, Delta blacks naturally assigned heroic stature to anyone who defied the white man's law.[69]

Delta blacks also fixed their admiration on black figures, both mortal and mythic, who without accepting the validity of white-imposed restrictions nonetheless managed to work within them and triumph over them. In the caste-bound Delta, the popularity of any black who defied white stereotypes was a given. Such a figure was the fabled John Henry, whose legendary battle with the steam drill was well known on both sides of the color line. John Henry's "man against machine" (i.e., incredible odds) struggle carried powerful inspirational symbolism for an entire race engaged in a seemingly hopeless struggle. A Tunica County tale credited John Henry not only with being able to carry a cotton bale under each arm and with single-handedly lifting a steamboat off a snag, but with building the fabled "Yaller Dog" railroad so prominent in Delta song and lore.[70]

Another heroic figure for Delta blacks was the resourceful "Shine," who supposedly escaped from the *Titanic*. Shine—whose name derived from the descriptive saying "so black he shines!"—was the fireman on the ill-fated vessel, which had, ironically, excluded black passengers, including the renowned prize fighter Jack Johnson. When the ship began to sink, Shine resisted the pleas of the captain to remain on board and of white passengers, both male and female, to save them in return for huge sums of money or sexual favors. (In one version Shine told the captain's daughter, "One thing about you white folks I couldn't understand: You all wouldn't offer me that pussy when we was all on land.") Shine is a more irreverent figure than John Henry. He is already getting drunk when the ship goes down: "When all them white folks went to heaven, Shine was in Sugar Ray's Bar drinking Seagram's Seven." Levine summarized the significance of both Shine and John Henry and distinguished them from the outlaw-hero figure by pointing out that their exploits were performed "in the name of the entire race." Unlike the trickster figure or the badman, who won temporary, individual victories, in Levine's view heroes like John Henry and Shine "defeated white society on *its* own rules" and in so doing "broke the molds that Negroes were supposed to conform to and created new rules and new possibilities."[71]

Such was also the case with flesh-and-blood heroes like Jack Johnson and Joe Louis. Clifton Taulbert remembered that for Glen Allan blacks "it was a sin to miss a Joe Louis fight." Watching a crowd gathered around a battery-powered radio in his aunt's window, young Taulbert realized that "Joe Louis with his fists, quickness, and punching power could say for them what they could never say for themselves."[72]

The dozens and a body of folk legend that celebrated the exploits of a variety of black heroes were but a part of a separate cultural sphere occupied by Delta blacks who alternated between public professions of Christian faith and private indulgences in the black arts or "voodoo." David Cohn related a number of incidents of voodooism among Delta blacks. Stakes driven into a crossroads at sunrise promised to keep enemies away. Women slashed men's coats to ensure their sexual fidelity. Roots chewed and spat upon the courthouse steps guaranteed acquittal at a criminal trial. Charms hidden in the limbs of trees restored sexual potency. The urine of a virgin was believed to cure an eye infection, although it often did the opposite. White observers were invariably amused or appalled when they learned of such practices in their midst, but for Delta blacks the practice of voodoo, as derived from their African past and reaffirmed during their experience in slavery, offered a sense of protection and control of their own destiny that was otherwise lacking in their daily lives.[73]

For all his racism and disdain for northern liberal critics of southern race relations, William Alexander Percy made the remarkable admission that, despite the proximity of the races in the South, "the sober fact is we understand one another not at all. Just about the time our proximity appears most harmonious something happens—a crime of violence, perhaps a case of voodooism—and to our astonishment we sense a barrier between. To make it more bewildering the barrier is of glass; you can't see it, you only strike it."[74]

David Cohn offered a similar assessment: "The Delta negro lives in the modern world. He goes to the moving-picture theatres, rides in automobiles, hears the radio, sees airplanes, and is conversant with the wonders of the white man's medicines. But he moves too, in a world of his own from which the white is jealously excluded; of which he knows nothing and cannot ever know. His questing mind is impotent to break through its shut windows and barred doors. His penetrating eye is powerless to perceive what is hidden from his untutored vision."[75]

Although the color line was the most fundamental barrier to interaction and understanding between the two major components of the Delta's population, it did not suffice on all occasions to identify the "place" of every resident or group within the surprisingly diverse population of the Delta. In addition to a number of descendants of Italian and other European immigrant groups imported as farm labor early in the twentieth century, the Delta was home to what was probably the most sizable cluster of Chinese-Americans anywhere in the nonmetropolitan South. The Chinese had been imported to the Delta in small numbers during the Reconstruction Era in the apparent hope that they might one day relieve Delta planters of their dependence on black labor. The Chinese quickly grew disenchanted with farming, however, and were soon operating small-scale mercantile enterprises catering to blacks.[76]

The clientele of these Chinese groceries was so impoverished and the volume of business per customer so low that whites seldom viewed Chinese merchants as competitors. Whites did object, however, to the initial disregard shown by the Chinese for the Delta's racial taboos. Not only did the Chinese appear to treat blacks with inappropriate courtesy, but Chinese males, faced with a severe scarcity of Chinese female companionship (because of severe restrictions on Chinese immigration that prevailed until World War II), consorted openly with black females and in a few cases even married them. Delta whites could hardly tolerate behavior so threatening to the unity and purity of white society and chose therefore to lump the Chinese with blacks and treat them accordingly. Hence, prior to World War II, Delta Chinese faced laws prohibiting intermarriage with whites and were subject to much the same kind of discrimination and intimidation as that encountered by blacks.[77]

Of crucial importance to Chinese leaders was the consignment of their children to separate schools, which, though publicly funded, were decidedly inferior to those available to whites. Determined to alter this situation, Chinese leaders consulted sympathetic whites, who urged them to adopt "white" behavior patterns in their dealings with blacks and, particularly, to curtail their unconcealed interracial sexual liaisons. In sum, as James Loewen explained it, Delta whites had no real economic interest in keeping the Chinese on the other side of the color barrier, but they were reluctant to allow them to cross over so long as the Chinese might behave in a manner injurious to the "racial integrity" of Delta society. Delta whites complained that it was often difficult to identify a Chinese child who was part black. As a result, whites were reluctant to accept Chinese children into their schools for fear that they might unknowingly allow "Chinese-Negro half-breeds" to associate with their children. In response to this concern, Delta Chinese leaders undertook a vigorous campaign of education and coercion to curb sexual interaction with blacks, and their efforts were facilitated by the lowering of barriers to Chinese immigration during World War II. The Chinese also began to take greater pains to demonstrate to whites their own feelings of prejudice toward blacks by making derogatory remarks about them and relating unflattering examples of black behavior to whites. At the same time, the Chinese retained a distinct air of deference in their dealings with whites, encouraging whites, for example, to call them by their first names, but taking pains to always address whites as "Mr." or "Mrs."[78]

Such behavior gradually convinced Delta whites that allowing the Chinese to cross the color barrier would no longer jeopardize white unity and the stability of Delta society. Beginning in the late 1930s (and continuing through the 1940s and early 1950s), the exclusion of Chinese pupils came to an end in Delta school systems, and local churches and restaurants, as well as civic groups, also opened their doors to the Chinese. The Delta Chinese hardly achieved entrée into the most exclusive inner circles of white society, but their willingness to live within the caste guidelines imposed by whites ultimately helped to win them at least the opportunity to cross the color line and enjoy access to a white world that continued to exclude blacks.[79]

As the case of the Delta Chinese suggested, the separate worlds on either side of the color barrier were far from monolithic. Class distinctions not only existed but played a major role in structuring both black and white society. On the white side of the line, upper-class status was far more a matter of birth than of economics or morality. Despite their prodigious efforts to assert their elite status through conspicuous consumption and what one commentator described as "behavior patterns characteristic of the newly rich," most Delta plantation owners had acquired their land and wealth too recently to qualify as aristocrats. The real white upper class in the Delta spread outward and downward from a tiny core of families whose entry into the Delta dated back to the antebellum era. In their shadow sat a much sterner, morally upright, deferential, and duly envious middle class. Finally there were the region's poor whites, a class disdained by both their white superiors and the entire spectrum of blacks, whose enmity they returned fully and often violently.[80]

The Delta's aristocracy presided over white society in the comfortable, laid-back fashion characteristic of those who feel they have nothing to prove. Hortense Powdermaker quickly sensed the power of the patrician William Alexander Percy's endorsement in Indianola, a town where she found no genuine members of the white upper class. After she reported on an initial meeting with an edgy and suspicious group of Indianola's leading white citizens, Percy responded with scornful laughter and told her, "Now you have just seen the flower of our Southland." Powdermaker was struck by the openness of Percy's contempt for the status-conscious middle-class whites in that community and by the way in which they deferred to Percy despite his obvious disdain for them. She also noted that Percy's chauffeur-driven but shabby automobile contrasted with the newer and shinier cars owned by Indianola's bourgeoisie. "As an aristocrat, he could 'afford' to drive such a car," she wrote.[81]

Openly covetous of upper-class status, the Delta's middle-class whites often seemed obsessed with establishing some claim to aristocracy through minute examination of their genealogies. In Indianola, Craig Claiborne's mother was forced to take in boarders, including, ironically, Dr. John Dollard, but despite their economic distress both of his parents insisted that they were genuine bluebloods. Claiborne's ne'er-do-well father secured a huge, diagrammed "family tree," which covered the better part of one wall in the Claiborne home. Likewise, Claiborne's mother taught him "that we were of noble blood and to the manor born" and urged him to "never forget that you are a Craig." Claiborne went on to international fame as a writer and food critic, but as a youth he found that his mother's grandiose genealogical assurances did little to dull the pain of having to shop on credit at a grocery where the family owed "hundreds and hundreds of dollars" or having to walk while other children rode around in automobiles.[82]

Recalling her interviews with Indianola whites, Powdermaker noted that "almost everyone boasted about having an ancestor who had been a Colonel in the Confederate Army, and tried to give an impression of being descended from men who had big plantations with a large number of slaves." Powdermaker realized that many, even most, of these claims were exaggerated but noted that even "lies" or "fantasies" can tell much about cultural values in a society. In this case she saw these aristocratic delusions as a manifestation of the absence of a middle-class tradition in the Delta. This absence seemed to force on middle-class whites the obligation of shouldering an aristocratic heritage that was really not their own. Powdermaker saw this "burden" manifested in several ways. An immigrant from Ohio who established an efficient and diversified planting operation but continued to wear overalls and reject any semblance of social elitism found himself and his wife all but ostracized by the local white community. Aristocratic pretensions fostered a deep-seated aversion to manual labor that led even white families on relief to retain their black servants whenever possible.[83]

The deference and envy with which the white middle class regarded the Delta aristocracy was in sharp contrast to the contempt that they heaped on the region's small group of lowly poor whites. Widely traveled and a friend and confidant of William Alexander Percy, David Cohn nonetheless had roots in the Delta's middle class. Cohn's greatest fear for his region was that the Delta's planter aristocracy faced a political revolution spurred by an influx of lower-income whites that had actually begun in the World War I era.

Such a revolt was certain to bring down the "last vestige of influence in public affairs" of the small cadre of whites who still clung "to the traditions of *noblesse oblige*." This laudable minority was composed of figures like Percy and other sworn foes of the Klan, the lynch mob, and the race-baiting politician. The toppling of such men could lead only to greater injustices to blacks and hence greater black out-migration. The result, according to Cohn, would be that "the whole character of this civilization will be completely altered; its racial and social habits changed, its pride trailed in the dust; its memories erased; and its flickering dreams of a better way of life extinguished."[84]

Cohn's paranoia about a lower-class white uprising illustrated the tendency of the Delta's middle class to dote on its aristocracy. The patrician Percy was actually more philosophical—though no less melodramatic—than Cohn about the political challenge from below. Resigned to seeing "the bottom rail on top," Percy rationalized that it might be "a strengthening experience to see evil triumphant, valor and goodness in the dust."[85]

Cohn's and Percy's apocalyptic vision of the destruction of the Delta's way of life pointed to a fundamental tension inherent in the complex web of economic, social, and political interaction that defined the Delta as a society. The relative wealth and social status of Delta planters was obvious enough, and their assertion of their own peculiar, class-based interests blatant enough, that the binding thread of white unity, the notion of *Herrenvolk* democracy, with its dogged though implausible insistence on the equality of all whites regardless of income or status, was stretched to the breaking point. Indeed, many Delta aristocrats readily professed a greater degree of respect and compassion for blacks than for whites on the lower rungs of the socioeconomic ladder. This attitude not only exacerbated tensions between whites in the Delta and those in the hills, but it also manifested itself within the white society of the Delta itself. Kathleen Knight remembered that as poor white sharecroppers her family sensed that the landlord "was just in a higher class than we were and so we just didn't feel as compatible with them as our common sharecropping neighbors."[86]

In their Delta enclave, planters were accustomed to absolute political and social deference from an economically dependent middle class as well, of course, as a disfranchised and socially repressed black laboring class. As for its near-outcast, lower-class whites, like the Delta's economic system, its closely related political and social structure held no place for a lower-income white population that possessed full legal and civil rights and was prepared to exercise them in an independent, class-interested manner. So long as blacks could not vote and there were no challenges from other whites, Delta planters could capitalize on their preeminent position within the area's white minority to wield their disproportionate influence in state politics and defend their regional and class interests. On the other hand, significant class-based squabbling among Delta whites would most certainly undermine the influence of the region's planters in state politics as well as the stability that was the key to planter dominance within the Delta.

Because poor whites lived for the most part in the rural areas of the county, white neighborhoods in Indianola provided little indication that class distinctions existed at all. In contrast to the superficial impressions of homogeneity conveyed by the white area, however, the black section of Indianola was a study in diversity. Dwellings ranged from modest cottages to tiny hovels, and a microscopic upper class lived in the midst of a large middle and lower class. As Powdermaker saw it, "In close proximity were the pious and the disreputable, known for their drinking, gambling and fighting; respectable women with Victorian standards and prostitutes; college graduates and peasants who believed in voodoo; the dusty blacks, the medium browns, the light creams; all thrown together because they were all Negroes. The contrasts gave a sense of drama, lacking in the one-class white section of town."[87]

According to Powdermaker, class was determined among blacks less by birth than by educational and economic status and one's reputation for sexual restraint. For the most part, a high school diploma was the absolute minimum for membership in the tiny black upper class, although a relatively prosperous landowner or businessman might achieve his position by virtue of his economic accomplishments. Teachers, school officials, doctors, and dentists were also accorded automatic membership in the black upper class. Powdermaker found that marital stability and legitimacy was also a vital manifestation of upper-class status. A reputation for chastity was essential to upper-class status for females and a properly legal—as opposed to common-law—marriage was equally important. Powdermaker cited the case of a woman who had lived in a common-law relationship for some time before marrying. In order to conceal this fact, she displayed her marriage license with the dates covered by stick-on, heart-shaped valentines. From the tiny upper class, status among Delta blacks moved downward through the upper- and lower-middle class to the lower class, its descent marked by decreases in economic and educational levels as well as by reputational morality and family stability.[88]

Although it did not function as an actual determinant of class, a lighter skin could also play a key role in upward social mobility among Delta blacks. As a rule, lighter-skinned blacks were more common at the highest level of black society and were considered highly desirable marriage partners, while extremely dark-skinned blacks were often shunned unless their economic standing made them desirable.[89]

Clifton Taulbert's aunt and a similarly light-skinned friend engaged in a fierce running debate about how much white blood would be needed to make each of them whites. Despite the higher status attached to a lighter complexion, David Cohn suggested that the Brazilian adage "money whitens" had some applicability to the class/caste system in the Delta when he offered the story of Wash Jackson, who as a young man had married a lighter-skinned woman. The couple had three children, also light-skinned. When the children were small, the woman left her husband, confiding to neighbors that she had no intention of disgracing herself by living with the "graveyard black" Wash any longer. The abandoned Wash soon took a job with a wealthy plantation owner, who, at his death, left his loyal employee a thousand dollars, a house, and twenty acres of land. Not long thereafter a letter arrived from Wash's wife, who wrote of her love and of their children crying every night to see their father. Apparently unmoved, Wash replied, "I ain't fade none."[90]

Although a lighter skin was a definite social advantage, ambitious Delta blacks saw education as the real key to their hopes of upward mobility for their children. Delta blacks invested a great deal of faith and not a little of their pitifully scarce monetary resources in the schooling of their children. The gross imbalance in facilities, teacher salaries, length of school terms, and operating budgets and the general white indifference, ambivalence, or outright hostility toward black education made it difficult to maintain even marginally adequate schools. Yet the same blacks whom whites dismissed as lazy and ignorant worked tirelessly and contributed generously to the upkeep and improvement of their schools. Many a school building was constructed, "finished off," and furnished solely through the donations of time and labor by blacks. Because the school terms were longer and the teachers and facilities superior, many black parents either moved into towns in the Delta or sent their children into the towns as boarders, often at considerable economic sacrifice, in order to further their children's chances at a better education and the better future it promised.[91]

Rural schools were often located in abandoned churches with shuttered windows that blocked out the light on cold days, when they had to be closed. Such schools often lacked tables, let alone desks, and had no blackboards. Large numbers of students spread across eight grades working on separate assignments and exercises at the same time were the rule rather than the exception. Such schools were often seriously affected by the weather. A wet fall delayed cotton picking and thus the beginning of the school year; it also made it difficult to gather sufficient wood suitable for heating the school when cold weather arrived. Extremely cold weather made it all but impossible to conduct normal classroom work, for all the children could do was huddle around the stove, which was often vented through a broken window pane.[92]

Clifton Taulbert's mother taught eight grades in a one-room plantation school. What she lacked in formal training, she made up for in energy and dedication, organizing a program whereby mothers could provide a hot lunch for the children each day and planning and staging an annual Christmas pageant wherein "the children of tired fieldhands became angels, shepherds, and kings." Taulbert recalled "the families crowded into the one-room building, their greased faces shining as they watched their children perform. I remember parents crying as the children recited their lines by memory."[93]

Despite the adversity they faced, a number of black parents continued to make whatever sacrifices necessary to see their children educated. Taulbert passed directly by the white school in Glen Allan each day as he began his daily hundred-mile roundtrip to the black high school in Greenville. Powdermaker detailed the case of a black woman who lived with her husband and eight children in a rickety two-room shack. Hanging in that shack was the picture of her oldest son in his graduation cap and gown. He had recently received a master's degree from a black university. His mother had pushed herself unmercifully, working in the fields and taking in washing to put him through school, and was now doing the same for his younger brothers and sisters, despite a "nervous breakdown" (possibly a severe case of exhaustion) that she had recently suffered. Among the blacks she studied, Powdermaker observed, "it is considered normal and natural for parents, especially mothers, to labor incessantly in order to win for their children the opportunities they themselves have lacked. Such efforts are so taken for granted that they rouse neither comment or criticism; nor are the children criticized for accepting the parents' sacrifices. Some mothers map out a program for their children's education years in advance and hold to it despite calamities and setbacks."[94]

Blacks received precious little help from whites in their efforts to educate their children. Whites in Delta counties benefited enormously from a statewide funding formula that allotted monies according to the total number of school age children regardless of color. White officials simply diverted a great percentage of the money that should have gone for black schools to the education of white pupils. In Bolivar and Tunica counties, for example, only 34 and 36 percent of the money appropriated for black schools was actually spent on them. In Washington County the ratio between per pupil expenditures for whites and those for blacks stood at seven to one in 1929–1930. (This discrepancy had actually grown worse as the twentieth century unfolded. The ratio had stood at five to one in 1908–1909.)[95]

In practical terms, the diversion of black school funds enhanced the quality of white education in the Delta relative not only to black education but to the education of whites in counties where the black population percentage was lower. By denying blacks their full share of school funds, white school systems in the Delta were in a position to offer pupils a longer school term and pay better salaries to their teachers. The fundamental explanation for such severe underinvestment in black education lay in the fact that Gavin Wright's observation concerning white southern entrepreneurs in the years before World War I remained truer still for Delta planters in the 1930s: "As low-wage employers in a high-wage country, they could not take steps to open communication and interaction with the outside world, without risking loss of labor."[96]

Dollard pointed out that white planters supported black churches far more readily than black schools, primarily because they believed that churches reinforced the status quo, while education contributed to black dissatisfaction. As one planter explained, "What I want here is Negroes who can make cotton, and they don't need education to help them make cotton." Moreover, education greatly increased the probability that young blacks would aspire to more than working in the cotton fields and therefore seek better opportunities elsewhere.[97]

Addressing this phenomenon, David Cohn noted that, where education for blacks was concerned, whites believed that "the Negro should be taught to work with his hands" rather than "to conjugate Latin verbs." This attitude rested on the conviction that a classical education did the young black in the Delta a disservice, causing him to "lose a sense of the realities about him or, in plain Delta language, to get out of his place." As a result, Cohn actually regretted the similarity between the curricula, if not the facilities, of the black and white schools and deplored the fact that, just as in the white schools, the blackboards of the black schools were "filled with diagrams of the Peloponnesian wars."[98]

Such a curriculum was not consistent with the restrictions that awaited the black high school graduate, who, in Cohn's words, often found "that he has been given a vision of a land whose gates are closed against him; of water with which he cannot quench his thirst; of food with which he cannot satisfy his hunger. The end is pain and confusion and bitterness." Cohn concluded that all programs for the betterment of blacks should be planned "with an eye to the cold realities of the situation. There is room and welcome in this Delta only for the Negro who 'stays in his place'."[99]

Cohn's observations coincided with the findings of Powdermaker, who encountered a number of relatively enlightened whites who realized that education for blacks was necessary, but nonetheless a threat to the stability of Delta society. One respondent summed up her feelings with the conclusion that "if you educate the niggers you ruin the South; if you don't educate them you ruin it too." Although she stood apart from those who opposed education for blacks, one woman cast the need for education in terms of improving the quality (but not the status) of black labor: "We must keep the darkies as workers because we can't do without them. But education is good for them. I don't think it's right to deny anyone education. I would certainly rather have a cook who could read and write than one who is completely illiterate." On the other hand, education as a means of elevating blacks above the status of laborers was anathema to the whites interviewed by Powdermaker. All too typical were the views of a white schoolteacher, described as "moderately liberal in her attitudes toward Negroes," who offered the fatalistic observation that, no matter how much education he received, "a million years from now, a nigger will still be a nigger in the South."[100]

The long-term experience of Delta blacks gave them little reason to dispute such a pronouncement. Without surrendering their dream of racial equality, black parents who had made so many sacrifices in behalf of their children also saw education as a means of social advancement within black society. The younger blacks who were the beneficiaries of this education apparently harbored greater expectations, however. One such young man described by Powdermaker was well educated, "temperate," and "strictly monogamous." In short, he had done "all the right things" that, had he been white, should have gained him the acceptance and respect of the white community. Yet he received no such acceptance or respect and could not even express his preferences at the polling place. Powdermaker offered this description of the young man's mood:

> He says, as many of his contemporaries say and feel, that sometimes he wonders how he can bear it any longer. He sees the futility of fighting, since he thinks there is no chance of winning now. He lives quietly, coming into relatively little contact with whites; does his job as well as possible; gets all the pleasure he can from his intra-Negro social life, his family, an occasional fishing trip, a movie now and then. At times his underlying bitterness finds vent in words. For the most part, it accumulates unexpressed.[101]

Such was not always the case. One of Powdermaker's informants, a college-educated mulatto, confided that "sometimes he'd like to be a Dillinger" and leave "a bloody trail of dead whites in his wake." Admitting that his philosophy was "if he makes the day, all right, and if he doesn't make it, all right too," and asserting that if he had a son he would teach him to shoot and give him guns, he confessed that he often felt as if "it would be better to die killing a white man than just to go on living." This young man's attitude reflected the frustrations of the educated, younger generation of blacks, who, having been exposed to experiences and ideas undreamed of by their parents, found that their heightened awareness and sensitivity had brought them neither fulfillment nor happiness. More often than not, instead of opening doors for young blacks, education had only increased their awareness of the doors that remained closed to them. If schooling assured them a higher social status and a somewhat more secure economic position in the white-dominated caste society of the Delta, it also made them them doubly sensitive to the injustices, insults, and abuse that their parents had been forced to accept as a simple matter of survival.[102]

One of the most irritating habits of the paternalistic upper-class whites in their dealings with blacks was to invoke the "beautiful tradition of the black mammy." Younger, educated blacks and members of the black upper class found this stereotype particularly demeaning. On one occasion black students even hissed a white speaker who invoked this figure, and on another blacks rejected the support of a would-be benefactor who prefaced his offer with a tribute to his father's "old black mammy." Powdermaker observed of the Delta's younger blacks: "They do not have to bear the lashes of an overseer, or live in a slave shanty, or step off the sidewalk if they see a white person coming. But in countless ways their self-respect and pride daily receive blows. Expecting more, demanding more, than their parents ever dreamed of, they are hurt in ways their grandparents could not have imagined."[103]

Higher levels of educational awareness among black youths had contributed to a difference in the attitudes of the older and younger generations toward upper-class whites. The parental generation had traditionally praised the "good white folks" who had helped them out in times of crisis and perhaps even enabled them to provide better educational opportunities for their children. Delta blacks of all generations realized that the paternalism of the better-element whites came with a great many strings attached. Younger, more educated blacks found it more difficult, however, to accept the sense of dependence and the often humiliating obligations of deference and obedience that the paternalistic relationship implied.

Blacks appeared to become less dependent on white assistance as the 1930s unfolded, not only because examples of the old individualized paternalism became noticeably less frequent but also because with the onset of the New Deal, federal agencies had begun to assume the provider's role once played by those whom Powdermaker called the "good white folks." Looking at poor families of both races in the New Deal South, Lorena Hickok Walsh agreed: "A lot of these people who used to look up that way to their paternalistic landlords and employers have now switched to the President and Mrs. Roosevelt." Another observer explained that the black sharecropper was "increasingly coming to recognize the federal government as an instrument for attaining a higher degree of security. 'De government' is displacing the paternalistic planter as 'his friend.'" Perhaps the best evidence for this shift in expectations—or transfer of dependence—came in the song of a young black girl overheard by Powdermaker: "Say, my Lord knows just how we've been fed. If it weren't for the President, we'd all be dead."[104]

As the 1930s began, the Yazoo-Mississippi Delta offered as comprehensive, predictable, and efficient a working model of the "southern way of life" as might be found. In order to survive, blacks had little choice but to adhere to ordained, stereotypical behavior patterns, which were then invoked in support of the dogma of caste that imposed them. Holding all the cards, whites enjoyed every advantage: tractable black labor that knew better than to challenge a command or quibble about a settlement; vulnerable black females who had little choice but to yield to the advances of white males; and, finally, the exhilaration of encountering absolute deference at every turn while returning not even the slightest acknowledgment or hint of respect. Such were the features of a caste-based social and economic system that filled the purses and boosted the egos of the Delta's white elite even as it ensured the continued subservience of its black masses and generally affirmed Rupert Vance's 1935 conclusion that "nowhere are antebellum conditions so nearly preserved than in the Yazoo Delta."[105]

Vance's judgment notwithstanding, as the 1930s drew to a close, observers detected some subtle but potentially significant threats to the status quo in the Delta. With blacks looking increasingly to Washington for assistance and support and with younger blacks growing noticeably restive and more openly critical of local whites, the remarkable stability of the Delta's caste-based society seemed destined to face some fundamental challenges, especially as New Deal farm programs (soon to be reinforced by a global military conflict) wrought major changes in the economy and demography of the Deepest South.

8 ▽ "We Are at the
▽ Crossroads"
▽
▽

As the 1930s began, the stability of Delta society depended on an intricate network of customs and control mechanisms that guaranteed the fundamental socioeconomic supremacy of all whites over all blacks, while assuring as well that the Delta's white planter elite would remain at the very top of the region's socioeconomic and political pyramid. The Great Depression plunged the Delta's economy into crisis, and the Roosevelt New Deal recovery program introduced the first ongoing federal presence in the region since the end of Reconstruction. The New Deal set in motion forces that would dramatically alter the Delta's agricultural system, and the influences unloosed by World War II reinforced these trends. Local whites managed to shape the Roosevelt administration's relief and recovery initiatives to their own needs and interests, however, and their subsequent manipulation of wartime agencies and programs helped to ensure that the planter elite remained in control. Still, although an economically transformed Delta emerged from the protracted trauma of depression and war with its controversial socioeconomic and racial hierarchy largely intact, a changing social and political climate in the nation at large promised to make the relationship between Washington and the region's white leadership an increasingly tense and contradictory one.

Well before the Great Depression, Delta planters had already begun to realize that, in the proper context, the federal government could function as an ally rather than an adversary. The extended period of civil war, military occupation, and conflict and the memories and myths of Reconstruction left Delta planters sensitive to the point of paranoia about the prospect of external interference in their affairs. Yet by the end of the 1920s, the federal government, through its support for flood-control efforts, had already played a major role in the Delta's transformation from a swampy wilderness to a modern cotton kingdom. The 1927 flood left death, destruction, and human dislocation in its wake and set off a near panic among Delta planters, who feared the loss of their labor, but the disaster brought a massive federal relief effort as well. Delta planters had rejected such assistance in 1890 for fear that it would lessen their control over local blacks. The experience of 1927 proved to be an eye-opening one, however; not only did Congress appropriate $325 million for a flood-control system for the region, but planters learned as well that, when properly directed, federal assistance programs could reinforce, rather than undermine, the existing economic order.[1]

As the flood waters began to recede, Delta political leader Walter Sillers, Jr., proposed that in addition to revamping the Delta's flood-control network, the federal government should take responsibility for revitalizing its economy. Sillers pointed out that "it would be folly for this government to expend millions upon millions to rebuild the levees and provide spillways and other adequate means to assure safety from future floods if at the same time the government is going to permit the abandonment of the territory it seeks to protect." Without the assurance of federal aid, Sillers feared, planters would be forced to "let their labor go, abandon their homes, and turn the country back to be grown up in a wilderness" because "Delta lands without labor are as useless as an automobile without an engine."[2]

Always concerned about the loss of labor, Delta planters discovered during the flood that federal aid could actually be used to restore the labor control that the high water had threatened to disrupt. Red Cross assistance and supplies, distributed in large part by local whites, sustained black laborers until the floodwaters receded, and the federal government not only allowed Mississippi officials to use national guardsmen to incarcerate the Delta's displaced black force but even took steps to discredit criticism of this practice. Walter White of the NAACP was appalled to find so much of the 1927 relief effort "in the hands of these Crackers." White warned that the planters would take the Red Cross supplies, which they received at no cost, and charge the homeless blacks for them with an eye toward using this indebtedness to hold onto their labor. With the Red Cross providing food and medical support, Myron McNeil contended, these planters had reason to "feel that they are being supported by the government in holding these people in a state of peonage."[3]

The Delta had no sooner emerged from the flood than it plunged into the Great Depression. As the Depression worsened, increasingly critical national attention focused on the system of tenancy that so dominated the Delta's agricultural economy. William Alexander Percy and other defenders of the sharecropping system cited its beneficial impact during hard times when, regardless of income or crop prospects, the tenant and his family could be assured that the planter would keep them clothed, housed, and fed. For most planters, however, the Depression only made it all the more imperative that they continue their policy of holding all costs, particularly those for tenant furnishings, to a minimum. In 1930 the Delta-based *Staple Cotton Review* touted a plan by which both stock and tenants could be maintained at the same fifteen cents per day cost "per head." The editor announced that, if any planter was interested in a copy of the plan, "we shall be glad to send it to him on request." A study of a representative sample of Delta plantations indicated a net profit of $615 per plantation even in the rock-bottom year of 1932, but the old system of paternalism seemed to count for little as general conditions worsened. Diarist Harry Ball noted in February 1932 that "the negroes are starving. They throng about us daily, begging for work and food."[4]

Individual acts of benevolence were by no means uncommon in the Depression-era Delta, but, as the New Deal's influence grew increasingly pervasive, the region soon presented a prime example of the process whereby planters accepted progressively less responsibility for their tenants and, in Pete Daniel's words, "the federal government took the place of the landlord." As this process unfolded, however, the design and implementation of government policies actually made not the Delta's impoverished sharecroppers but its relatively affluent planters the prime beneficiaries of the new federal paternalism.[5]

Although the acreage-reduction programs initiated by the Agricultural Adjustment Act of 1933 made a crucial contribution to revolutionizing the region's agricultural system, AAA's policies were administered for, and to a great extent by, planters or those sympathetic to their interests. The speedily implemented AAA "plow-up" acreage-reduction program of 1933 gave little attention to the problem of farm tenancy and the landlord-tenant relationship. AAA's contract made no direct reference to tenants, requiring producers to obtain the consent of "lien holders" and "persons who appeared to have an interest in the crop" before signing the contract. Payments for the plow-up went directly to planters, and AAA guidelines instructed landlords to divide them according to the percentage of the tenant's interest in the crop. Sharecroppers were to receive one-half the payment, a share tenant two-thirds or three-fourths, and a cash tenant the full amount.[6]

The most influential officials of the AAA cotton section argued that paying the planter and presuming that he would live up to his "moral obligation" to his tenants was the most pragmatic course of action. Tenants had little or no legal status, and payments directly to them would undermine their landlord's influence over them, thereby fostering potential social upheaval and engendering considerable opposition to the program from planters with close ties to the politically potent southern bloc in Congress. From the landlord's point of view (which essentially became that of the AAA's cotton section as well), the tenants were incapable of handling their money and were likely to "throw away" what they received, rather than apply it to their debts or spend it on essentials. Since the tenant normally looked to the landlord for "guidance" as well as credit, the simplest way to implement the new program was to route all payments through the landlord. Although commendable in its simplicity (if not its naiveté), this policy ensured that the tenant's new dependence on the federal government did not free him from his old dependence on the planter.[7]

Fewer than half of Bolivar County's farmers received any cash at all from the 1933 AAA cotton plow-up, and many whose names actually appeared on the AAA checks were unable to cash them because county agents delivered them directly to merchants or landlords, who simply applied them to the tenant's debts. One tenant was due $136 for plowing up five acres of cotton, but all he got was an itemized statement from the planter that this amount had been deducted from his account. Another reported that he had received $11 in cash and the remainder as a credit balance. Still another had received no indication that he had been given any credit, despite the fact that he received no check. A Mound Bayou cropper told of plowing up ten acres of cotton and being assured that he would receive $170 "credit." Yet at the end of the year, he was told he owed his landlord $42. More than one landlord appeared to be using the plow-up program as an excuse to force less productive tenants off his place. In one such case, a cropper claimed that his landlord had told him that "since I was a cripple I could make more if I plowed up the cotton," but according to the tenant, the landlord "didn't give me a cent of the money he got from the government." Perhaps hoping to induce the tenant to move on, the planter also suddenly refused to allow him to have a "truck patch" to grow vegetables for sale.[8]

When D. S. Wheatley of Greenwood wrote Secretary of Agriculture Henry A. Wallace in November 1933, he warned that "one of your most serious problems in the acreage reduction plan is the surplus tenant farmer who will be left without a farm to farm." Wheatley reminded Wallace that "the tenant farmers, white and black, have been worse used than any other class in our country" and called for a tenant protection clause in future AAA contracts.[9]

More attention to the question of payments to tenants actually did go into the planning of the 1934 AAA cotton program, but the "planters first" policy was difficult to overturn, particularly with much of the planning in the hands of Oscar Johnston, president of the massive Delta and Pine Land Company, whose thirty-eight-thousand-acre plantation spread over two counties in the Delta. Johnston was first appointed as finance director of AAA, and for more than a decade he filled a variety of other positions, all the while serving as the Roosevelt administration's chief expert on cotton policy. Johnston was clearly knowledgeable about large-scale cotton farming, but, as the chief administrative officer of the world's largest cotton plantation, he was by no means inattentive to the interests of the large planter.[10]

Under the 1934 AAA plan, each landlord received an acreage allotment based on 40 percent of his cotton production in the period 1928-1932. In return for removing this allotted acreage from cultivation, he collected a rental payment based on average yields of lint cotton on his land. The payment amounted to 3.5 cents per pound up to a maximum of eighteen dollars per acre. The landlord also received a "parity" payment of at least one cent per pound of the farm's assigned cotton allotment.[11]

Rental payments came in two equal installments, the first in March or April, just before planting, and the second in August or September, immediately before harvest. The timing of these payments promised to reduce the credit constraints under which cotton farmers operated. Yet this timing presented a problem for AAA administrators and an even greater one for farm workers, because a landowner could receive half the rental payments for which he was eligible before it became clear that he would either reduce his acreage or retain his tenants. Moreover, because he received the second half of the rental payment before the harvest, the most he stood to lose by violating the contract at that point was the parity payment, which represented only about 22 percent of the total income he was to receive from the government.[12]

AAA's policy was that "the benefits went with the land," and therefore sharecroppers received none of the rental payments (as opposed to cash tenants who collected all the rental, and share tenants, who were paid half). Parity payments were to be apportioned by the planter according to the tenant's share in the crop. As result, if he was not evicted or simply cheated, all a sharecropper could hope for from AAA (via his landlord) was half the parity payment—a half-cent per pound of cotton normally produced on 40 percent of his acreage. For a twenty-acre plot yielding two hundred pounds per acre in 1934, this would have amounted to only eight dollars. Again, this was the maximum a cropper could expect, while the planter received the other half of the parity payment plus a rental payment of 3.5 cents per pound of the cotton AAA estimated that he might have grown on the land taken out of production. In the long run, if the planter followed all AAA guidelines, the cropper received half of 60 percent of the crop he might otherwise have grown had there been no AAA program and one-eighth of the total benefits offered in exchange for not planting the remaining 40 percent.[13]

Any tenant bold enough to file an official charge that he had been cheated by his landlord was a prime target for eviction, because such complaints ultimately made their way back to planter-dominated AAA county committees. The vague wording of certain provisions of the act spelled even more trouble for a tenant, who had little hope in any event of a sympathetic hearing from his county committee. Ostensibly written to protect the tenant, Paragraph Seven read in part:

> The producer shall . . . endeavor in good faith to bring about the reduction of acreage . . . in such a manner to cause the least *possible* amount of labor, economic, social disturbance, and to this end, *insofar as possible*, he shall effect the acreage reduction as near ratable as *practicable* among tenants on this farm; (he) shall, *insofar as possible* maintain on this farm the normal number of tenants and other employees; [he] shall permit all tenants to continue in the occupancy of their houses on this farm, rent free, for the years of 1934 and 1935, respectively (*unless* any such tenant shall so conduct himself as to become a nuisance or a menace *to the welfare of the producer*).[14]

A welfare worker charged that, although Leflore County had some conscientious planters who encouraged their tenants to raise livestock and gardens and aspire to a measure of self-sufficiency, others simply agreed to furnish a tenant only to turn him off the land after the crop was "laid by." These unscrupulous planters would then take the entire crop as reimbursement for the furnish, leaving the destitute tenant to fend for himself: "By spring and the start of a new crop year, he is a sorry sight, mentally and physically, and lacks collateral needed to secure any credit whatsoever." Throughout the Delta, reported the welfare worker, there were "hundreds of cases in whose home you will find no sheets, pillow cases, towels, etc. The quilts have been used to sleep on for so long and necessarily have had to be washed so regularly that they are in shreds. You will also find these people with no underwear, and many times they have only one piece, the outer garment."[15]

Because AAA contributed to higher cotton prices, it made the cost of any labor compensated with a share of the crop relatively more expensive. At the same time, by encouraging acreage reduction and tenant displacement, AAA helped to expand the supply of day laborers and thus depress the wages paid to them. The AAA crop-reduction plan also encouraged planters to shift more of their acreage from tenant to wage labor, because AAA benefits derived from reductions in the acreage worked by wage labor did not have to be shared. All the planter had to do was to convince the AAA, whose county committees were already inclined to give him the benefit of the doubt, that he was cutting the amount of land farmed by wage hands when he was actually trimming the size of the plots assigned to tenants. This little bit of winked-at deception accomplished, the planter was in a position to enjoy the benefits of cheaper labor, higher prices, and a guaranteed subsidy, all supplied in some manner by the United States government.[16]

Between 1935 and 1939, the average benefit received by landlords per wage worker for each acre of land yielding 350 pounds of lint cotton was $21.36 as compared to a return of only $11.19 per sharecropper and $9.01 per share tenant. By replacing a sharecropper with a wage hand, the planter could improve his per-acre return by 91 percent; by similarly displacing a share tenant, he could boost this income by 137 percent. Over the same period, the absolute return per acre from shifting from sharecropper to wage hand grew from $1.75 in 1934 to $16.78 in 1939. The gain from replacing a share tenant with a wage hand rose in that same period from $10.41 to $19.16.[17]

Government acreage-reduction payments also made the decision to purchase planters, cultivators, and other equipment considerably less difficult. In 1934 and early 1935, Coahoma County planters spent over $250,000 on tractors. By the end of the 1930s, one planter in Washington County had already purchased twenty-two tractors and thirteen four-row cultivators capable of doing as much work as 130 tenant families. Mechanization made tenant displacement more tempting because it made wage labor more efficient. Planters also forced tenants to use tractors to plant and cultivate their cotton and charged them for the use of the tractor even if the tenant's preference was to continue to rely on mules.[18]

The technology to mechanize planting and cultivation of cotton had been available well before the Great Depression. The real bottleneck in the mechanization of cotton farming lay in providing an efficient, affordable, mechanical cotton picker. So long as a mechanized harvest was not achievable, the amount of acreage farmed by wage labor rather than sharecroppers would be determined by the planter's estimate of his chances of securing an adequate supply of hands at picking time. "Tenancy," explained Gavin Wright, was "the price" the planter paid for the "certainty of harvest labor." Planters were generally unwilling to risk complete dependence on day labor, but, by encouraging planters to reduce their tenant population, AAA automatically enlarged the pool of workers available for day labor. Moreover, if relief agencies cooperated, as they often did, by purging their rolls at picking time, an expanded harvest labor supply stood ready "for the picking," as one economist wrote.[19]

In addition to simply evicting their tenants, some landlords replaced a larger family with a smaller one, thereby reducing the amount of furnish they had to provide in order to secure the cultivation of the decreased acreage. Meanwhile, managing share tenants who could provide workstock and fertilizer found it increasingly difficult to rent a place to work, because their status under AAA was more favorable than that of the sharecropper, who could furnish only his labor. The reduced labor needs induced by AAA policies also discouraged the traditional moving about every year or so that had long characterized the sharecropping system. Tenants were too concerned about finding a new place to "crop" to be too quick to abandon their old homes even if the current landlord was abusive and unfair in his treatment of them. Under such conditions, it was not difficult for a hard-nosed landlord to convince a tenant to accept an agreement that would sign over all government funds to him. Some tenants even began to see debt in different terms, because owing a sizable amount to the landlord could actually serve as a form of security against displacement on some plantations.[20]

There was also evidence that some landlords simply reduced the acreage officially allotted to the tenant without actually taking any land out of production. One Bolivar tenant reported that, despite the fact that he was working exactly the same acreage as he had worked before, his landlord now counted it as 14.5 instead of 19.5 acres. Another reported that his landlord claimed he was farming only sixteen acres in cotton when he knew he had twenty acres. This latter tenant complained bitterly of inadequate furnishings, claiming he and his sisters were practically "naked" and that their food supply gave out on Thursday, but they were unable to get more until Saturday.[21]

By reducing their labor needs, AAA allowed planters to be more choosy about those with whom they contracted and generally made it less crucial for planters to deal honestly and generously with their tenants in order to retain them. Even so staunch a defender of the planter-paternalists as William Alexander Percy became alarmed at the cheating he observed under AAA. Percy insisted publicly that the landlords who swindled and abused their tenants were in the minority. Privately, however, he suggested that AAA official Oscar Johnston might have underestimated "the amount of dishonesty practiced by landlords in this section in their settlements with their tenants." Percy warned "that such dishonesty is widespread and disruptive of interracial relations, disintegrating to the planters, and conducive to making the tenant distrust or even hate the white man." Johnston assured Percy that he knew that "dishonest practices are widespread" and even added that he feared "such practices are the rule rather than the exception." Yet Johnston rejected the idea of greater federal supervision, and, because he knew of no way to legislate "morals into the unregenerate mass of our population," he saw no end to the cheating and exploitation of labor in the Delta "as long as man is made in his present image."[22]

Just as it winked at illegal evictions and dishonest settlements, AAA did nothing to discourage usury and other forms of profiteering. Investigators found the commissary system flourishing in the Delta, with prices 10 to 50 percent higher than at retail stores. Interest rates on advance credit purchases ranged from 6 to 30 percent. One report cited a case where interest was compounded at 25 percent daily, even though the debt itself ran for only a few days. The policies of the Farm Credit Administration's Farm Loan Banks had apparently made it more difficult for planters to borrow money at 6 to 8 percent and turn around and charge their tenants 20 percent or more on the same money, but, as an investigator noted, "legal intricacies" usually prevented a tenant or cropper from borrowing directly from these federal banks.[23]

The New Deal's Resettlement Administration and the Farm Security Administration oversaw programs designed to loan money directly to "worthy" tenants who aspired to become landlords or to relocate tenants in communities where they could find industrial employment. Both of these agencies seemed to promise much-needed assistance to struggling farm workers in the Delta, but both also encountered considerable opposition from Delta planters, who, despite their participation in the AAA acreage-reduction plan, remained hostile to any program that might affect the availability or tractability of labor.[24]

Meanwhile, the pervasiveness of planter influence on the AAA and other New Deal programs combined with the shrinking demand for labor to undercut the efforts of tenants—especially black tenants—to call attention to their plight. Numerous official tenant complaints about AAA abuses either fell into a bureaucratic black hole or found their way back to county committees whose planter membership quickly saw to it that neither rental contracts nor federal assistance was available to those who had filed them. Such consequences were profound indeed in a region where more than 90 percent of the tenants were blacks whose meager incomes depended entirely on white employers and/or government relief.[25]

Black tenants were not the only victims of AAA policies. Frank Smith described the impact of the New Deal farm program on his Uncle John, a white farmer who came back to the Delta in 1920 and made a down payment on a three-hundred-acre farm. In 1926 he lost this land to foreclosure and spent the next four years farming as a cash renter. In 1930 his good reputation enabled him to secure credit to buy a five-hundred-acre farm. He made a good crop each of the next three years, but depressed cotton prices prevented him from meeting a single note payment. Faced with foreclosure once again, he returned to cash renting, but, with the boost to cotton farming supplied by the AAA program, good land became harder to rent. Only twice in eight years was "Uncle John" able to work the same land two years in succession, and on several occasions he lost his tenants because he was unable to rent land by Christmas and thereby secure credit on his rental contract to provide his croppers with their customary Christmas advance. Feeling more than a little "snake-bit," Smith's uncle passed up chances to purchase land at good prices only to see it sell within a short time for a much higher figure.[26]

AAA created few such difficulties for well-established planters. A survey of payments in excess of ten thousand dollars by AAA to individuals in Mississippi showed the extent to which the Delta's large planters benefited from the program. In 1933 more than 25 percent of such payments nationwide went to plantation operators in the Delta. The following year the figure climbed to 35 percent, and it rose to 41 percent in 1935.[27]

Every AAA payment of ten thousand dollars or more in Mississippi in 1933 went to a plantation in twelve counties wholly or partly in the Delta, with the great majority concentrated in Washington, Bolivar, Sunflower, and Coahoma counties. The biggest beneficiary was Oscar Johnston's Delta and Pine Land Company, which received $114,840. The state penitentiary at Parchman was given more than $75,000. Several prominent Delta families drew large sums from AAA, including the Eastlands, who were paid over $26,000, and the Percys, whose Trail Lake operation received $16,422. Between 1933 and 1935, the Delta and Pine Land Plantation and other smaller ones managed by Oscar Johnston received nearly $400,000 in AAA funds. In 1936 AAA payments accounted for $68,000 of Delta and Pine Land's $153,000 net income. This pattern persisted throughout the 1930s as Delta planters continued to dominate published lists of those who received checks from AAA in excess of ten thousand dollars.[28]

Between 1933 and 1939, Bolivar County received nearly three million dollars in AAA rental and benefit payments. The same was true of Sunflower. Coahoma County farms received nearly two million dollars during the same period. Nearly half of the total AAA expenditures in Mississippi during these years went to farmers in fourteen of eighty-two counties, all of which were in or adjacent to the Delta. All of these counties had a population at least 60 percent black, and the tenancy rate was greater than 80 percent in all but two. A study of two dozen Delta plantations during the first four years of the New Deal revealed an average government-subsidized net profit of $9,870.[29]

The AAA program's advantages for landlords were obvious enough. On the other hand, the negative impact of AAA on farm laborers could be surmised from the fact that even though cotton prices began to rise, with planters monopolizing AAA payments, reducing tenant acreage, and shifting to day labor, increasing numbers of tenants and former tenants were in need of relief. Moreover, although relief expenditures grew, they continued to represent but a fraction of federal subsidy payments to planters. Relief expenditures in Bolivar County rose from $1,300 to $50,000 during 1933 and 1934, although AAA spent nearly $400,000 in the county during the same period. In Sunflower, relief spending climbed from $6,000 in 1933 to $32,000 in 1935 while the county received nearly $300,000 in AAA payments during the latter year. In addition to the Delta's destitute and unemployed, relief programs also benefited the planters, who realized that the more tenants they could get on relief, the lower their own expenditures for furnish. In November 1936, for example, two Bolivar County planters offered to provide mules for a WPA construction project, provided at least ten of their tenants were given jobs on the project.[30]

Although planters made good use of New Deal relief agencies when it served their purpose to do so, with the government paying thirty cents an hour for rural work relief and landlords offering farm labor only seventy-five cents for a fourteen-hour day, local whites did their best to get relief programs suspended at harvest time. In the mid-1930s a black newspaper reported that all WPA projects in the Delta had been suspended in order to provide "cotton pickers for distressed plantation owners after planters complained that federal projects used workers ordinarily available for picking cotton." The paper went on to charge that law enforcement officers in the Delta had been combing small towns and loading "unemployed" blacks "into trucks where they are carried to the plantations and forced to pick cotton. Those who refuse to go are jailed as 'vagrants.'"[31]

Although not set in the Delta, WPA project engineer John Faulkner's *Men Working* satirized the WPA and illustrated the manner in which planters urged tenants to turn to the federal government for support during the months between crops. When Hub Taylor's father was denied a loan by his landlord, who told him to apply to the "WP and A," Hub was furious: "The bastard. Thinks he can hire us for day hands and take all the parity checks and the crop too and then in the winter when we go to him for supplies he'll say, why don't you git on the WP and A? By God, we'll just git to the WP and A and let him have the crops. I wish we had two crops to let him have . . . and both of 'em was full of grass."[32]

New Deal investigators saw a "notable disregard for consistency" among planters "who have been glad to dump many of their workers on relief in recent years" and then raised "the cry that relief has demoralized the 'nigger.'" "They do not," these critical observers noted, "seem to feel that it is a reflection upon the cotton system when people prove anxious to cling to a $21 a month security [WPA wage] instead of plunging back into the zone of private employment at the rare times they can be used."[33]

When it became apparent in 1933 that some of the cotton planted by Leflore County landlords would not come up, they lost all or part of the line of credit that financed the furnish they supplied to their tenants. These planters then stopped furnishing the tenants, who were given only occasional work chopping and the promise of a chance to pick cotton. When local relief officials put some of these destitute former tenants to work in a mosquito control program, however, local planters grew fearful that they would be unable to get enough day labor when they needed it. A local planter accosted a welfare worker, telling him that such efforts were "ruining these people," who "should be made to get out and go to work as there were plenty of jobs." When he asked the planter where these jobs were to be had, however, the welfare worker reported, "He could not give me one name."[34]

Delta planters had once sought to recruit immigrant labor to reduce their dependence on blacks, but New Deal investigators and officials quickly discovered that Delta landlords favored black tenants over white ones. John Dollard explained that "low standards of living can be forced on the Negro by utilizing caste prerogatives to suppress any demand for change on his part." A government researcher agreed: "Plantation owners prefer the docile Negro cropper. They despise a white cropper who is so low that he submits to their overbearing supervision; and they cannot get along with one who talks back." A survey of Leflore County concluded that local planters had been forced to recruit white labor after the great black out-migration of the war years but that "this class of workers were never to the liking of the landlords and with the return of the Negro labor supply to the County the planters began to displace these white croppers. The white croppers and tenants were too shrewd traders and bargainers to suit the planters, and they always had arguments over their trades and accounts. They also would not 'crop' the land as ordered by their landlords." This "did not rest well" with the planters, and as rapidly as possible they put the white croppers off their holdings and substituted Negro croppers, whom they could more readily handle and "settle with!"[35]

A number of planters showed no hesitation in rejecting white tenants or day labor. When one New Deal official offered to provide a planter with eleven white families to pick cotton, the planter refused. One white tenant reported that, as he sought employment, he was rebuffed by one planter, who bluntly informed him: "I won't have any G—— damned white cropper on my place. Get off and stay off. All I want to work are niggers who will do what I tell them to."[36]

Planters also tried to use their influence over New Deal relief agencies to rid the Delta of potentially troublesome white tenants. One official reported that planters regularly urged him not to put poor whites on relief but to "starve them out. They are not worth feeding. We do not want them in our county." A Leflore County welfare worker complained to Mississippi governor Martin S. Conner that planters who refused to employ poor whites were also pressuring the local welfare board to discontinue relief work in order to force unwanted white farm labor out of the county. "As soon as the cotton season is over," the writer predicted, "you will find these same planters bringing pressure (and you know monied pressure is strong) on the members of the Board to apply for aid to help carry [black] 'hands' through the winter, as the crop was mortgaged and 'nothing was cleared.'"[37]

Twenty-two Leflore County Civil Works Administration workers complained to Harry Hopkins about powerful planters from that county who were getting CWA work for their black tenants and were also refusing to contract with white tenants. These men were not farm labor, and they assured Hopkins that they wanted "the Negro who follows public work for a living to have his CWA work, but we don't want farm labor white or black to rob us of what we believe to be rightfully ours."[38]

State and county relief officials steadfastly maintained that the decision to grant relief was not a matter of color. As was the case on the plantation, however, differences in the "standards of living" of the two races did come into play in the calculation of how much and what kind of relief would be offered. As a result, during June 1933, sixty-three Leflore County white families received an average of $12.16 in assistance, while fourteen black families were given only an average of $5.44. Despite the apparent pressure to deny relief to indigent whites, thereby driving them out of the county, those whites who did receive assistance had no reason to complain that they were being treated no better than blacks. Moreover, the amount of aid received by blacks was hardly sufficient to make them reluctant to return to farm work when they were needed.[39]

Inequities and abuses permeated the intricate framework of federal relief and recovery programs, but for all its shortcomings the New Deal contributed to some significant improvements in the quality of life for many Deltans. In the area around Frank Smith's hometown of Sidon, near Greenwood, the New Deal wrought many changes. Acreage reduction pushed tenants into both Sidon and Greenwood, and a nearby Farm Security Administration resettlement effort pulled in whites from the nearby hills. In Sidon itself a surplus commodity program helped to feed the destitute population, while WPA workers paved streets and WPA money sponsored Sidon's first library and a recreational program featuring both "round" and "square" dancing on the weekends. More important, however, in Smith's view was the fact that "the days of WPA, NYA, and distribution of surplus food commodities were the first that Sidon ever knew without sharp pockets of poverty and even just plain hunger in some corners of the community."[40]

When Turner Catledge visited Tunica County in 1935, he found that the New Deal had induced considerable prosperity in some circles. Three planters who, prior to the AAA acreage-reduction campaign, had been chronically in debt signed up in 1934 to reduce acreage, taking their marginal land out of cotton to grow corn and hay and pushing their tenants to raise gardens and keep hogs. The AAA payments, bolstered by price supports of twelve cents per pound, produced a profit for the landlords in 1934 and enabled them, for the first time in recent memory, to plant the next crop without having to borrow. The New Deal also brought joy to the Delta's financial community. A Tunica banker gleefully reported that clients were coming in to pay back loans long dismissed as uncollectible: "People come in here and ask to pay back interest on notes we literally have to fish out of the waste baskets." The banker vowed to fight "anyone who said we had not prospered" under the New Deal.[41]

Delta political leaders quickly realized that their communities could benefit considerably from tapping into the flow of New Deal funds. Walter Sillers, Jr., proposed to use Federal Emergency Relief Administration funds to establish a print paper mill at Rosedale. He also sought federal aid in restoring abandoned lands to be sold, "preferably to whites," in tracts of forty to one hundred acres on long-term, low-interest loans. Finally, he hoped to convince WPA administrators to support the construction of a hospital, pool, and playground at Rosedale. Not all his inquiries seemed to be motivated by purely altruistic concerns. When he learned that the FERA was planning to purchase lands in his area, he informed officials that he had "several tracts in mind which I would like to have ready to have offered just as soon as your development is ready to purchase." As a planter, Sillers was by no means disinterested in farm policy, and he warned in 1935 that the failure of the government to loan at least twelve cents per pound on that year's crops would mean "disaster to the South" because, if the crop was as large as expected, prices would fall as low as eight cents per pound.[42]

Although it benefited some considerably more than others, the New Deal brought a tremendous boost to the economy of Mississippi as a whole. Between 1933 and 1939, the federal government spent $450 million in the state and cleared or insured loans for an additional $260 million. This figure represented approximately $355 for each resident of the state in 1940. In response to this spending, federal income tax receipts almost quadrupled between 1934 and 1939. Bank deposits doubled during the 1930s, as did the value of farm real estate. Farm income rose by 134 percent. By 1934 federal aid had become the state's major source of revenue, and it was the major reason that the state's treasury showed a surplus by the end of 1935. With its reserve supplemented by new sales and beer and wine taxes, Mississippi could thank the federal government, which had, in the words of one scholar, "subsidized the poorest state in the Union into solvency" through "massive federal handouts . . . [including] work relief wages, cotton subsidy payments, veteran's bonuses, and direct relief."[43]

Although Delta blacks encountered all manner of discrimination at the hands of the New Deal, the slender benefits that finally trickled down to them nonetheless made a difference to many a family living on the very edge of starvation and despair. Some of the most significant progress by blacks during the New Deal came in Holmes County at Mileston, where an FSA project involving more than one hundred black farmers enabled a number of them to become independent landowners. These FSA beneficiaries ultimately formed the core of the Holmes County Movement, which played a prominent role in black political mobilization during the civil rights era.[44]

Of all the beneficiaries of the New Deal in Mississippi, however, no single group fared better than the planters of the Delta. Instead of considering all New

Deal programs as "anathema," as V. O. Key suggested, Delta planters embraced the ones that could be turned to their interests. Thanks to the New Deal, the Delta confirmed better than any southern subregion Gavin Wright's description of the South at the end of the 1930s as "planters' heaven . . . with generous government subsidies, protection against risk, ready financing for new machinery, and cheap harvest labor to make it all possible." Pete Daniel elaborated on Wright's description: "There was plenty of labor, the federal government cared for those who were without work or food, and the agricultural program favored landlords. With a few adjustments, a landlord could change the status of his sharecroppers and tenants, keep nearly all of the government money, transfer the furnish to the government, and save money toward a tractor." Finally, with more intensive fertilization and cultivation, Delta planters actually increased their yields as they reduced their acreage. For example, many of them produced a bale per acre in 1936.[45]

A careful study of the plantation system in the Delta shows that the 1930s were definitely a decade of change. Cotton acreage fell by more than 39 percent between 1930 and 1940. The Delta accounted for nearly half of all the state's tractors by 1940, and, although cotton acreage declined, yields per acre jumped by more than 40 percent in response to increased fertilization and more intensive farming of the most productive lands on the plantation. The number of sharecroppers shrank by 9.4 percent during the decade, but the truly drastic reductions occurred among share tenants. Their more favorable status under AAA made them more susceptible to eviction, and their number declined by 66.2 percent. The fact that acreage farmed by sharecroppers fell by 21.3 percent, a figure nearly two and one-third times as great as the decline in the number of croppers, suggests that the croppers who were not displaced were also employed as wage hands on the operator's remaining land. Overall, the percentage of cropland harvested by tenants of all sorts fell from 81.9 in 1930 to 58.2 in 1940.[46]

Despite these indications of dramatic change, the Delta of 1940 was still clearly recognizable as the Delta. More than 90 percent of the farms were still operated by tenants. A sample of 220 heads of farm labor households showed a 53 percent illiteracy rate. The Delta's farm labor force still consisted largely of emigrés. Only 35 percent of the heads of households of farm labor families in four sample counties had actually been born in the Delta. Labor turnover rates remained high; out of a sample of 129 sharecropper families, 59 had moved at least once between 1930 and 1940. Despite the economic advances made by some sharecroppers, the "furnish" system still flourished, and one survey of 129 croppers showed that nearly half of them were paying more than 10 percent interest on the furnish and other credit items they received. Sharecropping had declined precipitously doing the 1930s, but the move to partial- or full-wage labor status was not a voluntary one for most croppers; of those surveyed, 76 percent preferred working for a share of the crop to working for wages.[47]

That the modernization of agriculture held out little in the way of upward mobility for the area's workers became clear in the observations of a researcher who surveyed the area's farm economy in 1940: "The so-called agricultural ladder is largely non-existent in the Delta. Large operating units, high land values, the persistence of the caste system, the need for relatively large investments in operating equipment, and the importance of managerial skills reduce the probability of tenants, croppers, and wage workers ever rising to the status of ownership." Four years later a report on conditions in Coahoma County concluded that "the white [man's] control over his sharecroppers is fairly absolute. . . . Supervision of the farming activities of the sharecropper is very close; he has no opportunity to exercise any initiative."[48]

For all such evidence of continuity, however, as the 1940s began the Delta stood at the threshold of an era of profound economic change, much of it traceable directly or indirectly to the cumulative influence of New Deal farm policies acting in combination with the far-reaching and dramatic influences of World War II. Across the state, per capita income rose from $250 in 1940 to $627 in 1945. A new air base at Greenville and several other small installations in the area created some attractive job opportunities. Demographic changes were swift and significant. Overall, for example, the population of Coahoma County declined by 8.4 percent between 1940 and 1943 alone. The Delta's rural farm population fell by 19 percent during the 1940s as farm workers moved into cities and towns (the rural nonfarm population including towns of twenty-five hundred or less grew by 30 percent, and the urban population rose by 38 percent). The major concern for planters was the fact that during the 1940s 10 percent of the rural black population left the Delta, creating sporadic labor shortages and raising the prospect of a prolonged labor crisis.[49]

Although it by no means destroyed the reality of the Delta's reputation as "planters' heaven," World War II clearly contributed to a sense of trouble in paradise. In addition to drawing labor away from the region, the war also helped to loosen the economic constraints on black laborers who remained in the Delta. Planters soon realized that, because of war-induced wage increases, former sharecroppers could now make as much by working only a few days each week as they had once earned for a full week's work. Irritated planters in desperate need of cotton pickers could hardly endure the sight of blacks driving about the Delta enjoying their new leisure and flaunting their new sense of independence. Other planters complained that croppers simply moved into towns at the end of the summer when the planters stopped furnishing them and before their debts to the planter came due. Once in town these hands could take advantage of the higher wages available to them as day laborers and cotton pickers. Some planters were forced to allow tenants to stay on rent-free to keep them around through the cotton harvest. Even so, many who stayed on refused to pick or pull the less valuable "scrap" cotton that remained in the fields at the end of the picking season.[50]

Planters were also frustrated by the fact that black women receiving money from husbands in service were no longer forced to work in the fields or as domestics. Whites tried to convince these women that it was their patriotic duty as wives of servicemen to work in the fields and kitchens of the Delta. They also tried to enlist both black preachers and teachers in their efforts to get blacks to work on Saturdays and Sundays but enjoyed little success. White women were also receiving money from their soldier husbands, but this was not seen as a problem because most of them had never picked cotton, and in any event, as one Delta white explained, "You can't force white women to work."[51]

Longing for the days when cheap labor was more plentiful, some Delta planters expressed the hope that racial violence in urban areas in 1943 might "break the niggers loose in Northern cities" and cause them to "hit back for Mississippi." An AAA official in the Delta admitted that some local planters even stood ready to invest in "an organization that would encourage Race Riots in Northern Cities to get a plentiful supply of labor around after the war so (they) can have 2 croppers begging for each tract and plenty of extra help around for picking."[52]

As the foregoing observation suggested, when Delta planters complained of a scarcity of labor, what they often meant was a scarcity of labor willing to work at the wages and on the terms they offered. In 1942 Oscar Johnston lauded the efforts of Coahoma County planters to set the "wages for cotton pickers at $1.50 per hundred. This, I think, should be done throughout the Delta," he wrote, noting that on the Delta and Pine Land plantations at Scott and Deeson, pickers were receiving only one dollar per hundred because company officials saw no "reason or necessity for paying more than this."[53]

In order to maintain a stable labor supply at a wage they were willing to pay, Delta planters attempted to exert the same influence on federal agencies and programs that had served them so well throughout the New Deal Era. Planters hailed the passage of the 1942 Tydings Amendment, which empowered local draft boards to defer agricultural workers so long as they remained on the farm. Planters dominated the Delta's Selective Service boards and could therefore provide deferments to their "loyal" tenants while shifting others to the top of the list. Farm Security Administration officials even claimed that white opposition to their tenant purchase programs, which opened the door to landownership to blacks, led local boards to target FSA clients for the draft. Delta planters also relied heavily on the cooperation of the Selective Service officials. Early in 1943 Delta planters worked in conjunction with the American Legion and the Selective Service—the head of the Selective Service system in Mississippi was a Deltan—to find a means "that will not get us in trouble with federal authorities" whereby the threat of conscription could be used to prevent farm laborers from leaving the plantation.[54]

During 1942–1943 control over the mobility and distribution of labor resided with the United States Employment Service, which worked closely with the Farm Security Administration to provide transportation and shelter for workers shifted from areas of labor surplus to those where labor was scarce. Having long viewed the FSA as a menace to labor stability in the Delta, planters lobbied hard for Public Law 45, a 1943 measure that created the Emergency Farm Labor Supply program and transferred responsibility for the recruitment of farm labor to the Department of Agriculture. An amendment to the new law required the signature of the county extension agent before a worker could receive federal assistance to leave his county for alternative employment. Since county agents usually had close ties to the planter-dominated local Farm Bureau chapter and AAA committee, this amendment provided greater planter control over labor mobility. Delta planters also succeeded in getting the government to provide them with POWs and Hispanic labor to pick their cotton. They requested as well that Japanese-American internees be made available for this purpose, although not without some reservations. Several planters made it clear that they had no desire to see the Japanese-Americans remain in the Delta after the war. In that event, wrote one, "instead of having one racial problem we will have two." Sounding a bit prophetic, he warned that if the Japanese were brought to the Delta, "they will own a large proportion of the neighborhood before they have been here many years."[55]

Planters also capitalized on their political influence to turn to their advantage a program that employed black county agents in rural areas with relatively large black populations. Instead of advising and assisting struggling black farmers, however, in the Delta these black agents performed a host of "chores" for whites—"vaccinating livestock, servicing farm machinery, and spraying and pruning orchards."[56]

For all of the efforts of Delta planters to maintain a sizable and stable labor supply and hold down labor costs, wages for cotton picking rose from one dollar per hundred pounds in 1940 to as high as three dollars per hundred in 1944. Despite higher cotton prices than the previous year, however, cotton planters paid pickers less in 1945 than in 1944, thanks to a wage ceiling of $2.10 per hundred imposed by the federal government as a wartime emergency measure. Local chambers of commerce (from which blacks were excluded) carried on a vigorous lobbying effort in behalf of this ceiling policy, which saved area planters an estimated fifteen million dollars in wages. When a minimum wage for picking was suggested, however, the planters condemned the proposal as "outside interference." Although blacks were barred from membership in chambers of commerce, they were often forced to join the Farm Bureau (which also maintained an energetic prolandlord lobbying effort), even though they were not allowed to attend meetings. Landlords simply added Farm Bureau dues to their tenants' accounts, much as they had done with war bonds and Red Cross contributions.[57]

Many tenants never realized they were Farm Bureau members until they saw the deductions from their settlement checks. Others had joined because planters had led them to believe that the Farm Bureau was responsible for their parity checks. At the end of the war, an estimated 95 percent of the Farm Bureau members in Coahoma County were black.[58]

This statistic was particularly ironic given that Delta planters saw the Farm Bureau as their most potent weapon against efforts to agitate and organize their workers. The Southern Tenant Farmers Union, a biracial organization founded in 1934 largely to plead the cases of tenants victimized by AAA, was noticeably more active across the river in Arkansas until 1939, when Mississippi Delta blacks began to show more interest in the STFU. STFU organizers entered the Delta at considerable risk. One analyst described the typical Coahoma County planter as "suspicious of any stranger who wants to contact his Negro sharecroppers" and warned that "anyone who was suspected of organizing tenants into a union or discussing their 'rights' with them would find himself forcefully removed from the county."[59]

Throughout the 1940s the Farm Bureau and the planter-dominated Delta Council waged a campaign of spying, coercion, and harassment against the STFU. Dorothy Lee Black, office manager of the Delta Council, attempted to spy on an STFU meeting in 1942 and reported that various speakers had urged black tenants to unionize and seek wage-and-hour legislation and to demand the vote as well. One speaker "urged complete social equality of negroes and whites, and left no doubt in my mind that he favored intermarriage," while another delivered "one of the most abusive, vindictive and profane denunciations of plantation agriculture and those interested in commercial agriculture that I have ever heard."[60]

Researchers had encountered considerable dissatisfaction among younger blacks in the 1930s, and, although they were quick to assert that none of their own well-treated and contented black workers would join an organization like the STFU, Delta planters detected a growing sense of militance and aggressiveness among local blacks as the war progressed. Coahoma County blacks staged a brief strike in 1945 in protest of planters' efforts to limit wages for cotton pickers. A Department of Agriculture researcher who studied Coahoma County in 1944 concluded that "beneath the surface among the Negroes an important change is going on; even down to the sharecropper there is a feeling of discontent and a growing consciousness of exclusion from social, economic, and political participation. Furthermore, Negro leaders are becoming more fearless and ready to state what they believe to be the basic rights of the group." Black ministers often took the lead in this effort, and the report concluded that "it is actually coming to pass that the Negro church has become the means here and there for encouraging Negroes to resist the controls which the landlord has held over them."[61]

Sociologist Samuel Adams found a growing sense of race consciousness among Delta blacks during the war. Adams cited the influences of the radio, the movie theater, and the automobile in breaking down the isolation of Delta society and introducing a more sophisticated, secularized world view. Adams recorded a poem that urged blacks to take more pride in themselves:

> Think something of yourself, you crazy dunce,
> No matter if you was a slave once,

Every nation been a slave once.
They didn't draw up and act a dunce.
Think because you a nigger,
You just can't get no bigger.

A young black man told Adams: "I can't get nothing out of what no white man do; but boy I get a thrill out of what the colored do." Said another: "No whites can sing to suit me. When a nigger sings, he sing with more emotion. Ain't nothing no white man do sincere."[62]

If the war appeared to spur some blacks to be more assertive, the conflict stirred the racial anxieties of many whites and reinforced as well the growing anti-New Deal, anti-national Democratic party sentiment that was already clearly visible in the Delta and the South at large by the end of the 1930s. A Delta planter worried in 1942 that Eleanor Roosevelt's "association with the darkies" and her efforts to encourage the Democratic party to court black voters were signs of trouble ahead. He predicted that the time would soon come when black votes would be protected by federal law, "and we all know what that will mean in the South." Delta planter O. F. Bledose III compared the New Deal's programs aimed at helping tenants to acquire land to "the same promise the other Yankees made to the negroes during the other Civil War." Yet another planter, hearing of an interracial meeting reportedly held in Greenville in 1943, described Delta whites as "sitting right under the mouth of the gun" and facing their worst crisis "since prior to Reconstruction days." He claimed that he and his fellow planters were organizing vigilante groups to protect "their civilization and their way of life."[63]

"A prosperous farmer is the most conservative man on earth," an Alabamian observed, and the Delta clearly had its share of these, thanks in no small part to the generous policies of a Democratic administration that they nonetheless grew first to distrust and then to despise. In 1942 Delta planter James O. Eastland mounted a bitter anti-New Deal campaign to win the Senate seat left vacant by the death of Pat Harrison, a staunch Roosevelt supporter. Upon her return from a tour of the Deep South in 1942, author Lillian Smith reported that in the Delta she had found "reaction rising like a great wave." Smith explained further: "Cotton is 26 cents in the Delta now and the general attitude among the planters is that neither Mr. Roosevelt nor God Himself is going to keep them from making some money while the making is good. There is childish desperation in their attitude that would be awfully funny were they not so powerful. . . . This spring I find them on the defensive, very antagonistic to all liberal movements, growing so suspicious and antagonistic that I dared not tell them that I was on Rosenwald Fund business for their hospitality would not have been equal to such a strain being put on it!" Another commentator found Delta planters totally opposed to "every agency which would put ideas in the Negroes' heads" and determined to "muzzle every person who would criticize what they are doing."[64]

Planters who hoped that a measure of labor stability would return as soon as the war ended were soon disappointed. Returning black veterans were much less likely to accept shoddy and unfair treatment at the hands of landlords. Their protests were not always verbal. Some cotton pickers filled their sacks with green bolls or rocks before weighing. Planters who tried to curb such behavior with physical abuse seldom enjoyed much success. Said one observer, "The day when a man could protect the grade of his cotton and assume a clean-picked crop by threatening his labor with a single-tree or a trace chain is gone forever. The word spreads fast against that kind of planter nowadays and the first thing he knows, he can't get anybody to pick his cotton." Sensing that fairer and more humane treatment might be necessary to hold onto their labor, the Delta Council recommended in 1945 that the state legislature adopt a plan to improve black schools. The council's recommendations included a call for higher salaries for black teachers and a request for the establishment of a black junior college to train teachers in the Delta.[65]

Despite such evidence of moderation, however, some planters refused to abandon the older, more primitive methods of labor control. Such was the case with a Leflore County planter who was charged with holding a laborer in debt peonage. His none-too-contrite response was: "I'll kill the SOB before the year's out; I'm damned tired of people trying to get my negroes." Such blatant efforts to hold blacks against their will only emphasized the realization on the part of most Delta planters that, once they departed, their former workers would not return of their own volition. It was small wonder that this was the case. Concerns among planters about the loss of labor and the rise in farm wages notwithstanding, a 1947 survey showed nearly two-thirds of a sample of black families in Bolivar County receiving less than $750 in cash income. During 1946 only 57 percent of the families had savings on hand; for half of these, savings amounted to less than twenty-five dollars.[66]

Clearly the transformation of the Delta's agricultural system had not alleviated disparities in income and wealth, nor had it relieved Delta planters of their obsession with labor control and racial hegemony. A Coahoma County survey outlined both the extent and limitations of the changes that had come to the Delta as a result of the New Deal and World War II: "The planters are fairly quick to accept new ideas, probably more so today than 15 years ago. Their interest can be quickly enlisted in new farm practices, mechanization, political pressure, etc., if they can be made to see that their economic interests will thereby be enhanced." On the other hand, the report indicated that, while "a new cultural trait or complex that has any reasonable possibilities of making more money for the plantation owner is looked on with favor, any new element which threatens to upset the Negro-white relationship, particularly as it relates to the plantation labor force, is resisted immediately." The author of the report concluded that "the dominant white planter group lives in constant fear that some outside person or idea will threaten the *status quo* in respect to race relations."[67]

Despite their resistance to changes in its social and political structure, the Delta's leading planters soon reconciled themselves to the transformation of its economy. In 1946 Delta Council member W. T. Wynn summarized the impact of the war when he observed: "War does a lot of things. We have found out that our economics have been disrupted. If you walk over Delta farms, you will find one-third of your farms not in production. . . . Forty percent of the houses are vacant. Forty percent of the labor is lost. . . . I believe that in the next five to ten years you will see the greatest revolution that ever happened in this country, happen in this Mississippi Delta."[68]

Although the war-induced labor shortage seemed to give planters little choice but to proceed with rapid, full-scale mechanization, the absence of a viable mechanical picker actually forced some planters to retain or even expand their sharecropper force in order to assure themselves of an adequate supply of harvest labor. For such landlords a common pattern was to plant with tractors and turn the crop over to the hands once the cotton showed green in the rows. Still, wartime anxiety about labor shortages only dramatized the need for a workable cotton picker that could reduce man hours per bale by 80 percent compared to hand cultivation and harvesting.[69]

Growing fears of racial upheaval also sparked renewed white interest in a mechanical picker. From the Coahoma County plantation where a picker prototype was being tested, Richard Hopson wrote other local planters to stress both the economic and social implications of the cotton picker:

> I am confident that you are aware of the acute shortage of labor which now exists in the Delta and the difficult problem which we expect to have in attempting to harvest a cotton crop this fall and for several years to come. I am confident that you are aware of the serious racial problem which confronts us at this time and which may become more serious as time passes. . . . I strongly advocate the farmers of the Mississippi Delta changing as rapidly as possible from the old tenant or sharecropping system of farming to complete mechanized farming. . . . Mechanized farming will require only a fraction of the amount of labor which is required by the sharecrop system thereby tending to equalize the white and Negro population which would automatically make our racial problem easier to handle.[70]

The marketing of a self-propelled one-row cotton picker by International Harvester in 1947 signaled the beginning of the end for the "harvest bottleneck" to full-scale mechanization of cotton production. Seven percent of Delta cotton was picked by machines in 1950; as the trend toward the reduction of the labor force and increased reliance on machines became even more pronounced, crumbling and unoccupied tenant dwellings were soon a common sight. On the Delta and Pine Land Plantation, the number of occupied tenant houses fell from 850 to 525 between 1944 and 1947. A Bolivar County study focused on a plantation where only 400 of 1,450 acres in cotton had been cultivated with day labor in 1940. In 1951, 1,200 acres were being worked by day labor, while only 450 were being farmed by tenants and sharecroppers. Still, although as much as 70 percent of the cotton crop on this plantation was harvested mechanically, management remained reluctant to divest itself entirely of its tenant work force so long as there were periodic demands for hand labor to control weeds and grasses.[71]

As the 1950s began, however, if the Delta's economic metamorphosis was not yet complete, it was clearly well under way. The role of federal farm policy in sparking this economic revolution in the Delta can hardly be exaggerated. No marketing quotas or cotton allotments were in effect between 1944 and 1953. These were reimposed in 1953, however, and, in conjunction with the Soil Bank Program introduced in 1956, they contributed to a dramatic reduction in Delta cotton acreage. A survey of forty cotton plantations between 1953 and 1957 reflected this diminished cotton cultivation and the other changes in farming and management techniques that accompanied it. The proportion of cropland devoted to cotton fell from 59 to 32 percent, and the percentage of cotton acreage farmed by croppers dropped from 56 to 39 percent, while over the same span the amount of cotton worked by wage labor rose from 44 to 52 percent. The number of mechanical cotton pickers rose by 46 percent, and the portion of cotton land treated with herbicide more than doubled between 1953 and 1957 as well.[72]

Consolidation, diversification, and mechanization brought enormous overall changes to Delta agriculture during the 1950s. Average farm size tripled, the number of farms fell by one-third, and as the sixties began 15 percent of the farmers were planting 70 percent of the cotton. As cotton acreage fell dramatically, soybean acreage rose by 538 percent between 1949 and 1959. A decade that began with machines picking 7 percent of the Delta's cotton closed with mechanical pickers harvesting half the crop. As mechanization continued, many displaced heads of sharecropper families moved into full-time wage-hand status, with their dependents serving as seasonally employed cotton choppers and pickers.[73]

Despite the dramatic cuts in cotton acreage, modern technology and improvements in chemical fertilizers and herbicides enabled large-scale producers to achieve both higher levels of productivity and dramatic savings in production costs, while they benefited as well from government price supports keyed to the buying power of a bale of cotton in the years when per-acre yields were much lower. In 1957, for example, a *Wall Street Journal* report cited the case of Jo Prichard, who grew cotton on his thirty-three-hundred-acre Delta plantation at a cost of twenty-four cents per pound and sold it at a government-supported price of approximately thirty cents per pound.[74]

As planters reaped the benefits of mechanization and federal farm programs, rapidly diminishing employment opportunities for farm laborers contributed to a 54 percent decrease in the Delta's rural farm population between 1950 and 1960. Meanwhile, the area's urban population increased by 39 percent, as many of those who remained in the Delta moved into its larger cities and towns.[75]

With the number of people employed in agriculture declining dramatically, many Delta leaders began to embrace industrial development as the key to the region's postwar economic survival. Formed in 1935 as the Delta Chamber of Commerce, the Delta Council quickly emerged as the primary advocacy organization for the large-scale planting and business interests of the Delta. During the war the council moved from its initial emphasis on limited efforts to recruit agriculture-related industries to a recognition that more broadly based industrial growth might help to stem the war-induced population exodus. Affirming the conclusion of one observer that by the end of the war Delta planters had become "modern businessmen who are alert to every new development that may affect their interests," one council member warned that the Delta was lagging behind the rest of the state in its industrial progress: "We must have more (industry) to take care of our people or we're going to find that our population will be gone in a few years when we do get fully mechanized." The council quickly went on record in support of the recruitment of "sound and stable" industry and offered its endorsement of vocational training programs designed to make the Delta more attractive to such firms.[76]

Industrial development advocates were heartened by some early successes. In 1949 Cleveland became the new home of a Baxter Laboratories plant, whose construction was subsidized by municipal bonds issued under the state's Balance Agriculture with Industry (BAWI) program, and Belzoni attracted both a broom handle factory and a soybean processing facility. The traditionally conservative probusiness outlook and the up-front hostility of Delta planters to labor organizers of all sorts stood the region's leaders in good stead as they wooed runaway industries from the North. When the Alexander Smith Company faced a strike at its Yonkers, New York, plant, crusading editor Hodding Carter spearheaded a drive to bring the firm to Greenville. As Alexander Smith fled its union antagonists, Carter praised "the truly splendid one-hundred-year human and industrial record" of the firm. By 1953 the Alexander Smith Company occupied a brand new fifteen-acre plant, whose construction had been subsidized by a BAWI bond issue and whose workers showed not the slightest inclination to organize. Elsewhere, a "good supply of desirable workers" helped to lure "Strutwear, Incorporated," to Clarksdale. A decade after the close of the war, the Delta economy was still dominated by agriculture and its politics by agricultural interests. Yet, although less than 10 percent of the work force was employed in manufacturing as of 1960, intensified enthusiasm for industrial development had nonetheless spread throughout a region where a growing number of planters now realized that the mechanization of agriculture made a significant degree of industrialization not only acceptable but desirable.[77]

When Delta leaders endorsed industrial development as a means of stemming out-migration, they were referring to the loss of white residents. In eleven Delta-area counties, estimated white out-migration between 1955 and

1960 (27,441) nearly equaled the estimated total for blacks (27,939). The white exodus was offset somewhat by in-migration, but the net migration deficit for whites over this five-year period nonetheless stood at an estimated 8,974. To merchants and professionals in the cities and towns, the loss of this many white consumers spelled gloomy economic times ahead. Moreover, despite high levels of black out-migration, whites accounted for barely one-third of the Delta's population in 1960.[78]

With the prospect of a black political challenge looming ever larger as the 1950s drew to a close, the anticipated defense of the racial status quo in the Delta seemed to dictate the retention of as large a white population as possible. On the other hand, as civil rights pressures began to mount, few of the Delta's white leaders showed any interest in maintaining a black population in excess of the region's rapidly diminishing farm labor needs. Influential planters and businessmen realized, however, that development officials emphasized Mississippi's abundance of "friendly Anglo-Saxon labor," and they knew that the new firms wooed to the state would either employ no blacks or that blacks would be given only low-paying and distasteful jobs that whites might be unwilling to accept. Critics charged that Delta planters served on the state's Agricultural and Industrial Commission in order to assure that no unionized, nondiscriminatory, high-wage plants came to their area, but, in fact, few such industries expressed an interest in locating anywhere in Mississippi, least of all in the Delta. Many, such as the Alexander Smith Company, were fleeing the union pressures they had encountered in the North. Such firms had few qualms about adhering to "whites only" employment policies that prevented them from competing for labor with the Delta's planters.[79]

Although the cumulative influences of the New Deal and World War II brought dramatic changes to the Delta's economy, the transformation of Delta agriculture left the region's planter-dominated social and political framework fundamentally intact. Still, despite their success in making Washington's expanded presence in the area work for them, many Delta whites detected during the war what Pete Daniel called "subtle indications of impending challenges to segregation." For example, the Supreme Court's invalidation of the white primary in 1944 only exacerbated growing fears about federal interference in the Delta's racial affairs. Shortly before the close of the war, as they weighed the merits of a federally imposed wage ceiling for cotton pickers, several Delta planters admitted they were on the horns of a dilemma. "I am thoroughly convinced," said one, "that we are at the crossroads. This action is far bigger than control of picking cotton wages in the Mississippi Delta in 1945. We are here today definitely deciding as to whether or not we are going ahead and encourage government regulation." The planters finally decided that the benefits of a federally mandated wage ceiling outweighed the risk of greater government involvement in their region's internal affairs. The decision was not an easy one, however, for Delta planters foresaw the day when an increasingly intrusive Washington might turn its attention and its regulatory inclinations toward the economic inequities and racial injustices that were the dominant features of Delta life.[80]

The racial tensions aggravated by World War II mounted steadily in the early postwar years as the Democratic party grew increasingly responsive to labor unions and black voters and the Supreme Court continued its move to dismantle the machinery of disfranchisement and segregation. In the wake of the war, Delta planters seemed to be confronting a future in which they would be forced to fend off the civil rights initiatives of the same federal government whose agricultural and relief policies had thus far helped them to sustain their social and political dominion over an economically transformed Delta.

9 ▽ "A Man's Life Isn't Worth
  ▽ a Penny with a Hole in It"
  ▽

Although Delta planters had managed to preserve their way of life even as the New Deal and World War II brought significant changes in the way they made their living, close observers realized that the remarkable caste-based society that sustained the Delta's grossly unbalanced and exploitive plantation economy might soon become an indefensible anachronism in the face of the social and political changes that seemed to be sweeping across the nation and the world in the wake of World War II. Writing in 1935, David Cohn noted that "disturbing ideas crawl like flies around the screen of the Delta 'but' they rarely penetrate." Describing the Delta as a land of "almost complete detachment," Cohn added, "Change shatters itself on the breast of this society as Pacific breakers upon a South Sea reef." On the other side of the war, however, Cohn found a different Delta. Writing in 1947, he perceived that the people of his native region were no longer immune to "the changes and fears of the world." Beyond that, they were also subject to "special stresses" arising from the Delta's unpredictable economy and its racially imbalanced society where, as Cohn explained, the "Negro question" was "almost without counterpart in the United States."[1]

The racial tensions detected by Cohn were traceable in no small part to the economic, demographic, and ideological forces generated or intensified by World War II. Pete Daniel observed that "the war unleashed new expectations and, among many whites, taught tolerance." Yet, while military service and the war experience encouraged some Delta blacks and even a few whites to challenge the racial orthodoxy that was so clearly at odds with the nation's sense of wartime purpose, the threat posed by the war to both the economic and social stability of Delta society and to the interests of those who reaped the benefits of that stability also triggered a militant and occasionally violent counterreaction. Well before the civil rights confrontations of the 1960s, the Delta's white power structure was waging a determined and sometimes violent campaign against internal dissent even as it girded itself to repulse an external assault on a status quo that had served it so long and so well.[2]

Having already earned a reputation for combative journalism by virtue of his outspoken criticism of Huey Long in Louisiana, Hodding Carter and his wife, Betty, moved to Greenville in 1936 at the urging of David Cohn and William Alexander Percy. Within two years they had bought out a rival paper and formed the *Delta Democrat Times*. As he prepared to leave for military duty in December 1940, Hodding Carter paid a final visit to Percy and asked him what could be done to remake whatever part of the world could be saved. Percy replied: "You can't do anything on a grand scale . . . but you can work again for your own people in your own town. It isn't national leaders we need so much as men of good will in each of the little towns of America. So try to keep Greenville a decent place by being a correct citizen yourself. The total of all Greenvilles will make the kind of country we want or don't want."[3]

A few months later, after he had finished reading Percy's *Lanterns on the Levee*, Carter wrote him from Camp Blanding, Florida, praising his "beautiful and brave book." "When I get out of the army," Carter wrote, "I want only to get back to Greenville and do my best to preserve there the pattern you uphold. Maybe I can help."[4]

As John Kneebone has pointed out, Carter's postwar crusade for improved race relations "flowed out of the campaign against Nazism," but his service as editor of the Middle East edition of *Stars and Stripes* also allowed him to view firsthand the resentment among the native population engendered by British colonial and racial views. "Men with white skins are in the minority in this world," Carter wrote in 1945, adding that "in even smaller minority are white-skinned men who look upon darker skins with contempt."[5]

In 1944 Carter published *Winds of Fear*, a novel about a wounded white veteran, the son of a liberal newspaper editor, who returns to his hometown to find it gripped by racial hysteria that culminates in a lynching. Greenville recorded no such lynching, but it did outrage Carter by failing to establish an honor roll listing veterans of World War II because some whites objected to putting the names of blacks and whites together, even under separate headings. The whole incident created a "stench in the nostrils of the fair-minded," Carter complained. He also asked, "How in God's name can the Negroes be encouraged to be good citizens, to feel that they can get a fair break, to believe that here in the South they will some day win those things which are rightfully theirs—decent housing, better educational facilities, equal pay for equal work, a lifting of health standards, and all of the other milestones along an obstacle filled road—if we deny them so small a thing as joint service recognition?"[6]

Carter's fellow Deltan, veteran, and racial moderate, Frank E. Smith of Greenwood, concluded that "more men came home from World War II with a sense of purpose than from any other American venture." Decision-making in the war effort had given Smith the confidence that he was "capable of decisive action in the new world that the war had made." Observing the acceptance by other southern whites of racially integrated training programs at Fort Sill, Oklahoma, Smith had concluded "that changes in racial patterns would be generally accepted when authority backed acceptance and when resistance would mean resistance to compelling authority." Smith entered politics in 1947 and moved subsequently from the state senate to a congressional seat, which was eventually gerrymandered out from under him in 1962.[7]

A number of blacks who became civil rights leaders in Mississippi were also veterans of World War II. National Association for the Advancement of Colored People leader Aaron Henry of Clarksdale spent three years in the armed services, part of it in an experimentally integrated unit in Hawaii. An NAACP member who later worked with the Student Nonviolent Coordinating Committee, Cleveland's Amzie Moore reacted strongly when he was plucked from the segregated Delta and deposited in a segregated unit in the Pacific. Moore explained, "Here I'm being shipped overseas, and I been segregated from this man whom I might have to save or he save my life. I didn't fail to tell it." To make matters worse, one of Moore's responsibilities as a soldier was to assist in a move to counter Japanese propaganda by speaking to black servicemen and assuring them that conditions for black troops would improve in the United States after the war.[8]

When he returned to Mississippi, Moore determined to insulate himself from white repression by achieving as much economic independence as possible. He acquired a store, a gas station, and a brick house, but he quickly reassessed his attitude after visiting Mound Bayou to look over some property. He was taken to a home where a woman lived with fourteen children, all of whom were naked from the waist down. They were burning cotton stalks in a barrel to keep warm. They had no bed and no food. Moore recalled, "Just looking at that I think really changed my whole outlook on life. I kinda figured it was a sin to think in terms of trying to get rich in view of what I'd seen, and it wasn't over seven miles from me."[9]

When men like Carter, Smith, Henry, and Moore returned from the war committed to bringing significant changes to the Delta, they quickly encountered vigorous opposition from those who were determined to maintain the status quo. The war clearly contributed to escalating racial tensions in the Delta as blacks became more independent and assertive and whites viewed with alarm both the leftward drift of the national Democratic party and the inclination of Delta blacks to look to Washington for security and support. As a result, during the war the Delta's conservative white leadership grew increasingly fearful that the same federal government whose assistance had proven so vital in preserving their socioeconomic and political prerogatives might soon take action in behalf of those who wished to strip them of those prerogatives.

In the wake of the war, leading Delta planters seemed to believe that their best hope was to assert as vociferously as possible their claim on the continuing economic and political assistance of Washington even as they denounced with equal vigor the expanded regulatory and social welfare activities of the federal government. Fearful that agitation by organized labor and various civil rights groups might disrupt or "demoralize" their labor supply and perhaps lead to

federal intervention in the day-to-day affairs of the Delta, outspoken conservatives like Walter Sillers, Jr., urged their fellow planters to continue their
wartime efforts to "solicit" tenants to join the Farm Bureau in order to
"counter the adverse activities to our interests of the communist-inspired labor
unions and communist organizations."[10]

Sillers personified the marked changes in attitude toward the national
Democratic party that occurred among Delta planters and their counterparts
across the Deep South during the Roosevelt years. During the early years of
the New Deal, Sillers had worked tirelessly to maintain local support for the
Roosevelt administration. In 1934 he warned friends that "big business" was
trying to "destroy" Roosevelt and pointed out that without Roosevelt's aid
local planters "would be getting much less than 15 cents per pound for cotton,
which you know means bankruptcy and ruin, sorrow and disaster." Sillers contributed freely to Roosevelt's 1936 reelection campaign and urged others to do
the same.[11]

A decade later, Sillers had apparently forgotten his region's debt to Roosevelt and the New Deal, which he described as an attempt to take over the
Democratic party, "bring the South to her knees, and force upon us non-seg-
regation and social and political equality amongst the races." Sillers had hoped
that as president, border state native Harry Truman might prove sympathetic
to the white South's racial philosophy, but by 1947 he was writing of the Democratic party in the past tense, blaming its death on Franklin Roosevelt, who
replaced it with a "Communistic-Socialistic party called the New Deal."[12]

More than one observer of Delta society in the first decade after the war
concluded that Delta whites felt themselves trapped between their old race-
baiting political antagonists in the hills and their own black masses grown
increasingly restive—"a great sticky force gradually hardening," as one visitor
described them—and looking to Washington for socioeconomic and political
redress. Though V. O. Key felt he saw promising signs of progressive inclinations among the younger generation, by 1946 the overwhelming majority of
Delta whites responded to what they perceived as serious external as well as
internal threats to their "way of life" by rejecting criticism and suggestions for
reforms of any sort and vowing to defend the status quo at all costs. The fact
that most Delta whites believed they could and should "simply stand up against
the world and demand our rights" helped to explain why in 1946, as Key put
it, "many a Delta planter held his nose and voted for [Theodore G.] Bilbo."
Whereas his mere presence on the ballot had traditionally assured a strong
Delta turnout for his opponent, the strength of the Delta's support for the
uncouth, race-baiting Bilbo in his 1946 senatorial reelection bid only foreshadowed an emerging statewide political consensus in which the need for racial
unity overrode geographic and class differences.[13]

Not surprisingly, the quickened racial consciousness of blacks and white
concerns over the potential aggressiveness of returning black servicemen led
to escalating racial violence in the wake of the war. Amzie Moore and others

claimed that some Delta whites had formed a home guard to protect white women and that for a period of several months after the war black men were being killed at the rate of one per week. In June 1946 the body of Leon McTatie was discovered in a Sunflower County bayou. McTatie had been whipped to death, allegedly for stealing a saddle. Though his wife witnessed the affair and three of the defendants confessed to the beating, a grand jury deliberated less than ten minutes before freeing his accused slayers. In 1948 at Louise, a black tenant farmer was severely beaten by two whites because he asked for a receipt after paying his water bill.[14]

Racial paranoia and growing hostility to the national Democratic party led Delta whites to rally to the Dixiecrat banner in 1948. Delta politicians like Walter Sillers, Jr., hoped that the Dixiecrats would, in the words of Numan V. Bartley, "counter the growing attack on southern social institutions . . . and reassert the sovereign rights of states." Fielding Wright, the Dixiecrat vice-presidential nominee, was himself a Deltan from Rolling Fork. In fact, Wright may have actually fathered the movement when he devoted his inaugural address as governor to what Numan Bartley described as "a clarion call for a states' rights crusade."[15]

The strength of the Dixiecrat movement in the region foreshadowed the Delta's role as the birthplace of the Citizens' Council, an organization pledged to defend the Jim Crow system from any and all challenges. In November 1953 Robert B. Patterson, a former paratrooper, who managed a sixteen-hundred-acre Leflore County plantation, learned of the pending school desegregation cases that would lead to the *Brown v. Board of Education* decision a few months later. Professing to be "confused, mad, and ashamed," he urged friends and acquaintances to "stand together forever firm against communism and mongrelization." Patterson's alarm apparently seemed premature to most Mississippi whites at the time, but the *Brown* decision soon made his fears all too common, not only in the Delta but throughout the state. Circuit court judge Tom P. Brady of Brookhaven caught Patterson's attention when he denounced the decision in his May 1954 "Black Monday" speech to the Greenwood chapter of the Sons of the American Revolution. The Yale-educated Brady expanded his talk into a ninety-page pamphlet that became the first "bible" of the massive resistance movement. Laced with dogma about "amalgamation" and "communism," the pamphlet was a call to action for whites. What Brady proposed was not a wave of KKK-style terrorism but a nationally based program of "law abiding" resistance and education perhaps leading even to the formation of a third political party.[16]

Brady's summons to action appealed so strongly to Patterson that he determined to devote the remainder of his life to resisting desegregation. To that end his first step was to call together the manager of the Indianola cotton compress, a local Harvard-educated attorney, and a prominent banker. He subsequently recruited as well the mayor and other high-profile members of the local white community. Before the first public meeting convened, the Citizens'

Council's leadership was already in place, awaiting the rubber stamp of the rank-and-file.[17]

Along with the organizational effort went a mass mailing of form letters such as those sent out by former legislator Fred Jones, a council member who also served on the Sunflower County Board of Supervisors. Jones's letter raised the threat of an NAACP invasion with the troubling news that "Walter White, a Negro from the Society for Advancement of Colored People, will speak in Jackson early in November." Jones blamed this "aggressiveness" on white "complacency," adding that "White would not have dared to do this ten years ago."[18]

Patterson supplemented this letter-writing effort with a circular containing a "reading list" on desegregation, which contained publications from a number of organizations generally considered to be anti-Semitic as well as antiblack. Shortly after the first reading list appeared, Greenville editor Hodding Carter called on the council to "come out in the open." Carter added that, since "the most respectable citizens in each community" appeared to be leading these organizations dedicated to maintaining the "status quo," their secrecy was their "only unresponsible aspect."[19]

A few days later an Associated Press report indicated that Mississippi legislators were abuzz over a new organization committed to resisting racial integration and spreading from the Delta to counties throughout the state. One Humphreys County representative bragged that his county's council had about five hundred members, and he added, "They mean business." He provided no specifics as to the nature of this "business," but other Delta legislators had predicted violence, and one had even suggested that "a few killings" could be the proverbial ounce of prevention that might "save a lot of bloodshed later on." These remarks created such a stir that Delta representative Wilma Sledge of Sunflower County took the floor of the state legislature to dispel concerns about the possibly violent intentions of the councils. Sledge described the council's leadership as "the most prominent, well educated and conservative businessmen" with "motives and methods" that were both "laudable" and "timely."[20]

By 1961 Hodding Carter was considerably less sympathetic to the council, but he pointed out nonetheless that "no matter how dubious its aims, repugnant its methods, or despicable its philosophy," the Citizens' Council was not "made up of hooded figures meeting furtively in back alleys." Drawing its leadership not from "the pool hall" but from "the country club," the council's attitudes were those of middle- and upper-class whites, and its language was not the violent rhetoric of the lynch mob but "the careful embroidery of states rights and constitutionalism."[21]

Bartley concluded that lower-class whites "who wished to protect the white man's prerogatives were likely to prefer the Ku Klux Klan to the Citizens' Council." Although the council's differences with the Klan on the question of maintaining white supremacy proved to be ones of means rather than ends, the fiscally conservative, "neobourbon" values that lay behind the council's overall approach to defending the status quo reflected a definite orientation toward the interests of middle- and upper-class whites.[22]

Prior to 1958 the Delta whites supplied more than 75 percent of the funding for the Citizens' Council movement in Mississippi. With its planter-dominated society and economy and agriculture-dependent business and professional classes, the Delta was an ideal spawning ground for the council, which, as Bartley explained, appealed primarily "to the middle class of the towns and villages" but also drew considerable support from planters and farmers in the surrounding countryside. Throughout the Delta, Citizens' Council members were well positioned to pursue the organization's policy of inflicting severe economic suffering on, as one council leader put it, "members of the Negro race who are not cooperating."[23]

An incident in Yazoo City revealed the effectiveness of the Citizens' Council's economic bludgeoning of black activists. On August 6, 1955, the local NAACP chapter submitted a petition bearing fifty-three signatures to the school board. The document asked for immediate desegregation of all schools. Stunned that their supposedly well-treated, contented black citizenry would make such a move, the local Citizens' Council moved swiftly. The first step was to run a large advertisement in the Yazoo City *Herald* listing the names of the petitioners. (These had already been published in the paper's account of the incident.) Like other such NAACP efforts in Mississippi during the 1950s, most of the participants were black professionals, businessmen, and tradesmen who had achieved a measure of economic independence and could therefore resist the pressures from whites that were certain to come. It soon became obvious, however, that NAACP leaders had underestimated the amount of economic influence that local whites still enjoyed over members of the black middle class in Mississippi. One by one those who signed the petition began to lose their jobs or whatever "business" or "trade" they had with whites. Some blacks moved quickly to remove their names from the list. Others held out but eventually followed suit. Many of those who removed their names found it impossible to get their old jobs back, however; nor could they find new employment. Many left town altogether. Only those who were totally dependent on the black community for their incomes managed to survive economically. By the end of the year, only two names remained on the petition; both belonged to people who had left town.[24]

A plumber reported that, after completing half a job, he was told by his employer that he could finish the work if he would take his name off the petition. He refused initially, but even after relenting and taking his name off the list he was still unable to find work. He admitted, "I just didn't think it would be this hard." One signer, a grocer, lost a thriving business when white wholesalers cut off his supplies. An NAACP official admitted that the local chapter had lost members as a result of the petition drive. "We expected pressure," said another, "but not this much. We just weren't prepared for it."[25]

Describing the Citizens' Council as a restrained, "conservative" organization, Hodding Carter wrote in 1961 that "no act of racial violence in Mississippi has ever been directly connected to the Citizens' Council." Carter added, however, that "those incidents that have occurred may be indirectly traceable to the climate engendered by the council, but it is a theoretical relationship. The council has found it doesn't need to operate that way to get results."[26]

Delta blacks knew better. The relationship between white-on-black violence and the activities of the council was clearly more than a theoretical one. Such was certainly the case in the "heart of the Delta," in Humphreys County at Belzoni, where blacks outnumbered whites more than two to one in 1956 and where half the county's registered voters belonged to the Citizens' Council. The Humphreys County Citizens' Council's executive committee consisted of a tax consultant, an automobile salesman, two bankers, a store owner, an insurance salesman, and several planters. A local council leader denied even the use of economic pressure against blacks, saying that it would involve the council in a "conspiracy," but investigators heard numerous allegations, not only of economic coercion but of physical violence as well.[27]

Reverend George Lee, a black minister in Belzoni, who was trying to encourage black voter registration, was killed by a shotgun blast as he drove home one Saturday night in 1955. Local blacks claimed that Humphreys County sheriff Ike Shelton had insisted, until the FBI proved him wrong, that the buckshot pellets found in Reverend Lee's mouth were actually loose fillings from his teeth. Another Belzoni black activist, Gus Courts, was evicted from the building he rented for his grocery store when he refused to remove his name from the voting lists. Courts did not give in, however, even when a local bank president told him that, if he did not abandon his NAACP activities, "we'll force you out of the business." A local white who belonged to the council warned Courts, "They're planning to get rid of you," and Courts soon fell, wounded by gunshots in his own store. The only witness, a black woman, stuck to her claim that she had seen a white man fire the shots and soon found herself and her four children taken off relief by the state Welfare Department. Courts had to be dissuaded from returning to Belzoni when he was discharged from the hospital, and no new leader stepped forward to take his place. The local undertaker, formerly one of the town's most outspoken blacks, had even declined to provide an ambulance when Courts was shot.[28]

The manager of the Coca-Cola bottling plant in Belzoni offered this candid insight into the racist mentality that lay behind the Citizens' Council strength in the Delta:

Integration leads to intermarriage; then there won't be any whites left or nigras left: there'd be a race of mulattoes. If my daughter starts going to school with nigras now, by the time she gets to college she won't think anything of dating one of 'em. The nigra's life consists of sex, eating, and drinking. . . . This town is 70 percent nigra; if the nigra voted, there'd be nigra candidates in office.[29]

Such virulent racism and racial anxiety explained why the council had succeeded, as Hodding Carter wrote, "to a degree which is hard to convey to
someone who does not live in Mississippi" in forging white racial antipathy
into "a mold which includes the total rejection of any deviation from the status
quo and 'our way of life,' as defined by the Citizens' Council."[30]

In offering this observation, Carter summed up the attitude of the Delta's
own Senator James O. Eastland of Sunflower County, who quickly earned the
title of "spiritual leader of Southern resistance to school desegregation" and
drew national attention for his uncompromising stance. Although he was con-
summately political, Eastland's bluntness on the matter of segregation and
white supremacy was legendary. Virginia Durr related an illustrative incident—"an absolutely true story, a nasty story, but a true story." When a group
of Methodist churchwomen from Mississippi visited Washington to lobby
against the poll tax, they prevailed on her to escort them to the office of Senator
Eastland. After a brief exchange of pleasantries, they explained the purpose of
their visit to Eastland, whose turkey-like jowls suddenly turned purple as he
squawked, "I know what you women want—black men laying on you!" Mortally embarrassed, the ladies quickly explained to Alabamian Durr that the Eastlands had come to the Delta from the hills and had "made their money quite
recently." (Hardly an admirer of Eastland herself, Durr's translation was that
"Jim Eastland was common as pig tracks and that was just the kind of remark
he would make.")[31]

Dubbed the "symbol of racism in America" by a New York colleague,
Eastland was described in *Time* magazine in 1956 as "one of the most widely
unliked men in America." From the Senate floor he proclaimed his belief in
black inferiority and warned that the white people of Mississippi will "protect
and maintain white supremacy throughout eternity." Eastland had no qualms
about counseling defiance of the *Brown* decision, "an illegal, immoral, and sinful doctrine" handed down by a "crowd of racial politicians in judicial robes."
In Eastland's rationalized view, "Southern people will not be violating the
Constitution or the law when they defy this monstrous proposition."[32]

Within Mississippi itself Eastland was naturally the hero of the Citizens'
Council movement. In December 1955 he addressed the statewide convention,
urging his fellow whites to take the offensive. Citing an "Anglo-Saxon pre-
cept" that "resistance to tyranny is obedience to God," Eastland predicted that,
by overcoming the tyranny of the Supreme Court, southern whites would
achieve a status comparable to that of the participants in "those glorious events
in the history of freedom that led from Magna Charta to the American Revolution."[33]

For all their pretensions to civilized resistance on constitutional grounds
and professed devotion to blacks who stayed "in their place," for the majority
of Delta whites, the fear that the racial underpinnings of their way of life might
be weakening made them increasingly intolerant of dissent or nontraditional
behavior on the part of blacks or whites. The tensions accompanying the
Supreme Court's *Brown v. Board of Education* desegregation decision found

their ugliest manifestation in the murder of Emmett Till, a fourteen-year-old black youth, and in the acquittal of his slayers in the face of overwhelming evidence of their guilt. Although he lived in Chicago, Till was visiting his grandparents in Leflore County in August 1955. He quickly created a stir among local blacks by responding to whites with "yeah" and "naw" and by showing pictures of his "white girlfriend" back in Chicago.[34]

Standing in a crowd of black youths outside Roy Bryant's store at Money, Till was reportedly challenged to demonstrate his expertise with white women by asking Bryant's wife, who was tending the store, for "a date." As Till approached twenty-one-year-old Carolyn Bryant, his friends stared through the windows in disbelief. When the young white woman held out her hand to receive Till's payment for some candy, he reportedly grabbed her wrist and asked, "How about a date, baby?" Bryant testified that she jerked her hand away and walked toward the living quarters at the back of the store, where she knew she would find her sister-in-law, Juanita Milam. According to her testimony, Till grabbed her around the waist and told her, "You needn't be afraid of me, baby. I've been with white women before." At that point one of Till's cousins ran in and grabbed him, as the white woman ran out to get a pistol from her sister-in-law's car. Before leaving with a car full of blacks, Till reportedly sounded a "wolf-whistle" at her.[35]

Despite his wife's efforts to keep it from him, Roy Bryant learned of the incident several days later, and, knowing that the prevailing orthodoxy demanded swift retribution for such a breach of caste, he and J. W. Milam, his half-brother, resolved to give Till a "whipping." Bryant explained later that because of the time that expired before a black customer told him of the rumored incident, he feared that local blacks, who made up the majority of his customers, would lose respect for him if he failed to "deal with the Chicago boy" as soon as possible.[36]

At 2:00 a.m. on August 28, Milam and Bryant arrived at the home of Mose Wright, Till's grandfather, and told the old man that they wanted "that boy who did the talking down at Money." The two men entered the house, awakened young Till, and, despite the pleas of his grandparents, took him with them. Milam claimed after the trial that at this point he "had no idea o' killing him" but intended to "whip him, scare some sense into him, and send him back to Chicago." Milam and Bryant took Till on a seventy-mile drive searching for a particular bluff, "the scariest place in the Delta," where, they claimed, they planned to pistol-whip him to make him think they were going to throw him in. Failing to find the spot, they returned to Milam's place, took Till to the tool shed, and began to beat him. According to Milam, Till "never even whimpered" but instead taunted his abductors: "You bastards, I'm not afraid of you. I'm as good as you are. I've had white girls and my grandmother was a white woman." Milam also claimed that when Till took out his billfold and pointed to a picture of a white female he claimed was his "girl," he told him, "Boy, you ain't never going to see the sun come up again."[37]

After his acquittal Milam explained his reaction: "What could I do? . . .

He thought he was as good as any white man. . . . I'm no bully. I never hurt a niggah in my life. But I just decided it was time a few people got put on notice. As long as J. W. Milam lives and can do anything about it, niggahs are gonna stay in their place. Niggahs ain't gonna vote where I live. If they did they'd control government. They'd tell me where to stand and where to sit. They ain't gonna go to school with my kids. And when a niggah even gets close to mentioning sex with a white woman, he's tired o' livin'. . . . I'm gonna kill him." Milam explained further that he decided to make Till's death an example "just so everybody could know how me and my folks stand."[38]

Having made the decision, Milam and Bryant put Till back in the truck, drove to Boyle, and picked up a discarded gin fan. (The sun had risen by this time, but the two men were concerned primarily that anyone who saw them might think that they had stolen the fan.) They then drove to the Tallahatchie River and forced Till to undress. As he took aim, Milam asked Till, "Are you still as good as I am?" Milam had hoped to shoot the young man between the eyes, but his victim ducked, and the bullet struck him just above the right ear. Bryant and Milam then wired the fan to Till's neck and pushed him down the bank and into the river.[39]

The discovery of the body and the arrest of Milam and Bryant created a stir, not only locally but regionally and nationally as well. Local newspapers called for vigorous prosecution of the guilty parties, and even Robert Patterson, executive secretary of the Citizens' Council, publicly deplored the "very regrettable incident." Initially, as well, the local white power structure showed little sympathy for the defendants, and Breland and Whitten, the county's most powerful law firm, set their fee well above what Bryant and Milam could pay.[40]

As NAACP denunciations and a tidal wave of criticism from both black and white newspapers in the North began to mount, however, Delta whites quickly grew more defensive, especially after the announcement that Till's funeral in Chicago would be an open-casket affair. Till's mother explained that she wanted to "let the people see what they did to my boy!" Newsreel footage captured the ghastly, battered, swollen, and disfigured face of her son. NAACP spokesman Roy Wilkins denounced the murder as a "lynching" and observed that it appeared that the state of Mississippi had "decided to maintain white supremacy by murdering children."[41]

Whatever inclinations toward morality and justice white leaders in Tallahatchie County may have shown in the immediate aftermath of the killing were overwhelmed by their resentment of the criticism they received from the northern press and black activist groups. With civil rights pressures beginning to swell, justice took a back seat to white unity and supremacy, just as it had in numerous other instances down through the years. As national outrage mounted, Milam and Bryant gained crucial support when Sheriff H. C. Strider began to express doubt that the body in question was Till's. Then all five lawyers in Sumner reversed themselves and offered to provide the defense for the accused pair.[42]

Bryant and Milam's attorney, J. J. Breland, admitted that he finally took the case only after "Mississippi began to be run down." One of the defense attorneys confessed that his wife kept asking if Bryant and Milam were guilty: "I didn't want to have to lie to her. I just told her I didn't know." Sheriff Strider said much the same thing, claiming that the "last thing" he wanted to do was "to defend those peckerwoods" but, after the external attacks (many of them aimed at Strider himself) began, felt he "had no choice." Ultimately many local whites decided to "let the North know we are not going to put up with Northern negroes stepping over the line." Northern journalists, black and white, flocked to Sumner for the trial, which was also attended by Charles Diggs, a black congressman from Michigan.[43]

Sheriff Strider did little to gather evidence for the state and ultimately testified that he believed the body had been in the water too long to be Till's. Despite a vigorous prosecution effort, by the time a defense attorney told the jury that he was certain that "every last Anglo-Saxon one of you has the courage to set these men free," the outcome of the trial was no longer in doubt. Rumors persisted that each member of the sequestered jury had been contacted by the Citizens' Council to make certain that he would vote "the right way." Such contact was probably unnecessary, because the jury "deliberated" for only sixty-eight minutes, reportedly staying out that long only because of the advice of the sheriff-elect, who urged them to take enough time "to make it look good." The acquittal on murder charges in Tallahatchie County failed to clear up the matter of kidnapping charges in Leflore County, but, despite their admission that they had taken Till by force, a grand jury refused to indict Bryant and Milam for that crime.[44]

In the wake of the acquittal, most prominent whites in the area tried to distance themselves from the entire affair. They pointed out that the actual killing had been done by two "po whites" and that ten of the jurors were residents of the supposedly more violently racist hill section of Tallahatchie County. (Initially, prosecutors had believed that they stood a better chance of getting a conviction if they could impanel as many jurors as possible who did not know Bryant or Milam or live in the area where the killing took place.)[45]

The results of the trial brought a hailstorm of criticism from outside the South. The Pittsburgh *Courier* dubbed the date of the verdict "Black Friday" and condemned Mississippi as the "sin-hole of American civilization." Strider received threatening letters from all over the world, including one from Sydney, Australia, addressed only to "Sheriff Strider, U.S.A." that reached him five days after it was mailed. As for the defendants, Milam and Bryant, their three stores at Glendora, Money, and Sharkey lost so much of their traditional black patronage that they were either closed or sold within fifteen months of the trial.[46]

Shortly after their acquittal, the two men agreed to sell their story for thirty-five hundred dollars. They admitted guilt and described the crimes to writer William Bradford Huie, who published their accounts in several articles and a book, and the white community that had tried its best to act as though

Milam and Bryant could be innocent found itself "sold out." Neither man found Tallahatchie County hospitable thereafter. Milam had great difficulty securing farmland to rent, found it impossible to secure black labor, and had to hire white workers at higher wages. Finally, he reportedly turned to bootlegging and outraged the white citizenry of the county even more by loading a fully equipped moonshine still on his truck and driving down the main street and around the courthouse square in Charleston. Ultimately, both men and their families left Mississippi and moved to Texas.[47]

Many local whites prided themselves on the fact that both Bryant and Milam were forced to leave not only the county but the state after they had sold their confession to Huie. One white told proudly of encountering Roy Bryant at a stoplight in Texas and turning away from Bryant to stare straight ahead until the light changed and he could speed away. Despite their repudiation of the deeds of Bryant and Milam, however, the Delta's white elite continued to recognize the value of lower-class white atrocities as a deterrent to black activism. J. J. Breland, the Princeton graduate who had headed the defense team for Bryant and Milam, explained that "peckerwoods" like his clients played a useful role in defense of the caste system in the Delta. "Hell, we've got to have our Milams and Bryants to fight our wars and keep our niggahs in line." Breland warned that further pressures for integration would mean that "the Tallahatchie River won't hold all the niggers that'll be thrown in it" and expressed the hope that the "approved killing" of Emmett Till would "put the North and the NAACP and the niggers on notice."[48]

For all of the contempt many whites claimed they felt for them, the accused killers of Emmett Till were much safer in Tallahatchie County after the trial than were those who had testified against them. The black witnesses in the trial had little choice but to leave the Delta. Mose Wright, Till's grandfather, who exclaimed "Dar he!" as he sat in a courtroom where "every able-bodied white man you saw . . . had a .45 or a .38 strung on him" and pointed to Milam as the man who took his grandson, became a hero to blacks and sympathetic whites all over the world. The sixty-four-year-old Wright, a lifelong Delta resident, had proclaimed that he was "through with Mississippi" even before the trial ended. Wright was offered a "life-time" job in New York, but the story of his final departure from Mississippi with emotional good-byes to friends and "Dallas," whom he described as "the best dog in the seven states," was a poignant footnote to the entire tragic affair.[49]

Whatever remorse there may have been in Tallahatchie County in the wake of the Till murder, it was not sufficient to protect blacks from further white violence. On December 3, 1955, a white man who reportedly had been drinking shot and killed Clinton Melton, a black filling station attendant in Glendora. Melton was so respected among Tallahatchie County whites that the Glendora Lions Club endorsed a resolution of regret concerning the loss of "one of the finest members of the Negro race of this community." In the ensuing trial, several members of the jury voted "guilty" on the first ballot, but after

four hours of deliberation the final vote was for acquittal. A local newspaperman explained that the Till affair had created a siege mentality among Tallahatchie whites and "convinced them that they were all right and everyone else
was all wrong." What the incident demonstrated was "the fact that you can't
put one value on a Negro three hundred and sixty-four days a year and then
raise him up equal in court." Summarizing the perilous circumstances faced by
blacks, particularly those inclined to activism, in the Delta at the end of 1955,
Amzie Moore wrote a friend in Chicago: "It's ruff [*sic*] down here and a man's
life isn't worth a penny with a hole in it. I shall try to stay here as long as I can,
but I might have to run away up there."[50]

If Delta whites showed no tolerance for blacks who challenged the racial
status quo, neither did they respect the rights of those few whites who refused
to embrace every aspect of the "southern way of life" as it was practiced in the
Delta. Any breach of caste, regardless of whether it was part of some organized
civil rights activity or not, was certain to be met with white wrath and, quite
likely, violence as well. Providence Farm, a twenty-seven-hundred-acre spread
in the Delta section of Holmes County near Tchula, was actually an outgrowth
of an earlier failed cooperative farming effort at Delta Farm in Bolivar County.
It began operation in 1936, and in that same year A. E. Cox arrived, fresh from
Texas Christian University, to join the project. Ten years later Dr. David R.
Minter returned from World War II to open a small clinic on the farm and
serve as a sort of "medical missionary" to the poor blacks in this isolated section. Local planters had always been puzzled by Cox's and Minter's decisions
to pursue such unremunerative careers and accept such spartan lifestyles. (Such
behavior certainly offered a sharp contrast to that of a great many of the Delta's
more affluent whites.) They also found it difficult to understand how the farm
brought in much income, since it consisted only of Minter's clinic, a nonprofit
store, and a credit union for blacks offering interest rates considerably lower
than those demanded by local planters.[51]

The question about the Providence operation that proved most troubling
to local whites, however, was that of its racial policies. The farm hosted summer camps for black youths and Sunday religious meetings (with movies). Minter treated a host of black patients, and rumors floated about that interracial
swimming often took place in the farm's makeshift pool. Minter became more
controversial when he testified in behalf of Hazel Brannon Smith, a Lexington
newspaper editor sued for libel after criticizing the local sheriff for the allegedly unprovoked shooting of a black man while dispersing a Saturday night
black gathering. The sheriff denied that the man had even been shot, but Minter
testified that he had treated the young man's wounds. In an environment
charged by hostile reaction to the 1954 *Brown* decision, local Citizens' Council
leaders were anxious to rid the community of anyone so potentially subversive
of white supremacy.[52]

Their opportunity came on September 23, 1955, when a white girl
accused four Holmes County black teenage boys of whistling at her. The four

were hauled into the courthouse for questioning, which turned eventually to the sorts of activities that took place on Providence Farm. The answers were tape-recorded; word spread that the tapes would be played at Tchula High School the next evening, and more than five hundred people showed up. J. P. Love, a newly elected state legislator, chaired the meeting and announced that its purpose was to defend the "American Way of Life." After an invocation a hushed audience listened to the two-hour taped interrogation. A nineteen-year-old black male, who subsequently pleaded guilty to making "obscene remarks" to a white girl and received a six-month sentence to the county farm, testified that there had been "mixed swimming parties" at Providence. Minter denied this allegation, as well as the charge that he had publicly advocated integration or that he had only one waiting room for both races.[53]

On the matter of integration, Cox tried to make a distinction between what he believed and what he advocated to others, but, when the angry crowd pressed him to state his own personal position, he finally offered his opinion that segregation was inconsistent with Christianity. At this point from the buzzing audience came the shout, "This isn't a Christian meeting!" A planter then offered a motion that the Minters and Coxes be asked to move "for the best interests of the county." Most of those in attendance stood in support of this motion, and, when someone demanded that those in opposition also be required to stand, only two did so. One dissident thought the matter deserved more prayer before such action was taken. The other was the Reverend Marsh Callaway, pastor of a Presbyterian church in nearby Durant, who affirmed his support for segregation but criticized the meeting as improper, un-American, and un-Christian. Shortly thereafter his congregation requested unanimously that he resign.[54]

The Providence Farm incident drew considerable national as well as regional notice. The Minters and Coxes initially refused to leave despite harassment and a variety of threats. One man at the meeting had been heard to utter the opinion that a lynching was in order. The sheriff put Providence Farm under surveillance, and sheriff's department personnel took down the license numbers of visitors.[55]

The Citizens' Council quickly unleashed what had become its standard array of coercive measures against the Coxes and the Minters. The agent for the company that insured the clinic and household goods at Providence was a member of the council, and the Minters and Coxes quickly learned that all of their policies had been canceled. The pastor at the Presbyterian church attended by the couples apparently took note of the plight of his fellow minister at Durant and avoided the topic altogether, focusing his attention instead on matters like "infant baptism." Critics of the Coxes and Minters explained that the two couples had been "practicing social equality out there" and added that such reckless behavior had to be stopped in order to prevent "a lot of good niggers getting killed."[56]

In a response to these developments, Hodding Carter offered an editorial reminder "that Mississippi, including Holmes County, is still in the United States." Expressing certainty that Cox and Minter "have been the victims of false witness, given by frightened negroes," Carter pointed out that if the two families did leave Holmes County, "something else would leave with them, something very precious and American, something for which a great many Holmes County citizens apparently don't give a damn. That something is the Bill of Rights, the guarantees which alone distinguish us from the oppressed people of the totalitarian world." Carter's outrage notwithstanding, the pressures on the Coxes and Minters proved too great, and they soon left Holmes County for good.[57]

Holmes County whites also waged a persistent and virulent campaign of harassment against controversial journalist Hazel Brannon Smith. Smith had come to Holmes County in 1936, purchased a small paper in Durant, and thereafter acquired the Lexington *Advertiser*. Although staunchly conservative in her politics, she quickly established a reputation as a reformer, attacking the illegal liquor racket in Holmes County and interviewing the widow of a black man who died after a whipping at the hands of five white men later acquitted of the crime. Because the widow was a witness in the case at the time, the trial judge fined Smith fifty dollars, gave her a fifteen-day suspended jail sentence, and put her "under good behavior" for two years. Smith appealed the gag rule to the state supreme court, which ultimately upheld her appeal.[58]

Smith created even more of a stir in 1954 by denouncing the local sheriff, Richard Byrd, for shooting a black man without cause: "The laws in America are for everyone—rich and poor, strong and weak, black and white. The vast majority of Holmes County people are not rednecks who look with favor on the abuse of people because their skins are black. Byrd has violated every concept of justice, decency and right. He is not fit to occupy office." Sheriff Byrd subsequently filed a $57,500 libel suit and was awarded $10,000 by the jury, allegedly after each juror had dropped into a hat the amount of settlement he thought the sheriff should receive. The Mississippi supreme court again found in Smith's favor, and the damage award was denied.[59]

Smith confounded local whites by leading the life of a latter-day Scarlett O'Hara, tooling about town in a Cadillac convertible and living in splendor in an antebellum mansion. Still, her outspoken dedication to fairness kept her continually at odds with the white power structure in Holmes County. In the summer of 1954, a black teacher was shot in her own home by a well-known white man after she had objected to his damaging her yard by driving his car into it while turning around. Citizens' Council members urged Smith to suppress the story, but she refused. No arrest was made, however, and the teacher was fired, as was her husband, who worked at a local filling station.[60]

Outside Holmes County, Smith's reputation as a forthright and courageous editor grew rapidly, and she began to receive a host of journalistic awards. At home, however, she encountered only mounting hostility from the Citizens' Council. A burning cross appeared on her lawn, and her husband lost his job as administrator of the Holmes County Hospital because the council-dominated board of trustees felt his wife had become "a controversial person." The council also began an advertising boycott of Smith's newspaper and ultimately launched a weekly paper of its own to compete with the *Advertiser*.[61]

Smith summed up conditions as she saw them in a number of editorials, like the one in which she described the "dark cloud" of fear hanging over Mississippi and "dominating every facet of public and private life." As a result of this repressive climate, Smith wrote, "Almost every man and woman is afraid to try to do anything to promote goodwill and harmony between the races, afraid he or she will be taken as a mixer, as an integrationist or worse, if there is anything worse by southern standards."[62]

"My editorial policy," Smith explained, "is not to favor Negroes any more than anyone else, but to uphold equal protection of the law for all people, including Negroes. Unfortunately, some of my fellow Mississippians do not look upon Negroes as 'people', although they would be shocked if you told them that." Writing in 1963, Smith estimated that in addition to her husband's job and "nine years of our lives," her battle with the Citizens' Council had cost her two hundred thousand dollars.[63]

Smith's courageous commitment to fairness won her the Pulitzer Prize in 1964, but the Delta's most famous dissident (who also won the Pulitzer, in 1946) remained Greenville's Hodding Carter. Never one to mince words, Carter responded to the *Brown* decision with an emphatic "I told you so!" Carter added, "If ever a region asked for such a decision, the South did through its shocking, calculated, and cynical disobedience to its own state constitutions which specify that separate school systems must be equal. For seventy-five years, we sent Negro kids to school in hovels and pig pens."[64]

Black response to Carter's opinions on racial matters was sometimes difficult to gauge, but the editor was quick to brag about his paper's four thousand black subscribers. Although Carter adhered for a long time to the doctrine of separate but equal, his outspokenness on issues of simple fairness was surely appealing to local blacks, one of whom expressed his appreciation in a brief anonymous note: "Kind paper edder, pore it to white."[65]

There was certainly no mistaking the reaction of Mississippi's white supremacists to Carter's criticism. The infamous Theodore G. Bilbo denounced him as a "disgrace to the white race" and "the biggest liar in Mississippi and one of the biggest in the nation." After a white Bolivar County store owner shot and killed a black man in a dispute over a debt, the slayer, who was also a justice of the peace, was exonerated without a trial or even a coroner's jury. At that point, the Benoit town marshal urged a reporter for the *Delta Democrat-Times* to "tell *that* to your Mr. Carter."[66]

Carter's response was characteristically bold: "Well, Marshal, we got the word. We're repeating it now and later, whether or not any bully boys from Benoit or Bolivar County like it not." Decrying the "shameful laxity" of Bolivar officials, Carter explained that he had recently spent "three not altogether pleasant months in distant lands, trying to defend the South against the kind of nasty accusations for which this slaying and hearing provide bloody material. . . . Until we in Mississippi look upon law and crime without relation to the color or faith or nationality of the principals, we have no right to lift our heads and ask for equal treatment in the concert of states or the community of nations." In 1955 the Mississippi House of Representatives responded to a *Look* magazine article in which Carter attacked the Citizens' Councils by approving by a vote of eighty-nine to nineteen a formal resolution declaring that Carter had slandered Mississippi and sold out the South. At the time, Carter was out turkey hunting with friends, and he received a copy of a wire service report on the resolution dropped by a small plane. Carter's companions laughed at the report, but he responded angrily: "I herewith resolve by a vote of 1 to 0 that there are 89 liars in the State Legislature." Carter went on to urge those "89 character robbers" to "go to hell, collectively or singly, and wait there until I back down. They needn't plan on returning."[67]

In 1959, after a legislative investigating committee listed Carter as one of eleven Mississippians who belonged to Communist-front organizations, Carter responded with predictable defiance: "If the moral morons who apparently constitute a perpetual majority of the Mississippi legislature think they can drive me out of our state by resolutions, they've got another think coming. If any assorted half dozen of them believe they can do it by other means, all I ask is ten minutes notice so I can cut a crabapple switch, not that their kind gives anybody ten minutes."[68]

Carter's conflicts with the legislature reflected the general rise in racial tensions in Mississippi during the post-World War II years. These tensions also contributed to significant changes in the Delta's political relationship with the remainder of the state. Throughout the postwar period, Delta whites continued to associate their economic interests with those of Wall Street and the business and financial community in Jackson rather than with those of the small farmers in the Mississippi hills. Along with whites in other heavily black counties and the more affluent white voters in Jackson, in the postwar years Delta planters manifested what Numan V. Bartley and Hugh D. Graham described as "an uncompromising conservatism that could have been matched by few other areas of the nation." The economic component of this conservatism surfaced not only in the 1947 gubernatorial triumph of Deltan Fielding Wright, a corporate lawyer and future Dixiecrat vice-presidential nominee, but in the Delta's enthusiastic support in 1951 for the gubernatorial bid of Hugh L. White, a wealthy lumberman, who in 1936 had introduced Mississippi's Balance Agriculture with Industry program for economic development. In both cases the losing candidate was the less fiscally conservative and, in the words of Bartley and Graham, even "vaguely New Dealish" Paul B. Johnson, Jr.[69]

Calls for more progressive taxation had long been anathema to Delta planters. In the post-World War II period, however, such suggestions also met with a hostile response from a growing number of non-Delta politicians hoping to encourage industrial expansion in their districts by emphasizing Mississippi's good "business climate." As enthusiasm for industrial development grew and racial tensions mounted, neopopulist hill-county representatives, who had traditionally advocated expanded public services and improved educational facilities financed by higher taxes on both corporations and the more affluent residents of the Delta, soon found themselves drowned out by calls for fiscal responsibility and white solidarity in the face of the impending integrationist challenge.[70]

The Delta had given as much as 95 percent support to the Dixiecrats in 1948, and moderate Frank Smith won the area's congressional seat in 1950 only by pledging "to support the traditional viewpoint of the white electorate of the Delta on racial issues" while advocating economic development as the real solution to the state's racial problems. Staunchly conservative on both racial and economic issues, James O. Eastland of Sunflower County retained his seat in the United States Senate in 1954 by running with comparable strength in both the higher income areas of Jackson and the planter-dominated Delta. Race remained a paramount concern, but hostility to unions continued to flourish as well, especially as communities in the Delta and throughout the state expanded their courtship of low-wage, labor-intensive northern industries under the BAWI program. A visitor to the Delta reported in 1956 that Delta planters seemed to feel as strongly about labor organizers as they did about integrationists and noted that "whenever the talk turned to labor unions, the conversation was violent and burdened with hate and fear." In 1960 an amendment inserting antiunion, right-to-work provisions in the state constitution received enthusiastic support in the Delta, support exceeded only by that which it was accorded in the white-collar districts of Jackson.[71]

By the mid-1950s any white politician from any part of Mississippi could be assured of a positive response if he talked a lot about racial segregation and relatively little about tax reform or the expansion of public services. In 1955 gubernatorial hopeful Paul B. Johnson, Jr., sounded not at all New Dealish when he charged his opponent, J. P. Coleman, with consorting with labor unions. Noting that twenty years earlier Johnson's father had openly courted labor support, F. Glenn Abney concluded that "for the descendants of Bilbo and Vardaman, the concern for the common man was fast becoming race rather than economic welfare." The unequivocal subordination of regional and economic class divisions to racial solidarity proved nothing less than a boon to those who sought to protect the economic interests of Delta whites. Having established himself as "Mr. Delta" in Mississippi political circles, longtime Speaker of the Mississippi House of Representatives and Citizens' Council kingpin Walter Sillers, Jr., cooly dismissed efforts to introduce progressive taxation aimed at improving public education statewide by observing matter-of-factly in 1958 that "the people who have the children should pay the tax, and you know the favored few don't have many children."[72]

Fiscal and social conservatism had always been fundamental components of the political philosophy of Delta whites. Still, in the past these had at least been paired with a relatively restrained public posture on the race question that contrasted sharply with the blatant and sometimes bloodthirsty racial dema- goguery traditionally associated with white politicians who represented the hills. By the end of the 1950s, however, Mississippi had fallen under the spell of a thoroughly reactionary political consensus, one that synthesized the most extreme elements of the contrasting political philosophies and styles that had once distinguished the Delta from the hills. In conjunction with an increasingly broad-based statewide commitment to industrial recruitment, the absolute insistence of the state's segregationist leadership on the need for white unity in the face of integrationist pressures had subordinated the neopopulist impulses of the hill-county leadership to the economic conservatism of the Delta. Meanwhile, as racial tensions rose, mechanization dramatically reduced the labor demands of whites in the black-majority plantation counties. As a result, the rabid demagoguery that had always played so well with whites in the hills now found a more receptive audience in the Delta's jittery white minority, a group once known for their more pragmatic, labor-conscious approach to preserving the status quo in race relations.

The new mutual-defense alliance between whites in the Delta and whites in the hills manifested itself most clearly in the gubernatorial administration of Ross R. Barnett, whom Bartley and Graham described as "the ultimate cari- cature of the racist demagogues of the massive resistance period." Barnett not only defied federal authority by delaying the integration of Ole Miss in 1962, but he made a great public show of respect and support for Byron DeLa Beck- with, the Deltan accused of shooting black activist Medgar Evers. The melding of the minds of the Delta and the hills produced some striking policy devel- opments during the first legislative session of Barnett's administration. In addi- tion to approving the right-to-work amendment in 1960, the legislature also lowered the income tax while raising its own salaries, provided public funding for the Citizens' Council, enacted a host of anti-sit-in and anti-voter registra- tion measures, and capped these accomplishments by commending South Africa for "the determined stand of the government . . . in maintaining its firm segregation policy." The economic and racial consensus prevailing in Missis- sippi in the early 1960s was evident in the correspondence of Walter Sillers, Jr., and Ross Barnett. Sillers praised arch-segregationist Barnett for towering "head and shoulders" above his counterparts in other southern states. Barnett in turn conveyed his thanks to Sillers and other supporters of the right-to-work amendment who had "demonstrated to business and industry all over the nation in the most effective manner possible that we have an outstanding climate favorable to economic development."[73]

V. O. Key had observed in 1949 that Mississippi "only manifests in accen- tuated form the darker political strains that run throughout the south." Key's description was more accurate than ever by the early 1960s, as the economic differences between the Delta and the hills were shoved into the background while the leaders of the two regions joined forces to defend white supremacy with all the vehemence they could muster. This new political consensus emerged as the state moved toward a period of bitter confrontation in which the Delta, which stood out even in Mississippi as a citadel of white supremacy and black subservience, would become the target of a long-awaited assault on its well-defined system of caste and discrimination.[74]

10 ▽ "A Testing Ground
  ▽ for Democracy"
  ▽

Visiting the racially tense Mississippi Delta in the mid-1950s, Tris Coffin marveled at the way his planter hosts managed "to hold the conversation rigidly on small matters that no one cared about" as they sipped their mint juleps, seemingly oblivious to the escalating racial tensions that gripped their state and region. The Delta remained a bastion of Citizens' Council defiance as the 1960s began, but its gentry refused to let mounting evidence of a forthcoming assault on their way of life prevent them from making a great show of enjoying that way of life to the fullest. Ostentatious parties, famous for their "the devil with the cost" extravagance, were still the order of the day.[1]

Prior to the onset of continuous, large-scale civil rights demonstrations and organizational efforts in 1962, the major indication that the Delta's always lively social scene was in any measure affected by mounting racial tensions came in 1961 when the controversial Hodding Carter was asked to serve as master of ceremonies at the annual Delta Debutante Ball. Usually drawn from the older white families in the region, the debutantes attended five weeks of parties in addition to a gala "coming out" celebration where each was presented to the strains of a particular song. The Debutante Ball remained a pivotal event in the lives of the women of the Delta's white aristocracy, who represented "the highest ideals of the southern way of life." Determined that the biggest night in their daughters' lives should not be spoiled by the presence of someone whose loyalty to the southern way of life was open to question, a number of parents objected when they learned of Carter's scheduled participation in the event. A stand-in emcee presented several of the girls. The evening passed without incident, however, although tuxedo-clad policemen were stationed throughout the crowd, just in case.[2]

The impression that, even as mounting civil rights tensions gripped the state, it was not only "business" but "pleasure" as usual for most of the Delta's white elite seemed to confirm the existence of "the Delta mind," a sense of invincibility that, as V. O. Key saw it, could survive only among "men whose horizon was circumscribed by the Delta." The great show of confidence by

Delta whites in their ability to maintain the status quo was more than a mere manifestation of their provincialism, however. Over the span of nearly eighty years, the Delta's white minority had compiled an impressive record of neutralization and manipulation of federal policy initiatives, in large part because the region's black majority remained politically powerless and socially repressed. The blatantly coercive activities of the Citizens' Councils during the 1950s suggested that the Delta's white supremacists realized that their prospects for averting or repulsing an external assault on the Delta's way of life might well depend on whether that way of life faced an internal challenge as well. Consequently, the Delta's white elite responded to mounting evidence that the long-awaited Second Reconstruction was at hand with a vigorous reassertion of the tenets and prerogatives of a caste system that required it to remain, as Rupert Vance had described it three decades earlier, "affable and courteous with equals" but "commanding and forceful with inferiors" and to behave generally, in the words of Ralph McGill, as though it had "a God-given right to do as it pleases, unshaken by history or events." By the same token, those on the other side of the color line were expected, and if necessary forced, to respond to such arrogance with equally exaggerated deference and subservience.[3]

For all the talk in Washington about civil rights and obedience to the law, in the Delta of the early 1960s the white planter's word was still the law, and even his most audacious pronouncements stood as unchallenged statements of fact. Despite the increasingly critical national attention to which the Delta was being subjected, visitors and investigative reporters discovered at every turn conditions and situations that seemed more appropriate to the first half of the nineteenth century than to the last half of the twentieth.

When Nicholas Von Hoffman toured one of Delta planter Roy Flowers's plantations, he met elderly blacks like Fannie, age sixty-two or sixty-three, who, after being instructed to remove her hat and stop chewing her gum, assured Von Hoffman that she had never been beaten and pointed out that no one was ever driven away from Flowers's place, regardless of age or physical condition. Miz Mary, Flowers's sister-in-law, added at this point, "That's right, Fannie. They can all stay as long as they obey." Another tenant, Big Lee, denied that conditions were by any means unsatisfactory in the Delta: "It ain't what the rackets out. [It isn't as bad here as people are saying.] I been to Chicago. I got children there. I can't stand it. I likes it here fine." "Big Lee don't have nothing to do with civil rights," Flowers asserted, and added, "He don't want for anything." After Big Lee agreed, Flowers concluded the interview with a cheery summary: "They're happy. We're happy. Everybody's happy here."[4]

Roy Flowers's assertion of universal happiness among both blacks and whites in the Mississippi Delta and his ability to elicit the appropriate confirmation from people to whom he still referred as "my niggers" were indications of how effectively the system of caste continued to function in the Delta in the early 1960s. Even as Flowers spoke, however, his region stood on the threshold of an era of conflict and upheaval. The eruption of grassroots civil rights activism made it obvious enough that the remarkable stability of the Delta's racial hierarchy had less to do with the happiness and satisfaction of Delta blacks than with the historic effectiveness of Delta whites in maintaining, through the appropriate combinations of reward, coercion, and repression, a status quo that fed not only their bank accounts but their delusions of omnipotence as well.

Despite the assertions of Flowers and numerous other Delta whites, blacks had long made it clear that they were anything but happy with conditions in the Mississippi Delta. During the 1950s, however, organized civil rights protest activity in Mississippi had consisted largely of NAACP-instigated desegregation petitions and voter registration efforts. After such efforts were summarily crushed by overwhelming and unyielding white opposition, NAACP leaders contented themselves with membership drives and inspirational speeches and shunned most activities that even resembled direct protest. The conservative, middle-class orientation of the civil rights movement in Mississippi during the 1950s was in sharp contrast to the strategy favored by the young organizers who came to the state in the early 1960s under the banners of the Congress of Racial Equality (CORE) and the Student Nonviolent Coordinating Committee (SNCC). Unwilling to accept the conservatism of the NAACP approach and anxious to reach out to blacks at the grassroots level, these young organizers agreed to coordinate their activities and present a unified front by forming the Council of Federated Organizations (COFO).[5]

A 1962 COFO voter registration effort spread from McComb into the Delta but met with tremendous white resistance and relatively little numerical success. As of June 1962, 1.97 percent of the adult black population in Leflore County was registered to vote. In fact, between 1955 and 1962, only forty blacks had even bothered to attempt to register. In October 1962 the Leflore County Board of Supervisors decided to suspend the distribution of surplus food commodities, hoping thereby to discourage further voter registration efforts. SNCC responded with a massive food distribution campaign, soliciting donations in the North and becoming the only source of nourishment for many blacks in Leflore County. On a single day in February 1963, volunteers gave away more than nine thousand pounds of food. Hoping to force federal intervention, COFO leaders promised in the spring of 1963 to launch a saturation campaign for black voting rights in the Greenwood area, which had "elected itself the testing ground for democracy."[6]

The initial response of local blacks to these organizational efforts was less than enthusiastic, but the SNCC food drive helped to rally support for the registration campaign, and the patient organizational and inspirational work of SNCC organizer Sam Block finally began to pay off as well. At the height of its confrontational stage, the Greenwood registration effort attracted large numbers of participants who braved police dogs, beatings, verbal abuse, and economic intimidation to stand in long lines outside the registrar's office. With every imaginable delaying tactic employed by whites, however, this show of courage produced only a handful of new black voters. Civil rights leaders blamed the slow progress in voter registration on the failure of federal officials to support their efforts. Early in 1963 SNCC leaders filed suit charging that "the Federal Government has only weakly asserted its existing powers in our defense."[7]

Kennedy administration officials raised the hopes of civil rights activists on March 31, 1963, when they petitioned the federal courts for a restraining order that would require Greenwood leaders to release movement organizers from jail, cease their interference with registration efforts, allow blacks the right of peaceful assembly and protest, and "protect them from whites who might object." The elation among Mississippi activists prompted by this action proved short-lived. Within a week the Justice Department had cut a deal with Greenwood's white leadership, agreeing to withdraw the injunction in exchange for the release of the imprisoned activists and a vague promise not to interfere with future registration attempts.[8]

Justice Department officials rationalized their reluctance to push Greenwood authorities too hard by explaining that, without guarantees of support from local white authorities, Washington might have to assume responsibility for protecting every black who showed up to register anywhere in the far-flung Delta. The Justice Department did pressure local leaders to call off their police dogs and to allow blacks to at least attempt to register. Still, Greenwood whites relented but little on the matter of who would actually be allowed to join the electorate. Between June 1962 and January 1964, only thirteen new black names appeared on the registration lists. (This raised the percentage registration among eligible blacks from 1.97 to 2.07.)[9]

Washington's obvious inclination to back down in the face of the threat of physical violence left the civil rights movement in Mississippi "stalled on every front," as John Dittmer put it, by the end of the summer of 1963. In the Delta the Greenwood movement had been so thoroughly undermined by the Kennedy administration's concessions that whites seemed fully confident they could handle any future challenge SNCC might muster. Meanwhile, in Clarksdale, where Aaron Henry had organized an ambitious local protest movement, whites simply rejected black demands and packed the jails with demonstrators.[10]

In order to regain momentum and dramatize the plight of disfranchised blacks in Mississippi, COFO leaders decided to hold a "Freedom Election" that would coincide with the 1963 gubernatorial primary in Mississippi. The slate of candidates in this mock election included Aaron Henry for governor and Edwin King, a white chaplain at all-black Tougaloo College, for lieutenant governor. The purpose of this unofficial election was, as Robert Moses explained, to show "that if Negroes had the right to vote without fear of physical violence and other reprisals, they would do so." Although the vote was only symbolic, it was conducted in such an "atmosphere of fear" that one observer compared Mississippi to the "Soviet Union or Cuba under communism." Said one white worker, "When we talked to the Negroes, their eyes lit up like silver dollars; you could see they were frightened to be talking to us." Cognizant of what they were up against, SNCC workers decided that the best means of collecting the votes of black farm workers was to disguise themselves as cotton pickers and go directly into the fields in order to prevent white landlords from seeing their tenants engaging in even a symbolic protest against the status quo.[11]

Whether cast through the mail or marked in churches or the cotton field, the more than eighty thousand "freedom" ballots made a dramatic statement about the desire of Mississippi blacks for political participation. Beyond that, involvement with the Freedom Vote was a milestone for many Mississippi blacks, most of whom had never even worn a campaign button, much less cast a ballot. In the wake of the vote, COFO workers detected less fear among blacks about participating in civil rights activities. In fact, more than sixty thousand who cast ballots had been willing to give their names and addresses to COFO activists, who could, in turn, call on them to assist in future registration efforts.[12]

Throughout the 1950s black participation in civil rights activity in Mississippi had been limited largely to male members of the black middle class, who considered themselves the logical and appropriate spokesmen for their race. The Freedom Vote proved to be a pivotal event in the process whereby large numbers of less affluent and educated blacks of both sexes, within the Delta and throughout Mississippi, began to play a role in efforts to bring them their full rights and privileges as citizens of the United States. Neil McMillen saw the Freedom Election as the opening event in "a revolution within a revolution—the one, an external revolution, the revolt of black Mississippians against their former white oppressors; the other . . . . of black 'have nots' against their former leaders, the black 'haves.'" The Freedom Election paved the way for the 1964 Freedom Summer Project, which sought to focus national attention on Mississippi through the recruitment of white middle-class youth to be the foot soldiers in a new campaign for voter registration and grassroots community organization.[13]

The Freedom Election also set the stage for the formation, in the spring of 1964, of the Mississippi Freedom Democratic party, an organization that posed another challenge to white political dominance in the state. This move sprang from the desire of SNCC leaders to put conditions such as those in the Mississippi Delta in the national spotlight in the election year of 1964. MFDP duplicated the regular party structure down to the precinct level and sent a nearly all-black delegation to the Democratic convention in Atlantic City to challenge the seating of the regular party's all-white one.[14]

In some of the most dramatic testimony about racial brutality ever reported in the national media, MFDP members gave party officials a look at what life was like in Mississippi for blacks seeking to secure their civil and political rights. As President Lyndon B. Johnson frantically called a news conference in order to upstage the MFDP witnesses, Deltan Fannie Lou Hamer told of a beating she had received in the Winona, Mississippi, jail: "They beat me and they beat me with the long flat blackjack. I screamed to God in pain. My dress worked itself up. I tried to pull it down. They beat my arms until I had no feeling in them. After a while the first man grew numb from tiredness. The other man, who was holding me, was given the blackjack. Then he began beating me." As Mrs. Hamer broke into sobs, Johnson's hastily called news conference finally went on the air, but the networks replayed much of the remainder of the testimony that evening, and the newspapers gave it full play the following day.[15]

The MFDP bombshell was too powerful to ignore. Hoping to avoid a floor fight over the seating of the MFDP delegation, national party officials recognized the need to give at least the appearance of making concessions to them. Hence they offered to make Aaron Henry and the Reverend Ed King delegates-at-large to the convention and promised to introduce an essentially unenforceable resolution requesting that all the southern delegations be integrated thereafter. In spite of a great deal of pressure from Johnson, party officials, and even the Reverend Martin Luther King, the MFDP held firm. Their supporters on the credentials committee were more vulnerable to pressure and outright bullying by the White House, however, and MFDP support on the Credentials Committee shrank from eighteen votes to four, a total well short of that needed to secure a vote from the convention floor on the seating of the MFDP insurgents. Still, the Mississippi challengers refused to accept the at-large delegates concession, described by Mrs. Hamer as "a token of rights on the back row that we get in Mississippi. We didn't come all this way for that mess again."[16]

In the meantime Hamer and three other MFDP candidates had qualified to run in the June 2, 1964, Democratic congressional primary. Hamer opposed twelve-term incumbent Jamie Whitten. Whitten lived in part-Delta Tallahatchie County and had only become the Delta's congressional representative in 1962, after the state's Democratic political establishment used redistricting as a ploy to pit Whitten against the more moderate and therefore politically vulnerable Frank Smith, who had formerly represented the Delta in Congress.[17]

The final vote totals in the 1964 contest, 29,711 votes for Whitten and 386 for Hamer, were by no means surprising, but the campaign effort yielded many more signatures for another unofficial but symbolically important "freedom" registration effort as well as a number of carefully documented examples of white harassment and intimidation. A second Freedom Election paralleled the general election in 1964. In the wake of this election, the MFDP challenged the seating of the state's regular congressional delegation and urged that three of the black congressional candidates from the Freedom Election be seated instead. Congress ultimately rejected the MFDP request but not before a hundred out-of-state volunteers collected ten thousand pages of testimony on allegations of voter discrimination in Mississippi.[18]

MFDP's achievements remained largely symbolic in 1964, but the group had nonetheless succeeded in focusing national attention on the plight of Mississippi blacks and achieving a degree of mobilization and organization among blacks that most whites and many blacks would have thought impossible two years before. These achievements were all the more remarkable in light of the brutal and heavy-handed manner in which Delta whites, accustomed to generations of unfettered dominance, fought to restore by brute force a caste-based status quo they could no longer preserve by coercion and intimidation.

Lafayette Surney, a SNCC worker from Ruleville, swore that as soon as he arrived in Clarksdale in 1963 he was accosted by police chief Ben Collins, who warned him, "I'm going to kill you if it's the last thing I do!" After further harassment by Collins, Surney claimed he heard that Collins had hired someone to kill him. The following night he encountered a group of white men, one of whom showed him a gun and warned him, "This has two buckshots in it and both of them have your name on them. I'm going to blow this up your ass and blow it off." Surney claimed that, when he called Collins to report this incident, "He told me to go to hell and hung up!" A few days later, while Surney was involved in a voter registration effort at the court house, Collins allegedly warned him, "If you don't want to come up like your nigger loving friends in Philadelphia you'd better get back to the nigger section of town."[19]

The Coahoma branch of the NAACP also charged that Chief Collins had managed to get one man fired from a part-time job at the local Coca-Cola plant because he had helped to unload a truckload of food and clothing sent to those who had been thrown off the welfare rolls. A few weeks later, the same man was arrested as a result of a civil rights demonstration, charged with "vagrancy," and fined sixteen dollars.[20]

Aaron Henry recounted an incident that demonstrated the depth of the defiance among many whites and added to Collins's reputation as one of the most formidable antagonists faced by civil rights activists in the Delta. Henry claimed that he received a call from Attorney General Robert F. Kennedy, who told him, "I've got three good ones for you." The three were Allard Lowenstein, a congressional candidate in New York; Steven Bingham, son of the governor of Connecticut; and Franklin Roosevelt III, the grandson of the former president. All of them had visited Henry in Clarksdale and had been arrested by Chief Collins. When Henry arrived, Collins accosted him: "Nigger, ain't you gonna never get no sense? . . . Don't you know that these white guys ain't fooling around with you but for one reason, to get to your women?" When Henry identified the young men and suggested that they might have other motives, the undaunted Collins, "bull-headed as he could be" according to Henry, turned to the grandson of Franklin D. Roosevelt, the only married man of the trio, and asked, "Say, fellow, how many times have you sold your wife to a nigger?"[21]

If Clarksdale's Collins was known as the toughest lawman in the Delta, Greenwood, the home of James K. Vardaman, was easily the toughest town.

An elderly black woman who had lived "all over the Delta" claimed "there ain't nowhere in this whole world where a Negro has got it as bad as in Greenwood, Mississippi." A special report to the United States Commission on Civil Rights charged that Greenwood blacks lived in "a reign of terror." Greenwood and Leflore County law enforcement officers not only threatened to harm black protestors, but apparently followed through. A member of the sheriff's department reportedly warned a black man seated at a whites-only lunch counter: "Get your black ass up from there. You know what happened to Emmett Till!" On another occasion a bearded civil rights worker was arrested in Greenwood on a traffic charge, severely beaten, and kicked in the groin. His head was slammed repeatedly against the walls and bars of his cell, and his goatee was plucked out.[22]

After picketing at the Leflore County courthouse, Willis Wright encountered a motorcycle policeman who yelled, "You think wouldn't anybody run over you, don't you, you black mother fucker?" When the policeman found out that Wright had a part-time job at a local café, he grew even more irate: "You mean to tell me that you picket in the morning and work up there in the afternoon? . . . We'll see what we can do about that." The next day when Wright appeared at work, his employer met him, handed him his paycheck, and told him, "I will have to lay you off right now."[23]

The intensity of the hatred and cruelty exhibited by Greenwood whites was shocking even by the standards of Mississippi. Whites shot civil rights workers and tried to burn and bomb them out as well, but Greenwood mayor Charles Sampson suggested that COFO leaders themselves staged many of these incidents in the hope of gaining publicity and stirring up local blacks. Despite continuing protests, Sampson claimed that local blacks were actually well treated: "We give them everything. We're building a new swimming pool. We work very close with the nigger civic league. They're very satisfied." Police used the town's single police dog to break up a protest march, much to the delight of a crowd of vicious whites, one of whom explained to reporter Claude Sitton in language reminiscent of a Faulknerian character: "We killed two-month-old Indian babies to take this country. And now they want us to give it away to the niggers."[24]

In addition to heavy reliance on violence and economic reprisal, across the Delta the initial, almost instinctive, white reaction to black activism was often an attempt to reassert the rituals and stereotypes of the caste system. A white bank teller became enraged when black civil rights worker Sam Block tried to cash a check made out to "Mr. Sam Block." The teller not only refused to cash his check but angrily scratched through the "Mr.," muttering that anyone who would make out such a check had to be "a damned fool." As black civil rights workers sat in an Indianola courtroom, they were sprayed with an aerosol insect bomb by a white man, who announced loudly in the presence of the judge and the chief of police and to the delight of the whites in attendance that he had to "deniggarize" [*sic*] the area. Whites also brought a chimpanzee to the Leflore

County courthouse and hung around its neck a sign reading I WANT TO VOTE, TOO. The complexity of the caste system and the intricate interrelationship of its parts meant that a threat to any element of the status quo loomed as a threat to all. South of the Delta in McComb, a white farmer in overalls attacked a black voter registration worker, shouting, "You sonofabitch, you sonofabitch, you'll never marry my daughter."[25]

As they responded to the challenge to their caste superiority, Delta whites revealed a continuing obsession with the sexuality of blacks, both male and female. A white male civil rights worker was accompanied by a black female when he went to the Greenwood police station to swear out a warrant against a man who had beaten him. A white officer who stood sharpening a long pocketknife asked the man how he "liked screwing that nigger." As he continued to sharpen his knife, he observed, "Sounds like rubbing up against nigger pussy." Poking the young man in the ribs, he asked, "Think it's sharp enough to cut your cock off?" He then warned him to "get out of here before I do what I'd like to do." Both the officer and the desk sergeant pointed a pistol at the girl, struck her, cursed her, and threatened to put her in jail.[26]

A sixteen-year-old girl swore that, after enduring several beatings and being forced to describe her family as "black-ass niggers," she was accosted in her cell by a white man who asked her if she had ever been "dicked by a nigger man." When she replied "No, sir," the man told her he was going to "dick" her and forced her to allow him to fondle her breast. After she refused to pull up her dress for him, he threatened to "put a stick" in her vagina if she told anyone about the incident.[27]

Civil rights leaders had hoped that mounting public outrage would force Delta whites to curtail their acts of violence and accept the inevitability of integrated public facilities and black political participation. Yet, even after the activities of the Mississippi Freedom Democratic party and the Freedom Summer movement had focused national attention on racial conditions in Mississippi and Congress had passed both the Civil Rights Act of 1964 and the Voting Rights Act of 1965, Delta whites remained adamant in their resistance to any move that seemed to represent even the slightest step in the direction of racial equality. Freedom Democratic party chairman Lawrence Guyot charged that a small plane dropped flares and explosives on an FDP rally at Indianola in October 1964. The day before, near Marks, a campaign worker had been forced off the road, beaten, and urinated upon by four whites.[28]

When thirteen workers attempted to force a restaurant in Indianola to comply with the Civil Rights Act of 1964, they were billy clubbed, arrested, and charged with trespassing and resisting arrest. One of the cars used by the group belonged to a black man with an artificial leg, who also suffered from epilepsy. After he showed up at the police station to claim his car, the desk sergeant queried him as to whether he loaned it "voluntarily." He responded in the affirmative, and was ordered out of the station; when his artificial leg prevented him from moving fast enough to suit the officers, one of them began prodding him with his club, and another leapt forward, shouting, "I'll beat up that son-of-a-bitch!" After banging the man's head against the wall, the policeman dragged him back into the office, charged him with refusing to obey an officer, and threw him in jail.[29]

Lafayette Surney claimed that, after the Civil Rights Act went into effect, Ben Collins visited all the black restaurants in Clarksdale and threatened to close them if they served civil rights workers of either race. In the wake of the Civil Rights Act, the mayor of Greenwood refused to accept responsibility for the safety of those who attempted to desegregate businesses that formerly had catered only to whites. "We're not going to help them integrate any place," he warned, adding that "any business that voluntarily integrates in the Delta is ruined as far as local people are concerned." Greenwood restaurants transformed themselves into private "key clubs" that catered to "members" (i.e., whites) only. The "Crystal Grill" became the "Crystal Club" because, in the owner's view, desegregation would cost him 90 percent of his regular business. Because whites had to pay a "membership fee" in order to eat at his restaurant, he lost a good portion of his customers who were not permanent residents of the Greenwood area.[30]

Unlike other local hotels, the Holiday Inn, which was part of a national chain, agreed to accept black guests, but its restaurant was "closed for repairs" for an extended period. The attitude of Buff Hammond, who as police commissioner was supposedly charged with overseeing law enforcement, reflected the strength of segregationist defiance in Greenwood. Hammond predicted that "desegregation just won't happen until the Federal Government beats us to our knees. . . . They just aren't going to force those things on people who have any damn guts." School officials apparently shared this opinion. Both the Leflore County and Greenwood school systems refused to integrate in 1965 despite the fact that their refusal meant the loss of federal funds.[31]

As the civil rights movement began to force at least token desegregation of some facilities and businesses, an underground "civic group" in Greenwood attempted to intimidate blacks and use economic blackmail on whites who succumbed to integrationist pressures. Citing the example of one supermarket manager who remarked that "ninety-five percent of his business was already negro," this organization's newsletter suggested that "white people help him make it one hundred percent by not going in this store for anything."[32]

Not even the physicians who voted to integrate the local hospital escaped the wrath of Greenwood's arch-segregationists, who condemned the "race-mixing, dollar-loving doctors" and urged local citizens to pressure these physicians to reverse their stand and to "exert their wealth and influence to resegregate our hospital from TOP TO BOTTOM." Local segregationists also objected to the integration of the Leflore Theatre, which, because it "willingly integrated," deserved "the complete ostracizing of all white people." The Leflore Theatre was, in fact, integrated only for blacks who were willing to brave insults, intimidation, and outright physical abuse. Frank Smith reported that a "gang of toughs" often walked around both in and outside the theatre with baseball bats, occasionally shining flashlights in the faces of patrons to determine their identity. According to Smith, one of these rowdies was "Delay" (Byron DeLa) Beckwith, the accused murderer of Medgar Evers.[33]

Despite such distractions, a few whites continued to attend the theatre. Among them was Thatcher Walt, editor of the Greenwood *Commonwealth*. Thugs accosted Walt and his family as they left the theatre, and someone left a threatening note on his front porch. The next day Walt and his family fled town after he heard of a plot to kill him in order to dissuade other whites from patronizing the theatre. When Walt returned on Monday, he found that he was no longer employed by the *Commonwealth*, and he discovered as well that his home had been fired into with a shotgun. He soon realized that he had no chance of getting a job with any other Mississippi newspaper and was forced to move to Jacksonville, Florida, in order to find a paper that would hire him.[34]

As it lashed out at whites who went along with integration, the Greenwood group did not overlook local blacks. The message in the following warning was all too clear: "The world first heard the revolutionary cry of BLACK POWER shouted from the mouth of a sunbaked Ubangi named STOKLEY CARMICAL [*sic*] right here in Greenwood during the 'Mississippi March.' If any of you should allow yourselves to become intoxicated with this revolutionary brew, rest assured, you will be promptly sobered up with massive doses of BLACK POWDER, already in the hands of we white, Christian patriots. Do not be fools black men. We will live here with you in the future as we have in the past or we will fertilize the soil of our beloved Southland with your remains. Remember, the choice is yours and ours."[35]

Delta blacks had not only heard such threats before but seen them carried out in many cases. However, the success of the Freedom Vote and of the Freedom Democratic party as well indicated that local blacks were no longer willing to allow the area's white minority to use such tactics to deny them their rights. In fact, the Delta produced some truly remarkable examples of individual courage and leadership among people who had lived for years amid discrimination, poverty, and repression.

As the son of a shoe store owner, Aaron Henry was a product of the Delta's relatively conservative black middle class. Henry's mother had always upbraided him for bad behavior with the pronouncement that "white folks wouldn't do that." Henry explained that his mother believed "the morals or mores, the conduct of whites, was the thing that this country responded to, and that this was recommended, that you act like white folks." As a high school student, Henry finally lost patience with his mother's faith in whites. His work as a porter at the Cottonbowl Court motel, an all-white establishment, not only convinced Henry that whites were no more "moral" than blacks but that whites viewed him as little more than an "inanimate object." He related experiences similar to those described by Richard Wright in his autobiographical *Black Boy*: "And many a time a guy would call down for four cokes and whatever else he wanted, he was in bed with a gal, I'd knock on the door: 'Who is it? The por- ter?' 'Yea!' 'Come on in!' Both butt naked, you know, doing their thing and never stop." Reliving this experience many times led Henry finally to tell his mother that her reverence for white morality was misplaced: "Honey, you don't know what's happening."[36]

Henry's military experience gave him both confidence and a broader per- spective; he became a leading figure in the NAACP in Mississippi after his return from the war. Henry studied pharmacy at Xavier University in New Orleans, and his drugstore soon became a base of operations for civil rights activists in the Clarksdale area. He circulated a desegregation petition in the wake of the *Brown* decision, and his house was firebombed in 1955 in retalia- tion for his efforts to organize a voter registration campaign. As he played a key role in organizing local boycotts and sit-ins during the early 1960s, both his house and his drugstore were bombed again. By his own estimate, he was arrested thirty times. A leader in the MFDP who urged acceptance of Lyndon Johnson's compromise seating proposal at the 1964 Democratic Convention, Henry was viewed as too conservative by many SNCC members, but he was nonetheless identified in some quarters as the next black leader marked for exe- cution after the shooting of Medgar Evers in 1963.[37]

Although he received less publicity than Aaron Henry, Amzie Moore was a key figure in the transformation of the civil rights movement in the Delta from a conservative middle-class phenomenon to a broadly based grassroots movement. Deeply affected by his wartime experience and jolted out of his complacency by the sight of a black family's wretched poverty, Moore became active in the NAACP. It was at his urging that Bob Moses brought in SNCC volunteers to launch a voter registration drive. Like many of his contemporar- ies, Moore was impressed by the courage and activism of SNCC's leadership: "I found that SNCC was for business, live or die, sink or swim, survive or perish. They were moving, and nobody seemed to worry about whether he was gonna live or die." Having lived for years the life of a "marked man" in the Delta, Moore described the inspirational sight of SNCC workers standing in voter registration lines as armed whites drove by: "How they stood . . . how gladly they got in the front of that line, those leaders, and went to jail! It didn't seem to bother 'em. It was an awakening for me." Ironically, to the young SNCC volunteers, it was Moore who seemed to be "a pillar of strength." Described by Tracy Sugarman as "an intrepid man who had made an unalter- able decision," Moore remained steadfastly committed to the movement, play- ing a crucial role as a liaison between SNCC organizers and the black popula- tion they hoped to involve in voter registration efforts.[38]

One of the most successful efforts at grassroots black political organiza- tion in the Delta came in the form of the Holmes County Movement, a group that drew its strength from the county's eight hundred black landowners, many of whom achieved that status through participation in the FSA tenant purchase project at Mileston. One such owner of seventy acres of rich Delta earth was

Hartman Turnbow. A persistent young organizer from Leflore County finally interested Turnbow in "redishin" (his words) to vote in order to become "a first class citizen" with a higher standard of living, despite the fact that Turnbow was already an "ageable" man at the time.[39]

On May 9, 1963, Turnbow became the first of twelve blacks to register in Holmes County in a single day; he had stepped forward when an angry sheriff tried to intimidate the group by demanding to know who would be first. Turnbow was also the first to have his house firebombed and fired upon. He startled the two whites doing the shooting by returning the fire. Turnbow was quickly arrested for "arsony" when whites claimed he set the fire and did the shooting himself. With John Doar of the Justice Department serving as attorney in his behalf, Turnbow's appeal led to a dismissal of the charges. Subsequently, however, Turnbow's house was again riddled with gunfire, which narrowly missed a white civil rights worker from New York, who hurriedly vacated the premises and never returned. When the next shooting incident occurred, Turnbow was prepared. He had purchased a twelve-gauge automatic shotgun and loaded it with "them high velocity buckshot." When he heard the first shots he grabbed his own weapon and "turned it loose a time or two." According to Turnbow, he then contacted the FBI in Jackson whose agents pleaded with him, "Don't kill nobody, don't kill nobody." Turnbow responded that he intended to protect his home and that they should take steps to stop whites from shooting at his house, "cause I'm gonna git my gun and git busy and see who can I shoot." This warning apparently put an end to such incidents.[40]

Turnbow's overt militance was unusual for a Delta black of his generation. When asked why he suddenly developed a "rebellious" attitude toward the caste system and white repression, Turnbow responded, "I don't know where all that there braveness come from. I just found myself, I just found myself with it. Other words, the shootin' in my house. I had a wife, and I had a daughter, and I loved my wife just like a white man loves his'n, and I loved my baby daughter just like a white man loves his'n, and a white man will die for his'n, and I say I'll die for mine."[41]

Perhaps the most remarkable story of an "inside" agitator for racial equality in the Delta was that of Fannie Lou Hamer. Hamer's story of her life before she became a civil rights activist reveals much about the ignorance and drudgery that dominated the entire lives of many Delta blacks. She had started to work in the fields at age six and seldom attended school for more than four months in any one year. Hamer guessed that she had a total of perhaps six years of schooling, but she recalled, "There was never, never a time in April that kids would be in school when I was a kid."[42]

For most Delta blacks, life consisted of little but work "from one season to another." "They just chopped cotton," Hamer recalled. "Sometimes they'd have a week out, and then they'd be right back in the field and go over that cotton again." Hamer was the youngest of twenty children in a hardworking family that had risen from sharecropping to cash renting until a jealous white neighbor poisoned their livestock and forced them back to sharecropping. After Hamer married Perry "Pap" Hamer, a tractor driver, the couple spent the next twenty years working on plantations in Sunflower County.[43]

Hamer claimed that she did not learn until 1962, at age forty-five, that blacks were legally entitled to vote. She added that she never knew that Mississippi had a constitution until she was asked to copy and interpret a section of it as a part of her registration test. "We didn't know what was going on in the rest of the state, even, much less in other places," Hamer explained. "We could hear about the President, but it was kind of farfetched from us." Weary and isolated, Hamer learned of the possibilities of registering and voting at a "mass meeting" she had attended largely out of curiosity: "Well, I didn't know what a mass meeting was, and I was just curious to go to a mass meeting."[44]

Hamer's path to the ballot box was a long, frustrating one. She failed her first voter registration test, and on the way back from Indianola to Ruleville, the old school bus in which she and her would-be fellow registrants were riding was stopped by state patrolmen, who told the driver he had "too much yellow" on his bus. When she finally reached her home, her landlord had already learned of her registration attempt, and he warned her that, if she persisted in her efforts, she would "have to leave this place." Hamer left the plantation where she had lived for eighteen years and moved into Ruleville the same night, only to have night riders shoot into the house where she was staying. Undaunted, she asserted, "They kicked me off the plantation, they set me free. It's the best thing that could happen. Now I can work for my people." Before attempting to register again, she studied the state constitution and passed her test. Yet when she appeared to vote, she was disqualified because she could not produce her poll tax receipts for the previous two years.[45]

Hamer went on to become perhaps the most inspirational grassroots leader of civil rights activity in the South. Through her affiliation with SNCC, she traveled widely, leading groups in inspirational songs and telling in honest, forthright language of the abuses and tribulation suffered by southern blacks. Hamer's earnest, down-to-earth, straight-to-the-point rhetoric quickly established her as the folk philosopher of the Mississippi movement. Under severe harassment she once admitted: "Sometimes it seem like to tell the truth today is to run the risk of being killed. But if I fall, I'll fall five feet four inches forward in the fight for freedom. I'm not backing off that and no one will have to cover the ground I walk as far as freedom is concerned."[46]

Tracy Sugarman described a powerful impromptu speech Hamer delivered to an Indianola congregation. Her talk was filled with biblical quotations and allusions, and she concluded by issuing a passionate charge to a reluctant young minister: "You, Reverend Tyler, must be Moses! Leadin' your flock out of the chains and fetters of Egypt—takin' them *yourself* to register—*tomorra*—in Indianola!"[47]

Despite her sixth-grade education, Hamer proved all but impossible to intimidate. Charged with being a Communist, she retorted that she knew as much about communism as "a horse do about Christmas." Faced with intense pressure from liberal democrats to compromise on the issue of the seating of the Mississippi Freedom Democratic party delegates at the 1964 Democratic convention, she told a squirming Hubert Humphrey: "Senator Humphrey, I know lots of people in Mississippi who have lost their jobs for trying to register to vote. I had to leave the plantation where I worked in Sunflower County. Now if you lose this job of vice president because you do what is right, because you help the MFDP, everything will be all right. God will take care of you. But if you take it [the vice-presidential nomination] this way, why, you will never be able to do any good for civil rights, for poor people, for peace or any of those things you talk about."[48]

It was a measure of the prominence she achieved and, perhaps, of the changes she helped to bring to her state that four years after she failed in her first attempt to register to vote, *Mississippi* magazine listed her as one of the six "Women of Influence" in the state, carrying her picture next to that of Florence Sillers Ogden, the white Delta matron who regularly voiced her racist and segregationist views in a newspaper column entitled "Dis an' Dat." Ten years after her failed registration attempt, Ruleville held a Fannie Lou Hamer Day. The mayor, who had once jailed her husband for an overdue water bill, paid tribute to her as a champion of her people. At her death in 1977, she was eulogized far and wide, but her obituary in the *New York Times* was less significant than the action of the Mississippi House of Representatives, which voted 116-0 to praise her for devoting "her life to equality and justice for all" and serving as "a symbol to people across the nation in their struggle for human dignity."[49]

The "struggle for human dignity" in the Delta ultimately involved efforts to desegregate schools, theatres, lunch counters, swimming pools, waiting rooms, motels, and other public accommodations. With blacks constituting a solid majority of the population in every county, however, the removal of barriers to black voting seemed to pose the single greatest threat to white supremacy in the region, and, not surprisingly, whites resisted black voting and office-holding with all the resources they could muster. In response to the MFDP slate of candidates in the 1964 congressional elections, the Mississippi legislature passed a bill making it much more difficult for independents to qualify for elective office. A final response to the MFDP uprising was the passage of an "open primary" bill, which would have required all candidates for statewide office to run in a special "preferential election." If no candidate received a majority of votes, the two front runners would compete in a general election runoff; the intent of this legislation, passed in 1966 but killed by gubernatorial veto, was to prevent a black independent from winning a general election contest in which the white vote was split between the Democratic and Republican nominee.[50]

Despite these legislative precautions, the black-majority Delta remained vulnerable to black assaults on white political supremacy. In October 1965 the

Freedom Democratic party filed suit to force a more equitable distribution of the population among the state's congressional districts. The prevailing district alignments diluted black voting strength because the Delta lay within the Second District, which had 608,441 residents as compared, for instance, to only 295,072 in the Fourth. While the court considered this case, the legislature responded by redrawing congressional lines again, this time splitting the Delta three ways into two majority-white districts and a third with a 51 percent black population majority (but a white majority in voting-age population and registered voters). One non-Delta representative only noted the obvious when he charged that "we all know that the Negro situation was the main factor" in prompting the redistricting plan.[51]

Delta legislators also led the way in engineering changes from district to at-large county supervisor's elections and school board contests. Two separate bills required at-large school board elections in Coahoma, Leflore, and Washington counties. Both bills required that school board members own real estate worth five thousand dollars, a tidy sum when the average wealth of Delta blacks was taken into account. The legislature also passed a bill making the office of school superintendent an appointive rather than elective one in ten counties, four of them in the Delta, and allowing countywide referenda on the matter elsewhere.[52]

Such maneuvering notwithstanding, the mass enfranchisement of blacks prompted by the passage of the Voting Rights Act of 1965 quickly brought some startling changes to the political landscape of the Delta. As Table 4 shows, by 1968 black voter registration figures in the region were a far cry from the negligible numbers on the books no more than three or four years earlier. A case in point was Leflore County, where less than 2 percent of the black voting-

TABLE 4. Voter Registration in the Delta (Voting-Age Population), Summer 1968

County	Percent of Whites Registered	Percent of Blacks Registered	Black Registrants as a Percentage of All Registrants
Bolivar	70.6	53.0	54.4
Coahoma	90.5	67.3	55.5
Humphreys	91.2	48.3	46.8
Issaquena	100.0+	60.2	42.6
Leflore	80.0	73.0	54.7
Quitman	97.9	47.7	39.9
Sharkey	100.0+	50.2	20.0
Sunflower	85.5	41.9	43.0
Tunica	100.0+	37.4	50.7
Washington	77.3	43.9	37.1

Source: Voter Education Project, Southern Regional Council, Inc., *Voter Registration in the South* (Atlanta, 1968), mimeo, n.p.

age population had been registered in 1962 but 73 percent were on the rolls by the middle of 1968. On the other hand, however, Leflore was the only county lying wholly in the Delta that showed more than 50 percent black registration at this time. Moreover, white voter registration had also picked up considerably, in apparent response to the growth of the black electorate. At least 70 percent of the adult white population was registered in each of the ten core counties of the Delta, and official records showed that more than 100 percent were registered in three. Still, as of mid-1968 blacks already accounted for the majority of the registrants in four Delta counties and, of course, represented a majority of the potential electorate in every county.[53]

If these figures left any doubts as to their long-term implications, whites need only look to the results of the 1967 elections, in which twenty-two blacks won county-level offices across the state. The most notable of these was Robert Clark, who became the first black since the Reconstruction Era to serve in the Mississippi House of Representatives. Clark won his seat as an MFDP candidate from Holmes, the part-Delta county where the independent black landowners of the Holmes County Movement provided a ready-made organizational base and a 73 percent registration by blacks helped to offset the 100 percent-plus registration figures for whites.[54]

The affable and politically astute Clark had taught in the public schools and served as athletic director and business manager at a local junior college. Moreover, several members of his family had also taught in the county schools over the years. Hence he was well known and liked by local blacks at all socioeconomic levels. Working in close coordination with the MFDP, Clark ran a well-organized campaign that utilized as many as 150 bloc captains to inform voters about his candidacy.[55]

Clark's platform called for a more realistic welfare system, educational reform, industrial development, a compulsory school attendance law, an end to discriminatory law enforcement, and a host of other measures aimed at improving the lot of Mississippi blacks. Clark defeated twelve-year incumbent J. P. Love by 116 votes. Ironically, it was Love who had chaired the infamous "mass meeting" that led to the exile of the Minters and Coxes from Providence Farm near Tchula. Love attempted to block Clark from taking his seat by challenging his candidacy on a technicality, but legislative leaders urged him to reconsider, and he finally withdrew his challenge. When Clark strode past the statue of Theodore G. Bilbo in the lobby and took his seat in the legislative chamber, he met with a cold reception from his new colleagues, none of whom would eat with him at a legislative luncheon. He also found that his desk was in "no man's land" between an aisle and an empty seat in the legislative chamber. A dozen or so solons did, however, go so far as to shake hands with Clark; one even predicted that his new colleague would be "a good, humble legislator" and added, "If so, we'll work with him."[56]

After the creditable showing by blacks in 1967, the *Delta Democrat-Times* had concluded that the black vote had become "potent" in Mississippi. Despite their growing numerical strength, however, blacks continued to face intimidation and fraud. In the 1967 local elections in Sunflower, a small town only a few miles from Senator Eastland's home at Doddsville, illiterate blacks who wished to vote for an all-black slate of candidates had to ask a white official to mark their ballots. The local election commission had decided on the eve of the voting not to allow a black official to be present at the polls to assist black voters. Upon entering the polling place, blacks had to pass in front of the chief of police, and as they left they had to make their way through a crowd of whites. Despite these adverse circumstances, black turnout was 98 percent, although a similarly high turnout by whites left the black candidates sixty votes short.[57]

Such disappointments notwithstanding, black political leaders remained optimistic as black registration continued to climb, reaching 30 percent statewide by 1971 and giving blacks a clear electoral majority in twenty of the state's eighty-two counties. Expecting to build on the base established in 1967, over three hundred blacks sought elected positions across the state in 1971. Many of their campaigns showed an impressive degree of organization and determination. Still, black independent gubernatorial candidate Charles Evers received only 22 percent of the vote, and 259 of 309 black candidates were defeated. Robert Clark barely managed to retain his seat in the legislature. Black victories were restricted in large part to minor posts. Mississippi still had no black sheriff, school superintendent, or state senator. Only eight of seventy-four black candidates for county supervisor were elected. The election of fifty more black officials, bringing the total to 117, gave Mississippi more black officeholders than any southern state, but black turnout barely topped 50 percent, as compared to a 70 to 75 percent showing among whites. The effort to energize the black community had mobilized whites as well. Fearful of a black political takeover, whites flocked to the polls. Explained one Holmes County banker, "All my land and everything I own is in this county, and the same goes for my neighbors. If the blacks take control, we're finished. Now you don't expect us just to stand by and see that happen, do you?"[58]

The economic blackmail employed by the Citizens' Council in the mid-1950s was still apparent in 1971. Black applicants for loans were often directed to "go see Charles Evers." Moreover, many blacks in the Delta feared the loss of their jobs in the ongoing cotton harvest should they show too much interest in the election. A black legislative candidate from Tallahatchie County explained: "These are the poorest and most unsophisticated people in America. They only average $600 a year. They believe the boss can tell, so they vote how they are told."[59]

For the most part, blacks met with subtle intimidation rather than outright threats. In James Eastland's town of Doddsville, the only black polling official regularly left the room whenever a black voter asked for assistance, leaving the voter with no choice but to call out his or her choice to a white official. At a precinct in Bolivar County, where voting machines were used, three of the machines were manned by whites whom local blacks distrusted. The fourth

machine was supervised by a local white minister in whom blacks had a measure
of confidence. Many voters in this precinct required assistance, and when the
count was made white candidates bested blacks by a five to three margin in the
three machines operated by the suspect whites, while blacks carried the other
machine by three to one.[60]

There were charges of election day fraud and intimidation, and at least
four blacks had been slain in the Delta in the months prior to the 1971 elections.
The racial tensions generated by black political activism were further exacerbated by efforts to force desegregation of the public schools. Melany Neilson
recalled the strained atmosphere that prevailed in Holmes County as school
integration got under way in the late 1960s. Like most other white parents in
the area, Neilson's sent her to Central Holmes Academy, a hastily constructed
private school: "Private school tuition had spelled financial strain for most of
us: at home the parties stopped abruptly, we had to let Elsie [their black house-
keeper] go; and farmers across the county, heretofore sure of affluence even
though money was never readily available, moaned more loudly about the
unpredictable: the weather, the yield, the federal courts." The brake lines on
the family car were cut after Neilson's father refused to join the Klan, and she
noticed that suddenly "most everyone, even fine families, was using the word
'nigger' as often as 'colored.' . . . We came to expect this, to accept it. And
every time we spoke the word 'nigger,' each time a little more in condescension, we began to feel some power in the word itself." When Martin Luther
King, Jr., was killed, whites half anticipated a black uprising in the county, but
she explained that by the late 1960s "the familiar threat of violence did not
make us wonder . . . only the silence, the peaceful days, struck us as a strange
surprise."[61]

Discussing integration at Drew High School and his behavior toward
Ruth Carter, his first black classmate, Ole Miss football star Archie Manning
admitted, "It was a very tense situation. . . . I felt kind of sorry for Ruth; she
had to be scared stiff. I talked to her once or twice, but I wouldn't say that I
went out of my way to be friendly to her. You can't change the place you grew
up in or the way you grew up." Attempting to describe the atmosphere at Drew
High School when the seven Carter children became the first blacks to enroll,
a math teacher recalled, "There was no violence, no ugly incidents that made
headlines. . . . The people here aren't like that. The Carter children were simply ignored. No one would talk to them. At noon they wouldn't eat lunch in the
cafeteria, they'd eat on the gym steps. I think there was only one time I ever
saw one of those Carter children smile."[62]

By 1971 blacks at Drew High School outnumbered whites about four to
one. On May 25 Joetha Collier, a black girl who had just graduated from Drew
High, was shot and killed in front of a grocery store in the black section of
town. Three white men, two of them from Drew and one from Memphis, were
arrested and charged with the crime. Collier, who was apparently selected at
random by the killers, had won a good citizenship award at the graduation cer-

emony. She had been a member of both the girls' track and basketball teams. Her white principal described her as "a good girl. She was a black student but was a good girl."[63]

The Collier killing sparked protest marches leading to the arrest of at least thirty-seven persons and spawned sporadic rock throwing incidents that led Drew Mayor W. O. Williford to impose a dusk-to-dawn curfew. Aaron Henry placed Collier's killing in the context of white reaction to a voter registration drive then under way in the Delta, noting the shooting of another black at Ecru in northeast Mississippi and a similar shooting of a black by a white night watchman at Sumner in the Delta. Citing harassment, threats, and vandalism against registration workers, Henry declared, "Opposition to blacks registering to vote seems to have awakened the white community."[64]

Elsewhere, Rainey Poole, a black plantation worker with one arm, was beaten and shot to death outside a "white" nightspot in the Delta town of Louise. The search for Poole's body led to the dragging of the Sunflower River, which in turn yielded the bodies of two other black men whose families thought they were in Chicago. Angry blacks began a boycott of white businesses in the first concerted protest effort the little town had witnessed.[65]

The resort to violence in order to reassert their dominance was nothing new to Delta whites, but instead of intimidating local blacks such actions now elicited bitter protests and even threats of a violent counterresponse. Melany Neilson recalled that during Robert Clark's first campaign for the legislature a local white asked a black bag boy at the supermarket, "What's gonna happen if Clark's not around on election day?" and the young man replied without hesitation, "If Clark's not around ... then a lot of you white folk won't be either."[66]

In his study of the part-Delta county of Panola, Frederick M. Wirt noted that when the civil rights struggle began, whites still spoke of "their nigras": "It's not going to make all that much difference because our nigras aren't going to listen to what these outsiders are saying." Consequently, the initial reaction of whites to black political activism was one of "puzzlement and hurt."[67]

For all the distress it may have caused whites, however, black voting quickly forced white leaders to pay closer attention to blacks as individuals and as a group. Wirt found that, whereas when the civil rights era began most whites had little idea as to the identity of the real leaders among blacks, white politicians soon made it a point to learn more about patterns of influence in the black community as the number of black registered voters began to expand. By the end of the 1960s, Panola County planters were at least more cautious about any hint of economic reprisal against those tenants who might have registered to vote. One planter who had once been particularly adamant in his opposition to the idea of his employees voting reversed his position entirely when he decided to run for political office himself. Overt appeals to segregationist sentiments soon became a thing of the past. Blacks also noticed more attention being given to street repairs in their neighborhoods, and in rural areas gravel began to appear on roads where it had never been seen before. Black law enforcement officers were hired as well, although progress in this area was slow. Finally, for all of the evidence of continued prejudice on the part of individual whites, "Mr." and "Mrs." began to surface in reports concerning black activities, and the reports themselves began to appear with increased frequency.[68]

Melany Neilson described a similar situation in Holmes County, where "suddenly these politicians were making overtures to the black community: visits to black churches and juke joints, visits with [Robert] Clark and other local black leaders, handshakes and poses for photographs which made their way into the Lexington *Advertiser*. In one county race a former Citizens' Council member linked arms with blacks at a local church to sing "We Shall Overcome."[69]

For blacks some of the best evidence of a change for the better in race relations in the Delta was the sense that acts of violence and repression by law enforcement officials were noticeably less frequent. "This veil of fear has been lifted from our minds," said one influential black spokesman. "These officials see us now as a citizen, not as a Negro."[70]

Clearly, the civil rights movement made a major contribution to the improvement of black self-esteem in the Delta. To Endesha Ida Mae Holland, the pre-civil rights era Delta was "a testament to African-American inferiority." As for herself during this period, Holland wrote, "I had never read a book written by an African-American; I didn't know that Black people could write books. I never knew that Blacks had done any great things. I was always conscious of my inferiority and I always remembered my place—until the civil rights movement came to the town where I was born and grew up." By the end of the 1960s, Holland was involved in black studies—learning that "it was okay to be Black"—and on her way to a promising career as a playwright.[71]

If the civil rights movement encouraged Delta blacks to view themselves in a more positive light, its effect on basic white attitudes about blacks was less dramatic. The unleashing of the black vote had forced white politicians and public officials to treat blacks with more respect. Such behavior did not spread rapidly throughout the entire white population, however. Frederick Wirt heard numerous complaints about the failure of whites to respect the "dignity" of blacks and concluded that among whites in general there had been little change in "perceptions and cognitions of blacks as a race." Richard D. Chesteen found that, despite the progress that had been made, in the late 1960s many whites in Indianola still believed that "intellectually, morally, and health wise, blacks are inferior at this time."[72]

When asked by Howell Raines if the Mississippi Delta of the mid-1970s was different from what it had been twenty years before, Citizens' Council head Robert Patterson responded, "The change is almost indiscernible. We have public schools where white children that are not able to afford the private schools are forced to go to school with the Negroes. . . . The Negro in the

Delta doesn't overwhelm the white restaurants and so forth. Many restaurants have never had a black in them, or they may have one come in there just to show he can go in there. Some white civil rights person will bring him in there, but he doesn't come back. He doesn't want to go where he's not wanted."[73]

Patterson went on to explain that, in his view, the South was living "under a system of force. In other words, we're integrating because we're *forced* to integrate. . . . We're not submitting to it. We'll never submit any more than the Jews and the Arabs will ever submit to each other." Hodding Carter III was forced to agree with his longtime foe: "The medicine [of integration] is being taken, but a great number of people still think it's medicine."[74]

For two decades the Yazoo-Mississippi Delta lay at the center of the civil rights conflict in America. As a Dixiecrat stronghold, the birthplace of the Citizens' Council, and the site of the Emmett Till murder and numerous less-publicized outrages, the Delta earned a reputation as a citadel of white defiance. It invited the onslaughts of SNCC and other activist groups and was the breeding ground for the Mississippi Freedom Democratic party, whose 1964 challenge wedged the national Democratic party firmly between the rock of its historic dependence on the support of southern whites and the hard place of its stated commitment to civil rights for blacks.

The mixed results of twenty years of struggle were evident throughout the Delta by the early 1970s. On the one hand, there was a degree of black political participation, activism, and assertiveness unthinkable only a few years earlier. On the other hand, there was the enduring determination of a majority of whites to utilize every coercive measure at their disposal to restrict black influence on policy-making and, despite the legally mandated integration of public facilities, to minimize social interaction between the races. In most counties the white population of the public school consisted primarily of the children of white parents who could not borrow or beg the money to send their offspring to one of the speedily constructed private academies that soon dotted the Delta landscape.

The region's white elite, meanwhile, retired to their country clubs and "private" dining and drinking establishments, where they lamented the black "takeover" of the Delta. With an average of 68 percent of the black families in each Delta county trapped below the poverty line, however, blacks—who were hard pressed to exercise even the most fundamental civil and political rights they had fought so hard to gain—still thought more in terms of economic survival than political supremacy. A close observer of the 1971 elections concluded that "outright fraud and ballot-box stuffing were probably not necessary to defeat black candidates. Economic dependence and fear of economic pressures were sufficient."[75]

In an ironic historical parallel, the Voting Rights Act and the subsequent efforts to mobilize black voters had restored the black-majority Delta's status (circa 1880) as the area of the state where white supremacy seemed most vulnerable. Unfortunately, however, just as the loss of political rights by Delta

blacks at the end of the nineteenth century had been facilitated by the modernization of the region's economy and transportation network, their efforts to
reclaim these rights in the 1960s were frustrated by the labor market contrac-
tions resulting from mechanization and consolidation of Delta agriculture.
These changes had begun in the 1930s as a response to the federal acreage-
reduction and subsidy programs, which over the course of four decades helped
to revolutionize Delta agriculture while reinforcing the economic and political
dominance of the region by its large landholding planters. Hence the struggle
for civil rights in the Delta can be fully evaluated and understood only against
the larger backdrop of economic transformation and human upheaval induced
by the policies of the same federal government that had pledged itself to civil
and political equality for all Americans, including blacks in the Delta.

11 ▽ "Somebody Done Nailed Us
   ▽ on the Cross"
   ▽

Those who explained the failure of blacks in the Delta and else-where in the southern plantation belt to make more progress during the civil rights era often cited the enduring influence of paternalism, referring to the historic dependence of black tenants on their white landlords. In fact, however, it was a new form of paternalism, one introduced by the federal government, that played a major role in shaping events in the Mississippi Delta throughout the post-New Deal decades. Since the 1930s the Delta had moved increasingly into the federal orbit as Washington subsidized the reduction of cotton acreage and succeeded the planter as the primary source of support for the region's sea-sonally employed black laborers. It was Delta planters, however, who actually became the prime beneficiaries of these new government initiatives, which not only boosted their incomes through acreage-control payments and price supports but reduced their labor needs and relieved them of their responsibilities as providers as well. Meanwhile, the definite coercive advantage enjoyed by Delta whites derived not from the emotional legacy of the plantation but from the fact that continued white control of employment and public assistance made Delta blacks, in the words of one observer, "more vulnerable to reprisal and intimidation than at any time in their history."[1]

Even with the full commitment of federal influence and resources to the cause of civil rights, the struggle against a venerable and thoroughly pervasive system of caste would have been difficult enough. With federal agricultural policies contributing heavily to black unemployment and homelessness and with welfare assistance originating in far-off Washington but passing through the hands of the local segregationist establishment, the battle for black rights in the Delta was an uphill one indeed.

Despite their intense and long-standing fears of federal intervention in their racial affairs, by the civil rights era Delta planters could point to a long and beneficial relationship with a largely supportive Washington. Federal funds had played a vital role in the ongoing flood-control effort in the Delta. During the New Deal, AAA payments provided the wherewithal for the mechanization of cotton production as well as the incentive for the reduction of cotton acreage. Other New Deal relief programs shut down or revived according to the planter's need for labor. During the war, planters had used their influence with local draft boards to retain or control their labor, and cooperative federal officials had helped to prevent labor shortages from driving agricultural wages too high.

The restoration of price supports and the introduction of the Soil Bank program in the 1950s further boosted the economic fortunes of Delta planters at a time when they were rallying in resistance to any and all challenges to white supremacy. Although both the Dixiecrats and the Citizens' Council gave considerable lip service to "individualism" and "laissez faire," leaders of both groups were outspoken advocates of public assistance to private enterprise. Dixiecrat vice-presidential nominee Fielding Wright was an active supporter of Mississippi's Balance Agriculture with Industry program, which provided municipally subsidized buildings to new industries.[2]

When it came to federal support for agriculture, pious pronouncements about the virtues of laissez faire gave way to fervent assertions of Washington's obligation to assist the farmer. In 1952 when William Faulkner delivered an eloquent indictment of the growing dependence of Americans on federal assistance, he received a standing ovation from Delta Council members, who assumed the famous author was aiming his remarks not at them but at the poor and the black (who, if they heard Faulkner's speech that day, did so only as they served food or washed dishes). Described by Frank Smith as "an arch-conservative, whose views on national issues make the John Birch Society look like a branch of the ADA," Walter Sillers, Jr., served for many years as chairman of the Delta Council's resolutions committee and consistently called for "federal economy everywhere but in the Delta." Noting the selective, self-interested nature of the conservatism of black belt whites in the 1950s, Numan V. Bartley wrote that "the federal farm program, which lavished governmental benevolence upon the planter while providing little aid to the small farmer, approached the ideal." Equally ideal from the standpoint of the Citizens' Council was the backdrop of federally induced agricultural mechanization which rendered Delta farm laborers increasingly marginal or superfluous and left them especially susceptible to the council's efforts to use economic pressures against blacks inclined to activism and protest.[3]

A glance at the census reveals that modernization of agriculture in the 1950s had brought neither general economic, social, nor political progress to Delta blacks. Black farm laborers earned six hundred dollars per year in 1959 as compared to fifteen hundred dollars for whites. In 1960 median personal income for nonwhites exceeded five hundred dollars in only two of the Delta's counties, and approximately 80 percent of the dwellings in Tunica County had neither bathroom nor toilet facilities. Five percent of the farms accounted for 66 percent of the land in Coahoma County, and 7 percent of the farms represented 75 percent of the land in Issaquena. Given these conditions and the gen-

TABLE 5. Net Migration in Delta
Counties, 1950–1960

County	Percentage Migration
Bolivar	−13.8
Coahoma	−6.7
Humphreys	−17.5
Issaquena	−28.5
Leflore	−09.5
Quitman	−19.5
Sharkey	−17.1
Sunflower	−18.1
Tunica	−22.6
Washington	+11.0

Source: "The Mississippi Delta (Part 1)."

erally declining demand for farm labor, the high rates of out-migration indicated in Table 5 are hardly surprising.[4]

A 1959 survey found 17,563 sharecroppers in the Delta; five years later the figure was down to 8,788; and three years after that it was approaching zero. These figures reflected continuing and accelerated mechanization—by 1967 only 5 percent of Delta cotton was picked by hand—and reduced cotton acreage, both of which were direct results of federal policy and legislation. These influences brought about a drastic reduction of day labor employment as well. Seasonal jobs for choppers and pickers fell by more than 50 percent between 1965 and 1966.[5]

Demand for labor declined dramatically in response to the acreage-reduction incentives of the Federal Food and Fiber Act of 1965, which offered a payment of 10.5 cents per pound on projected yields for land diverted from cotton production. The act required at least a 12.5 percent reduction in acreage and allowed up to a 35 percent cutback. Follow-up crop-reduction programs introduced in 1966 and 1967 brought further contraction of the labor market. In 1967 the number of cotton choppers employed was less than one-fourth the number hired in 1964, and the number of days worked was also reduced considerably.[6]

These were ominous trends for Delta blacks. Those who had not joined in the massive out-migration of the 1950s and 1960s were often elderly, unskilled former sharecroppers reduced to wage labor status by mechanization. They were subsisting at the end of the 1960s on the periodic income they could earn as part-time cotton-choppers or weed-pullers, removing whatever grass survived the herbicides on which planters increasingly relied to keep their crops free of competing vegetation.

Another crucial influence for reduced agricultural employment in the

Delta was the one-dollar-per-hour minimum wage law that took effect on February 1, 1967. Such a law had long been the dream of liberal social scientists and planners, who saw it as a key to prying black farm workers from the grip of the archaic system of credit and paternalism that had throttled them since the end of the nineteenth century. At first glance a mandated wage of a dollar per hour might have seemed like a blessing to workers accustomed to receiving $3.50 for a twelve-hour day. In reality, however, the new minimum wage law simply worsened the plight of those whose situations were already the most woeful. Under the new statute, the occasional field hands who had once been assured of approximately thirty days' work in June or July (at $3.50 per day) became what one writer called an "absolute economic liability" to the planter. Chemical weed killers, already less expensive than hand labor, became in one estimate at least twelve times less expensive as soon as labor costs rose to a dollar per hour. Labor at such a rate was now, as one plantation manager put it, a "luxury we cannot afford."[7]

From the perspective of the wife of a day worker, the new wage law was anything but a blessing: "A dollar a hour ain't worth nothing when, maybe they give you one day, and then you're off for two weeks and like that. That dollar a hour ain't worth nothing. It would have been better if it had been 50 cents a day if you work every day." She explained that, in 1967 after the law went into effect, she and all her children had worked only one week, earning a total of $270.[8]

Unfortunately, those who had supported the minimum wage law had presumed that planters would maintain employment at pre-1967 levels. In fact, the new law succeeded in jerking the slack out of a system that was not yet fully mechanized and modernized. As Nicholas Lemann observed, "The minimum wage finally forced the planters of the Delta to drop their long-cherished self-conception as landed gentry presiding over a mild paternalistic system that lacked the relentless logic of capitalism." A year after the minimum wage took effect, a Delta planter explained: "Hell, last year was the first time we really found out what labor efficiency could mean. We knew we couldn't use any more casual labor because of the minimum wage, and now we're finding out we don't need as much specialized labor either. And they can do better than they have been doing, and they will."[9]

Many of those who could no longer find such sporadic employment were elderly social security and welfare recipients, but the contracted agricultural labor force also had no room for approximately twenty-five thousand able-bodied workers. It was no wonder that the region experienced an estimated net out-migration of twelve thousand in 1967 alone. Many planters allowed surplus workers to stay on in their shacks despite the lack of demand for their services, but as the exodus continued the smoke from abandoned tenant shacks torched by owners aiming to reclaim as much farm land as possible provided visible evidence that the revolution in agriculture had reached its final phase in the Delta.[10]

As they struggled to survive in an economy where their prospects for even sporadic employment grew worse each year, impoverished blacks receiving public assistance had to contend as well with the shift from federally distributed surplus commodities to food stamps. Prior to 1964 most of these low-income blacks had received monthly distributions of flour, canned goods, and other staples through the federal commodity program. As Delta counties moved to replace these commodities with food stamps, needy families found that they had to document their poverty in order to qualify for the stamps, which they then had to purchase and use like cash in grocery stores. For many, however, the stamps simply proved too expensive. Many of the older, poorer blacks were receiving Social Security, which had enabled them to sustain their meager existence as occasional laborers. This same income, however, proved to be a liability when they applied for food stamps because, according to a government-imposed formula, the cost of stamps and the amount of stamps available were tied to a client's income. This formula took no account of other expenses like rent, utilities, medical bills, and prescription costs.[11]

One family, consisting of two Social Security recipients who drew forty-one dollars each per month and a disabled forty-year-old woman who received no support, could not afford to pay the assigned fee of twenty-eight dollars for fifty dollars' worth of stamps. "I can't pay the doctor with food stamps," said one. The other allowed that "food stamps is all right if you is able to buy them. Well, I wasn't able to, not with the doctor. I owe the doctor now $177.40." Critics of the program cited other examples, such as that of the family with eight children and a monthly income of $455 that had to pay twenty-two dollars for ninety dollars in food stamps.[12]

Many poor blacks found their only alternatives were to borrow money from the planter to pay for food stamps—with the debt to be repaid from whatever future earnings a family member might receive from the planter—or to let the planter purchase the stamps and distribute them as he saw fit. This situation was difficult enough for a tractor driver earning a dollar per hour, but it fell with even greater weight on a female head of household who worked only occasionally for a planter like Senator James O. Eastland, who reportedly charged "interest" on such loans at "two bits on the dollar."[13]

Initially, the food stamp program made no allowance for the varying incomes of seasonal workers. In addition, many local merchants boosted their prices when the county shifted to food stamps. Others refused to provide "change" in the form of due bills for food stamp purchases, insisting instead that customers take additional items, which they often did not want. Overall, the most telling and painful result of the switch from commodities to food stamps was the statistic showing that, when Leflore County shifted to stamps in 1965, the number of recipients fell from 20,000 to 8,300. Elsewhere, while 3,205 Sunflower County families had been receiving commodities, scarcely half that number (1,683) were able to get food stamps. This latter figure was all the more alarming in view of the fact that approximately six thousand Sunflower County families actually lived below the federally designated poverty line.[14]

Although even the commodities program had been seen as a move to give low-income blacks more independence, local whites had retained control of the program, and planters were able not only to rely on these commodities as supplementary "furnish" but to regulate their distribution to individuals according to the inclination of potential recipients to remain docile and cooperative. Such was the case in 1962, for example, when the Leflore County Board of Supervisors voted to suspend the distribution of commodities in an effort to discourage local blacks from supporting the COFO voter registration drive. Moreover, despite promises of greater freedom and dignity for the recipient under the food stamp program, local planters were still called on to document the income and need of food stamp recipients.[15]

For many a worker, participation in the food stamp program meant double dependence on a planter who both certified his need and loaned him the money he needed to continue to receive the stamps. Planters like Sunflower County's Eastland, the staunchest segregationist in the United States Senate, often intervened to clarify the income status of seasonally employed day laborers. One family of ten was paying $78 for $118 worth of stamps until Eastland assured officials that the family had no income in winter and should therefore be eligible to receive $86 worth of stamps at the minimum charge of $3 per month. In the 1960s, as in the 1930s, Delta planters were able to utilize their influence over federal relief programs to support their workers during periods of slack labor demand or, if need be, to punish those who expressed dissatisfaction with the status quo by participating in civil rights activities.[16]

Meanwhile, as the food stamp program became increasingly controversial, a public outcry arose over the disparity in federal expenditures in the Delta. In 1967, for example, only $446,000 went for food relief and $8,676 to manpower development in Sunflower County, where human deprivation was both widespread and directly related to the scarcity of marketable skills. Less than 30 percent of Sunflower County's housing was considered "sound," but only $23,520 was spent on low-cost rural housing in 1967. Finally, the county had no free medical care and no free school lunch program. Federal funds in the amount of $92,000 made lunches available at twenty-five cents a day, but for a poor family with six or eight children, that figure might as well have been $25.00.[17]

No such parsimony was evident, however, in figures released by the Department of Agriculture identifying those who received payments in excess of five thousand dollars from the Agricultural Stabilization and Soil Conservation Service in 1967. These tabulations showed, on the contrary, that the United States government was considerably more generous to the Delta's planters than it was to its poor. Coahoma County's John B. McKee, for example, received more than a quarter of a million dollars from the government in 1967. Because it was the home of the powerful Senator Eastland, Sunflower

County attracted a great deal of attention as controversy over federal acreage-reduction subsidy payments, the food stamp program, and the impact of the dollar-per-hour minimum wage in agriculture came to a head in the Delta. Reports that Sunflower County planters received more than $10.2 million in cotton program payments in 1967, while federal food program expenditures in the county totaled less than 5 percent of that amount, put Eastland and other southern congressmen on the defensive. The fact that acreage-reduction payments to farmers amounted to a total twenty-three times greater than the expenditures to combat hunger in a county where 65 percent of the population was living in poverty was difficult to explain away.[18]

In 1966 seventy-seven Sunflower County planters received more than twenty-five thousand dollars in cotton program subsidies. The best known of these recipients was none other than "Big Jim" Eastland himself. Eastland received $168,524.52 in price support and acreage diversion payments and then sold the choice cotton that he did produce for an estimated $280,000.[19]

Federal farm payments in excess of fifteen thousand dollars amounted to nearly sixty million dollars in the Delta in 1967. For the state as a whole, ten "core" counties of the Delta accounted for just over half of such payments, slightly more than three-fourths of the payments above fifty thousand dollars and just over four-fifths of those over a hundred thousand dollars. Across the ten-county area, the ASCS made 280 payments over fifty thousand dollars and 69 that exceeded one hundred thousand dollars. This meant that 22 percent of all payments in excess of fifty thousand dollars for the entire nation were made in the Delta, which also accounted for 17 percent of the national total for payments above one hundred thousand dollars.[20]

As Delta whites sought to maintain their federally subsidized wealth while relying on both their Washington-enhanced economic clout and their strategic position within the welfare food chain to subvert federal civil rights initiatives, they could hardly have asked for two more effective political point men than Senator Eastland and Congressman Jamie Whitten. Eastland was known as the most committed segregationist in America, and Whitten was only slightly less rabid, having, for example, condemned the *Brown v. Board of Education* decision for starting the nation on the "downhill road to integration, amalgamation, and ruin." As chairman of the powerful House Appropriations Subcommittee on Agriculture, Whitten—known to some as "the permanent Secretary of Agriculture"—worked unceasingly to maintain and increase federal benefits to the large farmers he represented. In a typical year in the 1960s, federal farm payments in excess of five thousand dollars totalled $23.5 million in Whitten's district. This sum went to a group that represented about one-third of 1 percent of the population, while the 59 percent of his constituents living below the poverty level received a total of only four million dollars in food relief funds. In the Senate the generously subsidized Eastland was so adept at stonewalling civil rights measures that from 1956, when he became chairman of the Senate Judiciary Committee, until 1965 not a single piece of civil rights legislation was reported voluntarily out of his committee. (It was a tribute to Eastland's clout that it was nearly a year after the Voting Rights Act took effect before Attorney General Nicholas Katzenbach sent federal voting examiners into Eastland's Sunflower County.)[21]

So great was the influence of Delta planters in Washington that in 1962 representatives of the Delta Council could secure United States Department of Labor approval for a federally funded training program for twelve hundred tractor drivers and equipment operators in the Delta. Because the program promised to prevent damage to expensive machinery by inexperienced operators, it offered clear benefits to the region's large-scale planters, who would now have access to a pool of cheap labor whose skills had been sharpened at government expense. For the workers, on the other hand, there was no promise of higher wages, and it was difficult to see how their training in tractor and cotton-picker operation would enhance in the least their prospects for alternative employment. Ironically, however, before the plan received congressional approval, nervous Delta conservatives turned on their own piece of special-interest legislation and used their influence to kill it for fear that the measure might become, in the words of Jamie Whitten, "the entering wedge into Labor Department supervision of wage rates and hours in agriculture, which could upset the local economy."[22]

Officials of the Johnson administration expressed amazement at the rejection of the plan by the large planters, whose interests it so clearly promised to serve. Meanwhile, a disgusted but nonetheless deferential Secretary of Agriculture Orville L. Freeman could only listen politely as the powerful Whitten condemned federal interference in southern racial affairs and lectured him on Washington's absolute obligation to help agriculture achieve parity with other sectors of the economy.[23]

As a longtime beneficiary of governmental generosity, planter Roy Flowers of Coahoma County personified the manner in which, over three decades, federal agricultural and welfare policy had reinforced rather than undermined the wealth and power of reactionary Delta planters. Flowers, whose income was approximately one million dollars in 1966, received over $210,000 in federal payments in 1967. He had come to the Delta in 1908 as a store clerk earning twenty-five dollars per month. By the early 1960s, he claimed to own everything within forty-nine square miles, including seven thousand acres in cotton, four gins, a bank, the entire town of Mattson, and, in his own words, "more niggers than anybody in Mississippi."[24]

Like a number of the Delta's "self-made men," Flowers could actually trace his success back to the New Deal Era, when Franklin Roosevelt "put a support under the price of cotton, and we plowed up some cotton and he paid us for it." As time passed, Flowers continued to benefit from favorable government programs, and he bragged about his management style, which combined personal acts of paternalism on his plantation—Flowers was reputed to distribute silver dollars to his hands as they lined the turnrows—with skillful manipulation of federal and state programs: "I'll never have trouble with my niggers because I'm good to them. . . . I give 'em Christmas money, let 'em sign up for commodities . . . send my niggers to the charity hospital at Vicksburg. . . . It don't cost us so much."[25]

Most Delta whites refused to acknowledge any inconsistency in their objections to "wasteful" and "unnecessary" antipoverty efforts and their own eager acceptance of huge federal subsidy checks. Jamie Whitten opposed lowering the cost of food stamps, arguing that "when you start giving people something for nothing . . . I wonder if you don't destroy character more than you might improve nutrition." Whitten expressed no such concerns, however, about the effects of government farm payments on the character of their already well-heeled recipients. In 1965 half the local poverty board in Coahoma County resigned in protest of a two-million-dollar budget they considered excessive. In the same year, the Department of Agriculture divided the same amount of money among only twenty-seven of the county's large planters, none of whom offered any protest whatsoever.[26]

Powerful Delta whites could turn both federal aid to farmers and federal assistance to the poor to their own advantage because the Democratic party had long depended on the support of southern white voters. By the mid-1960s these voters were deserting the national Democratic party in droves, but powerful senate and house perennials like Eastland and Whitten remained in place, their ostensible allegiance to the Democrats belied by their votes and maneuvering against a host of civil rights and social welfare efforts.

Although southern congressional leaders like Eastland and Whitten were Democrats in name only, in deference to their seniority and crucial committee assignments, Johnson administration officials followed the lead of their New Deal predecessors by working within a regional socioeconomic and political framework almost certain to attenuate the reformist and redistributive potential of their programs. The rationale for this compromise was the need to secure congressional support for a host of other Great Society initiatives, but the results were bitterly frustrating for blacks in the Mississippi Delta and elsewhere (almost all of whom, given the opportunity, would have voted Democratic). Instead of assisting those who both needed its help and endorsed its goals, the Johnson administration rewarded those least in need of its aid and most in contempt of its principles. The result was a paradoxical phenomenon described by Walker Percy wherein, over the span of three decades, "planters [like Roy Flowers] who were going broke on ten cent cotton voted for Roosevelt, took federal money, got rich, lived to hate Kennedy and Johnson and vote for Goldwater—while still taking federal money."[27]

The reality of the "welfare for the wealthy" aspects of the farm program in the Delta did not escape Aaron Henry, state NAACP conference president, and Charles Evers, state NAACP director. In November 1967 they telegrammed President Lyndon B. Johnson to express their concern over the "alarming speed with which Senator James Eastland and [Agriculture] Secretary Orville Freeman make plans to declare North Mississippi a disaster area in order to get help to Mississippi cotton planters." Henry and Evers informed Johnson that they had been trying for months to get similar assistance for the "hungry, undernourished negro and white of the same area." The two reminded Johnson that "cotton planters have many resources . . . the impoverished almost none." They concluded with a pointed observation: "The concern of our state and national leaders about the minor problems of the rich and their unconcern about the overwhelming problems of the poor causes us to wonder if in fact the poverty program for the rich is not more important in their minds than the poverty programs for the poor."[28]

Washington's decision to allow the beneficiaries of the "poverty program for the rich" to oversee local administration of the poverty program for the poor clearly put Delta blacks at a disadvantage. Beyond that, blacks had to contend as well with the fact that the demise of the old plantation paternalism left a void that the new federal paternalism did not completely fill. Whereas the planter's need for labor was once the tenant's hedge against starvation, homelessness, and life-threatening illness, no such assurance existed for those who fell between the cracks of the various federal assistance programs.

The absence of adequate provision for the poor was nowhere more evident than in the area of health care, where the collapse of a labor-intensive agricultural system left penniless blacks to fend for themselves whenever illness or injury struck. Reacting to criticisms of health conditions among Delta blacks in the 1960s, Delta columnist Florence Sillers Ogden retorted: "Since time immemorial planters have taken care of the medical needs of their tenants. I farmed many years, some of them through the depression of the 30's. At one time, I had 45 families on my plantation. Not once did I ever refuse medical care for my people. I personally stood for all medical bills, as did every other farmer."[29]

Exaggeration or not, Ogden's claim was not without some foundation in fact; many planters once guaranteed their croppers' medical bills or maintained a "standing agreement" or "retainer" with a local physician. However, those days were gone forever by the mid-1960s. White hospitals operated on the "fee for services" system, and as one observer noted, "Cash and carry medicine doesn't work when there is no money." This was clearly the case with Mary, a fifteen-year-old who became ill in her eighth month of pregnancy. Mary reportedly went to the Bolivar County hospital around midnight after her plantation supervisor promised to call ahead and "make arrangements" for medical care. When she arrived, however, the hospital staff refused to admit her, claiming they had heard nothing from the supervisor. Mary sat in the waiting room, her illness worsening, until late afternoon the next day. By early evening, she was dead.[30]

Individual physicians followed the lead of the hospitals. Said one, "If there is a nigger in my waiting room who doesn't have $3 in cash, he can sit there and die. I don't treat niggers without money." Ailing blacks often spent whole days unattended in his waiting room, but, he added, "when I close up at night, out they go. I don't treat people who cannot pay for the service."[31]

Left with little choice, poor blacks could rely only on the resiliency of an immune system often weakened by improper diet. Said one, "If you don't have no money you just stays sick and hopes tomorrow'll be better." Such was the plight of Lula Mae, who lived with her eleven children in a three-room shack without electricity, running water, or a toilet. With two infant children suffering from diarrhea and so weak and dehydrated that they were unable to crawl out of the puddles of their own excrement, their mother explained with a degree of resignation shocking even by Delta standards: "There's nothing I can do for 'em. There's no doctor and I got no money for a hospital. All's I can do is wait and watch either they get better or they gonna die. I can't do nothin' but wait and pray." Another black mother explained: "You don't go to the doctor unless it's life or death. . . . You do what you can at home. You fight the fever with everything you've got. I waited too late for one of mine. He died."[32]

Even for those blacks who could pay or still get someone else to pay, there was no guarantee of adequate attention to their ailments. One black patient described his experience with a white physician in this manner: "Most often I sits on one side of the office and he sits on the other asking questions. There ain't no listening or thumping or looking in the mouth like white folks get." It was apparently quite common for black patients to get a diagnosis and a prescription without ever being touched. A civil rights leader charged, "The docs here ain't partial to laying on hands when it comes to treating the colored." White physicians often seemed to take the complaints of their black patients less seriously than those of their white ones. Doctors casually prescribed regular intercourse for twelve- and thirteen-year-old girls and told many a mature black woman complaining of the "miseries" that "if you haven't been pregnant for two years you can't expect to be healthy."[33]

For its impoverished blacks, the Delta combined an unfavorable health care environment with a startlingly unhealthy living environment. One physician testified that 81 percent of 501 Washington County children tested were anemic. A survey of 509 families in Washington and Sunflower counties showed that fully 60 percent of them were receiving less than two-thirds of the generally recognized minimum daily dietary requirement. This figure stood in stark contrast to a national figure of only 13 percent. Infant mortality statistics were similarly striking. The mortality rate for black infants in the Delta was 30 percent higher than for other Mississippi blacks and 109 percent higher than that for whites in the Delta. The infant mortality rate among black Mississippians actually rose as the farm economy modernized, climbing from 40.8 deaths per 1,000 births in 1946 to 55.1 in 1965. The Delta counties were at the cutting edge of this trend. The infant mortality rate increased by 13 percent in Bolivar County between 1960 and 1964 alone. Reliance on midwives was especially common among Delta blacks. Statewide in 1965, 40 percent of all black births had been attended by a midwife rather than a physician. For whites this figure was only 0.2 percent.[34]

For many black infants who survived, childhood was anything but a pleasant experience. One Delta mother offered this poignant summation of a day in the life of her offspring: "These children go to bed hungry and get up hungry and don't ever know nothing else in between." One of the more striking characters turned up by researchers was the old woman who lived with two dozen children and grandchildren in a three-room shack and explained that she always held back a little of her food money for snuff because "that-a-way the hunger don't hurt so bad when there's nothing left to eat." Another family in similar circumstances was that of Jacob Montgomery, a former tractor driver in failing health and facing eviction along with his wife and nine children. Only the two Montgomery children enrolled in Head Start received more than one meal a day, and one of the children, aged seventeen, had never been to school at all. Having lost an eye during infancy because of inadequate medical care, he had received an ill-fitting plastic replacement, which had caused an infection that sent a steady stream of pus down his cheek and threatened to travel up the optic nerve and invade his brain.[35]

Kenneth L. Dean, executive director of the Mississippi Council on Human Relations, sketched a chilling portrait of a severely impoverished, female-headed family with a large number of children and perhaps some dependent grandchildren. For such a family, breakfast consisted of grits, molasses, and biscuits. Lunch for the children might be bread and Kool-Aid or water. The adults would eat nothing. The evening meal might consist of baked beans and cornbread with occasional rice, peanut butter, or a canned meat substitute drawn from the commodities program. Lacking refrigeration, such a home might reveal rat- or roach-infested commodities stacked in the corner. The lack of toilet facilities meant that the odor of urine permeated the cold air blowing through cracks in the floor, cracks so large that children eating out of their hands or jar lids might drop food through the cracks. Its subsequent decay produced equally unpleasant odors to compete with the smell of urine.[36]

Dean described the members of one such family in detail: "Five of nine children were too filthy to get near, and it would not be advisable for them to be part of a regular school group, unless some provision was made for bathing. They were literally too filthy to touch, their bodies having gone unwashed for so long that their arms and legs reflected a blue-gray, clay-like color. This family is actually too poor to participate in a poverty program."[37]

A visiting team of physicians reported Delta children living under "such primitive conditions that we found it hard to believe we were examining American children of the twentieth century." The doctors reported seeing in "child after child" evidence of

> vitamin and mineral deficiencies; serious, untreated skin infections and ulcerations; eye and ear diseases, also unattended bone diseases secondary to poor food

intake; the prevalence of bacterial and parasitic disease as well as severe anemia, with resulting loss of energy and ability to live a normally active life; diseases of the heart and the lungs—requiring surgery—which have gone undiagnosed and untreated; epileptic and other neurological disorders; severe kidney ailments that in other children would warrant immediate hospitalization; and finally, in boys and girls in every county we visited, obvious evidence of severe malnutrition with injury to the body's tissues—its muscles, bones, and skin as well as an associated psychological state of fatigue listlessness and exhaustion. We saw children afflicted with chronic diarrhea, chronic sores, chronic leg and arm (untreated) injuries, and deformities. We had homes without running water, without electricity, without screens, in which children drink contaminated water and live with germ-bearing mosquitoes and flies everywhere around. We had homes with children who are lucky to eat one meal a day—and that one inadequate so far as vitamins, minerals, or protein is concerned. We saw children who don't get to eat fruit, green vegetables, or meat. They live on starches—grits, bread, Kool-Aid. Their parents may be declared ineligible for commodities, ineligible for the food stamp program, even though they have literally nothing. We saw children fed communally—that is by neighbors who give scraps of food to children whose own parents have nothing to give them. Not only are these children receiving no food from the government, they are also getting no medical attention whatsoever.[38]

Dr. Joseph Brenner of the Massachusetts Institute of Technology testified that he had spent a year in "the more backward or less developed areas of Kenya," where he saw villagers "living as best they could off a barren land, eating a diet composed entirely or almost entirely of carbohydrates with some little vegetable, with very rare intake of animal protein." Brenner informed the senators questioning him that "the condition of the people that I saw there was comparable to the children that I saw in Mississippi during my visit."[39]

Dr. Tom Levin, a psychiatrist, reported:

During the "picking" and "chopping" seasons, the mother will either carry her infant to the fields with her, or entrust its care to an older sibling or neighbor. Infants may be unhandled except when they are demanding and, even then, they must await the attentions of young siblings involved in play or a mother working in the fields or tired from such work. This pattern of mothering and handling has a profound effect upon the drives and hopes of the later adult. Passivity and limited aspirations are appropriate adaptations to the frustration and deprivation imposed upon both mother and child by their economic reality.[40]

Dr. Raymond Wheeler of Charlotte, North Carolina, believed that the major difference between the plight of the poor in his state and in Mississippi was the fact that in his own Mecklenburg County there were sympathetic officials who exhibited "compassion and concern" for the poor. As far as its poor blacks were concerned, Wheeler saw Mississippi as "a kind of prison in which live a great group of uneducated, semi-starving people from whom all but token public support has been withdrawn. They are completely isolated from the outside world. They have nowhere to turn for material aid or moral support. Their story needs to be told not merely for their sakes—but for the sake of all America." In the Mississippi Delta, Wheeler frequently heard charges of "an unwritten but generally accepted policy on the part of those who control the state to eliminate the Negro Mississippian either by driving him out of the state or starving him to death." Wheeler at first refused to believe these charges, but the more he saw of the severity of black suffering and the callousness of whites toward it, the more credible they became.[41]

Anyone familiar with the Delta's history of extensive efforts to recruit and retain black labor doubtless found it ironic that the region's whites were suddenly taking steps to drive blacks out, but mechanization and acreage reduction had reduced the Delta's labor needs dramatically, and black agitation for equal access to public facilities as well as the ballot box struck directly at the social and political supremacy that the Delta's white elite had once held so firmly in its grip. One observer explained sarcastically that the prospect of black voters electing black county supervisors, who might accept federal vocational retraining funds or take other steps that might cause more blacks to remain in the Delta, was a frightening one indeed for local whites: "In such a catastrophe Senator James O. Eastland would have to dig into the soil conservation payments and cotton parity price payments he receives annually from the federal government and pay for schools. That would be enough to cause a senator to make another speech about states' rights."[42]

Charges of an active conspiracy to drive blacks from the Delta seemed more plausible in light of the actions of local welfare officials who, as they cut back on payments to those attempting to register to vote, began to distribute information about the relatively generous welfare benefits available in Chicago and other northern cities. The loudest outcries about efforts to coerce black migration came, however, from black civil rights leaders, who cited a bill introduced in the Mississippi legislature in 1964 that made it a felony to become the parent of a second illegitimate child. Anyone convicted under this statute would face a prison sentence of one to three years unless he or she opted as an "alternative" to submit to sterilization. Critics argued that the proposed bill was an "experiment in genocide" and noted that the author of the original bill was a representative of Sunflower County and a part-time staff assistant to Senator Eastland. Supporters of the bill made no secret of their desire to force blacks to leave the state. Chortled one: "When the cutting starts, they'll head for Chicago." (Aaron Henry's reading of white attitudes during this period was "They wished we'd go back to Africa, but Chicago was close enough.")[43]

What SNCC representatives described as the "Mississippi Genocide Bill" passed the house but made it through the senate only after the sterilization provision was deleted and the offense was reduced from a felony to a misdemeanor with a lessened sentence of thirty to ninety days in jail or a $250 fine or both. As amended, the law—which remained in effect as of this writing—still acted as a coercive influence to leave the state and served the goal of stopping, as the bill's sponsor put it, "this black tide which threatens to engulf us."[44]

Further evidence that Delta whites looked on a black exodus as their "final solution" came from Sims Luckett, a Clarksdale lawyer: "I don't think that there is any true future for the Negro in this community unless and until we change the racial ratio. If we had—if half the Negroes in this community left tomorrow, the ones that are left behind would benefit immensely. . . . We've got to distribute the Negroes more evenly throughout the country."[45]

Mississippi whites reacted to charges of a conspiracy to starve blacks out with predictable indignation. Governor Paul B. Johnson, Jr., contested the findings on hunger and malnutrition with the assertion that the state's blacks were "so fat they shine." Columnist Florence Sillers Ogden proclaimed her indignance at the report on hunger, a report she described as "founded on misinformation and misstatement," "distorted," and "exaggerated beyond comprehension." She was most upset by the remarks of Dr. Joseph Brenner of the Massachusetts Institute of Technology, who compared conditions in the Delta "unfavorably with Darkest Africa," but she also dismissed the critical comments of Dr. Robert Coles, who was from Harvard: "We all know what Harvard thinks of Mississippi and what Mississippi thinks of Harvard."[46]

Senator Eastland rejected the criticism of conditions in the Delta presented by the visiting health team. He praised the Mississippi Public Health Service and responded to the gloomy picture witnesses had painted of schools in the Delta with a remarkably straight-faced assertion that "the truth is we have one of the finest public school systems in the United States." Eastland described Dr. Wheeler's charge of a conspiracy to drive blacks out of the state as "a totally untrue statement." Eastland continued, in rhetoric that Delta planters had been employing for decades, "I know of the people personally in the two counties which he visited. Nothing could be further from the facts. To tell you the truth, I live around Negroes. If they were all to leave the state and move out of the state, I would move out with them, because I have always associated and been around them." Elsewhere, in response to criticism that local whites were insensitive to the plight of the displaced workers, a Delta Council official called attention to a plan whereby Delta blacks who wished to do so could work in the off-season in the fruit and vegetable industry in Florida.[47]

As their economic and living conditions grew more desperate and Washington took little action to relieve their worsening plight, black farm workers and dispossessed tenants determined to take direct action in their own behalf. On May 31, 1965, a dozen tractor drivers and their families walked off the A. L. Andrews plantation near Tribbet, demanding an increase in their day wages. Their walkout involved eighty people and led to picketing by various support groups. This "strike" revealed the disadvantages faced by farm workers who sought to better themselves. Andrews obtained an injunction to hold picketing to a minimum and received assistance from the sheriff's department and prisoners in the county jail in evicting the strikers and dumping their furniture and other belongings on the side of the highway. The strikers eventually took up residence in tents in a settlement they called Tent City.[48]

Neighboring planters offered to send women and children from their own places to help Andrews with his cotton chopping, but given the diminished demand for farm labor by the mid-1960s he had little trouble replacing those who left. Although the strike appeared from the outset to have little chance of succeeding, the speed with which Delta planters rallied to the support of those whose plantations were struck indicated that such militance among Delta farm workers was nonetheless disconcerting to local landlords. After picketers turned away a busload of "day hand" workers at the Andrews plantation, an "unidentified white woman" fired a pistol over their heads.[49]

The strike received its most direct support from the Freedom Labor Union, an offshoot of the insurgent Mississippi Freedom Democratic party. Civil rights activists had high hopes for the protest, which they believed would spread across the Delta. Critics pointed out, however, that even if successful the efforts of the strikers to raise the wages of tractor drivers from six dollars a day and those of cotton choppers from three dollars a day to a minimum of $1.35 per hour would result in massive unemployment, because planters would simply move more rapidly to mechanize their operations and take fuller advantage of herbicides in order to avoid paying higher labor costs. Also, because so many tractor drivers lived virtually rent-free on the plantations where they worked, demands for a pay raise were certain to bring either eviction or an insistence on rental payments. Ultimately, however, the fundamental reason for the almost predictable failure of the strike was that it was an attempt to exploit white dependence on black labor at a time when, thanks to expanded federal acreage-reduction initiatives and the attendant move toward full-scale mechanization of cotton planting, planters found their dependence on black labor at an all-time low.[50]

The plantation strike was linked directly to a more militant action that occurred nearly a year later. This time, however, the target was not Delta planters but the Washington bureaucracy. By the end of 1965, a number of reports had already suggested that the following year would bring even more unemployment, destitution, and hunger to the Mississippi Delta. Promises of an expanded federal food distribution program failed to materialize, and Washington County welfare agents informed members of the striking farm labor families that they were no longer eligible for the commodities they had received while working on local plantations. Early in January 1966, the Washington County Board of Supervisors delayed action on a proposal to extend the free food program at no cost to the county.[51]

On January 24 the Mississippi Freedom Democratic party, the Mississippi Freedom Labor Union, and the Delta Ministry, the civil rights adjunct of the National Council of Churches, invited all the poor people in the state "to attend a conference aimed at securing more food, homes, and jobs." On January 29 seven hundred people met at Delta Ministry headquarters at Mount Beulah. Calling themselves the Poor Peoples Conference, they sent a telegram to President Lyndon B. Johnson explaining their displeasure with existing federal welfare programs. While at the meeting, the delegates learned that two elderly blacks had frozen to death in a plantation shack. As the conference came to a close, the delegates searched for a way to dramatize their plight and expressed interest in acquiring ground for a "new city" where they could build a new future offering self-determination and dignity as well as jobs and shelter.[52]

These plans took shape quickly; at 6:45 a.m. on January 31, four cars sped by a security guard and through the gate of the Greenville Air Force Base. This facility had been closed more than a year, and although its runways served as the municipal airport, its more than three hundred buildings stood empty. The group quickly forced its way into a locked building and hung out a sign reading, "This is our home, please knock before entering." Throughout the day others came, bringing stoves, mattresses, blankets, and food. A small snowman soon stood guard beside the door of the occupied building. Local officials decided not to intervene because the incident involved federal property, and air force officials were reluctant to take action because of the sensitive civil rights aspects of the incident. After the gates were locked, people joined the sit-in by scaling the fences around the base.[53]

The list of demands issued by the air-base squatters indicated they were aiming their protest not so much at their former employers as at the federal government. They demanded food: "We are here because we are hungry. Our children can't be taught in school because they are hungry. They can't even get the food in school because they have to buy it and don't have the money." They also demanded jobs: "We are here because we have no jobs. Many of us have been thrown off the plantations where we worked for nothing all our lives. We don't want charity. We demand our rights to jobs, so that we can do something with our lives and build us a future." With the cry for jobs came a call for job training, as well as income supplements and a food distribution program run not by white county supervisors but by the poor themselves.[54]

The protestors also called on the Office of Economic Opportunity to provide adequate funding for Project Head Start schools in the Delta, but they put special emphasis on their desire for land: "We are here because we don't have land. There are thousands of acres here that the government owns. We say we are supposed to be part of that government. We want the clear land and the unclear lands and we'll clear the unclear land ourselves." Having stated forthrightly their demands, the demonstrators asked President Johnson to make a choice: "Whose side are you on—the poor peoples' or the Millionaires'?"[55]

The commander of a small caretaker detachment stationed at the base tried to convince the group to vacate the building. He not only failed but claimed to have been kicked in the shins for his trouble. Throughout the night air police arrived from a number of bases around the United States. The next day a force of about 150 marched on the occupied building and carried the demonstrators from the building amidst a torrent of verbal abuse. The evicted squatters launched most of their taunts at the black airmen in the group. One black woman screamed, "You black fools. . . . All of you are fools. I don't care about your damn GI clothes; Uncle Sam ain't yours."[56]

Where the plantation strike was an attempt to wring concessions from an entrenched local white elite whose position had been bolstered by federal agricultural and welfare policies, the air-base sit-in was an effort to call Washington's attention to the plight of those whose positions had been undermined by these policies. At a press conference following the sit-in, Ida Mae Lawrence complained, "We ain't dumb, even if we are poor. We need jobs. We need food. We need houses. But even with the poverty program we ain't got nothin' but needs."[57]

Another protestor, Rev. Arthur Thomas, noted the power of Delta congressman Jamie Whitten on the House Agriculture Subcommittee and the clout wielded by Mississippi's John Stennis on the Senate Finance Appropriation Committee. "Those," he pointed out, "are the kinds of people who are supposed to represent the poor people in Congress." When a reporter asked Thomas if he were charging "the people who run the poverty programs" with "kow towing" to Mississippi's "power structure," Thomas responded, "That's what I'm saying. The poverty program and the Department of Agriculture. We Have No Government."[58]

Such dissatisfaction with Washington seemed to dictate a new strategy, that of pursuing self-determination for the poor blacks of the Delta. Isaac Foster announced that Tent City would become the site of an autonomous community of poor people. These plans led ultimately to the creation of "Freedom City" on four hundred acres of land near Greenville purchased with funds from an anonymous donor. Unita Blackwell explained, "We, the poor people of Mississippi, is tired. We're tired of it so we're going to build for ourselves, because we don't have a government that represents us."[59]

For a brief period, at least, the air-base sit-in did succeed in gaining national attention. Rev. Martin Luther King, Jr., telegrammed President Johnson seeking aid for the farm workers, pointing out that the "callous disregard of the federal government for their plight and the plight of tens of thousands of other poor Mississippi Negroes makes a mockery of all the humanitarian ideals this nation espouses throughout the world." Secretary of Agriculture Orville L. Freeman informed Secretary of Defense Robert S. McNamara that his department was working to meet the "critical needs" brought to light by the air-base sit-in. Freeman cited both a massive food distribution program and a job training effort developed in conjunction with the Department of Labor and the Office of Economic Opportunity. He stressed, however, the need for housing for these dispossessed workers, and he pressed McNamara (obviously with the Greenville Air Base in mind) to consider making "barracks or non-commissioned officer housing available on some kind of a lease basis at those military establishments where the personnel is being phased out or where an excess of housing exists." Ultimately, however, any hope of converting the Greenville base into housing for the homeless farm workers was snuffed out by Senator Stennis, who warned that if the base were not returned to the city of Greenville, "my only recourse will be through the HEW appropriations bill" then pending in Congress.[60]

Meanwhile, federal officials who flooded into the Delta in the wake of the sit-in were appalled not only at what they saw—"I felt as if I had been out of the country"—but at what they sensed. One confidential memo reported: "This many displaced people means a hell of a situation and it comes at a time when there's an awakening. These people are angry, frustrated—and knowledgeable. I've never seen the same seething resentment before."[61]

The role of the federal government in exacerbating the problems it was committed to solving was but one of the interlocking ironies that emerged from the upheaval that shook the Mississippi Delta during the 1960s. For a number of years, economists and social theorists had called for sweeping reform in the South's farm economy. Mechanization was needed to make production more efficient; acreage reduction would boost prices and support higher wages for those who remained in the farm labor force while others moved into industrial employment. The result was supposed to be a situation in which everybody won. The planter would reap greater profits through increased efficiency, and higher prices would more than offset reduced production. The cropper or farm laborer would benefit, either from higher wages or from employment in one of the new factories that would flock to the South once the strangle-grip of the farm tenancy system was broken.

Ultimately, the government not only delivered on all the proposed changes, but propped up cotton prices when acreage-reduction efforts failed to boost them to desired levels and then initiated an antipoverty effort to support those who found no demand for their services outside the pared-down farm economy. Yet, from the standpoint of the former cropper or day laborers, it was the federal government who was responsible for their plight. "Somebody done nailed us on the cross," lamented an elderly, dispossessed Sunflower County tenant. "Don't know who it is, but I believe it's the government."[62]

Delta blacks spoke so harshly of the federal government at the end of the 1960s not only because of the impact of the minimum wage and acreage-reduction measures but because, by allowing Mississippi whites to administer federal welfare programs, Washington was actually undermining black efforts to force local whites to adhere to federal civil rights laws. After the air-base sit-in, Ida Mae Lawrence expressed her frustration with a government that guaranteed her civil rights but allowed her to be punished for seeking them: "In November when they start qualifying you for commodities, they say you got to find out how many people you worked for and get them to sign for you as being poor. If they don't feel like signing, like maybe they don't like you for civil rights activities, you don't get commodities. But you still poor, whether the white boss says so or not." At one Delta welfare office, a white worker reportedly warned a black mother: "If you don't stop that freedom marching, I'm going to take your children from you." "The federal government ought to be ashamed of itself," Unita Blackwell charged. "The same men who pay us $3.00 a day and are bent on putting people off the land—that's the people who are on the poverty committee." Fannie Lou Hamer went even further when she claimed that "the people on those boards are the same people who were shooting at us in '63 and '64."[63]

The *National Observer* reported that only after considerable pressure from the federal government did the blacks living at Tent City begin to receive surplus commodities from Washington County officials. Unita Blackwell cited this case as "a perfect example of how government programs in the hands of local white folks can be used to break the people who are trying to better themselves. The whole idea is to keep them in line so they don't enter white schools, or register to vote, or do anything the white folks don't like."[64]

In the eyes of some critics, white officials made it as difficult to qualify for welfare assistance as to register to vote. In the Washington County food stamp office, a crowd of fifty to sixty blacks waiting to be served was a common sight. Many of these had traveled as far as thirty miles, often paying for a ride and not infrequently returning home with their applications unprocessed. Though apparently authorized to hire eight staff members, the office had only six, all of them white, to serve a clientele that was approximately 90 percent black.[65]

Delta whites were outraged when the tables were turned, albeit briefly, and the civil rights-oriented Child Development Group of Mississippi became the chief conduit for federal antipoverty funds in Mississippi. CDGM's clear ties to SNCC and its support for civil rights activities were a source of much irritation to whites in Mississippi, including Senators John C. Stennis and James Eastland. Charges of misuse of funds, often for political purposes, finally led the Office of Economic Opportunity to announce that CDGM would be replaced by a new organization, Mississippi Action for Progress, a twelve-person group chartered by Governor Paul B. Johnson and including white moderates such as Hodding Carter III, LeRoy Percy (a cousin of William Alexander Percy), and black NAACP leader Aaron Henry of Clarksdale. The leaders of this group were hardly reactionaries, but their charter bound them to act through Governor Johnson, a representative of the state's conservative white power structure. Republican critics also quickly pointed out that two of the MAP members were members of President Lyndon Johnson's "$1,000 a head" President's Club.[66]

With the active encouragement of the White House and the blessings of Senator Stennis, MAP forced the beleaguered remnants of the Mississippi Freedom Democratic party to soften their demands for grassroots empowerment as the two groups merged to form the pro-Johnson Loyalist coalition that unseated the segregationist regular state delegation at the 1968 Democratic national convention. Although the Loyalist victory represented a milestone for the forces of racial moderation, the taming of the MFDP signaled a return to the more conservative middle-class orientation that had marked the civil rights movement in Mississippi as the 1960s began.[67]

In the final analysis, the CDGAM-MAP controversy simply underscored the crucial linkage between control of federal funds and political power and momentum in Mississippi. The affair also demonstrated that, although they seemed to point in the same direction, federal agricultural, civil rights, and welfare initiatives in the Delta were often contradictory rather than complementary. On the one hand, civil rights legislation encouraged activism and the assertion of constitutional rights. So long as control of welfare funds and eligibility lists remained in the hands of Mississippi whites, however, civil rights protests and voter registration efforts were a risky proposition for the Delta's economically dependent blacks.

By the end of the 1960s, the interrelated influences of mechanization, federal acreage-reduction programs, and the minimum wage law had rendered Delta blacks largely superfluous to the economic interests of Delta whites, while the Voting Rights Act had transformed these former employees into an outright political liability. Despite their numerical advantage, however, continuing vulnerability to white coercion and the lack of an independent economic base made it difficult for blacks to mobilize and maintain the organizational structure needed to overcome white resistance to their political initiatives.

Black political gains came slowly, but by the end of the 1970s the sheer weight of the numbers finally began to take its toll. Air-base protest organizer Unita Blackwell became the first black female mayor in Mississippi when she was elected to lead the tiny Issaquena County town of Mayersville in 1977, and in 1979 black voters sent Clarksdale's Aaron Henry to join Robert Clark in the legislature. In the 1982 and 1984 congressional elections, conservative Republican Webb Franklin defeated Robert Clark in a campaign marked by heavy racial overtones and a voting pattern that adhered rigidly to the color line. In 1986 Mike Espy, a young black lawyer from Yazoo City, ousted Franklin by capturing 51 percent of the vote in a district where the voting-age population was 53 percent black. Ironically, Espy's ability to attract a larger share of the white vote than had Clark was attributable in part to the dissatisfaction of Delta whites with the farm program austerity measures introduced by the Reagan administration. Espy won reelection in 1988, and the following year his brother, Henry, became Clarksdale's first black mayor. By the end of the 1980s, there were eighteen black county supervisors, eighteen black mayors, two black sheriffs, and three black school superintendents holding office in the Delta area.[68]

The expansion of black officeholding was encouraging, but, more than a half century after the New Deal had first come to the Delta, the region's story was still one of dislocation, disparity, and dependence. The circumstances faced by many blacks elsewhere in the Delta differed little from those discovered in Tunica County, which captured fervent attention from the media and major political figures like Reverend Jesse Jackson, who described its infamous "Sugar Ditch" alley as "America's Ethiopia." Tunica's story was a familiar one in the Delta. Between 1960 and 1984, the number of farms in the county fell by 90 percent, while the average size grew by the same figure. Forty-five percent of its households lived in poverty, and the percentage of personal income attributable to government transfer payments was greater than that for agriculture and manufacturing combined. Health conditions remained deplorable; the county's infant mortality rate was nearly twice as high as that of Jamaica.[69]

Transfer payments were the chief source of income in all Delta counties in the 1980s. On average, more than 55 percent of the families in each county received less than ten thousand dollars in income in 1979. As had been the case historically, however, the region's poverty was still juxtaposed with relative affluence, much of it subsidized by federal funds. The percentage of families with less than ten thousand dollars in annual income was 80 percent higher in Delta counties than in the state's metropolitan counties, but the percentage of families receiving more than fifty thousand dollars per year (2.83) was nearly equal to the metropolitan average (2.96). Even Hinds County, where the capital city of Jackson is located, took a back seat in this latter category to Issaquena in the Delta, where 4.7 percent of the families received more than fifty thousand dollars and 53.9 percent less than ten thousand dollars, and where there was neither a public school system nor a hospital.[70]

These statistics suggest why the ten core counties of the Delta lost 33,265 nonwhites to out-migration between 1970 and 1980. To those who remained in the Delta, a forlorn and crumbling Freedom City was a compelling reminder of their dashed hopes. The Greenville Air Force Base was again occupied briefly in the 1980s, not by displaced farm workers but by a Boeing Aircraft repair operation. The air base was part of an eighteen-million-dollar subsidy package used to lure the Boeing plant to the Delta in 1985 after Boeing promised to create more than six hundred new jobs in an area with massive unemployment, but the company closed its Greenville facility in 1989, citing anticipated repair contracts that failed to materialize.[71]

Observers generally agreed that, however unintentionally, the minimum wage law had contributed heavily to the move toward increased mechanization and displacement of labor in the Delta. The same law also fell far short of its intended regulatory effect; a number of Delta farm workers still received wages well below the federal minimum as the result of either outright underpayment or suspect deductions for rent or for a "Christmas fund." Mechanics and tractor drivers rarely managed to avoid going in debt to the planter over the winter, and, while the accuracy of the planter's figures was more subject to challenge than in the pre-civil rights years, black workers in the Delta knew all too well that, in a labor surplus region, "if you get branded as 'trouble' you a can't find another job anywhere."[72]

Planters who flouted the law were occasionally discovered and forced to make restitution. Multimillionaire planter Roy Flowers, who had bragged to Nicholas Von Hoffman about his kindness to his workers, was forced to pay fifty thousand dollars in back wages when he was found guilty of ignoring the minimum wage and of overcharging his tenants for everything from house rent to cotton-picking sacks. Still, such was the power of intimidation and the continuing influence of planters over local affairs that some workers were reluctant to claim even court-ordered compensation. In 1978, when the two Yazoo County planters were ordered to repay more than forty thousand dollars in back wages, they warned workers who sought to collect what was due them that they were liable to lose their welfare or food stamp benefits. Said one planter, "Anybody drawing a check, I'm turning them in."[73]

With planters retaining their ability to affect the distribution of public social welfare benefits, it was small wonder that they also retained considerable influence over black farm workers. Those who attributed the hesitance of mechanics and tractor drivers to leave the plantation to their reluctance to cross "the Man" failed, however, to consider how few alternatives the economically stagnant Delta offered its unskilled black population. A sharecropper's son who was employed as a plantation mechanic explained, "As long as I can make it, I'm going to try and make it here. I know a few boys that left here and went to Greenwood and they didn't make a dime more than we make."[74]

Many of those who finally abandoned the Delta altogether seemed unable to shake the poverty and dependence that had marked their lives as sharecroppers. Robert Coles saw northbound refugees from Delta plantations carrying with them "a chronic state of mind, a form of withdrawn, sullen behavior that the word 'depression' only begins to describe."[75]

In 1986 Nicholas Lemann offered a provocative analysis of the origins of the American "underclass" in which he examined the spirit-numbing welfare culture of the northern urban ghetto. Lemann found many black families living on welfare in Chicago who had either worked in Mississippi as sharecroppers or were children of those who had, and he claimed to see a strong correlation between "underclass status in the North and a family background in the nascent underclass of the sharecropper South." In 1991 Lemann reiterated his belief that "among the migrants, people who had grown up in the sharecropping system—rural, poorly educated, often from unstable families—tended to fare worst in the North."[76]

Of this group, Lemann noted, it was those who had headed north after 1965 who seemed to encounter the most difficulty. By the 1960s, however, as Lemann himself acknowledged, the sharecropper system was "mostly dead in the South." At this point most former croppers who remained in the Delta were somehow managing to hang on as occasional day laborers, who also received a measure of welfare support. Even this tenuous status was difficult to maintain in the wake of the 1967 minimum wage law, and at the end of the sixties, thousands of blacks from the Delta and elsewhere had joined in a final "burst" of migration to northern cities, which were "far less hospitable" than they had been for migrants in earlier decades.[77]

Inner-city economic deterioration meant that refugees from the Delta found Chicago much less of a "promised land" in the 1960s than it had been in the 1940s. Still, Lemann's insightful analysis might also have taken note of the fact that for many, probably most, of the migrants of the sixties, the separation from sharecropping had been followed by a swift descent into an even more marginal and dependent existence, where their only hopes for economic survival lay with a welfare system and a smattering of seasonal jobs, both controlled by whites. If, as Lemann suggests, these later migrants faced material and psychological disadvantages that might be traceable to their sharecropper backgrounds, their difficulties were simply exacerbated by their inability to escape white coercion and supervision even after they were no longer part of the sharecropping system itself. For some Delta blacks the angry activism of the 1960s simply faded into a life on the edge of subsistence at the edge of a cotton field, while for others it eventually dissolved into the destructive monotony of a northern ghetto. The result in either case only underscored the tragic long-term consequences of Washington's willingness to grant local whites so much influence over the direction and flow of federal assistance into the Delta that, from the standpoint of the recipient, the paternalism that flowed from the banks of the Potomac might as well have originated on the banks of the Mississippi.

As was often the case with American assistance to other nations, in the Delta aid offered in the name of economic rehabilitation and human uplift was routed, in the interest of political expediency and stability, through those at the top of the region's socioeconomic structure. As a result, the story of the interaction of agricultural, civil rights, and social welfare policy in the Mississippi Delta is especially instructive. Regardless of region, nation, or hemisphere, when economic reform proceeds under safeguards against redistribution of wealth or power, social and political rights will prove difficult to extend and dangerous to exercise. Meanwhile, whether its story is told in the smudged ledgers of the landlord or the antiseptic memoranda of the bureaucrat, the phenomenon of economic and sociopolitical dependence is likely to remain as real and as debilitating as ever.

12 ▽ "The Blues Is a Lowdown
▽ Shakin' Chill"
▽

Although they appeared in the Mississippi Delta at the end of
the nineteenth century, not until the twentieth century was drawing to a close
did the blues gain widespread acceptance as a legitimate American musical
form. According to legend, the remarkable odyssey of the blues actually began
in 1903 at the railroad station in Tutwiler, Mississippi, where W. C. Handy
first heard "a lean, loose-jointed Negro" playing what Handy described as "the
weirdest music I ever heard." Another of Handy's early encounters with the
blues came when his band was performing for a dance at Cleveland and someone asked if he would mind if "a local colored band played a few dances."
Clearly Handy was not impressed by the appearance of the hometown aggregation: "They were led by a long-legged chocolate boy, and their band consisted of just three pieces, a battered guitar, a mandolin, and a worn-out bass."
Handy found the band's music "pretty well in keeping with their looks." It was
characterized by an "over and over" strumming that quickly "attained a disturbing monotony, the kind of foot-thumping, eye-rolling music associated
with cane rows and levee camps." Handy admitted that he found the music
more "haunting" than annoying, but, although he would gain fame as the dis-
coverer and popularizer of the blues, he doubted at the time that "anybody
besides small town rounders and their running mates would go for it."[1]
Handy was not the last observer who would underestimate and oversim-
plify the blues. Although they were rooted in the system of labor and social
relations that emerged in the Delta in the last quarter of the nineteenth century,
their influence eventually reached far beyond the levee camps and cotton fields
of the region. Not only did they offer invaluable insights into the lives of Delta
blacks, but their powerful and enduring legacy shaped the musical culture of
several generations of white youths who knew little of the roots of the blues
but nonetheless related to the sense of alienation and rebellion that permeated
the music of those who occupied the bottom strata of Delta society.[2]
Individual blues performances typically focused on male-female relationships and other intensely personal experiences with both pleasure and pain.

Yet, as an emotionally charged, deeply expressive, and unfailingly candid new music, the blues also offered an insider's perspective on the communal search for self-determination and stability that dominated the postemancipation experience of black southerners as a group.

The blues made their appearance almost simultaneously on the plantations and in the logging and levee camps throughout the Deep South. Although the blues flourished in a variety of locales, each of the music's several spawning grounds was a place where blacks came in search of a better life only to find themselves trapped in an endless cycle of hard work and meager reward amid almost intolerable living and working conditions. Given this reality, it is hardly surprising that the blues tradition developed so fully and rapidly in the Mississippi Delta, which, as Figure 1 illustrates, was clearly the principal source of blues performers during the music's formative years. While the historical context of the Delta is by no means adequate to explain the entire content of the blues, the relationship between the two is important to an understanding of both.[3]

In 1909 a visitor to the Delta overheard a black woman singing as she plowed a cotton field. He compared what he heard to the "lamentation of a

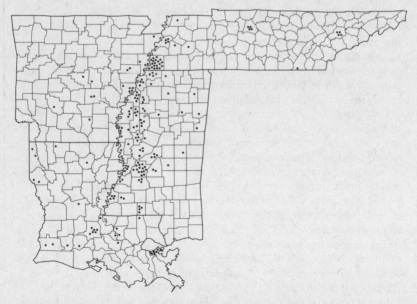

Figure 1. Birthplaces of Recorded Blues Performers, 1890–1920

Source: John F. Rooney, Jr., Wilbur Zelinsky, and Dean R. Louder, eds., *This Remarkable Continent: An Atlas of United States and Canadian Society and Cultures* (College Station, Texas, 1982), 243. Reprinted with the permission of George Carney.

creature in great distress and isolation" and concluded that her song "made me feel as if I were travelling through an African region and had just been to visit a colony of prisoners in confinement." A number of scholars, including Law-rence Levine, have identified certain central elements of the African "tradi-tional communal musical style" in the blues, but this new musical form actually evolved as part of a process whereby former slaves drew on both their African and American heritages to formulate a cultural response to the much-antici-pated but generally disappointing experience of emancipation.[4]

Structurally and stylistically, the blues drew on the same traditions and material that had provided the basis for the slave spirituals and work songs. The blues derived most directly, however, from the field hollers that could be heard throughout the nineteenth-century South, not only on the plantations but any-where blacks were engaged in hard manual labor. Linking the blues to the work environment of rural blacks in the Delta, blues performer Bukka White insisted, "That's where the blues start from, back across them fields. . . . It started right behind one of them mules or one of them log houses, one of them log camps or the levee camp. That's where the blues sprung from. I know what I'm talking about."[5]

Describing the field hollers, bluesman Son House recalled, "They'd sing about their girl friend or about almost anything—mule—anything. They'd make a song of it just to be hollering." Lawrence Levine cited the Coahoma County plowman who provided this example of a field holler suggestive of the blues-in-the-making, singing first to his mule:

> O-O-O, This donkey won't drink water.
> I'll knock him in the collar till he go stone blind . . .

And then to himself:

> The gal I'm lovin' she can't be found.

David Evans concluded that somewhere near the end of the nineteenth century the "free, almost formless vocal expressions" of the field hollers "were set to instrumental accompaniment and given a musical structure, an expanded range of subject matter and a new social context" in a remarkable creative process that gave birth to the blues.[6]

As the music matured, blues lyrics typically appeared in a configuration marked by twelve-bar, three-line stanzas with the first statement repeated in the second line and supplemented or extended in the third. Levine used Charley Patton's "Green River Blues" as a classic example:

> Some people say the Green River blues ain't bad.
> Some people say the Green River blues ain't bad.
> Then it must not have been the Green River blues I had.[7]

Across the South the blues emerged as blacks reached the final and unavoidable realization that the great promise of freedom was to be, if not denied, at least indefinitely deferred. Hence the Delta's misleading image as an attractive promised land for black farmers was no doubt crucial to its role as a breeding place for the blues. With its rich soil and intense demand for farm labor, the postbellum Delta had promised blacks the best opportunity available anywhere in the South to rise to independent landowning status. Lured by the chance to make a good crop under relatively good living conditions and to receive relatively good treatment from whites in the bargain, blacks had flooded into the Yazoo Basin, making it the premier testing ground for emancipation in the rural South of the late nineteenth century.

Among the black migrants who came to the Delta in the 1890s were Bill and Annie Patton and their twelve children. The Pattons had moved north from near Bolton and Edwards, anticipating that their large family work force would bring them an advantageous sharecropping contract with a labor-hungry Delta planter. Believing they had found such a planter in Will Dockery, they settled on his plantation on the banks of the Sunflower River east of Cleveland. Although the Pattons were but one of thousands of black families who moved to the Delta in search of a better life, their decision to locate at Dockery's proved to be a pivotal event in both the history and mythology of American music.[8]

By the time the Pattons arrived, their son Charley was already playing the guitar, much to the consternation of a God-fearing, quick-to-punish father. Charley had learned music from the Chatmon family at Bolton, but the Chatmons' repertoire consisted of popular, ragtime, and white-oriented country dance tunes that bore little relationship to the music that would emerge as the Delta blues. At Dockery's Patton fell under the influence of Henry Sloan, a guitarist whose primitive rhythms captivated the young newcomer. The Patton family got along reasonably well at Dockery's, but young Charley, despite frequent and severe whippings from his father, fell into the hedonistic lifestyle of the musician. He drank heavily, worked infrequently, and managed somehow to stay on good terms with several women who worked for local whites and therefore could keep him well supplied with food. In the process of drinking, fighting, abusing and exploiting women, and avoiding insofar as possible having to work for whites himself, Patton also earned a lasting place in the history of American popular music through his influence on a host of bluesmen whose work in turn left a major imprint on several distinct musical forms.[9]

By 1918, when his mentor, Henry Sloan, left the Delta for Chicago, Patton already had a reputation as the finest musician in the area. One artist who fell under his spell and that of his companion, Willie Brown, was Tommy Johnson. He finally settled in Boyle, a village near Cleveland that was connected to Dockery's by the Pea Vine railroad. After two years in the Delta, Johnson returned to south Mississippi and began sharing what he had learned from Patton and Brown. Blues legend Robert Johnson first encountered Willie

Brown in the mid-1920s, and it was through Brown that he met Charley Patton. Howlin' Wolf also moved to Dockery's in 1926 and soon became one of Patton's favorite protégés.[10]

The Delta's attraction for most blacks was the prospect of working rich land on favorable terms. For a small but gifted coterie of musicians, however, it also offered the chance to learn a new and increasingly popular music from those who had pioneered in it. Son House, who came to Robinsonville in Tunica County in 1930, soon fell under Charley Patton's influence. As a young man, Bukka White's ambition was to "come to be a great man like Charley Patton." Both House and White spent a great deal of time listening to Patton's recordings. White remembered being unable to squeeze into an overcrowded room in Clarksdale where a new Patton record was being played. The popularity of blues records among Delta blacks was reflected in their love of the phonograph. For most of them, the victrola was their most expensive and prized possession. As Pete Daniel pointed out, during the 1927 flood fleeing blacks were more likely to try to save their victrolas than anything else they owned.[11]

Blues records were precious commodities, but after a long, hard week in the fields, a Saturday night spent listening to live music at a blues jook joint or house party was a blessing indeed. W. C. Handy's doubts about the popular appeal of blues performers were soon dispelled by a shower of silver dollars that fell around the rag-tag aggregation he encountered at Cleveland. At that point, Handy confessed, he suddenly saw "the beauty of the primitive music. . . . It touched the spot. Their music wanted polishing, but it contained the essence." More important, Handy realized that "folks would pay good money for it," and overnight he became a composer: "Those country black boys at Cleveland had taught me something. . . . My idea of what constitutes music was changed by the sight of that silver money cascading around the splay feet of a Mississippi string band."[12]

Charley Patton protégé Roebuck Staples, who lived on Dockery's plantation from age eight to twenty, recalled that on a typical Saturday afternoon "everybody would go into town and those fellows like Charley Patton, Robert Johnson, and Howlin' Wolf would be playin' on the streets, standin' by the railroad tracks, people pitchin' 'em nickels and dimes, white and black people both. The train come through town maybe once that afternoon and when it was time, everybody would gather around there, before and after the train came, and announce where they'd be that night. And that's where the crowd would go." When the crowd arrived, the scene was one of noise, excitement, and bright lights: "They'd have a plank nailed across the door to the kitchen and be sellin' fish and chitlins, with dancin' in the front room, gamblin' in the side room, and maybe two or three gas or coal-oil lamps on the mantel piece in front of the mirror—powerful light."[13]

Such gatherings were raucous and, as often as not, violent. "Them country balls were rough!" Son House recalled: "They were critical, man! They'd start off good, you know. Everybody happy, dancing, and then they'd start to getting louder and louder. The women would be dipping that snuff and swallowing that snuff spit along with that corn whiskey, and they'd start to mixing fast, and oh, brother! They'd start something then!"[14]

As the blues evolved, performers from different localities developed distinctive vocal and instrumental styles. Robert Palmer has stressed this diversity of the blues, noting that any sense of a cohesive identity for the music would require intensive examination of the repertoires of dozens of musicians. Still, these early Delta blues had some definite identifying characteristics: "The Mississippi Delta's blues musicians sang with unmatched intensity in a gritty, melodically circumscribed, highly ornamented style that was closer to field hollers than it was to other blues. Guitar and piano accompaniments were percussive and hypnotic, and many Delta guitarists mastered the art of fretting the instrument with a slider or bottleneck; they made the instrument 'talk' in strikingly speechlike inflections."[15]

Both the structure and the lyric content of the new music suggested that the key to the emergence of the blues was the development of "new forms of self-conception" among blacks. "The blues," Levine wrote, "was the most highly personalized, indeed, the first almost completely personalized music that Afro-Americans developed." Bluesmen performed solo—or at least blues performances featured a single performer—singing in the first person of his own experiences, suffering, and dreams and receiving a collective acknowledgment from an audience that had shared many of these feelings and experiences. The blues emerged in an era when prevailing mass culture values stressed rugged individualism as the key to upward mobility, but the values they exalted were hardly those of Horatio Alger or, more appropriately, Booker T. Washington. Instead of "Up from Slavery," the message of the blues was "Up from Slavery, but Not Far."[16]

David Evans explained that emancipation replaced the well-defined anonymity of slavery with the "responsibility" of freedom and a deck stacked more in favor of failure than achievement. The new life in freedom was also marked by hard labor, institutionalized discrimination; the threat of violence, death, and imprisonment; and the frustrations of tenancy with the often peripatetic existence it entailed. Evans wrote: "If economic failure, breakup of the family, and a desire to escape through travel resulted from these conditions, it is no wonder." Nor was it any wonder, in turn, that these concerns emerged as principal themes in the blues.[17]

Whereas others described the blues in terms of their matter-of-factness about suffering and social injustice, William Barlow found a spirit of rebellion in the blues, arguing that blues musicians presented a "ground-level view of southern society" and insisting that both their behavior and the content of their music represented a rejection of the values of the dominant white culture. Instead of an overt protest, however, the blues offered an alternative lifestyle in which rambling, hedonism, aggressive sexuality, and a general disregard for authority were the norm. Barlow sensed within the blues "an ethos of revolt" that he attributed to "the emerging consciousness of a young generation seeking personal freedom, social mobility, and better compensation for their labor." He insisted that the blues were "not the result of a few isolated incidents of individual genius, but rather a broadly based cultural movement occupying the time and energy of large numbers of black agricultural workers in the South's cotton belt."[18]

The black work force in the cotton belt was anything but stable as the twentieth century began. The large-scale movement of blacks into the Delta was part of a regionwide, east-to-west, north-to-south flow of workers responding to the greater demand for their services in a region where the soil was fertile but difficult to clear and cultivate. Unfortunately, the wages or terms offered in the Delta, while often better than elsewhere in the rural South, were still much less attractive than those available in other parts of the nation. At the same time, the treatment of black labor, while perhaps superior to that in many other areas in the South, was decidedly inferior to that afforded elsewhere in the nation. As the farm wage gap between states like Mississippi and Ohio widened from twenty cents a day in 1880 to eighty cents a day in 1914, bright promise soon dissolved into bitter frustration, especially as centralized, streamlined, and impersonal plantation management increasingly consigned sharecroppers to a lifetime of hard labor with little hope of achieving either economic or personal independence from whites. Meanwhile, the prospect of political equality embodied in black-white political fusion efforts gave way to the reality of disfranchisement, lynching, and the hate-mongering of James K. Vardaman. Given these developments, it is hardly surprising that the blues emphasized dissatisfaction and alienation as well as an ongoing struggle in the face of overwhelming odds.[19]

As the completion of the Delta's railroad system sealed the region's transformation from untamed frontier to modern plantation kingdom, it also ushered in an era of declining social, economic, and political prospects, one that called for tough decisions by Delta blacks. Whereas they had always found it difficult to ignore the contradictions between their own circumstances and prospects and those of their white employers, the Delta's expanded railroad network also exposed many more Delta blacks to the contrast between black life in the Delta and the rosy promise of life in the urban North. The vision of a promised land to the north dominated the pages of the Chicago *Defender*, borne southward and sold by railroad porters traveling through the Delta. In addition to its role as the conduit for letters from relatives and friends already gone, the Illinois Central Railroad itself became a seductive symbol of the superiority of northern life. Moreover, the Delta's new railroad system put the majority of the region's blacks within twenty-four hours of Chicago, thereby providing both the temptation as well as the means to leave the Delta. Not sur-

prisingly, the railroad became a symbol of freedom and escape as references to
the Illinois Central permeated the Delta blues:

> That I. C. Special is the only train I choose,
> That's the train I ride when I get these I. C. blues.[20]

Linking the blues to the Great Migration, William Barlow saw "a clear
historical connection between the rebellious and restless spirit of this new
music and "the Afro-Americans' mass exodus out of the cotton belt." For all
the anger and dissatisfaction they may have expressed, however, with their
emphasis on rambling and impermanence as well as escape, the blues were no
more the music of those who had decided to leave than of those who had
decided to stay or, perhaps more so, those who were unable to decide. Certainly, by the second decade of the twentieth century, Delta blacks found themselves confronting a difficult choice. Should they uproot themselves and their
families (perhaps for the second time in a relatively short period), leave friends
and familiar surroundings, and depart for the golden streets of northern cities?
Or should they hang on in the Delta, hoping for the big crop year that might
free them from debt and give them the opportunity to become independent,
landowning farmers? As Neil McMillen has written, "The decision to vote
with one's feet, to leave in search of fuller participation in American life, was
perhaps the clearest and most frequently exercised expression of black discontent. But it was a relatively costly and wrenching option beyond the reach of
many and one that even some of the most alienated black Mississippians might
not choose to exercise." For many blacks the blues conveyed better than any
other medium available their agonizing struggle with the "wrenching option"
of northward migration.[21]

For most who did remain in the Delta, there was anything but stability and
promise in their existence. They became part of a forever shifting, essentially
rootless farm labor force, more concerned about survival than advancement,
their existence and outlook captured by the bluesman's resigned lament:

> Goin' no higher;
> Goin' no lower down.
> Gonna stay right here,
> Gonna stay right here,
> 'Til they close me down.[22]

Muddy Waters left the Stovall place in Coahoma County for Chicago in
1943 and seldom returned: "I wanted to get out of Mississippi in the worst way,
man. Go back? What I want to go back for?" It was Waters who popularized
the lines:

> If I feel tomorrow, the way I feel today,
> I'm gonna pack my bags and make my getaway.

Such lyrics suggested disappointment and might mean that the singer was at last ready to muster his courage for the trip north to the promised land of Chicago, or they might signal no more than a move to a nearby plantation. Such a move might not bring better economic conditions; indeed, it could well bring worse ones, especially if it primarily reflected a desire to escape the supervision and enforced regimen of efficiency that characterized the large "business plantations." Still, by changing plantations a black sharecropper could at least exercise what little control he retained over his own destiny. Moreover, merely "slipping" one plantation for another postponed a much tougher decision about a bigger move away from family, friends, familiar surroundings, and the assurance of at least minimal upkeep from a landlord. It was small wonder, then, that blues lyrics, while stressing movement, often expressed mixed feelings about it:

> Gotta mind to move,
> A mind to settle down.[23]

As Joel Williamson explained, the early blues should be seen as "the cry of the cast-out black, ultimately alone and lonely, after one world was lost and before another was found." When the blues were emerging in the late nineteenth and early twentieth centuries, Delta blacks were still struggling to disengage themselves from the dreams of independence and prosperity that had brought them or their parents to the region in the first place. In addition, they were also beginning to wrestle with the temptation to embrace a new dream, that of a better life in the urban North.[24]

Not surprisingly, the ambivalence, uncertainty, and restlessness that permeated the lives of Delta blacks was readily apparent in their music as well. Conflict and contradiction and the agony of making tough choices were apparent throughout the blues, not just in songs about rambling or escape but in those that dealt with personal relationships as well. For example, Charley Patton sang:

> Sometimes I say I need you;
> Then again I don't. . . .
> Sometimes I think I'll quit you;
> Then again I won't.[25]

By focusing on transience, uncertainty, and rebellion, the blues seemed to offer a disturbing contradiction to the reassurances provided by the teachings of the church. Moreover, blues performances appeared to compete with church services for the affections of Delta blacks, not so much because of their secular orientation but because they possessed a certain spiritual quality of their own and therefore threatened to usurp the communal, cathartic role that was otherwise the function of organized religious activity. Lawrence Levine explained

that, like "both the spirituals and folktales, the blues was an expression of experiences and feelings common to the group." Elsewhere, Li'l Son Jackson, a
bluesman-turned-gospel singer, identified the "sinfulness" of the blues in
terms of the sense of autonomy and individual responsibility for one's own fate
that they projected: "If a man feel hurt within side and he sing a church song
then he's askin' God for help. . . . If a man sing the blues it's more or less out
of himself. . . . He's not askin' no one for help. And he's not really clingin' to
no-one. But he's expressin' how he feel. . . . You're trying to get your feelin's
over to the next person through the blues, and that's what makes it a sin."[26]

The flesh-and-blood realism of the blues gave them a relevance that many
blacks found lacking in the scriptures or spirituals. Vicksburg bluesman Willie
Dixon explained, "I was raised on blues and spirituals, but after you wake up
to a lot of facts about life, you know, the spiritual thing starts to look kind of
phony in places."[27]

Lawrence Levine linked the anticlerical implications of the blues to what
he called the "decline of the sacred world view," a phenomenon he traced
through black humor as well. One need only note the scorn and ridicule heaped
on the stereotypical bed-hopping black minister in the Delta to make the connection. Bluesmen and the lyrics of the music they sang often expressed open
contempt for preachers. When drunk or angry, Robert Johnson would even
curse God openly, much to the consternation of his often frightened audience.
Not surprisingly, Johnson had little time for religion in his songs:

> If I had possession over Judgment Day. . . .
> I wouldn't give my woman the right to pray.

In "Preachin' the Blues," Son House vowed cynically to "be a Baptist preacher
and I sure won't have to work." House also placed the blues and religion
squarely at odds when he sang:

> Oh, up in my room,
> I bowed down to pray;
> Say, the blues come along,
> And they drove my spirit away.[28]

For all such evidence of conflict between the two, however, the blues actually coexisted quite peacefully with organized religion and appeared even to
complement it on occasion. Describing black tenant families, Jeff Titon wrote:
"If values and behavior did not conform to white middle-class standards, they
were well suited to the economic system and to the culture it carried. People
moved frequently, if not easily, from Saturday night dances to Sunday services;
structural and functional similarities made the transition more comfortable."
Clifton Taulbert recalled Sunday afternoon sessions where Glen Allan blacks,
many still wearing their church clothes, danced, drank beer, ate catfish, and

"lost themselves in the blues." Taulbert added, "They sang the blues with the excitement of a Sunday church service. . . . They knew it would be Monday in the morning, but this was their time, their Sunday, and they let the blues express the life they lived." Titon explained that "the blues sermon often proved as therapeutic as Sunday morning worship. The large number of singers and listeners who have testified to feeling better after blues performances indicates that the ceremonies were effective, that people were renewed."[29]

Like his clerical counterpart, the bluesman was a key figure, symbolic of a communal culture. Moreover, like the preacher, the bluesman entertained his audiences by expressing deeply felt, shared emotions in a manner that made him more than an entertainer. The murmurs of reinforcement and encouragement that buoyed John Dollard as he spoke to a black congregation in Indianola bore a strong similarity to the give-and-take between audience and performer at a blues session. As Levine observed, "Black musical performances properly speaking had no audience, just participants."[30]

Another scholar saw both the preacher and the bluesman in terms of the "privileges of their office: more money, greater social prestige, finer clothes and an attractiveness to women not shared by the common man. "Both preacher and bluesman filled their society's need for "entertainment, catharsis, recreation and ritual." Both promoted group solidarity and reinforced group values and traditions. Steeped in black culture, they represented "the two prime role models that have been generated within black society."[31]

Although the two worlds represented by the preacher and the bluesman seemed largely antithetical, they actually overlapped a great deal; many a bluesman moved into the pulpit, while not a few preachers found a second calling at the jook joint or country dance. Charley Patton not only recorded some religious songs but periodically renounced whiskey and women and turned to Bible study in preparation for a career in the pulpit. He reportedly fled via the back door of the church when he panicked at the thought of his first sermon, but he did preach successfully on several occasions. His conversions to the ministry never lasted, but he recorded a favorite sermon drawn largely from the book of Revelation and allegedly repeated it in a frenzy on his deathbed.[32]

Born into a deeply religious, "sanctified" Pentecostal family, Sonny Boy Williamson claimed to have been a minister himself at one time. He soon abandoned the pulpit, however, for the life of an itinerant musician, performing under a variety of pseudonyms. Frederick Jay Hay saw in the early recordings of Williamson a tendency not just to secularize but actually "sensualize" religion. "Eyesight to the Blind" described a woman whose sexual powers had all the healing capabilities of the Holy Spirit:

> You talk about your woman,
> I wish to God you could see mine. . . .
> Everytime she start loving,
> She brings eyesight to the blind.

Hay compared this message to that of "Amazing Grace": "I once was blind but now I see."[33]

In a sense the bluesman and the preacher may have also shared similar pressures to conform to widely held stereotypes. For the preacher this meant flamboyance, conviviality, and possibly an eye for women; for the bluesman it certainly meant an eye for women, but it demanded as well a reckless, rambling, hard-drinking lifestyle that made his music and his persona one and the same. The stereotype of the lazy, shiftless musician was hardly peculiar to the bluesman, but if they did not consciously cultivate this persona, Delta blues performers did nothing to dispel it. As Barry Lee Pearson explained, "The itinerant musician presented the image of being footloose and fancy free—a romantic alternative to the drudgery of sharecropping." Freddie Spruell's "Low Down Mississippi Bottom Man" depicted the bluesman stereotype to near perfection:

> Way down in the Delta, that's where I long to be,
> Where the Delta bottom women are sure goin' crazy over me.
> I'm lookin' for a woman who's lookin' for a low-down man.
> Ain't nobody in town get more low down than I can.[34]

When Tommy Johnson left Crystal Springs for the Delta, he was still a teenager and relatively innocent of the ways of the world. After a year or so of associating with Delta bluesmen, however, he was not only a compulsive womanizer but a hopeless alcoholic, so addicted that when whiskey was unavailable he would consume shoe polish or even Sterno or "canned heat." His "Canned Heat Blues," recorded in Memphis in 1928, was clearly autobiographical: "Canned heat don't kill me; crying babe I'll never die." Along with his degeneration into a "rambler" and a "rounder" came a surprisingly sudden maturity as a musician that Johnson attributed to a pact with the Devil. He repeated to anyone who would listen the story of his bargain at the crossroads:

> If you want to learn how to play anything you want to play and learn how to make songs yourself, you take your guitar and you go to where a road crosses that way, where the crossroad is. . . . Be sure to get there, just a little 'fore twelve o'clock that night so you'll know you'll be there. You have your guitar and be playing a piece sitting there by yourself. You have to go by yourself and be sitting there playing a piece. A big black man will walk up there and take your guitar and he'll tune it. And then he'll play a piece and hand it back to you. That's the way I learned how to play everything I want.[35]

A similar and even more powerful legend grew up around bluesman Robert Johnson. Son House recalled that as an adolescent Johnson would slip away from home late at night to attend one of the "balls" where House and Willie Brown were playing. When the two took a break, Johnson would pick up one of their guitars and attempt to play it, although, according to House, the results were usually anything but satisfactory: "Such another racket you never heard! It'd make the people mad, you know. They'd come out and say, 'Why don't y'all go in there and get that guitar away from that boy! He's running people crazy with it.' I'd come back in and I'd scold him about it. 'Don't do that, Robert. You drive people nuts. You can't play nothing.'"[36]

Frustrated, humiliated, and unenthusiastic about farm work, young Johnson finally ran away from home and stayed gone for approximately six months. He surfaced again one evening when House and Brown were playing, a guitar swung over his back. House took up where he had left off, taunting Johnson, "Well, boy, you still got a guitar, huh? What do you do with that thing? You can't do nothing with it." This time, however, Johnson responded self-confidently, "Let me have your seat a minute." House agreed, winking at Brown and warning Johnson that he "had better do something" once he was in House's seat. To House's and Brown's amazement, Johnson had mysteriously transformed himself into a guitarist par excellence: "He was so good! When he finished all our mouths were standing open. I said, 'Well, ain't that fast! He's gone now!'"[37]

One of Robert Johnson's relatives told a researcher that the suddenly gifted young bluesman had met the Devil at a certain crossroads in the Delta. "The Devil came there and gave Robert his talent and told him he had eight more years to live on earth." Almost certainly aware of the legend of Tommy Johnson's pact with the Devil, Robert Johnson did nothing to dispel the rumors or the reputation he developed as a dangerous, sinister, but also melancholy and darkly romantic musical genius. Johnson sang frequently about the Devil and the supernatural and often projected a deeply troubling, menacing personal image. Muddy Waters timidly peeked into a crowd in Friars Point to catch a glimpse of a musician he thought might be Robert Johnson: "I stopped and peeked over, and then I left because he was a dangerous man."[38]

The figure who carried the association with the Devil to its most obviously orchestrated extreme was William Bundy, who called himself "Peetie Wheatstraw," the "Devil's Son-in-law," or the "High Sheriff from Hell." Born near Memphis in 1902, Wheatstraw grew up across the river in the Arkansas Delta and doubtless influenced Robert Johnson as he did others, like Floyd "the Devil's Daddy-in-law" Council. Unlike Johnson's, however, Wheatstraw's attempts to link himself with the Devil became comical, little more than a caricature. In his "Peetie Wheatstraw Stomp," he bragged:

> Women all raving about Peetie Wheatstraw in this land. . . .
> I am Peetie Wheatstraw, the High Sheriff from Hell;
> The way I strut my stuff so well now you never can tell.
> He makes some happy some he make cry;
> Well, now he make one old lady, go hang herself and die.

The "High Sheriff from Hell" even appeared in novelist Ralph Ellison's *Invisible Man*: "My name is Peter Wheatstraw, I'm the Devil's only son-in-law, so roll'em! . . . All it takes to get along in this here man's town is a little shit, grit, and mother-wit. And man, I was born with all three. . . . I'm a piano player and a rounder, a whiskey drinker and a pavement pounder, I'll teach you some good bad habits."[39]

A legendary element in the folklore of the blues, the musician's bargain with the Devil has roots in African religious beliefs that are also preserved in voodoo. Actually more like the trickster figure of Afro-American lore than the sinister Devil or Satan depicted in the scriptures, Legba was a black man traditionally associated with the crossroads. (Robert Johnson played the role of trickster to the hilt, carrying a large rabbit's foot and performing all manner of acrobatics with his guitar.) Known for his manual dexterity, Legba was also a personification of male sexual potency, and this characteristic, combined with his freedom of movement and free and easy way with words, left him an appropriate symbol for the bluesman himself. Thus Legba became, in the view of Steve West, a figure who "frequents shadows on the limits of civilization and waits for those so disillusioned with life and vastly victimized by false promise that they would carry a guitar down to the crossroads at midnight and wait for the devil to work his magic."[40]

Although the pact with Satan soon took on the aspect of a folk legend turned musician's promotional gimmick, the fabled willingness of bluesmen to strike such a deal not only reinforced the stereotype of the blues as the devil's music but was perhaps the ultimate symbolic expression of black alienation. William Barlow saw in the mythology of the deal with the Devil "a defiance of the dominant white culture that enforces its social constraints with the help of its official religion, Christianity." The significance of the relationship between the official, white-sanctioned Christian code of morality and the aims and wishes of local whites was by no means lost on Delta blacks, as indicated by the heroic status accorded Roy, the condemned murderer who refused to repent, as well as the popularity of a number of folk-hero black "badmen" like Stagolee.[41]

The bluesman, a rounder, drifter, drinker, and womanizer who disdained work and any restraints on his morality or behavior, was the antithesis of what Delta whites wanted their black workers to be. It was not just the music but also the lifestyle of the blues musician that presented a problem for the white power structure. Refusal to work for the white man could be evidence of laziness, or it could suggest rebellion. One bluesman asked, "A black man, if he didn't work out in the fields, he was called lazy, no good. But who was he working for? You figure out who the lazy one was!" One observer allowed that a planter would "rather see a dog than a guitar player." Certainly, the image of a man who survived without working for whites was a socially desirable one within the black community, and a bluesman was just as likely to boast, "I's

Wild Nigger Bill frum Redpepper Hill, I never did work, an' I never will," as
a white country musician was to cite long years of hard labor on the farm.[42]

In addition to obtaining the best possible labor at the lowest possible cost,
Delta planters also hoped to convince blacks of their stake in a system that actually offered them minimal opportunity for advancement. As the personification
of alienation, the bluesman put in time everywhere but put down roots
nowhere and acknowledged no common interest whatsoever with white merchants or landowners. In many ways the image of the bluesman was comparable
to that of the boll weevil, a destructive little bug who brought ruin to many
cotton-growing areas of the South and set off near-panic among planters in the
Delta. The popularity of songs such as Charley Patton's "Mississippi Bo
Weavil [*sic*] Blues" suggested that, despite its potential for destroying them
along with whites, the boll weevil's capacity to bring ruin to the white man won
it the admiration of blacks, while its endless wandering in search of a home
struck a familiar chord as well.[43]

The sense of restlessness that pervaded the blues was also evident in the
prominent role accorded trains in many blues songs. Black firemen often used
the train's whistle to spread a mournful blues note across the flat fields of the
Delta:

> Mister I. C. engineer, make that whistle moan.
> Got the I. C. blues and I can't help but groan.[44]

One of the most famous "blues railroads" was the Yazoo and Mississippi
Valley, known more commonly as the "Yellow Dog." This short-line railroad
(which also figures prominently in Eudora Welty's *Delta Wedding*) earned its
place in history when W. C. Handy recorded his initial contact with the blues
and told of a young musician singing, "I'm goin' where the Southern cross the
dog." This famous crossing, where the Yellow Dog intersected the Southern
line, lay at Moorhead. Hence a bluesman wailed:

> If my baby didn't catch the Southern,
> She must've caught the Yaller Dawg. . . .
> The Southern cross the Dawg at Moorehead [sic],
> Man, Lawd on, she keeps through. . . .
> I swear ma baby's gone to Georgia;
> I believe I go to Georgia, too.[45]

As a means of escape for not only the individual but his or her lover as
well, the railroad was simultaneously a source of both reassurance and anxiety.
The "Pea Vine" was a winding little railroad that connected Dockery's plantation with the nearby towns of Cleveland and Boyle and with the river port
city of Rosedale. Although it was confined wholly to Bolivar County, in Char-

ley Patton's "Pea Vine Blues" even this little railroad seemed a tempting avenue of escape for a loved one:

> I think I heard the Pea Vine when she blows.
> Blowed just like my rider getting on board.[46]

The desire to move on, to escape mistreatment, and to be free was as pervasive in the blues as it was in the lives of Delta blacks. "I got rambling, I got rambling (all) on my mind," sang Robert Johnson, who played the role of rambler to the hilt. Johnny Shines recalled that Johnson "was a guy, you could wake him up any time and he was ready to go. . . . Say, for instance, you had come from Memphis to Helena, and we'd play there all night probably and lay down to sleep the next morning and hear a train. You say, 'Robert, I hear a train. Let's catch it.' He wouldn't exchange no words with you. He's just ready to go. We'd go right back to Memphis if that's where the train's going. It didn't make him no difference. Just so he was going."[47]

Bluesman Mott Willis described a similar lifestyle when he told of his own nomadic meanderings in the Delta: "I was just backwards and forwards, you know. . . . I moved around from place to place, you know; staying with different fellows playing. . . . Well, fact of the business, I've been all over that Delta just about." Delta sharecroppers were no strangers to moving themselves, but the apparently unrestricted mobility of the bluesman was as much the stuff of exotic fantasy for them as it was a source of irritation to white planters, who feared anyone or anything that stood to make their labor any more restless or dissatisfied than they already were.[48]

Another area in which the blues rejected prevailing white norms was that of sexuality. The double entendre of the blues was by no means difficult to decipher. Yet, despite their highly suggestive content, the lyrics of the blues flourished in a society where even the slightest hint of sexual aggressiveness on the part of black males could cost them their lives. Robert Johnson's "Terraplane Blues" was only one such song:

> I'm gonna heist your hood, mama,
> I'm bound to check your oil. . . .
> I'm going to get deep down in this connection,
> Keep on tangling with your wires,
> And when I mash down on your little starter,
> Then your spark plug will give me fire.[49]

Charley Patton's "Shake It and Break It (Don't Let It Fall, Mama)" suggested the joys of intercourse while standing and the potential enjoyment of sexual experimentation in general:

> You can shake it, you can break it, you can hang it on the wall.
> Throw it out the window, catch it 'fore it falls.

> You can break it, you can hang it on the wall.
> Throw it out the window, catch it fore it falls.
> My jelly, my roll, sweet mama, don't you let it fall.[50]

"Jelly roll" was a common metaphor for sex (or the sex organs) in the blues, whose lyrics often associated eating and the preparation of food with lovemaking. A desirable young woman was a "biscuit," her lover a "biscuit roller." A light-skinned, "coffee"-colored woman might be paired with a good "coffee grinder." James "Son" Thomas promised:

> When I marry, now I ain't gonner buy no broom.
> She got hair on her belly gonner sweep my kitchen, my dining room.

Robert Johnson's "Come On in My Kitchen" carried the same culinary/sexual implications. Even a forlorn blues song like Johnson's "Stones in My Passway" offered a boastful sexual metaphor:

> I got three legs to track on.
> Boys, please don't block my road.

The lyrics sung by male blues performers contained their share of posturing and exaggeration, but, when it came to attracting women, many bluesmen claimed a genuine advantage. One of them told Alan Lomax, "I got a home wherever I go." Another elaborated, "If I'd see a woman I wanted and she just absolutely—her husband couldn't carry her home. I'd pick that guitar hard and sing hard. And I've had women come up and kiss me and didn't ask me could they kiss me—kiss me right then. Just grab and kiss me."[52]

On his first recording trip, Robert Johnson seemed to confirm his image as a womanizing bluesman. Recording executive Don Law found Johnson a room in a boardinghouse and urged him to get some sleep in anticipation of the first day of recording. Law joined his wife for dinner at a hotel, only to be summoned to the police station, where Johnson, badly beaten and his guitar smashed, was being held for vagrancy. After bailing Johnson out, Law took him back to the boardinghouse, instructed him to stay in the house for the rest of the evening, and gave him forty-five cents for breakfast. Upon returning to the hotel, Law received another phone call. This time it was Johnson himself. When Law asked Johnson what was wrong, the bluesman replied, "I'm lonesome, and there's a lady here. She wants fifty cents and I lacks a nickel."[53]

After surveying numerous jokes in which blacks celebrated their sexual superiority to whites, Lawrence Levine examined this apparent embrace of what seemed to be a degrading white stereotype of blacks. Levine's commentary on this form of black humor might have been applied to the blues as well, because both reflected "an awareness that the pervasive stereotype of Negroes as oversexed hypervirile, and uninhibitedly promiscuous was not purely a negative image; that it contained envy as well as disdain, that it was a projection of desire as well as fear." By personifying this stereotype, bluesmen only enhanced their status as black folk heroes, because their menacing sexual aggressiveness and self-assurance combined with their disdain for menial labor to make them a symbol of resistance to white authority.[54]

Son Thomas was not only a bluesman but a folk sculptor of some renown. Thomas explained why the clay faces he created presented blacks as poised and proud:

> Tell me why if you see a statue of a man in a white person's yard it will be a black man. They make him black all over and have his lips red and his eyes white. Most of the time you see him, if he ain't got a fishing pole, he got a hoe. I reckon it's an invitation to work. Trying to make the colored folks work. When you see one with a hoe it's to let us know it's all we can do. Well, Old John did more than hoe—right around the house.[55]

William Ferris elaborated on Thomas's comments, explaining that "the theme of John, the yard boy, and his sexual relations with the white woman inside the 'big house' is widespread in Delta folktales, and like Thomas's clay faces, it counters the stereotyped white impression of blacks as depicted in their lawn statues."[56]

At its heart the assertive masculinity of the blues was often a matter of racial as well as personal pride. In "I Wonder When I'll Be Called a Man," Bill Broonzy asserted, "A Black man's a boy, I don't care what he can do." As he sang, Broonzy drew on his boyhood experiences in the Delta, his service in World War I, and his return to the plantation where the owner, instead of hailing him as a hero in the uniform of his country, merely said: "Boy, get you some overalls."[57]

Occasionally the blues suggested a direct relationship between racial and masculine aggression:

> Killed that old grey mule.
> Burned down that white man's barn. . . .
> I want you to love me or leave me.
> Anything you want me to do.
> Well, it's strange things happening,
> Someday might'a happen to you.[58]

By asserting masculine aggressiveness, the blues offered an outlet for the frustrations of the black male, whom Hortense Powdermaker saw "entangled in a mesh of contradictions. . . . He sees the whites, whose culture and concepts have been to a large measure imposed on him, breaking their own rules with impunity—or rather, evading them—choosing their wives from their own group, hedging them about by protections and taboos, and taking their mistresses from his. He sees the women of his own group consorting with men of both races. He cannot keep them for himself, nor can he in turn take women from another group."[59]

In "Long Black Song," Richard Wright told the story of Silas, an enraged black man who whipped his wife because he suspected she had given sexual favors to a white traveling salesman in exchange for a reduced price on a phonograph. (Wright's use of the phonograph may reflect his sense of its popularity among Delta blacks.) A hardworking landowner, Silas exploded in rage, fought with two white men, and met his death after whites surrounded his house and burned it down around him.[60]

Blues lyrics sometimes suggested what seemed to be "senseless," uncontrollable violence and rage. Furry Lewis sang:

> I believe I'll buy me a graveyard of my own;
> I'm goin' kill everybody that have done me wrong.

Other lyrics were more indirect:

> I feel my hell a-risin' every day.
> Someday it'll burst this levee and wash the whole wide world away.

Such sentiments invite comparisons with the sinister figures of black outlaw folklore; they bring to mind as well the examples of Roy, the "unprepared man," as well as James Coyner, the cold-blooded mutilator-killer described by David Cohn. Like these "bad niggers," both mythical and real, the bluesman's heroic status derived, as William Barlow saw it, from the desire of Delta blacks "to negate the feelings of powerlessness and to avenge victimization by the white social order."[61]

The important linkage between racial and masculine pride seemed to cast the black female as little more than a helpless sex object utterly defenseless against exploitation, abuse, and abandonment at the hands of every selfish, fast-talking black stud who came along. In "Low Land Moon," Lonnie Johnson warned:

> I'm going to buy me a shotgun, long as I am tall.
> I'm going to shoot my woman, just to see her fall.

In "Me and the Devil Blues" Robert Johnson sang casually that he intended to "beat my woman, until I get satisfied." In other Johnson songs, women were depicted as phonographs or automobiles, mere mechanical conveniences meant to provide pleasure or diversion for males.[62]

Such rhetoric was less a commentary on the helplessness of the black female than on the frequent perceptions of male powerlessness that surfaced in the angry, violent behavior of black men in the Delta. In "Long Black Song,"

Wright's Silas expressed his rage toward his wife by whipping her, but the real source of his anger was the white-dominated caste system and the emasculating sexual double standard it imposed on him: "From sunup to sundown Ah works mah guts out to pay them white trash bastards whut Ah owe em, n then Ah comes n fins they been in mah house! Ah can't go into their houses n yuh know Gawdam well Ah can't! They don have no mercy on no black folks; we's jus like dirt under their feet!" Facing certain death, vowing to fight to the end but realizing the futility of it all, Silas concludes, "It don mean nothin'! Yuh die ef yuh fight! Yuh die ef yuh don fight! Either way yuh die 'n it don mean nothin'."[63]

The masculine perspective dominated the early Delta blues because, in the formative period of the music, the Delta itself produced only a few female blues performers. The dangers and uncertainty of life as an itinerant musician were such that many female singers often chose church choirs or minstrel troupes over jook joints and house parties around the Delta. The handful of female blues artists who achieved prominence in the Delta, however, lived by the same rules—or with the same absence of rules—and projected feelings of rebellion, rootlessness, and alienation similar to those exhibited by their male counterparts.

An accomplished guitarist, Josie Bush was married briefly to another blues pioneer, Willie Brown. Bush's strong appeal to male audiences often led to violent arguments with her jealous husband while the two were performing together. Moreover, her attractiveness to her male listeners suggested that the sexual energy unloosed by the blues transcended gender. Such evidence abounds in the lyrics of the relatively small number of songs actually recorded by early female blues artists in the Delta. Louise Johnson's "On the Wall" urged women to "cock it on the wall," while Mattie Delaney claimed, "I asked him about it and he said all right, I asked him how long and he said all night." Delaney's "Down the Big Road Blues" was also a classic expression of rootlessness and alienation:

> I feel like crying,
> Ain't got no tears to spare,
> I had a happy home,
> And I wouldn't stay there.[64]

Blues singers often seemed reluctant to express commitments to places or people, but they also exalted the merits of an enduring male-female relationship and offered detailed descriptions of the pain and sorrow engendered by such a relationship gone sour. Hence Robert Johnson bragged about being a "Steady Rollin' Man" who rolled "both night and day," but he admitted that "you can't give your sweet woman everything she wants in one time." As a result, Johnson complained, "she get rambling in her brain, mmm some other man on her mind." In "From Four until Late," Johnson punned that a woman was "like a dresser, with a man always rambling through its drawers" but admitted, "A man is like a prisoner, and he's never satisfied." Meanwhile, from the female perspective, Louise Johnson moaned that "I never had no good man, I mean to ease my worried head," and Mattie Delaney, who sang about her "traveling mind," nonetheless conceded, "I can't go down that big road by myself."[65]

If male-female relationships were treated much more casually and the deterioration of such relationships much more matter-of-factly in the blues than in mainstream American popular music, this seemingly cold-blooded realism simply acknowledged the economically marginal, emotionally debilitating circumstances that could easily undermine otherwise solid relationships between black men and women in the Delta. (Under such circumstances, it was surely no coincidence that a stable, monogamous relationship was a key to higher class standing among Delta blacks.) Moreover, to express a desire for companionship on one's journey down that "big road" was merely to give voice to a basic human need. In the case of Delta blacks, whose journey often promised little but deprivation, humiliation, and denial, that need was especially intense.

The blues presented a strong reflection of the everyday life experiences of Delta blacks. Blues songs dwelt on hard work, violence, poverty, despair, wanderlust, loneliness, drunkenness, and incarceration, which were so much a part of black life in the Delta that any performer might be fairly well assured of a knowing response from his listeners should he even allude to one of these experiences in song.

The physical influences that shaped the lives of Deltans on both sides of the color line also figured prominently in the blues. In "Dry Spell Blues," Son House sang of the devastating effects of a drought and the resulting hard times. Muddy Waters's "Flood" conjured up visions of a gloomy, rainy day in the Delta:

> Go look at the weather,
> I believe it's goin' to be a flood. . . .
> I believe my baby's gon' quit me,
> Because I can feel it all in my blood.[66]

As these lyrics suggest, however, the appeal of the blues derived not just from their relevance to what was immediate and tangible but from their capacity to evoke a sentiment, a mood, a feeling, that had to be experienced to be fully understood. In Robert Johnson's "Preachin' Blues," the blues was a familiar but by no means welcome feeling:

> The blues, is a lowdown shakin' chill.
> You ain't never had them, I hope you never will.
> Well, the blues, is a aching old heart disease.
> Like consumption, killin' me by degree.[67]

Lonnie Johnson's "Devil Got the Blues" presented an even more intimidating portrait of the blues:

> The blues is like the devil,
> It comes on you like a spell.
> Blues will leave your heart full of trouble
> And your poor mind full of hell.[68]

Although the blues flowed directly from the life experiences of Delta blacks, the popularity of the music in the urban North, where successive generations of black migrants found alienation, frustration, and disillusionment in yet another promised land, suggests why the old bluesman made no reference to historical or geographical context when he explained that "it take a man that have the blues to sing the blues." Clearly the blues struck an affirmative chord with large numbers of people who had never seen a stalk of cotton or a mule, much less witnessed a lynching. Lawrence Levine insisted that "the rootlessness and alienation which were so well conveyed in the blues and work songs were not solely the reflection of Afro-American culture but of the larger society as well, which was at its heart rootless and deeply afraid of the rapid changes that were transforming it." Lawrence Goodwyn concluded that the discontented white farmers and tenants who rallied to the cause of populism in the 1890s did so because "in an age of progress and forward motion they had come to suspect that Horatio Alger was not real." As we have seen, Goodwyn's observation was even more applicable to black farmers and farm laborers in the Delta at the turn of the century. Living on the "periphery" of American society, Levine explained, blacks had little reason to embrace its "dreams and myths." As a result, they were "more able to accept the fact of their alienation, their isolation, their fears, and give unambiguous voice to the anguish of modern man."[69]

Levine's comment is better understood when one realizes that, despite the music's identification with the cotton fields and levee camps of the Delta, the context in which the blues emerged was shaped in no small part by the Delta's ties to the modern urban-industrial colossus, whose investment capital, transportation network, and economic doctrines were already well established in the region by the turn of the century. Insulated from popular retaliation by the rigidly enforced rules of caste and the legally mandated system of disfranchisement, Delta planters eagerly followed the lead of their northern industrialist counterparts by implementing centralized, cost-conscious management and supervisory techniques that effectively transformed sharecroppers into wage laborers, separating them from the product of their labor and dashing their dreams of economic independence. As this process unfolded, the blues gave voice to the emotions of increasingly alienated workers who could do little but stand and watch as their dreams of self-determination and progress fell prey to·

the seemingly paradoxical convergence of economic modernization and social and political retrogression in the Delta.

When Ralph Ellison observed that black culture embodied a great deal more than "the relatively spontaneous and undifferentiated responses of a people living in close contact with the soil," he went on to explain that "despite Jim Crow, Negro life does not exist in a vacuum, but in the seething vortex of those tensions generated by the most highly industrialized of western nations." Ellison's observation was especially pertinent to blacks in the Delta, where, significant contextual differences notwithstanding, the modernization of the plantation economy contributed to the disaffection of the work force in much the same fashion as the rise of an impersonal urban-industrial economy produced a similar result north of the Mason-Dixon line. As Alan Lomax explained, "Years before the rest of the world, the people of the Delta tasted the bittersweet of modern alienation so that the blues of those days ring true for all of us now."[70]

The more or less universal contemporary relevance of blues themes was clear enough, but for much of the twentieth century the white listening audience for the blues consisted largely of academics and urban intellectuals. During the 1920s and 1930s, recording companies found a strong and expanding demand for the stylings of previously little-known southern blues artists. Companies such as Okeh, Columbia, and Victor played a key role in expanding and solidifying the popularity of blues music, but they made little effort to market the blues to white listeners. Country music was the medium of choice for working-class southern whites, regardless of whether they remained in Dixie or headed north. Country artists like Jimmie Rodgers and Bob Wills drew heavily on black instrumental stylings, but, ironically, it was changes in the listening habits and stylistic preferences of a younger, more urban-based black audience that led initially to the broader exposure of whites to blues influences.[71]

The Delta continued to produce accomplished blues performers, but the ongoing exodus of blacks to northern cities encouraged musical stylists to develop a more relevant and sophisticated music calculated to appeal to the tastes of an increasingly urbanized black population. Such a form was "rhythm and blues," an electrically amplified, dance-oriented music that had all but overwhelmed the older traditional country blues by the end of World War II. Among Delta bluesmen only Howlin' Wolf and Muddy Waters succeeded in making the musical and instrumental adjustments that seemed to be necessary for significant commercial success.[72]

Prior to the 1950s, the popularity of rhythm and blues performers within the United States was defined almost wholly in terms of their appeal to black audiences. At the end of the 1940s, however, it became apparent that the musical tastes of white Americans were shifting dramatically. This shift was particularly apparent in the Delta and elsewhere in and around Memphis. For some time the affluent white youth of the Delta had been hiring black bands for dances at schools or country clubs, and by the 1950s jukeboxes were usually well stocked with newly introduced 45 rpm versions of rhythm and blues tunes, or "nigger music," as they were known to white youths captivated by their lyrical and rhythmic sensuality.[73]

Ike Turner of Clarksdale played piano in a rhythm and blues group called the Kings of Rhythm and also worked as a disc jockey at a local radio station. Turner and his cohorts could play the Delta blues in traditional fashion, but they drew as well on the inspiration of the contemporary "jump blues" bands they heard on radio and records. In March 1951 they joined forces with producer Sam Phillips of Memphis to record "Rocket 88," which Robert Palmer described as "a rocking little automobile blues, squarely in the tradition of Robert Johnson's 'Terraplane Blues.'" Palmer also noted that Phillips and others decided in retrospect that "Rocket 88" was the first rock and roll record. Certainly by the time that "Rocket 88" was recorded, "rock and roll," once known primarily to bluesmen as a euphemism for sex, had become a familiar phrase in rhythm and blues. It was perhaps not totally coincidental that another big rhythm and blues recording of 1951 (by the New York-based Dominos) was the overtly sexual "Sixty-Minute Man":

> I rock 'em and roll 'em all night long;
> I'm a sixty-minute man.[74]

Meanwhile, in June 1951 as "Rocket 88" climbed the charts, Cleveland, Ohio, disc jockey Alan Freed began "The Moon Dog House Rock 'n' Roll Party" where he played rhythm and blues records for both white and black listeners and called the music "rock and roll." At approximately the same time, "Sixty-Minute Man" became the first rhythm and blues tune to "cross over" to the pop charts, where it enjoyed a twenty-three-week stint. In the next few years, a number of rhythm and blues tunes captured the hearts of white youths, including Bill Haley's much more successful cover of Joe Turner's rhythm and blues hit "Shake, Rattle, and Roll." A few black performers like Fats Domino and Chuck Berry managed to establish themselves with white pop fans, but Sam Phillips realized that this new music would never reach its true commercial potential without white artists who could perform in what Bill Malone called "a convincing black style." A co-worker recalled Phillips saying repeatedly, "If I could only find a white man who had the Negro feel, I could make a billion dollars."[75]

Phillips finally found such a man in Elvis Aaron Presley from Tupelo, a town in the hills some eighty miles east of the Mississippi Delta. Never before had the musical culture of blacks and lower-class whites been so closely conjoined as they were in the early stylings of Presley, whose music bore the imprint of country and gospel music as well as the blues. This remarkable synthesis was apparent on Presley's first single, released by Phillips's Sun Records, consisting of "Blue Moon of Kentucky," a "bluegrass" number written by Bill Monroe, and "That's All Right, Mama," an old blues tune learned from Arthur "Big Boy" Crudup. Presley explained that he "dug the real low down Mississippi singers, mostly Big Bill Broonzy and Big Boy Crudup," although his family often scolded him for listening to such "sinful music."[76]

Similar influences shaped the music of Carl Perkins. As a member of the only white tenant family on a plantation in Lake County, Tennessee (just north of the Yazoo Delta), Perkins grew up listening to Bill Monroe and the Grand Ole Opry on radio as well as to the gospel singing of his neighbors. He learned his guitar style from an elderly black man named John Westbrook:

> I'd be so tired, chopping or picking cotton, whatever we was doin', and I'd take off for Uncle John's after we'd work hard all day. Looking back on it now, there's that old black man who was tired, much tireder than I was as a young boy, but yet he took time and sat on his porch and showed me the licks that he knew. I was dealing with a black angel. He didn't have to take time to show me anything. And under the circumstances of segregation back in those years, when he couldn't go get him a drink of water at the courthouse, he could have hated a little white boy like me, but he didn't. He loved me.[77]

Perkins's story and the experiences his family shared with the black families on the plantation suggested that the working-class white country music audience should have experienced little difficulty in relating to the blues. Although white tenant farmers and mill workers enjoyed advantages unavailable even to upper-class blacks, like blacks in the Delta and elsewhere, theirs was also a marginal world that offered little hope for economic or social advancement or meaningful political expression. Both groups suffered at the hands of an isolated regional labor market where limited opportunities for significant advancement engendered a perpetual restlessness of spirit and body that contributed to high rates of turnover in the cotton mill as well as the cotton patch. Surely no point of comparison between the blues and country music is so striking as the common emphasis on mobility, whether in the form of travel or aimless "ramblin'." Not surprisingly, country singers were as fascinated by trains as were bluesmen, and, more often than not, they were as ambivalent, longing for escape on the one hand, searching for a place to call home on the other. Although it was even less a music of overt protest than the blues, country music did provide a critical, alienated view of modern, urban-industrial society. Early country music stars like Jimmie Rodgers, and then later Hank Williams, personified the rootlessness and the overt sexuality, as well as the fatalistic and self-destructive genius, that were so readily associated with bluesmen like Robert Johnson.[78]

Like the blues, country music also reflected the tension between the teachings of the church and the temptations of the world. Jerry Lee Lewis, cousin of evangelist Jimmy Swaggart, briefly attended the Southwestern Bible Institute in Waxahatchie, Texas, before being expelled for rendering a "rockin'" version of "My God Is Real" during a chapel performance. Lewis periodically renounced "the devil's music" throughout much of his early career, and Malone noted that Lewis "often acted as if he had walked out of the pages of Wilbur J. Cash's *Mind of the South*: "He is the prototypical ambivalent southerner, embodying both hedonistic and puritanical traits." Malone was, of course, correct, but Lewis, who as a youth loved to play with black musicians around his Ferriday, Louisiana, home, was hardly more prototypically southern than a host of blues singers (not to speak of his rhythm and blues contemporary Little Richard) in this regard. Among the bluesmen Charley Patton, Sonny Boy Williamson, John Lee Hooker, and Muddy Waters, to name but a few, also had strong religious upbringing; and, as we have seen, like Jerry Lee, several bluesmen succumbed repeatedly, albeit briefly, to the "call to preach," in the process renouncing the blues as the instrument of the Devil.[79]

These similarities are indeed striking, but despite the common economic and cultural terrain they occupied, both country music and the blues were thoroughly commercialized by the post-World War II era, and in the final analysis it was the prospect of increased record sales rather than the breakdown of racial barriers to communication and understanding that brought them together under the rubric of rock and roll. Certainly, commercial influences were primarily responsible for the fact that during the 1940s, as Charles Gillett observed, country music "probably absorbed more elements of black music than were accepted into the mainstream pop of the time." In addition to the country performers who drew on black gospel influences, Ernest Tubb modernized the "white blues" style of Jimmie Rodgers through his electrified, "honky tonk" sound. Even the "mountain" music of Roy Acuff and Bill Monroe showed black influences, while the Delmore Brothers and several others served up offerings dubbed "hillbilly boogie." Then, as Gillett saw it, "when Hank Williams emerged on the new MGM label in the late forties, he shook all these black-influenced country styles together using as strong a beat as his recording supervisor would sanction." With young whites exhibiting a growing fascination with black music, country musicians not only began to perform rhythm and blues songs but sought as well to incorporate the distinctive, rocking beat into their country offerings.[80]

The exposure of young white "rockabilly" stars to black musicians came not only as a result of growing up within earshot of both the blues and black gospel music, but by virtue of the fact that many of these white performers began their careers with small independent recording companies that were also producing the songs of various rhythm and blues artists. As William Barlow explained: "Given the proliferation of R&B through independent record labels and disk jockeys in the postwar era, little wonder that young white musicians like Elvis Presley, Bill Haley, Jerry Lee Lewis and Buddy Holly began to copy the new black musical styles they heard all around them."[81]

Bill Malone observed that the early stars of rockabilly performed with a style that expressed "the macho complex so deeply imbedded in southern working class culture" and violated "conventional middle-class standards" as well. Clearly, then, the bluesman and the rockabilly star shared a great deal when it came to the styling and the imagery of their music. Moreover, if the early white southern rock and roll stars did succeed in implanting "much of the culture of the working-class South in the nation at large," this cultural implant was actually a hybrid, one that tapped a sense of alienation that flourished on both sides of the gaping chasm of misunderstanding and fear that continued to separate the races in the South.[82]

Youthful white rock and roll fans were hardly more aware than their concerned parents of the social and historical significance of the blues. Yet, the bluesy stylings—as well as the emphasis on sexuality, the physical and often ephemeral aspects of love, and the general rejection of prevailing community norms—that permeated early rock and roll won the hearts of white teenagers drawn to the ill-defined but undeniable sense of rebellion that it conveyed.[83]

As the true substance of rock and roll's appeal to American youth became apparent, guardians of the public morality sounded the alarm. In the spirit of the McCarthy era, some critics saw the music as part of the "Communist conspiracy." A Florida minister flayed Elvis Presley for reaching "a new low in spiritual degeneracy," although Elvis enjoyed the reputation of a proverbial choir boy compared to what Nick Tosches described as the "hellish persona" of "the Killer," Jerry Lee Lewis, whose behavior taxed the vocabulary of the most articulate minister and rendered similarly speechless the terrified parents of teenagers of either sex. The subversive, even revolutionary implications of rock and roll and its link to the blues were by no means lost on the defenders of the racial status quo. Throughout the South leaders of the massive resistance movement condemned rock and roll as "jungle music" and charged that it was part of an NAACP plot to pull white youths down to the level of blacks.[84]

That a music so potentially subversive in its social and political implications could succeed in threatening the Cold War decorum of the 1950s seems less surprising if one considers the interactive roles of technology, marketing, and, of course, the profit motive, in the rock and roll explosion. Richard Petersen argued, for example, that the adaptation of network radio programming to television that occurred during this period simply led radio stations to adopt the "Top Forty" format as the least expensive way of filling airtime. Because Top Forty charts were calculated on the basis of not only record sales but radio airplay and jukebox selections as well, a great many rhythm and blues records appeared on the charts, thereby demonstrating their popularity with transistor-radio- and juke-box-listening, 45-rpm-record-buying white teenagers, who represented the primary audience for rock and roll.[85]

Once they recognized the tremendous profit potential of the new music, the recording industry's management elite moved in and took rock and roll from the margin to the mainstream, where the unmistakable market appeal of its rebellious essence could be exploited. In the process, however, they quickly took steps as well to bring both the content and the packaging of the music under their control. As big-name firms regained control of the music distribution market, they muscled out the smaller labels that had launched rock and roll and sustained it through the early years of the rock and roll revolution. By the end of the 1950s, as Barlow wrote, "the primal 'roots' rock and roll of Little Richard, Fats Domino, Chuck Berry, Bo Diddley, Elvis Presley, and Jerry Lee Lewis was being replaced by the sanitized 'schlock rock' of Fabian, Paul Anka, and Frankie Avalon—or the clean-cut, white buck cover versions of Pat Boone." Charles Gillett agreed that recording-industry leaders "killed off the music but kept the name."[86]

Just when it seemed, however, that the blues influences in rock and roll would fall victim to the conservatism of the music industry, elements of the raw, revolutionary, blues-derived characteristics that had initially made rock and roll so appealing to American youth resurfaced during the "British invasion" of 1963. Ironically, it was only with the British invasion that rock music became the medium through which a small group of blues (rather than strictly rhythm and blues) performers actually became known to large numbers of American whites. Rock musicians from Great Britain, where whites far more readily accepted and appreciated the blues, gratefully acknowledged the influence of these Delta bluesmen, who thereby gained considerably greater recognition among American whites than they might otherwise have achieved.[87]

The Rolling Stones, the Animals, and the Yardbirds were among the British groups influenced by Muddy Waters. ("If it had not been for you, we would never be where we are today," telegraphed the Rolling Stones to Waters on his birthday in 1975.) Waters's appeal to American whites seemed directly related to the fact that these groups, particularly the Rolling Stones (who took their name from one of his songs), began recording his songs and praising his music. "Before the Rolling Stones," explained Waters, "people over here didn't know nothing and didn't want to know nothing about me. . . . If they'd buy my records, their parents would say, 'What the hell is this? Get this nigger record out of my house!' But then the Rolling Stones and those other groups come over here from England, playing this music, and now, today, the kids buy a record of mine, and they listen to it."[88]

Sonny Boy Williamson not only recorded with several British artists but also influenced the music of an American group called Levon and the Hawks, who went on to win almost universal acclaim as The Band. Unfortunately, Williamson died before a tour or a joint recording session could be arranged. Elsewhere, the distinctive guitar stylings that marked the recordings of Howlin' Wolf deeply affected a host of rock performers on both sides of the Atlantic. Wolf accompanied the Rolling Stones on their first appearance on the television show "Shindig," and their popular recording of his "Little Red Rooster" further affirmed rock and roll's debt to the blues.[89]

The linkage between rock and roll and the blues became more apparent at the end of the 1980s as the blues finally achieved significant popularity among middle-class white adults, who found in them the energy and grit that contemporary, mass-produced rock music appeared to have lost. A Grammy-winning album reissue of every known Robert Johnson recording quickly hit the Billboard Top Pop Album chart in 1990 and carried tributes to Johnson from Keith Richards ("Everybody should know about Robert Johnson") and Eric Clapton ("I have never found anything more deeply soulful than Robert Johnson"). A *Newsweek* writer's exuberant assessment of Johnson's musical legacy as "a powerful concentrate which, when diluted, became 35 years of rock and roll" merely indicated broader public appreciation of a relationship long acknowledged by rock pioneers such as Big Joe Turner, who conceded, "For a fact rock 'n' roll ain't no different from the blues, we just pepped it up a lot. Man, that music was in the blues bag all the time."[90]

One can hardly escape the irony in the fact that the blues, a music born of the incessant toil and demolished dreams of impoverished Delta blacks, exerted such a formative influence on rock and roll, a music that not only tapped the alienation and wanton energy of the relatively advantaged white youth of the 1950s but, despite the best efforts of the American economic and moral establishment to thwart it, continued to reflect and shape the sensibilities of succeeding generations. This irony was compounded by indications that as the blues gained a new audience with whites they seemed to lose their appeal among younger blacks who found rap, rhythm and blues, and other more contemporary forms of musical expression more attuned to their lifestyles, aspirations, and concerns.

There is precious little evidence that the commercially inspired fusion of black and white music that lay at the heart of rock and roll has made a significant contribution to interracial understanding or that the new generation of white blues fans has much appreciation of the context of human suffering from which this suddenly trendy music evolved. Still, as they see the promise of socioeconomic advancement that was once assumed to be nothing less than their national birthright give way to diminished hopes and frustrated expectations, a number of Americans of every race in every region may one day come to appreciate the difference between *hearing* the blues and *feeling* them. If so, just as the blues once so clearly chronicled the failure of Delta society to live up to its ideals (or to celebrate ideals consistent with the life experiences of the majority of its members), their remarkable musical legacy may eventually transcend geographic boundaries and racial barriers to focus critical popular attention on the discrepancies between the real and ideal in not only regional but national life as well.

13 ▽ "More Writers per
   ▽ Square Foot . . ."
   ▽

The Delta's reputation as the richest source of blues music and
musicians in the South was well established by World War II. Only after the
war, however, did observers begin to recognize that, despite the poverty, illiteracy, and rural isolation which afforded ready-made excuses for cultural arid-
ity, the Delta was also a flourishing center for literature and the arts. By the end
of the 1940s, the region could claim not only William Alexander Percy and
David L. Cohn but Pulitzer Prize-winning journalist and author Hodding Carter. Stark Young from Panola County was another of the region's prominent
literary figures. Young Greenvillian Shelby Foote was also beginning to gain
recognition for his work, as was Elizabeth Spencer of Carrollton in the edge
of the Delta. Writer and agent Ben Wasson and editor and critic Herschell
Brickell rounded out the Delta's literary scene.[1]

If the Delta had seemed a most unlikely literary oasis at the end of the
1940s, the same was hardly less true thirty years later. At that point, however,
the Delta's literary "who's who" had expanded to include Will Percy's adopted
son, Walker, as well as Ellen Douglas, Beverly Lowry, Charles Bell, Ellen Gilchrist, and Willie Morris, to name but a few.[2]

The locale within the Delta that produced the most writers and artists was
Greenville, which by the middle of the twentieth century enjoyed a reputation
as the most open and tolerant community in the Delta and perhaps in all of Mississippi as well. The state field director of the NAACP even went so far in 1965
as to describe Greenville as "the heaven of Mississippi." This perception of
Greenville was no doubt at odds with the experience of many black residents
and civil rights workers as well, but Greenville's reputation for moderation was
real enough to irritate segregationist whites in neighboring counties and serve
as a source of pride for most of the artistically and intellectually gifted figures
it produced. Long recognized as having "more writers per square foot than any
other city of its size," Greenville celebrated its own rich creative tradition in
1982 with a special festival, "The Time Has Come." When the outstanding
writers and artists in attendance were pressed as to the sources of Greenville's

creative heritage, they invariably cited the exceptional local tradition of tolerance and intellectual curiosity fostered by William Alexander Percy.[3]

Percy's devotion to literature and the arts derived in part from local tradition. Many of the Delta's early planter families had made a great show of their
musical, literary, and artistic interests. The pioneering Worthington family
had not only lived in a grand mansion but had taken great pride in possessing a
violin that reputedly belonged at one time to Paganini. Like many other females
in the plantation gentry, the Worthington girls dabbled in poetry:

Give me the level country of the Delta.
Give me horizons ever forest-rimmed,
Cloud-fires of sunset mirrored in the river, far to the north sky and water
    silver dimmed.
Duty or fate may take me far a-roving,
But I will come back, for the Delta land is home.[4]

Will Percy was quick to point out that although the nascent aristocracy of
the Delta lacked the splendid residences and fine furniture of more established
communities, excellent libraries abounded—"a library was as portable as a
slave." Certainly his own family was known for its love of good books. The
estate of his great-great grandfather, Charles Percy, who died in 1794, contained the works of fifty different authors. Charles's son, Thomas G., was also
a bookish young man; after attending Princeton, he contented himself with
reading, traveling, and tending his garden. He accumulated a huge library,
which ultimately passed into Will Percy's possession. After Thomas G. Percy
died, his three sons moved to the Delta, where they carved out a good life in
the swampy wilderness in Washington County.[5]

Lewis Baker offered this description of these pioneer Percys:

> The wealth that the Percys found in the Delta's swamps gave them the freedom
> to live the good life that Don Carlos and Thomas G. had pursued. They were free
> to travel, to enjoy fine food and drink, to appoint their rustic surroundings with
> a touch of elegance. Socially, their wealth placed them above the criticism of the
> community and allowed them to advocate independent and at times unpopular
> positions without losing their neighbors' respect. Wealth also left the Percys the
> leisure to live the life of the mind, a habit that reinforced their already healthy
> tendency to follow their own course. They usually knew what they wanted to do,
> and their wealth allowed them to do it. Their sovereignty over their own lives
> was their key to the good life.[6]

Although he was born into an upper-class Delta family that embraced the
tradition of at least a superficial respect for literature and the arts, Will Percy's
childhood interest in poetry—he composed his first serious poem at the age of
twelve—alarmed his parents. Concerned that the boy was developing little

interest in more practical subjects, his mother put him under the tutelage of the parish priest and arranged for him to study math and science under the supervision of the superintendent of the public schools. When he was fifteen, his parents made arrangements for him to enroll in the preparatory school at Sewanee. One look at the uniform he would be required to wear, however, led Will to enroll in the college instead. He began immediately to immerse himself in courses like literature and ethics and in extracurricular activities related to literature and writing. Even when he graduated from Sewanee, Will had no interest in a "practical" career. He jumped at the chance to defer any vocational decision by spending a year in Paris; the trade-off for his trips to the Louvre, piano and French lessons, and the free time for writing was his agreement to take fencing instruction.[7]

Percy, David Cohn, and a number of other literary and artistically minded Greenville students cited the influence of Miss Carrie Stern, a frustrated artist and poet, who as a teacher inspired several generations of pupils with her love of poetry and the arts. Cohn explained that cultural affairs in the Delta were "ordered and preempted by women," whose organized literary discussions, piano and violin recitals, and poetry readings usually reached a merciful and convenient conclusion just in time for the tea to be served. From the male perspective, manliness and a true passion for cultural pursuits resided at opposite poles. As Cohn put it, it was "suspect to read good poetry and catastrophic to one's reputation as a normally functioning male to write it." In his somewhat harsher appraisal of the cultural life of the region, Shelby Foote insisted that the Delta planter "had no use for art." He "left that up to his wife; and she had no use for it either."[8]

The sons and daughters of the Delta gentry almost invariably found their way into college, but, as Cohn observed, they rarely returned "with a passion for truth . . . an intellectual curiosity aroused and a desire to pursue beauty and wisdom for their own sakes." Given the superficiality of the Delta elite's interest in the arts and learning, it was not surprising that, although both of his parents expressed a passing interest in classical music and the great books, Will Percy's genuine zeal for both concerned both Camille and LeRoy Percy and raised a serious question about their boy's already suspect masculinity. Still, as the son of the influential and popular LeRoy Percy, Will enjoyed both the social and economic clout needed to encourage and legitimize creativity in Greenville and its environs. Having accepted at face value so much of the Delta aristocracy's professed interest in cultural pursuits, the young Percy took full advantage of the exposure to the arts and letters afforded him by his parents. He developed a keen personal interest that infected others, imbuing the Greenville community with a far greater appreciation for creative activity and independent thought than it might have ever developed otherwise.[9]

One of Percy's first protégés was Cohn, a Greenville native educated at the University of Virginia and Yale. The son of a successful merchant, Cohn quickly amassed considerable wealth in the business world, only to turn his back on that career and undertake one as a writer. After traveling widely, Cohn fell ill, returned to Greenville to recuperate, and wound up staying at the Percy home for two years. While Percy's guest, Cohn encouraged him to complete his autobiography despite the fact that drafts of the early chapters had received disappointing reviews from some of Percy's "highbrow" friends. After Cohn dismissed the criticisms that Percy had received and insisted that he continue, his tired and frail host resumed the writing of *Lanterns on the Levee*.[10]

Meanwhile, Cohn undertook the task of reacquainting himself with his birthplace after a twenty-year absence. The product of this process of rediscovery was *God Shakes Creation*, a vivid description of Delta life published in 1935 and revised and reissued in 1948 as *Where I Was Born and Raised*. Although there were some similarities, Cohn's treatment of the Delta proved to be noticeably different from Percy's. Cohn gave considerably more attention to the complexity of a society pervaded by paradox and contradiction, one that appeared relaxed and informal but was in fact governed by elaborate unwritten codes of behavior.

Hodding Carter came to Greenville at the urging of both Percy and Cohn and soon made his mark on the city. Carter was best known for courageous editorials that both tested and reinforced the local community's tolerance for dissenting opinions. He also wrote several nonfiction books, and his novel, *Flood Crest*, published in 1947, featured a manipulative villain named Cleve Pikestaff, who bore a strong resemblance to Theodore G. Bilbo. Carter also dabbled in poetry, producing *The Ballad of Catfoot Grimes and Other Verse*.[11]

The most successful local visual artist encouraged by Percy was Leon Koury, who read one of Percy's poems in *Scribner's* and, not realizing that Percy lived in Greenville, wrote him at the magazine. Percy invited Koury over but proved to be more impressed with the drawings on the back of his notebook than with the poems inside it. He encouraged Koury to continue his drawing and supplied him with the materials to do so. In the meantime Percy showed Koury's work to several artists, including William Van Dresser, who recognized Koury's potential as a sculptor. Percy was so impressed with Koury's modeling efforts that he enlisted the help of Greenville writer Ben Wasson in setting up a West Coast exhibition of Koury's work. Despite his failing health, Will continued to champion the arts and was the leading force in the formation of the Delta Art Association in 1938. He then led the effort to secure a fifteen-thousand-dollar grant for a local art center from the Federal Arts Project. In May 1939 the Delta Art Association held its first exhibit, featuring the works of Leon Koury.[12]

As he was encouraging local talent, a stream of nationally prominent literary figures passed through Percy's household. Vachel Lindsay paid a visit and proceeded to get drunk and shout one of his poems from Percy's front porch. Even William Faulkner showed up for a tennis match, albeit too drunk to play. Carl Sandburg, Stephen Vincent Benét, and fellow Deltan Stark Young also enjoyed Percy's hospitality. Walker Percy recalled that even black poet Langston Hughes visited his uncle, who introduced Hughes to an audience as "a man who's black and a poet and who has risen above the issues of race and ideologies." Hughes then proceeded to read what Walker Percy termed "the most ideologically aggressive poetry you can imagine."[13]

Will Percy's contributions as a patron of the arts should not be minimized. Percy not only encouraged a large number of his contemporaries but helped to forge a supportive context for succeeding generations of creative and imaginative people who came out of the Greenville area. Percy's influence was felt primarily in and around Greenville, however; a full understanding of the Delta's overall reputation as a haven for creativity requires attention to the entire region's historical experience and its physical and emotional environment as well.

In one hundred years, the Delta had risen from a swampy wilderness through its heyday as the New South's Old South to its post-New Deal status as a planter's paradise, where those who reaped the benefits of a rapidly modernizing plantation economy also managed to maintain their dominance in the social and political sphere. A late-emerging society and subculture, the Delta rapidly relived much of the South's past in full view of a curious and often critical audience of nonsoutherners and southerners as well. In a sense the Delta's experience was comparable to the meteoric rise of Wilbur J. Cash's "stout young Irishman" or Faulkner's devil-planter parvenu Thomas Sutpen, whose immorality and greed was too blatant for the tastes of a society where the passage of a little time had subordinated the memories of the brutal conquest of the frontier to a more appealing notion of civility and noblesse oblige.

When it came to history, the Delta was clearly a region in a hurry. One of Elizabeth Spencer's characters noted how quickly a farmer became a "planter" in the Delta: "A planter, working like a fiend in overalls and busted shoes and a straw hat. Got six nigger families at it from daylight to dark. I tell you, the stumps are still smoking in that man's first field." A number of writers have noted the "terrific compression" of the human experience that occurred in the Delta. Greenville native Shelby Foote remarked that one could see "a hundred years of history in twenty years in the Delta." Ellen Douglas saw the Delta as both a physical and philosophical frontier, one that had moved "from the state of innocence to the state of corruption in a very short time." Foote described the Delta as a region where "credit is easy and crashes are hard." He explained that both his grandfathers were millionaires at one point—his maternal grandfather was "a Viennese Jew" who took a job as a plantation bookkeeper and wound up marrying one of the planter's daughters—but at their deaths "both of them had scarcely the money to dig the hole to bury them in."[14]

John Faulkner caricatured the rages-to-riches-to-rags stereotype of the Delta in *Dollar Cotton*, the story of hill-country immigrant Otis Town, who, through hard work, shrewd dealing, and not a little cheating, rose quickly to the status of "Old Man Town" and then became "Old Man Towne" when his pretentious wife added a superfluous "e" to his name and forced him to build a stucco mansion, where her promiscuous daughter's suitors "sat in the imitation Louis XIV chairs, listening to Mrs. Towne's bad French and drinking Old Man Towne's good whiskey." Towne's empire collapsed when he overextended himself by buying huge parcels of land in Arkansas and then refused to sell his cotton for less than a dollar per pound.[15]

The Delta tantalized its writers and artists with an almost irresistible physical and human panorama. For David Cohn the Delta was "a land of excess. The hot sun, the torrential rains, the savage caprices of the unpredictable river. The fecund earth, the startlingly rapid growth of vegetation, the illimitable flat plains, and the vast dome of heaven arching over them: all these environmental influences seemed to breed in the people a tendency toward the excessive." Delta matron Florence Warfield Sillers simply described her region as the "most intemperate country in the world and the most alluring." Artist Byron Burford commented on the richness and diversity of life in a Delta that was influenced profoundly and perpetually by a river that, in addition to providing its own innately fascinating presence, brought showboats, circuses, and a host of emigrés from around the world. In the Delta, Syrian and Jew, Chinese and Italian, and black and white mingled and/or remained apart in ways that gave the region both a stratified and a fluid society, one simultaneously provincial and cosmopolitan.[16]

The river never affected life in the Delta so much as when it climbed out of its banks to, in the words of William Alexander Percy, "vex and sweeten the land it has made." Describing a Mississippi on the rampage, Faulkner explained that "the river was now doing what it liked to do, had waited patiently the ten years in order to do, as a mule will work for you ten years for the privilege of kicking you once." In *Tournament* Shelby Foote offered an all too familiar description of an oncoming flood that seemed like "an immense plate being slid over the ground, shallow, opaque, innocent looking, flecked with foam and littered with chicken coops and fence rails." As soon as the water had covered the land, it offered a view that Deltans were accustomed to seeing for days at a time: "a wide brown expanse" that looked like nothing so much as a "motionless, limitless, level sheet like rusty cast iron."[17]

Delta flood stories were legendary family treasures told and retold alongside tales of brushes with marauding Yankee invaders. Walker Percy's recollection of dead mules floating into the front room of the family home in Greenville was but one example. Year after year the floods came, and each time Deltans maintained a jaunty air, doing their best to reassure themselves that things would soon return to normal and that their way of life would resume.[18]

Delta blacks suffered the most from the floods, which not only uprooted them but threatened the region with the loss of their labor and therefore inclined whites to take steps to hold them against their will. These steps often led to charges of peonage and the virtual enslavement documented by several scholars and described by Richard Wright in his short story "Down by the Riverside."[19]

A number of writers and artists attempted to describe the environmental stimuli provided by a Delta that, as Neal Peirce put it, "has to be seen to be believed." One of Greenville native Beverly Lowry's characters noted that as she made her automotive descent into the Delta she could "see from sky to sky all around her, the whole sky like a bowl turned upside down over her head." As Eudora Welty's *Delta Wedding* opens, Laura McRaven realizes that the train she was riding has suddenly passed into the Delta: "Thoughts went out of her head and the landscape filled it. In the Delta, most of the world seemed sky. . . . The land was perfectly flat and level, but it shimmered like the wing of a lighted dragonfly. It seemed strummed, as though it were an instrument and something had touched it." Employing a similar analogy, Paul Simon would sing many years later of a Mississippi Delta that "shines like a National Guitar."[20]

Robert Penn Warren was struck by the "sad and baleful beauty" of the Delta. David Cohn saw the Delta landscape as "both beautiful and ugly." Season after season fields that were starred in spring with creamy or pinkish cotton blossoms disappeared under the undulating softness of the opening bolls, which in turn gave way to the dead stalks, brown, ugly, and rattling in the winter wind. Even ten-year-old Rhoda, an Ellen Gilchrist creation, noted the summer sun in the Delta "beating down a million volts a minute feeding the soybeans and cotton and clover, sucking Steele's Bayou up into the clouds, beating down on the road and the store, on the pecans, the elms and magnolias."[21]

Shelby Foote saw a Delta wilderness where "slow, circuitous creeks, covered with dusty scum and steaming in the heat" wound through the jungle undergrowth "each doubling back on itself in convulsive loops and coils like a snake fighting lice." In *The Married Land*, Greenville native Charles Bell described the Delta writhing like a pile of snakes: "waterways, swampways, woodways, coils within coils, so plain but cunning, so serpentine in its involutions around the heart." In his poetic vision, William Alexander Percy saw the Delta "blurred ash-blue" under a sun whose golden billows broke across its cotton fields with neither "shade or sound." Willie Morris recalled the Delta as "the *noisiest* land I ever knew," a land that "rustled, moaned, and made apocalyptic noises."[22]

In a Delta seething with human tensions, the landscape did seem to nurture a sense of impending crisis. Ellen Douglas described a summer dry spell, when thunderheads piled up "miles high in the afternoon sky" without yielding any rain while "dust devils—small whirlwinds that form in the dry furrows—go careening off across gray-green fields like living demons bent on some terrible work of destruction." "The environment in which I lived often weighed heavily on me," wrote David Cohn, noting that "the sun was too hot for too long, the rains too heavy, the soil too passionate for fruition, the vegetation too dense, the honeysuckle too sweet, the fields too flat." As a result, Cohn felt "there was a doom on the land where I was born and raised."[23]

Writing in 1983, Greenwood native James Harkness still found "something other worldly" about a landscape that implied "final things as if the horizons were not just an endpoint of vision but the edge of the world. At the end of day, the hazy red sun might be extinguishing itself for all time instead of just setting for the night. Drive a few hours here and you begin to comprehend all the South's lurid literary brouhaha about primeval soil and relentless/brooding/looming dome of sky, ibbity bibbity boo."[24]

The Delta's human landscape was even more intriguing than its physical one, perhaps because flamboyant, almost caricatured role playing from those at both ends of the spectrum was necessary to confirm and sustain the Delta's anachronistic and grossly inequitable social and economic order. In *Delta Wedding* Eudora Welty recognized the special sense of social class and family that prevailed among Delta planters. The marriage of Dabney Fairchild to Troy Flavin, a rough-edged plantation manager who had migrated to the area from the hills, was a less than joyous occasion for the ultra-clannish Fairchilds, who had yet to accept fully even Dabney's Virginia-born mother. Still, they staged the nuptials in typically extravagant Delta style, complete with lavish gifts like a Pierce-Arrow automobile and ostentatious decorations and accessories like shepherd's crooks imported from Memphis. In her short story "The Hitchhikers," Welty captured the impulsiveness of Delta whites who thought nothing of traveling fifty miles in search of a card game or covering a similarly great distance simply to spit off a particular bridge.[25]

In Tennessee Williams's *The Glass Menagerie*, Amanda Wingfield recalled her ostensibly privileged Delta girlhood with obvious embellishment: "I had malaria fever all that Spring. . . . I had a little temperature all the time—not enough to be serious—just enough to make me restless and giddy! Invitations poured in—parties all over the Delta! . . . I took quinine but kept on going, going! Evenings, dances! Afternoons, long, long rides! Picnics—lovely! So lovely that country in May—all lacy with dogwood, literally flooded with jonquils." Waxing similarly romantic and nostalgic, Ellen Gilchrist's LeLe Arnold recalled in "Traveler" the summer when she and her cousin attracted an endless, round-the-clock stream of suitors from all over the Delta, all of whom were ready for a good time whether it was to be had at the country club or the "bootlegger's shack."[26]

Gilchrist's story also captured the Delta aristocracy's tendency to produce free-spirited, flamboyant, and often tragic characters. LeLe spent the summer in the Delta with her cousin Baby Gwen Barksdale; made friends with a girl named Sarah, who had a wooden arm with flecking paint; swam across Lake Jefferson without a life vest; and generally made her bid for the staunchly contested title of "wildest girl in the Mississippi Delta." Another serious contender for this designation was Ellen Douglas's Nat Hunter Stonebridge, "always good company—if she keeps the drinking under control and doesn't set fire to the house." In a similar vein, Gilchrist's novel *The Annunciation* spun the tale of Amanda McCamey, "prettiest girl in Issaquena County," who became pregnant at fourteen with her cousin's child and, returning years later at her grandmother's death, made love to the same cousin (now a Chicagoan) again: "It doesn't matter. It's all right. It's raining and Grandmama's dead and you're supposed to fuck your cousin at your grandmother's funeral. Don't they know things like that in Chicago?"[27]

Ahead of Amanda lay a dissolved marriage, a flamboyant affair with a much younger man, and a second child, born on the night the baby's young father died in an automobile accident. As for Nat, for all of her good looks and libertine spirit, she remained lonely and harbored a deep inner sadness. At the conclusion of Douglas's *Where the Dreams Cross*, she strikes out for California, a most unlikely locale for another of her ill-fated efforts to put down roots.

Tennessee Williams lived for a time as a child in the Clarksdale home of his grandparents. More than any other writer who employed the Delta as a setting, he explored the materialism and self-indulgent excess and depravity that seemed to be so much a part of lives of the region's gentry. In *Cat on a Hot Tin Roof*, Big Daddy Pollit was yet another of the Delta's "self-made" men, having quit school at ten to go to work "like a nigger in the fields." Big Daddy rose from overseer to owner of "28,000 acres of the richest land this side of the Nile Valley" and an additional "ten million in cash in blue-chip stocks." Like many real-life Delta planters, however, Big Daddy had only a limited appreciation for most of the finer things his money could buy. Recalling with disgust Big Mama's buying spree on their ill-fated European tour (to Big Daddy, Europe was no more than a "great big auction" or "a big fire sale" spread out over a "bunch of old worn-out places"), Big Daddy vowed to get, or rather buy, himself a new female companion: "I don't care how much she costs, I'll smother her in—minks! Ha, Ha! I'll strip her naked and choke her with diamonds and smother her with minks and hump her from hell to breakfast."[28]

When Williams's Amanda Wingfield listed her beaux—"gentlemen all! . . . some of the most prominent young planters of the Mississippi Delta"—she also cited their financial pedigrees. Champ Laughlin went on to become a vice president of the Delta Planters Bank. Hadley Stevenson, who drowned in Moon Lake, left his widow "one hundred and fifty thousand in Government bonds." Bates Cutrere, who was killed in a shoot-out on the floor of the Moon Lake Casino, died with Amanda's picture in his pocket, leaving "eight or ten thousand acres, that's all" to a widow he never loved. Finally, there was Duncan J. Fitzhugh, the man with the "Midas touch," who became "the Wolf of Wall Street."[29]

When David Cohn cited "special stresses" that affected the people of the Delta, he noted the uncertainty that arose from the wobbly and unpredictable nature of the region's cotton-producing economy—"with all risked upon cotton, the winners taking large gains and the losers suffering bankruptcy." Cohn also gave particular emphasis to the "Negro question," which, as it existed in the Delta, was "almost without counterpart in the United States." These mounting racial anxieties caught the attention of a number of writers and artists on both sides of the color line.[30]

The tensions and contradictions of Delta society as seen from the perspective of Delta blacks were nowhere more apparent than in the blues, described by Paul Garon as a "fusion of music and poetry accomplished at very high emotional temperature." The powerful message of the blues often manifested itself in the literary realm. Ken Bennett detected the tension between religion and the blues in Faulkner's short story "That Evening Sun." In religious circles the setting sun warned that the hour of judgment was at hand; in the language of the blues, sunset brought out the male rounders and female prostitutes intent on asserting their sexuality. A homicidal black male— "Jesus," a stereotypical blues-style rounder—appeared in Faulkner's story to exact his revenge for his wife's suspected infidelity, which he described in typical blues double entendre: "I can't hang around white man's kitchen. . . . But white man can hang around in mine."[31]

Jesus's angry refrain here is much like that of Silas, the black husband in Richard Wright's "Long Black Song," who discovers that a white man has taken advantage of his wife: "From sunup to sundown Ah works mah guts out and pay them white trash bastards what ah owe em, n then Ah comes n fins they been in mah house! Ah can't go into their houses n yah know Gawdamn well Ah can't."[32]

Ralph Ellison saw a strong blues influence on Richard Wright's *Black Boy*: "The blues is an impulse to keep the painful details and episodes of a brutal experience alive in one's aching consciousness, to finger its jagged grain, and to transcend it, not by the consolation of philosophy but by squeezing from it a near-tragic, near-comic lyricism. As a form the blues is an autobiographical chronicle of personal catastrophe expressed lyrically. . . . Like a blues sung by such an artist as Bessie Smith, [*Black Boy*] evokes the paradoxical, almost surreal image of a black boy singing lustily as he probes his own grievous wound."[33]

A feminist perspective on black life in the Delta came from Endesha Ida Mae Holland, a playwright born in Greenwood. Holland's "Memories of the Mississippi Delta" was a semi-autobiographical story of black women struggling against poverty, racism, and sexual exploitation. Among her prominent characters was Aint Baby, a "Country Midwife" and "Whore House Keeper," who taught her daughter "that I could do more things than she had words for."[34]

For a number of years, upper-class whites in the Delta had considered themselves benefactors and defenders rather than exploiters of the huge black population on whose labor they depended. In "Hold On" Ellen Douglas used the story of a Delta white woman's struggle to save her black maid from drowning to raise questions about white guilt and black suffering. Douglas satirized the patronizing racism of Delta whites in "I Just Love Carrie Lee," a story-monologue wherein the narrator seemed to view her maid as her own personal property. In *Can't Quit You Baby*, Douglas presented a much more complex relationship between a white woman and her black domestic helper. Although the white employer sees her maid "Tweet" as a constant source of support and affection, an exasperated Tweet finally blurts out: "Hated you. . . . You ain't got sense enough to know I hated you. I hate you all my life, before I ever know you."[35]

In "Night Watch" Charles East explored the manner in which two white policemen in the Delta maintained a superficial adherence to the Delta's prevailing racial orthodoxy, each afraid to reveal to the other his misgivings about the cruelty and injustice he had seen visited on blacks. After he had provided his younger companion with an eyewitness account of the burning of a black prison escapee, a remorseful Mr. Joe thought, "If this boy had been there, . . . he'd have been the one to set the torch to him. I never could have. I went up there to Rome to see him burn, but so did everybody else."[36]

Meanwhile, the young Toler, who remembered his own inability to join his fellow white servicemen as they had kicked and beaten a black sergeant, sized up Mr. Joe, concluding that "he'd kick a nigger as soon as look at him" and speculating that Mr. Joe had probably wielded the torch at the lynching he had described. "What is it? What makes a man like that who could go and sit with his grandbabies and who would give you the shirt off his back if he thought you needed it?"[37]

In addition to their anxieties about racial upheaval, white Deltans lived in fearful anticipation of a day of moral judgment, which could not come soon enough for many who lived outside the region. Citing "an inverse ratio between the richness of the soil and the providence of the people who live on it," Shelby Foote conceded that, in contrast to the hills where "people put up preserves and took good care of the houses and everything," in the improvident Delta "nobody puts anything up and they don't take care of their houses. They figure that if they need some pole beans, they'll go down and buy them in a can." In *Dollar Cotton* John Faulkner captured the feeling of outrage at the unpunished profligacy and laziness of the Delta that pervaded the hill counties of Mississippi, where the Delta was seen as a land where men made "twice the cotton with half the exertion" required elsewhere, broke bread "that they did not sweat for," showed no respect for "a pocketed dollar," and "wallowed in riches that fell in their laps in unearned lavishness." Similar sentiments, reflected as a sense of guilt, lurked just beneath the surface of the Delta.[38]

The image of the Delta, conceded David Cohn, was that of "a land of *dolce far niente* where the sun shines, Negroes work, white men loaf on the verandas of white porticoed mansions, and money mysteriously rolls in." Cohn conceded that his region had rejected Calvinist morality and "the gospel of success with its repellent attributes of thrift and hard work." He illustrated the Delta's reputation for "success without diligence" with the story of a bookkeeper whose planter friend had fled Greenville to avoid a murder charge and proceeded to offer his plantation to the bookkeeper rent free. Failing to secure a loan for operating expenses in New Orleans, the dejected auditor fell into a poker game as he made his return via riverboat; his spirits improved markedly as his winnings mounted, and he stayed with the game until he had traveled well past Greenville in the process of winning a ten-thousand-dollar stake that launched his career as a wealthy and prominent planter. Here was a story that defied all the teachings of the fundamentalists and the moralists—success in this case was the result not of hard work, thrift, and clean living but of a murder and a poker game. "What," asked Cohn, "was one to believe?" So much a part of the Delta's mystique, stories such as this—or that of Jimmy Dick Hill, whose 12:00 a.m. triumph at the poker table led him to name his newly acquired plantation "Midnight"—were hardly the stuff of first-class parables about morality, diligence, and thrift.[39]

The Delta seemed besieged by tangible physical forces as well as moral ones. Flood and malaria were constant companions, and the horrible yellow fever epidemic of 1878 was an indelible element of Delta lore. The boll weevil menace loomed large—larger, in fact, than it ever became. By the end of World War II, the stability of Delta society faced a new threat. As Cohn noted, the war had opened the once-oblivious Delta to "the changes and fears of the world," and the inevitability of technological and social change overshadowed all of Delta life as the forties drew to a close. With its flood control, farm subsidy and welfare programs, the federal government had cleared the Delta's path to agricultural modernity, and at the midpoint of the twentieth century all signs pointed increasingly to a federal role in forcing a social transformation on the region as well. The invasion of the tractor and the mechanical cotton picker, as well as the automobile, the radio, and the television, also heightened the sense of anticipation that the Delta's day of reckoning was at hand. Anxiety about modernization penetrated even to the bottom layers of Delta society. Cohn quoted one black plowman who lamented the invasion of the Delta by the tractor: "I'd druther have a mule fartin' in my face all day long walkin' de turnrow than dem durned tractors." Complained another: "There ain't nothing about a tractor that makes a man want to sing. The thing keeps so much noise, and you so far away from the other folks. There ain't a thing to do but sit up there and drive."[40]

The Delta's black farm laborers also realized that mechanization of agriculture meant that their status was likely to decline even further—from that of a sharecropper, who could look to the planter for support for roughly eight months of the year to that of a wage hand, who worked for the planter only during peak labor periods and shifted for himself the rest of the time. A popular blues singer warned that not until "white folks" decided to "cut off so many trucks and tractors" and "work more mules and men" would "money get thick again."[41]

At the end of the 1940s, with the Delta poised on the brink of an era of unparalleled change, John W. Wilson described the region as the last stronghold of "the older vanishing culture," the place where "the conflict of the old culture with new forces appears in sharpest definition." Wilson noted the strong emphasis on decay that permeated the work of those who wrote in or near the Delta and observed as well the inability of characters created by these writers to cope with the complexities of modern life. Behind the outpouring of creativity he described, Wilson identified an awakened "consciousness of the changes that are shaping themselves and forcing themselves into the life of the region."[42]

As the examples of the Nashville Agrarians and similar cultural nationalist groups around the world suggest, this consciousness of impending change may elicit a conservative, even reactionary, response. Such was the case in the Delta with William Alexander Percy. William Faulkner described Percy as a "little boy closing his eyes against the dark of modernity," but, like Faulkner's, Percy's eyes were anything but closed where modernization was concerned. In fact, Richard H. King has argued that Will Percy can best be understood "against the background of the modernization of the South."[43]

Percy's cultural nostalgia led him to focus on decline and decay as one generation succeeded another. Hence he not only deplored the political ascendancy of the white masses but also stressed his own unworthiness in comparison to his father. As several observers have noted, Percy referred to himself in the subtitle of his autobiography as "a planter's son" when, in fact, he was at least as much a planter as his corporate lawyer father. Critics have scored Percy for his racism, citing his condescending view of blacks as childlike, frivolous characters who were perpetually in need of the guidance and oversight of whites. Percy's view of blacks as "younger brothers" and of whites, at least whites of his class, as benevolent paternalists, as well as his admiration of the "manners" or behavioral style that kept a potentially explosive biracial society operating relatively smoothly, seem all too typical of the short-sightedness of the Delta's white aristocracy. The thoughtful, well-traveled, and well-read Percy was anything but a Delta provincial, however.[44]

In fact, Percy saw the Delta's experience against a backdrop of modernization or westernization that threatened the simplicity and stability of premodern societies everywhere in the world. He visited Samoa in 1936 and wrote an unpublished essay, "The White Plague," in which he compared the loss of innocence on the part of Samoans as Western culture overwhelmed them to what was happening in the Delta as contact with whites underminded the simplicity and innocence of the region's blacks. This process, according to Percy, resulted inevitably in the degeneration of a "first-rate negro" into a "second-rate white man." Percy saw essentially the same thing happening to the Samoans: "They are eager to take our comfortable beds, ice boxes, radios, and victrolas, our varied and devitalized foods, our bicycles and automobiles, never suspecting that taking these, they must take, too, our weariness, our restlessness, our unhappy hearts."[45]

Percy's protégé, David Cohn, also expressed admiration for the ability of Delta blacks to satisfy their wants without embracing "the white man's passion for acquisition" and dreaded the day when blacks became infected with the virus of "let us then be up and doing." Percy's adopted son, Walker, developed this theme further, using black characters to represent a simplicity that was difficult to maintain amid the intimidating complexities of modern American life. In *Love in the Ruins*, Percy shows what happens when, as Lewis Baker put it, "blacks, by becoming like whites, have become vulnerable to the malaise of modern civilization."[46]

Instead of embracing the reactionary nostalgia of a Will Percy, intellectuals in developing regions facing the imminent challenge of economic and social modernization often attempt to separate those attributes of the native culture, lifestyle, and mindset that are pernicious and outmoded from those that are integral to the region's cultural identity and therefore worth preserving. Many of the Delta's writers offered a similarly ambivalent response to the prospect of sweeping changes in their society. Shelby Foote condemned the life of the Delta planter as "wretched" because of the abuses to other human beings that it involved: "Working people all day long for a dollar. That's no good life, and whatever you get out of it, it's not worth doing that to people." On the other hand, however, Foote conceded: "It was a decent society in many ways. It had virtues. People would genuinely help each other in any kind of distress. That's nearly always true in a backward country."[47]

Though mindful of the need for changes in "the Southern way of life," William Faulkner harbored grave misgivings about both the social and environmental consequences of modernization. Deploring the greed and cruelty that Delta society embodied, Faulkner linked the destruction of the Delta wilderness, which had been "deswamped and denuded and derivered in two generations," and the general conquest of the region by modernity to his own growing feelings of inadequacy and his fears about the nation and the world in general. Grieving for the "ruined woods" of the region, Faulkner's Ike McCaslin predicted that "the people who have destroyed it will accomplish its revenge." The pessimism of Faulkner's "Delta Autumn" carried over into many of his later works, including an article on Mississippi for *Holiday* magazine in which he made the Delta—and his interaction with it throughout his life—the focal point of the piece. The essay concludes with the Tallahatchie River bottom, where Faulkner hunted as a boy, disappearing under an artificial lake, whose bottom is "being raised gradually but steadily each year by another layer of beer cans and bottle caps and lost bass plugs."[48]

David Cohn shared many of Faulkner's concerns. The Delta Cohn described in 1935 was one where the "machine age" consisted of a "patient mule lost in prehistoric thought, followed by a plodding Negro down a turnrow." Twelve years later the situation had changed dramatically; now Cohn surveyed a Delta caught up in an economic, technological, and demographic revolution. As in his earlier volume, the twin influences of race and economics remained Cohn's primary concern. He described the mechanization of the cotton economy, a phenomenon that led to "vanishing mules and men" and contributed to a massive northward movement of Delta blacks. Cohn also predicted that the transformation of agriculture spelled doom for the old "paternalistic relationship" between whites and blacks, which "whatever its defects was often marked by human tenderness, understanding, and enduring friendships. As such it was without parallel in our national life."[49]

Cohn worried about blacks displaced by mechanization, as well as those

whose northward, or at least urbanward, trek was voluntary. These blacks were
no more prepared for urban life than the cities were to receive them. Perhaps
anticipating the opportunity to voice a well-aimed "I told you so!" or two,
Cohn warned that the "Negro problem" might be "transferred from the South
to other parts of the nation who have hitherto been concerned with it only as
carping critics of the South."[50]

Cohn's views on this matter were similar to those of his friend Hodding
Carter. Although he earned a national and international reputation as a courageous spokesman for racial harmony in the South and worked tirelessly to promote industrial development in his beloved Greenville, Carter was by no means
unaware of the downside of both economic and social change in the Delta. Mississippi governor Ross Barnett proved uncharacteristically perceptive when he
damned Carter as "a moderate by his own admission," for Carter was indeed a
moderate, one who deplored the cruelty, injustice, and repression he saw all
about him but also objected to the efforts of northern would-be reformers to
press for rapid and sweeping changes in the status quo.[51]

Carter worried that, however well intentioned, the South's critics often
did more harm than good by triggering the fear among southern whites "of
swift, drastic, and forcible change from without." In Carter's view it was only
because white southerners were "hag-ridden by this fear" that race-baiting,
rabble-rousing politicians like Theodore G. Bilbo retained their appeal: "Upon
this rotten meat does Bilbo feed and grow great in the eyes of resentful, frightened men." As a result Carter condemned members of the "hit and run school
of popular writing," who were caught up in the "old American sport" of "hunting the Southerner in his native habitat." Despite his own satirical treatment of
a Bilboesque character in his novel *Flood Crest* and his valiant efforts to thwart
Bilbo's reelection bid in 1946, Carter actually found himself defending "the
Man" as Bilbo, already dying of cancer of the mouth, came under fire from
northern critics for his questionable associations with war contractors and
faced allegations that black voters had been intimidated or otherwise prevented
from voting during the 1946 campaign.[52]

Struggling to reconcile his anguish over his region's racial inequities and
abuses with his antagonism toward the South's critics, Carter observed wryly
that the South "was the only place in the western world where a man could
become a liberal simply by urging obedience to the law." Yet, sounding more
than a little like Faulkner's Gavin Stevens, he also complained that, "unless the
Southerner measures up to the qualifications which the Northern liberals set
for liberalism, he is considered no liberal at all."[53]

Some of his critics labeled him "the Fence Rider," and Carter's moderation did force him to occupy an ideological no man's land on a number of occasions. Responding to the formation of the White Citizens' Council, Carter
wrote, "We've been battling the NAACP's own angry racism for a long
time. . . . We'll battle [Robert] Patterson's identical brand of hatred of dissim-
ilar people just as hard." Carter responded to the NAACP's involvement in the

Emmett Till controversy by suggesting that a "not guilty" verdict would please not only the negrophobes throughout the South but the NAACP, which seemed to him intent on making a scapegoat of Mississippi. Carter admitted that, if justice was not done in the matter, "we will deserve all the criticism we get." When the acquittal came, however, Carter criticized law enforcement officials for doing so little to locate evidence or witnesses, but he again placed much of the blame on the NAACP, whose "propaganda making" effectively "put on the defensive from the outset" the local white leaders, who "might otherwise have made an honest effort to do more."[54]

Carter could not resist the temptation to issue an "I told you so!" when the *Brown* decision came down, and he expressed his conviction "that the court could not have made a different ruling in the light of democratic and Christian principles and against the world background of today." Still, Carter conceded that, in this opinion, he probably differed from "many of our fellow southerners," and he added that "it would be tragic if in the deep South any widespread or concerted effort is made this fall or in the immediate future to enroll Negro children in hitherto all-white schools." As he urged blacks to embrace gradualism, Carter tried simultaneously to use the threat of black challenges to the dual school system to prod his fellow whites into providing equal facilities for "every educable child."[55]

Despite his initial misgivings about federally mandated desegregation and his preference for a "go slow" approach, Carter recognized that the *Brown* decision would eventually have to be implemented, and he worked to see this accomplished as peacefully as possible. He condemned the violent white response to black activism in the early 1960s, charging that responsibility for the murder of Medgar Evers lay with "what any poll would determine to be the most inflammatory newspapers, the sorriest legislature, and the most weak-kneed citizenry in our nation." At the end of the 1960s, however, Carter surveyed the changes that the civil rights movement had brought to the South and confessed to some significant misgivings. Declaring that "the Old South had something worth saving," he drew on a lifetime's experience in the Deep South to describe traditional relationships between the races as "brutal and loving, poignant and wry and ecstatically comical, wrong in the basic premise of superiority and inferiority and so right in a basic affection that made the abuses less bitter to the soul and less heavy upon the heart."[56]

Carter bemoaned the likelihood that relationships such as the one he enjoyed with the black playmates of his boyhood would be difficult to maintain now that "Little Black Sambo" had given way to "big black power." He found black impatience "understandable" but feared that this impatience bred a "deadly hate." The result was "a sad barrenness" and an "unbridgeable gulf" that went "hand in hand with the new black power."[57]

A frustrated Carter faced not only the prospect of alienation from the blacks whom he had sought to help but from the whites whose demagoguery and acts of violence and intimidation he attacked with such vengeance. Walter

Sillers, Jr., branded Carter as "unfit to live in a decent white society," while Theodore G. Bilbo charged that Carter was "as bitter an enemy to our customs, practices, ideals, and ways of life as any Russian refugee that ever landed in New York" and added for good measure that Carter "glowers [sic] in the praise that he gets from the nigger lovers and niggers of the North when he indicts the South." An anonymous "poet" identified himself with "the southern patriots," whose number was "legion," and informed Carter, "Your language is foreign to this, our region."[58]

Despite his anger at such personal attacks, Carter refused to sever his ties with his fellow white southerners, especially those in Greenville. He laughed off the news that he had been burned in effigy in nearby Glenn Allan after delivering a speech critical of southern race relations in Providence, Rhode Island, in 1961—finding it encouraging that he had only been burned in effigy, since white Mississippians had been known to "burn people in the flesh." Even in the wake of an incident in which his lawn was strewn with garbage as he and Betty Carter grieved for their son, who had killed himself in an apparent game of Russian roulette, Carter clung to the conviction that he could condemn the barbarism and injustice of the southern way of life without severing his ties with the white society to whose benefit that way of life operated. Responding to charges that he was out to destroy the "southern way of life, Carter revealed his ambivalence: "There's a lot of it I do want destroyed. There's a lot I want to keep."[59]

For all the national and international recognition they enjoyed, Hodding and Betty Carter were heavily involved in an array of local civic activities and were also fixtures on Greenville's hyperactive social circuit. The controversy over Carter's selection as master of ceremonies at the Delta Debutante Ball, after all, overshadowed his insistence on taking part in a ritual that so much reflected the social values of the region's white elite. In fact, save for his much more progressive stance on race, as one writer observed, Carter "largely symbolized the better-educated conservative, entrepreneurial profile of the Delta planter."[60]

Carter was hardly unique in his efforts to remedy the deficiencies he found in Delta society while reaffirming what he saw as the many virtues of the Delta's way of life. The desire to analyze, modify, and selectively preserve a regional heritage to which they felt such strong emotional ties had helped to fuel the creative energies of a host of writers from one end of the South to the other. For white writers in the Delta, however, this effort amounted to more than an occasional encounter with the romantic imagery of a seductive but safely distant southern past. Like Hodding Carter, many of the white "insiders" who wrote critically and perceptively about the problems of the Delta struggled on almost a daily basis to reconcile their abhorrence of the racism, poverty, and inequity that pervaded their region with their affinity for its physical appeal, human charm, and the comfortable and intellectually uncomplicated lifestyle it offered them.

For all her outspokenness and the resultant alienation from the local white community, early in her career even the fiery Hazel Brannon Smith behaved much like a Delta debutante, tooling around in a flashy convertible and living in Hazelwood, a grand antebellum style mansion described by neighbors as "a real *Gone-with-the-Wind*-type thing." Although he wrote with considerable disdain in 1965 of the conquest of the Delta by "the usual coalition of peckerwoods, super-patriots, and the Citizens' Council," Walker Percy was nonetheless present in December 1966 when his daughter made her debut, courtesy the Delta Debutante Society, in "the elaborately decorated Plantation Room of the Downtowner Motor Inn" in Greenville.[61]

As a seventeen-year-old Willie Morris dreamed of living the tranquil good life as a member of the Delta's landed elite. He fantasized about attending Ole Miss—"as all my friends planned to do"—and then returning to the huge plantation where his girlfriend lived "to preside there on the banks of the Yazoo over boll weevils big enough to wear dog tags, pre-Earl Warren darkies, and the young squirearchy from the plantations abutting on Carter, Eden, Holly Bluff Sidon and Tchula."[62]

A former Ole Miss sorority girl whose social and political awakening led her to work in the congressional campaigns of black legislator Robert Clark, Melany Neilson offered this insider's retrospective on what it had meant to her to be a youthful member of the Delta's white elite:

> The best of us were from fine families. We were bright, the star students, teachers' favorites. Our fathers were farmers, professionals, businessmen, young to middle aged, hopeful, full of promise. Our mothers were attractive, members of the Garden and Bridge clubs, Den Mothers, some of whom paid weekly visits to the beauty parlor and had their names written up in the Holmes County Herald society column. We had comfortable homes, cars, memberships at the local country club. We were the best because we expected to be; our privileges were granted, not earned, by an accident of birth.[63]

White Mississippians had long joked that they had no desire to farm but simply wanted to "live like a Delta farmer." Travel writers gushed about a planter lifestyle that "at its grandest has a seignorial sweep to it, a panorama of big country houses, gardens, and cooks at work" and "dozens of farm laborers behind $60,000 cotton pickers." However, more thoughtful observers were struck by the fact that Delta whites managed to enjoy life so much when, as Neal Peirce observed, "it takes a stranger driving through the Delta only an hour or two to see the human misery." Hodding Carter III offered a simple explanation: "Many local wealthy people live on the incredible fiction that they don't have poverty all around them. . . . It's an elaborate edifice you have to maintain if you want to live with yourself." One planter who was able to throw off this mindset did so only after returning from a European tour to see "more poverty between Memphis and Clarksdale than I had in all of Europe. . . .

Before, I guess, the shanties and little Negro children urinating from the porches had just blended into the landscape."[64]

Although they were struck by the ability of high-living Delta whites to look at the staggering poverty of Delta blacks without actually appearing to see it, a number of even the most critical visitors to the Delta were nonetheless captivated by the manners and lifestyles of the Delta's affluent whites. As he stressed the economic hardships visited upon Delta blacks, Rupert Vance also wrote admiringly of the "mansions" and lifestyles of the Delta's planter aristocracy. Tris Coffin found the julep-sipping Delta elite "a charming people," and even such demanding critics as Ralph McGill and Lillian Smith found the hospitality of the racist and politically reactionary Delta planters difficult to resist.[65]

Neal Peirce cynically traced the ancestry of many so-called Delta aristocrats to "some smart foreman a generation or two back who got hold of a piece of land and scratched his way to affluence." Still, Peirce conceded that Delta planters led "a good life." "They give lavish parties at home or the country club, charter air conditioned buses to take their friends to the football games in Memphis, jet off to New York for Broadway shows, or to Europe, or to places in the sun for long winter sojourns. Even those of less flamboyant tastes lead a very good life."[66]

The Philadelphia *Inquirer*'s Julia Cass noted in 1983 that Martin Luther King, visiting the Delta town of Marks in 1966, "literally wept at the poverty of the black people there." Cass added that "there are sights in Marks today that still would make you cry," yet she was clearly fascinated by the region's extraordinarily friendly and hard-partying planters. She reported on a gathering in the impoverished town of Tunica where, apparently unconcerned about the area's problems with poverty or infant mortality, one guest flaunted his Gila monster-skin tasseled loafers, while another talked about his trip to the Pribilof Islands, which he had taken merely "to satisfy his curiosity about a seal kill." Elsewhere, Rheta Grimsley Johnson took note of the Delta's widespread poverty but made no secret of her admiration for the "slow and civilized" lifestyle of its white elite.[67]

As a region where the vast black majority continued to live in poverty that was difficult to imagine, let alone accept, while a small, seemingly oblivious white minority enjoyed a pampered and gracious lifestyle that many found difficult to resist, the Delta seemed to have captured for posterity the essence of the troubling, but nonetheless intriguing, historical legacy of the Old South. As the comments of a number of both internal and external observers indicated, the Delta's southernness seemed very much a palpable, present-day, flesh-and-blood reality. As early as the 1930s, Rupert Vance had described the Delta as the "Deepest South" and "the heart of Dixie." Tony Dunbar found a Delta where "the real life of the plantations in the 1960s was so reminiscent of the lovely and terrible and glorified heritage of old Dixie that I could not get enough of it." In 1983 Julia Cass observed that "if any place in the South still seems southern, it is the Mississippi Delta." In 1990 Rheta Grimsley Johnson described the Delta as the last refuge of "the mythical South." Richard Ford, who lived in the Delta for a time, seemed to suggest that the Delta represented such a South in miniature when he observed that "what the South is to the rest of the country, the Delta is to Mississippi. It is the South's South."[68]

As an astute blend of caricature and analysis, Wilbur J. Cash's *The Mind of the South* drew belated criticism as a Piedmont-obsessed "hillbilly history" of the region, but the South dissected by Cash also bore considerable resemblance to the Delta described by David Cohn and a host of others. Like the Delta, Cash's South was a land of contradiction and excess featuring a remarkable juxtaposition of hedonism and piety, hospitality and violence. In the Delta, Cohn saw a "whiskey-drinking and Church-going society" that, despite the outward appearance of placidity, was nothing short of an "armed camp." Certainly Cash would have recognized the Delta banker's wife who recalled her Delta girlhood as a delightfully uncomplicated mixture of sex ("I was deflowered on a John Deere tractor. That doesn't sound very romantic, does it, but I assure you it was. We have such beautiful moonlight here.") and Sunday school ("Church was very important in my family. I went to Sunday school every week until I got out of college.").[69]

At its best the Delta exhibited the courtesy, generosity, hospitality, and pride that Cash identified as the primary virtues of an entire region. At its worst the Delta had more than its share of the exaggerated individualism, narrow concept of social responsibility, "excessive attachment to racial values," and "tendency to justify cruelty and injustice in the name of those values" that Cash identified as the most disturbing qualities of the South at large.[70]

Testimony to its enduring southernness abounded, but, however effectively it may have fueled the fantasies of tourists or first-time visitors, matched up with Cash's schizophrenic South, or filled the bill as Ford's Dixie in microcosm, the Delta could scarcely have sustained its reputation as a rich source of literary inspiration if the themes and circumstances that it offered were of none but regional significance. Reduced to its essence, the Delta's most intriguing characteristic—and, in the final analysis, perhaps that of the mythic, stereotypical Old South as well—was less a matter of its latitude than of its capacity to present such fundamentally unmoderated and starkly juxtaposed extremes of human behavior and the human condition. Neal Peirce asserted that "nowhere in America do the life styles of the privileged and less fortunate contrast so vividly." (The Delta, after all, had produced both Will Percy, well read and widely traveled even early in his youth, and Fannie Lou Hamer, who only discovered in middle age that she was legally entitled to vote.) V. O. Key observed in 1949 that "in the agrarian economy of the Mississippi sort no great middle class—not even an agrarian middle class—dulls the abruptness of the line between lord and serf." Rheta Grimsley Johnson described the Delta in 1990 as "the only place left in America with bona fide shacks and mansions side by side with not enough middle class to blunt the disparity," and another recent visitor noted that, "so often in the Delta, extremes stand side by side." The struggle to reconcile the Delta's contrasts and unravel its contradictions provided the central dynamic for its rich literary tradition. The major contributors to this tradition, however, discovered in the Delta's story the opportunity to pursue themes that were more universal than unique. William Faulkner, for example, used the Delta to explore transcendent questions of greed, cruelty, and the ravages of man and modernity against nature. Similarly, Tennessee Williams drew on the Delta to expose the materialism and depravity that may flourish behind the facade of wealth, status, and power in any society.[71]

Writing in 1964, Howard Zinn suggested that the embattled South represented not the antithesis but the "essence" of American society and could therefore function effectively as a mirror "in which the nation can see its blemishes magnified." If one accepts Zinn's argument, as "the South's South" the Delta actually functioned as a mirror within a mirror, capturing not just the South's but the nation's most controversial traits in mercilessly sharp detail. Hence, when one looked closely at the Delta's polarities of self-indulgence and suffering, what seemed at first glance to be a regional legacy that refused to fade began to suggest instead the bittersweet fruits of a larger, even more powerful and enduring national obsession with wealth, status, power, and pleasure. Behind the seductive and disarming Old South facade of the Delta, the American Dream had been not so much perverted as simply pursued to its ultimate realization in a setting where human and natural resources could be exploited to the fullest with but little regard for social or institutional restraint.[72]

Although the Old South myth is often treated as an escapist alternative to the frantic pace and hollow materialism of modern life, in reality the plantation imagery associated in fiction and film with *Gone with the Wind* and in real life with the Mississippi Delta may actually represent not so much the antithesis of the American scramble for success as the ultimate attainment of that success itself. Although Faulkner's *Absalom, Absalom!* was not set in the Delta, it was nonetheless about the Delta in much the same way as it was about the rest of the nation as well. Having been turned away from the front door of an imposing Tidewater mansion, Thomas Sutpen vows to have such a house himself. Utterly ruthless in his determination to fulfill this ambition, Sutpen personifies a South (and suggests an America) destroyed by its own single-minded pursuit of wealth and status and its insensitivity "to the evil done to men and nature" in the process. As F. Gavin Davenport observed, the story of Sutpen and his dream reveals that "the cavalier myth contributes to and encourages the very exploitation and crass worship of material goods" many "Southern traditionalists" believed that it opposed. Even better than the fictional account of Thomas Sutpen, the flesh-and-blood story of the Delta attests to the richness of Davenport's insight.[73]

While Sutpen's saga ended in the ashes of his once grand plantation home, however, the Delta emerged from a historical experience driven by similar extremes of greed and social ambition with the big house still standing. As a result the Delta offered tourists and travel writers the opportunity to escape into the "South of fiction and fantasy," as Johnson called it, while allowing more thoughtful observers to consider the implications of the Delta story for a larger society in which material success frequently counted for more than moral failure and human and environmental costs were all too often no object at all.

▽ Epilogue:
▽ An American Region
▽

The Delta's capacity to provide a literary as well as a musical window on American society at large should come as no surprise. Despite its image as an isolated, self-sustaining, ultra-southern anachronism, many of the Yazoo-Mississippi Delta's primary identifying qualities, especially the enduring contrasts in lifestyles and living conditions that it presents, are less a reflection of its Old South beginnings than a postbellum experience characterized by more than a century of consistent and close interaction with the pervasive influences of the modern American economic and political system.

As the 1990s began, the relationship between conditions in the Delta and the economic and political climate in the nation at large was more obvious than ever. Nicholas Lemann observed in 1991 that Clarksdale whites saw the town's black community as "a welfare colony floating on a tide of federal transfer payments, sapped of the will to work." As had been the case almost continuously since the New Deal Era, however, by no means all the Delta's recipients of public subsidies were black. A white developer of low-income housing conceded as much when he observed that "if you took away the farmer's government subsidy payment, the welfare, and the unemployment check, this whole place would blow away."[1]

Despite congressionally imposed limits of fifty thousand dollars per person in annual subsidy payments, Delta planters still sought on occasion to collect massive amounts of federal money. In August 1990 the *New York Times* reported on the case of Richard Flowers and his partner, who reportedly oversaw a fourteen-thousand-acre planting operation in the Delta and managed, through a sophisticated organizational scheme that involved thirty-seven interlocking corporations and fifty-one trusts, to claim eligibility for $1.3 million in federal payments. Even plantations whose subsidies did not exceed the fifty-thousand-dollar limit seemed to be thriving. Consolidation and a virtual corporate invasion—among others, the Stovall plantation, where J. W. Fowler fumed about his losses to the Yankees and Muddy Waters once ran a jook joint, was now operated by the Prudential Corporation—put the size of the average cotton farm in Coahoma County at approximately two thousand acres, while rising cotton prices promised profits in the neighborhood of $100 per acre.[2]

The Delta's ties to Washington went well beyond farm subsidies and welfare checks. Tony Dunbar observed "an overriding fact of life in the Delta" when he noted that "there is very little that is not touched by the federal government. What to plant, when to plant it, where to plant, whom to hire, how to house farm workers, how to finance the farm, not to mention public welfare, the schools, and local government itself are all strongly influenced by the federal government."[3]

Economic-development leaders had hoped for years to stimulate local industries and businesses in order to reduce the Delta's dependence on outside capital and federal programs, but such efforts met with relatively little success. Many of those concerned about the economic problems of the region had expressed high hopes for the catfish industry, which by 1990 employed approximately six thousand workers in Mississippi, many of them in the Delta area. Catfish processing did indeed seem to be the long-sought "home-grown" industry that had eluded the Delta for so long, but the events of 1990 indicated that the catfish was unlikely to become the symbol of the Delta's economic salvation. The predominantly black work force at the Delta's several catfish-processing plants had encountered stiff resistance and considerable harassment as they pushed for union representation in 1986. The primary motivation for unionization was the desire for better wages and working conditions, but changes in these areas came slowly, so slowly that workers at the Delta Pride plant at Indianola went out on strike in September 1990. "It's a hellhole," charged one striking worker who was making $4.02 per hour after three years with the company. "It stays nasty. . . . All day long they're harassing you, treating you like animals. They're right in your face with a stopwatch." Some workers complained of standing in blood and fish intestines for hours on end. Others told of having to get permission from a supervisor before going to the bathroom and of male supervisors following females into the toilets. Rumors persisted that white male supervisors had sought sexual favors from female workers in exchange for better jobs or wages.[4]

Assessing the situation at Delta Pride, a local black leader concluded that "the only thing that's changed from the plantation is the crop. . . . Instead of cotton, it's catfish." An Indianola minister agreed, accusing Delta Pride of following "the plantation approach, which assumes that labor is disposable." Certainly, for workers paid on a piecework basis, the parallels between picking cotton at three dollars per hundred and filleting fish at three dollars per fifty-pound tub were obvious enough. Moreover, following the example of local planters, who once relied on commodities and food stamps to subsidize their workers, at Delta Pride (where the average annual wage was more than forty-four hundred dollars below the minimum poverty-level income for a single parent with three children) the personnel department assisted employees in applying for welfare.[5]

The Delta Pride strike also seemed to evoke memories of the ill-fated 1965 cotton-choppers' strike on the Andrews Plantation. Certainly the workers were confronting similar disadvantages in terms of their low skill levels and the abundance of underemployed labor in the area. In reality, however, the Delta Pride strike had less to do with the persistence of the plantation mentality among Delta whites than with the sobering realities of employment in any slow-growth, low-wage, low-skill industry not only in the South but anywhere in the nation in the 1990s. With the market for catfish showing signs of saturation, the quest for continuing profits entailed a redoubled emphasis on worker productivity in conjunction with stubborn resistance to significant wage increases. The Delta's distinctive economic and cultural context may have strengthened management's hand and stiffened its resolve during the three-month strike, but the fundamental disadvantages confronting workers at Delta Pride could actually be found throughout a manufacturing sector beset by slow growth, global competition, automation, and industrial migration to cheaper labor markets. (The strikers were exultant after finally winning modest wage concessions from Delta Pride in December 1990, but the settlement came amid reports of lagging sales and warnings of lower prices at the pond bank for catfish producers.) The Delta's susceptibility to such national and global economic trends became even more apparent in August 1991 when the Schwinn Bicycle Company, considered one of the area's most progressive and generous employers, shocked state and local development leaders by suddenly announcing that the ongoing recession had forced it to shut down its Greenville plant and rely more heavily on its Taiwanese manufacturing facility.[6]

The relationship between the fortunes of the Delta and the political and fiscal climate in the nation at large was also evident in the saga of the Lower Mississippi Development Commission. Created by Congress in October 1988, ostensibly to recommend solutions to the woeful economic and social problems that prevailed throughout the lower Mississippi area, the nine-member commission spent eighteen months compiling data for a report on the needs of the region. Although the area's difficulties were already well publicized, the commission's findings nonetheless revealed human suffering and institutional deficiencies of staggering proportions. The poorest of the 214 counties in the study area was Tunica, where nearly 53 percent of the population lived below the poverty line, while Humphreys County, where twenty-nine of every one thousand babies died before their first birthday, had the area's highest infant mortality rate. Overall, eleven of the fifteen counties with the highest frequency of infant deaths lay wholly or partly within the Yazoo Delta, and all of these had higher infant death rates than Chile or Malaysia.[7]

Meanwhile, overwhelming evidence of hard-core unemployment, severe educational deficiencies, and the utter absence of local capital or entrepreneurial expertise left little cause for optimism. Commission member Webb Franklin, a former Republican congressman from the Delta, predicted that the region would benefit from the migration of "smokestack industries" from the North, but consistent indications of "redlining" of areas with large black populations by many firms suggested that Franklin might be unrealistic in his expectations. Beyond questions of race was the matter of the geographically isolated, educationally and institutionally underdeveloped Delta's fundamental unattractiveness as a potential location for business or industry. One observer concluded that "people on Wall Street see more attractive investments in Venezuela than in the Mississippi Delta."[8]

Conditions such as these seemed to call for drastic measures, such as a massive neo-New Deal recovery program along the lines of the Appalachian Regional Commission. Whereas the ARC had been launched in the relatively supportive social and political context of 1965, however, the mood of the Congress and the White House was dramatically different in 1990. Bowing to the social and fiscal conservatism that gripped official Washington, commission members took pains to characterize their recommendations, in the words of Delta congressman Mike Espy, as "politically possible and not terribly expensive." As Espy's remarks implied, the commission's report, which appeared on the same day as a presidential-congressional summit conference aimed at reducing the massive federal budget deficit, emphasized local, state, and regional self-help initiatives as the primary remedy for the Delta's woes. Such recommendations appeared to fly in the face of the commission's own findings relative to the Delta's massive human and material deficiencies, but a White House official praised the group for submitting a "good solid report" that "doesn't take the approach of looking for the federal government to heal all the ills in this area." Even the minimal commitment the report requested from Washington was too much, however, for the Bush administration, which sought to project a "caring attitude" without actually "endorsing" the report or its recommendations.[9]

As had been the case historically, a reluctance to commit federal funds to relieve human suffering in the Delta did not necessarily reflect a consistent commitment to frugality in other government programs or initiatives. As the commission began to release its findings, Congress debated the number of B-2 bombers to purchase at $500 million apiece, and the estimated $250 billion savings and loan bailout moved into high gear. Shortly after the report appeared, the United States undertook a massively expensive commitment of troops and equipment to the defense of United States interests in the Persian Gulf.[10]

Although Congress and the White House had little time and less money to devote to the problems of the region, Tony Dunbar observed that "an optimism flows through the black communities of the Delta that is completely at odds with economic reality." Similarly, Nicholas Lemann found that among Clarksdale blacks "nearly everyone has the feeling of being on a communal upward trajectory," adding that "the transition from a plantation economy to a welfare economy doesn't look like such a bad trade from the black perspective." Lemann's fascinating account of the experiences of black migrants who fled the Delta for Chicago in the 1940s and came back in the 1970s and 1980s

chronicled the remarkable odyssey of a people who had abandoned one promised land for another only to return to the first. Upon resettling in the Delta,
these migrants found it much improved and generally more to their liking than
a Chicago whose onetime allure had long since succumbed to a choking tangle
of economic stagnation and social pathology. Ironically, however, returnees
also found that many of the problems they hoped to leave behind in Chicago
were already awaiting them in the Delta. The spray-painted symbols of Chicago gangs marked poorer neighborhoods in the larger towns of the region.
Meanwhile, gang-related violence was becoming distressingly commonplace,
as were broad-daylight muggings on the days when social security and welfare
checks arrived. Cocaine circulated freely, and even residents of smaller towns
complained of an influx of drug dealers. "We caught it from Chicago; the hard
stuff is here," complained one Leland resident. Having fled its oppression and
suffering to pursue a better life in the urban North, returning migrants found a
changed Delta far more hospitable than the one they had left. Unfortunately,
however, the same Delta whose barriers to black advancement had once made
the promise of full participation in American life seem so remote could now
offer little protection from the perils of such participation, including the contagion of social deterioration that seemed to be spreading outward so rapidly
from what had once been the great land of hope just up the I.C. line.[11]

Traditional wisdom has long held that isolation from the major currents
of the American political and socioeconomic mainstream was primarily responsible for the human and material extremes that were the key to the Delta's image
as a region. Typically, this "isolation" theory has also been offered to explain
the Delta's enduring southernness, although by the 1990s one also heard it in
conjunction with the designation of the Delta as an American "Third World,"
a region that had somehow been bypassed by the progressive economic, social,
and political forces that seemed to have had such a positive impact on American
society at large. In reality, however, many of the human and material extremes
that were the keys to the Delta's identity either as the "South's South" or
"America's Ethiopia" were shaped not by its isolation but by pervasive global
and national economic influences and consistent interaction with a federal government whose policies often confirmed the Delta's inequities and reinforced
its anachronistic social and political order as well.

Recent statistical trends pointing to rapidly widening gaps in income and
opportunity throughout the United States suggest that the economic and social
polarization that is synonymous with the Mississippi Delta may be observed
wherever and whenever the pursuit of wealth, pleasure, and power overwhelms
the ideals of equality, justice, and compassion and reduces the American Dream
to a self-indulgent fantasy. As socioeconomic disparity and indifference to
human suffering become increasingly prominent features of American life, it
seems reasonable to inquire whether the same economic, political, and emotional forces that helped to forge and sustain the Delta's image as the South writ
small may one day transform an entire nation into the Delta writ large.

▽ Notes
▽
▽

Preface

[1]My observations were recalled in Tony Dunbar, *Delta Time: A Journey through Mississippi* (New York, 1990), 166. See also Rupert B. Vance, *Human Geography of the South* (New York, 1935), 266, 270.

[2]David L. Cohn, *Where I Was Born and Raised* (Boston, 1948), 12.

[3]Ibid., 42.

[4]Dunbar, *Delta Time*, 5.

[5]Ibid., xx.

[6]Lawrence Levine, *Black Culture and Black Consciousness: Afro-American Folk Thought from Slavery to Freedom* (Oxford, London, and New York, 1978); Immanuel Wallerstein, "What Can One Mean by Southern Culture?" in Numan V. Bartley, ed., *The Evolution of Southern Culture* (Athens, Ga., 1988), 4.

Introduction: "Pure Soil, Endlessly Deep, Dark, and Sweet"

[1]Arthell Kelley, "Some Aspects of the Geography of the Yazoo Basin, Mississippi" (Ph.D. diss., University of Nebraska, 1954), 13–14; Robert L. Brandfon, *Cotton Kingdom of the New South: A History of the Yazoo Mississippi Delta from Reconstruction to the Twentieth Century* (Cambridge, Mass., 1967), 24–29; Robert W. Harrison, *Alluvial Empire: A Study of State and Local Efforts toward Land Development in the Alluvial Valley of the Lower Mississippi River* (Little Rock, 1961), 5, 20. The counties lying wholly within the Yazoo Delta are Bolivar, Coahoma, Humphreys, Issaquena, Leflore, Quitman, Sharkey, Sunflower, Tunica, and Washington. Other counties that are situated partially within or adjacent to the Delta include Carroll, Holmes, Panola, Tallahatchie, Warren, and Yazoo. Unless otherwise indicated, statistical computations relating to "the Delta" refer only to the area encompassed by the former group of counties. In cases where material from diaries, correspondence, or plantation records originating in counties not wholly within the Delta has been used, every effort has been made to ascertain that the specific physical origins of the material lay wholly within or immediately adjacent to the Delta and that the material is representative of conditions within the Delta itself. The tenth core county, Humphreys, was created in 1918.

[2]Brandfon, *Cotton Kingdom of the New South*, 26–28.

[3]Kelley, "Some Aspects of the Geography," 36.

[4]Cohn, *Where I Was Born and Raised*, 26.

[5]Kelley, "Some Aspects of the Geography," 41; William Alexander Percy, *Lanterns on the Levee: Recollections of a Planter's Son* (Baton Rouge, 1973), 4; Cohn, *Where I Was Born and Raised*, 26; Brandfon, *Cotton Kingdom of the New South*, 29.

[6]Edgar J. Cheatham, Jr., "Washington County, Mississippi: Its Antebellum Generation" (M.A. thesis, Tulane University, 1950), 1–6.

[7]Cheatham, "Washington County," 6.

[8]Ibid., 6–7; Cohn, *Where I Was Born and Raised*, 26.

Chapter 1. Plantation Frontier

[1]Irene Long Shurden, "A History of Washington County, Mississippi, to 1900" (M.A. thesis, Mississippi College, 1963), 12; John Edmund Gonzales, "Flush Times, Depression, War, and Compromise," in Richard Aubrey McLemore, ed., *A History of Mississippi*, vol. 1 (Hattiesburg, Miss., 1973), 284–85.

[2]Kelley, "Some Aspects of the Geography," 48–49; Cheatham, "Washington County," 23–26. There is disagreement as to whether William W. Blanton and his family moved to their plantation, where Greenville is presently situated, in 1818 or 1828. See O. M. Blanton, "The Mother of Greenville," and Mrs. H. B. Theobald, "Reminiscences of Greenville," in *Memoirs of Henry Tillinghast Ireys: Papers of the Washington County Historical Society, 1910–1915* (Jackson, Miss., 1954), 49, 51.

[3]Cheatham, "Washington County," 34.

[4]Ibid., 31–32, 41; Cohn, *Where I Was Born and Raised*, 25.

[5]Ibid., 72, 108, 110; *Seventh Census of the United States, 1850* (Washington, 1853), 447; Charles S. Sydnor, *Slavery in Mississippi* (New York, 1933), 188; Andrew Alexton Ewing, "Elite Control in Washington County: 1850–1880" (M.A. thesis, Jackson State University, 1982), 16.

[6]Cheatham, "Washington County," 108–11; Gail Criss and Charlotte Hill, "A Demographic Study of Bolivar County in 1850," and Ann D. Clifton, "A Demographic Study of Bolivar County in 1860," *Journal of the Bolivar County Historical Society* 1 (March 1977), 3–9, 10–20. See also Herbert Weaver, *Mississippi Farmers, 1850–1860* (Gloucester, Mass., 1968), 28.

[7]Patricia A. Kell, "The Aristocracy in Late Antebellum Mississippi" (M.A. thesis, Lamar University, 1977), 76, 83, 102.

[8]Percy L. Rainwater, "The Autobiography of Benjamin Grubb Humphreys, August 26, 1808–December 20, 1882," *Mississippi Valley Historical Review* 21 (January 1934–March 1935), 241; Cheatham, "Washington County," 17.

[9]Vernon L. Walters, "Migration into Mississippi, 1798–1837" (M.A. thesis, Mississippi State College, 1969), 161.

[10]Ibid., 162.

[11]Paul C. Cameron to Thomas Ruffin, January 1, 1834, in J. G. De Roulhac Hamilton, ed., *The Papers of Thomas Ruffin*, vol. 2 (Raleigh, N.C., 1918), 108–9; James W. Williamson to Paul C. Cameron, September 23, 1856, Cameron Family Papers,

Southern Historical Collection (hereinafter cited as SHC), University of North Carolina, Chapel Hill.

[12]William L. Barney, *The Secessionist Impulse: Alabama and Mississippi in 1860* (Princeton, 1974), 146; John Hebron Moore, *The Emergence of the Cotton Kingdom in the Old Southwest: Mississippi, 1770–1860* (Baton Rouge, 1988), 127.

[13]Weaver, *Mississippi Farmers, 1850–1860,* 120.

[14]William K. Scarbrough, "Heartland of the Cotton Kingdom," in Richard A. McLemore, ed., *A History of Mississippi,* vol. 1 (Hattiesburg, Miss., 1973), 349–50.

[15]Andrew J. Polk to Paul C. Cameron, June 20, 1854, Cameron Family Papers.

[16]Stovall Plantation Records, Ledger 1, John D. Williams Library, University of Mississippi, Oxford, Miss.

[17]Everard G. Baker Diary, October 13, 1858, SHC; Wade Hampton II to Mary Fisher Hampton, March 11, 1855, Wade Hampton III to Mary Fisher Hampton, April 10, 1858, in Charles E. Cauthen, ed., *Family Letters of the Three Wade Hamptons, 1782–1901,* (Columbia, S.C., 1953), 38–39, 59–60.

[18]"Crop, Amounts of Crops of Cotton, Average Price, Expenses, Crop and Nett [*sic*] Yield, 1856–58," Stovall Plantation Records, John D. Williams Library.

[19]William Mason Worthington to Albert Worthington, November 10, 1857, Amanda Worthington to Albert Worthington, December 28, 1857, January 17, 1858, Worthington Family Papers, Mississippi Department of Archives and History (hereinafter cited as MDAH), Jackson, Miss.

[20]H. E. Merritt to My Dear Uncle, February 27, 1857, box 2, Sterling Neblett to W. H. E. Merritt, December 11, 1857, box 37, W. H. E. Merritt Papers, William R. Perkins Library, Duke University, Durham, N.C.

[21]Sterling Neblett to W. H. E. Merritt, December 11, 1857, W. H. E. Merritt Papers.

[22]Andrew Jackson Donelson to Andrew Jackson Donelson, Jr., November 30, 1857, Andrew Jackson Donelson Papers, Manuscripts Division, Library of Congress, Washington, D.C.

[23]Sterling Neblett to W. H. E. Merritt, December 11, 1857, H. E. Merritt to My Dear Father, February 26, 1859, box 37, W. H. E. Merritt Papers; Martha Rebecca Blanton to My Dear Parents, January 25, 1859, Martha Rebecca Blanton to My Dear Sisters, February 8, 1861, Blanton Family Papers, John D. Williams Library.

[24]Paul C. Cameron to Thomas Ruffin, March 21, 1857, in Hamilton, ed., *Papers of Thomas Ruffin,* vol. 2, pp. 549–50.

[25]James H. Ruffin to Thomas Ruffin, April 30, 1833, in Hamilton, ed., *Papers of Thomas Ruffin,* vol. 2, pp. 77–78.

[26]Rush G. Miller, "John G. Jones: Pioneer Circuit Rider and Historian," *Journal of Mississippi History* 39 (February 1977), 26–27; Amanda Worthington to Robert Tilford, April 22, 1838, Worthington Family Papers.

[27]"Flux or Dysentery at Prairie, 1854," Stovall Plantation Records, John D. Williams Library; Everard G. Baker Diary, May 23, 1860–October 15, 1861.

[28]Willie D. Halsell, "Migration into and Settlement of Leflore County, 1833–1876," *Journal of Mississippi History* 9 (October 1937), 223; Cheatham, "Washington County," 8; William Otey to Dearest Real (his wife), October 27, 1852, Wyche-Otey Papers, SHC.

[29]Cheatham, "Washington County," 13.

[30]Wade Hampton to Mary Fisher Hampton, March 11, November 17, 1855, in

Cauthen, ed., *Letters of the Three Wade Hamptons*, 38–40; Moore, *Emergence of the Cotton Kingdom*, 123; Sydnor, *Slavery in Mississippi*, 195; Scarborough, "Heartland of the Cotton Kingdom," 348; Paul C. Cameron to Thomas Ruffin, February 1, 1858, in Hamilton, ed., *Papers of Thomas Ruffin*, vol. 2, pp. 582–83.

[31]Cameron to Ruffin, February 1, 1858, in Hamilton, ed., *Papers of Thomas Ruffin*, vol. 2, pp. 582–83.

[32]Amanda Worthington to Robert Tilford, April 22, 1838, Worthington Family Papers.

[33]J. F. Griffin to Dear Nefew [*sic*], March 20, 1853, Micajah Wilkinson Papers, Hill Memorial Library, Louisiana State University, Baton Rouge, La.

[34]Wade Hampton II to Mary Fisher Hampton, April 25, November 17, 1855, in Cauthen, ed., *Letters of the Three Wade Hamptons*, 39–40; Griffin to Dear Nefew [*sic*], March 20, 1853, Micajah Wilkinson Papers; "Mark Oliver Interview," in George P. Rawick, ed., *The American Slave: A Composite Autobiography*, Supplement, ser. 1, vol. 9 (Mississippi Narratives, pt. 4) (Westport, Conn., 1977), 1660–61.

[35]Amelia Glover to James L. Alcorn, October 5, 1850, James L. Alcorn Papers, SHC.

[36]Lillian Pereyra, *James Lusk Alcorn: Persistent Whig* (Baton Rouge, 1966), 22–23.

[37]Ibid., 21.

[38]Martha Rebecca Blanton to My Dear Parents, March 12, 21, 1857, Blanton Family Papers.

[39]Sam Worthington, "Antebellum, Slaveholding Aristocracy of Washington County," in William D. McCain and Charlotte Capers, eds., *Memoirs of Henry T. Ireys: Papers of the Washington County Historical Society, 1910–1925* (Jackson, Miss., 1954), 350–51.

[40]Ibid., 350–52; Kell, "Aristocracy in Late Antebellum Mississippi," 64.

[41]"Early Settlers," in Wirt Williams, ed., *History of Bolivar County* (Jackson, Miss., 1948), 5.

[42]Charles Allen to Dear Parents, November 29, 1856; Charles Allen to Cher Parents, April 1, 1857, James Allen Papers, SHC, 1 roll, microfilm.

[43]"Prince Johnson Interview," in Rawick, ed., *American Slave*, Supplement, ser. 1, vol. 8 (Mississippi Narratives, pt. 3) (Westport, Conn., 1977), 1167–74.

[44]William Faulkner, *Absalom! Absalom!* (New York, 1936).

[45]Worthington, "Antebellum, Slaveholding Aristocracy," 351–52.

[46]Ibid., 352.

[47]Charles S. Sydnor, *The Development of Southern Sectionalism, 1819–1848* (Baton Rouge, 1948), 25; Cheatham, "Washington County," 127–28.

[48]Amanda Worthington to Albert Worthington, January 17, 1858, Worthington Family Papers.

[49]J. F. Griffin to Dear Nefew [*sic*], July 10, 1855, Micajah Wilkinson Papers.

[50]Martha Rebecca Blanton to Dear Parents, November 14, 1857, Blanton Family Papers.

[51]Wade Hampton II to Mary Fisher Hampton, January 6, 1855, in Cauthen, ed., *Letters of the Three Wade Hamptons*, 38; Amanda Worthington to Albert Worthington, January 17, 1858, October 20, 1857, Worthington Family Papers; Caroline Stern, "A Remembrance of Miss Pauline Pleasants Mosby," in McCain and Capers, ed., *Memoirs of Henry Tillinghast Ireys*, 153.

[52]Minerva Cook Diary, MDAH, typescript, 25. (The chronology of this diary is not continuous with pagination, and all entries are not precisely dated.)

[53]Ibid., 41.

[54]Ibid.

[55]Ibid., 25.

[56]Frederick Law Olmsted, *A Journey in the Back Country* (New York, 1970), 81, and *The Cotton Kingdom: A Traveller's Observations on Cotton and Slavery in the American Slave States* (New York, 1953), 444.

[57]Olmsted, *Cotton Kingdom*, 439.

[58]Joseph Holt Ingraham, *The South-West by a Yankee,* vol. 2 (Ann Arbor, 1966), 281; Newstead Plantation Diary, June 12, 1858, SHC; W. T. Lamb to Paul C. Cameron, November 24, 1860, Cameron Family Papers; Everard G. Baker Diary, January 15, 1862.

[59]Panther Burn Plantation Records, MDAH.

[60]William R. Elley Plantation Book, MDAH.

[61]Betty Vaughn Maxwell, "The Operation of Doro Plantation, 1852–1862" (M.A. thesis, Mississippi State College for Women, 1968), 61; Minerva Cook Diary, 29–49.

[62]Minerva Cook Diary, 66.

[63]Charles S. Sydnor, "Life Span of Mississippi Slaves," *American Historical Review* 35 (April 1930), 566–74; Kenneth M. Stampp, *The Peculiar Institution: Slavery in the Antebellum South* (New York, 1975), 319–20; Olmsted, *Cotton Kingdom*, 439; Wade Hampton III to Mary Fisher Hampton, November 2, 1857, in Cauthen, ed., *Letters of the Three Wade Hamnptons,* 50; Paul C. Cameron to J. H. Ruffin, February 1, 1858, in Hamilton, ed., *Papers of Thomas Ruffin,* vol. 2, p. 582; Stovall Plantation Records, Ledger 2, John D. Williams Library, *passim.*

[64]Olmsted, *Cotton Kingdom*, 442; Sydnor, *Slavery in Mississippi*, 69; Clifton, "Demographic Study of Bolivar County," 13.

[65]"Noah Rogers Interview," in Rawick, ed., *American Slave,* Supplement, ser. 1, vol. 9 (Mississippi Narratives, pt. 4) (Westport, Conn., 1977), 1879; "Delia Hill Interview," in Rawick, ed., *American Slave,* ser. 2, vol. 11 (Arkansas Narratives, pt. 7, and Missouri Narratives) (Westport, Conn., 1972), 179–80 (Missouri).

[66]Ullrich B. Phillips, ed., *Plantation and Frontier Documents: 1849–1863,* vol. 2 (Cleveland, 1909), 113–15.

[67]Scarborough, "Heartland of the Cotton Kingdom," 334.

[68]Moore, *Emergence of the Cotton Kingdom,* 100–101.

[69]Scarborough, "Heartland of the Cotton Kingdom," 337.

[70]J. F. Griffin to Dear Nefew [*sic*], March 20, 1853, Micajah Wilkinson Papers.

[71]Scarborough, "Heartland of the Cotton Kingdom," 337.

[72]John Hebron Moore, ed., "Two Documents Relating to Plantation Overseers of the Vicksburg Region, 1831–1832," *Journal of Mississippi History* 16 (January 1954), 31; Charles Allen Plantation Book, August 5, 18, 1861, MDAH.

[73]Ibid., March 20, April 22, 1862.

[74]H. E. Merritt to My Dear Uncle, February 27, 1857, box 37, W. H. E. Merritt Papers; Olmsted, *Cotton Kingdom*, 440; Scarborough, "Heartland of the Cotton Kingdom," 334–35.

[75]Olmsted, *Cotton Kingdom*, 442.

[76]"Charity Jones Interview," in Rawick, ed., *American Slave,* Supplement, ser. 1,

vol. 8 (Mississippi Narratives, pt. 3), 1192; "Joe Clinton Interview," in Rawick, ed., *American Slave,* ser. 2, vol. 8 (Arkansas Narratives, pts. 1 and 2) (Westport, Conn., 1972), 35 (pt. 2); "Noah Rogers Interview," in Rawick, ed., *American Slave,* Supplement, ser. 1, vol. 9 (Mississippi Narratives, pt. 4) (Westport, Conn., 1977), 1877–80; Minerva Cook Diary, 12.

[77]"Ellen Cragin Interview," in Rawick, ed., *American Slave,* vol. 8 (Arkansas Narratives, pts. 1 and 2) (Westport, Conn., 1972), 44–45 (pt. 2); "Elvira Boles Interview," in Rawick, ed., *American Slave,* Supplement, ser. 2, vol. 2 (Texas Narratives, pt. 1) (Westport, Conn., 1979), 336–38.

[78]"Ellen Cragin Interview," 44–45.

[79]"Marie Hervey Interview," in Rawick, ed., *American Slave,* vol. 9 (Arkansas Narratives, pts. 3 and 4) (Westport, Conn., 1972), 231 (pt. 3); "Ruben Laird Interview," in Rawick, ed., *American Slave,* Supplement, ser. 1, vol. 8 (Mississippi Narratives, pt. 3) (Westport, Conn., 1977), 1299.

[80]"Susan Jones Interview," in Rawick, ed., *American Slave,* Supplement, ser. 1, vol. 8 (Mississippi Narratives, pt. 3) (Westport, Conn., 1977), 1257.

[81]"Delia Hill Interview," 181–82.

[82]Wilbur J. Cash, *The Mind of the South* (New York, 1941), 28–30.

Chapter 2. "The Stern Realities of War"

[1]Brandfon, *Cotton Kingdom of the New South,* 29; "A Survey of Mississippi," *Debow's Review* 23 (December 1857), 649.

[2]Brandfon, *Cotton Kingdom of the New South,* 35; Robert W. Harrison, "Levee Building in Mississippi before the Civil War," *Journal of Mississippi History* 12 (April 1950), 80–92.

[3]Anna Alice Kamper, "A Social and Economic History of Antebellum Bolivar County, Mississippi" (M.A. thesis, University of Alabama, 1942), 50; Herbert Weaver, "The Agricultural Population of Mississippi, 1850–1860" (Ph.D. diss., Vanderbilt University, 1941), 122, Appendix 6, Chart 52; Kell, "Aristocracy in Late Antebellum Mississippi," 57, 59, 63, 71, 76–77, 83, 102; William L. Barney, *The Secessionist Impulse: Alabama and Mississippi in 1860* (Princeton, 1974), 145–46; Moore, *Emergence of the Cotton Kingdom,* 124–5, 129.

[4]Weaver, *Mississippi Farmers,* 39, 81; U.S. Department of the Interior, *Eighth Census of the United States,* vol. 2, *Agriculture* (Washington, 1864), 232, 247; Scarborough, "Heartland of the Cotton Kingdom," 346–47.

[5]Lee Soltow, *Men and Wealth in the United States, 1850–1870* (New Haven and London, 1975), 157–68.

[6]Barney, *Secessionist Impulse,* 146; David Nathaniel Young, "The Mississippi Whigs, 1834–1860" (Ph.D. diss., University of Alabama, 1968), 46, 49, 51, 67, 166–83; Donald M. Rawson, "Party Politics in Mississippi, 1850–1860" (Ph.D. diss., Vanderbilt University, 1964), 23, 80, 89, 117, 132, 204–5, 210, 264, 290, 300, 307–9.

[7]Gavin Wright, *Old South, New South: Revolutions in the Southern Economy since the Civil War* (New York, 1986), 270; William Kirkland to Octavia Otey, November 18, 1860, Wyche-Otey Family Papers.

[8]Paul C. Cameron to Thomas H. Ruffin, January 28, 1861, in Hamilton, ed., *Papers*

of *Thomas Ruffin*, vol. 3 (Raleigh, N.C., 1920), 116; Barney, *Secessionist Impulse*, 145, 319–20, 288.

⁹Kell, "Aristocracy in Late Antebellum Mississippi," 56; Bern Keating, *A History of Washington County, Mississippi* (Greenville, Miss., 1976), 34; James L. Alcorn, "Schedule of Property (Mississippi)," James L. Alcorn Papers; Pereyra, *James Lusk Alcorn*, 43–44.

¹⁰R. L. Dixon to Harry St. John Dixon, January 12, 1861, Harry St. John Dixon Papers, SHC; Pereyra, *James Lusk Alcorn*, 44.

¹¹Keating, *History of Washington County*, 35.

¹²Ibid., 35–36.

¹³Shelby Foote, *The Civil War: A Narrative from Fredericksburg to Meridian* (New York, 1963), 63.

¹⁴"Recollections of Samuel Wragg Ferguson," Heyward and Ferguson Family Papers, SHC.

¹⁵Anne B. Finlay, "One Woman's Experience, 1862–1865," in McCain and Capers, eds., *Memoirs of Henry T. Ireys*, 205.

¹⁶Ibid., 206.

¹⁷James L. Alcorn to Amelia Alcorn, December 18, 1862, in Percy L. Rainwater, ed., "Letters of James Lusk Alcorn," *Journal of Southern History* 5 (May 1939), 201–2; Frank E. Smith, *The Yazoo River* (New York, 1954), 144.

¹⁸Everard G. Baker Diary, December 26, 1862.

¹⁹Stovall Plantation Records, Ledger 4, August 1862–June 1865; Keating, *History of Washington County*, 36–43.

²⁰Keating, *History of Washington County*, 36–43.

²¹Ibid., 41–43; R. L. Dixon to Harry St. John Dixon, March 6, 1863, Harry St. John Dixon Papers.

²²Smith, *Yazoo River*, 148–50.

²³Margaret Holt Guinn, *Pocock Pickle: Louisa's 1863 Journal* (Bolivar County Historical Society Sesquicentennial Edition, 1986), 21. See also Florence Burrus, "Reminiscences of the Civil War," *Journal of the Bolivar County Historical Society* 2 (1978), 17–18.

²⁴Walter Sillers, "Incidents of the War in Bolivar County as Experienced by a Ten-Year-Old Boy and as Given by Him," in Williams, *History of Bolivar County*, 148–49.

²⁵Ibid., 148–53.

²⁶"The Journal of Lettie Vick Downs in the Year 1863," John D. Williams Library, March 15, 1863–July 27, 1863, typescript.

²⁷Ibid., September 24, 1863.

²⁸"Ruben Laird Interview," 1300; "Henretta Gooch Interview," in Rawick, ed., *American Slave*, Supplement, ser. 1, vol. 8 (Mississippi Narratives, pt. 3) (Westport, Conn., 1977); 842; "Lizzie Dunn Interview," in Rawick, ed., *American Slave*, ser. 2, vol. 8 (Arkansas narratives, pts. 1 and 2) (Westport, Conn., 1972), 221; "Elvira Collins Interview," in Rawick, ed., *American Slave*, Supplement, ser. 1, vol. 7 (Mississippi Narratives, pt. 2) (Westport, Conn., 1977), 479.

²⁹James L. Alcorn to Amelia Alcorn, November 25, 1862, December 18, 1862, in Rainwater, ed., "Letters of James Lusk Alcorn," 199, 201.

³⁰Pereyra, *James Lusk Alcorn*, 62–64; James L. Alcorn to Amelia Alcorn, May 3, 1864, January 21, 1865, in Rainwater, ed., "Letters of James Lusk Alcorn," 205, 208; Smith, *Yazoo River*, 130–31.

[31]Smith, *Yazoo River,* 133.

[32]"Excerpts from the Diary of Mrs. Myra Smith," December 23, 1863, May 28, 1865, MDAH.

[33]Amanda Worthington Diary, February 25, December 6, 1862, Worthington Family Papers.

[34]Ibid., April 20–25, 1863; Worthington, "Antebellum, Slaveholding Aristocracy," in McCain and Capers, eds., *Memoirs of Henry T. Ireys,* 364.

[35]Worthington, "Antebellum, Slaveholding Aristocracy," in McCain and Capers, eds., *Memoirs of Henry T. Ireys,* 361–62.

[36]Maxwell, "Operation of Doro Plantation," 80; James L. Alcorn to Amelia Alcorn, December 18, 1862, November 25, 1862, in Rainwater, ed., "Letters of James Lusk Alcorn," 201–2.

[37]"Virginia Harris Interview," in Rawick, ed., *American Slave,* Supplement, ser. 1, vol. 8 (Mississippi Narratives, pt. 3) (Westport, Conn., 1977), 941; "Letha Taylor Meeks Interview," in Rawick, ed., *American Slave,* ser. 2, vol. 11 (Arkansas Narratives, pt. 7 and Missouri Narratives) (Westport, Conn., 1972), 253–54 (Missouri); "R. H. Howard Interview," in Rawick, ed., *American Slave,* Supplement, ser. 1, vol. 8 (Mississippi Narratives, pt. 3) (Westport, Conn., 1977), 1051; Burrus, "Reminiscences of the Civil War," 17; Smith, *Yazoo River,* 146; Sillers, "Incidents of the War," in Williams, ed., *History of Bolivar County,* 151.

[38]Wade Hampton III to Mary Fisher Hampton, January 14, 1864, in Cauthen, ed., *Letters of the Three Wade Hamptons,* 102; Smith, *Yazoo River,* 135–37.

[39]Annie Jacobs, "Recollections of Doro Plantation," MDAH.

[40]"Adeline Hodge Interview," in Rawick, ed., *American Slave,* Supplement, ser. 1, vol. 1 (Alabama Narratives, pt. 1) (Westport, Conn., 1977), 182–83.

[41]"Milly Henry Interview," in Rawick, ed., *American Slave,* ser. 2, vol. 14 (North Carolina Narratives, pt. 1), 400; Jon'a Pearce to Hon'l Jas. A. Seddon, November 3, 1863, in Ira Berlin et al., eds., *Freedom: A Documentary History of Emancipation, 1861–1867,* ser. 1, vol. 1, *The Destruction of Slavery* (Cambridge, 1985), 775.

[42]"Charity Jones Interview," 1192; "Mark Oliver Interview," 1668–69; "Ellen Cragin Interview," 45; "Cindy Anderson Interview," in Rawick, ed., *American Slave,* Supplement, ser. 1, vol. 6 (Mississippi Narratives, pt. 1), 67.

[43]William J. Cooper Diaries, May 16, June 9, 16, July 16, 1865, SHC.

[44]"Ruben Fox Interview," in Rawick, ed., *American Slave,* Supplement, ser. 1, vol. 7 (Mississippi Narratives, pt. 2) (Westport, Conn., 1977), 773; "Needham Love Interview," in Rawick, ed., *American Slave,* ser. 1, vol. 9 (Arkansas Narratives, pts. 3 and 4) (Westport, Conn., 1977), 292 (pt. 4).

[45]A. G. Paxton, "Recollections of Deer Creek," in McCain and Capers, eds., *Memoirs of Henry T. Ireys,* 110; James L. Alcorn to Amelia Alcorn, January 2, 1865, in Rainwater, ed., *Letters of James Lusk Alcorn,* 206–7.

[46]James L. Alcorn to Amelia Alcorn, January 21, 1865, in Rainwater, ed., "Letters of James Lusk Alcorn," 207–8.

[47]Ibid.

[48]Jean Smith to Martha Rebecca Blanton Smith, September 28, 1865, Blanton Family Papers.

[49]Jacobs, "Recollections of Doro Plantation," 168–69.

[50]Henry Tillinghast Ireys, "Autobiography," in McCain and Capers, ed., *Memoirs of Henry T. Ireys,* 31.

[51]Brandfon, *Cotton Kingdom of the New South,* 40–41.

[52]Robert Somers, *The Southern States since the War, 1870–1871* (University, Ala., 1965), 255.

[53]Ibid., 256.

[54]Ibid., 257.

[55]Mrs. L. A. Little, "Sketch of Life in Bolivar County in 1872," in Williams, ed., *History of Bolivar County,* 165–68.

[56]Henry T. Crydenwise to Dear Parents, December 11, 1866, Henry T. Crydenwise Papers, William R. Perkins Library, Duke University; Wade Hampton III to Mary Fisher Hampton, May 14, 1866, in Cauthen, ed., *Letters of the Three Wade Hamptons,* 120.

[57]Henry T. Crydenwise to Dear Parents, March 3, 1866, Henry T. Crydenwise Papers.

[58]Ibid., June 25, 1866; Sarah Crydenwise to My Dear Mother, July 31, 1866, June 5, 1866, Henry T. Crydenwise Papers.

[59]Henry T. Crydenwise to Dear Parents, November 11, 1866, Henry T. Crydenwise Papers.

[60]Friar's Point (Miss.) *Coahomian,* November 10, 1865; George C. Benham, *A Year of Wreck, a True Story, by a Victim* (New York, 1880), 9, 12, 17 (this work was actually written under a pseudonym); Whitelaw Reid, *After the War: A Tour of the Southern States, 1865–1866* (New York, 1965), 414.

[61]James L. Alcorn to Amelia Alcorn, March 22, 1865, James L. Alcorn Papers.

[62]Wright, *Old South, New South,* 18.

Chapter 3. A "Harnessed Revolution"

[1]Henry T. Crydenwise to Dearest Brother Charles, March 21, 1866, Henry T. Crydenwise Papers.

[2]Vernon Lane Wharton, *The Negro in Mississippi, 1865–1890* (New York, 1965), 117.

[3]J. Pearce to William Sharkey, July 15, 1865, Governor William Sharkey Correspondence, RG 27, MDAH; William C. Harris, *Presidential Reconstruction in Mississippi* (Baton Rouge, 1967), 95.

[4]Pearce to Sharkey, July 15, 1865, Sharkey Correspondence.

[5]Harris, *Presidential Reconstruction,* 94–95; William E. Bayley to Commanding Officer, July 1, 3, 1865, Letters Received, Bureau of Refugees, Freedmen, and Abandoned Lands, Records of the Assistant Commissioner for the State of Mississippi (hereinafter cited as BFRAL), John D. Williams Library, microfilm, roll 8.

[6]Harris, *Presidential Reconstruction,* 94.

[7]Eric Foner, *Reconstruction: America's Unfinished Revolution, 1863–1877* (New York, 1988), 69; Clifton L. Ganus, Jr., "The Freedman's Bureau in Mississippi" (Ph.D. diss., Tulane University, 1953), 24, 184–228.; W. F. Griffin to Stuart Eldridge, August 21, 1865, C. B. Foster to T. S. Free, December 15, 1865, BFRAL, microfilm, roll 30; James T. Currie, *Enclave: Vicksburg and Her Plantations, 1863–1870* (Jackson, Miss., 1980), 147.

[8]C. B. Foster to T. S. Free, December 15, 1865, BRFAL, microfilm, roll 30.

[9]P. F. Howell to Alfred W. Ellet, February 6, 1865, A. W. Ellet Papers, William R. Perkins Library, Duke University.

[10]Currie, *Enclave*, 152–53; P. F. Howell to Alfred W. Ellet, April 30, 1866, Ellet Papers. See also Edward Ellet to A. W. Ellet, April 6, 1866, Ellet Papers.

[11]C. B. Foster to T. S. Free, December 15, 1865, BRFAL, microfilm, roll 30; John T. Trowbridge, *The Desolate South, 1865–1866: A Picture of the Battlefields and of the Devastated Confederacy* (New York, 1956); 194; Wade Hampton III to Mary Fisher Hampton, January 12, 1866, in Cauthen, ed., *Letters of the Three Wade Hamptons*, 118.

[12]George Corliss to Stuart Eldridge, April 9, 1866, BRFAL, microfilm, roll 13; Wharton, *Negro in Mississippi*, 65.

[13]Harris, *Presidential Reconstruction*, 98; Ross H. Moore, "Social and Economic Conditions in Mississippi during Reconstruction" (Ph.D. diss., Duke University, 1938), 54–57.

[14]William Slider, "Articles of Agreement Made and Concluded this 3d day of February, 1866 . . . ," BRFAL, microfilm, roll. 50.

[15]George W. Gift, "Cotton under High Culture," in *Report of the Commissioner of Agriculture for the Year 1867* (Washington, 1868), 416–17.

[16]Harris, *Presidential Reconstruction*, 137–40; Wharton, *Negro in Mississippi*, 84–89.

[17]Harris, *Presidential Reconstruction*, 147–51.

[18]Works Progress Administration, Negro Anecdote 241, Warren County, WPA County History Collection, MDAH; Everard G. Baker Diary, July 17, 1866, May 29, 1867; Leon F. Litwack, *Been in the Storm So Long: The Aftermath of Slavery* (New York, 1979), 434–35, 444.

[19]George Collins to Anne Collins, December 29, 1866, Anne Cameron Collins Papers, SHC; Litwack, *Been in the Storm So Long*, 437.

[20]"The State of Mississippi, Sunflower County," January 11, 1867, BRFAL, microfilm, roll 50.

[21]Stovall Plantation Records, Ledgers 1, 7 (1868), and 5 (1869–71).

[22]"Contract for Hire, January 1, 1867," "State of Mississippi, County of Washington, September 7, 1868," BRFAL, microfilm, roll 50.

[23]Harris, *Presidential Reconstruction*, 71; Benham, *Year of Wreck*, v.

[24]Currie, *Enclave*, 159; *Debow's Review* 35 (new ser.) (December 1866), 667–68.

[25]Currie, *Enclave*, 158–59.

[26]Wright, *Old South, New South*, 87–89; Foner, *Reconstruction*, 211; Harris, *Presidential Reconstruction*, 173.

[27]Litwack, *Been in the Storm So Long*, 447–49; Foner, *Reconstruction*, 172–74; Wright, *Old South, New South*, 85–86; Wharton, *Negro in Mississippi*, 69; Thad K. Preuss to Merrit Barber, February 29, 1868, W. J. Manning to S. C. Greene, May 2, 1868, BRFAL, microfilm, roll 32; Samuel Goozee to John Tyler, October 31, 1868, BRFAL, microfilm, roll 33.

[28]Wharton, *Negro in Mississippi*, 58; Harris, *Presidential Reconstruction*, 88.

[29]Everard G. Baker to Messrs Irby and Ellis and Mosely, October 22, 1865, enclosed in Benjamin G. Humphreys to General M. Force, November 3, 1865, in Ira Berlin et al., *Freedom: A Documentary History of Emancipation, 1861–1867*, ser. 1, *The Black Military Experience* (Cambridge, 1982), 747–49.

[30]*Appleton's Annual Cyclopedia and Register of Important Events for the year 1867*, vol. 7 (New York, 1868), 518.

[31]Henry T. Crydenwise to Dear Parents, April 3, 1866, C. B. Foster to T. S. Free, December 12, 1865, BRFAL, microfilm, roll 30.

[32]George Corliss to Stuart Eldridge, April 9, 1866, BRFAL, microfilm, roll 13; Currie, *Enclave*, 155.

[33]George Collins to Anne Collins, February 9, 1867, Anne Cameron Collins Papers.

[34]William C. Harris, *The Day of the Carpetbagger: Republican Reconstruction in Mississippi* (Baton Rouge, 1979), 66–67.

[35]John R. Skates, *Mississippi: A Bicentennial History* (New York, 1979), 114.

[36]Appleton's *Cyclopedia*, 1867, 518; Harris, *Day of the Carpetbagger*, 26–28.

[37]Currie, *Enclave*, 172–73.

[38]Thad K. Preuss to Merrit K. Barber, January 31, 1868, BRFAL, microfilm, roll 32; Harris, *Day of the Carpetbagger*, 168; Currie, *Enclave*, 173.

[39]Allen Huggins to S. C. Greene, April 30, May 31, 1868, BRFAL, microfilm, roll 32; Samuel Goozee to John Tyler, October 31, 1868, BRFAL, microfilm, roll 33; Andrew Jackson Donelson to Elizabeth Donelson, September 11, 1869, Andrew Jackson Donelson Papers; George Collins to Anne Collins, July 22, 1871, January 6, 1872, Anne Cameron Collins Papers.

[40]Everard G. Baker Diary, July 5, 1872.

[41]James W. Garner, *Reconstruction in Mississippi* (New York, 1901), 295; Foner, *Reconstruction*, 357.

[42]Lester Milton Salamon, "Protest, Politics, and Modernization in the American South: Mississippi as a Developing Society" (Ph.D. diss., Harvard University, 1971), 166–71; Michael W. Fitzgerald, *The Union League Movement in the Deep South: Politics and Agricultural Change during Reconstruction* (Baton Rouge, 1989), 174.

[43]Harris, *Day of the Carpetbagger*, 274; Salamon, "Protest, Politics, and Modernization," 207; Foner, *Reconstruction*, 409–10.

[44]Jean Smith to My Dear Sisters, January 12, 1870, Blanton Family Papers.

[45]J. R. Dixon to Harry St. John Dixon, June 2, 1867, November 5, 1869, January 29, 1870, Harry St. John Dixon Papers.

[46]J. R. Dixon to My Dear Willie, January 18, 1870, J. R. Dixon to Harry St. John Dixon, January 29, 1870, Harry St. John Dixon Papers.

[47]Garner, *Reconstruction in Mississippi*, 180.

[48]Warren A. Ellem, "Who Were the Mississippi Scalawags?" *Journal of Southern History* 38 (May 1972), 228, 224, 233.

[49]Friar's Point *Deltan*, February 3, 24, 1869, quoted in Thomas N. Boschert, "The Politics of Expediency: Fusion in the Mississippi Delta, Late Nineteenth Century" (M.A. thesis, University of Mississippi, 1985), 54.

[50]Harris, *Day of the Carpetbagger*, 251–52.

[51]Ibid., 640–41.

[52]Wharton, *Negro in Mississippi*, 175–76; Richard N. Current, *Those Terrible Carpetbaggers: A Reinterpretation* (New York, 1988), 307–9; Ellem, "Who Were the Mississippi Scalawags?" 236.

[53]Salamon, "Protest, Politics, and Modernization," 207; Foner, *Reconstruction*, 535; Harris, *Day of the Carpetbagger*, 606; C. L. Hardeman to John C. Burrus, December 11, 1875, John C. Burrus Papers, MDAH.

[54]Foner, *Reconstruction*, 537–44.

[55]Ibid., 542; Michael Perman, *The Road to Redemption: Southern Politics, 1869–1879* (Chapel Hill and London, 1984), 147–48; Harris, *Day of the Carpetbagger*, 507, 542.

⁵⁶Salamon, "Protest, Politics, and Modernization," 207; Brandfon, *Cotton Kingdom*, 41–43.

⁵⁷George Collins to Paul C. Cameron, November 19, 1872, Cameron Family Papers; Brandfon, *Cotton Kingdom*, 42.

⁵⁸Brandfon, *Cotton Kingdom*, 42–46.

⁵⁹Ibid., 44–45; David H. Donald, "The Scalawag in Mississippi Reconstruction," *Journal of Southern History* 10 (November 1944); 455; Lewis Baker, *The Percys of Mississippi: Politics and Literature in the New South* (Baton Rouge, 1983), 9–10; Ellem, "Who Were the Mississippi Scalawags?" 239.

⁶⁰Harris, *Day of the Carpetbaggers*, 681, 679; Baker, *Percys of Mississippi*, 8–10; Foner, *Reconstruction*, 558.

⁶¹Foner, *Reconstruction*, 559, 563; Mary Fisher Robinson, "A Sketch of James L. Alcorn," *Journal of Mississippi History* 12 (January 1950), 41.

⁶²Foner, *Reconstruction*, 559.

⁶³Ibid., 560; Current, *Those Terrible Carpetbaggers*, 322.

⁶⁴Current, *Those Terrible Carpetbaggers*, 324; Foner, *Reconstruction*, 561–62.

⁶⁵Foner, *Reconstruction*, 562.

⁶⁶Ibid., 603, 109.

⁶⁷Ibid., 110, 410; Barbara Jeanne Fields, "The Advent of Capitalist Agriculture: The New South in a Bourgeois World," in Thavolia Glymph and John J. Kushma, eds., *Essays on the Post-bellum Southern Economy* (College Station, Texas, 1985), 85–87.

⁶⁸Foner, *Reconstruction*, 663; Salamon, "Protest, Politics, and Modernization," 214–15.

⁶⁹Skates, *Mississippi*, 118.

Chapter 4. Conquering the Plantation Frontier

¹*Appleton's Annual Cyclopedia and Register of Important Events of the Year 1879*, new ser., vol. 4 (New York, 1883), 63.

²Ibid., 634–35. See also Nell Irvin Painter, *Exodusters: Black Migration to Kansas after Reconstruction* (New York, 1977), 216–20; Greenville *Times*, June 28, 1879.

³Harris, *Day of the Carpetbagger*, 485; Wharton, *Negro in Mississippi*, 71.

⁴Wharton, *Negro in Mississippi*, 94.

⁵J. R. Dixon to Harry St. John Dixon, June 25, 1869, Harry St. John Dixon Papers; Newstead Plantation Diaries, January 15, 1879, SHC, microfilm; C. L. Hardeman to John C. Burrus, December 11, 1875, John C. Burrus Papers.

⁶George Collins to Anne Collins, March 6, 1877, Anne Cameron Collins Papers.

⁷Foner, *Reconstruction*, 405–6.

⁸Harris, *Day of the Carpetbagger*, 277.

⁹Duncan Cameron to Paul C. Cameron, January 23, 1871, Cameron Family Papers; Wharton, *Negro in Mississippi*, 87; Foner, *Reconstruction*, 429.

¹⁰J. R. Dixon to Harry St. John Dixon, August 16, 1867, Harry St. John Dixon Papers; Fitzgerald, *Union League*, 174.

¹¹Sydney Nathans, "Gotta Mind to Move, A Mind to Settle Down: Afro-Americans and the Plantation Frontier," in William J. Cooper et al., eds., *A Master's Due: Essays in Honor of David Herbert Donald* (Baton Rouge, 1985), 208–10; Harris, *Day of the Carpetbagger*, 575.

¹²Somers, *Southern States since the War*, 249.

¹³Department of the Interior, Census Office, *Report on the Productions of Agriculture*, Tenth Census, vol. 3 (June 1, 1880), (Washington, 1883), 66–67; Wharton, *Negro in Mississippi*, 63; Pereyra, *James Lusk Alcorn*, 183.

¹⁴Nathans, "Gotta Mind to Move," 210.

¹⁵Roger L. Ransom and Richard Sutch, *One Kind of Freedom: The Economic Consequences of Emancipation* (Cambridge, 1977), 91; *Report on the Productions of Agriculture*, Tenth Census, 66–77; Eugene W. Hilgard, "Cotton Production in Mississippi," *Report on Cotton Production in the United States*, Part 1, *Mississippi Valley and Southwestern States* (Washington, 1883), 154.

¹⁶Hilgard, "Cotton Production in Mississippi," 154; *Report on the Productions of Agriculture*, Tenth Census, vol. 3 (June 1, 1880), 67.

¹⁷Hinds County *Gazette*, August 31, 1866, quoted in Moore, "Social and Economic Conditions," 66; W. W. Williams to Mrs. O. A. Otey, September 29, 1869, Wyche-Otey Papers.

¹⁸Andrew Jackson Donelson to Martin Donelson, December 14, 1868, March 10, April 1, December 21, 1869, Andrew Jackson Donelson Papers.

¹⁹Ibid., August 16, 1870. See Memphis (Tenn.) *Public Ledger*, August 30, 1871. (Copy of "Trustee Sale" notice supplied to the author by Thomas N. Boschert.)

²⁰Wade Hampton III to Mary Fisher Hampton, June 3, 1866, Wade Hampton III to Mrs. Thomas L. Preston, April 27, 1875, in Cauthen, ed., *Letters of the Three Wade Hamptons*, 122, 151; Newstead Plantation Diaries, February 27, March 1, 3, 1875. See also entries for November 9, 15, 22, 1873.

²¹George Collins to Paul C. Cameron, January 19, 1871, Cameron Family Papers.

²²George Collins to Anne and Rebecca Collins, December 28, 1871, Annie R. Cameron to Anne Collins, December 28, 1871, George Collins to Anne Cameron, January 6, 1872, Anne Cameron Collins Papers.

²³George Collins to Paul C. Cameron, February 27, 1879, Cameron Family Papers.

²⁴Ibid.

²⁵George Collins to Anne Collins, December 20, 1880, November 3, 1882, Anne Cameron Collins Papers.

²⁶David H. Donald, "A Generation of Defeat," in Walter J. Fraser, Jr., and Winfred B. Moore, Jr., eds., *From the Old South to the New: Essays on the Transitional South* (Westport, Conn., 1981), 14–15; Moore and Young to Paul C. Cameron, October 27, 1883, Cameron Family Papers.

²⁷Pereyra, *James Lusk Alcorn*, 182–85.

²⁸*Report on the Productions of Agriculture*, Tenth Census, vol. 3, pp. 66, 231; Hilgard, "Cotton Production in Mississippi," 72.

²⁹Hilgard, "Cotton Production in Mississippi," 73; *Report on the Productions of Agriculture*, Tenth Census, vol. 3, pp. 195, 122–23, 231.

³⁰Nathans, "Gotta Mind to Move," 207; John C. Hudson, "The Yazoo Mississippi Delta as Plantation Country," *Proceedings of the Tall Timbers Ecology and Management Conference* 16 (Tallahassee, 1979), 70; Will H. Dockery, "Bolivar County, Mississippi, in 1888," Bolivar County *Democrat*, August 6, 1936; Friar's Point *Gazette*, July 22, November 25, 1881. See also F. W. Goff Diary, 1875–1876, January 1, 1876, MDAH.

³¹Robert W. Harrison, "Levee Building in Mississippi before the Civil War," *Journal of Mississippi History* 12 (April 1950), 80–92; Brandfon, *Cotton Kingdom*, 34–40.

³²Jackson *Daily Clarion*, January 1, 1865, quoted in Moore, "Social and Economic Conditions," 70; Harrison, "Levee Building," 97.

[33]Harrison, *Alluvial Empire*, 97–99.

[34]Arthell Kelley, "Levee Building and the Settlement of the Yazoo Basin," *Southern Quarterly* 1 (July 1963), 300; Gary B. Mills, "New Life for the River of Death: Development of the Yazoo River Basin, 1873–1977," *Journal of Mississippi History* 41 (November 1979), 288.

[35]Brandfon, *Cotton Kingdom*, 66–67.

[36]Ibid., 68–71.

[37]Hudson, "The Yazoo Mississippi Delta," 76–77; Brandfon, *Cotton Kingdom*, 73.

[38]Neil R. McMillen, *Dark Journey: Black Mississippians in the Age of Jim Crow* (Urbana, 1989), 186–87; Maurice Elizabeth Jackson, "Mound Bayou: A Study in Social Development" (M.A. thesis, University of Alabama, 1937); Janet Sharp Hermann, *In Pursuit of a Dream* (New York, 1981), 219–44.

[39]Brandfon, *Cotton Kingdom*, 74–75, 80.

[40]Ibid., 108.

[41]Ibid., 109–11.

[42]*Ibid.*, 73; Thomas J. Pressly and William H. Scofield, eds., *Farm Real Estate Values in the United States by Counties, 1850–1959* (Seattle, 1965), 53–54.

[43]United States Bureau of the Census, *Eleventh Census of the United States, 1890*, vol. 5, *Statistics of Agriculture, 1895*, 156–59.

[44]Columbus *Democrat* and Summit *Sentinel*, quoted in Painter, *Exodusters*, 156; Wharton, *Negro in Mississippi*, 110.

[45]Wharton, *Negro in Mississippi*, 95; McMillen, *Dark Journey*, 141.

[46]Department of the Interior, Census Office, Tenth Census, *Statistics of the Population*, vol. 1 (Washington, 1883), 397–98; Department of the Interior, Census Office, Eleventh Census, *Report on the Population of the United States* (Washington, 1985), 504–5.

[47]Linton Weeks, *Clarksdale and Coahoma County: A History* (Clarksdale, Miss., 1982), 55, 57.

[48]Harris, *Day of the Carpetbagger*, 709.

[49]W. B. Roberts, "After the War Between the States," in Williams, ed., *History of Bolivar County*, 163.

[50]Friar's Point *Gazette*, April 15, September 16, 23, 1881.

[51]Ibid., April 15, October 7, 1881.

[52]Rosedale *Weekly Leader*, November 5, 1886.

[53]J. Morgan Kousser, *The Shaping of Southern Politics: Suffrage Restriction and the Establishment of the One-Party South* (New Haven, Conn., 1974), 17; Katie Burrus to John C. Burrus, July 9, 1888, Burrus Papers; Bolivar County *Review*, August 29, 1889; Walter Sillers to Florence Sillers, September 1, 1890, Walter Sillers Papers, Roberts Memorial Library, Delta State University, Cleveland, Miss.

[54]William F. Holmes, "The Leflore County Massacre and the Demise of the Colored Farmer's Alliance," *Phylon* 34 (September 1973), 267–74.

[55]*The New Coahomian*, January 12, 1889.

[56]Holmes, "The Leflore County Massacre," 272.

[57]Ibid., 273.

[58]J. S. McNeily to Walter Sillers, July 4, 1890, Sillers Papers.

[59]Kousser, *Shaping of Southern Politics*, 6–7.

[60]Ibid., 259; Bolivar County *Review*, September 1, 1893.

[61]Albert D. Kirwan, *Revolt of the Rednecks, Mississippi Politics: 1876–1925* (Lexington, Ky., 1951), 66, 71.

⁶²J. S. McNeily to Walter Sillers, July 4, 1890, Walter Sillers Papers; Kousser, *Shaping of Southern Politics*, 143–45.

⁶³Memphis *Commercial Appeal*, September 26, 1895; Bolivar County *Democrat*, January 11, 1895. Years later, Walter Sillers remained on guard against any effort to establish "mixed black and white politics," noting that "social equality" was likely to ensue should there be any "breaking of the white ranks." See Walter Sillers to John Sharp Williams, January 25, 1922, John Sharp Williams Papers, Manuscripts Division, Library of Congress.

⁶⁴Clark L. Miller, "Let Us Die to Make Men Free: Political Terrorism in Post-Reconstruction Mississippi, 1877–1896" (Ph.D. diss., University of Minnesota, 1983), 622, 625; Kirwan, *Revolt of the Rednecks*, 78–79; Eric C. Clark, "Legislative Apportionment in the 1890 Constitutional Convention," *Journal of Mississippi History* 42 (November 1980), 299.

⁶⁵Kirwan, *Revolt of the Rednecks*, 80; Guy B. Hathorn, "Suffrage, Apportionment, and Elections in the Mississippi Constitutional Convention of 1890" (M.A. thesis, University of Mississippi, 1942), 45, 50; Miller, "Let us Die to Make Men Free," 625.

⁶⁶Kirwan, *Revolt of the Rednecks*, 83; Eric C. Clark believes the discrepancy cited by Kirwan may have resulted from the use of the 1880 state census rather than the 1890 United States Census in drawing up the apportionment plan. See Clark, "Legislative Apportionment," 313.

⁶⁷C. Vann Woodward, *Origins of the New South, 1877–1913* (Baton Rouge, 1951), 340–41.

⁶⁸See V. S. Naipaul's conversation with William Winter in Naipaul, *A Turn in the South* (New York, 1989), 217. See also Clark, "Legislative Apportionment," 301, 313.

⁶⁹Thomas N. Boschert, "Politics of Expediency," 167–211.

⁷⁰Ibid., 192–93, 204–5.

⁷¹Nathans, "Gotta Mind to Move," 207.

⁷²Ibid., 214.

⁷³John Sharp Williams to L. T. Carpenter, June 10, 1907, John Sharp Williams Papers, Library of Congress. Hereinafter, the collection of John Sharp Williams Papers at the Library of Congress will be designated LC, while those located at the John D. Williams Library at the University of Mississippi will be designated UM.

⁷⁴Pressly and Scofield, *Farm Real Estate Values*, 54–55; Nathans, "Gotta Mind to Move," 216–17.

⁷⁵These statistics were compiled by the NAACP. They were broken down by county and provided to the author by Professor Neil McMillen, University of Southern Mississippi.

⁷⁶This debate revolves around C. Vann Woodward's *The Strange Career of Jim Crow* (New York, 1955). For a recent summary of the debate, see Howard N. Rabinowitz, "More than the Woodward Thesis: Assessing *The Strange Career of Jim Crow*," *Journal of American History* 85 (December 1988), 842–56.

⁷⁷C. Vann Woodward, *Thinking Back: The Perils of Writing History* (Baton Rouge, 1986), 74. For a recent discussion of this long-standing debate, see James C. Cobb, "Beyond Planters and Industrialists: A New Perspective on the New South," *Journal of Southern History* 54 (February 1988), 45–68.

⁷⁸Goodspeed Publishing Company, *Biographical and Historical Memoirs of Mississippi*, vol 1 (Chicago, 1891), pt. 1, pp. 553–54, 647–48, and pt. 2, pp. 1004–5. Plantation-bred Will Mason Worthington founded and served as president of the Bank of Greenville (Unidentified clipping, February 16, 1897, Worthington Family Papers).

[79]Foner, *Reconstruction*, 298; Brandfon, *Cotton Kingdom*, 52–61.

[80]Baker, *Percys of Mississippi*, 7–8, 17–19.

[81]Bolivar County Tax Records, 1883, MDAH, RG 29, microfilm, roll 29; *Biographical and Historical Memoirs*, vol. 1, pt. 1, pp. 553–54; Bolivar County *Review*, October 2, 1890; *The New Coahomian*, March 9, 1889; Friar's Point *Gazette*, February 11, 1887.

[82]Greenville *Times*, April 8, 1877.

[83]Ibid., March 18, 1882; William F. Holmes, *The White Chief: James Kimble Vardaman* (Baton Rouge, 1970), 20, 27–29; Donald, "A Generation of Defeat," 16.

[84]Woodward, *Thinking Back*, 74; *Biographical and Historical Memoirs*, vol. 1, pt. 1, pp. 276–77.

[85]Percy, *Lanterns on the Levee*, 68–69.

[86]Ibid., 69; William F. Holmes, "William Alexander Percy and the Bourbon Era in Mississippi Politics," *Mississippi Quarterly* 26 (Winter 1972–73), 74, 87.

[87]*Biographical and Historical Memoirs*, vol. 2, pt. 2, p. 767, and vol. 1, pt. 1, p. 552; Holmes, "William Alexander Percy," 81, 87.

[88]Woodward, *Origins of the New South*, 1, 18.

[89]Brandfon, *Cotton Kingdom*, 20.

[90]David L. Cohn, "Drunk on Cotton," in David L. Cohn, unpublished autobiography, John D. Williams Library.

Chapter 5. New South Plantation Kingdom

[1]Hudson, "The Yazoo-Mississippi Delta as Plantation Country," 82.

[2]Department of Commerce, Bureau of the Census, *Thirteenth Census of the United States*, vol. 5, *Agriculture* (1909–1910) (Washington, 1914), 884, 798–801; Brandfon, *Cotton Kingdom*, 132, 138–39.

[3]Brandfon, *Cotton Kingdom*, 136; McMillen, *Dark Journey*, 258; Department of Commerce, Bureau of the Census, *Fourteenth Census*, vol. 2, *Population:* 1920 (Washington, 1922), 533–40.

[4]Brandfon, *Cotton Kingdom*, 135; Department of Commerce, Bureau of the Census, *Thirteenth Census*, vol. 6, *Agriculture* (1909–1910) (Washington, 1914), 872–79.

[5]E. A. Boeger and E. A. Goldenweiser, "A Study of the Tenant Systems of Farming in the Yazoo-Mississippi Delta," United States Department of Agriculture, Bulletin 337 (Washington, 1916), 6–7.

[6]Ibid., 1–2.

[7]Ibid., 12.

[8]Brandfon, *Cotton Kingdom*, 114–27.

[9]Ibid., 128–29.

[10]Ibid., 130, 17.

[11]Harold D. Woodman, "Postbellum Social Change and Its Effects on Marketing the South's Cotton Crop," *Agricultural History* 56 (January 1982), 224.

[12]Harold D. Woodman, "Post-Civil War Southern Agriculture and the Law," *Agricultural History* 53 (January 1979), 331.

[13]Brandfon, *Cotton Kingdom*, 134; "Bledsoe Plantation, Shellmound, Leflore County, Mississippi," in "Reports, Speeches, and Articles Relating to Farm Management, 1902–1920," in James R. Grossman, ed., *Black Workers in the Era of the Great Migration* (Frederick, Md., 1985), microfilm, roll 22.

[14]"Bledsoe Plantation," in "Reports, Speeches, and Articles Relating to Farm Management," roll 22.

[15]Ibid.

[16]"An Account of Runnymede Plantation," in "Reports, Speeches, and Articles Relating to Farm Management," roll 22.

[17]Ibid.; "Bledsoe Plantation," "Dunleith Plantation, Washington, County," in "Reports, Speeches, and Articles Relating to Farm Management," roll 22.

[18]"Bledsoe Plantation," in "Reports, Speeches and Articles Relating to Farm Management," roll 22.

[19]Ibid.

[20]McMillen, *Dark Journey*, 145.

[21]Ibid., 142–43, 367n.

[22]Ibid., 150.

[23]Ibid., 145; LeRoy Percy to J. E. Braxton, March 6, 1907, Percy Family Papers, MDAH; Walter Sillers, Jr., to N. S. Spencer, December 31, 1919, Walter Sillers Papers.

[24]Pinckney S. George to LeRoy Percy, May 13, 1907, Percy Papers.

[25]Alfred H. Stone, "A Plantation Experiment," in *Studies in the American Race Problem* (New York, 1908), 127–28.

[26]Ibid., 131–45.

[27]"Cultural Reconnaissance Survey of Coahoma County, Mississippi," Bureau of Agricultural Economics, U.S. Department of Agriculture, December 1944, Arthur Raper Papers, SHC.

[28]"Labor Management on Some Plantations in the Yazoo-Mississippi Delta," in "Reports, Articles, and Speeches Related to Farm Management," roll 22; Stone, "A Plantation Experiment," 145; Wright, *Old South, New South*, 86.

[29]Lois B. Lawrence, "Movin'," Warren County Negro Anecdote, WPA County History Collection, MDAH.

[30]Ibid.

[31]Ibid.

[32]Wharton, *Negro in Mississippi*, 96; LeRoy Allen Memoirs, copy in possession of the author.

[33]LeRoy Percy to J. B. Ray, January 18, 1907, Percy Family Papers.

[34]Ibid., January 18, 1907, March, 23, 1908, Percy Family Papers.

[35]LeRoy Percy to Mr. Hawkins, n.d., LeRoy Percy to H. G. Goepel, July 19, 1907, LeRoy Percy to S. J. McPeak, Percy Family Papers.

[36]LeRoy Percy to J. B. Ray, December 28, 1906, Percy Family Papers.

[37]LeRoy Percy to George Hebron, January 20, 1908, Percy Family Papers.

[38]LeRoy Percy to B. R. Allen, February 19, 1908, Percy Family Papers.

[39]Baker, *Percys of Mississippi*, 31.

[40]LeRoy Percy, "A Southern View of Negro Education," *Outlook* 86 (August 3, 1907), 730–32.

[41]Baker, *Percys of Mississippi*, 27.

[42]LeRoy Percy to James L. Watkins, February 20, 1908, LeRoy Percy to John T. Savage, March 9, 1907, Percy Family Papers.

[43]"Don't Go to the Mississippi: Revelations of Adolfo Rossi," November 4, 1904, Percy Family Papers.

[44]Baker, *Percys of Mississippi*, 30; Mary Grace Quackenbos Report, 1907, Records of the State Department, National Archives (hereinafter cited as NA) Washington, D.C., RG 59, microfilm, roll 539.

⁴⁵Baker, *Percys of Mississippi*, 30; LeRoy Percy to George S. Edgell, December 19, 1906, Percy Family Papers.

⁴⁶LeRoy Percy to George S. Edgell, December 19, 1906, LeRoy Percy to Umberti Pierini, October 20, 1906, Le Roy Percy to Will Dockery, March 8, 1907, Percy Family Papers.

⁴⁷Wright, *Old South, New South*, 77.

⁴⁸Nathans, "Gotta Mind to Move," 218.

⁴⁹Woodman, "Post-Bellum Social Change," 229.

⁵⁰Department of the Interior, Census Office, *Twelfth Census*, vol. 5, *Agriculture*, pt. 1 (Washington, 1902), 96–97; Department of Commerce, Bureau of the Census, *United States Census of Agriculture: 1925*, pt. 2, *The Southern States* (Washington, 1927), 842–51.

⁵¹McMillen, *Dark Journey*, 186–89.

⁵²Henry W. Ball Diary, June 5, 1903, MDAH.

⁵³Quoted in Frank Shay, *Judge Lynch: His First Hundred Years* (Montclair, N.J., 1969), 103–4.

⁵⁴Quoted in McMillen, *Dark Journey*, 234.

⁵⁵NAACP lynching statistics supplied by Professor Neil McMillen.

⁵⁶McMillen, *Dark Journey*, 227, 232.

⁵⁷James R. Grossman, *Land of Hope: Chicago, Black Southerners, and the Great Migration* (Chicago, 1989), 148; Carl F. Grindstaff, "Migration and Mississippi" (Ph.D. diss., University of Massachusetts, 1970), 101. See also Jack Temple Kirby, "The Southern Exodus, 1910–1960: A Primer for Historians," *Journal of Southern History* 49 (November 1983), 585, 600.

⁵⁸McMillen, *Dark Journey*, 268–69; National Urban League Migration Survey, Research Department, "Migration Study, Draft, Early," John D. Williams Library, 1 roll, microfilm.

⁵⁹Nathans, "Gotta Mind to Move," 221; William Barlow, *Looking Up at Down: The Emergence of Blues Culture* (Philadelphia, 1989), 6; Matthew Barton, "Big Bill Broonzy," in Alan Lomax, *Blues in the Mississippi Night—The Story of the Recording* (?, 1990), n.p.

⁶⁰National Urban League, "Migration Study."

⁶¹Ibid.

⁶²Walter Sillers to Memphis *Commercial Appeal*, n.d., Walter Sillers Papers; National Urban League, "Migration Study."

⁶³National Urban League, "Migration Study."

⁶⁴Ibid.

⁶⁵Grossman, *Land of Hope*, 109; McMillen, *Dark Journey*, 273.

⁶⁶Grossman, *Land of Hope*, 3, 107, 52.

⁶⁷National Urban League, "Migration Study."

⁶⁸Grossman, *Land of Hope*, 55; Florette Henri, *Black Migration: Movement North, 1900–1920* (Garden City, N.Y., 1975), 130.

⁶⁹National Urban League, "Migration Study"; Grossman, *Land of Hope*, 154.

⁷⁰LeRoy Allen Memoirs, copy in possession of the author.

⁷¹Dorothy Dickins, *A Nutritional Investigation of Tenants in the Yazoo-Mississippi Delta* (Mississippi Agricultural Experiment Station, Bulletin 254, A & M College, Mississippi, 1928), 1–28.

⁷²Ibid., 32–33.

[73] Ibid., 35.

[74] John Miller MacLachlan, "Mississippi: A Regional Social-Economic Analysis" (Ph.D. diss., University of North Carolina, 1937), 495; Wayne Flynt, *Poor But Proud: Alabama's Poor Whites* (Tuscaloosa, Ala., 1989), 84.

[75] Dickins, *Nutritional Investigation*, 9–10.

[76] Richard Wright, *Black Boy* (New York, 1966), 150–51.

[77] Beulah Amidon Ratliff, "Mississippi: Heart of Dixie," *The Nation* 114 (May 17, 1922), 588.

[78] J. W. G. Rateree to U.S. District Attorney, March 22, 1928, Department of Justice Central Files, Assorted Peonage Files, RG 60, NA.

[79] Affidavit of Sam Edwards, December 23, 1931, United States of America, Southern District of Alabama, Department of Justice Central Files, Assorted Peonage Files, RG 60, NA. For other accounts of peonage in the Delta, see Pete Daniel, *The Shadow of Slavery: Peonage in the South, 1901–1969* (London, 1973), 146–47.

[80] John Wilson McRaven, Jr., to Will Henry McRaven, May 5, 1922, May 26, 1923, Will Henry McRaven Papers, MDAH.

[81] Percy, *Lanterns on the Levee*, 257.

[82] Ibid., 258; Baker, *Percys of Mississippi*, 138.

[83] Baker, *Percys of Mississippi*, 139.

[84] Daniel, *Shadow of Slavery*, 153.

[85] Pete Daniel, *Deep 'n as It Come: The 1927 Mississippi River Flood* (New York, 1977), 108.

[86] Richard Wright, "Down by the Riverside," in Richard Wright, *Uncle Tom's Children* (New York, 1965), 54–102.

[87] Myron S. McNeil to Attorney General, June 27, 1927, Records of the Department of Justice, RG 60, NA

[88] Oscar Johnston to V. E. Cartledge, June 30, 1927, Oscar Johnston Correspondence, Delta and Pine Land Papers, Mitchell Memorial Library, Mississippi State University, Starkville, Miss.

Chapter 6. A World Apart

[1] Brandfon, *Cotton Kingdom*, 138.

[2] Elizabeth Spencer, *This Crooked Way* (New York, 1952), 28.

[3] New York *World*, November 14, 1907.

[4] William L. Hemphill Manuscript, June 1905, Hemphill Family Correspondence, 1905, William R. Perkins Library.

[5] Ibid.

[6] Ibid.

[7] William Faulkner, *Go Down Moses* (New York, 1973), 364; Spencer, *This Crooked Way*, 28.

[8] Florence Ogden Sillers Memoirs, Walter Sillers Papers.

[9] Ibid.

[10] Ibid.

[11] "Some Excerpts from a Very Interesting Diary of the Late Henry W. Ball," September 5, 1890, W. A. Percy Library, Greenville, Miss., typescript.

[12]Ibid.

[13]Ibid.

[14]Daniel, *Deep 'n as It Come,* 5, 10; Henry W. Ball Diary, May 5, 1927.

[15]Fred Chaney, "A Refugee's Story," Fred Chaney Papers, W. A. Percy Library, typescript.

[16]Henry W. Ball Diary, July 13, 1927.

[17]Joe Rice Dockery Interview with John Griffin Jones, December 13, 1979, MDAH; James Hand to Mother, May 7, 1927, letters in Roberts Memorial Library, Delta State University, Cleveland, Miss.

[18]Joe Rice Dockery Interview with John Griffin Jones, December 13,1979, MDAH.

[19]Daniel, *Deep 'n as It Come,* 128; Cohn, *Where I Was Born and Raised,* 56.

[20]Cohn, "Drunk on Cotton," in Cohn, unpublished autobiography.

[21]Ibid.

[22]LeRoy Percy to Drs. Gayden, Dodson, and Sauls, October 16, 1908, Percy Family Papers.

[23]Ibid., November 10, 1908.

[24]Cohn, "Drunk on Cotton," in Cohn, unpublished autobiography.

[25]Ibid.

[26]G. Clay to John C. Burrus, June 1, 1887, Duffin Brothers and McGhee to J. C. Burrus, April 7, 1899, Burrus Papers.

[27]Charles B. Allen, Jr., to Charles B. Allen, March 1, 1899, James Allen Papers, MDAH.

[28]LeRoy Percy to John G. Jones, December 3, 1908, Percy Family Papers.

[29]Cohn, "It Ain't What I Owes," in Cohn, unpublished autobiography; MacLachlan, "Mississippi: A Regional Social and Economic Analysis," 512.

[30]Cohn, "It Ain't What I Owes," in Cohn, unpublished autobiography.

[31]LeRoy Allen Memoirs, copy in possession of the author.

[32]Ibid.

[33]Ibid.

[34]John Faulkner, *Dollar Cotton* (New York, 1942), 229–31.

[35]Cohn, "It Ain't What I Owes," in Cohn, unpublished autobiography.

[36]Clive Metcalf Diary, November 19, 21, December 26, 29, 1889, SHC.

[37]M. Parham to J. M. Andrews, January 9, 1887, February 29, 1892, James M. Andrews Papers, Louisiana State University, Baton Rouge, La.

[38]Walter Sillers to A. J. McClaurin, July 6, 1916, Walter Sillers Papers.

[39]Walter Sillers to W. B. Roberts, July 5, 1921, Walter Sillers Papers.

[40]Ibid.

[41]Virginia Estes Causey, "Glen Allan, Mississippi: Change and Continuity in a Delta Community, 1900 to 1950" (Ph.D. diss., Emory University, 1983), 80; Shelby Foote Interview with Orley B. Caudill, June 9, 1976, *New York Times* Oral History Program, Mississippi Oral History Collection, microcard 150–51.

[42]Joe Rice Dockery Interview with John Griffin Jones, December 13, 1979, MDAH.

[43]Ibid.

[44]Clive Metcalf Diary, July 30–31, August 3, 5, 7, 10–11, 14, 19–21, 1889.

[45]LeRoy Percy to Walker Percy, June 24, 1907, Leroy Percy to William Alexander Percy, October 8, 1907, Percy Family Papers.

[46] LeRoy Percy to Edward Holland, June 27, 1908, Percy Family Papers.

[47] Baker, *Percys of Mississippi,* 133–34.

[48] LeRoy Percy to Walker Percy, July 2, 1908, Percy Family Papers.

[49] Smith, *Yazoo River,* 293.

[50] Kate Burrus to Dear Cousin, July 2, 1884, Burrus Papers; Walter Sillers to Florence Sillers, September 1, 1890, Walter Sillers Papers; Clive Metcalf Diary, December 28, 1888, February 3, March 31, 1889.

[51] Florence Warfield Sillers Memoirs, Walter Sillers Papers.

[52] Ibid.

[53] Henry W. Ball Diary, July 21, 22, 1887.

[54] Ibid., July 26, 28, 30, 1887.

[55] Ibid., December 9, 31, 1887, January 6, 1888, January 27, 1892.

[56] Ibid., December 9, 1887.

[57] Florence Warfield Sillers Memoirs, Walter Sillers Papers.

[58] Ibid.

[59] Henry W. Ball Diary, May 20, 1887.

[60] Baker, *Percys of Mississippi,* 32.

[61] John Sharp Williams to Lem Motlow, January 26, 1914, Williams Papers, UM; John Sharp Williams to Dr. E. B. Pool, May 27, 1907, John Sharp Williams Papers, LC.

[62] George C. Osborn, John *Sharp Williams, Planter-Statesman of the Deep South* (Baton Rouge, 1943), 436–37.

[63] Ibid., 319, 437.

[64] Percy, *Lanterns on the Levee,* 238–41.

[65] Causey, "Glen Allan," 85.

[66] James F. Brieger, comp., "Hometown, Mississippi," bound typescript in John D. Williams Library, 1980, 195–96.

[67] Faulkner, *Dollar Cotton,* 257.

[68] See Henry H. Moss, "Sectionalism in Mississippi, 1817–1832" (M.A. thesis, University of Mississippi, 1934).

[69] Brandfon, *Cotton Kingdom,* 65.

[70] Ibid., 74.

[71] Clark, "Legislative Apportionment in the 1890 Constitutional Convention," 300.

[72] Wharton, *Negro in Mississippi,* 238; Kirwan, *Revolt of the Rednecks,* 167–68.

[73] Lyda Shivers, "A History of the Mississippi State Penitentiary" (M.A. thesis, University of Mississippi, 1930), 48–49.

[74] Holmes, *White Chief,* 31–32.

[75] Ibid., 151–42.

[76] Brandfon, *Cotton Kingdom,* 137.

[77] Kirwan, *Revolt of the Rednecks,* 138–39.

[78] Ibid., 140–41; LeRoy Percy to E. H. Woods, March 28, 1907, Percy Family Papers.

[79] Kirwan, *Revolt of the Rednecks,* 263.

[80] Ibid., 263–64.

[81] Ibid., 123, 127–29.

[82] LeRoy Percy to J. S. McNeily, March 9, 1906, Percy Family Papers.

[83] LeRoy Percy to H. C. Nall, May 9, 1905, LeRoy Percy to Messrs. Britton and Koontz, December 19, 1904, Percy Family Papers.

[84]Charles Scott to LeRoy Percy, May 1, 1905, LeRoy Percy to Charles Scott, May 4, 1905, Percy Family Papers.

[85]Ibid.

[86]V. O. Key, Jr., *Southern Politics in State and Nation* (New York, 1949), 233.

[87]Key, *Southern Politics*, 232–33; Baker, *Percys of Mississippi*, 26.

[88]Alfred H. Stone, "The Negro in the Yazoo Mississippi Delta," *Publications of the American Economic Association*, 3rd ser., vol. 3 (New York, 1902), 240, 272.

[89]LeRoy Percy to Editor, Minneapolis *Bellman*, December 19, 1906, Percy Family Papers.

[90]Kirwan, *Revolt of the Rednecks*, 146–47.

[91]LeRoy Percy to John Sharp Williams, June 22, 1907, LeRoy Percy to Frank C. Armstrong, March 9, 1907, Percy Family Papers.

[92]John Sharp Williams to L. T. Carpenter, June 10, 1907, John Sharp Williams to Charles E. Hooker, Jr., June 10, 1907, John Sharp Williams to R. A. Barnett, May 27, 1907, John Sharp Williams Papers, LC; LeRoy Percy to R. W. Banks, March 31, 1911, John Sharp Williams to Woodrow Wilson, April 13, 1914, John Sharp Williams Papers, UM.

[93]LeRoy Percy to W. P. Brown, July 8, 1907, Percy Family Papers.

[94]Leroy Percy to Theodore Roosevelt, August 10, 1907, Percy Family Papers.

[95]Kousser, *Shaping of Southern Politics*, 235.

[96]Baker, *Percys of Mississippi*, 52.

[97]Percy, *Lanterns on the Levee*, 149; LeRoy Percy to John R. Goge, August 7, 1911, Percy Family Papers.

[98]LeRoy Percy to C. P. Mooney, March 30, 1922, Percy Family Papers; Baker, *Percys of Mississippi*, 98.

[99]Baker, *Percys of Mississippi*, 105, 102.

[100]Dick Cox to LeRoy Percy, March 5, 1922, Percy Family Papers.

[101]John Sharp Williams to Otho C. Stubblefield, June 20, 1922, box 116, John Sharp Williams Papers, LC.

[102]John Sharp Williams to Walter E. Stokes, January 9, 1922, box 116, John Sharp Williams Papers, LC; John Sharp Williams to H. W. Phillips, February 10, 1921, John Sharp Williams Papers, UM.

[103]Baker, *Percys of Mississippi*, 148–49; John Sharp Williams to LeRoy Percy, December 21, 1929, Percy Family Papers; John Sharp Williams to Lucille Banks, January 11, 1930, John Sharp Williams Papers, UM.

[104]Kirwan, *Revolt of the Rednecks*, 295–96.

[105]See Paul M. Gaston, *The New South Creed: A Study in Southern Mythmaking* (Baton Rouge, 1983), 70–71; untitled manuscript in Walter Sillers Papers. Sillers was heavily involved in stock speculation himself. See Walter Sillers, Jr., to B. E. Eaton, May 15, 1926, Walter Sillers Papers.

[106]Francis Glenn Abney, "The Mississippi Voter: A Study of Voting Behavior in a One-Party, Multifactional System" (Ph.D. diss., Tulane University, 1969), 147–56.

[107]Steven Alan Patterson, "Mississippi's Four Constitutions: A Study of Political Response to Societal Change" (M.A. thesis, University of Mississippi, 1974), 86–91.

[108]Oscar Johnston to Oscar O. Wolfe, Jr., April 28, 1932, Oscar Johnston Correspondence, Delta and Pine Land Papers.

Chapter 7. "The Deepest South"

[1] Rupert B. Vance, *Geography of the South* (New York, 1935), 266, 270. There was ample statistical data to confirm Vance's observations. For example, although the percentage of those filing income tax returns showing less than a thousand dollars in net income was more than twice the national norm, the Delta's percentage of those receiving ten thousand dollars or more in net income (2.7 percent) was practically equal to the national rate (2.9 percent) and nearly twice the state average. For evidence of the Delta's economic disparities, see Charles Felder Reynolds, Jr., "The Economic and Social Structure of the Yazoo-Mississippi Delta" (Ph.D. diss., University of Virginia, 1946), 36, 42, 44, 63, 102.

[2] John Dollard, *Caste and Class in a Southern Town*, 2nd ed. (New York, 1949); Hortense Powdermaker, *After Freedom: A Cultural Study in the Deep South* (New York, 1968).

[3] Dollard, *Caste and Class*, 107–8.

[4] Cohn, "It Ain't What I Owes That Worries Me," in Cohn, unpublished autobiography.

[5] Powdermaker, *After Freedom*, 91, 94.

[6] Dollard, *Caste and Class*, 110–11.

[7] Hortense Powdermaker, *Stranger and Friend: The Ways of an Anthropologist* (New York, 1966), 184.

[8] Frank E. Smith, *Congressman from Mississippi* (New York, 1964), 14; Smith, *Yazoo River*, 182; McMillen, *Dark Journey*, 134.

[9] Nathans, "Gotta Mind to Move," 215.

[10] Causey, "Glen Allan," 32.

[11] Powdermaker, *After Freedom*, 105–6; Ralph Ellison, "Richard Wright's Blues," *Shadow and Act* (New York, 1964), 89–90; Danny Collum, "Stepping Out into Freedom," reprinted from *Sojourners* (December 1982), n.p., copy in possession of the author.

[12] Winthrop D. Jordan, *The White Man's Burden: Historical Origins of Racism in the United States* (London, 1974), 19, 82.

[13] Dollard, *Caste and Class*, 161.

[14] Ibid., 161–62.

[15] Powdermaker, *After Freedom*, 167–68.

[16] Jordan, *White Man's Burden*, 19.

[17] Willie Morris, *North toward Home* (Oxford, Miss., 1982), 79.

[18] Faulkner, *Dollar Cotton*, 262–63.

[19] Clifton Taulbert, *Once upon a Time When We Were Colored* (Tulsa, Okla., 1980), 106; Endesha Ida Mae Holland, "Memories of the Mississippi Delta," *Michigan Quarterly Review* 26 (Winter 1987), 246.

[20] Dollard, *Caste and Class*, 170–71.

[21] Ibid., 142.

[22] Powdermaker, *After Freedom*, 194.

[23] Dollard, *Caste and Class*, 381.

[24] "Against Lynch Law: A Resolution Published in the Bolivar County *Democrat* on the 30th Day of April 1904," Walter Sillers Papers, typescript.

[25] Cohn, *Where I Was Born and Raised*, 282; Powdermaker, *After Freedom* 194–95.

[26]Cohn, *Where I Was Born and Raised,* 282.

[27]Morris, *North toward Home,* 79; Dollard, *Caste and Class,* 136, 140.

[28]Dollard, *Caste and Class,* 136, 169.

[29]Dollard Interview with William R. Ferris, March 14, 1975, transcript in possession of the author.

[30]Dollard, *Caste and Class,* 369.

[31]Morris, *North toward Home,* 77–78, 88, 90.

[32]Ibid., 90.

[33]Ibid., 379.

[34]Cohn, *Where I Was Born and Raised,* 193–94.

[35]Dollard, *Caste and Class,* 125.

[36]Powdermaker, *After Freedom,* 27–28; Dollard, *Caste and Class,* 330–31, 358; Nicholas Lemann, *The Promised Land: The Great Migration and How It Changed America* (New York, 1991), 34–35.

[37]Powdermaker, *After Freedom,* 339–45; Dollard, *Caste and Class,* 309.

[38]Morris, *North toward Home,* 79.

[39]Dollard, *Caste and Class,* 342–52; Powdermaker, *After Freedom,* 336–47.

[40]Wright, "The Ethics of Living Jim Crow," in Wright, *Uncle Tom's Children,* 14–15.

[41]Dollard, *Caste and Class,* 247–48.

[42]Powdermaker, *Stranger and Friend,* 176.

[43]Powdermaker, *After Freedom,* 285; Taulbert, *Once upon a Time,* 91, 94, 105–6.

[44]Dollard, *Caste and Class,* 243–44.

[45]Powdermaker, *After Freedom,* 216.

[46]Holland, "Memories of the Mississippi Delta," 246.

[47]Powdermaker, *After Freedom,* 218.

[48]Ibid., 336.

[49]Levine, *Black Culture and Black Consciousness,* 350; William Reynolds Ferris, Jr., "Black Folklore from the Mississippi Delta" (Ph.D. diss., University of Pennsylvania, 1969), 174.

[50]Ferris, "Black Folklore," 181.

[51]Ibid.

[52]Ibid., 164; Dollard, *Caste and Class,* 273–74; Dollard, "The Dozens: Dialect of Insult," *The American Imago* 1 (1939), 3–25.

[53]Levine, *Black Culture and Black Consciousness,* 356–58.

[54]Richard M. Dorson, "Negro Tales from Bolivar County," *Southern Folklore Quarterly* 19 (March 1955), 108–9.

[55]John W. Roberts, *From Trickster to Badman: The Black Folk Hero in Slavery and Freedom* (Philadelphia, 1989), 188; Dorson, "Negro Tales," 106.

[56]Levine, *Black Culture and Black Consciousness,* 414.

[57]Ibid., 415.

[58]Ibid., 418.

[59]Ibid., 419–20.

[60]Roberts, *From Trickster to Badman,* 182; Levine, *Black Culture and Black Consciousness,* 326.

[61]Allison Davis, Burleigh B. Gardner, and Mary R. Gardner, *Deep South: An Anthropological Study of Caste and Class* (Chicago, 1959), 533–34.

[62]Ibid., 534.

[63] Ibid., 538, 535, 533–34.

[64] Cohn, *Where I Was Born and Raised*, 159.

[65] Ibid., 68.

[66] Ibid., 75, 70.

[67] Sam Rembert to Sillers and Sillers, March 5, 1920, Walter Sillers, Jr., Papers, Roberts Memorial Library.

[68] McMillen, *Dark Journey*, 203.

[69] Ibid., 203–5; Cohn, *Where I Was Born and Raised*, 112.

[70] Levine, *Black Culture and Black Consciousness*, 420; H. C. Tinney, "How Big John Henry Built the 'Yaller Dog' Railroad," Tunica County Folklore Collection, WPA County History Material, MDAH.

[71] Levine, *Black Culture and Black Consciousness*, 420, 429–40.

[72] Taulbert, *Once upon a Time*, 52.

[73] Cohn, *Where I Was Born and Raised*, 80.

[74] Percy, *Lanterns on the Levee*, 299.

[75] Cohn, *Where I Was Born and Raised*, 100–101.

[76] James W. Loewen, *The Mississippi Chinese: Between Black and White* (Cambridge, Mass., 1971), 9–31.

[77] Loewen, *Mississippi Chinese*, 61, 63.

[78] Cohn, *Where I Was Born and Raised*, 156–57; Loewen, *Mississippi Chinese*, 73–80.

[79] Loewen, *Mississippi Chinese*, 93–98.

[80] "Cultural Reconnaissance Survey," 3, 18; Dollard, *Caste and Class*, 75–82; Powdermaker, *After Freedom*, 14–22.

[81] Powdermaker, *Stranger and Friend*, 141–43.

[82] Craig Claiborne, *A Feast Made for Laughter* (Garden City, N.Y., 1982), 35, 52.

[83] Powdermaker, *Stranger and Friend*, 185–86.

[84] Cohn, *Where I Was Born and Raised*, 201.

[85] Percy, *Lanterns on the Levee*, 149–53.

[86] Powdermaker, *Stranger and Friend*, 14. On *Herrenvolk* democracy, see George M. Frederickson, *The Black Image in the White Mind: The Debate on Afro-American Character and Destiny, 1817–1914* (New York, 1971), 61; Flynt, *Poor But Proud*, 89.

[87] Powdermaker, *Stranger and Friend*, 147.

[88] Powdermaker, *After Freedom*, 66–67, 149–51; Powdermaker, *Stranger and Friend*, 164. Dollard found the black upper class too tiny to merit discussion. His description of the black middle class resembles Powdermaker's analysis of the black upper class. See Dollard, *Caste and Class*, 85–89.

[89] Powdermaker, *After Freedom*, 64, 175–79.

[90] Taulbert, *Once upon a Time*, 106. See Carl F. Degler, *Neither Black Nor White* (New York, 1971), 105; Cohn, "Wash Jackson," in Cohn, unpublished autobiography, John D. Williams Library.

[91] Dollard, *Caste and Class*, 194–97; Powdermaker, *After Freedom*, 210–12.

[92] Dollard, *Caste and Class*, 196, 308–10.

[93] Taulbert, *Once upon a Time*, 27.

[94] Ibid., 37; Powdermaker, *After Freedom*, 213.

[95] McMillen, *Dark Journey*, 74, 77.

[96] Wright, *Old South, New South*, 78.

[97] Dollard, *Caste and Class*, 248; McMillen, *Dark Journey*, 93.

[98] Cohn, *Where I Was Born and Raised*, 157–58.

[99] Ibid., 158–59.

[100] Powdermaker, *After Freedom*, 301–2.

[101] Ibid., 321–22.

[102] Ibid., 332.

[103] Ibid., 333, 345–46.

[104] Ibid., 138; Richard Lowitt and Maurine Beasley, eds., *One-Third of a Nation: Lorena Hickok Reports on the Great Depression* (Urbana, 1981), 215; "Cultural Reconnaissance Survey," 31.

[105] Vance, *Human Geography*, 270.

Chapter 8. "We Are at the Crossroads"

[1] Boschert, "Politics of Expediency," 192–93; Daniel, *Deep 'n as It Come*, 150.

[2] Walter Sillers, Jr., to Pat Harrison, June 9, 1927, Walter Sillers, Jr., Papers.

[3] Daniel, *Shadow of Slavery*, 154; Myron S. McNeil to Attorney General, June 27, 1927, Department of Justice, RG 60, NA.

[4] Vance, *Human Geography*, 271; E. L. Langsford and B. H. Thibodeaux, *Plantation Organization and Operation in the Yazoo-Mississippi Area*, U.S. Department of Agriculture, Technical Bulletin 682 (Washington, 1939), 35–36; Henry W. Ball Diary, February 19, 1932.

[5] Pete Daniel, "The Transformation of the Rural South, 1930 to the Present," *Agricultural History* 55 (July 1981), 236.

[6] David Eugene Conrad, *The Forgotten Farmers: The Story of Sharecroppers in the New Deal* (Urbana, 1965), 52.

[7] Ibid., 52–54.

[8] Roger D. Tate, "Easing the Burden: The Era of Depression and New Deal in Mississippi" (Ph.D. diss., University of Tennessee, 1978), 90–91; Stanley Van Vliet White, "Report of Survey of Factors Contributing to the Economic Insecurity of Workers in the Mississippi Delta Cotton Region," Harry Hopkins Papers, Franklin D. Roosevelt Library, Hyde Park, N.Y.

[9] Pete Daniel, *Breaking the Land: The Transformation of Cotton, Tobacco, and Rice Cultures since 1880* (Urbana, 1985), 97.

[10] Lawrence J. Nelson, "Oscar Johnston, the New Deal, and the Cotton Subsidy Payments Controversy, 1936–1937," *Journal of Southern History* 40 (August 1974), 400–401.

[11] Conrad, *Forgotten Farmers*, 55–56.

[12] Ibid., 55, 79.

[13] Ibid., 59–60.

[14] Ibid., 8.

[15] Harold C. Hofsommer, "Survey of Rural Problem Areas: Leflore County, Mississippi, Cotton Growing Area of the Old South," Bureau of Agricultural Economics Report, RG 83, NA.

[16] Wright, *Old South, New South*, 228–29.

[17] Warren C. Whatley, "Labor for the Picking: The New Deal in the South," *Journal of Economic History* 43 (December 1983), 920.

[18]Tate, *Easing the Burden*, 84; White, "Report of Survey of Factors."

[19]Wright, *Old South, New South*, 235.

[20]Daniel, *Breaking the Land*, 101; White, "Report of Survey of Factors"; Conrad, *Forgotten Farmers*, 78–79.

[21]White, "Report of Survey of Factors."

[22]William Alexander Percy to Oscar Johnston, November 8, 1938, Oscar Johnston to William Alexander Percy, November 10, 1938, Oscar Johnston Correspondence, Delta and Pine Land Papers.

[23]White, "Report of Survey of Factors."

[24]Tate, "Easing the Burden," 95, 98; Jack Temple Kirby, *Rural Worlds Lost: The American South, 1920–1960* (Baton Rouge, 1987), 57–60.

[25]Conrad, *Forgotten Farmers*, 80–81.

[26]Smith, *Congressman from Mississippi*, 19–20.

[27]U.S. Congress, Senate, *Payments under Agricultural Adjustment Program*, 74th Cong., 2nd. sess., 1936, 26, 28, 29, 33–35, 47, 48, 55, 56; New Orleans *Times-Picayune*, April 8, 1936.

[28]Tate, "Easing the Burden," 81–82, 84; Nelson, "Oscar Johnston," 407.

[29]Tate, "Easing the Burden," 85–86; Langsford and Thibodeaux, "Plantation Organization and Operation," 35–36.

[30]Tate, "Easing the Burden," 91; Elizabeth R. Varner to Buford Yerger, November 23, 1935 Walter Sillers, Jr., Papers.

[31]*Louisiana Weekly*, September 18 [1936], quoted in White, "Report of Survey of Factors"; Hofsommer, "Survey of Rural Problem Areas."

[32]John Faulkner, *Men Working* (New York, 1941), 31.

[33]White, "Report of Survey of Factors."

[34]Hofsommer, "Survey of Rural Problem Areas."

[35]Dollars, *Caste and Class*, 13; Hofsommer, "Survey of Problem Areas"; White, "Report of Survey of Factors."

[36]Hofsommer, "Survey of Rural Problem Areas."

[37]Daniel, *Breaking the Land*, 89; Hofsommer, "Survey of Rural Problem Areas."

[38]Tate, "Easing the Burden," 124.

[39]Hofsommer, "Survey of Rural Problem Areas."

[40]Smith, *Congressman from Mississippi*, 22.

[41]Tate, "Easing the Burden," 87–88.

[42]Walter Sillers, Jr., to Will M. Whittington, March 4, 1935, January 5, 1935, Walter Sillers, Jr., to Pat Harrison, October 14, 1935, Walter Sillers, Jr., to C. B. Braun, March 7, 1935, Walter Sillers, Jr., to Pat Harrison, August 5, 1935, Walter Sillers, Jr., Papers.

[43]Tate, "Easing the Burden," 194–204.

[44]Salamon, "Politics, Protest, and Modernization," 214–15.

[45]Key, *Southern Politics*, 243; Wright, *Old South, New South*, 236; Daniel, *Breaking the Land*, 100.

[46]Wright, *Old South, New South*, 233; Frank J. Welch, *The Plantation Land Tenure System in Mississippi* (State College, Miss., 1943), 38, 45.

[47]Welch, *Plantation Land Tenure System*, 19, 28, 32, 35, 47.

[48]Ibid., 32; McMillen, *Dark Journey*, 128.

[49]Tate, "Easing the Burden," 198; John Ray Skates, Jr., "World War II and Its

Effects, 1940–1948," in McLemore, ed., *History of Mississippi*, vol. 2, 120–39, and "World War II as a Watershed in Mississippi History," *Journal of Mississippi History* 37 (May 1975), 131–42; "Nelson L. LeRay, George L. Wilbur, and Grady B. Crowe, "Plantation Organization and Residential Labor Force, Delta Area Mississippi," (State College, Miss., 1960), 13; "Cultural Reconnaisance Survey"; Richard H. Day, "The Economics of Technological Change and the Demise of the Sharecropper," *American Economic Review* 57 (June 1967), 443.

⁵⁰Nan Elizabeth Woodruff, "Pick or Fight: The Emergency Farm Labor Program in the Arkansas and Mississippi Deltas during World War II," *Agricultural History* 64 (Spring 1990), 75; Fred Young to Ransom Aldrich and Walter Sillers, Jr., January 18, 1943, Walter Sillers, Jr., Papers.

⁵¹J. G. Prichard to Mrs. W. M. Black, October 1, 1942, Walter Sillers, Jr., Papers; Daniel, "Going among Strangers," 895.

⁵²Daniel, "Going among Strangers," 894.

⁵³Oscar Johnston to Mrs. W. M. Black, September 26, 1942, Walter Sillers, Jr., Papers.

⁵⁴Walter W. Wilcox, *The Farmer in the Second World War* (Ames, Iowa, 1947), 185–86; Woodruff, "Pick or Fight," 80; Daniel, "Going among Strangers," 891; Fred Young to Ransom Aldrich and Walter Sillers, January 18, 1943, Walter Sillers, Jr., Papers.

⁵⁵Woodruff, "Pick or Fight," 77–79, 82; Merrill R. Pritchett and William L. Shea, "The Enemy in Mississippi (1943–1946)," *Journal of Mississippi History* 41 (November 1979), 367–69; W. P. Kretcschner to Walter Sillers, Jr., July 1, 1942, July 8, 1942, Walter Sillers, Jr., Papers; Oscar Johnston to E. B. Whitaker, May 2, 1942, Oscar Johnston Correspondence, Delta and Pine Land Papers.

⁵⁶J. Lewis Henderson, "In the Cotton Delta," *Survey Graphic* 36 (January 1947), 51.

⁵⁷Woodruff, "Pick or Fight," 83; "Cultural Reconnaisance Survey"; Henderson, "In the Cotton Delta," 108.

⁵⁸Henderson, "In the Cotton Delta," 108.

⁵⁹"Cultural Reconnaisance Survey." For specific examples of Delta blacks' complaints to the STFU about the AAA, see J. R. Butler to Zero Mumford, November 16, 1939, J. R. Butler to Curley Williams, November 20, 1939, and see also "Eviction Problems Acute in Yazoo-Mississippi Delta," press release, December n.d., 1939, *Papers of the Southern Tenant Farmers Union, 1934–1970* (microfilm, 60 rolls, Glen Rock, N.J., 1971), roll 13.

⁶⁰Dorothy Lee Black to Walter Sillers, Jr., November 12, 1942, Walter Sillers, Jr., Papers.

⁶¹Daniel, "Going among Strangers," 892; "Cultural Reconnaisance Survey."

⁶²Samuel C. Adams, Jr., "The Acculturation of the Delta Negro," *Social Forces* 26 (December 1947), 203.

⁶³John W. Brunini to Dorothy Lee Black, October 14, 1942, J. W. Bradford to Walter Sillers, Jr., April 2, 1943, Walter Sillers, Jr., Papers; George B. Tindall, *The Emergence of the New South, 1913–1945* (Baton Rouge, 1967), 707.

⁶⁴Tindall, *Emergence of the New South*, 707; Tate, "Easing the Burden," 165; Rose Gladney, "A Letter from Lillian Smith," *Southern Changes* 9 (December 1987), 33; McMillen, *Dark Journey*, 314.

⁶⁵Kenneth Williams, "Mississippi and Civil Rights, 1945–1954" (Ph.D. diss., Mississippi State University, 1985), 181; Jay R. Mandle, *The Roots of Black Poverty: The Southern Plantation Economy after the Civil War* (Durham, N.C., 1978), 90.

⁶⁶Joseph T. Hill, FBI Report, February 2, 1945, Classified Subject Files, Central Files, Correspondence, General Records of the Department of Justice, RG 60, NA; Robert Daryl Lewis, "Delta Council: Transformer of an Agrarian Mind" (M.Ed. thesis, Delta State University, 1984), 38–39; Dorothy Dickins, *The Labor Supply and Mechanized Cotton Production*, Mississippi Agricultural Experiment Station Bulletin 463 (State College, Miss., 1949), 17, 19.

⁶⁷"Cultural Reconnaisance Survey."

⁶⁸Lewis, "Delta Council," 38–39.

⁶⁹Robert C. McMath, Jr., "World War II and the Rural South: Death Knell for Traditional Community Life?" Paper presented at the annual meeting of the Southern Historical Association, Memphis, Tenn., 1982.

⁷⁰Lemann, *Promised Land,* 49–50.

⁷¹Wright, *Old South, New South,* 236; Jack Temple Kirby, *Rural Worlds Lost: The American South, 1920–1960* (Baton Rouge, 1987), 72; Harold A. Pedersen and Arthur F. Raper, *The Cotton Plantation in Transition,* Mississippi State College Agricultural Experiment Station (State College, Miss., 1954), 16, 26.

⁷²Nelson LeRay, Jr., and Grady B. Crowe, *Labor and Technology on Selected Cotton Plantations in the Delta Area of Mississippi, 1953–1957,* Mississippi State Agricultural Experiment Station Bulletin 575 (State College, Miss., 1959), 5–23.

⁷³Morris M. Lindsey, "An Economic Analysis of Custom Work on Farms in the Yazoo-Mississippi Delta," *Mississippi State Agricultural Experiment Station Bulletin* 667 (State College, Miss., 1963), 5–6; Ralph Alewine, Jr., "The Changing Characteristics of the Mississippi Delta," in U.S. Department of Labor, Manpower Administration, "Farm Labor Developments," May 1968, mimeo, 32–33, 35.

⁷⁴*Wall Street Journal,* July 3, 1957.

⁷⁵Day, "Economics of Technological Change," 443.

⁷⁶Lewis, "Delta Couuncil," 41. See also Don A. Newton, "Industry and the Delta," *Delta Review* 1 (Spring 1964), 29–31, 62.

⁷⁷Lewis, "Delta Council," 52; Hodding Carter, *Where Main Street Meets the River* (New York and Toronto, 1953), 208; U.S. Bureau of the Census, *Census of Population, 1960,* vol. 5, pt. 26 (Washington, 1962), 187–93.

⁷⁸U.S. Bureau of the Census, *Census of Population, 1960, Subject Reports: Mobility for States and State Economic Areas* (Washington, 1963), 179, and *U.S. Census of Population, 1960, Selected Area Reports: State Economic Areas* (Washington, 1963), 33.

⁷⁹As agricultural mechanization continued to reduce the demand for black labor and civil rights pressures mounted, by the 1960s development leaders in Yazoo City admitted that they had put forth little effort to create jobs for blacks and thereby slow black outmigration. James C. Cobb, *The Selling of the South: The Southern Crusade for Industrial Development, 1936–1980* (Baton Rouge, 1982), 116. See also Bill P. Joyner and Jon P. Thames, "Mississippi's Efforts at Industrialization: A Critical Analysis," *Mississippi Law Journal* 38 (1967), 476–77 and Salamon, "Protest, Politics, and Modernization," 369.

⁸⁰Daniel, *Going among Strangers,* 910; *Smith v. Allwright* 321 U.S. 64; Delta Council Board of Directors Meeting, July 12, 1945, Walter Sillers, Jr., Papers.

Chapter 9. "A Man's Life Isn't Worth a Penny with a Hole in It"

[1]Cohn, *Where I Was Born and Raised,* 41, 40, x–xi.

[2]Daniel, "Going among Strangers," 910.

[3]Hodding Carter, "I Love My Town," *Rotarian* 109 (October 1966), 31.

[4]Hodding Carter to William Alexander Percy, March 23, 1941, Hodding and Betty Werlein Carter Correspondence, 1941, Mitchell Memorial Library.

[5]John T. Kneebone, *Southern Liberal Journalists and the Issue of Race, 1920–1944* (Chapel Hill and London, 1985), 192–93.

[6]Hodding Carter, *Winds of Fear* (New York, 1944); James E. Robinson, "Hodding Carter: Southern Liberal, 1907–1972" (Ph.D. diss., Mississippi State University, 1974), 80–81.

[7]Smith, *Congressman from Mississippi,* 59, 281–300.

[8]Howell Raines, *My South Is Rested: The Story of the Civil Rights Movement in the Deep South* (New York, 1985), 233.

[9]Ibid., 233–34.

[10]Walter Sillers, Jr., to Oscar Johnston, April 23, 1947, Walter Sillers, Jr., Papers.

[11]W. C. Roberts to A. F. Toler, October 10, 1936, Walter Sillers, Jr., to J. Lake Roberson, September 12, 1934, Walter Sillers, Jr., to Mrs. W. T. Burt, September 14, 1934, Walter Sillers, Jr., Papers.

[12]Walter Sillers, Jr., to M. W. Schwartz, December 29, 1947, Walter Sillers, Jr., Papers. See also Thomas R. Melton, "Walter Sillers and National Politics (1948–1964)," *Journal of Mississippi History* 391 (August 1977), 213–25.

[13]Key, *Southern Politics,* 244–49; William D. McCain, "Theodore Gilmore Bilbo and the Mississippi Delta," *Journal of Mississippi History* 31 (February 1969), 1–27.

[14]*New York Times,* February 7, 1982; James A. Burran III, "Racial Violence in the South during World War II (Ph.D. diss., University of Tennessee, 1977), 263–65; Williams, "Mississippi and Civil Rights," 54. In some accounts the victim in the case is referred to as Leon "McAtee" rather than "McTatie."

[15]Numan V. Bartley, *The Rise of Massive Resistance: Race and Politics in the South during the 1950s* (Baton Rouge, 1969), 22, 23.

[16]Neil R. McMillen, *The Citizens' Council: Organized Resistance to the Second Reconstruction, 1954–1964* (Urbana, 1971), 16–18.

[17]Ibid., 18–21.

[18]Ibid., 21.

[19]Quoted in ibid., 24.

[20]Ibid., 24–25.

[21]Hodding Carter, "Citadel of the Citizens' Council," *New York Times Magazine,* November 12, 1961, 23.

[22]Bartley, *Rise of Massive Resistance,* 17–20, 242–43.

[23]Ibid., 104; Ellet Lawrence to All Council Officers and Members, Race Relations Collection, John D. Williams Library; McMillen, *Citizens' Council,* 209.

[24]David Halberstam, "A County Divided Against Itself," *Reporter* 13 (December 15, 1955), 30.

[25]Ibid., 31–32.

[26]Carter, "Citadel of the Citizens' Council," 125.

[27]Charles J. Lapidary, "Belzoni, Mississippi," *New Republic* 134 (May 7, 1956), 12.

[28]Ibid., 12–13.

²⁹Ibid., 12.
³⁰Carter, "Citadel of the Citizens' Council," 125.
³¹"Authentic Voice," *Time* (March 26, 1956), 2; Hollinger F. Barnard, ed., *Outside the Magic Circle: The Autobiography of Virginia Foster Durr* (Tuscaloosa, Ala., 1985), 171–72.
³²"Authentic Voice," 26.
³³"We've Reached an Era of Judicial Tyranny: An Address by Senator James O. Eastland of Mississippi before the Statewide Convention of the Association of Citizens Councils of Mississippi" (Winona, Miss., 1955?).
³⁴Hugh Stephen Whitaker, "A Case Study in Southern Justice: The Emmett Till Case" (M.A. thesis, Florida State University, 1963), 104. For a briefer account of the Till affair, see Stephen J. Whitfield, *A Death in the Delta: The Story of Emmett Till* (New York, 1988).
³⁵Whitaker, "Case Study," 104–5.
³⁶Ibid., 106
³⁷Ibid., 109–14; Henry Hampton and Steve Fayer, eds., *Voices of Freedom: An Oral History of the Civil Rights Movement from the 1950s through the 1980s* (New York, 1990), 14.
³⁸Whitaker, "Case Study," 114.
³⁹Ibid., 114–15.
⁴⁰Ibid., 119–21.
⁴¹Memphis *Commercial Appeal*, September 1, 1955; Whitaker, "Case Study," 122–24.
⁴²Whitaker, "Case Study," 124–25.
⁴³Ibid., 47, 128, 140–49.
⁴⁴Ibid., 153–55, 159.
⁴⁵Ibid., 142–44.
⁴⁶Ibid., 157, 160, 163–65.
⁴⁷Ibid., 160–62.
⁴⁸Ibid., 162; Whitfield, *Death in the Delta*, 54–55.
⁴⁹Hampton and Fayer, *Voices of Freedom*, 11; Whitaker, "Case Study," 166.
⁵⁰Whitaker, "Case Study," 172–74; Amzie Moore to James P. Kizart, December 20, 1955, Amzie Moore Papers, box 1, Wisconsin Historical Society, Madison, Wis.
⁵¹Hodding Carter, "Racial Crisis in the Deep South," *Saturday Evening Post* 228 (December 17, 1955), 75; William Lee Miller, "Trial by Tape Recorder," *Reporter* 15 (December 15, 1955), 27.
⁵²Carter, "Racial Crisis in the Deep South," 75.
⁵³Miller, "Trial by Tape Recorder," 28.
⁵⁴Ibid., 29.
⁵⁵Ibid., 29; A. E. Cox to J. P. Coleman, October 3, 1955, A. E. Cox Collection, Mitchell Memorial Library.
⁵⁶Miller, "Trial by Tape Recorder," 27.
⁵⁷*Delta Democrat-Times*, September 30, 1955; Hodding Carter to David R. Minter, October 24, 1956, Carter Correspondence, 1936.
⁵⁸Hodding Carter, "Woman Editor's War on Bigots," in Hodding Carter, *First Person Rural* (Garden City, N.Y., 1963), 218–19.
⁵⁹Ibid., 220–22.
⁶⁰Ibid., 221.

[61] Ibid., 223–24.

[62] James W. Silver, *Mississippi: The Closed Society*, 2nd ed. (New York, 1966), 39.

[63] Hazel Brannon Smith to Stephen W. Burks, July 28, 1963, Allard Lowenstein Papers, F352, SHC.

[64] *Delta Democrat-Times*, May 18, 1954.

[65] Letter to the Editor, n.d., 1953, Hodding Carter Correspondence, 1953, Hodding and Betty Werlein Carter Papers.

[66] John Gibson to Hodding Carter, June 12, 1946, Carter Correspondence, 1946; Hodding Carter, "Bloodstained Whitewash," *Saturday Review* 36 (May 23, 1953), 14.

[67] Carter, "Bloodstained Whitewash," 14; Robinson, "Hodding Carter," 204–5.

[68] Robinson, "Hodding Carter," 225–26.

[69] Numan V. Bartley and Hugh D. Graham, *Southern Politics and the Second Reconstruction* (Baltimore and London, 1975), 72.

[70] On the combination of racial and economic conservatism that characterized Mississippi's "emerging modernization consensus," see Jesse L. White, Jr., "Mississippi Electoral Politics, 1903–1976: The Emerging Modernization Consensus" (Ph.d. diss., Massachusetts Institute of Technology, 1979), vol. 2, pp. 599–602.

[71] Smith, *Congressman from Mississippi*, 88–89; Bartley and Graham, *Southern Politics and the Second Reconstruction*, 72; Tris Coffin to Jonathan Daniels, March 24, 1956, Jonathan Daniels Papers, SHC.

[72] Abney, "Mississippi Voter," 161; Smith, *Congressman from Mississippi*, 280; Jackson *Daily News*, March 16, 1958. See also Charles N. Fortenberry and F. Glenn Abney, "Mississippi: Unreconstructed and Unredeemed," in William C. Havard, ed., *The Changing Politics of the South* (Baton Rouge, 1972), 504–5.

[73] Bartley and Graham, *Southern Politics and the Second Reconstruction*, 71, 73; Walter Sillers, Jr., to Ross Barnett, September 27, 1960, Ross Barnett to Dear Friend and Fellow Official, September 6, 1961, Walter Sillers, Jr., Papers.

[74] Key, *Southern Politics*, 229.

Chapter 10. "A Testing Ground for Democracy"

[1] Tris Coffin to Jonathan Daniels, March 24, 1956, Jonathan Daniels Papers, SHC; "Dum vivamus biberimus et edimus," *Delta Review* 1 (Summer 1964), 26–27.

[2] George Patterson, "The Debutante Story," *Delta Review* 1 (Spring 1964), 17–18, 23, 48.

[3] Key, *Southern Politics*, 238; Atlanta *Constitution*, October 22, 1962.

[4] Nicholas Von Hoffman, *Mississippi Notebook* (New York, 1964), 82–84.

[5] John Dittmer, "The Politics of the Mississippi Movement, 1954–1964," in Charles W. Eagles, ed., *The Civil Rights Movement in America* (Jackson, Miss., 1986), 72–74.

[6] Neil R. McMillen, "Black Enfranchisement in Mississippi: Federal Enforcement and Black Protest in the 1960s," *Journal of Southern History* 43 (August 1977), 31; Seth Cagin and Phillip Dray, *We Are Not Afraid: The Story of Goodman, Schwerner, and Chaney and the Civil Rights Campaign for Mississippi* (New York, 1988), 192.

[7] Steven F. Lawson, *Running for Freedom: Civil Rights and Black Politics in America since 1941* (New York, 1991), 88–89; McMillen, "Black Enfranchisement," 363.

[8]Dittmer, "Politics of the Mississippi Movement," 78.

[9]Taylor Branch, *Parting the Waters: America in the King Years, 1954–1963* (New York, 1988), 718–25; McMillen, "Black Enfranchisement," 363.

[10]Dittmer, "Politics of the Mississippi Movement," 79.

[11]Joseph A. Sinsheimer, "The Freedom Vote of 1963: New Strategies of Racial Protest," *Journal of Southern History* 55 (May 1989), 233, 238.

[12]Ibid., 240–41, 243.

[13]Neil R. McMillen, "Commentary," in Eagles, ed., *Civil Rights Movement in America*, 95.

[14]Len Holt, *The Summer That Didn't End* (London, 1966), 154.

[15]Ibid., 168–69.

[16]Ibid., 169–74.

[17]Smith, *Congressman from Mississippi*, 281; Memphis *Commercial Appeal*, June 3, 1964.

[18]Memphis *Commercial Appeal*, June 3, 1964; Neil R. McMillen, "The Development of Civil Rights," in McClemore, ed., *History of Mississippi*, vol. 2 (Hattiesburg, Miss., 1973), 170–71.

[19]Affidavit II, Office Harassment—Clarksdale, Congress of Racial Equality Papers, Addendum, 1944–1968, ser. 3 (Frederick, Md., 1983), microfilm, roll 23.

[20]"Coahoma County Branch NAACP, September 7, 1963," Article 2: "Chief Fires Negro Then Arrests Him for Not Having a Job," Congress of Racial Equality Papers, Addendum, 1944–1968, ser. 3, microfilm, roll 23.

[21]Aaron Henry Interview with Neil R. McMillen and George Burson, May 1, 1972, *New York Times* Oral History Program, Mississippi Oral History Collection, John D. Williams Library, microcard 131.

[22]Hugh Stephen Whitaker, "A New Day: The Effects of Negro Enfranchisement in Selected Mississippi Counties" (Ph.D. diss., Florida State University, 1965), 71–74.

[23]"Affidavit, Willis Wright, Firing of Voter Registration Applicant, Greenwood, Miss.," Student Nonviolent Coordinating Committee Papers (hereinafter cited as SNCC Papers), Library and Archives, Martin Luther King, Jr., Center for Nonviolent Change, Atlanta, Ga.

[24]Cagin and Dray, *We Are Not Afraid*, 193.

[25]Ibid., 83, 157; Whitaker, "New Day," 184.

[26]Whitaker, "New Day," 75–76. See also Odessa Brooks Affidavit, SNCC Papers.

[27]Statement: Carrie Triplett, November 11, 1969, Delta Ministry Papers, "Police Brutality" File, Mitchell Memorial Library.

[28]"Text of Telegram to Democratic National Committee from Lawrence Guyot, Chairman, Freedom Democratic Party," Allard Lowenstein Papers.

[29]"The Civil Rights Bill in Sunflower County," James W. Silver Papers, John D. Williams Library, typescript.

[30]Affidavit 2: Office Harassment—Clarksdale; *Wall Street Journal*, August 27, 1964.

[31]*Wall Street Journal*, August 27, 1964; Whitaker, "New Day," 109.

[32]"A Delta Discussion—Issue 6," Race Relations Collection, John D. Williams Library, typescript.

[33]"A Delta Discussion—Issue 2 of a Series," Race Relations Collection, typescript; Frank E. Smith to Hodding Carter, July 24, 1964, Carter Correspondence, 1964.

[34]Frank E. Smith to Hodding Carter, July 24, 1964, Carter Correspondence; Frank E. Smith to James W. Silver, July 21, 1964, John W. Silver Papers.

[35]"A Delta Discussion—Issue 5 of a Series," Race Relations Collection.

[36]Henry Interview with McMillen and Burson, May 1, 1972.

[37]Ibid.; "It Takes Guts to Work for LBJ in Mississippi," *New Republic* 151 (October 1964), 6–7; Lemann, *Promised Land*, 46.

[38]Raines, *My Soul Is Rested*, 235–37; Tracy Sugarman, *Stranger at the Gates: A Summer in Mississippi* (New York, 1966), 72–73.

[39]Salamon, "Protest, Politics, and Modernization," 214–15, 449–52; Raines, *My Soul Is Rested*, 260.

[40]Salamon, "Protest, Politics, and Modernization," 454; Raines, *My Soul Is Rested*, 261–65.

[41]Raines, *My Soul Is Rested*, 266.

[42]Fannie Lou Hamer Interview with Neil McMillen, April 14, 1972, *New York Times* Oral History Program, Mississippi Oral History Collection, microcard 130.

[43]Ibid.; Collum, "Stepping Out into Freedom."

[44]Hamer Interview with McMillen, April 14, 1972; Raines, *My Soul Is Rested*, 249.

[45]Raines, *My Soul Is Rested*, 250–51; Hamer Interview with McMillen, April 14, 1972; *New York Times*, March 16, 1977.

[46]*New York Times*, March 16, 1977; Collum, "Stepping Out into Freedom."

[47]Sugarman, *Stranger at the Gates*, 120–21.

[48]Edwin King, "Go Tell It on the Mountain," reprint from *Sojourners* (December 1982), n.p., copy in possession of the author.

[49]Raines, *My Soul Is Rested*, 254; Jackson *Clarion-Ledger*, March 18, 1977.

[50]Frank R. Parker, *Black Votes Count: Political Empowerment in Mississippi after 1965* (Chapel Hill and London, 1990), 34–40, 51–66. See also Frank R. Parker, "Mississippi's 'Massive Resistance' to Black Political Empowerment after Passage of the Voting Rights Acts, 1965 to 1970," paper prepared for presentation at the sixteenth annual meeting of the National Conference of Black Political Scientists, Chicago, Ill., April 2–5, 1986.

[51]Parker, *Black Votes Count*, 41–51.

[52]Ibid., 40, 55.

[53]Voter Education Project, Southern Regional Council, Inc., *Voter Registration in the South: Summer 1968* (Atlanta, 1968), mimeo, n.p.

[54]Leslie Burl McClemore, "The Mississippi Freedom Democratic Party: A Case Study of Grassroots Politics" (Ph.D. diss., University of Massachusetts, 1971), 381–82.

[55]Ibid., 382–83.

[56]Ibid., 384–86; "Mississippi: The Last Citadel," *Newsweek* (January 15, 1968), 23.

[57]Robert Analavage, "Bitter Defeat in Sunflower," *National Guardian* (May 13, 1967), clipping in Fanny Lou Hamer Papers, John D. Williams Library, microfilm, roll 7.

[58]Jack Bass and Walter Devries, *The Transformation of Southern Politics: Social Change and Political Consequence since 1945* (New York, 1976), 208; Lester Salamon, "Mississippi Post-Mortem: The 1971 Election," *New South* 27 (Winter 1972), 45.

[59]Neal R. Peirce, *The Deep South States of America: People, Politics, and Power in the Seven Deep South States* (New York, 1972), 185.

[60]Salamon, "Mississippi Post-Mortem," 46–47.

[61]U.S. Commission on Civil Rights, *The Voting Rights Act: Ten Years After* (Washington, 1975), 178–80; Melany Neilson, *Even Mississippi* (Tuscaloosa, Ala., 1986), 35, 38–39.

[62]Paul Zimmerman, "The Patience of a Saint," *Sports Illustrated* 54 (June 8, 1981), 99.

[63]*Delta Democrat-Times,* May 26, 1971.

[64]*Delta Democrat-Times,* May 26, 27, June 6, 1971.

[65]Tony Dunbar, *Our Land, Too* (New York, 1971), 229–30.

[66]Neilson, *Even Mississippi,* 37.

[67]Frederick M. Wirt, *The Politics of Southern Equality: Law and Social Change in a Mississippi County* (Chicago, 1970), 303, 319.

[68]Ibid., 166–67.

[69]Neilson, *Even Mississippi,* 43.

[70]Wirt, *Politics of Southern Equality,* 166–68.

[71]Holland, "Memories of the Mississippi Delta," 246.

[72]Wirt, *Politics of Southern Equality,* 318–20; Richard Dallas Chesteen, "Change and Reaction in a Mississippi Delta Civil Community" (Ph.D. diss., University of Mississippi, 1975), 147.

[73]Raines, *My Soul Is Rested,* 301–2.

[74]Ibid., 302; Peirce, *Deep South States,* 164.

[75]Salamon, "Mississippi Post-Mortem," 47. Insofar as the relationship between economic progress and political empowerment was concerned, the effects of poverty on Delta blacks were compounded by the relative affluence of many of their white antagonists. When the nonmetropolitan counties of Mississippi were considered, the Delta's percentage of the state's families with incomes in excess of fifty thousand dollars in 1970 (22.9) was actually greater than its percentage of the families with incomes less than 75 percent of the poverty level (20.5). U.S. Bureau of the Census, *Census of Population: 1970,* vol. 1, *Characteristics of the Population, Part 26: Mississippi* (Washington, 1973), 190–91, 202–310.

Chapter 11. "Somebody Done Nailed Us on the Cross"

[1]Cagin and Dray, *We Are Not Afraid,* 182.

[2]Bartley, *Rise of Massive Resistance,* 34.

[3]Joseph Blotner, *Faulkner: A Biography,* vol. 2 (New York, 1974), 1416–17; Smith, *Congressman from Mississippi,* 280; Bartley, *Rise of Massive Resistance,* 243–44.

[4]"The Mississippi Delta (Part 1)," COFO Publication 2, and "The Mississippi Delta (Part 2)," COFO Publication 3, SNCC Papers, typescripts.

[5]Ralph W. Alewine, Jr., "The Changing Characteristics of the Mississippi Delta," in U.S. Department of Labor, Manpower Administration, "Farm Labor Developments," May 1968, mimeo, 32–37.

[6]Ibid., 37; Foster Davis, "The Delta: Rich Land and Poor People," *Reporter* (March 24, 1966), 42; William M. Seabron to David B. Filvaroff, February 7, 1966, box 85, Employment, Records of the Secretary of Agriculture RG 16, NA.

[7]Hodding Carter, Jr., "Negro Exodus from the Delta Continues," *New York Times Magazine,* March 10, 1968, 26.

[8]Des Moines *Register,* February 27, 1968.

[9]Lemann, *Promised Land,* 319; Carter, "Negro Exodus."

[10]Alewine, "Changing Characteristics of the Mississippi Delta," 38–39; Carter, "Negro Exodus from the Delta Continues," 26.

¹¹Carter, "Negro Exodus from the Delta Continues," 120; Des Moines *Register,* February 25, 1968.

¹²Des Moines *Register,* February 25, 1968; U.S. Congress, Senate, Subcommittee on Employment, Manpower, and Poverty of the Committee on Labor and Public Welfare, *Examination of the War on Poverty,* pt. 2: *Jackson, Mississippi,* 90th Cong., 1st. sess., April 10, 1967, p. 725.

¹³Des Moines *Register,* February 25, 1968.

¹⁴Ibid., U.S. Congress, Senate, Subcommittee on Employment, Manpower, and Poverty of the Committee on Labor and Public Welfare, *Examination of the War on Poverty: First Session on Hunger and Malnutrition in America,* 90th Cong., 1st sess., July 11–12, 1967, p. 271.

¹⁵Tony Dunbar, *Our Land, Too* (New York, 1971), 76–83.

¹⁶Des Moines *Register,* February 25, 1968.

¹⁷Ibid., February 25, 28, 1968.

¹⁸U.S. Congress, Senate, Committee on Appropriations, *Hearings on H.R. 16913,* 90th Cong., 2nd sess., March 29, April 26, 1968, pp. 561–69, 1492; Des Moines *Register,* February 25, 1968.

¹⁹Des Moines *Register,* February 25, 28, 1968.

²⁰U.S. Congress, Senate, Committee on Appropriations, *Hearings on H.R. 16913,* 561–619, 1492.

²¹Congressional Quarterly Service, *Congress and the Nation: A Review of Government and Politics,* vol. 2: *1965–1968* (Washington, 1969), 339, 359, 373, 729; Alan Ehrenhalt, ed., *Politics in America: The 100th Congress* (Washington, 1987), 822–23; Peirce, *Deep South States of America,* 202; Steven F. Lawson, *In Pursuity of Power: Southern Blacks and Electoral Politics, 1965–1982* (New York, 1985), 21.

²²New York *Times,* February 4, 1962.

²³"Memo for the Files, the Secretary," February 17, 1965, box 92, Farm Program, Records of the Secretary of Agriculture, NA.

²⁴Committee on Appropriations, *Hearings on H.R. 16913,* 569; Nicholas Von Hoffman, *Mississippi Notebook* (New York, 1964), 79–81.

²⁵Von Hoffman, *Mississippi Notebook,* 81, 84–86.

²⁶Nick Kotz, *Let Them Eat Promises: The Politics of Hunger in America* (Englewood Cliffs, 1969), 92; Donald C. Mosley and D. C. Williams, Jr., "An Analysis and Evaluation of a Community Action Anti-Poverty Program in the Mississippi Delta" (College of Business and Industry, Mississippi State University, Starkville, Miss., 1967); Leon Howell, *Freedom City: The Substance of Things Hoped For* (Richmond, 1969), 17; Lemann, *Promised Land,* 316.

²⁷Walker Percy, "Mississippi: The Fallen Paradise," *Harper's* 230 (April 1965), 169–70.

²⁸Charles Evers and Aaron Henry to Lyndon B. Johnson, November 21, 1967, box 96, Food Stamp Program, Records of the Secretary of Agriculture, NA.

²⁹Jackson *Daily News,* June 25, 1967.

³⁰Subcommittee on Employment, Manpower, and Poverty, *Examination of the War on Poverty: First Session on Hunger and Malnutrition in America,* pp. 262–63.

³¹Ibid., 264.

³²Ibid., 264, 265, 271.

³³Ibid., 264.

³⁴Ibid., 13, 227, 260, 281–82, 294.

³⁵Ibid., 49, 290.

[36]Subcommittee on Employment, Manpower, and Poverty, *Examination of the War on Poverty*, pt. 2, pp. 713–14.

[37]Ibid., 714.

[38]Subcommittee on Employment, Manpower, and Poverty, *Examination of the War on Poverty, First Session on Hunger and Malnutrition in America*, p. 46.

[39]Ibid., 19.

[40]Subcommittee on Employment, Manpower, and Poverty, *Examination of the War on Poverty*, pt. 2, p. 868.

[41]Subcommittee on Employment, Manpower, and Poverty, *Examination of the War on Poverty: First Session on Hunger and Malnutrition in America*, pp. 27, 52.

[42]Victor Ullman, "In Darkest America," *Nation* 205 (September 4, 1967), 180.

[43]"Genocide in Mississippi," Student Non-Violent Coordinating Committee Papers, 1959–1972, microfilm, 73 reels (Sanford, N.C., 1982), reel 19; Lemann, *Promised Land*, 49.

[44]*Delta Democrat-Times*, May 21, 1964; Lawrence Guyot and Mike Thelwell, "The Politics of Necessity and Survival in Mississippi," *Freedomways* 6 (Spring 1966), 130; Miss. Code Ann. & 97-29-11 (1972 & Suppl. 1990).

[45]Howell, *Freedom City*, 18.

[46]Foster Davis, "Darkness on the Delta," *Reporter* (September 21, 1967), 37; Jackson *Daily News*, June 25, 1967.

[47]Subcommittee on Employment, Manpower, and Poverty, *Examination of the War on Poverty: First Session on Hunger and Malnutrition in America*, p. 64; B. F. Smith to Betty W. Carter, February 28, 1966, "Unpublished Ms. Notes on DM," Hodding and Betty Werlein Carter Papers.

[48]Jackson *Clarion-Ledger*, June 1, 1965, June 4, 1965; Chattanooga *Times*, June 7, 1965.

[49]Jackson *Clarion-Ledger*, June 4, 1965.

[50]Claude Ramsay, "A Report on the Delta Farm Strike," box 1, James W. Silver Collection, John D. Williams Library.

[51]Howell, *Freedom City*, 27–28.

[52]Ibid., 29.

[53]Ibid., 30–32; Memphis *Commercial Appeal*, February 1, 1966.

[54]"Why We Are at the Greenville Air Force Base," January 31, 1966, SNCC Papers.

[55]Ibid.

[56]Memphis *Commercial Appeal*, February 2, 1966; "Events at the Airbase," SNCC Papers, typescript; Howell, *Freedom City*, 37.

[57]"We Have No Government," transcript of a press conference held in the Greenville office of the Delta Ministry, February 1, 1966, SNCC Papers.

[58]Ibid.

[59]Ibid.; Howell, *Freedom City*, 43; *National Observer*, February 21, 1966.

[60]Lemann, *Promised Land*, 319–20; Orville L. Freeman to Robert S. McNamara, February 5, 1966, Employment, box 85, Records of the Secretary of Agriculture.

[61]"Secret' Crisis in the Delta," *Newsweek* (March 7, 1966), 27–29.

[62]Davis, "Darkness on the Delta," 42.

[63]"We Have No Government"; Robert E. Anderson, Jr., "Welfare in Mississippi: Tradition vs. Title VI," *New South* 22 (Spring 1967), 69; Marvin Hoffman and John Mudd, "The New Plantations," *Nation* (October 24, 1966), 413.

[64]*National Observer*, February 21, 1966.

[65]James Edwards to William M. Seabron, October 19, 1967, box 96, Food Stamp Program, Records of the Secretary of Agriculture.

[66]Jackson *Daily News,* September 30, 1966; "Shriver Drops CDGM," *New Republic* (October 15, 1966), 7; *New York Times,* October 19, 1966; Washington *Evening Star,* November 9, 1966.

[67]Dittmer, "Politics of the Mississippi Movement," 91–92.

[68]Jackson *Clarion-Ledger,* September 27, 1981, June 7, 1989; Bill Minor, "Congressman Espy from Mississippi," *Southern Changes* 8 (December 1986), 1; Lemann, *Promised Land,* 331; Tony Dunbar, *Delta Time* (New York, 1990), 70.

[69]M. C. Farray, "Tunica, Mississippi: Profile," typescript in possession of the author; Memphis *Commercial Appeal,* May 4, 7, 8, 1986.

[70]U.S. Bureau of the Census, *County and City Data Book: 1983* (Washington, 1983), 306, 320

[71]Mississippi Research and Development Center, *Handbook of Selected Data for Mississippi* (Jackson, 1983), 17; Jackson *Clarion-Ledger,* December 17, 1980, August 25, 1985, November 30, 1988.

[72]Jackson *Clarion-Ledger,* December 17, 1980.

[73]Ibid., February 17, 1978, December 17, 1980; *Delta Democrat-Times,* June 27, 1968, clipping, Delta Ministry "Coahoma County" folder, Mitchell Memorial Library.

[74]Jackson *Clarion-Ledger,* December 17, 1980.

[75]Subcommittee on Employment, Manpower, and Poverty, *Examination of the War on Poverty: First Session on Hunger and Malnutrition in America,* p. 53.

[76]Nicholas Lemann, "The Origins of the Underclass," *Atlantic Monthly* 257 (June 1986), 41–43, 47, and *Promised Land,* 287.

[77]Lemann, *Promised Land,* 287.

Chapter 12. "The Blues Is a Lowdown Shakin' Chill"

[1]W. C. Handy, *Father of the Blues: An Autobiography* (London, 1957), 76–77.

[2]David Evans, "Blues," in Charles Reagan Wilson and William Ferris, eds., *Encyclopedia of Southern Culture* (Chapel Hill, 1989), 959–98.

[3]Evans, "Blues," 995.

[4]Michele Bernardinelli, "Report on Italian Peonage Matters in Mississippi, March 1909," in Department of Justice, Central Files, Classified Subject File Correspondence, RG 60, box 10803, NA; Levine, *Black Culture and Black Consciousness,* 223–24.

[5]Levine, *Black Culture and Black Consciousness,* 221; David Evans, *Big Road Blues: Tradition and Creativity in the Folk Blues* (Berkeley, Los Angeles, and London, 1982), 43.

[6]Ibid.; Evans, "Blues," 996; Levine, *Black Culture and Black Consciousness,* 218.

[7]Levine, *Black Culture and Black Consciousness,* 222.

[8]Barlow, *Looking Up at Down,* 33–35; Robert Palmer, *Deep Blues* (New York, 1981), 48–50.

[9]Palmer, *Deep Blues,* 50–53; Barlow, *Looking Up at Down,* 35.

[10]Barlow, *Looking Up at Down,* 35–46; Palmer, *Deep Blues,* 62–63.

[11]Palmer, *Deep Blues,* 62; Pete Daniel to the author, May 28, 1991.

[12]Handy, *Father of the Blues*, 77.

[13]Palmer, *Deep Blues*, 61–62.

[14]Peter Guralnick, *Feel like Going Home: Portraits in Blues and Rock 'n' Roll* (New York, 1989), 50.

[15]Palmer, *Deep Blues*, 44.

[16]Levine, *Black Culture and Black Consciousness*, 221.

[17]Evans, *Big Road Blues*, 40.

[18]Barlow, *Looking Up at Down*, 6.

[19]Wright, *Old South, New South*, 66.

[20]Houston A. Baker, Jr., *Blues, Ideology, and Afro-American Literature: A Vernacular Theory* (Chicago and London, 1984), 11; Paul Oliver, *Blues Fell This Morning: The Meaning of the Blues* (London, 1960), 70.

[21]Barlow, *Looking Up at Down*, 6; McMillen, *Dark Journey*, 271–72.

[22]Nathans, "Gotta Mind to Move," 220.

[23]Guralnick, *Feel like Going Home*, 67; Evans, *Big Road Blues*, 19.

[24]Joel Williamson, *The Crucible of Race: Black-White Relations in the American South since Emancipation* (New York, 1984), 213.

[25]Charley Patton, "Bird Nest Bound," quoted in Evans, *Big Road Blues*, 19.

[26]Levine, *Black Culture and Black Consciousness*, 237.

[27]Ibid.; Larry Neal, "The Ethos of the Blues," *Black Scholar* 3 (Summer 1972), 45. See also Giles Oakley, *The Devil's Music: A History of the Blues* (New York, 1978), 50–51.

[28]Levine, *Black Culture and Black Consciousness*, 154–89, 261, 326–30, 519; Steve West, "The Devil Visits the Delta: A View of His Role in the Blues," *Mississippi Folklore Register* 19 (Spring 1985), 12; Robert Johnson, "If I Had Possession over Judgment Day," in Michael Taft, *Blues Lyric Poetry: An Anthology* (New York and London, 1983), 148; Son House, "Preachin' the Blues," in Eric Sackheim, comp., *The Blues Line: A Collection of Blues Lyrics* (New York, 1969), 212.

[29]Jeff Todd Titon, *Early Downhome Blues* (Urbana, 1977), 33; Taulbert, *Once upon a Time*, 45–46.

[30]Levine, *Black Culture and Black Consciousness*, 234.

[31]Frederick Jay Hay, "The Delta Blues and Black Society: An Examination of Change (1900–1960) in Style and Community" (M.A. Thesis, University of Virginia, 1981), 119.

[32]Palmer, *Deep Blues*, 59: Barlow, *Looking Up at Down*, 39.

[33]Hay, "Delta Blues," 129–30.

[34]Barry Lee Pearson, *"Sounds So Good to Me": The Bluesman's Story* (Philadelphia, 1984), 66; Palmer, *Deep Blues*, 107–8.

[35]Palmer, *Deep Blues*, 59–60.

[36]Samuel Charters, *Robert Johnson* (New York, 1973), 17.

[37]Ibid., 18.

[38]Palmer, *Deep Blues*, 113, 111.

[39]Peetie Wheatstraw, "Peetie Wheatstraw Stomp" and "Peetie Wheatstraw Stomp No. 2," in Taft, *Blues Lyric Poetry*, 298. See also West, "Devil Visits the Delta," 18–20; Ralph Ellison, *Invisible Man* (New York, 1972), 134.

[40]Palmer, *Deep Blues*, 59–60; West, "Devil Visits the Delta," 13.

[41]Barlow, *Looking Up at Down*, 50, 21.

[42]Pearson, *"Sounds So Good to Me,"* 67.

[43] Charley Patton, "Mississippi Bo Weavil Blues," in Taft, *Blues Lyric Poetry*, 210. See also Oakley, *Devil's Music*, 58–59.

[44] Oliver, *Blues Fell This Morning*, 70.

[45] Handy, *Father of the Blues*, 74; Oliver, *Blues Fell This Morning*, 74.

[46] Charley Patton, "Pea Vine Blues," in Taft, *Blues Lyric Poetry*, 211–12.

[47] Robert Johnson, "Ramblin' on My Mind," in Taft, *Blues Lyric Poetry*, 146; Palmer, *Deep Blues*, 117–18.

[48] Evans, *Big Road Blues*, 189.

[49] Robert Johnson, "Terraplane Blues," in Taft, *Blues Lyric Poetry*, 147.

[50] Paul Oliver, *Screening the Blues: Aspects of the Blues Tradition* (London, 1968), 199.

[51] William R. Ferris, "The Blues Family," *Southern Exposure* 5 (Summer/Fall 1977), 22; Robert Johnson, "Come On in My Kitchen" and "Stones in My Passway," in Taft, comp., *Blues Lyric Poetry*, 149.

[52] Alan Lomax, "The Land Where the Blues Began: A Transcript and Study Guide to the Film" (Jackson, Miss., 1982)," 11.

[53] Liner notes, "Robert Johnson/King of the Delta Blues Singers," Columbia Records, CL1654.

[54] Levine, *Black Culture and Black Consciousness*, 338.

[55] *James "Son" Thomas Exhibition of Clay Sculpture, January 17–February 22, 1985, University Art Gallery, New Mexico State University, Las Cruces, N.M.*

[56] Ibid.

[57] Russell J. Linnemann, "Country Blues: Mirror of Southern Society," *Western Journal of Black Studies* 9 (1985), 185.

[58] Lomax, "Land Where the Blues Began," 18.

[59] Powdermaker, *After Freedom*, 192–93.

[60] Wright, "Long Black Song," 126.

[61] Furry Lewis, "Furry's Blues," in Taft, *Blues Lyric Poetry*, 169; Barlow, *Looking Up at Down*, 22.

[62] Lonnie Johnson, "Low Land Moon," and Robert Johnson, "Me and the Devil Blues," in Taft, *Blues Lyric Poetry*, 140, 150.

[63] Wright, "Long Black Song," 118–19, 125.

[64] Louise Johnson, "On the Wall," and Mattie Delaney, "Down the Big Road Blues," in Taft, *Blues Lyric Poetry*, 144, 76.

[65] Robert Johnson, "I'm a Steady Rollin' Man" and "From Four Until Late"; Louise Johnson, "All Night Long Blues"; and Mattie Delaney, "Down the Big Road Blues," all in Taft, *Blues Lyric Poetry*, 149, 144, 76.

[66] Son House, "Dry Spell Blues—Part 1," in Taft, *Blues Lyric Poetry*, 112–13; Muddy Waters, "Flood," quoted in Palmer, *Deep Blues*, 168–69.

[67] Robert Johnson, "Preachin' Blues," in Taft, *Blues Lyric Poetry*, 148.

[68] Lonnie Johnson, "Devil's Got the Blues," in Taft, *Blues Lyric Poetry*, 143.

[69] Lomax, "Land Where the Blues Began," 6; Lawrence Goodwyn, *The Populist Moment: A Short History of the Agrarian Revolt in America* (Oxford, London, and New York, 1978), 320; Levine, *Black Culture and Black Consciousness*, 283.

[70] Ralph Ellison, "Richard Wright's Blues," in Ellison, *Shadow and Act* (New York, 1972), 88–89; Lomax, "Land Where the Blues Began," 11.

[71] Levine, *Black Culture and Black Consciousness*, 226–28; Bill C. Malone, *Southern Music, American Music* (Lexington, Ky., 1979), 97–98.

[72]Ibid.

[73]Ibid.; Palmer, *Deep Blues*, 222–23.

[74]Palmer, *Deep Blues*, 223–25.

[75]Ibid., 224–25; Malone, *Southern Music*, 101–2; Nick Tosches, *Country: Living Legends and Dying Metaphors in America's Biggest Music* (New York, 1985), 45.

[76]Charlie Gillett, *The Sound of the City: The Rise of Rock and Roll*, rev. ed. (New York, 1983), 28.

[77]Dave McGee, "Carl Perkins," *Rolling Stone* (April 19, 1990), 75.

[78]For a thorough discussion of the themes of country music, see Bill C. Malone, *Country Music USA: A Fifty-Year History* (Austin, 1975).

[79]Patrick Carr, "Killer Verite," *Southern* 3 (July/August 1989), 75; Malone, *Southern Music*, 103.

[80]Gillett, *Sound of the City*, 8; Robert Palmer, "The 50s," *Rolling Stone* (April 19, 1990), 46.

[81]Barlow, *Looking Up at Down*, 336.

[82]Malone, *Southern Music*, 105.

[83]Barlow, *Looking Up at Down*, 337.

[84]Jim Curtis, *Rock Eras: Interpretations of Music and Society, 1954–1984* (Bowling Green, Ohio, 1987), 39; Tosches, *Country*, 100, 73; Gillett, *Sound of the City*, 17–18.

[85]Richard Petersen, "Why 1955? Explaining the Advent of Rock Music," *Popular Music* 9 (January 1990), 113.

[86]Palmer, "The 50s," 48; Barlow, *Looking Up at Down*, 336–37; Gillett, *Sound of the City*, 168.

[87]Malone, *Southern Music*, 99.

[88]The Rolling Stones to Muddy Waters, April 4, 1975, in *Muddy Waters* (pamphlet accompanying "Muddy Waters: The Chess Box" (recordings, 1990), 24; Palmer, *Deep Blues*, 259–60.

[89]Palmer, *Deep Blues*, 262–63; Guralnick, *Feel like Going Home*, 28.

[90]*Robert Johnson: The Complete Recordings* (pamphlet accompanying "Robert Johnson: The Complete Recordings" [1990]), 21, 23; "There's Blues in the News," *Newsweek* (November 12, 1990), 72–74; Guralnick, *Feel like Going Home*, 61.

Chapter 13. "More Writers per Square Foot . . ."

[1]Baton Rouge *Morning Advocate* (Magazine Section), September 14, 1952, clipping in Hodding and Betty Werlein Carter Papers (Publications 1952); Delta Farm Press, March 6, 1947, clipping in Subject File, "Delta, The," MDAH; Holmes Adams, "Writers of Greenville, Mississippi, 1915–1950, *Journal of Mississippi History* 32 (August 1970), 229–44.

[2]*Delta Democrat-Times*, May 2, 1982.

[3]Ibid.; *New York Times*, May 4, 1982; Whitaker, "New Day," 67; Holmes Adams, "Writers of Greenville, Mississippi, 1915–1950," *Journal of Mississippi History* 32 (August 1970), 229.

[4]"The Delta Heart," in Worthington Family Papers.

[5]Percy, *Lanterns on the Levee*, 7; Baker, *Percys of Mississippi*, 1–5.

[6]Baker, *Percys of Mississippi*, 5.

[7] Ibid., 59–62.

[8] Cohn, *Where I Was Born and Raised,* 16–17; Richard Tillinghast, "Interview with Shelby Foote," in William C. Carter, ed., *Conversations with Shelby Foote* (Jackson, Miss., 1989), 228.

[9] Cohn, *Where I Was Born and Raised,* 16; Baker, *Percys of Mississippi,* 59–63.

[10] Lewellyn Lee Jordan, "A Biographical Sketch of David L. Cohn" (M.A. thesis, University of Mississippi, 1963), 47–53; David L. Cohn, "Eighteenth Century Chevalier," *Virginia Quarterly Review* 21 (August 1955), 561–75; Baker, *Percys of Mississippi,* 168.

[11] Hodding Carter, *Flood Crest* (New York, 1947) and *The Ballad of Catfoot Grimes and Other Verses* (Garden City, N.Y., 1964).

[12] Baker, *Percys of Mississippi,* 162–63.

[13] John G. Jones, Interview with Walker Percy, August 10, 1981, in John G. Jones, *Mississippi Writers Talking* 2 (Jackson, Miss., University Press of Mississippi, 1982), 18.

[14] Elizabeth Spencer, *This Crooked Way* (New York, 1952), 129; Tillinghast, "Interview with Shelby Foote," 221; Robert L. Phillips, ed., *Mississippi Writers in Context: Transcripts of "A Climate for Genius," A Television Series* (Jackson, Miss., 1976), 29; John Carr, "It's Worth a Grown Man's Time: An Interview with Shelby Foote," in Carter, ed., *Conversations with Shelby Foote,* 38.

[15] Faulkner, *Dollar Cotton,* 165.

[16] Cohn, *Where I Was Born and Raised,* 320; Florence Warfield Sillers Memoirs; Jackson *Daily News,* May 6, 1982.

[17] Percy, *Lanterns on the Levee,* 3; William Faulkner, "The Old Man," in Faulkner, *Three Famous Short Novels* (New York, 1961), 115–16; Shelby Foote, *Tournament,* 2nd ed. (Birmingham, Ala., 1987), 103.

[18] Walker Percy, "Uncle Will's House," *Architectural Digest* 41 (October 1984), 44.

[19] Richard Wright, "Down by the Riverside," in Wright, *Uncle Tom's Children,* 54–102. See also William Howard, "Richard Wright's Flood Stories and the Great Mississippi River Flood of 1927: Social and Historical Backgrounds," *Southern Literary Journal* 26 (Spring 1984), 44–62.

[20] Peirce, *Deep South States of America,* 227; Beverly Lowry, *Emma Blue* (Garden City, N.Y., 1982), 187; Eudora Welty, *Delta Wedding* (New York, 1974), 4; Paul Simon, quoted in Dunbar, *Delta Time,* xviii.

[21] Robert Penn Warren, *Segregation: The Inner Conflict in the South* (New York, 1956), 4; Cohn, *Where I Was Born and Raised,* 31; Ellen Gilchrist, "Revenge," in Gilchrist, *In the Land of Dreamy Dreams* (Boston, 1981), 115.

[22] Shelby Foote, *Jordan County: A Landscape in Narrative* (New York, 1954), 242; Charles Bell, *The Married Land* (Boston, 1962), 397; William Alexander Percy, "In the Delta," in *The Collected Poems of William Alexander Percy* (New York, 1950), 191; Morris, *North toward Home,* 138.

[23] Ellen Douglas, "Hold On," in Douglas, *Black Cloud, White Cloud* (Boston, 1963), 162; David L. Cohn, "Growing Up in Greenville," in Cohn, unpublished autobiography, John D. Williams Library.

[24] James Harkness, "Mississippi Footprints," *American Spectator* 19 (February 1986), 24.

[25] Eudora Welty, "The Hitchikers," in *The Collected Stories of Eudora Welty* (New York, 1980), 62–74.

[26]Tennessee Williams, *The Glass Menagerie* (New York, 1966), 65–66; Ellen Gilchrist, "Traveller," in Gilchrist, *Land of Dreamy Dreams*, 145.

[27]Gilchrist, "Traveler," 151; Ellen Douglas, *Where the Dreams Cross* (Boston, 1968), 302–3; Ellen Gilchrist, *The Annunciation* (Boston, 1983), 3, 58.

[28]Tennessee Williams, *Cat on a Hot Tin Roof*, in *Five Plays by Tennessee Williams* (London, 1962), 40, 45, 51.

[29]Williams, *Glass Menagerie*, 10.

[30]Cohn, *Where I Was Born and Raised*, x–xi, 320.

[31]Palmer, *Deep Blues*, 19; Ken Bennett, "The Language of the Blues in Faulkner's 'That Evening Sun,'" *Mississippi Quarterly* 38 (Summer 1985), 339–42; William Faulkner, "That Evening Sun," in *Collected Stories of William Faulkner* (New York, 1950), 292.

[32]Richard Wright, "Long Black Song," 118–19.

[33]Ellison, "Richard Wright's Blues," 78–79.

[34]Holland, "Memories of the Mississippi Delta," 256–58.

[35]Ellen Douglas, "I Just Love Carrie Lee" and "Hold On," in Douglas, *Black Cloud, White Cloud*, 117–41, 142–232, and *Can't Quit You Baby* (New York, 1988), 254.

[36]Charles East, "Night Watch," in Charles East, *Where the Music Was* (New York, 1965), 166.

[37]Ibid., 162.

[38]Tillinghast, "Interview with Shelby Foote," 220; Faulkner, *Dollar Cotton*, 259–60.

[39]Cohn, *Where I was Born and Raised*, 30; Cohn, "It Ain't What I Owes that Worries Me," in Cohn, unpublished autobiography, John D. Williams Library.

[40]Cohn, *Where I Was Born and Raised*, x, 299; Samuel C. Adams, Jr., "The Acculturation of the Delta Negro," *Social Forces* 26 (December 1947), 203.

[41]Sleepy John Estes, "Workin' Man Blues," in Taft, *Blues Lyric Poetry*, 87.

[42]John W. Wilson, "Delta Revival," *English Journal* 38 (March 1949), 124.

[43]Richard H. King, "Mourning and Melancholia: Will Percy and the Southern Tradition," *Virginia Quarterly Review* 43 (Spring 1977), 254.

[44]Baker, *Percys of Mississippi*, 158–59; Bertram Wyatt-Brown, "Walker, Will, and Honor Dying: The Percys and Literary Creativity," in Winfred B. Moore, Jr., and Joseph F. Tripp, eds., *Looking South: Chapters in the Story of an American Region* (Westport, Conn., 1989), 229–58.

[45]William Alexander Percy, "The White Plague," Percy Family Papers, typescript; Baker, *Percys of Mississippi*, 159–60.

[46]Cohn, *Where I Was Born and Raised*, 33–36; Baker, *Percys of Mississippi*, 193. On Will Percy's influence on his adopted son, see Suzanne B. Watkins, "From Physician to Novelist: The Progression of Walker Percy" (Ph.D. diss., New York University, 1977), 25–36. See also Walker Percy to Shelby Foote, August 4, 1970, Walker Percy Correspondence, SHC.

[47]Tillinghast, "Interview with Shelby Foote," 228. For a general discussion of the responses of southern writers to modernization, see James C. Cobb, "Southern Writers and the Challenge of Regional Convergence: A Comparative Perspective," *Georgia Historical Quarterly* 73 (Spring 1989), 1–25.

[48]Michael Grimwood, *Heart in Conflict: Faulkner's Struggles with Vocation* (Athens, Ga., and London, 1987), 254–63; Faulkner, *Go Down Moses*, 364, and "Mississippi" in James B. Merriwether, ed., *Essays, Speeches, and Public Letters* (New York, 1965), 36.

[49]Cohn, *Where I Was Born and Raised*, 41, 299–327.

378   *Notes*

[50]Ibid., 327–30.

[51]Silver, "Mississippi: The Closed Society," 44.

[52]Robinson, "Hodding Carter," 120, 90–91.

[53]John T. Kneebone, *Southern Liberal Journalists and the Issue of Race, 1920–1944* (Chapel Hill and London, 1985), 216.

[54]"The Fence Rider," anonymous typescript, n.d., Walter Sillers, Jr., Papers; Kneebone, *Southern Liberal Jouralists,* 222; Robinson, "Hodding Carter," 212–13.

[55]Robinson, "Hodding Carter," 263. Carter is quoted in Harry D. Marsh, "Hodding Carter's Newspaper on School Desegregation, 1954–1955," *Journalism Monographs* no. 92 (May 1985), 6–8.

[56]Hodding Carter, Jr., "The Old South Had Something Worth Saving," *New York Times Magazine,* December 4, 1966, p. 170.

[57]Ibid., 179.

[58]Smith, *Congressman from Mississippi,* 87; Bilbo Speech, John Gibson, telegram to Hodding Carter, June 12, 1946, Carter Correspondence, 1946; "The Fence Rider," Walter Sillers, Jr., Papers.

[59]Betty W. Carter, Interview with Orley B. Caudill, August 17, 1977, University of Southern Mississippi, Oral History Collection, transcript in Carter Papers; Robinson, "Hodding Carter," 207, 249.

[60] Gary Boulard, "'The Man' versus 'The Quisling': Theodore Bilbo, Hodding Carter, and the 1946 Democratic Primary," *Journal of Mississippi History* 51 (August 1989), 207. On Hodding Carter's affection for Greenville, see Carter, "I'll Never Leave My Town," *Saturday Evening Post* 232 (June 4, 1960), 19–20, 58, 61.

[61]Jackson *Clarion-Ledger,* January 5, 1986; *Delta Democrat-Times,* January 2, 1967; Walker Percy, "Mississippi: The Fallen Paradise," *Harper's* 230 (April 1965), 170.

[62]Morris, *North toward Home,* 140–41.

[63]Neilson, *Even Mississippi,* 36.

[64]Ron Hollander, "Down Home in the Delta," *Town and Country* 138 (March 1984), 119; Peirce, *Deep South States,* 231–32.

[65]Vance, *Human Geography of the South,* 266; Coffin to Daniels, March 24, 1956; Atlanta *Constitution,* October 22, 1962; Gladney, "A Letter from Lillian Smith," 33.

[66]Peirce, *Deep South States,* 227.

[67]Philadelphia *Inquirer,* August 25, 1983; Rheta Grimsley Johnson, "The Delta Remains Home to the Mythical South," Memphis *Commercial Appeal,* July 8, 1990, sec. B, p. 1.

[68]Dunbar, *Delta Time,* xviii; Philadelphia *Inquirer,* August 25, 1983; Johnson, "The Delta Remains Home"; W. Hampton Sides, "Interview: Richard Ford," *Memphis* 10 (February 1986), 42.

[69]Cash, *Mind of the South,* 439–40. On Cash, see C. Vann Woodward, "The Elusive Mind of the South," *American Counterpoint: Slavery and Racism in the North-South Dialogue* (Boston, 1971), 261–83. Cohn, *Where I Was Born and Raised,* 15; Dunbar, *Delta Time,* 98.

[70]Cash, *Mind of the South,* 426.

[71]Key, *Southern Politics,* 240; Peirce, *Deep South States,* 227; Johnson, "The Delta Remains Home." See also *New York Times,* April 21, 1991; *Wall Street Journal,* October 3, 1989.

[72]Howard Zinn, *The Southern Mystique* (New York, 1964), 263.

[73]F. Garvin Davenport, *The Myth of Southern History: Historical Consciousness in Twentieth-Century Southern Literature* (Nashville, 1970), 99.

Epilogue: An American Region

[1] Lemann, *Promised Land*, 330; Dunbar, *Delta Time*, 122.

[2] *New York Times*, August 6, 1990; Atlanta *Constitution*, October 18, 1990; Dunbar, *Delta Time*, 230.

[3] Dunbar, *Delta Time*, 136.

[4] Michael Alexander, "Fishy Business," *Southern Exposure* 14 (September/October, November/December 1986), 32–34; Atlanta *Journal and Constitution*, October 30, 1990.

[5] St. Louis *Post-Dispatch*, October 16, 1989; Atlanta *Journal and Constitution*, October 30, 1990; *New York Times*, December 10, 1990.

[6] Memphis *Commercial Appeal*, December 16, 1990; Jackson *Clarion-Ledger*, August 11, 1991.

[7] Jackson *Clarion-Ledger*, May 10, 1990; Memphis *Commercial Appeal*, October 17, 1989.

[8] Jackson *Clarion-Ledger*, May 10, 1990; Los Angeles *Times*, May 13, 1990.

[9] Memphis *Commercial Appeal*, May 21, 1989, May 14, 1990; Jackson *Clarion-Ledger*, May 10, 1990.

[10] *Wall Street Journal*, October 13, 1989.

[11] Tony Dunbar, *Delta Time*, 207, 237; Lemann, *Promised Land*, 336–37.

Index

▽

▽

▽